THE LIFE OF MAHOMET

THE
LIFE OF MAHOMET

FROM ORIGINAL SOURCES

by
SIR WILLIAM MUIR, K.C.S.I
LL.D., D.C.L., PH.D. (BOLOGNA)

WITH AN INTRODUCTION TO THE REPRINT
by
RAM SWARUP

VOICE OF INDIA
NEW DELHI

Third edition: London 1894
First Indian reprint: 1992
Second Indian reprint: 2002

ISBN: 978-81-85990-76-7

Published by Voice of India, New Delhi – 110 002.
Printed at Replika Press Pvt. Ltd.

INTRODUCTION TO THE REPRINT

(Muir on what *Lives of Muhammad* should be like—Muir's *Life* for thinking Muslims—Missionary angle—Similarities between Christianity and Islam—Christianity as Islam without Muhammad—Debate—"Idolatry" as common enemy—Monotheism—its origin—Pre-Islamic Arab— Prophetism, an adjunct of Monotheism—Genesis of Religious intolerance—Yogic spirituality—Advaita—Reincarnation—Christianity and Islam as Intruders—Europe, Americas, the Middle East, Africa seeking their spiritual roots—How Hinduism can help them in their self-discovery).

Sir William Muir's *The Life of Mahomet* was first published in 1861 in four volumes, a pioneering study based wholly on orthodox original sources. An abridged edition came out in 1876. The third edition was published with important alterations in one volume in 1894. The present volume is a reprint of this edition. After Muir's *Life* many Lives of the Prophet have appeared, but it still remains a classic and in some ways has not yet been surpassed in comprehensiveness and in the wealth of material. Thanks to Archeology and other related disciplines, today we know a great deal more about Pre-Islamic Arabian culture, but ever since Muir there has been no addition in the source material relating to the Prophet's life. This was exhausted long ago by early Muslim writers and all this was taken into account by Muir.

Muir belonged to the highest rung of British officialdom in India, but his reputation as an outstanding Arabist and Islamist has proved the most enduring. But he was also a believing Christian and his scholarly labours had a missionary motivation at heart. The motivation gave him a certain direction and a certain way of looking at things, but it did not compromise his scholarship. In fact, he thought that for the very success of the Missionary enterprise, a good biography of the Prophet, based on unimpeachable sources respected by orthodox Muslim scholars, was a first necessary step. While discussing the inaccuracies of Washington Irving's *Life of Muhammad*, he stressed the need for a "life of the Prophet of Arabia which is based on sound, orthodox Muslim sources."

In his various articles which he wrote during mid-1840s and which appeared in the *Calcutta Review*, we easily get to know what he expected his *Life* to be and to achieve. He wanted it to oppose two kinds of Lives that were current: one was by Missionary writers who were careless about their facts, slipshod in their scholarship, hostile in intent, unsympathetic in treatment, and uninhibited in expressing their opinions. For example, A. Sprenger, his contemporary, a Missionary and an Islamist of great repute, regarded Muhammad as having a "weak and cunning mind." Muir disagreed and argued that such a man "could never have accomplished the mighty mission which Mahomet wrought." Others called Islam "a spurious faith," and its founder "a false prophet" and a "counterfeit Messiah." Muir probably shared these opinions, but he discouraged their too open expression. He thought that if the Missionaries used such epithets, how could they get the hearing of the Muslims? He probably also thought that stating facts should do, for they would speak for themselves.

He also wanted his *Life* to oppose Biographies of the Prophet written by native Muslim writers which were current among devout Muslims. These were highly fanciful and extravagant and were based on fabricated traditions of which the early biographers of the Prophet were quite innocent. For illustration, Muir discussed a biography of the Prophet, *moulud sharif* or "The Ennobled Nativity" written by Ghulam Imam Shahid, an Indian Muslim, during the 1840s. It was very popular among the Muslims and it had already seen a dozen editions. In this biography, the author, an ornate writer, informed us how Allah wishing to manifest himself formed the "light of Muhammad a thousand years before creation;" how when the light was at last transferred to the womb of Ameena, Muhammad's mother, "200 damsels of the Coreish died of envy;" how angels rejoiced at his birth; how, as he came out of the womb he was already circumcised; and how he repeated the kalima.

Muir tells us that early traditions relating to the Prophet's nativity contain no such material. He wanted his *Life* to be faithful to this early tradition, and he thought that such a biography would be respected by the Muslims and would therefore serve the Missionary cause better. He argued: "If we can from their own best sources, prove to them that they are deceived and superstitious in many important points... we shall have gone a great way to excite honest inquiry and induce the sincere investigator to follow our lead." He wanted to present this biography to "thinking Mohammedans, who are turning their attention to the historical evidence of their faith; and are comparing them with those of Christianity." In this way, he thought, rather fondly, that "thinking Muslims" would come to prefer Christianity to their own faith. How the stories of the Immaculate Conception, the Virgin Mother, the Only Begotten Son will satisfy their historical sense is not made clear. In fact, some of the "thinking Mohammedans" on whom Muir so much relied remained unmoved by Muir's labour of love. Sayyad Ahmed (later Sir Sayyad), who wrote his own Biography of the Prophet in reply to Muir's, argued whether the Biblical miracles of Moses and Jesus should not be considered from the same rational viewpoint. But in their turn, the Christians were dogmatic and they had learnt to believe that while the miracles of Jesus were historical and well attested, those found in rival faiths were irrational.

II

As Missionary scholars studied Islam, mostly with a view to convert Muslims, they found that there was a lot in common between it and their own faith. Both were Judaic in origin and orientation, and both had common prophets. The Biblical prophets including Jesus are highly honoured in the Quran. Both shared a common God and a common line of prophets, and both believed in Revelation from the same God. In fact, the prophet of Islam claimed that he communicated with the same God who communicated with Moses and Jesus, and that he was merely reviving the old religion of Ibrahim, the common patriarch of them all. In this revival, he expected the Jews and the Christians to play their part and enlist under his banner. He felt that he was sent to the "people of the Book" as much as to the Arabs. "O ye people of the Book! our Apostle has come to you to explain to you much of what you have hidden of the Book," Allah told them (Quran 5.18). But by and large, they disappointed him. However, the Prophet still kept his hope, particularly in the Christians. On one occasion, Allah assured him that though the Jews and the idolaters are "the strongest in enmity" towards him, but those who call themselves Christians, "you will find the nearest in love...[and] when they hear what has been revealed to the Prophet, you will see their eyes gush with tears at what they recognize as truth therein" (Quran 5.85, 86).

The Missionaries in turn felt a similar affinity towards Islam and expected much from it. With so much in common — "a one and living God; Mosaic traditions; nay, a belief in Christ," as Sir Robert B. Edwardes, Commissioner and Governor-General's Agent at Peshawar put it—the Muslims should find no difficulty in converting to Christianity. In fact, according to him they should do very well as converts, and in support he quoted his Bible: "For if thou were cut out of the live tree which is wild by nature, and were grafted contrary to nature into a good live tree: how much more shall these, which be the natural branches, be grafted into their own live tree" (Romans 11.24).

But not all shared this bright vision and Muir was one of them. He agreed that Christians had many advantages in the contest. "We have no infidel view to oppose; the existence of sin, and its future punishment is allowed; the necessity of revelation, and even the Divine origin of the Old and New Testament dispensation, are conceded; the most of the attributes of God, the immaculate conception of Christ, the miracles which attested His mission, are all admitted," Muir said. But he still felt that this convergence was of no avail. For, the Muslims believed in Jesus not because of the Bible but because of the Quran, and his study of the Quran had convinced him that the "object of Mahomet was entirely to supersede Christianity", and that the conditions upon which he "permitted Christianity to exist were those of sufferance."

He argued that since the Quran has taken much from the Bible, it therefore abounds with approaches to truth. And this very fact fortifies the Muslims in their present position. "It is a melancholy truth," Muir said, that "a certain amount of light and knowledge often renders only the more difficult to drive the bigot from his prejudices." As a result, the supposed advantages, the points common to both, "are thus turned into a barrier against us, into a thick impenetrable veil which effectually excludes every glimmer of the true light," Muir added.

III

Some Missionaries wondered why Islam should have in the first instance succeeded at all considering that Christianity was already there in the field and the good news was already known. They believed that the founder of Islam came into contact with a corrupt form of Christianity and that had he known the purer type, the story would have been very different. Isaac Taylor says in his *Ancient Christianity*, Vol I, that the Christianity which Muhammad and his Khalifahs knew "was a superstition so abject, an idolatry so gross and shameless, church doctrines so arrogant, church practices so dissolute and so puerile, that the strong-minded Arabians felt themselves inspired anew as God's messengers to reprove the errors of the world, and authorized as God's avengers to punish apostate Christendom." Muir expresses the same thought and regrets that a purer Christianity like the one represented by the Anglican Church was not there at hand when Muhammad appeared on the scene.

Sir Monier Williams, a Sanskritist with deep missionary concerns, speculated in the same vein: "If only the self-deluded but fervent-spirited Muhammad, whose soul was stirred within him when he saw his fellow town-men wholly given to idolatry, had been brought into association with the purer form of Christianity... he might have died a martyr for the truth, Asia might have numbered her millions of Christians, and the name of Saint Muhammad might have been in the calendar of our Book of Common Prayer... Think, then, of the difference in the present condition of the Asiatic world, if the fire of Muhammad's eloquence had been kindled, and the force of his personal influence exerted on the side of veritable Christianity" (*Modern India*,1878).

A new opportunity came again for Christianity when Europe, and particularly England, dominated the world during the last few centuries. During this while, one would have expected, according to Muir, that Christian Europe would have improved its advantages for evangelizing the East, that "Britain, the bulwark of religion in the West, would have stepped forth as its champion in the East, and displayed her faith and her zeal where they were most urgently required." But, alas! it was not to be so and, Muir continues, "England was then sadly neglectful of her responsibility; her religion was shown only at home and she was careless of the spiritual darkness of her benighted subjects abroad; her sons, who adopted India as their country, so far from endeavouring to impart to its inhabitants the benefits of their religion, too often banished it from their own minds, and exhibited to heathens [Hindus] and Mohammadans the sad spectacle of men without faith...[and] their lives too often presented a practical and powerful, a constant and a living, argument against the truth of our holy faith."

IV

Though so much alike and having the same origin, Christianity and Islam quarrelled. They quarrelled as soon as they came face to face. For centuries they fought with fire and sword. At one time, it seemed that Islam had won and it was knocking at the door of Europe. But after much labour and luck, the tide was turned. In the long interval of armed peace that followed, Europe greatly improved its weaponry and its military position could not be challenged. Meanwhile, it also added another weapon to its arsenal—ideological warfare.

Islam had no way of meeting this challenge. It could not deal with Christians in the old way, the only way it knew, the way of the sword. It had to listen to the "arguments" of the Christian West with respect and even allow some sort of freedom and physical security to the Christians and the Jews in the countries it dominated.

Meanwhile, many things had taken place in Europe. It had passed through a period of rationalism and it began to discuss Christianity with a new freedom. As a result, it was now less Christian, and it did not apply the Spanish solution to the Muslim problem.

But it did recognize the usefulness of Christianity for the empire, and the Missionaries had a fairly free field. They were still discouraged from a too blatant use of force, but they were well-endowed and they had great political prestige; they often worked in collusion with the white administrators. They fully utilized these advantages.

They had also developed what they call *Apologetics*, the art of establishing the truths of Christianity and controverting those of other faiths.

The Muslims were new to the art of religious discussion—their *forte* had been of a different kind—and initially they were at a disadvantage. But they picked up the art soon, and did quite well. The Missionaries tried to prove Jesus with the help the Quran, Muslims tried to prove Muhammad's mission with the help of the Bible. The former argued that Christianity was Islam without Muhammad—no great matter according to them; that Muhammad himself had recognized Jesus as an Apostle and Muslims should have no difficulty in going a bit further and recognize him as the only Son and the Saviour. The latter argued that Muhammad's mission was prophesied in the Bible itself and in recognizing him as the last spokesman of God, Christians would only be true to their own scriptures.

Thus they bluffed each other and the game continued for some time. But they could not always keep the mask on. The Missionaries often let out that Islam was only an inferior reproduction of Christianity, an imitation of the original but not the original itself, and that Muhammad was obviously a pretender; Muslims argued that Muhammad's revelation was the last one and the Judaic and Christian revelations already stood abrogated. There is in fact a belief among the Muslims based on a *hadis* that Jesus in his Second Coming will be born a faithful Muslim, will fight for Islam, "judge Christians, break crosses, kill swine, and abolish *jizia*" (*Sahih Muslim*, 287)—*jizia* would be rendered superfluous as all Christians would become Muslims.

The controversy was sharp, as it often is between creeds which are alike in beliefs and aims and methods—like Stalinists and Trotskyites. Both claimed to believe in the same God, but each claimed sole heirship to his throne. Muir found in Islam "a subtle usurper, who climbed into the throne under pretence of legitimate succession, and seized upon the forces of the crown to supplant its authority." He also found in it a "dangerous adversary" who "has borrowed so many weapons of Christianity." Muslims argued that had the Jews and the Christians not falsified their scriptures, they would have long back joined the banner of Islam.

The debate had some interesting features. Each side was *rational* about the faith of the other, but not about its own. As a result, though Muslims fully utilized the rational critique to which Christianity was subjected by Europe during its recent Age of Reason, they had no use for it for themselves. Hence Muslims yet know no real self-criticism except to say that they are not Muslim enough!

Another feature was that even though the language of the debate was often sharp, its parameters were limited; they consisted of a single God who communicates with his followers through a privileged single medium, and who exercises an unbending enmity towards heathens and infidels. Throughout the debate, these premises remained unquestioned and no awareness was shown of the concerns of a deeper spirituality.

Though Christianity and Islam quarrelled between themselves, their real and ultimate target remained "Idolatry"— their name for all non-Semitic religions, which means all religions of the past and most religions of the present. The Missionary writers highly appreciated Islam's role in "cleansing the world from the scourge of idolatry, and for preparing the way for the reception of a purer faith." Similarly, Islam recognized Christians as "people of the

Book," no small honour and no small point of security. This recognition allowed the Christians to practise their faith under certain disabilities and also provided some sort of physical security to their persons, something which was denied by Muslim Arab rulers to their own blood brothers, who had to submit to a choice between Islam and death.

V

It is well-known that Christians and Muslims derived their much-vaunted Monotheism from the Jews, but the Jews themselves were not monotheists in the beginning. Like other neighbouring peoples, they had their tribal god towards whom they felt a special loyalty but it did not occur to them yet to deny the gods of others. True, the gods sometimes quarrelled as their followers quarrelled, yet it was still far from the thought of the Jews to deny "other" gods. That other gods did not exist or were false, and that their god alone was true and enjoyed some sort of universal sovereignty, was a later development. This development had to wait till the arrival of their Prophets, beginning with Moses.

It seems that the early Jews did not know Jehovah according to the Biblical testimony itself. "By name Jehovah was I not known to them," says the Bible (Exodus 6.3). Probably, the Jews borrowed Egyptian Gods, at least in some measure, while they were in Egypt and they continued worshipping them even during the days of their wanderings in the desert. There are also indications that the new religion, whatever it was and whenever adopted, was imposed against great opposition and with great ferocity. While Jehovah revealed himself to Moses as the only God of the Jews, they were worshipping another God under the symbol of a Bull (Has it something to do with *Nandi* of Hinduism?), a mode they had probably adopted in Egypt. "Slay every man his brother, and every man his companion, and every man his neighbour," ordered Jehovah to those who truly followed him. Three thousand men were killed in a day and a new religion was inaugurated or an old one established.[1] The killers were consecrated and they became the priestly class, the Levites.

---

[1] But Jehovah continued to be worshipped under the form of a Bull or Golden Calf for quite many centuries. There are repeated reference to this fact in the Old Testament (Numbers 23.22; 24.8; Hosea 8.5, 6; 13.2; 1Kings 12.28-30). Jehovah also continued to be worshipped as a brazen serpent till Hezekiah destroyed it (2Kings 18.4).

Some thinkers believe that Moses had borrowed the idea of a single God while in Egypt under the influence of Akhnaton's religious reforms. But this God was too mild and pacific, and would not do for the new life of the Jews. Therefore, during their wanderings, they adopted another God, the God of Midianites, a Volcano God. And that is how they acquired a god who was both militant as well as single. He became the God of the Jews and they became His people. Freud says that a God of this nature was "better suited to a people who were starting out to occupy a new homeland by force." He promised them "a land flowing with milk and honey," while he urged them to exterminate its inhabitants "with the edge of the sword" (Exodus 3.8 ; Deuteronomy 13.15).

As events settled, many Jewish scholars tried to allegorize the events of Exodus and ethicalize their God. The Talmuds, as these commentaries are called, contain much that is noble and inspiring. But the Biblical tradition still remained strong. Its God could not shed his jealousy and his exclusive character, and it continued to regard the Gods of other people as "abominations."

In course of time, this God in all his exclusiveness and jealousy was adopted by Christianity and Islam. In fact, in their hands, he became still more exclusive and jealous. He also became more ambitious and bellicose. While with the Jews, he remained their God alone; but, except spasmodically, he refused to be the God of others. Other people had to make do with their own Gods, howsoever "false," and these Gods had to be content with their own followers, howsoever benighted and out of grace with Jehovah. But things changed with the advent of Christianity and Islam. Through them, Jehovah came into his own and He offered to be the God of all. He asked his followers to go in all directions and preach His name, to "go out into the highways and hedges, and compel people to come in." He armed them and asked them to declare from the housetops several times a day that He alone was true and that other Gods were false. Others could refuse this invitation or call at their own peril, spiritual and physical. As His followers became more powerful, the peril became increasingly more physical.

There was another difference. Though the Jewish God was single, yet he spoke through many mouths. Moses was probably the most important, but a plurality of prophethood was recognized. It is unfortunate that the Judaic religion could not take full advantage of this principle. As the Mosaic-Monotheistic tradition was too strong, in practice the Prophetic message tended to be the same—more of the same Mosaic God. For the same reason, even movements like those represented by the Essenes, influenced by Hinduism-Buddhism, could not break away sufficiently from that tradition. But the principle of plurality of prophethood is in itself important, and some day it may become a source of significant spiritual changes.

Pre-Islamic Arabs

Monotheism of the Semitic kind was also unknown to Pre-Islamic Arabs.[2] They very well knew the Jews and the Christians but they had no particular attraction for their God. They had their own Gods and they were perfectly satisfied with them. The more religious of the Arabs who sought a deeper contact with their Gods often retired to the hills in their vicinity and engaged themselves in fasts and vigils. Muhammad also did it and in this he was following a long-established practice of his people.

But they were surrounded by neighbours who followed a faith which had a single God and a single Prophet. Traders returning from these lands brought news of how powerful and rich they were and how they were connected with the most powerful Empire of the time. Thus monotheism and prophetism were already prestigious creeds and they could not be without attraction for some persons.

Muhammad was one of those persons who were attracted by the new creed. He adopted the God of his powerful neighbours and claimed that He communicated with him as He had earlier communicated with Abraham, Moses and Jesus; that in fact his communication updated earlier communications and even abrogated them. He told his people that they had been worshipping false Gods, and that they should now take to the true one of his preaching. In his preaching, he also insisted that he was not only the latest but also the last apostle of this true God.

There was a long struggle. The Prophet harangued, castigated, mocked, denounced, fulminated against the traditional Gods of his people but without being able to move them. In the process, at one stage, he even felt isolated. In this state of mind, he recognized the

---

[2] Among the Arabs and the Phoenicians, *el, eloah, elohim, lah,* were common names for a God. But following the political fortunes of his votaries, a *lah,* a God also became *al-lah, the* God, and underwent enlargement without showing any corresponding moral improvement.

traditional deities as worthy intermediaries. The Meccans were pleased and offered to make up. But the prophet began to have doubts and thought that the conciliatory verses were inspired by Satan. These are called Satanic verses which, thanks to Salman Rushdie episode, are widely talked about but without many knowing what these are about. But from a deeper spiritual angle, these were probably the most Angelic of the Quranic verses.

The Prophet took up haranguing and ridiculing again. He appealed to the Arabs' patriotic feeling that his was an Arabic revelation, something which God had hitherto neglected to send, and that he was sent to the Arabs as their prophet, the only prophet ever sent to them. But the people argued that he was a poet, or a soothsayer, or was plainly out of his mind. He insisted that he was a prophet. It is not certain what the Meccans objected to, whether to the idea of a a single God or to Muhammad being His prophet, but the tussle continued, and he held out threats against their disbelief. He told them what they were heading for. Verily the day was not far off when they would cry in vain: "Yea! a warner came to us, and we called him liar...Had we but listened or had sense we had not been amongst the fellows of the Blaze"— the Quranic name for Hell.

As the Prophet gained strength, he supplemented spiritual threats with physical ones, while the Arabs observed constraints of their tribal code. The Meccans were waylaid, their caravans looted and eventually Mecca itself was invaded. The traditional idols were pulled down and their shrines were converted into houses of the new God. The Arabs were given an option between conversion and death. The story of Arab resistance to the new religion and how it broke down under superior force is ably shown by Sita Ram Goel in his *Hindu Temples: What Happened to Them,* Part II. Those interested in the subject may find it there.

But force alone would not have sufficed. The new creed was also found attractive economically and politically. The believers were promised not only houris in paradise but they were also given a share in the booty accruing from new religious wars that were becoming the order of the day; they also had a share in the large revenues coming from a fast expanding Muslim Empire. Every Arab was drafted as a soldier of Islam and his name was put on payroll. Umar regularized the system. Every Arab was a partner in the revenues derived from the loot and exploitation of the newly conquered lands — Muslim brotherhood in action. The scales were fixed according to one's nearness to the Prophet. The widows of Muhammad received an annual allowance of 10,000 dirhams each; the famous Three Hundred of the Battle of Badr had 5,000 dirhams each; those of the Pledge of the Tree received 4,000 each; every one who had converted to Islam before the Battle of Badr got 4,000 each, and their children 2,000 dirhams each; and so on, they graduated downwards to 200 dirhams. Wives, widows, and children had each their share. Every Muslim had a share in this classification. Officers of the Arab Occupation Armies in different cantonment areas of the Empire received yearly from 6,000 to 9,000 dirhams; and every boy, as soon as born, received 100 dirhams each; every Muslim had the title to be entered on the payroll, with a minimum annual allowance of ten pieces, rising with advancing age to its proper place. For a fuller account of the Civil List (*Diwan*), one can refer to the *Tarikh-i-Tabari*.

These stipends were hereditary, and they created a class of people who lived on the fat of the land they occupied. They laid the foundation of a thorough imperialism which was more durable than any other the world has known in the past. And this is how a people who had been hitherto upright and chivalrous, became a great scourge and cruel invaders and rulers. Their ethical code suffered a great decline.[3] They began to live on the labour and sweat of others.

But the greatest decline was in the concept of their Godhead which was at the root of all other kinds of degradation. Their new God was "one"; it was male; it was exclusive and intolerant; it took pride in refusing "partnership" with "other" Gods—whatever that may mean. It was also different from their accustomed Gods in another important sense: their traditional Gods spoke to them directly, but the new one dealt with them through an intermediary.

Pagan Arabs were a tolerant people. In fact, many Christians and Jews had found shelter with them; they were fleeing away from

---

[3] Margoliouth shows how and when it happened, how "men who had never broken an oath learnt that they might evade their obligations... men to whom the blood of the kinsmen had been as their own began to shed it with impunity in the cause of God; ... [how] lying and treachery in the cause of Islam received divine approval, hesitation to perjure oneself in that cause being represented as a weakness... [how] Moslems became distinguished by the obscenity of their language... [how] coveting of goods and wives (possessed by Unbelievers) was avowed without discouragement from the Prophet" (*Mohammed and the Rise of Islam, p.149).*

the intolerance of their own fellow religious men in the neighbouring countries. But as soon as the Pagan Arabs became Muslim, it was a different thing. Jews and Christians were turned out of the land of Arabia. Pagan Arabia accepted Jews and Christians but rejected their God for itself; Muslim Arabia embraced their God but rejected His people. This is a measure of the difference between the two approaches: Pagan and Semitic. Paganism has multiple Gods but believes in one humanity; Semitic religions have one God but at least two humanities: believers on one hand and unbelievers or infidels or heathens on the other. The division is not just social, or racial, or cultural; it is *metaphysical*. Believers owe nothing to infidels, not even ordinary ethical behaviour. The Quran requires that Muslims "are vehement against misbelievers, but kind amongst themselves" (48.29).

VI

Prophetism

The theory of a single God had a necessary adjunct in the theory of a single Prophet or Saviour or Interpreter. The two theories have a family likeness and go together. In fact, as the Semitic God was becoming one, he was also becoming exclusive in his communication. Even when he had a chosen people, these people had no direct approach to Him. He told them that He will send them a prophet and "will tell him what to say and he will tell the people everything I command. He will speak in my name and I shall punish anyone who refuses to obey him."

In due course, the intermediary became more than a medium. In Christianity, he became the Saviour; in Islam, he became the Intercessor and also the last Prophet through whom God ever spoke.

Claims began to be made on his behalf, claims almost as tall as for the God he represented. In fact, the God tended to become redundant and the intermediary took his place, who in turn was represented by his own nominees. The New Testament says: "Salvation is to be found through him (Jesus) alone; in all the world there is no one else whom God has given who can save us" (Acts 4.12). At another place it says: "God puts all things under Christ's feet and gave him to the Church as the supreme Lord over all things." Such claims are offensive to man's rational as well as to his spiritual sense, but they have proved highly profitable to those who speak in the name of these intermediaries. Now they represent a great vested interest.

Intolerance

Intolerance must be the fruit of such bitter seeds. Other Gods must be dethroned, and so must also die those who speak in the name of other Gods (Deuteronomy 18.18-19).

The Semitic God is jealous, and so is his sole prophet. Just like his God, he too can brook no rivals. Jesus tells us that "all who came before me are thieves and robbers" (John 10.8). He warns his flock again and again against rival claimants. "Beware of false prophets who come to you in sheep's clothing, but inwardly are ravenous wolves"(Matthew 7.15; or 24.4). Muhammad admitted some prophets in the past in order to give his own prophethood an ancestry, but he abolished further prophethood. He was the latest and also the last prophet, the seal of Prophecy.

The fact is that intolerance is inbuilt into the basic Semitic approach and cursing comes naturally to it. The Bible is full of curses invoked on rivals — gods, prophets, apostles, doctrines. For example, Paul told his Galatian followers that "should anyone preach to you a gospel contrary to that which we preached to you, let him be accursed." This tradition has continued and has been the strongest element in Christianity, whether Catholic or non-Catholic. For example, the "Articles of Religion" of the Anglican Church lays down: "They also are to be had accursed that presume to say, That every man shall be saved by the Law or Sect which he professeth... For holy Scripture set out unto us only the Name of Jesus Christ, whereby men must be saved."

Christians claim that Jesus is an incarnation. One is not sure what he incarnated, but it is not difficult to see that Christianity incarnated a new religious intolerance, a tradition which Islam also faithfully continued. Religious intolerance was there before, but it was spasmodic and it was not supported by a theology. It was with the coming of Christianity and Islam that religious bigotry and arrogance descended on the earth on a large scale and with a new power. They know so little about themselves but they claim to know everything about God, and in imposing their definition upon others, they have killed millions of people. They have been even more fanatic about their founders. "If you won't believe that you're redeemed by *my* redeemer's blood, I'll drown you in your own," says the Christian, to put it in the language of Aldous Huxley. The same is true of Muslims. In their practice, Muhammad has been more central to their religion than their One God. You could jest about this God but woe unto him who jests about the Prophet. His punishment is death.

Some apologists of Islam say that Islam was better in the beginning and that intolerance is a latter-day growth. But it is not so. According to Margoliouth, "Islam was intolerant in the beginning as it is to-day." Intolerance is part of its very creed. It is a declaration of war, a battle-cry against non-Muslims and their Gods, and historically it began so and continues to be so. Five times a day, a pious Muslim is expected to declare that the Gods of others are false and that only *his* God is true.

If religious tolerance is a value, Christianity as well as Islam lack it badly. Wherever they have gone, they have carried fire and sword and oppressed and destroyed so far as it lay in their power. They demolished and occupied the temples and shrines of others. Any tolerance shown was an exception, intolerance was the rule. Hindus know to some extent what the Muslims did, but the Christian record in this matter has not been less thorough. For that one has to know the history of Christianity in Europe,[4] North Africa, Americas, and even in South India under the Portuguese and the French. As Ishwar Sharan observes in his *The Myth of Saint Thomas and the Mylapore Shiva Temple*, "Aurangzeb is nobody in comparison to St. Xavier when it comes to temple-breaking and bloodshed." Their record has been matched only recently by Communism, considered a Christian heresy by thinkers like Bertrand Russell. In China, the communist regime destroyed half a million Buddhist shrines. (Were the Buddhists there also in the habit of hoarding their gold in their shrines, thus attracting communist expropriatory justice and getting them destroyed in the process? Or was it a rare example of an act purely motivated by an ideology? Probably Stalinist historians of the JNU would like to explain.)

[4] Christian history in Europe is full of great vandalism in which Christian "saints" played a most conspicuous role. St. Maurillius burnt idols in Gaul; St. Firminus of Amiens destroyed them wherever he found them; St. Columban and St. Gall destroyed shrines, groves and images on the Continent, especially in Germany, and St. Augustine in England. Another Saint, Gregory, also a monk, destroyed, among many pagan temples, two Vaishnava temples in Syria, built by Hindu colonists there, in 304 A.D., even long before Christianity was adopted by the Roman Emperor.

VII

It is obvious that this ideology of a single god, a single prophet, a single revelation, a single church or *ummah,* and also of a single life and single judgement (Hebrews 9.27) is very different from the one the world at large has known in the past or even at the present. Historically speaking, it is more of an aberration, a local vogue which consolidated itself through conquest and propaganda, and it could impose itself in no other way. It is different not only from polytheism, a religious expression at a more popular level, but also from mystical religions expressing man's more intensive search for a spiritual life. It is certainly different from the spirituality known in the East by Hermetics, Stoics, Pythagoreans, Taoists and Vedantists; it is different from them in most matters, particularly in its concept of deity, man, and nature; it is different in its definitions, modes, theory and praxis.

Man is a born worshipper and has an innate need for God. Therefore, all peoples and cultures have a God in one form or another. But the word does not mean the same thing everywhere, even within a single culture; it represents different grades and levels. Ordinarily, the concept of God is much mixed up with man's lower needs and nature and God is sometimes no more than a glorified Pharaoh or Caligula. But such a God cannot last long unless this meaning is frozen and made enduring with the help of a theology. More often, a God has to have other, more humane qualities and serve more humane ends. He has to be a helper and a guide and provide solace and succor to man in his difficulties — and sometimes even in his more questionable designs, like his designs against his enemies who may have done no wrong to him.

This much of God is enough for most people, but it will not do for all. Some seek a deeper meaning, a more final explanation of life, a higher law of conduct; they seek to find out Who they are, Where they come from, Where they are going. In short, they raise questions about their origins, their self-identity, their true home. They seek a transformed life; they seek to be led from the unreal to the real, from darkness to light, from death to immortality.

All higher spirituality in general and Hindu spirituality in particular has concerned itself with these questions. It has found that questions about Gods are ultimately questions about one's own true Self. It has also found that man lives for the most part in his external self, in his desires, hates, ego and nescience, and that this veils his true soul-life. It has found that in order to uncover this higher life, man has to purify his instruments of knowing, and develop new powers of the soul, like faith, *tapas*, self-restraint, harmlessness, truthfulness, steadfastness, forgiveness; he has to develop powers of concentration and meditation; he has to develop devotion, spiritual discrimination, detachment, equal-mindedness and universality.

As he goes within, he enters into new realms and realities hitherto unknown. He meets many psychic formations and spiritual beings of various grades of purity and power corresponding to his own purity, needs and readiness. He also meets desire-gods and ego-gods and if sufficient purity is not established in the soul, he may identify himself with one of them; he may then declare that *his god* is *the God*, and he may prophetically demand that his God be worshipped by all.

On this journey, the pilgrim sees God or Gods as powers of the soul, and he also finds that the qualities that satisfy and nourish the soul the most are also the most God-like—the *daivi sampad* of the Gita. Here the deity does not take particular pride in being single or object to being multiple, for it knows that it is both. Here there is no "jealous" God at war with "other" Gods; here Gods are friends, and each images all. Here the soul also discovers that it is kin to the deity, and like unto that which it worships.

Here a man may come to know that he is one with the Father, but that is not enough. He must also know that this is true of all. But Christian Theology says that while Jesus was one with God, the rest are one with Adam. The exclusive Sonship is also a gratuitous, and non-spiritual one.

Here one also does not find the "one" God of Semitic persuasion, but one discovers a new togetherness of all things, a unity holding all. The soul sees itself in all. Here a man is one with all humanity; in fact, with all living beings and even with all elements. Here one feels friendliness towards all. There are no infidels and heathens here.

Yoga

It is not all just a "funny feeling," as an American Jesuit friend described it. It is a deeper spirituality, a deeper conception of God that develops when one knows how to dive deep into oneself. It is science and art of inward journey developed by the Hindus and called by them *Yoga*. We cannot discuss the subject adequately here, but we have already mentioned some of its features above and that should suffice for our purpose here. Yoga is a special contribution made by religions belonging to the *Sanatana Dharma* family.

Hindu spirituality seeks Self-Knowledge, or *atma-jnana*. This also leads to the highest knowledge of Gods. In fact, without *atma-vada*, there cannot be developed *deva-vada*. Here the deity is known in deep meditation by a mind at its most luminous and intuitive, *dhyana-gamya* and *buddhi-gamya*; he is seated in the cave of the heart (*guhahitam*, and *hridayastha*), or he resides inside the lotus-plexus situated between the two eyes (*ajnachakrabja-nilaya*), or in the thousand-petalled *chakra* in the crown of the head (*sahasradala-padmastha*). All these are Yogic concepts based on a deep knowledge of man's inner topography, his spiritual body in touch with larger subtle worlds and spiritual cosmic forces and powers. There is nothing analogous to them in most other religions. Jehovah and Allah are non-Yogic Gods,[5] belonging to non-Yogic religions — religions which are more like ideologies than spiritualities. They are self-regarding Gods and embody an intolerant idea. They do not project a too happy psyche., and as their source is not a *dhyana-bhumi* sufficiently deep and pure, they would hardly do for the Gods of developed spiritualities. Readers who are interested in this approach to the problem may refer to our Introduction to *Inner Yoga* by Sri Anirvan.

---

[5] It is not that Semitic religions had no better model. They must have known the surrounding Hermetic, Pythagorean, even Vedantic and Buddhist traditions but they fought off these influences. For example, early Christianity had a Gnostic tradition which opposed Jehovah, the Biblical God — male, one, and jealous. The *Secret Book of John*, a Gnostic work, says that when Jehovah "in his madness", declared that "I am God, and there is no other beside me", he was "ignorant of... the place from which he came", and that in declaring that he was a jealous God and there was no other God, he proves " that another God does exist; for if there was no other one, of whom would he be jealous?" Similarly, another Gnostic work said that when Jehovah boasted that there was no other God, "he sinned against all the immortal ones."

The story of Islam is no different. Prophetic Islam is inimical to mystic ideas. In the beginning, some Sufis courted martyrdom, but eventually they bought peace and safety by surrendering to Prophetic Islam. There have been some outstanding Sufis, but by and large the Sufi movement has been part of a larger aggressive apparatus, just like Christian Missions of Imperialism. Though Islam persecuted "infidels", destroyed their temples, enslaved and looted them, we find no Sufis protesting. In fact, they were often beneficiaries of this vandalism. They fully took part in Islamic jihad. R.M.Eaton's *Sufis of Bijapur*, published by Princetone University (1978), illustrates i' amply. No wonder, the book has been banned by the Government of India.

The "oneness" attributed to these non-Yogic Gods is different from the "oneness" of a Yogic God. The oneness of the latter is like the oneness of the sky which pervades all, which is everywhere and is in all; it contains everything, though it is contained by none; it is *advaita*, undifferentiated reality, not the monadity of numbered things. A Yogic God is a *unity*, not a *unit*; it is compatible with "other" Gods, includes them, and is manifested by them. The *advaitic*-God of the Yogas and the Puranas is not the *monad*-God of the Bible and the Quran.

Reincarnation

A spirituality based on Yoga also makes a man aware of the great law of *karma* of inscrutable working; through it he becomes aware of the forces of inertia and the forces of transformation; he becomes aware of many lives he has lived and the many lives he has yet to live. This is called the doctrine of Incarnation, Rebirth. But behind these repeated births, this spirituality also makes one aware of a state of the soul which is free and untainted, pure and immortal.

According to the doctrine of Reincarnation, it is the soul which carries the body and not the body which carries the soul. According to this belief, the soul exists before it takes on a body and after it quits it. This belief is universal and is widely shared. It is found among people who are called "primitive" as well as those who are called "civilized." It is found among the Eskimos, Australians, Melanesians, the Poso Alfur of Celebes in Indonesia, among Algonquians, Bantus, Finns and Lapps, old Teutonics and Druids, the Lithuanians and Lettish people, among the old Greeks and Romans and the Chinese. Plato believed that the soul is immortal and it participates in many incarnations. The doctrine was preached by Pythagoreans, and the teachers of Orphic mystery; it was named by them *metensomatosis*, or "changing of bodies", almost in the language of the Gita. It was also preached by Manicheans who once formed the most formidable opposition to Christianity. It holds a central place in Taoism and in all great religious systems forming part of *Sanatana dharma*.

In short, the doctrine has the support of the spiritual intuition of most mankind, ancient or modern. It is strange that Semitic religions could do without it. There was a time when the belief was held by Christianity too, but it was given up at an early stage, strangely enough, first at the wishes of Empress Theodora. It was again condemned at the Council of Constantinople (543 A.D.) as an Origenist error. "If anyone says or thinks that human souls had a previous existence—*anathema sit*," the Council declared.

It had to do it. Following Plato, Basilides, Origen and many other early Christian writers believed that souls in their original purity pre-existed, that any punishment of hell was temporary, to be followed by the general restoration of all souls to their former state (*apokatastasis*). But this belief went completely against some of the most fundamental doctrines of Christianity: the doctrines of one life and one judgement, of pre-election, of some saved but many condemned to suffer eternal punishment in hell. Therefore, reincarnation had to be given up.

The idea could not have a better fate in Islam. The idea is known here as *tanasukh* and we meet it only amongst the Druzes, and some heretic sects such as Ali Ilahis, who ask men not to fear death because death is like the dive the duck makes. But the idea is incompatible with mainstream Islam and, indeed, with all religious ideologies that lack spiritual spaces and believe in one life, and one judgement.

There are many other differences between Semitic religions and the spiritualities based on Yoga.The latter are little concerned, as one can easily find, with Vicarious Atonement, Begotten Sons, Last Prophets, Special Covenants, Chosen Churches or Ummas, proxies and surrogates, Missions and Jihad, threats of hell and promises of a paradise, which are the staples of the former.

There is no wonder that Yoga is unwelcome to prophetic religions. It is subversive of dogmas and special claims, and is too universal in spirit. Only recently, in 1989, the Vatican issued a 23-page document, approved by Pope John Paul, to its monastries and convents warning them against the lure of "Eastern meditation practices" which obscured "the Christian conception of prayer, its logic and requirements."

VIII

A New Thinking

Over most of the world, there is a new thinking on religious questions. In many countries, there is also a growing awareness that their present religions were imposed on them and that they themselves belonged to a different religious tradition. Ralph Borsodi, an

American educationist and social thinker, in his *The Challenge of Asia* observes that "everywhere in the world excepting in Asia Minor, the three great Semitic religions—Judaism, Christianity and Islam—are intruders;" that "indigenous Asia is Brahmanist, Confucianist, Buddhist, Taoist; indigenous Europe is pagan;" that "in Europe, Christianity is a superimposition;[6] in Asia, Islam is."

As in many other things, Europe also leads this stir. It is witnessing a revival of its ancient religion; it is remembering its past and it is trying to throw off the yoke of Christianity and revive its old religious tradition that expressed itself in the language of Gods. Last year, the Pagans of Great Britain held a meeting attended by 300 representatives. They had met a year before, but their meeting was not allowed to be held by the Fundamental Christian Coalition. This time however they were able to hold their deliberations undisturbed. As reported in *Hinduism Today* (February, 1991), they said at the meeting that Christianity has buried them with a theology that has masculanized God, separated man from Divinity, and robbed the land of its sacredness. They promised to return divinity to the land and treat it as a friend, not an enemy.

They also found that their old religion was part of a larger religious system which once prevailed in other parts of the world as well. Nigel Pennick, author and thinker, found great similarity between old European Paganism and Hinduism. He said that Hinduism represented the Eastern expression of this universal tradition and foresaw the possibility that Hindus might come to accept Europe's Pagans as a European branch of Hinduism.

Prudence Jones, the spokesperson for the U.K. Pagan Federation, said the same things. She observed that all the world's indigenous and ethnic religions have three features in common: they are nature-venerating, seeing nature as a manifestation of Divinity; secondly, they are polytheistic and recognize many Gods, many Manifestations; the third feature is that they all recognize the Goddess, the female aspect of Divinity as well as the male. She showed how European Paganism was similar to Hinduism, Shintoism, and the North American tradition. She thought that apart from doctrinal similarity, it would be useful for the European Pagans to

---

[6] Christianity conquered Europe "from above", but many parts still continued to be pagan for quite some time. The Baltic States, for example, were pagan till the time of the Crusades. These were eventually conquered by the Order of Knights Templars, initially formed to fight the Saracens.

be affiliated with a world Hindu organization which would give them legal protection — remember, that Paganism in Europe is still a heresy and it has no legal rights and protection. She emphasized that European Pagan religion is the native, indigenous religion of Europe, and religions with doctrines like Christianity came later.

Americas

Among the indigenous peoples of two Americas, there is a growing awareness of their old identity. The ancient New World has a great message to give to the new Old World; it has to tell us about the mystery of the Mother Earth, tell us that we not only come *to* the Earth but we also come *from* the Earth. But one wonders if it is articulate enough culturally and, in fact, if enough of its old authentic religious tradition still survives to become the basis of a new revival. Indigenous America is poor, deprived, demoralized and not conscious enough of its spiritual heritage. In Central and Southern America, where there is still considerable native population left, things are no better. They are by far under the tutelage of Christian priests and functionaries who have ruled the roost for centuries. Now these priests are opposed, sometimes even violently, by lay Christians, by Evangelists from the North, and by radical Christianity which calls itself Liberation Theology. But they are sides of the same coin, and it has brought no relief to indigenous religions. Indigenous culture is as much opposed by the orthodox church as by the radical one. The former used to sell Jesus as a Saviour, the latter sell him as a liberator. The aim of both is the same: to keep indigenous America in cultural bondage. Old America will never rise politically unless it rises culturally and it revives its old religion.

Countries under Islam

The condition of countries now dominated by Islam is a difficult one. People here have yet to win the basic struggle for intellectual freedom. Once this is done, the rest would be a question of time. The people will be free to inquire into the dogmas of Islam, and look at the life and revelations of their Prophet more critically; they will also know more about other religious traditions including their own past religions. This may bring the necessary corrective and may even topple the Islamic apple-cart.

However, despite discouraging conditions, some advanced thinkers in Muslim countries have shown awareness of the fact that

Islam was an imposition on their country. For example, Tawfiq al-Hakim, a well-known dramatist and social thinker of Egypt, was writing in the twenties and the thirtees of this century on this subject. Quite understandably, he had to do it guardedly. He said that the "classical Arab", his name for Islam, was inadequate for "spiritual" Egypt, which he identified with Pharaonic golden age. He also found that Hinduism and Pharaonic Paganism of ancient Egypt were congruent and had been in contact. He thought that the responsibility for articulating a spiritual alternative to Europe's materialism lay on neo-Pharaonist Egypt and Hindu India. There is a highly informative and analytic article on the subject by Dennis Walker, a young Australian Arabist.

Iran, another ancient country which lost its individuality when it was conquered by Islam, also shows signs that it is aware of its "Aryan" past. But it has made two mistakes. First, it thought it could combine its pride in its ancient religion and culture with its present-day Islam; secondly, it underestimated the power of Ayatollahs, the fanatic Muslim priests. It has to realize that it cannot revive its religious and cultural individuality so long as Islam holds it down.

The African continent has been under the attack of the two monolatrous religions, Christianity and Islam, for centuries. Under this attack, it has already lost much of its old culture. Recently, the attack has very much intensified and indigenous Africa is almost on the verge of losing its age-old religion. Some time ago, there was an article in the London *Economist* praising it for taking this attack with such pagan *tolerance*. But there was no word of protest against intolerance practised against its people's religion. Thanks to the powerful Missionary lobby in the United Nations, there is a Universal Declaration of Human Rights which states that everyone has a right to embrace the religion of his choice. But where is a similar Declaration which says that tolerant philosophies and cultures have a right to protect themselves against aggressive, systematic proselytizing ? Are its well-drilled legionaries, organized round a fanatic and totalitarian idea, to have a free field ? Should not the Missionary Apparatus, a threat not only to Africa but to the whole Third World, be wound up? Has the UNO no obligation in this regard ?

Within what is now known as the Indian Sub-continent and Greater India itself, Islam is very powerful. But there is no doubt that once Hinduism comes into its own and begins to speak for itself, those who were forced to leave it under very special circumstances will return to their old fold.

IX

Hinduism

Hinduism can help all peoples seeking religious self-renewal, for it preserves in some way their old Gods and religions;[7] it preserves in its various layers religious traditions and intuitions they have lost. Many countries now under Christianity and Islam had once great religions; they also had great Gods who adequately fulfilled their spiritual and ethical needs and inspired in them great acts of nobility, love and sacrifice. But for many centuries they have been under great attack and much has been said against them while they gracefully retired to give the new totalist deity a chance to give whatever it had to offer. The results have been disastrous. Religious bigotry descended upon the earth; the concept of "one" God brought in the concept of two humanities and religious aggression became the highest duty and morality. Religion itself became dogmatic and lost its inwardness and vision. People both individually and collectively felt empty inside.

Now in their search for meaning, many peoples are turning to their old Gods. But during the long period of neglect, they lost the knowledge which could revive those Gods. Hinduism can help them with this knowledge.

We have discussed this problem in our *The Word As Revelation: Names of Gods*, and we need not dwell upon it here. Suffice it to say that in this book we have shown that, spiritually speaking, monotheism has no natural superiority over polytheism and, in point of historical fact, it has been worse. We also said that Hinduism has still the knowledge of the archetypal spiritual consciousness which expresses itself in the language of Many Gods, and therefore can help countries which are seeking their lost Gods. We said that those Gods are not lost but have merely gone out of manifestation, and that they can reappear again if properly invoked; that it could be a rewarding pilgrimage if we journeyed back to them to make our heart's offerings.

---

[7] This very fact gives some Missionaries great hopes. They feel that they can do to Hinduism what they did to old classical religions. The late Fr. J. Monchanin, the founder of Sachidananda Ashram in Tiruchirapalli (now presided over by Fr. Bede Griffiths), and a Missionary of the De Nobili school, says that the problem of Christianizing India is "of the same magnitude as the Christianization, in former times, of Greece", and he finds that "the Christianization of Indian civilization is to all intents and purposes an historical undertaking comparable to the Christianization of Greece."

We said that it will help the pilgrim nations in many ways. They have been taught to regard their past as a benighted period of their history, but a more understanding approach to their old Gods will make for a less severe judgement on their past and their ancestors. It will fill the generation gap, not the one we generally talk about, but the deeper one of historical rootlessness of nations. Gods provide an invisible link between the past and the present of a nation; when they go, the historical link also snaps. The peoples of Egypt, Iran, Greece, Germany, Scandinavian and Baltic countries are quite ancient but as they lost their Gods, they also lost their sense of historical identity.

We also said that what is true of Europe is also true of Africa and South America. The countries of these continents have recently gained political freedom, but it has done little to help them to regain their spiritual identity. If they wish to rise in a deeper sense, they must recover their soul, their Gods, their roots in their own psyche. If they need any change, and there is no doubt they do, it must come from within themselves as a part of their own experience. They have to make the best use of their own psychic and spiritual gifts. They cannot rise through imported deities, saviours and prophets.

X

Muir thought that comparative studies of Christianity and Islam and their founders would also yield an indirect benefit. Writing in the *Calcutta Review* in 1845, he said that as "the Hindu, sickened by idolatry (Islam's and Christianity's common name for Hinduism), turns to the other two religions which surround him, and inquires into their respective claims...we must be ready at hand to meet him with the proofs of our most holy faith... the comparison of the two religions, Christianity and Islam, cannot fail to be of essential service, under God's blessings, to lead to practical results."

Muir deserves our thanks for thinking so much of debates and "proofs" in establishing the superiority of his faith. This was a language quite new to Islam and until not long ago also to Christianity. It does not however appear that the Hindu was sickened by his own religion, and that he was impatient to join one of the two Semitic religions. But he had certainly been under a great barrage of attack of the two monolatrous religions, and anything which improved his level of information and education about them was a welcome development. Muir's book was and still is a great help to such Hindus who care to know more about the Prophet of Islam, and, indeed, about Islam itself — for no other creed is so synonymous with its founder. Voice of India, therefore, deserves our thanks for bringing out a reprint of Muir's *The Life of Mahomet* as it did a few years ago of D.S. Margoliouth's *Mohammed and the Rise of Islam*. That too carried our Introduction, in which we had discussed the importance of such studies for India and the need for her to develop her own scholarship and perspective. We had also pointed out that hitherto we have looked at Hinduism through the eyes of Islam and Christianity, but that it is high time that we now also learn to look at them through the eyes of Pagan religions in general and of Hinduism in particular. The two Introductions may best be read together.

Phag Day,
March 19, 1992.

Ram Swarup

PREFACE

The Life of Mahomet, by Sir William Muir, was first published in four volumes in the year 1861, with profuse notes and references, as well as introductory chapters on the Early History of Arabia, and an Essay on the 'Sources for the Biography of Mahomet—the Coran and Tradition.' In the second (1876) and third (1894) editions these introductory chapters, although of the highest interest in themselves, were omitted, as not being immediately relevant to the biography of the Arabian Prophet. Moreover, most of the notes and all the references to original authorities were left out, the curious readers being referred for the latter to the first and larger form of the work. The text itself remained practically unaltered in all three editions.

The present text is a revision in some matters of detail of that of the third edition. All the learned author's expressions of opinion and the view he took of particular events have, of course, been left unaltered. The changes which have been made have been in respect of the form rather than of the substance.

In the first place, the orthography of the Arabic proper names has been brought into line with modern usage. The name Mahomet was adopted by Principal Muir to designate the Prophet, 'following the established usage of Christendom, and had the further advantage of always distinguishing him from other persons of the same name, in whose case he wrote it Mohammad or Muhammad (first edition, p. 16). The objection to this is that we now place the accent on the first syllable of the name Mahomet instead of the second, thus giving it an entirely wrong sound. Moḥammad has, therefore, been used for all persons of that name in this edition. Other names which have become naturalised in English have been retained as in Muir, *e.g.* Mecca not *Makka;* Caliph, not Khalīfa; Medīna, not Al-Madīna (*op. cit.* p. vi.). On the other hand, I have put Aṭ-Ṭā'if instead of Muir's Tayif; 'Ā'isha for Ayesha; Az-Zubeir for Zobeir; and so on. Absolute consistency in these matters is not attainable.

In the matter of the transliteration from Arabic into Roman letters, the system of the Royal Asiatic Society has been generally followed. Thus *dh* is put for Muir's *dz*, *ḍ* for *dh*, *ẓ* for *tz*, *ḳ* for *c* or *ck*. The heavier sound of *t* is represented by *ṭ*, and of *s* by *ṣ;* and the guttural *h* by *ḥ*. The (to a European) unpronounceable letter *'ain* is denoted by the 'rough breathing': the lighter *hamza* being generally omitted, unless when it falls between two vowels. The long vowels are denoted by the long mark. The final *h* of the feminine is left out, although thus a final *a* may either correspond to a final *h* or final *y*, as in Selama, Mūsa. No system of transliteration is perfect, and the present one aims only at enabling the reader correctly to pronounce the proper names, and, if he wishes, to turn them back into their Arabic original.

In the first edition of the Life the references were made to *manuscript* copies of the histories of Ibn Hishām, Aṭ-Ṭabari, and Ibn Sa'd, which are quite inaccessible to the ordinary reader. Since that date excellent editions of all these have been published, and to these the references are made in the present revision. In the case of the *Maghāzi* of Al-Wāḳidi the condensed translation by the famous Professor Wellhausen is referred to as being more convenient and easy of reference than the Arabic text of Von Kremer, as well as because the latter is not available after the beginning of the fourth year of the Hijra. On some points the edition of Ibn

Ḳoteiba's *Kitāb al-Maʿārif* by the late Dr Ferdinand Wüstenfeld has also been referred to, as it groups together facts which occur separately in the histories which follow the order of time. References have not been given to the *Dīwān*, or Poems of Ḥassān ibn Thābit, recently published in the Gibb Memorial Series, as it is easily obtainable, and much of the material will be found in the Biographies cited above.

The text of the work has been left practically as it stood in the third edition. In a few cases a phrase has been changed so as to bring it nearer the original, and a variant account occurring in one of the old sources has been added. All such additions are enclosed within square brackets.

I have to thank Professor Margoliouth, D.Litt., of Oxford, for his kindness in giving me the advantage of his advice in regard to the system of transliteration to be followed and the authorities to which reference should be made. For the arduous task of the compilation of the Index, I owe thanks to M. G. W.

T. H. W.

THE UNIVERSITY, GLASGOW

CONTENTS

INTRODUCTION

PART FIRST

MOḤAMMAD TILL THE HIJRA

CHAPTER I

CHAPTER II

CHAPTER III

CHAPTER IV

CHAPTER V

CHAPTER VI

CHAPTER VII

PART SECOND

MOḤAMMAD AT MEDĪNA

CHAPTER VIII

CHAPTER IX

CHAPTER X

CHAPTER XI

CHAPTER XII

CHAPTER XIII

CHAPTER XIV

CHAPTER XV

CHAPTER XVI

CHAPTER XVII

CHAPTER XVIII

CHAPTER XIX

CHAPTER XX

CHAPTER XXI

CHAPTER XXII

CHAPTER XXIII

CHAPTER XXIV

CHAPTER XXV

CHAPTER XXVI

CHAPTER XXVII

CHAPTER XXVIII

CHAPTER XXIX

CHAPTER XXX

CHAPTER XXXI

CHAPTER XXXII

CHAPTER XXXIII

CHAPTER XXXIV

CHAPTER XXXV

CHAPTER XXXVI

CHAPTER XXXVII

ARABIAN CALENDAR

Arabian Months	Corresponding Months
Moḥarram	April
Ṣafar	May
Rabīʿ I.	June
Rabīʿ II.	July
Jumāda I.	August
Jumāda II.	September
Rajab	October
Shaʿbān	November
Ramaḍān	December
Shauwāl	January
Dhu'l-Ḳaʿda	February
Dhu'l-Ḥijja	March

The Arabian month is lunar, and the year was originally corrected by the intercalation of a month every third year. The reckoning was thus luni-solar until, at the Farewell pilgrimage, Moḥammad, by abolishing intercalation, made the Muslim or *Hijra* year a purely lunar one.

This table gives the months as they stood at the time of Moḥammad's flight to Medīna, and they were so maintained, by intercalation, with little variation till the Farewell pilgrimage. After that the year is of course shorter by about eleven days than the solar year.

The calculation is according to M. C. de Perceval.[1]

[1] For the results of more recent investigations, *cf.* S. D. Margoliouth *Mohammed and the Rise of Islam*, pp. xix., xx.

INTRODUCTION

CHAPTER I

SOURCES FOR THE BIOGRAPHY OF MOHAMMAD. THE KOR'ĀN AND TRADITION

Ancient story, legendary, traditional, or contemporary

CONFIDENCE in a narrative must vary with the medium through which it has been transmitted. The exploits of Hercules carry less conviction than the feats of the heroes of Troy; while, again, the wanderings of Ulysses and the adventures of the early founders of Rome are regarded with incomparably less trust than the history of the Peloponnesian war or the fortunes of Julius Cæsar. Thus there are three great divisions of ancient narrative. Legendary tales are based upon visionary materials, and it is doubtful whether they shadow forth facts or only myths and fancies. Tradition and the rhapsodies of bards have for their object actual or supposed events; but the impression of these events is liable to become distorted from the imperfection of the vehicle which conveys them. It is to contemporary history alone, or to history deriving its facts from contemporary records, that we accord a reliance which, proportioned to the means and the fidelity of the observer, may rise to absolute certainty.

Rise of Islām belongs to all three classes

The narrative which we now possess of the origin of Islām does not belong exclusively to any one of these classes. It is *legendary*, for it contains multitudes of pure myths, such as the 'Light of Moḥammad and the 'Cleansing of his Heart.' It is *traditional*, since the main material of the story was handed down by oral recitation not generally recorded until Islām had attained to a full growth. But it possesses also some of the elements of *History*, because there are certain contemporary records of undoubted authenticity, to which we can refer. Moreover, Muslim tradition is of a peculiar and systematic character, bearing in some respects an authority superior to that of common tradition.

From such imperfect and incoherent materials it might be supposed difficult, if not impossible, to frame a uniform and consistent biography of the Arabian Prophet, the various points of which shall be supported by sufficient evidence or probability. It will be my attempt to elucidate this topic; to inquire into the available sources for such a narrative; and the degree of credit to which they are severally entitled.

Sources specified

We have two main sources from which to draw materials for the life of Moḥammad and rise of Islām—the ḲOR'ĀN and TRADITION. Two minor classes may be added, namely, contemporary documents and Arab poetry; but these have been, for the most part, transmitted also by tradition, and may with propriety be treated as coming under the same head. What dependence, then, can be placed on these sources? What is their individual merit as furnishing historical evidence, and what their comparative value in relation to each other? The solution of these questions will form the subject of this Essay.

Value, absolute and comparative

How preserved during Moḥammad's lifetime

The Ḳor'ān consists exclusively of the revelations or commands which Moḥammad professed, from time to time, to receive through Gabriel, as a message direct from God; and which, under alleged divine direction, he delivered to those about him.[1] At the moment of inspiration or shortly after, each passage was recited by Moḥammad before the friends or followers who happened to be present, and was generally committed to writing by some one amongst them, at the time or afterwards, upon palm-leaves, leather, stones, or such other rude material as conveniently came to hand.[2] These divine

[1] According to the orthodox doctrine, every syllable of the Ḳor'ān is of divine origin, eternal and 'uncreate' as the Deity itself. Some of the earliest rhapsodies, indeed (as the 91st, 100th, 102nd, and 103rd Sūras, or chapters), do not seem to have been intended as revelations at all. But when Moḥammad's die was cast of assuming the Most High as the immediate speaker, then these earlier Sūras also came to be regarded as emanating directly from the Deity. Hence Moḥammadans rigidly include *every word* of the Ḳor'ān, at whatever stage delivered, in the category of 'Thus saith the Lord.' And it is one of their arguments against our Scriptures, that they are not exclusively oracles professing to proceed directly from the mouth of God.

[2] The Prophet himself neither read nor wrote. His being an *Ummī*

messages continued throughout the three-and-twenty years of his prophetical life, so that the last portion did not appear till near the time of his death. The canon was then closed; but the contents during the Prophet's lifetime were never as a whole systematically arranged or even collected together. We have no certain knowledge how the originals were preserved. That there did not exist any special depository for them, is evident from the mode in which, after Moḥammad's death, the various fragments had to be sought for. Much of the Ḳor'ān possessed only a temporary interest, arising out of circumstances which soon ceased to be important; and it is doubtful whether the Prophet intended such passages to be used for public or private worship, or even maintained in currency at all. Such portions it is little likely he would take any pains to preserve. Whether he retained under his own eye and custody the more important parts, we have no indication; perhaps he regarded them as sufficiently safe in the current copies, guarded by the miraculous tenacity of the Arab memory. The later, and the more important, revelations were probably left with the scribes who recorded them, or laid up in the habitation of some one of the Prophet's wives.[1] However this may have been, it is very certain that,

(unlearned) is held to enhance the marvel of his revelation. At Medīna, he had many Arabic amanuenses; some of them occasional as 'Alī and 'Othmān, others official as Zeid ibn Thābit, who also learned Hebrew for the purpose. In Al-Wāḳidi's collection of despatches, the writers are named, and they amount to fourteen. Some say there were four-and-twenty followers whom Moḥammad used as scribes; others as many as forty-two. In his early Meccan life, he could not have had these facilities; but even then Khadīja, Waraḳa, 'Alī, or Abu Bekr, who could all read, might have recorded his revelations. At Medīna, Obei ibn Ka'b is mentioned as one who used to do so. Another, 'Abdallah ibn abi Sarḥ, was excepted from the Meccan amnesty, because he had falsified revelations dictated by the Prophet before the Flight.

It is also evident that the revelations were recorded, because they are called in the Ḳor'ān itself *Kitāb*, *i.e.*, 'what is written' or 'Scriptures.' The name *Ḳor'ān* signifies simply 'recitation,' and does not necessarily imply a written original.

[1] If the originals were retained by Moḥammad himself, they must needs have been in the custody of one of his wives; since at Medīna the Prophet had no special house of his own, but dwelt by turns in the abode of each of his wives. 'Omar committed his exemplar (as we shall see) to the keeping of his daughter Ḥafṣa, one of the widows of Moḥammad, and this may have been done in imitation of the Prophet's own practice. The

when Moḥammad died, there was nowhere any deposit of the complete series, and it may be doubted whether the *original* transcripts themselves were anywhere preserved.

Committed to memory by early Muslims;

But the preservation of the various Sūras, during the lifetime of Moḥammad, was not altogether dependent on any such archives. The divine revelation was the corner-stone of Islām. The recital of a passage from it formed an essential part of daily prayer public and private; and its perusal and repetition were enforced as a duty and privilege fraught with religious merit. Such is the universal voice of early tradition, and may be gathered also from the revelation itself. The Ḳor'ān was accordingly committed to memory more or less by *every* adherent of Islām, and the extent to which it could be recited was one of the chief distinctions in the early Muslim empire.[1] The custom of Arabia favoured the task. Passionately fond of poetry, but without the ready means for committing to writing the effusions of their bards, the Arabs had long been used to imprint these, as well as the tradition of genealogical and tribal events, on the living tablets of the heart. The recollective faculty was thus cultivated to the highest pitch; and it was applied, with all the ardour of an awakened spirit, to the Ḳor'ān. Such was the tenacity of their memory, and so great their power of application, that several of his followers could, during the Prophet's lifetime, repeat with scrupulous accuracy the whole as then in use.[2]

but not in any fixed order of parts

We are not, however, to assume that the entire Ḳor'ān was at this period repeated in any fixed order. The present compilation, indeed, is held by the Muslims to follow the arrangement prescribed by Moḥammad; and early tradition

statement made by Sale, that the fragmentary revelations were cast promiscuously into a chest, is not borne out by any good authority that I have met with.

[1] Thus, among a heap of warrior martyrs, he who had been the most versed in the Ḳor'ān was honoured with the first burial. The person who in any company could most faithfully repeat the Ḳor'ān was of right entitled to be the *Imām*, or conductor of the public prayers (a post ordinarily implying also military command) and to pecuniary rewards. Thus after the usual distribution of the spoils taken on the field of Al-Ḳādisīya, A.H. 14, the residue was divided among those who knew most of the Ḳor'ān.

[2] Four or five such persons are named; and several others also who could very nearly repeat the whole before Moḥammad's death.

might appear to imply some known sequence.[1] But this cannot be admitted; for had any fixed order been observed or sanctioned by the Prophet, it would unquestionably have been preserved in the subsequent collection. Now the Ḳor'ān, as handed down to our time, follows in the disposition of its several parts no intelligible arrangement whatever, either of subject or time; and it is inconceivable that Moḥammad should have enjoined its recital invariably in this order. We must even doubt whether the number of the Sūras was determined by Moḥammad as we now have them.[2] The internal sequence at any rate of the contents of the several Sūras cannot, in most cases, have been that intended by the Prophet. The constant chaotic mingling of subjects, disjoined as well by chronology as by the sense; a portion

[1] Thus we read of certain Companions, who could repeat the whole Ḳor'ān in a *given time*, which might be held to imply some usual connection of the parts; but the original tradition may have intended such portions only as were commonly used in public worship, and these may have followed, both in copying and repetition from memory, some understood order; or the tradition may refer to a later period when the order had been fixed by means of 'Omar's compilation. There was no fixed order observed (as with 'Lessons' in Christian worship) in the portions of the Ḳor'ān recited at the public prayers. The selection of a passage was dependent on the will and choice of the Imām. Thus Abu Hureira one day took credit to himself for remembering which Sūra the Prophet had read the day before; and on urgent occasions we hear of a *short* Sūra being used. It is only in private recitals that the whole, or large portions, of the Ḳor'ān are said to have been recited consecutively.

The common idea of the Moḥammadans, that the Ḳor'ān was fixed by Moḥammad as we have it now, originates in the tradition that Gabriel had an annual recitation of the whole Ḳor'ān with the Prophet, as well as in the desire to augment the authority of the book as it now stands.

[2] But there is reason to believe that the chief Sūras, including all passages in most common use, were fixed and known by name or other distinctive mark. Some are spoken of, in early and well-authenticated traditions, as having been so referred to by Moḥammad himself. Thus he recalled his fugitive followers at the discomfiture of Ḥonein, by shouting to them as 'the men of the *Sūrat al-Baḳara*' [Ibn Isḥāḳ has not this expression] (*i.e.* Sūra ii.).

Several persons are stated by tradition to have learnt by heart a *certain number* of Sūras in Moḥammad's lifetime. Thus 'Abdallah ibn Mas'ūd learned seventy Sūras from the Prophet's own mouth, and Moḥammad on his death-bed repeated seventy Sūras, 'among which

produced at Medīna sometimes immediately preceding a passage revealed long before at Mecca; a command put in some places directly after a later one which cancels or modifies it; or an argument suddenly disturbed by the interjection of a sentence foreign to its purport; all this forbids us to believe that the present, or indeed any complete, arrangement was in use during Moḥammad's lifetime.

Fragments from which Ḳor'ān compiled, faithfully preserved

On the other hand, there is no reason to doubt that several at least of the Sūras are precisely the same, both in matter and order, as Moḥammad left them;[1] and that the remainder, though often resembling a mosaic of various material rudely dovetailed together, are yet composed of genuine fragments, generally of considerable length, each for the most part following the connection in which it was recited in public, and committed to memory or to paper from the mouth of the Prophet by his followers.[2] The irregular inter-

were the Seven long ones.' These traditions signify a recognised division of at least some part of the revelation into Sūras, if not a usual order in repeating the Sūras themselves.

The liturgical use of the Sūras by Moḥammad must, no doubt, have in some measure fixed their form, and probably also their sequence. But I fail to follow Sprenger in his conclusions as to 'double' Sūras, and Sūras 'in groups' (*mathāni* and *naẓāir*).

[1] Where whole Sūras were revealed at once, this would naturally be the case; but short passages were often given out in driblets, and even single verses, as occasion required. With regard to these, it is asserted in some traditions that Moḥammad used to direct his amanuensis to enter them 'in the Sūra which treated of such and such a subject.' This, if authentic (and it is probably founded on fact), would indicate that Moḥammad intended the Ḳor'ān to be arranged according to its matter, and not chronologically. There are also several Sūras which, from the unity of subject, or from the form of composition, are evidently complete and integral. Such are the history of Joseph, Sūra xii.; and the psalm descriptive of Paradise, Sūra lv., quoted in Ch. iv.

The traditions just cited as to the number of Sūras which some of the Companions could repeat, and which Moḥammad himself repeated on his death-bed, also imply the existence of such Sūras in a complete and finished form.

[2] Anecdotes are told of persons who, in reciting the Ḳor'ān, from an imperfect memory, or when tired, omitted passages—passing from one to another, because of the similar termination, and of others who, having been guilty of such omission, could spontaneously correct themselves. (*Homoioteleuta* are of very frequent recurrence in the Ḳor'ān from the rhythm of the verses being often formed by the repetition of set phrases at their close, such as the attributes of God, &c.) These anecdotes

position and orderless disposal of the smaller fragments have indeed frequently destroyed the sequence, and produced a perplexing confusion. Still, the fact remains, that the fragments themselves were strictly and exclusively Moḥammad's own composition, and were learned or recorded under his instructions; and this fact stamps the Ḳor'ān, not merely as formed out of the Prophet's own *words* and *sentences*, but to a large extent as his in relation to the *context* also.

Ability to write common both at Mecca and Medīna

However retentive the Arab memory, we should still have regarded with distrust a transcript made entirely from that source. But there is good reason for believing that many fragmentary copies, embracing amongst them the whole Ḳor'ān, or nearly the whole, were during his lifetime made by the Prophet's followers. Writing was without doubt generally known at Mecca long before Moḥammad assumed the prophetical office. And at Medīna many of his followers were employed by the Prophet in writing his letters or despatches.[1] Though himself delighting in the title of the 'illiterate Prophet,' and abstaining, whether from inability or design, from the use of penmanship, he by no means looked with a jealous eye upon the art. The poorer captives taken at Bedr were offered their release on condition that they taught a certain number of Medīna citizens to write. And although the people of Medīna were not so generally educated as those of Mecca, yet many are noticed as having been able to write before Islām.[2] The ability thus existing, it may be safely inferred that the verses so indefatigably committed to memory would be likewise committed carefully to writing.

Transcripts of portions of Ḳor'ān common among early Muslims

We also know that when a tribe first joined Islām, Moḥammad was in the habit of deputing one or more of his followers to teach them the Ḳor'ān and the requirements of the faith. We are frequently informed that they carried *written* instructions with them on the latter point, and they would naturally provide themselves also with transcripts of the

certainly suppose a settled order of the parts repeated; and though the period referred to is subsequent to Moḥammad's death, yet the habit of such connected repetition was most probably formed during his lifetime, and before the collection into one volume.

[1] Aṭ-Ṭabari I., 1782.

[2] Thus, to cite one out of a score of instances, Al-Wāḳidi says that 'Abu'l-'Abbās used to write Arabic before the rise of Islām, while as yet writing was rare among the Arabs.'

more important parts of the Revelation, especially those upon which the ceremonies of Islām were founded, and such as were usually recited in the public service. Besides the reference in the Ḳor'ān to its own existence in a written form, express mention is made, in the account of 'Omar's conversion, of a copy of the 20th Sūra, as used in his sister's family.[1] This refers to a period preceding, by three or four years, the emigration to Medīna. If transcripts of the revelations were made, and in common use, at that early time when the followers of Islām were few and oppressed, it is certain that they must have multiplied exceedingly when the Prophet came to power, and his Book formed the law of Arabia.

But incomplete and fragmentary

But such transcripts were (like the portions committed to memory) mere fragments compiled and put together with little or no connection of subject and date. The Sūras used in public worship, or for private perusal and recitation, would be those of which the greatest number of copies existed. Transcripts of the earliest Sūras, and of those of evanescent interest, if extant at all, would be few in number.

State of Ḳor'ān up to the year after Moḥammad's death.

Such was the condition of the text during Moḥammad's lifetime, and such it remained for about a year after his death, imprinted upon the hearts of his people, and fragmentary transcripts increasing daily. The two sources would correspond closely with each other; for the Ḳor'ān, even during the Prophet's lifetime, was regarded with a superstitious awe as containing the very words of God; so that any variations would be reconciled by a direct reference to Moḥammad himself,[2] and after his death to the originals, or to copies, or to the memory of the Prophet's confidential friends and amanuenses.

Ḳor'ān collected A.H. XI.-XIV. by Zeid; his text authoritative during the Caliphate of 'Omar

It was not till the overthrow of Museilima, when great carnage took place amongst the Muslims at Al-Yemāma, and large numbers of the best reciters of the Ḳor'ān were slain, that a misgiving arose in 'Omar's mind as to the uncertainty which would be experienced regarding the text, when all

[1] 'The Ḳor'ān . . . none shall touch the same, excepting such as are clean,' lvi., 80. This passage was referred to by the sister of 'Omar when at his conversion she refused to let him take her copy of Sūra xx. into his hands.

[2] We meet with instances of such references made in case of doubt to Moḥammad by 'Omar, Ibn Mas'ūd, and Obei ibn Ka'b.

those who had stored it in their memories should have passed away. 'I fear,' said he, addressing the Caliph Abu Bekr, that slaughter may again wax hot amongst the reciters of the Ḳor'ān, in other fields of battle; and that much may be lost therefrom. Now, therefore, my advice is, that thou shouldest give speedy orders for the collection of the Ḳor'ān. Abu Bekr agreed, and thus made known his wishes to Zeid ibn Thābit, the Prophet's chief amanuensis: 'Thou art a young man and wise; against whom no one amongst us can cast an imputation; and thou wast wont to write down the inspired revelations of the Prophet of the Lord. Wherefore now search out the Ḳor'ān, and bring it together.' So new and unexpected was the enterprise that Zeid at first shrank from it, and doubted the propriety, or even lawfulness, of attempting that which Moḥammad had neither himself done nor commanded to be done. At last, yielding to the joint entreaties of Abu Bekr and 'Omar, he sought out the Sūras and fragments from every quarter, and 'gathered them together, from date-leaves, and tablets of white stone, and from the breasts of men.'[1] By the labours of Zeid, these scattered and confused materials were within two or three years reduced to the order and sequence in which we now find them, and in which it is said that Zeid used to repeat the Ḳor'ān in the presence of Moḥammad. The original copy thus prepared was committed by 'Omar to the custody of his daughter Ḥafṣa, the Prophet's widow. The compilation of Zeid, as embodied in this exemplar, continued during 'Omar's Caliphate to be the standard and authoritative text.

Recension in 'Othmān's Caliphate A.H. XXX.

But variety of expression either prevailed in the previous transcripts and modes of recitation, or soon crept into the copies which were made from Zeid's edition. The Muslim world was scandalised. The Revelation as sent down from heaven was ONE, but where was now its unity? Ḥodheifa, who had warred in Armenia and Adherbaijān and had observed the different readings of the Syrians and of the men

[1] Other traditions add, fragments of parchment or paper, pieces of leather, and the shoulder and rib bones of camels and goats. Leather was frequently used for writing, and many of Moḥammad's treaties and letters were recorded on it. There is a curious tradition regarding a man who used a leather letter, received from Moḥammad, for the purpose of mending his bucket, and whose family were thence called the 'children of the *cobbler*.'

of Al-'Irāḳ, was alarmed at the number and extent of the variations, and warned 'Othmān to interpose, and 'stop the people, before they should differ regarding their Scripture, as did the Jews and Christians.' The Caliph was convinced, and to remedy the evil had recourse again to Zeid, with whom he associated a syndicate of three of Ḳoreish. The original copy of the first edition was obtained from Ḥafṣa's depository, the various readings were sought for throughout the empire, and a careful recension of the whole set on foot. In case of difference between Zeid and his coadjutors, the voice of the latter, as conclusive of the Ḳoreishite idiom was to be followed, and the collation thus assimilated exclusively to the Meccan dialect.[1] Transcripts were multiplied and forwarded to the chief cities in the empire, and previously existing copies were all, by the Caliph's command, committed to the flames. The original was returned again to Ḥafṣa's custody.

Which remains unaltered to the present day

The recension of 'Othmān has been handed down to us unaltered. So carefully, indeed, has it been preserved, that there are no variations of importance—we might almost say no variations at all—to be found in the innumerable copies scattered throughout the vast bounds of the empire of Islām. Contending and embittered factions, taking their rise in the murder of 'Othmān himself within a quarter of a century from the death of Moḥammad have ever since rent the Moḥammadan world. Yet but ONE ḲOR'ĀN has been current amongst them; and the consentaneous use by all of the same Scripture in every age to the present day is an irrefragable proof that we have now before us the very text prepared by command of the unfortunate Caliph.[2] There is probably

[1] It is one of the maxims of the Muslim world (supported perhaps by Sūra xi. 2) that the Ḳor'ān is incorruptible, and that it is preserved from error and variety of reading by the miraculous interposition of God himself. In order, therefore, to escape the inconsistency of a revision, it is held that the Ḳor'ān, as to external form, was revealed in *seven dialects* of the Arabic tongue, so that no change was made in the integrity of the text. [The expression, however, means no more than this—that the words of the Sūras were not fixed, but might be recited in an indefinite number of ways. *Cf.* Nöldeke's *Geschichte des Qorāns*, ed. by F. Schwally, p. 47 ff.]

[2] The Muslims would have us believe that some of the *self-same copies*, penned by 'Othmān or by his order, are still in existence. The copy which the Caliph held in his hand when he was murdered is said to have been preserved in the village of Antartus on the Coast of Syria.

in the world no other work which has remained twelve centuries with so pure a text. The various readings are wonderfully few in number, chiefly confined indeed to differences in the vowel points and diacritical signs. But these, invented at a later date, can hardly be said to affect the text of 'Othmān.[1]

I. Was 'Othmān's text a faithful reproduction of Zeid's?

Assuming, then, that we possess unchanged the text of 'Othmān's recension, it remains to inquire whether that text was an honest reproduction of Zeid's, with the simple reconcilement of unimportant variations. There is the fullest ground for believing that it was so. No early or trustworthy tradition throws suspicion upon 'Othmān of tampering with the Ḳor'ān in order to support his own claims. The Shī'a, indeed, of later times pretend that 'Othmān left out certain Sūras or passages which favoured 'Alī. But this is incredible.

Others hold that leaves of it were treasured up in the Mosque of Cordova, and Edrīsi describes the ceremonies with which they were treated; they were finally transferred to Fez or Telemsan. Ibn Baṭūṭa, when in the fourteenth century he visited Al-Baṣra, declares that this MS. was then in its Mosque, and that the marks of the Caliph's blood were still visible (according to tradition) at the words 'God shall avenge thee against them' (Sūra ii. 138). Other of 'Othmān's originals are said to be preserved in Egypt, Morocco, and Damascus, as well as at Mecca and Medīna. The Medīna copy has a note at the end, relating that it was compiled by the injunctions of 'Othmān; and the compilers' names are also given. But it appears very unlikely that any of 'Othmān's copies can have escaped the innumerable changes of dynasty and party to which every part of the Muslim world has been subjected. Any very ancient copy might come to be called that of 'Othmān. [The oldest copies of the Ḳor'ān belong probably to the third century of the Hijra; a few may belong to the second. *Cf.* Nöldeke's *Geschichte des Qorāns*, 1860, p. 325.]

[1] There are, however, instances of variation in the letters themselves, not confined always to difference in the dots, but extending sometimes to the *form* of the letters also; these too, however, are immaterial. This almost incredible purity of text, in a book so widely scattered over the world, and continually copied by people of different tongues and lands, is without doubt owing mainly to 'Othmān's recension and to the official promulgation and maintenance of his edition. To countenance a various reading was an offence against the State, and as such would still to this day be punished. We need not wonder then that, with such means resorted to, perfect uniformity of text has been maintained. To compare (as the Muslims are fond of doing) their pure text with the various readings of our Scriptures, is to compare things between which there is no analogy.

Reasons for believing that it was so

When 'Othmān's edition was prepared, no open breach had taken place between the Omeiyads and the 'Alids. The unity of Islām was still unthreatened. 'Alī's pretensions were as yet undeveloped. No sufficient object can, therefore, be assigned for the perpetration by 'Othmān of an offence which Muslims would have regarded as one of the blackest dye. Again, at the time of the recension, there were still multitudes alive who had the Ḳor'ān by heart as they had heard it originally delivered; and copies of any passages favouring 'Alī—had any ever existed—must have been in the hands of his numerous adherents, both of which sources would have proved an effectual check upon any attempt at suppression. Further, the party of 'Alī, immediately on 'Othmān's death, assumed an independent attitude, and raised him to the Caliphate. Is it conceivable that, when thus arrived at power, they would have tolerated a mutilated Ḳor'ān—mutilated expressly to destroy their leader's claim? Yet we find that they continued to use the same Ḳor'ān as their opponents, and raised no shadow of an objection against it.[1] The insurgents, indeed, made it one of their complaints against 'Othmān that he had caused the revision, and ordered all previous copies of the sacred volume to be burned; but these proceedings were objected to simply as in themselves unauthorised and sacrilegious. No hint was dropped of ulterior object, or of any alteration and omission. Such supposition, palpably absurd at the time, is altogether an afterthought of the Shī'a sect.

[1] So far from objecting to 'Othmān's revision, 'Alī multiplied copies of it. Among other MSS. supposed to have been written by 'Alī himself, one is said to have been preserved at Meshhed 'Alī as late as the fourteenth century, which bore his signature. Some leaves of the Ḳor'ān, said to have been copied by him, are now in the Lahore *Tosha-Khana;* others in the same repository are ascribed to the pen of his son, Al-Ḥosein. Without leaning on such uncertain evidence, it is sufficient for our argument that copies of 'Othmān's Ḳor'an were notoriously *used and multiplied by 'Alī's partisans*, and have been so used and multiplied to the present day. 'Alī was, moreover, deeply versed in the Ḳor'ān, and his memory (if tradition be true) would amply have sufficed of itself to detect, if not to restore, any passage that had been tampered with. 'Alī said of himself: 'There is not a verse in the Ḳor'ān of which I do not know the matter, the parties to whom it refers, and the place and time of its revelation, whether by night or by day, whether in the plains or upon the mountains.'

II. Was Zeid's edition a faithful copy of Moḥammad's revelations?

We may then safely conclude that 'Othmān's recension was, what it professed to be, namely, the reproduction of the text of Zeid, with a more perfect conformity, it is true, to the dialect of Mecca, and the elimination of the various readings prevalent throughout the realm, but still a faithful reproduction. The most important question yet remains, viz. *Whether Zeid's collection was itself an authentic and exhaustive collection of Moḥammad's Revelations.* The following considerations warrant the belief that it was authentic and in the main as complete as at the time was possible.

Reasons for believing it was so: *First.*—Sincerity and faith of Abu Bekr and early Muslims

First.—Abu Bekr, under whose direction it was undertaken, was a sincere follower of Moḥammad, and an earnest believer in the divine origin of the Ḳor'ān. His faithful attachment to the Prophet's person, conspicuous for the last twenty years of his life, and his simple, consistent, and unambitious deportment as Caliph, admit no other supposition. Believing the revelations of his friend to be the revelations of God himself, his first object would be to secure a pure and complete transcript of them. A similar argument applies with equal force to 'Omar, under whose Caliphate the revision was completed. From the scribes employed in the compilation, to the humblest Believer who brought to Zeid his little store of writing on stones or palm-leaves, all would be influenced by the same earnest desire to reproduce the very words their Prophet had declared to be his message from the Lord. A similar guarantee existed in the feelings of the people at large, in whose soul no principle was more deeply rooted than an awful reverence for the supposed word of God. The Ḳor'ān itself contains frequent denunciations against those who should presume to 'fabricate anything in the name of the Lord,' or conceal any part of that which He had revealed. Such an action, declared to be the height of impiety, we cannot believe that the first Muslims, in the early ardour of their faith and love, would have dared to contemplate.

Second.—Ḳor'ān as delivered by Moḥammad, yet fresh in memory of his followers

Second.—The compilation was made within two or three years of Moḥammad's death. We have seen that some of his followers had the entire revelation (excepting perhaps some obsolete fragments) by heart; that *every* Muslim treasured up portions in his memory; and that there were official Reciters of it, for public worship and tuition, in all countries to which Islām extended. These formed a living link between the Revelation fresh from Moḥammad's lips, and Zeid's collection. Thus the people were not only sincere in wishing for a faithful copy of the Ḳor'ān; they were also in possession of ample means for realising their desire, and for testing the accuracy and completeness of the book now placed in their hands.

Third.—It must have corresponded with numerous transcripts in daily use

Third.—A still greater security would be obtained from the copies of separate portions made in Moḥammad's lifetime, and which must have greatly multiplied before the Ḳor'ān was compiled. These were in the possession, probably, of all who could read. And as we know that the compilation of Zeid came into immediate and unquestioned use, it is reasonable to conclude that it embraced and corresponded with every extant fragment; and *therefore*, by common consent, superseded them. We hear of no fragments, sentences, or words omitted by the compilers, nor of any that differed from the received edition. Any such would undoubtedly have been preserved and noticed in those traditional repositories which treasured up the minutest and most trivial acts and sayings of the Prophet.

Fourth.—Internal evidence of simplicity and faithfulness of compilers

Fourth.—The contents and arrangement of the Ḳor'ān speak forcibly for its authenticity. All the fragments have, with artless simplicity, been joined together. The patchwork bears no marks of a designing genius or moulding hand. It testifies to the faith and reverence of the compiler, and proves that he dared no more than simply collect the sacred remains and place them in juxtaposition. Hence the interminable repetitions; the wearisome reiteration of the same ideas, truths, and doctrines; scriptural stories and Arab legends, told over and over again, with little or no verbal variation; hence also the pervading want of connection, and the startling chasms between adjacent passages. Even the frailties of the Prophet, as noticed by the Deity, have with evident faithfulness been entered in the Ḳor'ān. Not less undisguised are the many passages contradicted or abrogated by later revelations.[1] Thus the editor plainly contented himself with compiling and copying in a continuous form, but with scrupulous

[1] Though the convenient doctrine of abrogation is acknowledged in the Ḳor'ān, yet the Muslim doctors endeavour as far as possible to explain it away. Still they are obliged to allow that the Ḳor'ān contains no fewer than 225 verses cancelled by later ones.

accuracy, the fragmentary materials within his reach. He neither ventured to select from repeated versions of the same incident, or to reconcile differences, or by the alteration of a letter to connect abrupt transitions of context, or by tampering with the text to soften discreditable appearances. In fine, we possess every internal guarantee of confidence.

Recension of Abu Bekr's edition, why required?

But it may be objected,—If the text of Zeid was pure and universally received, how came it to be so soon deteriorated as to require, in consequence of its variations, an extensive recension? Tradition does not afford sufficient light to determine the cause of these discrepancies. They may have been due to various readings in transcripts that remained in the possession of the people, or have originated in the diverse dialects of Arabia, and different modes of pronunciation and orthography; or have sprung up naturally in the already vast domains of Islām, before strict uniformity was officially enforced. It is sufficient for us to know that in 'Othmān's revision recourse was had to the *original* exemplar of the first compilation, and that there is otherwise every security, internal and external, that we possess the text which Moḥammad himself gave forth and used.

Ḳor'ān may not contain some passages once revealed but subsequently cancelled,

While, however, it is maintained that we now have the Ḳor'ān *as it was left* by Moḥammad, there is no ground for asserting that passages, once put forth as inspired, may not at some subsequent period have been changed or withdrawn *by the Prophet himself*. On the contrary, repeated examples of withdrawal are noticed in tradition; and alterations (although no express instances are given) seem to be clearly implied. The Ḳor'ān itself recognises the withdrawal of certain passages, after they had been promulgated as a part of the Revelation: 'Whatever verses We cancel, or *cause thee to forget*, We give thee better in their stead, or the like thereof' (Sūra ii. 100).

Any passages which Moḥammad, finding to be inconvenient, or otherwise inexpedient for publication, withdrew before coming into circulation, will, of course, not be found in our present Ḳor'ān; nor would an altered passage remain but in its altered form. But this does not in any measure affect the value of the Ḳor'ān as an exponent of Moḥammad's opinions, or at least of the opinions he finally professed to hold; since what we now have, though possibly corrected and modified by himself, is still *his own.*

Nor some obsolete, suppressed, or ephemeral passages

It is, moreover, not impossible that verses which had been allowed to fall into abeyance and become obsolete, or the suppression of which Moḥammad himself desired, may have been sought out by the blind zeal of his followers, and, with pious veneration for everything believed to be the word of God, entered in Zeid's collection. On the other hand, many early passages of ephemeral interest may, without design on the part of Moḥammad, have disappeared in the lapse of time; and, no trace being left, must necessarily have been omitted from the compilation.

CONCLUSION.—Ḳor'ān authentic record of Moḥammad's revelations

The conclusion, which we may now with confidence draw, is that the editions of Zeid and 'Othmān were not only faithful, but both of them, so far as the materials went, complete; and that whatever omissions there may have been, were not on the part of the compilers intentional. The real drawback to the inestimable value of the Ḳor'ān as a contemporary and authentic record of Moḥammad's character and actions, is the want of arrangement and connection which pervades it; so that, in inquiring into the meaning and force of a passage, no certain dependence can be placed upon adjacent sentences as the true context. But, bating this serious defect, we may upon the strongest presumption affirm that every verse in the Ḳor'ān is the genuine and unaltered composition of Moḥammad himself, and conclude with at least a close approximation to the verdict of Von Hammer: *That we hold the Ḳor'ān to be as surely Moḥammad's word, as the Moḥammadans hold it to be the word of God.*

Importance of Ḳor'ān as contemporary evidence of Moḥammad's words and character

The importance of this deduction can hardly be overestimated. The Ḳor'ān becomes the groundwork and the test of all inquiries into the origin of Islām and the character of its Founder. Here we have a storehouse of *Moḥammad's own words recorded during his life*, extending over the whole course of his public career, and illustrating his religious views, his public acts, and his domestic character. By this standard of his own making, we may safely judge his life and actions, for it must represent either what he actually thought, or what he affected to think. And so true a mirror is the Ḳor'ān of Moḥammad's character, that the saying became proverbial among the early Muslims, *His character is the Ḳor'ān.* 'Tell me,' was the curious inquiry often put to 'Ā'isha, as well as to Moḥammad's other widows, 'tell me something about the Prophet's disposition.' 'Thou hast the Ḳor'ān,' replied 'Ā'isha; 'art thou not an Arab, and readest the Arabic tongue?' 'Yea, verily.' 'Then why take the trouble to inquire of me? For the prophet's disposition is no other than the Ḳor'ān itself.' Of Moḥammad's biography the Ḳor'ān is the keystone.

[A source second only to the Ḳor'ān would be the Dīwān or Poems of Ḥassān ibn Thābit, if we could be certain that in any given instance these were genuine. These poems have been edited recently (1910) in the Gibb Memorial Series. The verses of other contemporary poets, such as Al-Ash'a (*cf.* Ibn Hishām, p. 255 f.), would be of first-rate value, if their authenticity were established.]

TRADITION, the chief material of early Muslim history

Having gained this firm position, we proceed to inquire into the credibility and authority of the other source of early Moḥammadan history, viz. TRADITION. This must necessarily form the chief material for the biography of the Prophet. It may be possible to establish from the Ḳor'ān the outlines and some of the details of his life, but tradition alone enables us to determine their relative position, and to weave them into the tissue of intermediate affairs.

Described

Moḥammadan tradition consists of the sayings of the friends and followers of the Prophet, handed down by an alleged chain of narrators to the period when they were collected, recorded, and classified. The process of transmission was for the most part oral. It may be sketched as follows.

Habits of the early Muslims favoured growth of tradition

After the death of Moḥammad, the main employment of his followers was arms. The pursuit of pleasure, and the formal round of religious observances, filled up the intervals of active life, but afforded scanty exercise for the higher faculties of the mind. The tedium of long and irksome marches, and the lazy period from one campaign to another, fell listlessly upon a simple and semi-barbarous race. These intervals were occupied, and that tedium beguiled, chiefly by calling up the past in familiar conversation or more formal discourse. On what topic, then, would the early Muslims more enthusiastically descant than on the acts and sayings of that wonderful man who had called them into existence as a conquering nation, and had placed in their hands 'the keys both of this World and of Paradise'?

Lapse of time invested Moḥammad with supernatural attributes

Thus the converse of Moḥammad's followers would be much about him. The majesty of his character gained greatness by contemplation; and as time gradually removed him farther from them, the lineaments of the mysterious mortal who was wont to hold familiar intercourse with the messengers of heaven rose into dimmer but more gigantic proportions. The mind was unconsciously led on to think of him as endowed with supernatural power and surrounded by supernatural agency. Here was the material out of which Tradition grew luxuriantly. When there was at hand no standard of fact whereby these recitals might be tested, the Memory was aided by the unchecked efforts of the Imagination; and as days rolled on imagination gained the ascendancy.

Superstitious reverence with which traditions of *Companions* were regarded by succeeding generation

Such is the influence which the lapse of time would naturally have upon the minds and the narratives of the 'COMPANIONS' of Moḥammad—more especially of those who, being young when he died, lived long into the next generation. And then another race sprang up who had never seen the Prophet, who looked up to his contemporaries with a superstitious reverence, and listened to their stories of him as to the tidings of a messenger from the other world. 'Is it possible, father of 'Abdallah! that thou hast been with Moḥammad?' was the question addressed by a pious Muslim to Ḥodheifa, in the Mosque of Al-Kūfa; 'didst thou really see the Prophet, and wert thou on terms of familiar intercourse with him?' 'Son of my uncle! it is indeed as thou sayest.' 'And how wert thou wont to behave towards the Prophet?' 'Verily, we used to labour hard to please him.' 'Well, by the Lord!' exclaimed the ardent listener, 'if I had been but alive in his time, I would not have allowed him to put his blessed foot upon the earth, but would have borne him on my shoulders wheresoever he listed.' On another occasion, the youthful 'Obeida listened to a Companion who was reciting before an assembly how the Prophet's head was shaved at the Pilgrimage, and the hair distributed amongst his followers; the young man's eyes glistened as the speaker proceeded, and he interrupted him with the impatient exclamation: 'Would that I had even a single one of those blessed hairs! I would cherish it for ever, and prize it beyond all the gold and silver in the world.' Such were the natural feelings of fond devotion with which the Prophet came to be regarded by the generation which followed the 'Companions.'

Successors belong to latter half of first century

As the tale of the Companions was thus taken up by their followers, distance began to invest it with an increasing charm, while a living faith and warm imagination were fast degenerating into superstitious credulity. This new generation is termed in the language of the patristic lore of Arabia, SUCCESSORS. Here and there a *Companion* survived till near the end of the first century; but, for all practical purposes, they had passed from the stage long before its close. Their first *Successors*, who were in some measure also their contemporaries, flourished in the latter half of the same century, and some of the older may have survived for a time even in the second.[1]

Wants of expanding empire required enlargement of code of Ḳor'ān

Meanwhile a new cause was at work, which gave to the tales of Moḥammad's Companions a fresh and an adventitious importance. The Arabs, a simple and unsophisticated race, found in the Ḳor'ān ample provisions for the regulation of their affairs, religious, social, and political. But the aspect of Islām soon underwent a mighty change. Scarcely was the Prophet buried when his followers issued forth from their barren Peninsula resolved to impose the faith of Islām upon all the nations of the earth. Within a century they had, as a first step, conquered every land that intervenes from the banks of the Oxus to the farthest shores of Northern Africa, and enrolled the great majority of their peoples under the standard of the Ḳor'ān. This vast empire differed widely from the Arabia of Moḥammad's time; and that which sufficed for the patriarchal simplicity of the early Arabs was found altogether inadequate for the multiplying wants of

[1] Companions, termed *Aṣḥāb* اصحاب; their followers, or *Successors*, *Tābi'ūn* تابعون. For practical purposes, the age of Companions may be limited to the first half or three-quarters of the 7th century A.D. Thus, supposing a Companion to have reached his sixty-third year in A.D. 674, he would have been only twenty years of age at the Prophet's death, and but ten years of age at the time of the Flight. A margin of ten or twelve additional years may be left for cases of greater age and unusual memory.

their descendants. Crowded cities, like Al-Kūfa, Cairo, and Damascus, required elaborate laws for the guidance of their courts of justice: widening political relations demanded a system of international equity: the speculations of a people before whom Literature was throwing open her arena, and the controversies of eager factions on nice points of doctrine, were impatient of the narrow limits which confined them:—all called loudly for the enlargement of the scanty and naked dogmas of the Revelation, and for the development of its rudimental code of ethics.

Ḳor'ān at first sole authoritative rule of conduct

And yet, by the first principles of Islām, the standard of Theology, Politics, and Law was the Ḳor'ān alone. By the divine Revelation, Moḥammad himself ruled. To it in his teaching he always referred. From the same infallible source he professed to derive his opinions, and upon it to ground his decisions. If he, the Messenger of the Lord, and the Founder of the faith, was thus bound by the heavenly Revelation, how much more the Caliphs, his uninspired successors! But new and unforeseen circumstances were continually arising, for which the Ḳor'ān had made no provision. It no longer sufficed for the needs of society. How, then, was the deficiency to be supplied?

Deficiency supplied by the SUNNA, or sayings and practice of Moḥammad

The difficulty was resolved by adopting the CUSTOM ('SUNNA') of Moḥammad; that is, his *sayings* and his *practice*, as supplementary of the Ḳor'ān. The recitals regarding the life of the Prophet now acquired an unlooked-for value. *He* had never held himself infallible, except when directly inspired of God; but this new doctrine assumed that a heavenly and unerring guidance pervaded every word and action of his prophetic life. Tradition was thus invested with the force of law, and with something of the authority of inspiration. It was in great measure owing to the rise of this theory, that, during the first century the cumbrous recitals of tradition so far outstripped the dimensions of reality. The prerogative now claimed for Tradition stimulated the growth of evidence, and led to the preservation of every kind of story, spurious or real, touching the Prophet. Before the close of the century it had imparted an incredible impulse to the search for traditions, and had in fact given birth to the new profession of *Collectors*. Men devoted their lives to the business. They travelled from city to city, and from tribe to tribe, over the whole Moḥammadan world; sought out by personal inquiry every vestige of Moḥammad's biography yet lingering among the *Companions*, the *Successors*, or their descendants; and committed to writing the tales and reminiscences with which these were wont to edify their wondering and admiring auditors. They also established in every leading city schools of tradition, in which they held lectures, and recited their Collections with the string of authorities on which they rested. Each circle of pupils took notes from their master's oral delivery; and thus the compilations of the most popular Collectors were preserved and spread abroad.

Legendary tales of strolling story-tellers

I need here only allude to another body of so-called tradition, namely, the legendary tales of the strolling minstrel or story-teller. This personage has always been popular in the East, and in the early days of Islām had special opportunities for the exercise of his vocation. As he travelled from city to city and village to village, crowds gathered around, and hung upon his lips while he recited in glowing terms some episode of the Prophet's life, his birth and childhood, the heavenly journey, or the Battle of Bedr. Great latitude both in detail and colouring was allowed to these story-tellers, whose object was at once to entertain and edify. Such tales, no doubt, formed the groundwork of the biographical legends so popular all over the Moḥammadan world. They are still recited on special occasions (as the birth and childhood of Moḥammad in the first ten days of Rabī' I.); and they form the staple of the modern biographies of the Prophet. It is needless to add that, being utterly uncritical, they are possessed as historical sources of no authority whatever.[1]

General collections of biographical tradition

It was soon found that the work of collecting and circulating authoritative traditions too closely affected the public interests and the political aspect of the empire to be left entirely to private responsibility and individual zeal. About a hundred years after Moḥammad, the Caliph 'Omar II. issued circular orders for the formal collection of all extant tradition. The task, thus begun, continued to be vigorously prosecuted; but we possess no authentic remains of any

[1] See Sprenger, i. 341; and for samples of these legends as current at the present time, an article by myself in the *Calcutta Review* on Biographies of Moḥammad for India, No. xxxiv., Art. 6.

compilation of an earlier date than the middle or end of the second century of the Hijra. Then, indeed, ample materials had been amassed, and they have been handed down to us both in the shape of *Biographies* and of *General collections* which bear upon every imaginable point of Moḥammad's character, and record the minutest incidents of his life.

Tradition not recorded as a rule till latter part of 1st century

It thus appears that the traditions we now possess remained generally unrecorded for at least the greater part of a century. It is not, indeed, asserted that some of Moḥammad's sayings may not have been noted down in writing during his lifetime, and from that source copied and propagated afterwards. But the evidence in favour of any such record is meagre, suspicious, and contradictory. And few and uncertain as are the statements of the practice, there was a motive to invent them in the additional credit with which the traditions of a Companion supposed to have committed them to writing would be invested. It is indeed hardly possible that, if the writing down of Moḥammad's sayings had prevailed as a custom during his life, we should not have had frequent intimation of the fact, with notices of the writers, and special references to the nature, contents, and peculiar authority of their records. But no such references or quotations are anywhere to be found. It cannot be asserted that the Arabs trusted so implicitly to their memory that they regarded oral to be as authoritative as recorded narratives, and therefore had these existed would not have cared to notice them; for we see that 'Omar was afraid lest even the Ḳor'ān, believed by him to be divine and itself the subject of heavenly care, should become defective if left to the memory of man. Just as little weight, on the other hand, should be allowed to the tradition that Moḥammad *prohibited* his followers from the practice of noting down his words. The truth appears to be that there was at the first no such practice; and that the story of the prohibition, though spurious, embodies the afterthought of serious Moḥammadans as to what Moḥammad *would have said* had he foreseen the loose and fabricated stories that sprang up, and the danger his people would fall into of allowing *Tradition* to supersede the Ḳor'ān. The risks of Tradition, in truth, were as little thought of as its value was perceived, till many years after Moḥammad's death.

Even if memoranda were recorded in Moḥammad's lifetime, none connected with extant tradition

But even admitting all that has been advanced, it would prove no more than that *some of the Companions used to keep memoranda* of the Prophet's sayings. Now, unless it were possible to connect any given traditions with such memoranda, the concession would be useless. But it is not, so far as I know, demonstrable of any single tradition or class of traditions now in existence, that they were copied from such memoranda, or have been derived in any way from them. To prove, therefore, that *some* traditions were at first recorded, would not help us to a knowledge of whether any of these still exist, or to discriminate between them and such as rest on a purely oral basis. The very most that could be urged from the premises is, that our present collections *may* contain some traditions founded upon a recorded original, and handed down in writing. The entire mass of extant tradition rests in this respect on the same uncertain ground, and the uncertainty of any one portion (apart from internal evidence of probability) attaches equally to the whole. In fine, it cannot, with the least show of likelihood, be confidently affirmed of any tradition that it was recorded till nearly the end of the first century of the Hijra.

Mohammadan tradition affected by bias and prejudice

We see, then, how entirely Tradition, as now possessed, rests its authority on the *memory* of those who handed it down; and how dependent it must have been upon their convictions and their prejudices. For, in addition to the frailty of the faculty itself rendering such evidence notoriously infirm, and to the errors and exaggerations which must distort a narrative transmitted orally through many witnesses, there exist in Moḥammadan tradition abundant indications of actual fabrication; and there may everywhere be traced the indirect but not less powerful and dangerous influence of a latent bias, which insensibly gave colour and shape to the stories of their Prophet treasured up in the memories of Believers. To form an adequate conception of the value and defects of Tradition, the nature and extent of these influences must be thoroughly understood; and for this purpose the reader should possess an outline of the political aspect of the empire of Islām from the death of Mohammad to the period at which our *written* authorities commence. Such an outline I will now endeavour to supply.

Historical review necessary

During first two Caliphates, faction unknown

Moḥammad survived for ten years the era of his Hijra or flight to Medīna. The Caliphates of Abu Bekr and 'Omar occupied the thirteen succeeding years, during which the new-born empire, animated by the ruling passion of universal dominion, was unbroken by schism. The distorting medium of Faction had not yet interposed betwixt us and Moḥammad. The chief tendency to be dreaded in tradition as transmitted through this period, or originating in it, is one which was then perhaps even stronger and more busy than in the approaching days of civil broil, namely, the disposition to exalt the character of Moḥammad, and endow it with super-human attributes.

A.H. 23-35. First effect on tradition of 'Othmān's murder not unfavourable

The weak and vacillating policy of 'Othmān gave birth to the attack of the conspirators on Medīna, which, ending in the murder of the aged Prince, caused a fatal rent in the unity of the empire, and left it a prey to contending factions of new competitors for the Caliphate. The immediate effect of this disunion was not unfavourable to the historical value of Tradition. For although each party would be tempted to colour its recollections by their own factious bias, they must still do so in the face of a hostile criticism. And, while as yet there were alive on either side eye-witnesses of the Prophet's actions, both parties would be cautious in advancing what might be liable to dispute, and eager to denounce and expose any false statement of their opponents.[1]

A.H. 35-60. Omeiyad Caliphate favourable to truthful tradition

The Caliphate of 'Alī, after a troubled and doubtful existence of four and a half years, was terminated by assassination, and the opposing faction of the Omeiyads then gained undisputed supremacy. During the long reign of Mu'āwiya, *i.e.* to 60 A.H., and indeed, more or less through-

[1] 'Othmān (when Caliph) commanded, saying: 'It is not permitted to any one to relate a tradition as from the Prophet, which he hath not already heard in the time of Abu Bekr or 'Omar. And verily nothing hinders me from repeating traditions of the Prophet's sayings (although I be one of those endowed with the most retentive memory amongst all his Companions) but that I have heard him say, *Whoever shall repeat of me that which I have not said, his resting-place shall be in Hell.*' This tradition, if well founded, gives pretty clear intimation that, even before 'Othmān's murder, fabricated traditions were propagated by opponents to shake his authority, and that the unfortunate Caliph endeavoured to check the practice by forbidding the currency of traditions not already known in the reign of his two predecessors.

out the Omeiyad rule, the influence of the reigning power directly opposed the interested dogmas of the adherents of Moḥammad's immediate family. The authority of a line deriving its descent from Abu Sufyān, so long the grand opponent of the Prophet, may have softened the asperity of Tradition regarding the conduct of their progenitor, while it aided in the chorus of glory to Moḥammad. But it would be tempted to none of those distorting elements the object of which was to make out a divine right of succession in favour of the descendants of the Founder of Islām ; and which, for that end, invested their heroes with virtues, and attributed to them actions, which never had existence. Such in the process of time were the motives, and such the practice, of the partisans of the houses of 'Alī and of Al-'Abbās, the Son-in-law and Uncle of Moḥammad. In the early part, however, of the Omeiyad succession, these insidious tendencies had but little room for play. The fiction of divine right, even had it been thought of, contradicted too directly the knowledge and convictions of the early Muslims to have met with support. The unqualified opposition of a large section of Moḥammad's most intimate friends to 'Alī himself, shows how little ground there was for regarding him as the peculiar favourite of Heaven. The Khawārij, or sectarians of the theocratic principle and the extreme opponents of the Omeiyads, went the length of condemning and rejecting 'Alī for the scandalous crime of parleying with the denounced Mu'āwiya. It is hence evident that the extravagant pretensions of the 'Alids and 'Abbāsids were not entertained, or even dreamt of, in the early days of the Omeiyad Caliphate.

Type cast in first century, never materially altered

During the first century the main fabric of Tradition grew up, and assumed permanent shape. Towards its close, all surviving traditions began to be systematically sought out, and openly put on record. The type then moulded could not but be maintained, at least in its chief features, ever after. Subsequent sectaries might strive to recast it; their efforts could secure but partial success, because the only standard they possessed had been formed under Omeiyad influence. In the traditional impress of this period, although the features of the Prophet were magnified into majestic and supernatural dimensions, yet the character of his friends and followers, and the general events of early Islām, were undoubtedly preserved with very tolerable accuracy, and thus a broad basis of historical truth maintained.

'Alids and 'Abbāsids conspire to supplant Omeiyad line;

But in the latter part of the first century an undercurrent of great volume and intensity commenced to flow. The adherents of the house of 'Alī, beaten in the field and in all their attempts to dethrone the Omeiyads, were driven to other expedients; and the keystone of their machinations was the divine right of the family of the Prophet to both temporal and spiritual rule. They established secret associations, and sent forth emissaries in every direction, to decry the Omeiyads as godless usurpers, and canvass for the 'Alid pretender of the day. These claims were ever and anon strengthened by the mysterious report that the divine Imām or Leader of 'Alī's race was about to step forth from his hidden recess, and stand confessed the Conqueror of the world. Such attempts, however, issued in no more permanent results than a succession of rebellions, massacres, and fruitless civil wars, until another party leagued themselves in the struggle. These were the 'Abbāsids, who desired to raise to the throne a descendant of the Prophet's uncle, Al-'Abbās. They combined with the 'Alids in denouncing as usurpers the reigning dynasty, which, though sprung from Ḳoreish, was but distantly relating to Moḥammad. By their united endeavours they at length succeeded in supplanting the Omeiyads, when the 'Alids found themselves over-reached, and an 'Abbāsid Caliph was raised to the throne.

And for that object fabricate and pervert tradition

It is not difficult to perceive how much Tradition must have been affected by these unwearied conspirators. Perverted tradition was, in fact, the chief instrument employed to accomplish their ends. By it they blackened the memory of the forefathers of the Omeiyads and exalted the progenitors of the 'Abbāsids. By it they were enabled almost to deify 'Alī, and to assert their principle that the right of empire vested solely in the near relatives of the Prophet, and in their descendants. For these ends no device was spared. The Ḳor'ān was glossed over, and tradition coloured, distorted, and fabricated. Their operations were concealed. Studiously avoiding the eye of anyone likely to oppose them, they canvassed in the dark. Thus they were safe from criticism; and the stories and glosses of their traditional schools gradually acquired the character of presumptive evidence.

In the 132nd year of the Hijra, the 'Abbāsids were installed in the Caliphate; and the factious teaching, which had hitherto flourished only in the distant satrapies of Persia or, when it ventured near the throne, lurked in the purlieus of crowded cities, now stalked forth with the prestige of sovereignty. The Omeiyads were pursued even to extirpation, and their names and descent overwhelmed with obloquy.

Accession of the 'Abbāsids, A.H. 132

It was under the auspices of the first two 'Abbāsid Caliphs that the earliest biography of which we have any remains was composed; that, namely, of IBN ISḤĀḲ. It is cause for little wonder that this author followed in the steps of his patrons; and that, while lauding their ancestors, he sought to stigmatise the Omeiyads and to denounce those of their forefathers who acted a prominent part in the first scenes of Islām.

Under whom first biography of Moḥammad compiled

The fifth Caliph from this period was the famous Al-Ma'mūn who, during a reign of twenty years, countenanced with princely support the pursuits of literature. He effected a combination with the followers of 'Alī who had been bitterly persecuted by his predecessors;[1] and he adopted with enthusiasm the peculiar teaching of the Mo'tazila—a sect whom the learned Weil applauds as the *Rationalists* of Islām. But however freely this Caliph may have derided the doctrine of the 'eternity of the Ḳor'ān,' and in opposition to orthodox believers asserted the freedom of the human will, he was not a whit less bigoted or intolerant than his predecessors. He not only declared 'Alī to be the noblest of mortals, and Mu'āwiya the basest, but he denounced and punished anyone who should venture to speak evil of the one, or attribute good to the other. He made strenuous efforts to impose his theological views upon all. He went so far as to establish even a species of inquisition, and visited with penalties those who dared to differ from him. Unhappily for us, this very reign was the busiest age of the traditional writers, and the period at which (excepting only that of Ibn

Intolerant Caliphate of Al-Ma'mūn. A.H. 198-218

[1] When the 'Abbāsids reached the throne, they cast aside the 'Alid platform from which they had made their fortunate ascent. They were then obliged in self-defence to crush with an iron hand every rising of the 'Alids, who found to their cost that they had become the unconscious tools for raising to power a party which had in reality as little fellow-feeling with them as with the Omeiyads. They deserved their fate.

Its baneful influence on tradition

Isḥāḳ) the earliest extant biographies of Moḥammad were composed. It was under Al-Ma'mūn that AL-WĀḲIDI, IBN HISHĀM, and AL-MADĀ'INI, lived and wrote.[1] Justly, indeed, may we grieve over this as a coincidence fraught with evil to the interests of historical truth. 'We look upon it,' says Weil, 'as a great misfortune, that the very three oldest Arabic histories, which are nearly the only sources of authority for the first period of Islām, were written under the government of Al-Ma'mūn. At a period when every word in favour of Mu'āwiya rendered the speaker liable to death, and when all were declared outlaws who would not acknowledge 'Alī to be the most distinguished of mankind, it was not possible to compose, with even the smallest degree of impartiality, a history of the Companions of Moḥammad and of his successors.'

General collections of tradition made under similar influences

But besides the biographers of Moḥammad, the *Collectors of general tradition*, who likewise flourished at this period, came within the circle of 'Abbāsid influence, and some of them under the direct patronage of Al-Ma'mūn. This class, as shown above, travelled over the whole empire, and searched after every kind of tradition which bore the slightest relation to their Prophet. The mass of narrations gathered by this laborious process was sifted by a pseudo-critical canon, founded on the repute of the narrators forming the chain from Moḥammad downwards; and the approved residuum was published under the authority of the Collector's name. Such collections were far more popular than the biographical or historical treatises. They formed, in fact, and still form, the groundwork of the different theological schools of Islām; and, having been used universally and studied continuously from the period of their appearance, exist to the present day in an authentic and genuine shape. Copies of them abound in all Muslim countries; whereas the early biographies can only be procured with difficulty.

Two schools; *Sunni* and *Shī'a*

The six standard *Sunni* collections were compiled exclusively under the 'Abbāsid Caliphs, and the earliest of them partly during the reign of Al-Ma'mūn. The four canonical collections of the *Shī'a* were prepared somewhat later, and

[1] [The Caliphate of Al-Ma'mūn lasted from 198 to 218 A.H. (813-833 A.D.). Al-Wāḳidi died in 207 A.H., Ibn Hishām in 218, and Al-Madā'ini in 215 or 225 or 231.]

are incomparably less trustworthy than the former, because their paramount object is to build up the divine *Imāma* or headship of 'Alī and his descendants.

[The oldest and one of the best collections of Traditions, although it is not reckoned among the six, is that of the Imām Mālik ibn Anas, of Medīna, who died in the year 179 A.H. (795 A.D.). Many editions of it have appeared, including one lithographed at Fez.]

Service rendered by Collectors

That the Collectors of tradition rendered an important service to Islām, and even to history, cannot be doubted. The vast flood of tradition, poured forth from every quarter of the Muslim empire, and daily gathering volume from innumerable tributaries, was composed of the most heterogeneous elements; without the labours of the traditionists it must soon have formed a chaotic mass in which truth and error, fact and fable, would have mingled together in undistinguishable confusion. It is a legitimate inference from the foregoing sketch, that Tradition in the Second century embraced a large element of truth. That even respectably derived traditions often contained much that was exaggerated and fabulous, is an equally sure conclusion. It is proved by the testimony of the Collectors themselves, that thousands and tens of thousands of traditions were current in their times which possessed not even the shadow of authority.

Immense proportion of fictitious tradition current in second century

The prodigious amount of base and fictitious material may be gathered from the estimate even of Moḥammadan criticism. To quote again from Dr Weil: 'Reliance upon oral traditions, at a time when they were transmitted by memory alone, and every day produced new divisions among the professors of Islām, opened up a wide field for fabrication and distortion. There was nothing easier, when required to defend any religious or political system, than to appeal to an oral tradition of the Prophet.

Rejected even by Moḥammadan Collectors

The nature of these so-called traditions, and the manner in which the name of Moḥammad was abused to support all possible lies and absurdities, may be gathered most clearly from the fact that Al-Bukhāri, who travelled from land to land to gather from the learned the traditions they had received, came to the conclusion, after many years' sifting, that out of 600,000 traditions, ascertained by him to be then current, only 4,000 were authentic! And of this selected number, the European critic is compelled, without hesitation, to reject at least one-half.'[1] Similar appears to have been the experience of other intelligent compilers of the day. Thus Abu Dā'ūd, out of 500,000 traditions which he is said to have amassed, threw aside 495,200, and retained as trustworthy only 4,800.[2]

Anecdote of Al-Bukhāri

The heavenly vision which induced Al-Bukhāri to commence his pious and herculean task is significant of the urgent necessity which then existed for searching out and preserving the grains of truth scattered here and there amid the chaff. 'In a dream I beheld the Messenger of the Lord (Moḥammad), from whom I seemed to be driving off the flies. When I awoke I inquired of an interpreter of dreams the meaning of my vision. *It is*, he replied, *that thou shalt drive away lies far from him*. This it was which induced me to compile the *Ṣaḥīḥ*.'[3] And well, indeed, in the eyes of Moḥammadans, did he fulfil the heavenly behest; for to this day, the ṢAḤIḤ AL-BUKHĀRI is regarded by them as one of the most authentic treasuries of tradition.

Collectors, though unsparing in rejection of untrustworthy traditions, did not discriminate by any intelligent canon

It is evident, then, that some species of criticism was practised by the Collectors; and that, too, so unsparingly that out of every hundred traditions on an average ninety-nine were rejected. But the European reader will be grievously deceived if he at all regards such criticism, rigorous as it was, in the light of a sound and discriminating investigation into the credibility of the traditional elements. It was not the *subject-matter*, but simply the *names* responsible for it, which decided the credit of a tradition. Its authority must rest first on some Companion of the Prophet, and then on the character of each individual in the long chain of witnesses through whom it was handed down.[4] If these were unim-

[1] *Gesch. Chalifen*, ii. 290; *I. Kh.* ii. 595. [A French translation of Al-Bukhāri is in course of publication under the title, *Les Traditions islamiques*, by O. Houdas and W. Marçais, Paris, 1902 f.]

[2] Even of this number a portion is spoken of as doubtful. 'I wrote down,' says Abu Dā'ūd, '500,000 traditions respecting the Prophet, from which I selected those, to the number of 4,800, contained in this book. I have entered herein the authentic, *those which seem to be authentic, and those which are nearly so. Op. cit.* ii. 291; i. 589.

[3] Ṣaḥīḥ means *True*.

[4] Out of 40,000 men, who are said to have been instrumental in handing down Tradition, Al-Bukhāri and Muslim acknowledged the authority of only 2,000 by receiving their traditions. Later Collectors were less scrupulous.

peachable, the tradition *must be received.* No inherent improbability, however glaring, could exclude a narration thus attested from its place in the authentic collections. The compilers would not venture upon the open sea of criticism, but steered slavishly by this single canon. They dared not inquire into internal evidence. To have arraigned the motives of the first author or subsequent rehearsers of a story, discussed its probability and brought it to the test of historical evidence, would have been a strange and uncongenial task. The spirit of Islām would not brook free inquiry and real criticism. Implicit faith in Moḥammad and in his followers spurned the aids of investigation and of evidence. *Thus saith the Prophet of the Lord*, and every rising doubt must be smothered, every question vanish. If doubts did arise, the sword was unsheathed to dispel and silence them. The temporal power was so closely welded with the dogmas of Islām, that it had no option but to enforce with a stern front and iron hand an implicit acquiescence in those dogmas. Upon the apostate Muslim the sentence of death—an award resting on the Prophet's authority—was rigorously executed by the civil power; and between the heterodoxy of the free-thinker, and the lapse of the renegade, there existed but a vague and narrow boundary. To the combination, or rather the *unity*, of the spiritual and political elements in the unvarying type of Moḥammadan government, must be attributed the absence of candid and free investigation into the origin and early incidents of Islām, which so painfully characterises the Muslim mind even to the present day. The faculty of criticism was annihilated by the sword.

Political element of Islām extinguished free inquiry and real criticism

Upon the other hand, there is no reason to doubt that the Collectors were sincere and honest in doing that which they professed to do. It may well be admitted that they sought out in good faith all traditions actually current, inquired carefully into the authorities on which they rested, and recorded them with scrupulous accuracy. The sanctions of religion were at hand to enforce diligence and caution. Thus Al-Bukhāri, who, as we have just seen, commenced his work on a supposed divine monition, was heard to say 'that he never inserted a tradition in his *Ṣaḥīḥ*, until he had made an ablution, and offered up a prayer of two *rak'as*.' The prepossessions of the several Collectors would undoubtedly influ-

But Collectors were honest in accomplishing what they professed ence them in accepting or rejecting the chain of witnesses to any tradition; but there is no reason to suppose that they at all tampered with the traditions themselves. Thus a Shī'a collector would cast aside a tradition received from 'Ā'isha through an Omeiyad channel; whilst one of Omeiyad predilections would discard every traditional chain in the links of which he discovered an emissary of the house of 'Alī. But neither the one nor the other would venture to *fabricate* a tradition; or to tamper with a narration, whatever its purport or bearing might be, if only it were attested by a chain of unexceptionable names.

Guarantees and evidence of their honesty

The honesty of the compilers is warranted by the style and contents of their works. The series of witnesses, by which each tradition is traced up through each stage of transmission to one or other of the Prophet's Companions, is invariably prefixed; and we cannot but admit the authority which even the names of at least the later witnesses in such a chain would impart.[1] These could not be feigned names, but were the names of real characters, many of them personages of note. The traditional collections were openly published, and the credit of the compilers would have been endangered by the fabrication of such evidence. The Collector was likewise, in general, the centre of a school of traditional learning which, as it were, challenged the public to test its authorities. So far, then, as this kind of attestation can give weight to hearsay, that weight may be readily conceded. Again, the simple manner in which the most contradictory traditions are accepted, and placed side by side, is guarantee of sincerity. All that could be collected was thrown together with scrupulous fidelity. Each tradition, though the bare repetition, or possibly the direct opposite, of a dozen preceding it, is noted down unquestioned, with its special chain of witnesses; whilst no account whatever is made of the most violent improbabilities, of incidents plainly fabulous, or even of patent con-

[1] A tradition is always given in the direct form of speech in which it is supposed to have been originally uttered. Thus: 'A informed me, saying that B had spoken to the effect that C had told him, saying D mentioned that he heard E relate that he had listened to F, who said, *I heard G inquiring of 'Ā'isha, "What food did the Prophet of the Lord like?" and she replied, "Verily, he loved sweetmeats and honey, and greatly relished the pumpkin."*'

tradictions.[1] Now this is evidence at least of honest design. Pains would otherwise have been taken to exclude or soften down opposing statements; and we should not have found so much allowed to be credible tradition, which either on the one hand or on the other must have crossed the views and prejudices of the compiler. If we suppose *design*, we must suppose at the same time a less even-handed admission of contrary traditions.

How far do the collections of tradition contain elements of truth?

Conceding, then, the general honesty of the Collectors in making their selection, upon an untenable principle indeed, yet *bonâ fide* from existing materials, let us now turn to their selected compilations, and inquire whether they contain any authentic elements of the life of Moḥammad; and if so, how and to what extent these have become commingled with adventitious or erroneous matter.

Fragmentary and isolated character of each tradition prevents application of ordinary tests

In the first place, how far does the present text afford ground for confidence that its contents are identical with the supposed evidence originally given by contemporary witnesses? To place the case in the strongest point of view, we shall suppose a class of traditions purporting to have been *written down* by the Companions, and to have been recorded afresh at every successive stage of transmission. There is a peculiarity in traditional composition which, even upon this supposition, would render it always of doubtful authority; namely, that each tradition is short and abrupt, and completely isolated from every other. The isolation extends not simply to the traditions themselves as finally compiled by the Collector, but to their whole history and descent throughout the long period preceding their collection. At every point each tradition was completely detached and independent; and this, coupled with the generally brief and fragmentary character of the statements made in them, deprives us of the checks and critical appliances which are brought to bear on a continuous composition. There is little or no context whereby to judge the soundness of a tradition. Each witness in the chain, though professing simply to repeat the words of the first narrator, is in effect an independent

[1] The biographers of Moḥammad, when they relate contradictory or varying narratives, sometimes add an expression of their own opinion as to which is preferable. They also sometimes mark doubtful stories by the addition: 'The Lord knoweth whether this be false or true.'

authority; and we cannot tell how far, and at what stages, variations may or may not have been allowed, or fresh matter interpolated by any of them. Even were we satisfied of the integrity of all the witnesses, we are unacquainted with their views of the liberty with which tradition might be treated. The style of the narrations marks them for the most part as communicated, at the first, with the freedom of social conversation, and with much of the looseness of hearsay; and a similar informality and looseness may have attached to any of the steps in their subsequent transmission.

Each tradition was regarded as a unit, to be accepted or rejected as a whole

Again, each tradition was not only isolated, but was held by the Collectors to be an *indivisible unit*, and as such received or rejected. If the traditional links were unexceptionable, the tradition must be accepted *as it stood*, whole and entire. There could be no sifting of component parts. Whatever in each tradition might be true, and whatever might be fictitious,—the probable and the fabulous,—composed an indissoluble whole; so that the acceptance or rejection of one portion involved the acceptance or rejection of every portion, as equally credible or undeserving of credit. The power of eradicating interpolated words, or of excluding such parts of a tradition as were evidently unfounded or erroneous, was thus renounced. The good seed and the tares were reaped together, and the latter vastly predominated.

Exclusive oral character deprives early tradition of check against error and fabrication

Such is the uncertainty that would attach to tradition, even if we should concede that it had been recorded from the first. But (as we have seen) there is no ground for believing that the practice of writing down traditions was observed in the first days of Islām, or became general until many years, perhaps the greater part of a century, had elapsed. The existence of an early record would have afforded *some* check; but as the facts stand, there is no check at all. A record would have at least fixed the terms in which the evidence was given; whereas tradition purely oral is affected by the character and habits, the associations and the prejudices, of each witness in the chain of repetition. No precaution could hinder the commingling in oral tradition of mistaken or fabricated matter with what at the first may have been trustworthy evidence. The flood-gates of error, exaggeration, and fiction were thrown wide open; and we need only look to the experience of every country and every age, to be satisfied that but little dependence can be placed on the recital of historical incident, and none whatever upon supernatural tales, conveyed for any length of time through such a channel. That Islām forms no exception to the general principle is amply proved by the puerile extravagances and splendid fabrications which adorn or disfigure the pages of its early history. The critical test applied by the Collectors had no reference whatever to these pregnant sources of error; and, though it may have rejected multitudes of the more recent fabrications, it failed to place the earlier traditions upon any certain basis, or to supply the means of discerning between the actual and the fictitious, the offspring of the imagination and the sober evidence of fact.

Tradition as tested by Ḳor'ān

It remains to examine the traditional collections with reference to their contents and internal probability. And here we fortunately have in the Ḳor'ān a standard of comparison which has been already proved a genuine and contemporary document.

Main historical and biographical outlines agree

We find accordingly that in its main historical outlines the Ḳor'ān is at one with the received traditional collections. It notices, either directly or incidentally, those topics which, from time to time, most interested Moḥammad; and with these salient points, tradition is found upon the whole to tally. The statements and allusions of this description in the Ḳor'ān, though themselves comparatively few, are linked more or less with a vast variety of important incidents which refer as well to the Prophet individually and his domestic relations, as to public events and the progress of Islām. A just confidence is thus imparted that a large amount of historical truth has been conveyed by tradition.

Disagreement in certain important points, as power to work miracles

Upon the other hand, there are subjects in which the Kor'ān is at variance with Tradition. For example, there is no position more satisfactorily established by the Ḳor'ān than that Moḥammad did not in any part of his career perform miracles, or lay claim to the power of performing them. Yet tradition abounds with miraculous acts belying the plain declaration of the Ḳor'ān. Moreover, such miracles, if at all based on fact, would undoubtedly have been mentioned in the Ḳor'ān itself, which omits nothing, however trivial, calculated to strengthen the prophetical claim. Here, therefore, in matters of simple narration and historical incident, we find tradition discredited by the Ḳor'ān.

Perplexing alternative

The result of the comparison, then, is precisely that already arrived at, *a priori*, from the foregoing historical review. But though it strengthens our conclusion, the comparison does not afford us much help in the practical treatment of Tradition itself. Excepting in a limited number of events, it furnishes us with no rule for eliminating falsehood. Facts which we know from the Ḳor'ān to be well founded, and tales which we know to be fabricated, are indiscriminately woven together; and of both the fabric and colour are so uniform, that we are at a loss for any means of distinguishing the one from the other. The biographer of Moḥammad continually runs the risk of substituting for the realities of history some puerile fancy or extravagant invention. In striving to avoid this danger he is exposed to the opposite peril of rejecting as pious fabrication what may in reality be important historical fact.

Opinion of Sprenger too favourable to tradition

It is, indeed, the opinion of Sprenger that 'although the nearest view of the Prophet which we can obtain is at a distance of one hundred years,' and although this long vista is formed of a medium exclusively Moḥammadan, yet our knowledge of the bias of the narrators 'enables us to correct the media, and to make them almost achromatic.'[1] The remark is true to some extent; but its full application would carry us much beyond the truth. The difficulties of the task cannot without danger be underrated. To bring to a right focus the various lights of Tradition, to reject those that are fictitious, to restore to a proper direction the rays reflected by a false and deceptive surface, to calculate the extent of aberration, and make due allowance for a thousand disturbing influences;—this is indeed a work of entanglement and complication, which would require for its perfect accomplishment a finer discernment, and deeper analytic power, than human nature can boast. Nevertheless, it is right that an attempt should be made, and it is possible that, by a comprehensive consideration of the subject, and careful discrimination of the several sources of error, we may reach at the least a fair approximation to the truth. With this view I will endeavour to lay down some principles which

Attempt to frame tests discriminating what is reliable in tradition

[1] *Sprenger's Mohammad*, p. 68.

may prove useful to the inquirer in separating the true from the false in Moḥammadan tradition.

Traditional evidence *ex parte.* Tests must depend on internal examination

The grand defect in the traditional evidence consists in its being wholly *ex parte.* It is the statement of witnesses, in which the license of partiality and self-interest is unchecked by any opposing party, and the sanction even of a neutral audience is wanting. But what is thus defective in the process, may in some measure be corrected or repaired by close scrutiny of the record. By analysing the evidence, and considering the position and qualifications of the witnesses, we may find internal grounds for credit or for doubt; while, in reference to some classes of statements, it may even appear that a Muslim public would itself supply the place of an impartial censor. In this view, the points on which the probability of a tradition will mainly depend appear to be *first,* whether there existed a bias in the mind of the nation at large on the subject narrated; *second,* whether there are traces of any special interest, prejudice, or design, on the part of the narrator; and *third,* whether the narrator had opportunity for personally knowing the facts. These topics will perhaps best be discussed by considering the *Period* to which a narration relates, and then the *Subject* of which it treats.

Two divisions; *period* and *subject* of events narrated

I. PERIOD. *First.*—Before Moḥammad's entry on public life. Witnesses younger, most of them much younger, than Moḥammad

I. A.—The PERIOD to which a tradition purports to refer is a point of vital importance. The original authors of all reliable tradition were the *Companions* of Moḥammad himself. But Moḥammad was above threescore years old when he died; and few of his then surviving Companions, from whom tradition has come down, were of equal age,—hardly any of them older. In proportion to their years, the number of aged men was small and the period short during which they outlived Moḥammad; and these are precisely the considerations by which their influence, in the formation of tradition, must be limited also. The great majority were young; and in proportion to their youth was the number that survived longest, and gave the deepest impress to tradition.[1] We may, then, fix the term of Moḥammad's

[1] Abu Bekr, for instance, was within two years of Moḥammad's age; but then he survived him only two-and-a-half years. Most of the elderly Companions either died a natural death, or were killed in action before

own life as the extreme backward limit within which our witnesses range themselves. In other words, we have virtually no original witnesses who lived at a period anterior to Moḥammad; few, if any, were born before him; the great majority, many years after him. They are not, therefore, trustworthy authorities for events preceding Moḥammad's birth, or for details of his childhood; few of them, even, for the incidents of his youth. They could not by any possibility possess a personal knowledge of these things; and to admit that they gained their information at second-hand is to impair the value of their testimony as that of contemporary witnesses.

Personal knowledge cannot go farther back than his youth at earliest

Attention not attracted till Moḥammad had publicly assumed prophetic office

B.—Again, the value of evidence depends upon the degree in which the facts were noticed by the witness at the time of their occurrence. If attention was not specially attracted, it would be in vain to expect a full and careful report; and after the lapse of many years, the utmost that could be looked for would be a bare general outline. This principle applies forcibly to the biography of Moḥammad up to the time when he became the prominent leader of a party. Before, there was nothing remarkable about him. A poor orphan, a quiet, inoffensive citizen, he was perhaps of all the inhabitants of Mecca the least likely to have the eyes of his neighbours turned upon him, and their memory and imagination busy in noting the events of his life, and conjuring up anticipations of coming greatness. The remark may be extended, not merely to the era when he first laid claim to inspiration (for that excited the regard of a few only among his earliest adherents); but to the entire interval preceding the period when he stood forth *publicly* to assume the prophetic rank, oppose polytheism, and enter into open collision with the chiefs of Mecca. Then, indeed, he began to be narrowly watched; and thenceforward the Companions of the Prophet are not to be distrusted on the score at least of insufficient attention.

the practice of tradition came into vogue. Thus Al-Wāḳidi: 'The reason why many of the chief men of the Companions have left few traditions, is that they died before there was any necessity for referring to them. The chiefest among the Companions, Abu Bekr, 'Othmān, Ṭalḥa, &c., gave forth fewer traditions than others. *There did not issue from them anything like the number of traditions that did from the younger Companions.*'

C.—It follows that, in traditions affected by either of the foregoing rules, circumstantiality will be a strong token of fabrication. And we shall do well to adopt the analogous canon of Christian criticism, that any tradition whose origin is not strictly contemporary with the facts related *is worthless exactly in proportion to the particularity of detail.*[1] This will relieve us of a vast number of extravagant stories, in which the minutiæ of close narrative and sustained colloquy in early passages of the Prophet's life are preserved with the pseudo-freshness of yesterday.

For events prior to Moḥammad's public life circumstantiality ground of suspicion

D.—It will, however, be just to admit an exception for the main outlines of Moḥammad's life, which under ordinary circumstances his friends and acquaintance would naturally remember or might learn from himself, and would thus be able in after days to call up with tolerable accuracy. Such, for instance, are the death of his father, his nurture as an infant by the Beni Sa'd, his mother's journey with him to Medīna, and the expedition with his uncle to Syria while yet a boy. A still wider exception must be allowed in favour of public personages and national events, even preceding Moḥammad's birth; because the attention of the people at large would be actively directed to these topics, while the patriarchal habits of the Arabs and their spirit of clanship would be propitious to tenacious recollection. Thus the conversation of Moḥammad's grandfather with Abraha, the Abyssinian invader, is far more likely to be founded on fact than any of the much later conversations which Moḥammad himself is said to have had with the monks on either of his journeys to Syria; and yet the leading facts regarding these journeys there is no reason to doubt.

Exception in favour of leading outlines of Moḥammad's life

Public events,

Under the same exception will fall those genealogical and historical facts, the preservation of which for several centuries by the memory alone, is so wonderful a phenomenon in the story of Arabia. Here poetry, no doubt, aided the retentive

And national history

[1] The remarks of Alford are strikingly in point: 'As usual in traditional matter, on our advance to later writers, we find more and more particular accounts given; the year of John's life, the reigning Emperor, &c., under which the Gospel was written.' *Greek Test. Proleg.* p. 56. But Christian traditionists were mere tyros in the art of discovering such particulars in comparison with Muslims, at the talisman of whose pen distance vanishes, and even centuries deliver up the minutest details which they had engulfed.

faculty. The rhapsodies of the bard were at once caught up by his admiring clan, and soon passed into the mouths even of the children. In such poetry were preserved the names of the chieftains, their feats of bravery, their glorious liberality, the unparalleled nobility of their breeds of camel and horse. Many of these odes became national, and carried with them the testimony, not of the tribe alone, but of the whole Arab family. Thus poetry, the passion for genealogical and tribal reminiscences, and the singular capacity of imprinting them indelibly on the memory for generations, have secured to us the interwoven details of many centuries with a minuteness and particularity that would excite suspicion were not their reality in many instances established by other evidence and by internal coincidence.[1]

Second period.—From entrance on public life to taking of Mecca, *i.e.* B.H. 10 to A.H. 8

E.—A second marked section of time is that which intervenes between Moḥammad's entrance on public life and the taking of Mecca. Here, indeed, we have two opposing parties, marshalled against each other in mortal strife, whose statements might have been a check one upon the other. But during this interval (*i.e.* for some 18 years), or very shortly after, one of the parties came wholly to an end. Its chief leaders were nearly all killed in battle, and the remainder went over to the victors. We have therefore no surviving evidence whatever on the side of the Prophet's enemies. Not a single advocate was left to explain their actions, often misrepresented by hatred, or to rebut the accusations of Moḥammad and his followers. On the other hand, we have no witnesses of any kind against Moḥammad

No surviving evidence on side of Meccans; or against Moḥammad and his party

[1] M. Caussin de Perceval, who, with incredible labour, has sought out and arranged these facts into a uniform history, thus expresses his estimate of the Arab genealogical traditions: 'J'ai dit que toutes les généalogies arabes n'étaient point certaines; on en trouve en effet un grand nombre d'évidemment incomplètes. Mais il en est aussi beaucoup d'authentiques, et qui remontent, sans lacune probable, jusqu'à environ six siècles avant Mahomet. C'est un phénomène vraiment singulier chez un peuple inculte et en général étranger à l'art de l'écriture, comme l'étaient les Arabes, que cette fidélité à garder le souvenir des ancêtres. Elle prenait sa source dans un sentiment de fierté, dans l'estime qu'ils faisaient de leur noblesse. Les noms de aïeux, gravés dans la mémoire des enfants, étaient les archives des familles À ces noms se rattachaient nécessairement quelques notions sur la vie des individus, sur les événements dans lesquels ils avaient figuré; et c'est ainsi que les traditions se perpétuaient d'âge en âge.'—*Essai sur l'Histoire des Arabes*, I. p. ix.

and his party, whose one-sided assertions might perhaps otherwise have been often liable to question. The intemperate and unguarded language of the fathers of tradition is sufficient proof that, in speaking of adversaries, their opinion was seldom impartial, and their judgment not always unerring.

To what degree Meccan party, as finally incorporated with Muslim, proved a check upon misrepresentation

F.—It may be urged in reply that the great body of the hostile Meccans who eventually went over to Islām would still form a check upon any material misrepresentation of their party. It may be readily admitted that they did form some check on the perversion of public opinion in matters not vitally connected with the credit of Islām and its Founder. Their influence would also tend to preserve the reports of their own individual actions, and perhaps those of their friends and relatives, in as favourable a light as possible. But this influence at best was partial. It must be borne in mind that the enemies of the Prophet who now joined his ranks acquired at the same time, or very shortly after, all the *esprit de corps* of Islām.[1] And, long before the stream of tradition commenced, these very men had learned to look back upon the heathenism of their own career at Mecca with horror and contempt. The stains of a Believer's previous life were, on his conversion, washed away, and imparted no tarnish to his subsequent character. He had sinned 'ignorantly in unbelief'; but now, both in his own view and in the eyes of his comrades, he was *another man*. He might now, therefore, well speak of his mad opposition to 'the Prophet of the Lord' and the divine message, with as hearty a reprobation as others; nay, the violence of reaction might make his language even stronger. Such are the witnesses who constitute our only check upon the *ex parte* story told of the long struggle with the idolaters of Mecca.

Evidence against opponents of Moḥammad to be received with caution

G.—It is therefore incumbent upon us, in estimating the folly, injustice, and cruelty of the Unbelievers at Mecca, to make much allowance for the hostile tendency of the evidence. On the other hand, looking to the merit of suffering for the faith, we may suspect exaggeration in the tales of hardship and persecution endured by Believers at their hands.

[1] Thus Abu Sufyān, leader in the last stage of opposition to Moḥammad, became shortly after a zealous Muslim, and fought under the banners of his own son in the first Syrian campaign.

Above all, the history of those who died in unbelief, before the conquest of Mecca, and under the ban of Moḥammad, must be subject to a rigid criticism. For such men as Abu Jahl and Abu Lahab, hated and cursed by the Prophet, what Believer dare be the advocate? To the present day, the hearty ejaculation, *The Lord curse him!* is linked by every Muslim with the name of those 'enemies of the Lord, and of his Prophet.' What voice would be raised to correct the pious exaggerations of the faithful in the stories of their execrable deeds, or to point out just causes of provocation which they may have received? Impious attempt, and mad perversity! Again and again was the sword of 'Omar brandished over the neck of a luckless offender for conduct far more excusable and far less offensive to Islām.

So also with Jewish, Christian, and Pagan tribes of Arabia

H.—Precisely similar limitations must be brought to bear on the evidence against the Jewish inhabitants in the vicinity of Medīna, whom Moḥammad either expatriated, brought over to his faith, or utterly extirpated. The various Arab tribes also, whether Christian or Pagan, whom Moḥammad at different times of his life attacked, come more or less under the same category.

Similar considerations apply to disaffected inhabitants of Medīna

I. The same considerations apply also, though in a modified form, to the 'Hypocrites,' or disaffected population of Medīna, who covertly opposed the claim of Moḥammad to temporal authority over that city. The Prophet did not wage the same war of defiance with these as he did with his Meccan opponents, but sought to counteract their influence by skilful tactics. Neither was this class so suddenly rooted out as the idolaters of Mecca; they rather vanished gradually before the increasing authority of Islām. Still its leaders are held in abhorrence by the traditionists, and the historian must keep a jealous eye on the testimony against them.

II. SUBJECT-MATTER; *personal*, *party*, or *national* bias

II.—THE SUBJECT-MATTER of tradition itself, both as regards the motives of its authors and the views of early Muslim society at large, will help us to an estimate of its credibility. The chief aspects in which this argument may be treated refer to *personal*, *party*, and *national* bias.

1. *Personal* ambition of being associated with Moḥammad

A.—*Individual* prepossession and self-interested motives would cause exaggeration, false colouring, and even invention. Besides the more obvious cases falling under this head, there is a fertile class which originates in the ambition of the narrator to be associated with Moḥammad. The name of the Prophet threw a halo around every object connected with it; while his friendship imparted a rank and dignity acknowledged by the universal voice of Islām. It is difficult to conceive the reverence and court enjoyed by his widows, friends, and servants. Interminable inquiries were put to them; and their responses received with implicit deference. All who possessed personal knowledge of the Prophet, and especially those who had been honoured with his familiar acquaintance, were admitted by common consent into the envied circle of Muslim aristocracy; and many a picturesque scene is sketched by traditionists of the crowds which listened to these men as they delivered their testimony in the Mosques of Al-Kūfa or Damascus. The sterling value of such qualifications would induce imitation. Some who may have had but a distant and superficial knowledge of Moḥammad would be tempted, by the consideration it imparted, to counterfeit a more perfect intimacy; and the endeavour to support their equivocal position by particularity of detail would lead the way to loose and unfounded narratives of the life and character of the Prophet. Equally misleading was the ambition, traceable throughout the traditions of Companions, of being closely connected with any of the supposed mysterious visitations or supernatural actions of Moḥammad. To have been *noticed* in the Revelation was the highest honour that mortal man could aspire to; and in any way having been linked with the heavenly phases of the Prophet's life, reflected a divine lustre on the fortunate aspirant.[1] Thus a premium was put upon the invention or exaggeration of superhuman incidents.

Exaggeration of personal merit in the service of Moḥammad

B.—Under the same head are to be classed the attempts of narrators to exaggerate their labours and exploits, and to multiply their losses and perils in the service of the Prophet. The tendency thus to appropriate a special, and often an altogether unwarrantable, merit is obvious on the part of

[1] Thus 'Ā'isha's party having been long delayed when with the Prophet on a certain expedition, the verse permitting the substitution of sand for lustration was in consequence revealed. The honour conferred upon her father by this indirect connection with a divine revelation is thus eulogised: 'This is not the least of the divine favours poured out upon you, ye house of Abu Bekr!'

many of the Companions.[1] A reference to this tendency may even occasionally tend to exculpate the Prophet from questionable actions. For example, Ibn Omeiya, in narrating his mission by Moḥammad to assassinate Abu Sufyān, so magnifies the dangers and exploits of his adventure as might have involved that dark mission itself in suspicion, were there not collateral proof to support it.

Small chance of exaggerations and fictions being checked

It may be objected,—Would not untrue or exaggerated tales like these receive a check from other parties, free from the interested motives of the narrator? They would to some extent. But to prove a negative position is generally difficult, and it would not often be attempted without some strong impelling cause, especially in the early spread of Islām, when the public mind was in the highest degree impressible and credulous. Such traditions, then, were likely to be opposed only when they interfered with the private claims of others, or ran counter to public opinion, in which case they would fall into discredit and disuse. Other-

[1] We have many examples of the glory and honour lavished upon those who had suffered persecution. Thus when 'Omar was Caliph, Khabbāb showed him the scars of the stripes he had received from the unbelieving Meccans twenty or thirty years before. 'Omar seated him upon his couch, saying that there was but one man more worthy of this favour than Khabbāb (as having been also tortured), namely, Bilāl. But Khabbāb replied : 'And why is he more worthy? He had his friends among the idolaters whom the Lord raised up to help him. But I had none. I well remember one day they kindled a fire, and threw me therein upon my back ; and a man stamped with his foot upon my chest, my back being all the while upon the ground. And when they uncovered my back, lo ! it was blistered and white.'

The same principle led the Muslims to magnify the hardships which *Moḥammad himself* endured ; such as 'Ā'isha's strange exaggeration of the Prophet's poverty and frequent starvation, which she carries so far as to say that she had not even oil to burn in her chamber while Moḥammad lay dying there. The subsequent affluence and luxury of the conquering nation, also, led them by reaction fondly to contrast it with their former simplicity and want, and even to weep at the remembrance. Thus of the same Khabbāb it is recorded : He had his winding-sheet made ready of fine Coptic cloth ; he compared it with the wretched pall of Ḥamza (killed at Oḥod), and contrasted his own poverty when he possessed not a dīnār, with his present condition : 'and now I have in my chest by me in the house 40,000 pieces of gold. Verily, I fear that the sweets of the present world have hastened upon us. Our companions have received their reward in Paradise ; but truly I dread lest my reward consist in these benefits I have obtained after their departure.'

wise they would be carried down upon the traditional stream of mingled legend and truth, and with it find a place in the unquestioning record of the Second century.

C.—We have undoubted evidence that the bias of PARTY effected a deep and abiding impress upon tradition. Where this spirit tended to produce or embellish a tale adverse to the interests of another party, and the denial of the facts involved nothing prejudicial to the honour of Islām, endeavour might be made to rebut the fictitious statement, and the discussion so produced would subserve the purity of tradition. But this could seldom occur. The tradition would often affect that section alone in whose favour it originated, and therefore would not be controverted. The story would probably at the first be confined within the limits of the party which it concerned, and no opportunity afforded for its contradiction until it had taken root and acquired a prescriptive claim. Under any circumstances, the considerations advanced in the preceding paragraph are equally applicable here; so that without doubt a vast collection of exaggerated tales have come down to us, owing their existence to party spirit.

2. *Party.* Party traditions come into general currency

By the bias of party is not to be understood simply the influence of faction, but likewise the partiality and prejudice of lesser circles forming the ramifications of Muslim society. The former we are less in danger of overlooking. Where the full development of faction laid bare the passions and excesses to which it gave rise, the reader is on his guard against misrepresentation; he receives with caution the darkened or resplendent phases of such characters as 'Alī and Al-'Abbās, Mu'āwiya and Abu Sufyān. But, though on a less extensive scale, the influences of tribe, family, and the smaller associations of party clustering around the several heroes of Islām, were equally real and effective. The spirit of clanship, which ran so high among the Arabs that Mohammad endeavoured in vain at Medīna to supplant it by a so-called 'Brotherhood,' perpetuated the confederacies and antipathies of ante-Moḥammadan Arabia far down into the annals of Islām, and often exerted, as in the rivalries of the Ḳeis and Moḍar Clans, a potent influence upon the destinies of the Caliphate itself. It cannot be doubted that these combinations and prejudices imparted a strong and

Prejudicial influence of such associations as Tribe, Family, Patron. &c.

often a deceptive hue to the sources of tradition. As an example, may be specified the rivalry which led the several families or parties to claim the earliest converts to Islām until in the competition they arrived at the conclusion, and consequently propagated the tradition, that some of their patrons or ancestors were Muslims before Moḥammad himself.

3. *National* bias; common to whole of Islām; therefore most fatal

D.—We now come to the class of motives incomparably the most dangerous to the purity of Tradition, namely, those which were *common to the whole Muslim body.* In the previous cases the bias was confined to a fragment, and the remainder of the nation might form a check upon the fractional aberration. But here the bias was universal, pervading the *entire medium* through which we have received tradition, and leaving us, for the correction of its divergencies, no check whatever.

Tendency to exalt Moḥammad, and ascribe to him supernatural attributes

To this class must be assigned all traditions the object of which is to glorify Moḥammad, and to invest him with supernatural attributes. Although in the Ḳor'ān the Prophet disclaims the power of working miracles, yet he implies that there existed a continuous intercourse between himself and the agencies of the other world. The whole Ḳor'ān, indeed, assumes to be a message from the Almighty, communicated through Gabriel. Besides being the medium of revelation, that favoured angel is often referred to as bringing directions from the Lord for the guidance of his Prophet in the common concerns of life. Familiar intercourse with heavenly messengers, thus countenanced by the Prophet, was implicitly believed by his followers, and led them even during his lifetime to regard him with superstitious awe. On a subject so impalpable to sense and so congenial with imagination, it may be fairly assumed that reason had little share in controlling the fertile productions of fancy; that the conclusions of his susceptible and credulous followers far exceeded the premises granted by Moḥammad; that even simple facts were construed by excited faith as pregnant with supernatural power and unearthly companionship; and that, after the object of their veneration had passed from their sight, fond devotion perpetuated and enhanced the fascinating legends. If the Prophet gazed into the heavens, or looked wistfully to the right hand or to the left, it was Gabriel with whom he was holding mysterious converse. Passing gusts raised a cloud from the sandy track; the pious Believer exulted in the conviction that it was the dust of the Archangel with his mounted squadrons scouring the plain, as they went before them to shake the foundations of some doomed fortress. On the field of Bedr, three stormy blasts swept over the marshalled army; again, it was Gabriel with a thousand horse flying to the succour of Moḥammad, while Michael and Seraphil each with a like angelic troop wheeled to the right and to the left of the Muslim front. Nay, the very dress and martial uniform of these helmed angels are detailed by the earliest and most trustworthy biographers with as much *naïveté* as if they had been veritable warriors of flesh and blood; while the heads of the enemy were seen to drop off before the Muslim swords had even touched them, because the unseen scimitars did the work more swiftly than the grosser steel of Medīna! Such is the specimen of the vein of legend and extravagance which runs throughout even the purest sources of tradition.

Difficulty of discriminating what originated with Moḥammad in such tales

It will frequently be a question, extremely difficult to decide, what portions of these supernatural stories either originated in Moḥammad himself, or received his countenance; and what portion owed its birth, after he was gone, to the excited imagination of his followers. No doubt, facts have not seldom been adorned or distorted by a superstitious fancy. The subjective conceptions of the fond believer have been reflected back upon the biography of the Prophet, and have encircled even the realities of his life, like the figures of our saints, with a lustrous halo. The false colouring and fictitious light so deluge the picture, as often to place its details altogether beyond the reach of analytical criticism.[1]

Miracles

E.—To the same universal desire of glorifying their Prophet, must be ascribed the miraculous tales with which even the earliest biographies abound. They are such as the

[1] The corpse of Sa'd ibn Mo'ādh lay in an empty room. Moḥammad entered alone, picking his steps carefully, as if he walked in the midst of men seated closely on the ground. On being asked the cause, he replied: 'True, there were no men in the room, but it was so filled with angels, all seated on the ground, that I found nowhere to sit down, until one of the angels spread out his wing for me on the ground, and I sat thereon' It is almost impossible to say what in this is Moḥammad's own, and what has been concocted for him. Other supernatural tales connected with the same occasion will be seen below.

following: A tree from a distance moves towards the Prophet, ploughing up the earth as it advances, and then similarly retires; oft-repeated attempts at murder are miraculously averted; distant occurrences are instantaneously revealed, and future events foretold; a large company is fed from victuals hardly adequate for the supply of a single person; prayer draws down immediate showers from heaven, or causes their equally sudden cessation. A frequent class of miracles is for the Prophet to touch the udders of dry goats which immediately distend with milk; or to make floods of water well up from parched fountains, gush forth from empty vessels, or issue from betwixt his fingers. With respect to all such stories, it is sufficient to say that they are opposed to the clear declarations and pervading sense of the Ḳor'ān.[1]

That it mentions a miracle does not altogether discredit a tradition

It by no means, however, follows that, because a tradition relates a miracle, the collateral incidents are thereby discredited. It may be that the facts were fabricated to illustrate or embellish a popular miracle; but it is also possible that the miracle was invented to adorn, or to account for, well founded facts. In the former case, the supposed facts are worthless; in the latter, they may be true and valuable. In the absence of other evidence, the main drift and apparent design of the narrative is all that can here guide the critic.

Tales and legends, how far ascribable to Moḥammad

F.—The same propensity to fabricate the marvellous must be borne in mind when we peruse the childish tales and extravagant legends put by tradition into the mouth of Moḥammad. The Ḳor'ān, it is true, imparts a far wider basis of likelihood to the narration by Moḥammad of such tales, than to his assumption of miraculous powers. When the Prophet ventured to place such fanciful fictions as those of 'Solomon and the Genii,'[2] of 'The Seven Sleepers,'[3] or 'The Adventures of Dhu'l-Ḳarnein,'[4] in the pages of a *divine* Revelation, to what puerilities might he not stoop in the familiarity of social converse! It must, on the other hand, be remembered that Moḥammad was taciturn, laconic, and reserved, and is therefore not likely to have given forth more than an infinitesimal part of the masses of legend and fable which tradition represents as gathered from his lips. These

[1] *Cf.* esp. xiii. 27 ff.; xvii. 92 ff.
[2] xxvii. 16 ff. [3] xviii. 8 ff. [4] xviii. 82 ff.

are probably the growth of successive ages, each of which added its contribution to the nucleus of the Prophet's pregnant words, if indeed there ever was such a nucleus at all. For example, the germ of the elaborate pictures, and gorgeous scenery of the Prophet's heavenly journey lies in a very short and simple recital in the Ḳor'ān.[1] That he subsequently expanded this germ, and entertained or edified his Companions with the minutiæ which have been brought down to us by tradition, is *possible*. But it is also possible, and (by the analogy of Moḥammad's miracles) far more probable, that the vast majority of these fancies have no other origin than the heated imagination of the early Muslims.[2]

Supposed anticipations of Moḥammad by Jews and Christians

G.—Connected indirectly with Moḥammad's life, but more immediately with the foundations of Islām, is another class of narrations which would conjure up on all sides prophecies regarding the Founder of the faith and anticipations of his approach. These probably, for the most part, depended upon some general declaration or incidental remark of the Prophet himself, which his enthusiastic followers deemed themselves bound to prove and illustrate. For example, the Jews are often accused in the Ḳor'ān of wilfully rejecting Moḥammad, although, in point of fact, 'they recognised him as they did one of their own sons.'[3] Tradition provides us, accordingly, with an array of Jewish rabbins and Christian monks, who found it written in their books that the last of the Prophets was at this time about to arise at Mecca, and asserted that not only his name, but appearance, manners, and character were therein depicted to the life, so that recognition could not but be certain and instantaneous; and among other particulars, that the very city of *Medīna* was named as the place where he would take refuge from the persecution of his people. Again, the Jews are in the Ḳor'ān accused of grudging that a Prophet should arise among the Arabs, and that their nation should thus be robbed of its prophetic dignity; and so, in fit illustration, we have repeated

[1] xvii. i.

[2] Sprenger holds that the narrative, in its main features emanated from Moḥammad himself, because (says he) *There is no event in his life, on which we have more numerous and genuine traditions than on his night journey.* The fact is significant, but the conclusion doubtful.

[3] ii. 141; vi. 20.

stories of Moḥammad having been recognised by the rabbins, and of attempts made by them to kill him; and this, too, long before he had any suspicion himself that he was to be a prophet, nay *during his very infancy!* It is enough to have alluded to this class of fabrications.

Anticipations of Islām

H.—Such unblushing inventions will lead us to treat with caution the whole series of tales in which it is pretended that Moḥammad and his religion were *foreshadowed*, so that pious men anticipated, long before the Prophet arose, many of the peculiar rites and doctrines of Islām. It was a fond conceit of Moḥammad that Islām is as old as Adam, and has been from the beginning the faith of all good men, who looked forward to him as the Prophet charged with winding up all previous dispensations. It was therefore natural for his credulous followers to carry out this idea, and to invest the memory of any serious-minded man or earnest inquirer who preceded Moḥammad with some of the dawning rays of the divine effulgence about to burst upon the world.

History of ancestors, and early Arabia, borrowed from Jews

I.—To the same spirit we may attribute the palpable endeavour to make Moḥammadan tradition and the legends of Arabia *tally with the Scriptures of the Old Testament, and with Jewish tradition.* This canon has little application to the biography of Moḥammad himself, but it has a wide and most effective range in reference to the legendary history of his ancestors and of early Arabia. The desire to regard the Prophet of Islām as a descendant of Ishmael, and possibly the endeavour to prove it, began even in his lifetime. Many Jews, versed in the Scriptures, and won over by the inducements of Islām, placed themselves at the service of Moḥammad and his followers. Jewish tradition had long been well known in Medīna and in the countries over which Islām early spread, and the Muslim system was now made to fit upon it; for Islām did not ignore, but professed merely to supersede, Judaism and Christianity, as the whole does a part, or rather as that which is complete swallows up the inchoate. Hence arose such strange anachronisms as the attempt to identify Ḳaḥṭān with Joktan[1] (between whom, at the most moderate estimate, fifteen centuries intervene); and thus also were cast the earlier links of the Abrahamic genealogy of Moḥammad, as well as numberless tales of Ishmael and the

[1] Gen. x. 25 f.

Israelites, all in a semi-Jewish semi-Arab mould. These, though professing to be original traditions, can generally be recognised as mere plagiarisms from rabbinical lore, or as Arabian legends forced into accommodation with them.

Traditions as to Jewish and Christian Scriptures being mutilated and interpolated

J—Of analogous nature may be classed such traditions as affirm that Jews and Christians mutilated or interpolated their Scriptures. After repeated examination of the Ḳor'ān, I have been unable to discover any grounds for believing that Moḥammad himself ever expressed a doubt in regard either to the authority or the genuineness of the Old and New Testaments, as extant in his time.[1] He was profuse in assurances that his system was in close correspondence with both, and that he had been foretold by former prophets. As compliant Jews and Christians were at hand to confirm his words, and as the Bible was little known among the generality of his followers, these assurances were implicitly believed. But as Islām spread abroad and began to include countries where the Holy Scriptures were familiarly read, the discrepancies between them and the Ḳor'ān became patent. The sturdy believer, with an easy conscience, laid the blame at the door of the dishonest Jews and Christians, the former of whom their Prophet had accused in the Ḳor'ān of 'hiding' and 'dislocating' the prophecies regarding himself; and, according to Muslim wont, a host of stories with details of Jewish fabrication soon grew up, exactly suited to the charge.[2]

Why such extravagant and unfounded traditions not contradicted

If it appear strange that extravagant and unreasonable tales of the kind described in the last few paragraphs should not have been contradicted by the more upright and reasonable Muslims of the first age, and thus nipped in the bud, it must be remembered that criticism and freedom of opinion were stifled under the crushing dogmas of Islām. Any

[1] The reader will find all passages of the Ḳor'ān relating to the Scriptures in a little work called *The Coran and the Testimony it bears to the Holy Scriptures*, published by the S.P.C.K. [Passages which seem to infer the contrary are iv. 48; 'Some of the Jews pervert the words from their proper places,' etc.]

[2] As examples, take the following. A Copt, reading his uncle's Bible, was struck by finding two leaves closely glued together. On opening them, he discovered copious details regarding Moḥammad, as a Prophet immediately about to appear. His uncle was displeased at his curiosity and beat him, saying that the Prophet had not yet arisen.

simpleton might fancy, and every designing man could with ease invent, such tales; when once current, the attempt to disprove them would be difficult and dangerous. Supposing that they contradicted no well-known fact or received dogma, by what arguments were they to be rebutted? If anyone had contended that human experience was opposed to the marvellous foreknowledge of the Jews regarding the person of Moḥammad, he would have been scouted as an infidel. Honest inquiry, such as might touch the foundations of Islām, was not tolerated. Who would dare to argue that the ascription of a miracle to Moḥammad was in itself improbable, that the narrator might have laboured under a false impression, or that in the Ḳor'ān itself miraculous powers were disclaimed by the Prophet? The argument would have placed the neck of the honest inquirer in jeopardy; for it has been already shown that the faith and the polity of Islām were one, and that free opinions and heresy were synonymous with conspiracy, treason, and rebellion.[1] And thus, under the shelter of the civil arm and the fanatical credulity of the people, these marvellous legends grew up in perfect security from the attacks of doubt and of rational inquiry.

Traditions unfavourable to Moḥammad become obsolete

K.—The converse is likewise true; that is to say, traditions, founded upon good evidence, and undisputed because notorious in the first days of Islām, gradually fell into disrepute, or were entirely rejected, because they appeared to dishonour Moḥammad or countenance some heretical opinion. The nature of the case renders it impossible to prove this position so fully as the preceding, since

[1] Take as an illustration the following. On the expedition to Tebūk, Moḥammad prayed for rain, which accordingly descended. A perverse doubter, however, said: 'It was but a chance cloud that happened to pass.' Shortly after, the Prophet's camel strayed; again the doubter said: 'Doth not Moḥammad deem himself a Prophet? He professeth to bring intelligence from the Heavens; yet is he unable to tell where his own camel is!' 'Ye servants of the Lord!' exclaimed his comrade, 'There is a plague in this place, and I knew it not. Get out from my tent, enemy of the Lord! Wretch, remain not in my presence!' Moḥammad had, of course, in due time, *supernatural* intimation conveyed to him, not only of the doubter's speech, but of the spot where the camel was; and the doubter afterwards repented, and was confirmed in the faith. 'Omar's sword was readily unsheathed to punish such sceptical temerity, and Moḥammad himself once and again visited it in the early part of his Medīna career with condign punishment.

there can have survived but little trace of such traditions as were early and entirely dropped. But we discover vestiges of a spirit that would necessarily produce such results, working even in the second and third centuries. We find that the momentary lapse and compromise of Moḥammad with the idolatry of Mecca is well supported by the earliest and the best authorities. But theologians began to deem it dangerous or heretical to suppose that Moḥammad should have thus degraded himself 'after he had received the truth'; and the occurrence is therefore denied, or entirely omitted, by some of the earliest and by most of the later biographers, though the facts are so patent that the more candid fully admit them.[1] The principle thus found in existence in the second and third centuries, may be presumed to have been at work also in the first.

Pious frauds allowable in Islām

L.—The system of *pious frauds* is not abhorrent to the axioms of Islām. Deception, in the current theology, is under certain circumstances allowable. The Prophet himself, by precept as well as by example, encouraged the notion that to tell an untruth is on some occasions allowable; and what occasion would approve itself as more justifiable, nay meritorious, than that of furthering the interests of Islām? Early Muslims would suppose it to be fitting and right that a divine religion should be supported by the evidence of miracles, and they no doubt believed that they were doing God service by building up such testimony in its favour. The case of our own religion, whose purer morality renders such attempt the less excusable, shows that pious fabrications of this description easily commend themselves to the conscience, wherever there is the inclination and the opportunity for their perpetration.

Difficulty of distinguishing conscientious witnesses

There were indeed conscientious men among the early Muslims, who would have scrupled at such pious fraud; but these are the very individuals from whom we have the fewest traditions. We read of some cautious and scrupulous

[1] The author of the *Mawāhib al-Ledunīya* traces the omission of the passage to fear of heresy and injury to Islām. 'It is said that this story is of an heretical character and has no foundation. But it is not so; it is really well founded.' 'Again [another author] rejects it on the ground that if it had really happened, many of those who had believed would have become apostates, which was not the case.'

Companions who, perceiving the difficulty of reciting accounts of their Prophet with perfect accuracy, and perhaps offended at the effrontery of the ordinary propagators of garbled and unfounded traditions, abstained entirely from repeating the sayings of the Prophet.[1] But regarding those Companions from whom the great mass of tradition is drawn, and their immediate successors, it does not appear that we are now in possession of any satisfactory means for dividing them into separate classes, of which the trustworthiness would vary to any great extent. With respect, indeed, to some, it is known that they were more constantly than others with Moḥammad, and had therefore better opportunities for acquiring information; some, like the garrulous 'Ā'isha, were specially given to gossiping tales and trifling frivolities; but none of them, so far as we can judge, was free from the tendency to glorify the Prophet at the expense of careful recital, or could be withheld from the marvellous by the most palpable violations of probability or reason. Such at least is the impression derived from their evidence in the shape *in which it has reached us.*

[1] Thus 'Omar declined to give certain information, saying: 'If it were not that I feared lest I should add to the facts in relating them, or take therefrom, verily I would tell you.' Similar traditions are given regarding 'Othmān. Ibn Mas'ūd was so afraid of repeating Moḥammad's words wrongly, that he always guarded his relation by the conditional clause—'He spake something like this, or near unto it;' but one day, as he repeated a tradition, the unconditional formula of repetition—'*Thus spake the Prophet of the Lord*'—escaped his lips, and he became oppressed with anguish, so that the sweat dropped from his forehead. Then he said: 'If the Lord so will, the Prophet may have said more than that, or less, or near unto it.' Again, Sa'd was asked a question, and he kept silence, saying: '*I fear that if I tell you one thing, ye will go and add thereto, as from me, a hundred.*' Thus also one inquired of Ibn az-Zubeir: 'Why do we not hear thee telling anecdotes regarding the Prophet, as such and such persons tell?' He replied: 'It is very true that I kept close by the Prophet from the time I first believed (and therefore am intimately acquainted with his words); but I heard him say, "Whosoever shall repeat a lie concerning me, his resting-place shall be in hell-fire."' So in explaining why several of the principal Companions had left no traditions, Al-Wāḳidi writes: 'From some there are no remains of tradition regarding the Prophet, although they were more in his company, sitting and hearing him, than others who have left us many traditions; *and this we attribute to their fear*' (of giving forth erroneous traditions).

Examples of capricious fabrication

M.—The aberrations from fact hitherto noticed are presumed to have proceeded from some species of bias, the nature of which I have been endeavouring to trace. But the testimony of the Companions, as delivered to us, is so unaccountably fickle and capricious that, even where no motive whatever can be guessed at, and where there were the fullest opportunities of observation, traditions often flatly contradict one another. For instance, a score of persons affirm that Moḥammad dyed his hair: they mention the substance used; some not only maintain that they were eye-witnesses of it during the Prophet's life, but after his death produced relics of hair on which the dye was visible. A score of others, possessing equally good means of information, assert that he never dyed his hair, and that, moreover, he had no need to do so, as his grey hairs were so few that they might be counted.[1] Again, with respect to his *Signet ring*—a matter involving no faction, family interest, or dogma—tradition is most discordant. One party relate that, feeling the want of a seal for his despatches, the Prophet had a signet ring prepared for that purpose of pure silver. Another party assert that Khālid ibn Sa'īd made for himself an iron ring plated with silver; and that Moḥammad, taking a fancy to it, appropriated it to his own use. A third tradition states that the ring was brought by Ibn Sa'īd from Abyssinia; and a fourth that Mo'ādh had it engraved for himself in the Yemen. One set of traditions hold that Moḥammad wore this ring on his right hand, another on his left; one that he wore the seal inside, others that he wore it outside; one that the inscription upon it was *The truth of God*, while the rest declare that it was *Moḥammad, Prophet of God.* These traditions all refer to one and the same ring; because it is repeatedly added that, after Moḥammad's death, it was worn

[1] Even the exact number of his white hairs is given by different authorities variously, as 17, 18, 20, or 30. Some say that when he oiled his head these appeared; others that the process of oiling concealed them. As to the colour used, the accounts also differ. One says he employed Henna and Katam which gave a reddish tinge, but that he liked yellow best; another mentions a jet-black dye, while others say the Prophet forbade this; *e.g.* Moḥammad said: 'Those who dye their hair black like the crops of pigeons, shall never smell the smell of Paradise.' 'In the day of judgment the Lord will not look upon him who dyes his hair black.'

by Abu Bekr, by 'Omar, and by 'Othmān, and was lost by the latter in the well Arīs.[1] There is yet another tradition that neither the Prophet nor any of his immediate successors ever wore a ring at all. Now these varying narratives are not given doubtfully, as conjectures which might either be right or wrong; but they are told with the full assurance of certainty, and with such minute circumstantiality as to leave the impression on the simple reader's mind that each of the narrators had the most intimate acquaintance with the subject.

Unsupported tradition is insufficient evidence

To what tendency, then, or habit of mind, but sheer love of story-telling, are we to attribute such gratuitous and wholesale inventions? In fine, we may from all that has been said, conclude that tradition cannot be received with too much caution, or exposed to too rigorous a criticism; and that no important statement should be accepted as securely proved by tradition alone, unless there be some farther ground of probability, analogy, or collateral evidence in its favour.

III. Considerations confirming tradition

III.—We now proceed to the considerations which should be regarded as *confirming* the credit of a tradition.

Agreement between independent traditions

A.—General agreement between traditions independent one of another, or which, though traceable to a common origin, have descended by different chains of witnesses, may be regarded as a presumption of credibility. The sources of tradition were numerous; and the stream reaches us through many separate channels. Evidence of this description may therefore afford a cumulative presumption that matter common to many separate traditions was currently reported or believed at the period immediately succeeding the Prophet's death. But, on the other hand, close agreement may be a ground of distrust; it may argue that, though attributed to different sources, the traditions really belong to one and the same family, perhaps of spurious origin, long subsequent to the time of Moḥammad. If the uniformity be so great as to exclude circumstantial variety, it will be strong ground for believing that either the common source of such traditions is not of old date, or that the channels of their conveyance have not been kept distinct. Some degree of incidental discrepancy must be looked for, and will improve

[1] Aṭ-Ṭabari, i. 2856 f.

rather than injure the character of the evidence. Thus the frequent variations as to the day of the week on which remarkable events occurred are just what we should expect in independent traditions having their origin in hearsay; and the simplicity with which these are placed in juxtaposition speaks strongly for the honesty of the Collectors as having gathered them *bonâ fide* from various and independent sources, as well as having refrained from any attempt to blend or harmonise.

Agreement between portions of independent traditions

A like argument may be applied to the several parts of a tradition. Certain portions of distinct versions of the same subject-matter may agree almost verbally together, while other portions may contain circumstantial variations; and it is possible that the latter may have a *bonâ fide* independent origin, which the former could not pretend to. Thus the story of Moḥammad's infantile days, which professes to have been derived from his nurse Ḥalīma, has been handed down to us in three distinct traditions. 'These three accounts,' says Sprenger, 'agree almost literally in the marvellous, but they differ in the facts.'[1] The *marvellous* was derived from a common source of fabrication, but the *facts* from original authorities. Hence the uniformity of the one, and the variation in the other.

Verbal coincidence may point to a common written original

Verbal coincidence may sometimes involve a species of evidence peculiar to itself; it may point to a common *recorded* original of date older probably than that at which most of the other traditions were reduced to writing. There being no reason to believe that any such documents were framed till some considerable time after Moḥammad's death, they can assume none of the merit of contemporaneous remains. But they may claim the advantage of a greater antiquity of record than the mass of ordinary tradition, as in the history by Az-Zuhri of the Prophet's military conquests, recorded probably before the close of the first century.

Correspondence with the Ḳor'ān valuable confirmation

B.—Correspondence at any point with facts mentioned in the Ḳor'ān will generally impart credit to the traditional narrative. Some of the most important incidents connected with Moḥammad's battles and campaigns, as well as a variety of domestic and political matters, are thus attested. Such apparent confirmation may, however, be deceptive, for the

[1] *Mohammad*, p. 78, note 3.

allusion in the Ḳor'ān may have *given rise* to the tradition. The story may have originated in some illustrative supposition or paraphrastic comment on the text; and, gradually changing its character, been transmitted to posterity as a recital of fact. Take for example the following verse in the Ḳor'ān (v. 14): *Remember the favour of thy Lord unto thee, when certain men designed to stretch forth their hands upon thee, and the Lord held back their hands from thee.* By some this passage is supposed to refer to Moḥammad's escape from Mecca; but, the craving after the circumstantial and marvellous not being satisfied with this reasonable interpretation, several different occasions have been given on which the *hand* of the enemy, in the very act of brandishing a sword over Moḥammad's head, was miraculously stayed by Gabriel.[1] Again, the discomfiture of the army of Abraha shortly before the birth of Moḥammad, is thus poetically celebrated in Sūra cv.: *And did not the Lord send against them flocks of little birds, which cast upon them small clay stones, and made them like unto the stubble of which the cattle have eaten?* This seems only a highly coloured metaphor setting forth the general destruction of the army by the ravages of smallpox or some similar pestilence. But it has afforded a starting-point for the extravagances of tradition, which gives a detailed statement of the species of bird, the size and material of the stones, the mode in which they

[1] In the attack upon the Beni Ghaṭafān, we learn from Al-Wāḳidi that whilst Moḥammad was resting under a tree, the enemy's leader came stealthily up, and, snatching his sword, exclaimed: 'Who is there to defend thee against me this day? 'The Lord,' replied the Prophet. Immediately Gabriel struck the foe a blow upon his chest, which caused the sword to fall from his hand; thereupon Moḥammad in his turn seized the sword and retorted the question on his adversary, who forthwith became a convert; 'and *with reference to this*,' it is added, '*was Sūra* v. 14 *revealed*.'

The tale is a second time clumsily repeated by the biographers almost in the same terms, on the occasion of his expedition to Dhāt ar-Riḳā'; and here Ibn Isḥāḳ adds: 'With special reference to this event, Sūra v. 14 was revealed; but others attribute the passage to the attempt of 'Amr ibn Jaḥsh, one of the Beni an-Naḍīr,' who (as is pretended) tried to roll down a stone upon the Prophet from the roof of the house in which he sat. Ibn Hishām, p. 663.

Thus we have three or four different incidents to which the text is applied, *some of which are evidently fabricated to suit the passage itself.*

struck the enemy, the kind of wound inflicted, &c., as if the portent had but just occurred within sight of the narrators; and yet the whole has evidently no other foundation than the verse above quoted, which the credulous Muslims, interpreting literally, deemed it necessary to clothe with ample illustration. Such are examples of the numberless legends which, though purely imaginary, have been reared upon a Ḳor'ānic basis.[1]

Disparagement of Moḥammad

C.—When a tradition contains statements which, *from the Muslim's point of view*, would reflect unfavourably on the Prophet, that will be held in its favour. Such would be the tradition of an indignity shown to him by his followers, or an insult from his enemies after his emigration (for then the period of humiliation had passed); his failure in any enterprise or laudable endeavour; anything, in fine, at variance either in fact or doctrine with the principles and tendencies of Islām, then there will be strong reason for admitting it as authentic; because, otherwise, it seems hardly possible that a tradition of the kind could be fabricated, or, having been fabricated, that it could obtain currency among the followers of Moḥammad. At the same time we must be careful not to apply the rule to all that is considered *by ourselves* discreditable or opposed to morality. Cruelty and revenge, however ruthless, *when practised against infidels*, were regarded by the first followers of Islām as highly meritorious; and the rude civilisation of Arabia admitted with complacency a coarseness of language and behaviour, which we should look upon as reprehensible indecency. These and similar exceptions must be made from this canon of otherwise universal application.

Treaties contemporaneously recorded

D.—There is embodied in tradition a source of information far more authentic than any yet alluded to, though unfortunately of very limited extent,—I mean the transcripts of treaties purporting to have been dictated by Moḥammad, and engrossed in his presence.

Their authority far superior to that of ordinary tradition;

It has been already shown that ordinary traditions were not recorded in his lifetime; and that, even were we to admit an occasional resort to early notes or memoranda, there is no evidence regarding their

[1] As illustrative of similarly fabricated stories in the early history of the Church, the legend of St Paul's battle with the wild beasts may be referred to as growing out of 1 Cor. xv. 32. See Stanley *in loco*.

subsequent fate, nor any criteria for distinguishing traditions so derived from those that originated and were long sustained by purely oral means. To a very different category belong the treaties of Moḥammad. They consist of compacts entered into with surrounding tribes, which were at the time reduced to writing, and attested by one or more of his followers. They are of course confined to the period succeeding the Prophet's acquisition of political influence, and from their nature limited to the recital of a few simple facts. But these facts again form valuable points of support to the traditional outline; and, especially where they detail the relations of Islām with the neighbouring Jewish and Christian tribes, are of the highest interest.

Especially in regard to Jewish and Christian tribes

In Al-Wāḳidi's biography is a section expressly devoted to the transcription of such treaties, and it contains two or three scores of them. Over and again, the author (at the end of the second or beginning of the third century) states that he had copied these from the *original* documents, or recorded their purport from the testimony of those who had seen them. 'They were still in force,' writes Sprenger, 'in the time of Harun al-Rashid (A.H. 170-193), and were then collected.'[1] This is quite conceivable, for they were often recorded upon leather, and would invariably be preserved with care as charters of privilege by those in whose favour they were concluded. Some of the most interesting, as the terms allowed to the Jews of Kheibar and to the Christians of Nejrān, formed the basis of political events in the Caliphates of Abu Bekr and 'Omar; the concessions made in others to Jewish and Christian tribes are satisfactory proof that they were not fabricated by Muslims; while it is equally clear that they would never have been acknowledged if counterfeited by a Jewish or a Christian hand. Whenever, then, there is fair evidence in favour of such treaties, they may be placed, as to historical authority, almost on a par with the Ḳor'ān itself.

Written details of embassies preserved in several tribes

The narrative of official deputations to Moḥammad is sometimes stated to have been derived from the family or tribe which sent the embassy, and which had preserved a written memorial of the circumstances. Accounts so obtained may undoubtedly be viewed as founded on fact,

[1] *Mohammad*, p. 63.

for the family or clan would naturally treasure up in the most careful way any memorials of the manner in which the Prophet had received and honoured them, although there would, no doubt, be a tendency in such statements to self-aggrandisement.[1]

Poetical remains have special authority. I. Those ascribed to a period before the rise of Moḥammad

E.—Another traditionary source, supported by authority peculiar to itself, consists of the verses and poetical fragments attributed to the time of Moḥammad. Some of these profess to be the composition of persons who died before the Prophet, as Abu Ṭālib, his uncle; others, of those who survived him, as Ḥassān ibn Thābit, the poet of Medīna. There can be no question as to the great antiquity of these remains, though we may not always be able to fix with exactness the period of their composition. With respect to those which purport to be of date preceding the Prophet's rise to power, when we consider the poetical habits of the nation, their faculty of preserving poetry by memory,[2] the ancient style and language of the pieces themselves, and the likelihood that carefully composed verses were from the first committed for greater security to writing, it cannot certainly be deemed improbable that such poems or fragments should in reality have been composed by the parties to whom they are ascribed. It is, on the other hand, quite possible that poetry of date long after the death of Moḥammad, but descriptive of some passage in his life, may gradually have come to be regarded as composed by a contemporary poet upon the occasion, or as the actual effusion of the actors in the scene to whom, by poetical fiction, the

[1] Thus Al-Wāḳidi: 'My informant, Moḥammad ibn Yaḥya, relates, *that he found it in the writings* of his father, that,' &c.; and again, ''Amr al-'Odhri says, he *found it written in the papers* of his father, that,' &c.; proceeding with the narrative of a deputation from the tribe to Moḥammad.

[2] Burckhardt's testimony shows that the faculty still remains. 'Throughout every part of the Arabian desert, poetry is equally esteemed. Many persons are found who make verses of true measure, although they cannot either read or write; yet as they employ on such occasions chosen terms only, and as the purity of their vernacular language is such as to preclude any grammatical errors, these verses, after passing from mouth to mouth, may at last be committed to paper, and will most commonly be found regular and correct. I presume that the greater part of the regular poetry of the Arabs which has descended to us, is derived from similar compositions.'—*Notes on the Bedouins*, I. 251; see also p. 373.

modern author attributes it. As a general rule, it may be laid down that wherever there is betrayed an anticipation of Moḥammad's prophetical dignity or victories, the poetry may at once be concluded as an afterthought, triumphant Islām having reflected some rays of its refulgence upon the bare points of its early career. Tried by this rule, there are fragments which may be ascribed, as more or less genuine, to the men whose names they bear; but there is also much which, from patent anachronism either in fact or spirit, is evidently the composition of a later age.[1]

Poets who survived Moḥammad

Pieces said to have been recited by poets who survived Moḥammad, there is every reason for believing to be the composition of the persons to whom they are ascribed. But whether they were composed before the Prophet's death, even when so represented, is a more difficult question; and their authority will in some measure depend on the answer. Under any circumstances they must be of great value, as the work of Moḥammad's contemporaries. Wherever they bear upon historical events, they are of much use as adding

[1] The following glaring anachronism shows with what caution poetry of this class must be received. When Moḥammad with his followers performed the pilgrimage to Mecca under the treaty of Ḥodeibiya, the leader of his camel, as he encircled the Ka'ba, shouted verses of hostile defiance against Ḳoreish, who had retired by compact to the overhanging rocks and thence viewed the Prophet and his people. Among these verses was the couplet: 'We shall slay you on the score of the interpretation of it (the Ḳor'ān), as we slew you on the score of its revelation' (*i.e.* for rejecting it). Now this evidently belongs to a period long subsequent, when, Islām having been broken up into parties, men fought against each other for their several 'interpretations' of the Ḳor'ān, and looked back to the struggle with the idolaters of Mecca as to a bygone era. Yet the verses are ascribed both by Al-Wāḳidi and Ibn Isḥāḳ to the Ḥodeibiya armistice, *i.e.* a period anterior even to the conquest of Mecca. Ibn Hishām, p. 789.

As a further example, I may refer to the rhetorical contest held before Moḥammad between his own followers and the embassy of the Beni Temīm. Anticipations of universal conquest are developed in the orations of the Moḥammadan party. Thus the threat is used by Thābit ibn Ḳeis that the Muslims '*would fight against all the world till they were converted.*' This was language appropriate only to the time when the Arabs had issued from Arabia. The speeches and poems were, no doubt, composed afterwards as suitable to the occasion, and, like the orations of classical history, attributed to the speakers of the original scene. Ibn Hishām, p. 935.

confirmation to the corresponding traditions; for, whether handed down by writing, or by memory alone, their poetical form is a material safeguard against change or interpolation. As examples, may be specified the odes of Ḥassān ibn Thābit on the 'Battle of the Ditch,' and on 'the taking of Mecca'; and the poem of Ka'b ibn Mālik, descriptive of the oath of fealty by the Medīna converts at the 'Second pledge of Al-'Aḳaba,' in which are mentioned the names of the twelve leaders chosen by the Prophet. Besides illustrating specific facts, this early poetry is often instructive, from its exhibition of the *spirit* of the first Muslims towards their unconverted brethren, and the biting satire employed against the enemies of Islām.

Their poetry useful as confirmatory of tradition

But while these poetical pieces attest many facts we are already acquainted with, they reveal none which, without them, we should not otherwise have known. They are valuable because *confirmatory* of tradition, and, as the earliest literary remains of a period which contained the germ of such mighty events, they deserve our best attention; but they give us little fresh insight into the history or character of the Prophet.

Conclusion

Such, then, are the criteria which should be applied to Moḥammadan tradition. It is obvious that the technical rule of 'respectable names,' used by the Collectors as the connecting chain of evidence, can carry no authority with us; that every tradition, separately subjected to close examination, must stand or fall upon its own merits; and that, even after its reception as *generally* credible, the component parts are still severally liable, upon a close scrutiny of internal evidence, to suspicion and rejection. The sure light of the Ḳor'ān will be the pole-star of the historian; and by it he will judge tradition. Where in its absence tradition stands alone, he will maintain a jealous guard against the misleading tendencies which I have endeavoured to explain, and will reject whatever bears their traces. In the remainder he will find ample and trustworthy materials for the biography of the Prophet.

EARLY BIOGRAPHIES.

I will now notice briefly the EARLY HISTORIANS OF MOḤAMMAD. We have seen that towards the end of the

Az-Zuhri and other compilers of biographical collections

first century the general practice of recording tradition was first systematically set on foot. One of the persons known to have been employed in the task was Az-Zuhri, who died A.H. 124, aged 72. It has been even stated that both he and his master 'Orwa (who died as early as A.H. 94) composed regular biographies of Moḥammad; but the grounds are uncertain. Be this as it may, there is no doubt that Az-Zuhri at least made separate collections of the traditions bearing on various episodes of the Prophet's life, certainly on that relating to his military career. It is conjectured by Sprenger, that such compilations gave rise to the uniformity of narrative and coincidence of expression observable in many parts of the various biographies of Moḥammad, and especially in the history of his expeditions and battles. The supposition is probable; at all events the work of Az-Zuhri was one of such sources. He lived at the court of the Omeiyad Caliphs, and there is every reason to believe that his accounts are as unbiassed as could be expected from any Muslim author. There is nothing of Az-Zuhri extant in independent form, but he is largely quoted by subsequent biographers; and their account of Moḥammad's military operations is probably in great part the reproduction of materials collated by him.

Biographies compiled in second century A.H.

Two other authors are mentioned as having written biographies of Moḥammad early in the second century, MŪSA IBN 'OḲBA and ABU MAS'HAR. Neither of their works is extant; but the latter is extensively referred to by Aṭ-Ṭabari. To these may be added, as no longer available, the histories of ABU ISḤĀḲ, who died A.H. 188, and AL-MADĀ'INI, who survived to the beginning of the third century. Though the latter published many works on the Prophet, not one of them is now known to exist.

Extant biographies

The earliest biographical writers whose treatises are extant more or less in their original state are:—I. Ibn Isḥāḳ; II. Ibn Hishām; III. Al-Waḳidi, and his Secretary Ibn Sa'd; IV. Aṭ-Ṭabari. These works, though professing, like the traditional collections, to be composed exclusively of trustworthy traditions, differ from them in the following particulars.[1]

Difference from ordinary collections

[1] Biographical works are called *Siyar* (pl. of *Sīra*), while the *Collections* of tradition are termed *Ḥadīth*.

First.—The traditional matter is confined to biographical subjects, and is arranged in chronological order. Commencing with anticipatory and genealogical notices, the work advances to the birth of Moḥammad, and traces with some degree of method the various periods of his life. To each stage a separate chapter is devoted; and all traditions which have any bearing whatever on the subject, are thrown together in that chapter, and arranged with more or less of intelligible sequence. The practice of the Collectors as to the quotation of their authorities is generally observed; namely, that each separate tradition must be supported by its original witness, and the chain of witnesses specified by name which connects the biographer with that authority. This induces the same motley and fragmentary appearance which marks the traditional *Collections.* The biography of Moḥammad, in fact, resembles a collection of 'table talk.' It is a compilation rather than an original composition.

First.—Confined to biographical matter chronologically arranged

Second.—Traditions are sometimes fused together, or reduced into a uniform story. Such is more particularly the case in descriptions of Moḥammad's military life, where the expeditions are often detailed in an unbroken narrative, the authorities for which are generally thrown together at the beginning.

Second.—Traditions sometimes formed into connected narrative

Third.—This process at times induces some degree of critical examination of the several traditions so collected. Where the authorities differ, we find the biographer occasionally stating his opinion as to which is the correct exposition of fact. Verbal differences are sometimes mentioned, and various readings noted. Satisfactory evidence is thus afforded of the labour bestowed by the biographers in bringing together all authentic tradition which could illustrate their subject, and of the accuracy with which they recorded it.

Third.—A measure of critical collation

The following account of the four authors whose works are more or less extant will enable the reader to form an estimate of their value as biographical authorities.

I. MOḤAMMAD IBN ISḤĀḲ is the earliest biographer of whom any extensive remains, the authorship of which can certainly be distinguished, have reached us. He died A.H. 151, that is, some twenty years after the overthrow of the Omeiyad dynasty. His work was published under the auspices and influence of the 'Abbāsid Princes, and was in

MOḤAMMAD IBN ISḤĀḲ

fact composed 'for the use' of the Caliph Al-Manṣūr, the second of that line. Its accuracy has been impugned. But from the portions which have come down to us there seems no ground for believing that Ibn Isḥāḳ was less careful than other traditionists; while the high character generally ascribed to him, and the confidence with which he is quoted by later authors, leave little doubt that the aspersions cast upon him have no good foundation.

Testimonies to his authority

In the biographical dictionary of Ibn Khallikān we find the following testimonies in his favour: 'Moḥammad ibn Isḥāḳ is held by the majority of the learned as a sure authority in traditions, and none can be ignorant of the high character borne by his work, *the Maghāzi* (military expeditions). *Whoever wishes to know the early Muslim conquests*, says Az-Zuhri, *let him refer to Ibn Isḥāḳ;*' and Al-Bukhāri himself cites him in his history. Ash-Shāfi'i said: *Whoever wishes to obtain a complete acquaintance with the early Muslim conquests, must borrow his information from Ibn Isḥāḳ.* Sufyān ibn 'Oyeina declared that he never met any one who cast suspicions on Ibn Isḥāḳ's recitals; and Sho'ba ibn al-Ḥajjāj, was heard to say, '*Moḥammad ibn Isḥāḳ is the Commander of the Faithful*, meaning that he held that rank as a traditionist. . . . As-Sāji mentions that Az-Zuhri's pupils had recourse to Moḥammad ibn Isḥāḳ, whenever they had doubts respecting the exactness of any of the traditions delivered by their master; such was the confidence they placed in his excellent memory. It is stated that Yaḥya ibn Ma'īn, Aḥmed ibn Ḥanbal, and Yaḥya Sa'īd al-Ḳaṭṭān, considered Moḥammad ibn Isḥāḳ as a trustworthy authority, and quoted his traditions in proof of their legal doctrines. . . . It was from Ibn Isḥāḳ's works that Ibn Hishām extracted the materials of his biography of the Prophet, and every person who has treated on this subject has been obliged to take Ibn Isḥāḳ for his authority and guide.'[1]

Ibn Isḥāḳ one of the two chief sources of subsequent biographies

These testimonies are conclusive of the popularity of Ibn Isḥāḳ in the Muslim world, and of his general fidelity as a writer. But the surest proof of his character and authority is that his statements have been embodied in all subsequent biographies of the Prophet, excepting that of Al-Wāḳidi, who

[1] Ibn Khallikān (De Slane), vol. ii. p. 677 f.

in comparison with others quotes sparingly from him; and that in fact the two works of Ibn Isḥāḳ and Al-Wāḳidi contain between them the chief materials on which later writers have drawn for authentic details of the Prophet's life.

No copy of Ibn Isḥāḳ's biography, in its original form, is now available. But the materials have been so extensively adopted by Ibn Hishām, and wrought into his history in so complete and unaltered a form, that we have probably not lost much by the absence of the work itself.

Not extant, but largely available in Ibn Hishām

II. IBN HISHĀM, who died A.H. 213 (or 218), made the labours of Ibn Isḥāḳ the basis of his biography of Moḥammad. Copies of this work are extant, and are known to the European historians of the Prophet. The following extract from Ibn Khallikān will place before the reader all that it is necessary to know regarding the life of this author: 'Ibn Hishām, the author of the *Sīrat ar-Rasūl*, or *Biography of the Prophet*, is spoken of in these terms by Abu'l-Ḳāsim as-Suhaili, in his work entitled *Rauḍ al-Unuf*, or *The Fresh Pastures*, which is a commentary on the *Sīra*, and was composed in the year 569 A.H. (1173-4 A.D.). He was celebrated for his learning, and possessed superior information in genealogy and grammar. His native place was Old Cairo, but his family were of Al-Baṣra. He composed a genealogical work on the tribe of Ḥimyar and its princes; and I have been told that he wrote another work, in which he explained the obscure passages of poetry cited in [Ibn Isḥāḳ's] biography of the Prophet.[1] His death occurred at Old Cairo A.H. 213. This Ibn Hishām is the person who extracted and drew up the "History of the Prophet" from Ibn Isḥāḳ's work, entitled "The Wars and Life of Moḥammad." As-Suhaili explained its difficulties in a commentary, and it is now found in the hands of the public under the title of *Sīrat ibn Hishām*, *i.e.* "The Biography of Moḥammad, by Ibn Hishām."'[2]

IBN HISHĀM: His character

There is reason to suspect that Ibn Hishām was not quite so trustworthy as his great authority Ibn Isḥāḳ. Certainly there is one instance which throws suspicion upon him as a witness, disinclined at least to tell the *whole* truth. We find in Aṭ-Ṭabari *a quotation from Ibn Isḥāḳ*, in which is described the temporary lapse of Moḥammad into idolatry; and the same incidents are also given by Al-Wāḳidi from other

Suspicion of his candour and fidelity

[1] [Haji Khalfa, 7308 and 1347.] [2] Ibn Khallikān, vol. ii. p. 128.

original sources. But no notice whatever of the fact appears in the biography of Ibn Hishām, though it is professedly based upon the work of Ibn Isḥāḳ. His having thus studiously omitted all reference to so important an incident, for no other reason apparently than because he fancied it to be discreditable to the Prophet, cannot but lessen our confidence generally in this book. Still, it is evident from a comparison of his text with the quotations made by Aṭ-Ṭabari from the same passages of Ibn Isḥāḳ (the two ordinarily tallying word for word with each other) that whatever he did excerpt from his author was faithfully and accurately quoted.

Arrangement and composition

The arrangement and composition of Ibn Hishām are careful, if not elaborate. The traditions are well classified, and the narrative proceeds with much of the regularity of an ordinary biography. The frequent fusion of traditions, however, renders it sometimes difficult to single out the separate authorities, and to judge of them on their individual merits.[1]

Al-Wāḳidi His charracter and writings

III. AL-WĀḲIDI, or, as his full name runs, *Moḥammad ibn 'Omar Al-Wāḳidi*, was born at Medīna about A.H. 130, and died A.H. 207. He studied and wrote exclusively under the 'Abbāsids. He enjoyed their patronage, and passed a part of his life at their court, having in his later days been appointed a Ḳāḍi of Baghdad. In judging, therefore, of his learning and prejudices, we must always bear in mind that the influence of the 'Abbāsid dynasty bore strongly and continuously upon him. His traditional researches were vast, and his works voluminous. The following is from Ibn Khallikān: 'Al-Wāḳidi was a man eminent for learning, and the author of

[1] 'Even of this work copies are rare.'—*Sprenger*. The fact is that the literary public among Moḥammadans do not affect the early and original sources of their Prophet's life, and hardly ever use them. They prefer the modern biographies with their marvellous tales.

An abridged edition of Ibn Hishām was made at Damascus A.H. 707 (A.D. 1307) by one Aḥmed ibn Ibrāhīm. The abridgment consists chiefly in the omission in each case of the long series of witnesses leading up to the Companion who first gave forth the tradition. A beautiful manuscript, ***in the handwriting of the abbreviator himself***, was met with by Dr Sprenger in Delhi, and has been used both by Dr Sprenger and myself. I have placed a portion of this valuable MS., with an English abstract of its contents, in the India Office Library.

[The standard edition of the Arabic text of Ibn Hishām is that of Ferdinand Wüstenfeld, 1858-1860, and it has been translated into German by Gustav Weil, 1864.]

some well-known works on the conquests of the Muslims, and other subjects. His *Kitāb ar-Ridda*, a work of no inferior merit, contains an account of the apostacy of the Arabs on the death of the Prophet, and of the wars between his followers and Ṭoleiḥa, Al-Aswad, and Museilima, the false prophets. . . . His Secretary, Moḥammad ibn Sa'd, and a number of other distinguished men, delivered traditional information on his authority. He held the post of Ḳāḍi in the eastern quarter of Baghdad, and was appointed by the Caliph Al-Ma'mūn to fill the same office at 'Askar al-Mahdi. The traditions received from him are considered of feeble authority, and doubts have been expressed on the subject of his veracity. Al-Ma'mūn testified a high respect for him, and treated him with marked honour.'[1]

The 'Maghāzi' his only work extant in original form

Notwithstanding the extraordinary fertility of his pen, none of the works of Al-Wāḳidi have reached us in their original form, with the exception of the *Maghāzi*, or 'History of the Wars of the Prophet,' a copy of which was recently discovered in Syria, and has now been published in the *Bibliotheca Indica*.[2]

But results of his labours preserved by his Secretary Moḥammad ibn Sa'd

Happily, his Secretary, IBN SA'D, profited by the labours of his master, and through him we enjoy largely the results. The Secretary is thus described by Ibn Khallikān: 'Moḥammad ibn Sa'd was a man of the highest talents, merit, and eminence. He lived for some time with Al-Wāḳidi in the character of a Secretary, and for this reason became known by the appellation "The Secretary of Al-Wāḳidi."' . . . He composed an excellent work in fifteen volumes on the different classes of Moḥammad's Companions and the Successors; it contains also a history of the Caliphs, brought down to his own time. He left also a smaller edition. His character as a veracious and trustworthy historian is universally admitted. It is said that the complete collection of Al-Wāḳidi's works remained in the possession of four persons,

[1] Ibn Khallikān, vol. iii. p. 61 f.

[2] [Under the title *History of Muhammad's Campaigns*, by Aboo 'Abd Ollah Moḥammad 'bin Omar al-Wákidy, edited by Alfred von Kremer, Calcutta, 1856. A German translation, with slight abbreviations, has been published by Julius Wellhausen, under the title *Muhammed in Medina. Das ist Vakidi's Kitab alMaghazi*, Berlin, 1882. To this last work the references for this period will be made instead of to the Calcutta text.]

the first of whom was his Secretary, Ibn Sa'd. This distinguished writer displayed great acquirements in the sciences, the traditions, and traditional literature; most of his books treat of the traditions and law. The Khaṭīb Abu Bekr, author of the 'History of Baghdad,' speaks of him in these terms: 'We consider Moḥammad ibn Sa'd as a man of unimpeached integrity, and the traditions which he delivered are a proof of his veracity, for, in the greater part of the information handed down by him, we find him discussing it passage by passage.' At the age of sixty-two he died at Baghdad, A.H. 230, and was interred in the cemetery outside the Damascus gate.'[1]

The Secretary of Al-Wāḳidi

His works

In the fifteen volumes here noticed, the Secretary is supposed to have embodied the researches of his master, together with the fruits of his own independent labour. The first volume has, fortunately for the interests of literature and truth, been preserved to us in an undoubtedly genuine form. It contains the *Sīra* or 'Biography of Moḥammad,' with detailed accounts of the learned men of Medīna, and of all the Companions of the Prophet who were present at Bedr. This treatise (if we except some special narratives, as portions of the military expeditions) is composed entirely of detached traditions, which are arranged in chapters according to subject, and in fair chronological order. The chain of authority is generally traced in detail to the fountain-head for each tradition, separately; and so carefully is every fragment of a tradition bearing on each subject treasured up and gathered together, that we often find a dozen or more traditions reiterated in detail one after another, though they are all couched perhaps in precisely the same words, or in expressions closely resembling one another. We likewise meet continually with the most contradictory authorities placed side by side without any remark; and sometimes (but the occasion is comparatively rare) the author gives his opinion as to their relative credibility.[2]

Composed mainly of detached traditions

[1] Ibn Khallikān, vol. iii. p. 64 f.

[2] For a copy of this invaluable volume we are indebted to the indefatigable research of Sprenger, who discovered it in a library at Cawnpore. This manuscript is written in an ancient but very distinct character, and is in excellent preservation. It was transcribed at Damascus A.H. 718 (A.D. 1318), by a scholar named Al-Ḥaḳḳari, who traces up, link by link,

Authority of Al-Wāḳidi and his Secretary

Al-Wāḳidi is said to have been a follower of the 'Alid sect. Like others, he probably yielded to the prevailing influences of the day, which tended to exalt the Prophet's son-in-law as well as all the progenitors of the 'Abbāsid race. But there is not the slightest ground for doubting that his character is equal, if not superior, to that of any other historian of his time. Of the biography, at all events, compiled by his Secretary, Sprenger has well vindicated the authority and faithfulness. 'There is no trace,' says he, 'of a sacrifice of truth to design, or of pious fraud, in his work. It contains few miracles; and even those which are recorded in it admit of an easy explanation.' Concurring generally in this praise, I do not hesitate to designate the compilation as the fruit of an honest endeavour to bring together the most credible authorities current at the end of the second century, and to depict the life of Moḥammad with as much truth as from such sources was possible; it is marked by at least as great sincerity as we may expect to find in any extant Moḥammadan author. But Sprenger's admiration carries him too far, when he affirms that the miracles it contains are either few in number or of easy explanation. They are, on the contrary, nearly as numerous as those we find in Ibn Hishām. It is very evident that the criticism of Al-Wāḳidi and his Secretary extended little, if at all, beyond that of their contemporaries. They were mere compilers of current traditions; and these, if attested by reputable names, were received, however fabulous or extravagant, with a blind and implicit credulity.

At-Ṭabari

IV. At-Ṭabari, or *Abu Ja'far ibn Jarīr at-Ṭabari*,

from the pupil to the master (by whom it was successively taught, or by whom copied) the guarantee of the authenticity of the volume, till the chain reaches to the Secretary, Moḥammad ibn Sa'd himself. This rare MS. having come into my possession was presented (with a careful digest of its contents in English) to the India Office Library. A beautiful transcript, made for my own use at Delhi, I purpose depositing in the Library of the University of Edinburgh, where it may readily be consulted. There is but one other copy believed to be extant, which is in the Library of Gotha.

[Ibn Sa'd's *Great Book of the Classes* (Ṭabaḳāt) which includes biographies of famous Muslims down to his own time, has been published at Leyden. The first part deals with the life of Moḥammad down to the Hijra; the second with his Raids. Both of these are referred to in the foot-notes as 'Ibn Sa'd.']

flourished in the latter part of the third century of the Muslim era. The following is from Ibn Khallikān: 'Aṭ-Ṭabari was an Imām (or leader) in many various branches of knowledge, such as Ḳoranic interpretation, traditions, jurisprudence, history, &c. He composed some fine works on various subjects, and these productions are a testimony of his extensive information and great abilities. He was one of the *Mujtahid Imāms* (Defenders of the Faith) as he judged for himself and adopted the opinions of no particular doctor. . . . He is held to merit the highest confidence as a transmitter of traditional information, and his history is the most authentic and the most exact of any. . . . He was born A.H. 224 at Amul in Tabarestān, and he died at Baghdad A.H. 310.'[1]

Volume with biography of Moḥammad

Aṭ-Ṭabari, happily styled by Gibbon 'the Livy of the Arabians,' composed annals not only of Moḥammad's life, but of the progress of Islām. The Arabic original of the latter has long been known, but it commences only with the Prophet's death. Of the previous chapters, hitherto available only through an untrustworthy Persian translation, no trace, until a very few years ago, could anywhere be found.

discovered by Sprenger

Here again the literary world is indebted to Dr Sprenger, who, having been before the Mutiny deputed by the Indian Government to examine the libraries of Lucknow, succeeded in tracing, from amongst a heap of neglected manuscripts, a portion of the long-lost volume.[2] It begins with the birth of Moḥammad: but it terminates with the siege of Medīna, that is, five years before the Prophet's death. The discovery of this portion of Aṭ-Ṭabari in its original language is, after that of Al-Wāḳidi and his Secretary, the most important event affecting the biography of Moḥammad which has occurred for many years. It has a marked bearing on the

[1] Ibn Khallikān (De Slane), vol. ii. p. 597.

[2] The fortunate discovery is thus described by Sprenger: 'One of the most important books which it was my good luck to find during my late mission to Lucknow is the fourth volume of the history of Tabari (who died in A.H. 310), of which I believe no other copy is known to exist. It is a volume in a small quarto of 451 pages, fifteen lines in a page. Ten pages are wanting. The writing is ancient and bold, and though not without errors, generally very correct. I should say, from the appearance, the copy is 500 years old. The intrinsic merits of the work are not so great as might be expected. Two-thirds of the book

sufficiency and completeness of Ibn Isḥāḳ (as known to us through Ibn Hishām) and of Al-Wāḳidi. The estimate given by Sprenger (not an exaggerated one), that two-thirds of the work of Aṭ-Ṭabari are composed of extracts quoted formally from Ibn Isḥāḳ and Al-Wāḳidi, proves not only that these two biographers were in his day held as trustworthy, but likewise that they were the *standard writers* and the *chief authorities* on the subject, up to at least the close of the third century. The remaining materials of Aṭ-Ṭabari, derived from a variety of sources, possess, as observed by Sprenger, a peculiar interest, because accessible in no other quarter. Yet these sources in no case bear the character of a complete and authoritative biography, but only of occasional or miscellaneous fragments, nor do they bring to light any new or important features in Moḥammad's life. Quoted by Aṭ-Ṭabari, they are sometimes valuable as supplementary to the accounts given by Ibn Isḥāḳ and Al Wāḳidi, or confirmatory of them; but they are oftener symptomatic of the growth of a less honest and scrupulous selection than that of the earlier Collectors. Now, as Aṭ-Ṭabari was an intelligent and diligent historian, and evidently neglected no useful and trustworthy sources within his reach, we are entitled to conclude that, beside Ibn Isḥāḳ and Al-Wāḳidi, there were available in Aṭ-Ṭabari's time no other authoritative works, or sources of essential importance, relating to the biography of Moḥammad. Had any existed, they must have been within reach, and if so would unquestionably have been made use of in his Annals.

Especially as proving completeness of our other authorities, Ibn Isḥāḳ and Al-Wāḳidi

To the three biographies, then, of IBN HISHĀM, of AL-WĀḲIDI as rendered by his Secretary, and of AṬ-ṬABARI, the judicious historian of Moḥammad will, as his original authorities, confine himself. He will also receive

Historical sources recounted

consist of extracts from Ibn Ishac and Wakidy, and only one-third or thereabouts contains original traditions. Some of these are very valuable, inasmuch as they contain information not to be found anywhere else.' I have been fortunate enough to secure this MS. also, and have placed it with that of Al-Wāḳidi and Ibn Hishām in the India Office Library. It has been used in editing the complete works of Aṭ-Ṭabari now being printed at Leyden.

[This edition is now complete. It is arranged in three series. The biography of Moḥammad is comprised in Series I., vol. iii. and part of vol. iv.]

with a similar respect, such traditions in the general Collections of the earliest traditionists, Al-Bukhāri, Muslim, At-Tirmidhi, and others, as may bear upon his subject. But he will reject as evidence all later authors, to whose so-called traditions he will not allow any historical weight whatever.

No subsequent works carry historical weight

In the absence of any History or Collection of traditions, compiled *before* the accession of the 'Abbāsids, the works above specified present us with all the credible information regarding the Arabian prophet which mankind are ever likely to obtain. It is clear that our authorities compiled with zeal and assiduity all traditions which could illustrate their subject. They were contemporary with those tradition-gatherers who compassed sea and land in the enthusiastic search after any trace of Moḥammad yet lingering in the memories, or in the family archives, of his followers. Whatever authentic information really existed must already have become public and available. It cannot be imagined that, in the unwearied search of the second century, any trustworthy tradition could have escaped the Collectors; or, supposing this possible, that it could have survived that age in an unrecorded shape. Every day diminished the chance that any stray traditions should still be floating downward on the swift and troubled current of time. Later historians could not by any possibility add a single source of information to what these authors have given us. What they did add, and that abundantly, consisted of worthless and fictitious matter, gathered from the spurious traditions and romances of later times. After the era of our three biographers the springs of fresh authority absolutely fail.

Opinion of Sprenger

The verdict of Sprenger is therefore just, and of the deepest importance: 'To consider late historians like Abulfeda as *authorities*, and to suppose that an account gains in certainty because it is mentioned by several of them, is highly uncritical; and if such a mistake is committed by an Orientalist, we must accuse him of culpable ignorance in the history of Arabic literature.'

Early writers alone authoritative

Our early authors were, besides, in an incomparably better position than men in later days, for judging of the character and authenticity of each tradition. However blind their reception of the supposed authorities that lay far back close to the fountain-head, they must have possessed the ability, as we are bound to concede to them the intention and desire, to test the credit and honesty of the tradition-mongers of their own age, and of that immediately preceding. An intimate acquaintance with the character and circumstances of these would often afford grounds for distinguishing recently fabricated or mistaken narratives from ancient and *bonâ fide* tradition; and for rejecting many infirm and worthless stories, which later historians, with an indiscriminate appetite, have greedily devoured.

Review

I have thus, as proposed, endeavoured to sketch the original sources for the biography of Moḥammad. I have examined the Ḳor'ān, and have admitted its authority as an authentic and contemporary record. I have inquired into the origin and history of Moḥammadan tradition, and shown that it contains the elements of truth; and I have endeavoured to indicate some canons, by which fact may be distinguished from the legend and fiction commingled with it. I have enumerated those early biographical compilations which can alone be regarded as worthy of attention, and have shown that no later authors are possessed of an original and independent authority. The principles thus laid down, if followed with sagacity, perseverance, and impartiality, will enable the inquirer to arrive at a fair approximation to historical fact. Many Gordian knots regarding the Prophet of Arabia will remain unsolved, many paradoxes still vainly excite curiosity and baffle explanation. But the groundwork of his career will be laid down with confidence; the details will be substantially filled in with all reasonable amplitude; and the student will be able to determine with certainty the leading features of his life and character.

CHAPTER II

ARABIA BEFORE THE TIME OF MOḤAMMAD

Geographical outline of Arabia

ARABIA is usually described as a triangle, having a right angle at the Strait of Bāb al-Mandeb. It may be more correct to regard it as of an oblong shape. The sides bounded by the Red Sea on one hand, and by the Persian Gulf and Euphrates on the other, are the longest; while the southern side protracted towards the Strait of Ormuz, and washed by the Indian Ocean, is broader than the northern, of which the Syrian confine is narrowed by the westerly bend of the Euphrates.

Western Coast

Along the western side of the peninsula a chain of lofty mountains follows closely the line of the coast, from whence the mariner sees its dismal and repulsive rocks of reddish sandstone and porphyry, at times pressing near enough to be laved by the waves of the sea, at times receding so as to form a broad margin of low land, called the Tihāma. Between the sea and the crest of this range is the mountainous region of the Ḥijāz, within which lie Mecca and Medīna. The hills, as you recede from the coast, rise one above another, with vales or *Wādīs* between them, till the granite peaks of the chief range overtop the whole. The traveller who has toiled up the weary ascent finds to his surprise that, instead of a similar declivity on the eastern side, he has reached the level of a grand plateau, the Nejd or elevated central steppe of Arabia, stretching away towards the Persian Gulf.

Arid and inhospitable character of the soil

In this great peninsula, 1,400 miles in length, and half as many in breadth, there is not a single river deserving the name. The south-west quarter, indeed, abounds in perennial streams which, watering its fields and groves, have given to it the name of the Yemen, 'Araby the Blest.'[1] But elsewhere the leading feature is a weary waste of sand and rock. The floods lose themselves in the thirsty land, and seldom or never reach the sea. But underneath the dried-up channels a stratum of water is often found which supports a rich vegetation, and breaks out here and there in springs. Such are the wādīs or oases[2] of the desert, which, contrasting with the wild bleak wilderness around, charm the traveller by an indescribable freshness and verdure.

Early historical notices of Arabia

Until the 7th century, when Muslim conquest drew aside the veil, Central Arabia was an unknown land. Only on the extreme northern and southern confines did it touch the outer world. In ancient times notices of Arabia are few and meagre. In the days of Jacob we find Arab traders carrying the spiceries of Gilead on their camels down to Egypt. During the reign of Solomon a naval station was formed at Elath, the modern Acaba; the 'kings of Arabia' and its merchantmen supplied Judæa with the rarities of the East; and so widely throughout the peninsula was the fame of the Jewish monarch noised abroad, that the queen of Sheba came from the far south to visit him. In the reign of Augustus, Ælius Gallus, starting with a Roman army from the northern shores of the Red Sea, penetrated to the south probably as far as Ma'reb and Saba; but after some months was forced, by treachery and scarcity of water, to retrace his steps. Comparatively modern as is this expedition in the annals of Arabia, not a vestige of it is traceable in the national traditions and poetry of Arabia; and (stranger still) with very few exceptions it has been found impossible to identify the many names recorded by Pliny and Strabo in their account of the invasion with any known localities or tribes.[3]

Caravan trade

But though thus hidden for long ages from external view, we know that a great stream of trade was all the time passing through the peninsula, which made the Arabs in fact the

[1] [Al-Yemen really means 'the South Land.' 'The Blest' is from the Latin Felix, which again comes from the Ἀραβία Εὐδαίμων of Strabo, which itself is a mistranslation of Yemen as if it were Yumn, 'good fortune.']

[2] [Oasis is probably nothing else than the Arabic word *wādī*, though it has come to mean something different.]

[3] [But *cf.* Caussin de Perceval, *Essai sur l'Histoire des Arabes*, vol. i. p. 73.]

carriers of the world between the east and west. In those days the sea was dreaded, and commerce confined almost exclusively to the land. A continent, now the greatest obstacle to traffic, was then its chief facility. The steppes of Central Asia and Arabia were the ocean of the ancients, and companies of camels their fleets. But the way was long and perilous; and hence the necessity for caravans travelling at fixed periods and by determined routes. 'The course of the caravan,' says Heeren, 'was not a matter of free choice, but of established custom. In the vast steppes of sandy deserts, which they had to traverse, nature had sparingly allotted to the traveller a few scattered places of rest, where under the shade of palm trees, and beside the cool fountains at their feet, the merchant and his beast of burden might enjoy the refreshment rendered necessary by so much suffering. Such places of repose became *entrepôts* of commerce, and not unfrequently the sites of temples and sanctuaries, under the protection of which the merchant prosecuted his trade, and to which the pilgrim resorted.[1]

Two routes through Arabia

Through Arabia there were two main routes between Syria and the Indian Ocean. One struck north from Ḥadramaut to Gerra, the modern Lachsa, on the Persian Gulf, and thence by Palmyra to Palestine and Tyre. The western (with which we are more immediately concerned) started from the same quarter, and ran parallel with the Red Sea, avoiding on the one hand the parched deserts of Nejd, and the impracticable cliffs of the coast upon the other. Mecca, the ancient Macoraba, was probably the half-way station between Arabia Felix and Arabia Petræa. The traffic afforded a wide field of employment to the Arab tribes. Some settled in the various emporia, and became traders on their own account. Others, without abandoning their nomad habits, were carriers of the trade.

Mercantile prosperity of Arabia

The commerce assumed great dimensions, and enriched the nation. About 600 B.C. Ezekiel's denunciation of haughty Tyre marks the busy intercourse which then replenished the Phenician markets with the products of Arabia and the East.[2]

[1] *Heeren's Researches: Africa*, vol. i. p. 23. The concluding sentence bears upon the origin and rise of Mecca. But it will still be a question, which had the priority, the temple or the mercantile station?

[2] Ezek. xxvii. 19-24, which Heeren translates: '*Wadan and Javan*

Several centuries later, we learn from Roman writers that the Arabs of the Ḥījāz still carried on the same traffic; and, which is remarkable, the number of stages from Ḥaḍramaut to Ayla, given by them as seventy, corresponds exactly with the number at the present day. From the stately ruins which in the Syrian desert still denote the sites of ancient emporia, some conception may be formed of the prosperity and wealth of the merchant princes inhabiting them. And, no doubt, at the southern terminus also there were in Yemen and Ḥaḍramaut cities which might vie, though in a ruder and simpler way, with the queenly Palmyra.

Failure o the trade and disastrous results

It was an evil hour for Arabia when Roman enterprise, early in the Christian era, established a maritime traffic from Egypt direct to the Yemen and the East, and thus inflicted a fatal blow on the caravan trade of the peninsula. The land commerce melted away, and the mercantile stations were deserted. Such, after the lapse of sixteen centuries, is the tale which the ruins of Petra, Jerash, and Philadelphia still attest. The drying up of the tide of merchandise which from time immemorial had fertilised Arabia, and the abandonment of many populous cities dependent on it, cannot fail to have caused widespread disorganisation and distress. The Bedawi carriers might betake themselves to their desert wastes again; but the settled population, with no such resource, were forced to emigrate in quest of sustenance elsewhere. To this cause may most probably be traced those great emigrations from the south of Ḳoḍā'a and Azd tribes, which tradition tells us took place in the second century. These all tended northwards, some to Mecca and Syria, some to Central Arabia, and others to the Persian Gulf and Al-Ḥīra.

Emigration northwards

brought thee, from Sanaa, sword blades, cassia and cinnamon, in exchange for thy wares. The merchants of Saba and of Raama traded with thee; the best spices, precious stones, and gold brought they to thee for thy wares. Haran, Canna, Aden, Saba, traded with thee.' He adds: 'Some of these places, as Aden, Canna, and Haran, all celebrated seaports on the Indian Sea, as well as Saba (or Mariaba) and Sanaa still the capital of Yemen, have retained their name unchanged to the present day; the site of others, as Wadan, on the Straits of Bab el Mandeb, rest only on probable conjecture. These accurate statements of the prophet at all events prove what a special knowledge the inhabitants of Palestine had of Happy Arabia, and how great and active the intercourse with that country must have been.'—*Heeren's As. Res.* vol. ii. p. 98

Kingdoms of Ghassān and of Al-Ḥīra

There were but a few points at which, in ancient times, Arabia touched the outer world. The northern region, stretching from Syria to the Euphrates, was occupied in the 2nd century by some of those tribes which had, according to native tradition, about that time immigrated from the south, and of whom we frequently hear in the later annals of the Roman empire. To the west in the Syrian desert, with their capital at Palmyra, was the dynasty of the Ghassānids; and to the east, on the banks of the Euphrates, the kingdom of Al-Ḥīra; the former, as a rule, adhered to the Roman, the latter to the Persian, empire. At some points we can even identify the heroes of Arab story with those of western history. Thus, 'Odheina and Zebbā of Tadmor are, without doubt, the Odenathus and Zenobia of Palmyra. In the marvellous tales of Zebbā, her beauty, wealth, and knowledge of many languages, and her capture at the tunnel which she had constructed under the Euphrates, we can dimly read the story of Zenobia, her splendid reign, her rebellion and defence of Palmyra, and her seizure by the Romans as she endeavoured to escape across the river. The princes of Al-Ḥīra, again, are often mentioned by the Greek and Roman historians, in the wars of the 5th and 6th centuries, as adherents of the Persian cause. Suddenly as a thunder-cloud their troops would darken some fated spot on the Roman border, and sweeping in their train devastation, captivity, and death, as suddenly disappear, scorning pursuit, and leaving no trace, but in their ravages, behind.

Their decadence in the seventh century

The dynasty of Palmyra, with the western tribes, had embraced Christianity in the time of Constantine; to the east our Faith was later of gaining ground, and indeed was not adopted by the court of Al-Ḥīra till near the end of the 6th century. Early in the 7th, that kingdom fell from its dignity as an independent power, and became a satrapy of Persia. The Ghassānid rule also broke up into various petty sections, and eventually merged into the Roman empire. The Persian inroads in the reign of Phocas and early years of Heraclius, gave the Syrian tribes a shock from which they never recovered. Thus the decadence of kingdoms on both sides of the desert was destined to smooth the victorious path of the Arabian conqueror.

Turning now to the south, we find Ḥaḍramaut and the

Kingdom of Ḥaḍramaut and the Yemen

Yemen ruled by the Ḥimyarites, a dynasty of which tradition carries the origin back into the obscurity of ages. In the 4th century an embassy from Constantius visited this court, headed by a Christian bishop. In 523 A.D. the throne was seized by a bigoted and dissolute usurper. A proselyte to Judaism, he perpetrated frightful cruelties on the Christians of the neighbouring province of Nejrān who refused to embrace his faith. Trenches filled with combustible materials were lighted, and the martyrs cast into the flames. Tradition gives the number thus miserably burned, or slain by the sword, at twenty thousand. However exaggerated, there can be no doubt of the bloody character of the tyrant's reign. An intended victim escaped to the court of Justinian, and, holding up a half-burned Gospel, invoked retribution. At the Emperor's desire the Negus crossed from Ethiopia and defeated the usurper; and thus the Ḥimyarites were supplanted by a Christian government under an Abyssinian viceroy. But African rule was distasteful to the people; an appeal was made to Persia, and before the end of the 6th century the Abyssinians were expelled, and the Yemen sank into a simple dependency of Persia.

Arabia before Moḥammad unknown to the outer world

Thus, whether we look to the north or the south, it was but the farther outskirts of the Peninsula which came into even casual contact with the civilised world. The rest of Arabia was absolutely unknown; and excepting through the medium of countrymen engaged in merchandise, or settled on the confines of Syria, the Arabs themselves had but little knowledge of anything beyond their own deserts. For any community of interest with nations beyond, they might have been at the very antipodes of the Roman empire. It is not till the 5th century that native tradition, as preserved by Moḥammadan writers, begins to shed a fitful and shadowy light upon the political and religious condition of the country. Before, therefore, turning to Mecca, we shall take a rapid survey of Arabia at the period of Moḥammad's appearance.

Political condition of the Peninsula

The habits of the nomad tribes roaming over the Peninsula are singularly changeless; and Arabia, as we find it in the 6th century, differs little from the Arabia of Abraham and of Job. The leading feature has ever been impatience of restraint, and the consequent independence of the clan, the family, and the individual. The affairs of each tribe, or combination of tribes, are guided by a Sheikh, their popular representative; but there is no bond that of necessity holds them permanently together, and dissentients may secede at pleasure. With a code of honour bordering on jealousy, personal hostility and tribal warfare are ever liable to occur; new combinations arise, and old ones disappear; some cling to their ancestral haunts, and some, with characteristic restlessness, roam abroad, or even migrate to distant parts. On the other hand, a strong cohesive power, counteracting these disintegrating tendencies, conserves the tribal constitution, binds together the members of each body, and interests them in its safety and honour. So strong, indeed, is this conservatism, that after the lapse of twelve centuries we find at the present day some tribes, as the Beni 'Adwān and Hawāzin, the same in name and lineage, and inhabiting the same localities, as in the days of Moḥammad.

Political and religious state of Arabia

Subdivision and independence of Arab tribes a formidable obstacle to union

The first peculiarity, then, which attracts our attention is the subdivision of the Arabs into innumerable bodies, governed by the same code of honour and morals, exhibiting the same manners, speaking for the most part the same language, but each independent of the others; restless and often at war amongst themselves; and even where united by blood or by interest, ever ready on some insignificant cause to separate and give way to an implacable hostility. Thus at the era of Islām the retrospect of Arabian history exhibits, as in the kaleidoscope, an ever-varying state of combination and repulsion, such as had hitherto rendered abortive any attempt at a general union. The freedom of Arabia from foreign conquest was owing not so much to the difficulties of its parched and pathless wilds, as to the endless array of isolated clans, and the absence of any head or chief power which might be made the object of subjugation. The problem had yet to be solved, by what force these tribes could be subdued, or drawn to one common centre; and it was solved by Moḥammad, who struck out a political system of his own, universally acceptable because derived from elements common to all Arabia; vigorous, because based upon the energy of a new religious life; rapidly and irrepressibly expansive, because borne forward by inducements, irresistible to an Arab, of war and plunder.

Small prospect of religious reform

The prospects of Arabia before the rise of Moḥammad were as unfavourable to religious reform as they were to political union or national regeneration. The foundation of Arab faith was a deep-rooted idolatry, which for centuries had stood proof, with no palpable symptom of decay, against every attempt at evangelisation from Egypt and Syria.

Christianity neutralised by Judaism

Several causes increased the insensibility of Arabia to the Gospel. A broad margin of hostile Judaism on the northern frontier neutralised the effects of Christian teaching, and afforded shelter to the paganism beyond. Thus Jewish influence spread far towards the south, and was there supported by the powerful Jewish settlement in the Yemen, which at times even sought to proselytise the neighbouring tribes.

Combination with Judaical legends

But more than this, the idolatry of Mecca had formed a compromise with Judaism, and had admitted enough of its legends, and perhaps of its tenets also, to steel the national mind against the appeal of Christianity. Idolatry, simple and naked, may be comparatively powerless against the attacks of reason and the Gospel; but, aided by some measure of truth, it can maintain its ground against the most urgent persuasion. To advance the authority of Abraham for the worship of the Ka'ba, and vaunt his legacy of divinely inculcated rites, would be a triumphant reply to the invitations either of Judaism or of Christianity. Moreover, the Christianity of the 7th century was itself decrepit and corrupt. It was disabled by contending schisms, and had substituted the puerilities of superstition for the pure and expansive faith of the early ages.

Unsettled frontier to the north

Northern Arabia, long the battle-field of Persia and the Empire, was peculiarly unfavourable to Christian effort. Alternately swept by the armies of the Chosroes and of Constantinople, of Al-Ḥīra and the Ghassānids, the Syrian frontier presented little opportunity for the advance of peaceful Christianity.

Habits of the Arabs opposed to Christianity

The vagrant habits of the Nomads themselves eluded the importunity of missionary endeavour; while their haughty temper and vindictive code equally resented the peaceful and forgiving precepts of the Gospel. A nominal adhesion to Christianity, as to any other religion, may indeed be obtained without participation in its spirit or subjection to its moral requirements; but such formal submission could have resulted alone from the political supremacy of a Christian power, not from the persuasion of a religious agency. Let us inquire, then, what political inducements at this time bore upon Arabia from without.

Political influence of Christianity from without. 1. From the *North*

To the *North*, we find that Egypt and Syria, representing the Roman empire, exercised at the best but a remote influence upon Arabian affairs; and even that was neutralised by the victories of Persia. The weight of Constantinople, if ever brought to bear directly upon Arabia, was but lightly and transiently felt. The kingdom of Ghassān, on the borders of Syria, was indeed at once Arabian and Christian, but it yielded to Al-Ḥīra the palm of supremacy, and never exercised any important bearing on the affairs and policy of central Arabia.

2. From the *North-east*

Turning to the *North-east*, we observe that the prospects of Christianity had improved by the conversion of the court of Al-Ḥīra and many of its subject tribes. But Al-Ḥīra itself was only a vassal; for its native dynasty had lately been replaced by the direct government of Persia, a strong opponent of Christianity. Thus the authority of Pagan Persia over the northern and eastern Arabs more than counterbalanced the influence of Christianity in the west.

3. From the *South*

To the *South*, the Faith had suffered an important loss. The prestige of a Christian monarchy, though but an Ethiopian, was gone; and in its room had arisen a Persian satrapy, under the shadow of which the ancient Ḥimyarite idolatry, and once royal Judaism, flourished apace.[1] On the *West* there lay the Christian kingdom of Abyssinia, but it was divided from Arabia by the Red Sea; and the Negro race, even if brought into closer contact, could never have exercised much influence upon the Arab mind.

4. From the *West*

The peninsula presented no prospect of hopeful change

Thus the star of Christianity was not in the ascendant: in some respects it was declining. There was no hope from external aid; and, apart from such aid, the strong influence of Judaism, and almost universal submission to national idolatry, rendered the conversion of Arabia a doubtful and a

[1] Gibbon attaches, perhaps, too much importance to the change: 'This narrative,' he says, 'of obscure and remote events is not foreign to the decline and fall of the Roman empire. If a Christian power had been maintained in Arabia, Moḥammad must have been crushed in his cradle, and Abyssinia would have prevented a revolution, which has changed the civil and religious state of the world.'—*Decline and Fall*, chap. xlii.

distant prospect. During the youth of Moḥammad, the aspect of the Peninsula was strongly conservative; perhaps never at any previous time was reform more hopeless.

Causes are sometimes conjured up to account for results produced by an agent apparently inadequate to effect them. Moḥammad arose, and forthwith the Arabs were aroused to a new and a spiritual faith; hence the conclusion that Arabia was fermenting for the change, and prepared to adopt it. To us, calmly reviewing the past, pre-Islāmite history belies the assumption. After five centuries of Christian evangelisation, we can point to but a sprinkling here and there of Christian converts;—the Beni'l-Ḥārith of Nejrān; the Beni Hanīfa of Al-Yemāma; some of the Beni Ṭai' at Teimā; and hardly any more. Judaism, vastly more powerful, had exhibited spasmodic efforts at proselytism; but, as an active and converting agent, the Jewish faith was no longer operative. In fine, viewed in a religious aspect, the surface of Arabia had been now and then gently rippled by the feeble efforts of Christianity; the sterner influences of Judaism had been occasionally visible in a deeper and more troubled current; but the tide of indigenous idolatry and Ishmaelite superstition, setting strongly from every quarter towards the Ka'ba, gave ample evidence that the faith and worship of Mecca held the Arab mind in a rigorous and undisputed thraldom.

Arabia obstinately fixed in the profession of idolatry

Yet, even amongst a people thus enthralled, there existed elements which a master mind, seeking the regeneration of Arabia, might work upon. Christianity was well known; living examples there were amongst the native tribes; the New Testament was respected, if not revered, as a book that claimed to be divine; in most quarters it was easily accessible, and some of its facts and doctrines admitted without dispute. The tenets of Judaism were even more familiar, and its legends, if not its sacred writings, known throughout the peninsula. The worship of Mecca was founded upon patriarchal traditions common at once to Christianity and Judaism. Here, then, was ground on which the spiritual fulcrum might be planted; a wide field in close connection with the truth, inviting scrutiny and upward movement. No doubt, many an Arab heart, before Moḥammad, had responded to the voice, casually heard it

Still material prepared by Judaism and Christianity

may be, of Christianity and of Judaism: many an honest Bedawi spirit confessed of the law that it was just and good: many an aspiring intellect, as the eye travelled over the spangled expanse of heaven, concluded that the universe was supported by ONE great Being; and in time of need, many an earnest soul had accepted with joy the Christian sacrifice. Ḳoss, bishop of Nejrān, was not the first, nor perhaps the most eloquent and earnest, of Arab preachers who sought to turn their fellows from the error of their ways, and reasoned with them of righteousness, temperance, and judgment to come.

It was Moḥammad who worked the material into shape

The material for a great change was here. But it required to be wrought; and Moḥammad was the workman. The fabric of Islām no more necessarily grew out of the state of Arabia, than a gorgeous texture grows from the slender meshes of silken filament; or the stately ship from unhewn timber of the forest; or the splendid palace from rude masses of rock. Had Moḥammad, stern to his early convictions, followed the leading of Jewish and Christian truth, and inculcated upon his fellows their simple doctrine, there might have been a 'SAINT MOḤAMMAD'—more likely a 'MOḤAMMAD THE MARTYR'—laying the foundation stone of the Arabian Church. But then (so far as human probabilities and analogy indicate) Arabia would not have been convulsed by his preaching to its centre, or even any considerable portions of it converted. Instead of all this, he, with consummate skill, devised a machinery, by the adaptive energy of which he gradually shaped the broken and disconnected masses of the Arab race into an harmonious whole, a body politic endowed with life and vigour. To the Christian, he was as a Christian; to the Jew he became as a Jew; to the idolater of Mecca, as a reformed worshipper of the Ka'ba. And thus, by unparalleled art and a rare supremacy of mind, he persuaded the whole of Arabia, Pagan, Jew, and Christian, to follow his steps with docile submission.

Such a process is that of *the workman shaping his material.* It is not that of the material shaping its own form, much less (as some would hold) moulding the workman himself. It was Moḥammad that formed Islām; it was not Islām, or any pre-existing Muslim spirit, that moulded Moḥammad.

CHAPTER III

PRE-HISTORICAL NOTICES OF MECCA

WE shall in this chapter consider such mythical and traditional notices of Mecca as may throw light on the origin of the Ka'ba and its worship, and on the ancestry of Moḥammad.

Legendary founding of Mecca by Ishmael

Native legend ascribes the building of the Ka'ba to Abraham.[1] Hagar (so the story runs) wandering in the desert with her boy, reaches at length the valley of Mecca. In the agony of thirst she paces hurriedly to and fro between the little hills of the Ṣafā and the Merwa, seeking for water. Ishmael, whom she had left crying on the ground, kicks around him in childish passion, when behold the spot bubbles forth beneath his feet in a clear stream of sweet water. It is the well Zemzem. Amalekites and Arab tribes from the Yemen, attracted by the fountain, settle there; Ishmael grows up amongst them, and marries the daughter of their chief. In fulfilment of the divine command received in a vision, Abraham is about to offer up his son upon an eminence in the neighbourhood, when his arm is stayed and a vicarious sacrifice accepted. On a subsequent visit, the patriarch, assisted by his son, erected the temple where it now stands, and reconstituted the primeval rites of pilgrimage.

Traditional history to 4th century

Descending from this myth, we find little more than bare genealogical tables (borrowed palpably from the Jews) in which it is sought to trace up generation by generation the Ḳoreishite stock to Abraham. It is not till we reach the Christian era that tradition commences, and soon begins to teem with tales and legends in which, mingled with a mass of fiction, there may be grains of fact. The guardianship of

[1] Aṭ-Ṭabari, i. 270 ff., 1130 ff.; Ibn Sa'd, p. 21 ff.

Ka'ba (belonging to the Ḳoreishite ancestry in virtue of descent from Ishmael) was usurped by the tribe of Jurhum, which remained long in possession of the temple and supremacy of Mecca.[1] In the 2nd century some of the numerous tribes migrating (as we have seen) from the Yemen northwards, settled in the vicinity. Most of these passed on eventually to Medīna, Syria, and Al-Ḥīra; but a remnant, called Khozā'a, remained behind, and in their turn seized upon the government of Mecca.[2] The Jurhum dynasty was thus ousted in the 3rd century, and their last king, on retiring from Mecca, buried in the well Zemzem his treasures; among these were two gazelles of gold, and swords and suits of armour, of which we shall hear more hereafter.

Ḳoṣai assumes government; middle of 5th century

For 200 years the Khozā'a remained masters of Mecca, certain inferior offices of the Ka'ba being alone retained by families of the original stock. It was reserved for Ḳoṣai, a bold adventurer of Ḳoreish, to supplant the usurpers, and by force of arms resume for its rightful owners the supreme control of Mecca.[3] Gathering his kindred around him, he settled them in the sacred valley, enlarged the city, and assigned to each family a separate quarter. Near the Ka'ba he built a council-house in which, under his presidency, was transacted all important business. From thence caravans set out; there the returning traveller first alighted; and there, when war was waged, the banner was mounted and consigned to the standard bearer by Ḳoṣai or his sons. Ḳoṣai also assumed the chief offices connected with the local worship. The keys of the Ka'ba were in his hands; the giving of drink to the pilgrims and providing them with food were his sole prerogative, which, administered with princely hospitality, invested his name in the eyes of all Arabia with a peculiar lustre. The assumption of these functions consolidated the power of Ḳoṣai as the Sheikh of Mecca and chief of the surrounding territory; and tradition adds that 'his ordinances were obeyed and venerated, as people obey and venerate the observances of religion, both before and after his death.' This same Ḳoṣai was ancestor, at the fifth remove, of the Arabian Prophet.

[1] Ibn Hishām, p. 71 f. [2] *Ibid.* p. 75.

[3] Aṭ-Ṭabari, i. 1092 ff; Ibn Sa'd, p. 36 ff.

Rites of the Ka'ba

The ceremonies of pilgrimage thus handed down by Ḳoṣai were substantially the same as we find them in the time of Moḥammad; and, with some modifications introduced by Moḥammad himself, the same as practised at the present day. The centre of them all is the Ka'ba, to visit which, to kiss the Black Stone imbedded in the eastern corner, and to make seven circuits round the sacred edifice, is at all times and seasons, meritorious. The 'Lesser pilgrimage' (otherwise called '*Omra*), in addition to these acts, includes the passing to and fro with hasty steps seven times between the eminences of the Ṣafā and the Merwa. This may be performed with merit at any season of the year, but especially in the sacred month of Rejeb. Before entering the holy territory, the votary assumes the pilgrim garb, and at the conclusion of the ceremonies shaves his head and pares his nails.

Lesser pilgrimage

Greater pilgrimage

The 'Greater pilgrimage' can be performed only in the holy month Dhu'l-Ḥijja. In addition to the ceremonies of the Lesser, it embraces the tour of 'Arafāt, a small granite hill in the mountains, ten or twelve miles east of Mecca. The pilgrims, starting from Mecca on the 8th of the month, stay the following day at 'Arafāt, and having ascended the hill, hasten back the same evening three or four miles to Al-Muzdelifa. Next day, returning half-way to Mecca, they stay at Mina, where they spend the two or three succeeding days. Small stones are cast by the pilgrims at certain objects in the Mina valley, and the pilgrimage is concluded by the sacrifice of victims there.

Sacred environs of Mecca and four holy months

The *Ḥaram* or sacred tract several miles round Mecca was hallowed and inviolable, and had from time immemorial been so regarded. Four months of the year were held sacred; three consecutive, and one separate.[1] During this period war was by unanimous consent suspended, hostile

[1] The consecutive months were the last two of the Old year, and the first of the New; the other was the seventh, *Rejeb*.

An innovation was introduced (as is said, by Ḳoṣai) by which the first month of the year might be commuted into the second, *i.e.* Moḥarram into Ṣafar. Ḳoṣai may have wished, by abridging the long three months' recess of peace, to humour the warlike Arabs, as well as to obtain for himself the power of holding a month either sacred or secular as might best suit his purpose. The office of intercalation and commutation was called *Nasā'*; and the person holding it, *Nāsī'*.

feeling was suppressed, and amnesty reigned throughout Arabia. Pilgrims from every quarter could then safely repair to Mecca, and fairs in various parts were thronged by those whom merchandise, or the contests of poetry or social rivalry, brought together.

The luni-solar year of Mecca

There is reason to suppose that the year was originally lunar, and so continued till the beginning of the fifth century, when in imitation of the Jews it was turned, by the interjection of a month at the close of every third year, into a luni-solar period. If by this change it was intended to make the season of pilgrimage correspond invariably with the autumn, when a supply of food for the vast multitude would be easily procurable, that object was defeated by the remaining imperfection of the cycle; for the year being still shorter by one day and a fraction than the real year, each recurring season accelerated the time of pilgrimage; so that when, after two centuries, intercalation was altogether prohibited by Moḥammad, the days of pilgrimage had moved from October gradually backward to March.

Origin of the Ka'ba and its worship

In reviewing the history of Mecca, the origin of the temple and of the local worship demands further scrutiny. Muslim belief attributes both to Abraham, and connects part of the ceremonial with Biblical legend; but the story i. plainly a fable. The following considerations strengthen the conviction that Mecca and its rites cannot possibly claim any such origin. *First.*—There is no trace of anything Abrahamic in the essential elements of the superstition. To kiss the Black Stone; to make the circuit of the Ka'ba, and perform other observances at Mecca, Arafāt, and the vale of Mina; to keep the sacred months and to hallow the sacred territory—have no conceivable connection with Abraham, or with the ideas which his descendants would be likely to inherit from him. Such rites originated in causes foreign to the country chiefly occupied by the children of Abraham; they were either strictly local; or, in so far as based on the idolatry prevailing in the south, were imported by immigrants from the Yemen.

No Abrahamic element in its chief ceremonies

Remote antiquity of the Ka'ba

Second.—A very high antiquity must be assigned to the main features of the religion of Mecca. Although Herodotus does not refer to the Ka'ba, yet he names as one of the chief Arab divinities, ALILAT; and this is strong evidence of the worship at that early period of *Al-Lāt*, the great idol of Mecca.[1] He likewise alludes to the veneration of the Arabs for stones. Diodorus Siculus, writing about half a century before our era, says of Arabia washed by the Red Sea, 'there is, in this country, a temple greatly revered by the Arabs.' These words must refer to the Holy House of Mecca, for we know of no other which ever commanded such universal homage. Early *historical* tradition gives no trace of its first construction. Some authorities assert that the Amalekites rebuilt the edifice, which they found in ruins, and retained it for a time under their charge. All agree that it was in existence under the Jurhum tribe (about the time of the Christian era), and, being injured by a flood of rain, was then repaired. Tradition represents the Ka'ba as from time immemorial the scene of pilgrimage from *all* quarters of Arabia:—from the Yemen and Ḥaḍramaut, from the shores of the Persian Gulf, the deserts of Syria, and the distant environs of Al-Ḥīra and Mesopotamia, men yearly flocked to Mecca. So extensive a homage must have had its beginnings in an extremely remote age; and a similar antiquity must be ascribed to the essential concomitants of the local worship—the Ka'ba with its Black Stone, the sacred territory, and the holy months. The origin of a superstition so ancient and so universal must be looked for within the peninsula itself, and not in any foreign country.

Wide extent of the worship

Third.—The native systems of Arabia were Sabeanism, Idolatry, and Stone-worship—all closely connected with the religion of Mecca. There is reason for believing that *Sabeanism*, or the worship of the heavenly bodies, existed from an early period in Arabia. The book of Job contains historical notices of the system, and certain early names in the Ḥimyar dynasty imply its prevalence. As late as the fourth century, we find sacrifices offered in the Yemen to the sun, moon, and stars. The seven circuits of the Ka'ba were probably emblematical of the revolutions of the planetary bodies; and we are told that a similar rite was observed in other Arabian fanes. Again the practice of idolatry overspread the whole peninsula. We have authentic records of ancient idol shrines scattered in various quarters from the Yemen to Dūma and even as far as Al-Ḥīra, some of

Connection with systems native to Arabia

1. Sabeanism

2. Idolatry

[1] Herod. iii. 8.

them subordinate to the Ka'ba and having similar rites. A system thus widely diffused and thoroughly organised, may well be regarded as of indigenous growth. The most singular feature in this worship was the adoration paid to unshapen stones. Muslims hold that this practice arose out of the Ka'ba rites. 'The adoration of stones among the Ishmaelites,' says Ibn Isḥāḳ, 'originated in the custom of men carrying a stone from the sacred enclosure of Mecca when they went upon a journey, out of reverence for the Ka'ba; and whithersoever they went they set it up and made circuits round about it as about the Ka'ba, till at last they adored every goodly stone they saw, forgot their religion, and changed the faith of Abraham and Ishmael into the worship of images.' The tendency to stone-worship was undoubtedly prevalent throughout Arabia; but it is more probable that it gave rise to the superstition of the Ka'ba with its Black Stone, than took its rise therefrom.

3. Stone-worship

Supposed history of Mecca and its religion

Thus the religion of Mecca is, in all essential points, connected strictly with forms of superstition native to Arabia, and we may naturally conclude that it grew out of them. The process may be thus imagined. Mecca owed its origin to the convenient position which it held between the Yemen and Petra. We have seen that, from ancient times, the merchandise of the East passed through Arabia; and the vale of Mecca lay midway upon the great western route. A plentiful supply of water attracted the caravans; it became a halting place, and then the *entrepôt* of commerce; a mercantile population grew up in the vicinity, and change of carriage took place there. The carrier's hire, the frontier customs, the dues of protection, and the profits of direct traffic, added capital to the city which may have rivalled, though in a primitive and simple style, the emporia of Petra, Jerash, and Philadelphia. The earliest inhabitants were natives of the Yemen, and the ever-flowing traffic maintained a permanent intercourse between them and their original home. From the Yemen, no doubt, they brought with them, or subsequently received, Sabeanism, Stone-worship, and Idolatry. These were connected with the well Zemzem, the source of their prosperity; and near to it they erected their fane, with its symbolical Sabeanism and mysterious Black Stone. Local rites were superadded; but it was the Yemen, the cradle of the Arabs, which furnished the essential elements of the system. The mercantile eminence of Mecca, while it attracted the Bedawīn from all parts of Arabia by the profits of the carrying trade, by degrees imparted a national character to the local superstition, till at last it became the religion of all Arabia. When the southern trade deserted this channel, the mercantile prestige of Mecca vanished and its opulence decayed, but the Ka'ba continued the national temple of the Peninsula. The floating population betook themselves to the desert; and the native tribes (the ancestry of Ḳoreish) were overpowered by such southern immigrants as the Jurhum and Khozā'a dynasties; till at last Ḳoṣai arose to vindicate the honour, and re-establish the influence, of the house of Mecca.

How reconciled with the legend of Abrahamic origin

But, according to this theory, how shall we account for the tradition current among the Arabs, that the temple owed its origin to Abraham? This was no Muslim fiction, but the popular belief long before the time of Moḥammad. Otherwise, it could not have been referred to in the Ḳor'ān as an acknowledged fact; nor would certain spots around the Ka'ba have been connected, as we know them to have been, with the names of Abraham and Ishmael. It seems probable that Abrahamic tribes were early commingled with the Arabs coming from the South, and that a branch descended from Abraham and Ishmael, may have settled at Mecca and there become allied with the Yemenite race. Abrahamic legends still surviving in the land would be resuscitated and strengthened by intercourse with the Jews. The mingled stock from Syria and from the Yemen required such a modification of the local religion as would correspond with their double descent. Hence Jewish legends would naturally be grafted upon the indigenous worship, and rites of sacrifice would now for the first time be introduced, or at any rate now first associated with the memory of Abraham.

Supposed origin of this legend

Abrahamic legend combined with the local superstition

The Jews were also largely settled in Northern Arabia, where they acquired a considerable influence. There were extensive colonies about Medīna and Kheibar, in Wādi al-Ḳora, and on the shores of the Ælanitic gulf. These maintained a constant and friendly intercourse with Mecca and the Arab tribes, who looked with respect and veneration upon their religion and their holy books. When once the loose conception of Abraham and Ishmael as great forefathers of the race was superimposed upon the superstition of Mecca, and had received the stamp of native currency, it will easily be conceived that Jewish tradition and legend would be eagerly welcomed and readily assimilated with native legend and tradition. By a summary adjustment, the story of Palestine became the story of the Ḥijāz. The precincts of the Ka'ba were hallowed as the scene of Hagar's distress, and the sacred well Zemzem as the source of her relief. The pilgrims hasted to and fro between the Ṣafā and the Merwa in memory of her hurried steps in search of water. It was Abraham and Ishmael who built the temple, imbedded in it the Black Stone, and established for all Arabia the pilgrimage to 'Arafāt. In imitation of him it was that stones were flung by the pilgrims as if at Satan, and sacrifices offered at Mina in remembrance of the vicarious sacrifice by Abraham. And so, although the indigenous rites may have been little if at all altered by the adoption of Israelitish legends, they came to be viewed in a totally different light, and to be connected in Arab imagination with something of the sanctity of Abraham the Friend of God.[1] The gulf between the gross idolatry of Arabia and the pure theism of the Jews thus bridged over, it was upon this common ground Moḥammad took his stand, and proclaimed to his people a

Vantage ground thus gained by Moḥammad

[1] To the same source may be traced the doctrine of a Supreme Being, to whom gods and idols were alike subordinate. The title *Allah Ta'āla*, THE MOST HIGH GOD, was used long before Moḥammad to designate this conception. But in some tribes, the idea had become so materialised that a portion of the votive offerings was assigned to the great God, just as a portion was allotted to their idols. The notion of a supreme Divinity represented by no sensible symbol is clearly not cognate with any of the indigenous forms of Arab superstition. It was borrowed directly from the Jews, or from some other Abrahamic race among whom contact with the Jews had preserved or revived the knowledge of the 'God of Abraham.'

Familiarity with the Abrahamic races also introduced the doctrine of the immortality of the soul, and the resurrection from the dead; but these were held with many fantastic ideas of Arabian growth. Revenge pictured the murdered soul as a bird chirping for retribution against the murderer; and a camel was sometimes left to starve at the grave of his master, that he might be ready at the resurrection again to carry him. A vast variety of Biblical language was also in common use, or at least sufficiently in use to be commonly understood. Faith, Repentance,

new and spiritual system, in accents to which the whole Peninsula could respond. The rites of the Ka'ba were retained, but stripped of all idolatrous tendency, they still hang, a strange unmeaning shroud, around the living theism of Islām.

Heaven, and Hell, the Devil and his angels, the heavenly Angels, Gabriel the messenger of God, are specimens acquired from some Jewish source, either current or ready for adoption. Similarly familiar were the stories of the Fall of man, the Flood, the destruction of the cities of the plain, &c.—so that there was an extensive substratum of crude ideas bordering upon the spiritual, ready to the hand of Moḥammad.

CHAPTER IV

THE FOREFATHERS OF MOḤAMMAD

Civil polity based on the habits of the Bedawīn

THE social institutions of Mecca did not essentially differ from those of the wandering Bedawīn. They were to some extent modified by their settled habitation and by the pilgrimage and surroundings of the Ka'ba. But the ultimate sanctions of society, and the springs of political movement, were in reality the same at Mecca then as exist in Arabia at the present day.

General principles of Bedawī government

It must be borne in mind that at Mecca there was not, before the establishment of Islām, any *government* in the common sense of the term. No supreme authority existed whose mandate was law. Every separate tribe was a republic governed by public opinion; and the opinion of the aggregate tribes, who chanced for the time to act together, the sovereign law. There was no recognised exponent of the popular will; each tribe was free to hold back from the decree of the remainder; and no individual was more bound than his collective tribe to a compulsory conformity with even the unanimous resolve of his fellow-citizens. Honour and revenge supplied the place of a more elaborate system. The former prompted the individual, by the desire of upholding the name and influence of his clan, to a compliance with the general wish; the latter provided for the respect of private right, by the unrelenting pursuit of the injurer. In effect, the will of the majority did form the general rule of action, although there was continual risk that the minority might separate and assume an independent, if not a hostile, attitude. The law of revenge, too, though in such a society perhaps unavoidable, was then, even as now, the curse of Arabia. The stain of blood once shed was not easily effaced:

its price might be rejected by the heir, and life demanded for life. Retaliation followed retribution: the nearest of kin, the family, the clan, the confederate tribes, one by one in a widening circle, identified themselves with the sufferer, and adopted his claim as their own; and thus a petty affront or unpremeditated blow not unfrequently involved whole tribes and tracts of country in protracted and bloody strife. Still, in a system which provided no legal power to interfere in personal disputes, it cannot be doubted that the law of retaliation afforded an important check upon the passions of the stronger; and that acts of violence and injustice were repressed by fear of retribution from the relatives or adherents of the injured party. The benefit of the custom was further increased by the practice of *patronage* or guardianship. The weak resorted to the strong for protection; and when the word of a chief or powerful man had once been pledged to grant it, the pledge was fulfilled with chivalrous scrupulosity.

Offices conferring authority on Chiefs of Mecca

At first sight it might appear that, under this system, a Chief possessed no shadow of authority to execute either his own wish or that of the people. But in reality his powers, though vague and undefined, were large and effective. The position of Chief always secured an important share in forming and giving expression to public opinion; so that, excepting rare and unusual cases, he swayed the councils and movements of his tribe. It was mainly by the influence derived from the offices attaching to the Ka'ba and the Pilgrimage, that the Chiefs of Mecca differed from the Sheikhs of the nomad tribes, and exercised a more regular and permanent rule.

Ḳoṣai, A.D. 440, and his descendants

We have seen that about the middle of the 5th century Ḳoṣai had concentrated the chief of these offices in his own person. When he became old and infirm, he resigned them into the hands of his eldest son, 'Abd ed-Dār.[1] From him they descended to his sons and grandsons; but the latter, who succeeded to the inheritance in the beginning of the 6th century, were too young effectually to maintain their rights. 'Abd Menāf, another son of Ḳoṣai, had been the powerful rival of his brother; and the sons of 'Abd Menāf inherited their father's influence. The chief were, Al-Muṭṭalib, 'Abd

[1] Ibn Hishām, p. 84 f.; Aṭ-Ṭabari, i. 1098 f.; Ibn Sa'd, p. 42.

Discord among Ḳoṣai's descendants

Shams, Naufal, and Hāshim.[1] These conspired to wrest from the descendants of 'Abd ed-Dār the hereditary offices bequeathed by Ḳoṣai. Hāshim took the lead, and grounded his claim on the superior dignity of the family of 'Abd Menāf. But the descendants of 'Abd ed-Dār refused to cede their rights, and an open rupture ensued. Ḳoreish was equally divided, one portion siding with the claimants, and the other with the actual possessors of the offices. The respective factions, having bound themselves by the most stringent oaths, were already marshalled in hostile array, when unexpectedly truce was called. The conditions were to give Hāshim and his party the offices of providing food and water for the pilgrims, while the descendants of 'Abd ed-Dār retained custody of the Ka'ba and Council-hall, and the right of mounting the banner on its staff in war. Peace was restored upon these terms.

The offices amicably divided

Hāshim born A.D. 464

HĀSHIM,[2] thus installed in the office of entertaining the pilgrims, fulfilled it with princely magnificence. He was himself rich, and many Ḳoreish had also by trading acquired much wealth. He appealed to them as his grandfather Ḳoṣai had done: '*Ye are the neighbours of God, and the keepers of His house. Pilgrims to the temple are His guests;*

[1] This was the branch from which Moḥammad descended. The following table illustrates the family influences which affected not only the position of the Prophet, but the destinies of the Caliphate long ages after:—

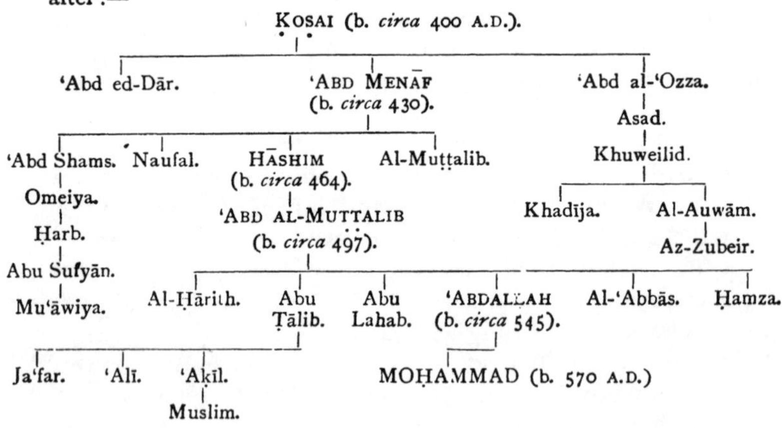

[2] Ibn Hishām, p 87; Aṭ-Ṭabari, i. 1088 f.; Ibn Sa'd, p. 43 f.

and it is meet that ye entertain them above all other guests. Ye are especially chosen unto this high dignity; wherefore honour His guests and refresh them. For, from distant cities, on their lean and jaded camels, they come unto you fatigued and harassed, with hair dishevelled and bodies covered with the dust and squalor of the way. Then invite them hospitably, and furnish them with water in abundance.' Hāshim set the example by a munificent provision, and the Ḳoreishites were forward to contribute, every man according to his ability. Water sufficient for the great assemblage was collected in cisterns close by the Ka'ba, and at the stations on the route to 'Arafāt. The distribution of food commenced upon the day on which the pilgrims set out for Mina and 'Arafāt, and continued until they dispersed. During this period, that is, for five or six days, they were entertained with pottage of meat and bread, butter and barley, and with the favourite national repast of dates.

Feeds the people of Mecca in a famine

Thus Hāshim supported the credit of Mecca. But his name is even more renowned for the splendid charity by which in a time of famine he relieved the necessities of his fellow-citizens. Journeying to Syria, he purchased an immense stock of flour, and conveyed it upon camels to Mecca. The provisions were cooked, the camels slaughtered and roasted, and the whole divided among the citizens. Destitution and mourning were turned into mirth and plenty; and it was (the historian adds) 'as it were the beginning of new life after the year of scarcity.'

Commercial treaties of Hāshim and his brothers

The foreign relations of Ḳoreish were conducted by the sons of 'Abd Menāf. With the Roman authorities, and the Ghassānid prince, Hāshim himself concluded a treaty; and he is said to have received from the Emperor a rescript authorising Ḳoreish to travel through Syria in security. 'Abd Shams made a treaty with the Negus, in pursuance of which Ḳoreish traded with Abyssinia; Naufal and Al-Muṭṭalib entered into an alliance with the king of Persia, who allowed the merchants of Mecca to traffic in Al-'Irāḳ and Fars, and with the kings of Ḥimyar, who encouraged their commercial operations in the Yemen. Thus the affairs of Ḳoreish prospered in every direction. To Hāshim is also ascribed the credit of establishing upon a uniform footing the mercantile expeditions of his people, so that every winter a caravan set out for the Yemen and Abyssinia, while in the summer a second visited Gaza, Ancyra, and other Syrian marts.

Hāshim challenged by Omeiya, who is vanquished and exiled

The success and glory of Hāshim exposed him to the envy of Omeiya, the son of his brother 'Abd Shams. Omeiya was opulent, and he expended his riches in a vain attempt to rival the splendour of his kinsman's munificence. The Ḳoreishites perceived the endeavour, and turned it into ridicule. Omeiya was enraged. *Who*, said he, *is Hāshim?* and he defied him to a trial of superiority.[1] Hāshim would willingly have avoided a contest with one so much his inferior both in years and dignity; but the Ḳoreishites, who loved such exhibitions, would not excuse him; he consented, therefore, but with the stipulation than the vanquished party should lose fifty black-eyed camels, and be ten years exiled from Mecca. A Khozā'ite soothsayer was appointed umpire; and, having heard the pretensions of both, pronounced Hāshim to be the victor. Hāshim took the fifty camels, slaughtered them in the vale of Mecca, and fed with them all the people present. Omeiya set out for Syria, and remained there the period of his exile. The circumstance is carefully noted by Moḥammadan writers as the first trace of that rivalry between the *Hāshimite* and *Omeiyad* factions, which in after ages shook the Caliphate.

Hāshim marries *Selma* at Medīna, who bears him a son A.D. 497

Hāshim was now advanced in years when, on a mercantile journey to the north, he visited Medīna with a party of Ḳoreish. As he traded there, he was attracted by the graceful figure of a female, who from an elevated position was directing her people beneath to buy and sell for her. She was discreet and comely, and made a tender impression upon the heart of Hāshim. He inquired of the citizens whether she was single, and they answered that she had been married, but was now divorced. The dignity of the lady, they added, was so great amongst her people that she would not marry, unless it were stipulated that she should remain

[1] It is difficult to express the idea implied by such a contest. It was a vainglorious practice, which consisted in one person challenging another, and claiming to be more noble and renowned, brave or generous. than he. Each disputant adduced facts and witnesses to prove his ambitious pretensions, and the arbiter adjudged the palm at his discretion.

mistress of her own concerns, and have at pleasure the power of divorce. This was SELMA, daughter of 'Amr, of the Khazraj tribe. Hāshim thereupon demanded her in marriage; and she consented, for she was well aware of his renown and noble birth. She accompanied him to Mecca, but returned to Medīna where she give birth to a son, who remained with his mother at Medīna.

Al-Muṭṭalib fetches his nephew 'Abd al-Muṭṭalib from Medīna,

Hāshim, dying a few years after on a mercantile expedition to Gaza, left his dignities to his brother Al-Muṭṭalib, who, when Hāshim's son had grown into boyhood, set out for Medīna to fetch him thence.[1] On his return, as the inhabitants of Mecca saw him pass with a lad by his side, they concluded that he had purchased a slave, and exclaimed, '*Abd al-Muṭṭalib!*—'lo, the servant of Al-Muṭṭalib!' 'Out upon you!' said he; 'it is my nephew, the son of Hāshim.' And as each scrutinised the features of the boy, they swore —'By my life, it is the very same.' In this incident is said to have originated the name of 'ABD AL-MUṬṬALIB, by which the son of Hāshim was thereafter called.

who maintains possession of paternal estate,

In due time 'Abd al-Muṭṭalib was installed by his uncle in possession of his father's property; but Naufal, another uncle, interposed, and violently deprived him of it. 'Abd al-Muṭṭalib, on reaching years of discretion, appealed to his tribe for aid to resist this usurpation of his rights; but they declined to interfere. He then wrote to his maternal relatives at Medīna, who no sooner received the intelligence than eighty mounted men of his mother's clan started for Mecca. 'Abd al-Muṭṭalib went forth to meet them, and invited them to his house; but their chief refused to alight until he had called Naufal to account. Proceeding straightway to the Holy house, he found him seated there among the chiefs of Ḳoreish. Naufal arose to offer welcome; but the stranger refused his welcome, and drawing his sword declared that he would plunge it into him unless he forthwith reinstated the orphan in his rights. The oppressor was daunted, and agreed to the concession, which was then ratified by oath before the assembled Ḳoreish.

eventually succeeds to the office of entertaining pilgrims,

Some years after, on the death of Al-Muṭṭalib, 'Abd al-Muṭṭalib succeeded to the office of entertaining the pilgrims. But for a long time he was destitute of power and influence;

[1] Ibn Hishām, p. 88 ff.; Aṭ-Ṭabari, i. 1082 f.; Ibn Sa'd, p. 48 ff.

and, having at the time but one son to assist him in the assertion of his claims, he found it difficult to cope with the opposing faction of Ḳoreish. It was during this period that he discovered the ancient well Zemzem. Finding it laborious to procure water for the pilgrims from the scattered wells of Mecca and store it in cisterns by the Ka'ba, and perhaps aware by tradition of the existence of a well in the vicinity, he made diligent search, and at last chanced upon the venerable masonry. It was a remnant of the palmy days when a rich and incessant stream of commerce flowed through Mecca. Centuries had elapsed since the trade had ceased, and with it had followed the decline of Mecca, and neglect of the well. In course of time choked up, the remembrance of it had become so indistinct that even the site was now unknown.

and discovers the well Zemzem

Claim of Ḳoreish negatived by oracle

As 'Abd al-Muṭṭalib, aided by his son Al-Ḥārith, continued digging deeper, he came upon the two golden gazelles, with the swords and suits of armour buried there by the Jurhumite king more than three centuries before. Ḳoreish, envying him these treasures, demanded a share; and they even asserted their right to the well itself, as the possession of their common ancestor Ishmael. 'Abd al-Muṭṭalib was not powerful enough to resist the claim; but he agreed to refer it to the decision of the arrows of HUBAL, the god whose image was set up within the Ka'ba. Lots were cast, one for the Ka'ba and two for the respective claimants. The gazelles fell to the share of the Ka'ba, and the swords and suits of armour to 'Abd al-Muṭṭalib, while the arrows of Ḳoreish were blank. Acquiescing in the divine decree, they relinquished their pretensions to the well. 'Abd al-Muṭṭalib beat out the gazelles into plates of gold, and fixed them by way of ornament to the door of the Ka'ba. He hung up the swords before the door as a protection to the treasures within; but at the same time added a more effectual guard in the shape of a golden lock and key. The plentiful flow of fresh water, soon apparent in the well Zemzem, was a great triumph to 'Abd al-Muṭṭalib. All other wells in Mecca were deserted, and this alone resorted to. From it 'Abd al-Muṭṭalib supplied the pilgrims; and the water itself soon shared the sacredness of the Ka'ba and its rites. The fame and influence of 'Abd al-Muṭṭalib now waxed greater and greater; a large family of powerful sons

Zemzem gives forth abundant spring

added to his dignity; he became, and continued to his death the virtual chief of Mecca.[1]

'Abd al-Muṭṭalib's son, *'Abdallah*, ransomed from sacrifice by one hundred camels

But a strange calamity now threatened to embitter 'Abd al-Muṭṭalib's prosperity.[2] During his early troubles, while supported by an only son, he had felt so bitterly his weakness in contending with the large and influential families of his opponents, as to vow that, if Providence should ever grant him ten sons, he would devote one of them to the Deity Years rolled on, and the rash father at last found himself surrounded by the longed-for number, the sight of whom daily reminded him of his vow. He bade his sons accompany him to the Ka'ba; each was made to write his name upon a lot, and the lots were made over to the intendant of the temple, who cast them in the usual mode. The fatal arrow fell upon 'ABDALLAH, the youngest and the best beloved. The vow devoting him to the Deity must needs be fulfilled, but how else than by the sacrificial knife? His daughters wept and clung around him, and he was willingly persuaded to cast lots between 'Abdallah and ten camels, the current fine for bloodshed. If the Deity should accept the ransom, the father need not scruple to spare his son. But the lot a second time fell upon 'Abdallah. Again, and with equal fortune, it was cast between him and twenty camels. At each successive trial the anxious father added ten camels to the stake, but the Deity appeared inexorably to refuse the vicarious offering, and to require the blood of his youngest son. It was now the tenth throw, and the ransom had reached a hundred camels, when the lot at last fell upon them. The father joyfully released 'Abdallah from his impending fate, and slaughtered the hundred camels between the Ṣafā and the Merwa. The inhabitants of Mecca feasted upon them, and 'Abd al-Muṭṭalib's family refusing to partake, the residue was left to the beasts and to the birds. This 'Abdallah was the father of Moḥammad.

'Abd al-Muṭṭalib challenged by Ḥarb, son of Omeiya

The prosperity and fame of 'Abd al-Muṭṭalib excited the envy of the house of Omeiya, whose son Ḥarb challenged his rival to a trial of their respective merits. The Abyssinian king declined to be the umpire, and the judgment was committed to a Ḳoreishite, who declared that 'Abd al-Muṭṭalib

[1] Ibn Hishām, p. 91; Aṭ-Ṭabari, i. 1088.
[2] Ibn Hishām, p. 97; Aṭ-Ṭabari, i. 1074 f.; Ibn Sa'd, p. 53 f.

was in every respect superior. Ḥarb was deeply mortified, and abandoned the society of his opponent, whose companion he had previously been. Thus the ill-feeling between the families of Hāshim and Omeiya was perpetuated and increased.

His league with the Beni Khozā'a

'Abd al-Muṭṭalib gained an important accession of stability to his party by concluding a defensive league with the Khozā'ite tribe, still inhabitants of Mecca. They came to him and represented that, as their quarters adjoined, such a treaty would be advantageous for both. 'Abd al-Muṭṭalib was not slow in perceiving this. With ten of his adherents he met the Beni Khozā'a at the Ka'ba, and there they mutually pledged their faith. The league was reduced to writing, and hung up in the Holy House. No one from the family of Omeiya was present, or indeed knew of the transaction until thus published. The compact was permanent, and in after times proved of essential service to Moḥammad.

The viceroy of the Yemen invades Mecca A.D. 570,

In the year 570 A.D., or about eight years before the death of 'Abd al-Muṭṭalib, occurred the memorable invasion of Mecca by Abraha, Abyssinian viceroy of the Yemen.[1] This potentate had built at Ṣan'ā a magnificent cathedral whither he sought to attract the worship of Arabia; and, thwarted in the attempt, vented his displeasure in an attack on Mecca and its temple. Upon this enterprise he set out with a considerable army. In its train was an elephant;—a circumstance for Arabia so singular that the commander, his host, the invasion, and the year, are still called by the epithet of 'the Elephant.' Notwithstanding opposition from various Arab tribes, Abraha victoriously reached Aṭ-Ṭā'if, three days east of Mecca. The men of Aṭ-Ṭā'if, ever jealous of Mecca, protested that they had no concern with the Ka'ba, and furnished the Abyssinians with a guide, who died on the way to Mecca. Centuries afterwards, wayfarers marked their abhorrence of the traitor by casting stones at his tomb as they passed. Abraha then sent forward a body of troops to scour the Tihāma and carry off what cattle they could find. They were successful in the raid, and among the plunder secured two hundred camels belonging to 'Abd al-Muṭṭalib. An embassy was despatched to the inhabitants of Mecca:

[1] Ibn Hishām, p. 29 ff.; Aṭ-Ṭabari, i. 950 f.; Ibn Sa'd, p. 55 f.

Abraha,' the message ran, 'had no desire to do them injury. His only object was to demolish the Ka'ba; that performed, he would retire without shedding the blood of any man.' The citizens had already resolved that it would be vain to oppose the invader by force of arms; but the destruction of the Ka'ba they refused on any terms to allow. At last the embassy prevailed on 'Abd al-Muṭṭalib and the other chiefs of Mecca to repair to the Viceroy's camp, and there plead their cause. 'Abd al-Muṭṭalib was treated with distinguished honour. To gain him over, Abraha restored his plundered camels; but he could obtain no satisfactory answer regarding the Ka'ba. The chiefs offered a third of the wealth of the Tihāma if he would desist from his designs against their temple, but he refused. The negotiation was broken off, and the deputation returned to Mecca. The people, by the advice of 'Abd al-Muṭṭalib, made preparations for retiring in a body to the hills and defiles about the city on the day before the expected attack. As 'Abd al-Muṭṭalib leaned upon the ring of the door of the Ka'ba (so the tradition runs), he prayed to the Deity thus aloud: 'Defend, O Lord, thine own House, and suffer not the Cross to triumph over the Ka'ba!' This done, he relaxed his hold, and, betaking himself with the rest to the neighbouring heights, watched what the end might be. Meanwhile a pestilential distemper had shown itself in the camp of the Viceroy. It broke out with deadly pustules and blains, and was probably an aggravated form of smallpox. In confusion and dismay the army commenced retreat. Abandoned by their guides, they perished among the valleys, and a flood (such is the pious legend) sent by the wrath of Heaven swept multitudes into the sea. Scarcely any recovered who had once been smitten by it; and Abraha himself, a mass of malignant and putrid sores, died miserably on his return to Ṣan'ā.[1]

and threatens the Ka'ba

Is discomfited by the pestilence

[1] Al-Wāḳidi, after describing the calamity in the fanciful style of the Ḳor'ān, adds: '*And that was the first beginning of the smallpox.*' The word signifies likewise 'small stones,' and the name as applied to the smallpox is probably derived from the gravelly appearance and feeling of the pustules. The name, coupled with its derivation, probably gave rise to the poetical description of the event in the Ḳor'ān: *Hast thou not seen how thy Lord dealt with the army of the Elephant? Did he not cause their stratagem to miscarry? And he sent against them flocks of little birds which cast upon them small clay stones, and made them like*

Ḳoreish found the *Homs*

The unexpected and seemingly miraculous disappointment of the magnificent preparations of Abraha increased the reverence with which throughout Arabia Ḳoreish were looked upon. They became vainglorious, and sought to mark their superiority by the assumption of special immunities. 'Let us,' they said, 'release ourselves from some of the observances imposed upon the multitude; and forbid ourselves some of the things which to them are lawful.'[1] Thus they gave up the yearly pilgrimage to 'Arafāt, and the ceremonial return therefrom, although they still acknowledged these acts to be, as an essential part of the 'religion of Abraham,' binding upon others; they also refused the use of cheese and butter while in the pilgrim garb; and, abandoning tents of camels' hair, restricted themselves to tents of leather. Upon pilgrims who came from beyond the Sacred limits, they imposed new rules for their own aggrandisement. Such visitors, whether for the Greater or the Lesser pilgrimage, were forbidden to eat food brought from without the holy boundary; and were compelled to make the circuit of the Ka'ba either naked, or clothed in vestments provided only by the citizens who formed the league. This association, whose members were called collectively The Ḥoms, that is, the strict or vigorous people, included Ḳoreish, the Beni Kināna a collateral branch, and the Khozā'a. To them the privileges of the league were restricted. All others were subjected to the humiliation of soliciting from them food and raiment. There is some doubt whether these innovations were only now begun or existed from an earlier period. But, however introduced, they give proof that the worship of the Ka'ba was active and vigorous, and that its directors exercised a wonderful influence over the whole of Arabia. The practices then enforced were superseded only by Islām; and (assuming the latest date assigned for their introduction) they were maintained for more than half a century. The reverence for the Ka'ba, which permitted the imposition of customs so un-

Strength and universality of the Ka'ba worship

unto the stubble of which the cattle have eaten.—Sūra cv. Gibbon says of this passage that it is 'the seed' of the marvellous details of Abraha's defeat. But it must have been partially at least the other way.

[1] [Ibn Hishām (p. 126 f.) says he does not know whether this happened before the year of the Elephant or after it.]

reasonable and oppressive, must necessarily have been grossly superstitious as well as widely prevalent.

Position of parties

Before proceeding with our history, let us for a moment review the state of parties in Mecca towards the latter days of 'Abd al-Muṭṭalib. There arose, as we have seen, upon the death of Ḳoṣai, two leading factions, the descendants respectively of his sons, 'Abd ed-Dār and 'Abd Menāf.

Low state of the descendants of 'Abd ed-Dār

The house of 'Abd ed-Dār originally possessed all the public offices; but in the struggle with Hāshim they were stripped of several important dignities; their influence had departed, and they were now fallen into a subordinate and insignificant position. The offices retained by them were still undoubtedly valuable; but, divided among separate members of the family, the benefit of combination was lost; and there was no steady and united effort to improve their advantages towards the acquisition of social influence and political power. The virtual chiefship of Mecca, on the other hand, was now with the descendants of 'Abd Menāf. Among these, again, two parties had arisen—the families, namely, of his sons Hāshim and 'Abd Shams. The grand offices of giving food and water to the pilgrims secured to the house of Hāshim a commanding and permanent influence under the able management of al-Muṭṭalib, and now of 'Abd al-Muṭṭalib who, like his father Hāshim, was regarded as the chief of the Sheikhs of Mecca. But the branch of Omeiya, son of 'Abd Shams, with its numerous and influential connections, were jealous of the power of the Hāshimites, and repeatedly endeavoured to humble them, and bring discredit on their high position. One office, the Leadership in war, indeed, was secured by the Omeiyad family, and contributed much to its splendour. The Omeiyads were, moreover, rich and successful in commerce, and by some are thought to have exceeded in influence and power even the stock of Hāshim.

Prosperity of the descendants of 'Abd Menāf

The Hāshimites

The Omeiyads

The birth of Moḥammad

But the 'Year of the Elephant,' had already given birth to a personage destined, within half a century, to eclipse the distinctions both of the Hāshimite and the Omeiyad race, and to the narration of this momentous event we shall now proceed.

THE LIFE OF MOHAMMAD

PART FIRST

MOHAMMAD TILL THE HIJRA

CHAPTER I

THE BIRTH AND CHILDHOOD OF MOHAMMAD[1]

A.D. 570

Description of Mecca

WITHIN the great mountain range which skirts the Red Sea, and midway between the Yemen and the Syrian border, lies Mecca with its holy Temple. The traveller from the seashore approaches the sacred valley by an almost imperceptible rise of about fifty miles, chiefly through sandy plains and defiles hemmed in by low hills of gneiss and quartz, which reach in some places the height of four or five hundred feet. Passing Mecca, and pursuing still an eastward course, he proceeds with the same gentle rise between hills of granite through the valley of Mina, and in five or six hours arrives at the Mount of 'Arafāt. Onwards the hills ascend to a great height, till about eighty miles from the sea the granite peaks of Jebel Ḳora crown the range, and Aṭ-Ṭā'if comes in sight thirty miles farther east. Between Jebel Ḳora and Aṭ-Ṭā'if the country is fertile and lovely. Rivulets every here and there descend from the hills; the plains are clothed with verdure, and adorned by large shady trees. Aṭ-Ṭā'if is famous for its fruits. The grapes are large and of a delicious flavour; and there is no want of variety to tempt the appetite, for peaches and

Fertility of Aṭ-Ṭā'if

[1] Ibn Hishām, p. 102 ff.; Aṭ-Ṭabari, i. 1073 ff.; Ibn Sa'd, p. 58 ff.

pomegranates, apples and almonds, figs, apricots and quinces, grow in abundance and perfection. Far different is it with the frowning hills and barren valleys for many a mile round Mecca. Stunted brushwood and thorny acacias occasionally relieve the eye, and furnish a scanty repast to the camel; but the general features are rugged rocks without a trace of foliage, and sandy stony glens from which the peasant looks in vain for the grateful returns of tillage. Even at the present day, after the riches of Asia have for twelve centuries been poured into the city, and a regular supply of water is secured by a conduit from the springs of 'Arafāt, Mecca can hardly boast a garden or cultivated field, and only here and there a tree.

Sterility of Mecca

Valley of Mecca

In its immediate vicinity the hills are formed of quartz and gneiss; but a little to the east, grey strata of granite appear, and within one or two miles of the city, lofty and rugged peaks shoot upwards in grand masses. The valley is about two miles in length. The general direction and slope are from north to south; but the upper or northern extremity on the way to 'Arafāt bends eastward; while at the lower end, where the three roads from the Yemen, Jidda, and Syria meet, there is a still more decided curve to the west. Here the valley opens out to the breadth of half a mile; and in this spacious amphitheatre, shut in by rugged hills, lies the city with the Ka'ba in its centre. Rocks rise precipitously all around, reaching on the eastern side a height of five hundred feet. It is here that the craggy defiles of Abu Ḳobeis, the most lofty of the hills encircling the valley, overhang the quarter of the town in which 'Abd al-Muṭṭalib and his family lived. Within three furlongs to the north-east of the Ka'ba, there is still pointed out to the pious pilgrim the spot of Moḥammad's birth; and hard by, the quarter in which 'Alī resided; both built upon the rocky slope.

Climate

Though within the tropics, Mecca has not the advantage of tropical showers. The rainy season begins about December, but the clouds do not at any time discharge their precious freight continuously or with regularity. Sometimes the rain descends with excessive violence and inundates the little valley with floods from 'Arafāt. Even in summer, rain is not unfrequent. The seasons being thus uncertain, the calamities of drought occasionally arise. The heat, especially in autumn, is oppressive. Surrounding ridges make the valley close and sultry; and the sun, beating with violence on bare gravelly soil, reflects an intense and distressing glare. The native of Mecca, acclimated to the narrow vale, may regard with complacency its inhospitable atmosphere; but the traveller even in winter complains of stifling warmth and suffocating closeness.[1]

Fond veneration with which it is regarded by the Arabs

Such is the spot, barren and unpromising, on which the Arabs look with fondest reverence as the cradle of their destiny and arena of the remote events which gave birth to their faith. Here Hagar alighted with Ishmael, and in search of water hurried to and fro between the little hill of the Ṣafā, a spur of Abu Ḳobeis, and the eminence of the Merwa, an offshoot from the opposite range. Here the Beni Jurhum established themselves upon the failing fortunes of the ancestors of Ḳoreish; and from hence they were expelled by the Khozā'ite invaders from the south. It was in this pent-up vale that Ḳoṣai nourished his ambitious plans, and, in the neighbouring defiles of Mina, asserted them in a mortal struggle with his rivals; and here he established Ḳoreish in their supremacy. It was hard by the Ka'ba that his descendants, the children of Abd ed-Dār and of 'Abd Menāf, were drawn up in battle array to fight for the sovereign prerogative. Here it was that Hāshim exhibited his princely liberality; and on this spot that 'Abd al-Muṭṭalib toiled with his solitary son till he discovered the ancient well of Zemzem. Thousands of such associations crowd upon the mind of the weary pilgrim, as the minarets of the Ka'ba rise before his longing eyes; and, in the long vista of ages reaching even to Adam, his imagination pictures multitudes of pious devotees in every age and from all quarters of the globe, flocking to the little valley, making their seven circuits of the holy house, kissing the mysterious stone, and drinking of the sacred water. Well then may the Arab regard the fane, and its surrounding rocks, with awe and admiration.

'Abdallah (born A.D. 545) marries Āmina

At the period of Abraha's retreat from Mecca (as narrated in the Introduction), 'Abd al-Muṭṭalib, now above 70 years

[1] Sprenger thinks the population may have been at this time 12,000. The number seems large; but materials for even the loosest estimate are wanting.

of age, enjoyed rank and consideration as the foremost chief of Mecca. Some months previous to that event, he had taken his youngest son 'ABDALLAH,[1] then about four-and-twenty years of age, to the house of Uheib [Wahb], a distant kinsman descended from Zuhra, brother of the famous Ḳoṣai; and there affianced him to ĀMINA, the niece of Uheib, under whose guardianship she lived. At the same time 'Abd al-Muṭṭalib, notwithstanding his advanced age, bethought him of a matrimonial alliance on his own account, and married Hālah, the cousin of Āmina and daughter of Uheib; of this late marriage, the famous Ḥamza was the firstfruits.[2]

Death of 'Abdallah

As was customary in a marriage at the home of the bride, 'Abdallah remained there with her for three days. Not long after, he left his wife with child, and set out on a mercantile expedition to Gaza in the south of Syria. On his way back he sickened at Medīna, and was left behind by the caravan with his father's maternal relatives. 'Abd al-Muṭṭalib, on learning of 'Abdallah's sickness, despatched his son Al-Ḥārith to take care of him. Reaching Medīna, Al-Ḥārith found that his brother had died about a month after the departure of the caravan. He returned with these tidings, and his father and brethren mourned for 'Abdallah. He was but five-and-twenty years of age, and Āmina had not yet been delivered. He left behind him five camels fed on wild shrubs,[3] a flock of goats, and Um Aiman, a slave-girl (called also *Baraka*), who tended the infant borne by his widow. This little property, and the house in which he dwelt, were all the inheritance Moḥammad received from his father; but, little as it was, the simple habits of the Arab required no more; and, instead of being evidence of poverty, the possession of a female slave was rather an indication of prosperity and comfort.

Āmina delivered of a son, August, A.D. 570

Passing over, as fabulous and unworthy of credit, the marvellous incidents related of the gestation of the infant, it may suffice to state that the widowed Āmina gave birth to

[1] Ibn Hishām, p. 100 ff.; Aṭ-Ṭabari, i. 1078 f.; Ibn Sa'd, p. 58. 'Abdallah, or *Servant of God* (corresponding with the Hebrew *Abdiel*), was a name common among the ante-Moḥammadan Arabs.

[2] Aṭ-Ṭabari, i. 1081.

[3] That is to say, not reared at home, and therefore of an inferior kind.

a son in the autumn of the year 570 A.D. The materials are too vague and discrepant for any close calculation. But we are told that the event occurred about fifty-five days after the attack of Abraha; and we may accept, as an approximation, the date carefully computed by Caussin de Perceval, namely, the 20th of August.

Joy of 'Abd al-Muṭṭalib

No sooner was the infant born, than Āmina sent to tell 'Abd al-Muṭṭalib. The messenger carrying the good tidings reached the chief as he sat in the sacred enclosure of the Ka'ba, in the midst of his sons and the principal men of his tribe; and he was glad (so the simple tradition runs), and arose and those that were with him, and visited Āmina, who told him all that had taken place. Then he took the young child in his arms, and went to the Ka'ba; and as he stood beside the Holy house, he gave thanks to God. The child was called MOḤAMMAD.

The child is called Moḥammad

Derivation of the name

This name was rare among the Arabs, but not unknown. It is derived from the root *ḥamada*, and signifies 'The Praised.' Another form is AḤMED, which having been erroneously employed as a translation of '*The Paraclete*' in some Arabic version of the New Testament, became a favourite term with Muslims, especially in addressing Jews and Christians; for it was (they said) the title under which the Prophet had been in their books predicted.

The infant was not nursed by his mother,

It was not the custom for the better class of women at Mecca to suckle their children. They procured nurses for them, or gave them out to nurse among the neighbouring Bedawi tribes, where was gained the double advantage of a robust frame, and the pure speech and free manners of the desert.[1] Thus the infant Moḥammad, shortly after his birth, was made over to Thuweiba, the slave of his uncle, Abu Lahab, who had lately suckled Ḥamza.[2] Though nursed by her for

but for a few days by Thuweiba

[1] The practice is still common among the Sherīfs of Mecca. At eight days old the infant is sent away and, excepting a visit at the sixth month, does not return to his parents till eight or ten years of age. Burckhardt names several tribes to which the infants are thus sent; and among them the *Beni Sa'd*, the very tribe to which the infant Moḥammad was made over. See *Journal Asiatique* for Jan. 1882, p. 18; where there is notice of an Arabic inscription in Hauran, five centuries before Moḥammad.

[2] [Thuweiba is not mentioned by Ibn Hishām, except in one of the MSS. (E) used by Wüstenfeld.]

a very few days, the Prophet retained in after-life a lively sense of the connection thus formed. Both he and Khadīja were wont to express in grateful terms their respect for her. Moḥammad used to send her periodically clothes and other presents until the 7th year of the Hijra, when tidings were brought of her death. Then he inquired after her son, his foster-brother; but he, too, was dead, and she had left no relatives.

Entrusted to Ḥalīma, a woman of the Beni Sa'd

When Thuweiba had nursed the child for several days, a party of the Beni Sa'd (a tribe of the Hawāzin) arrived at Mecca with ten women who offered themselves as nurses. They were soon provided with children, excepting Ḥalīma who was at last with difficulty persuaded to take the infant Moḥammad; for it was to the father that the nurses chiefly looked for reward, and the charge of the orphan child had been already declined. Tradition encircles Ḥalīma's journey home with a halo of auspicious fortune, but such legend it is not here our province to relate.

Remains among the Beni Sa'd till five years old

The infancy and part of the childhood of Moḥammad were spent with Ḥalīma among the Beni Sa'd. At two years of age she weaned and took him to his home. Āmina was delighted with the healthy and robust appearance of her infant, who looked like a child of double the age, and said: 'Take him with thee back again to the desert; for I fear the unhealthy air of Mecca.' So Ḥalīma returned with him to her tribe. When another two years were ended, some strange event occurred which greatly alarmed his nurse. It was probably a fit of epilepsy; but Muslim legend has invested it with so many marvellous features as makes it difficult to discover the real facts. It is certain that the apprehensions of Ḥalīma and her husband were aroused; for Arab superstition is wont to regard the subject of such ailments as under the influence of an evil spirit. They resolved to rid themselves of the charge, and Ḥalīma carried the child back to its mother. With some difficulty, Āmina obtained from her an account of what had happened, calmed her fears, and entreated her to resume the care of her boy. Ḥalīma loved her foster-child, and was not unwillingly persuaded to take him back once more to her encampment. There she kept him for about a year longer, and with such care that she would not suffer him to move out of her sight.

Is seized with a fit

But uneasiness was again excited by fresh symptoms of a suspicious kind; and she set out finally to restore the boy to his mother when he was about five years of age. As she reached the outskirts of Mecca, he strayed from her, and she could not find him. In her perplexity she repaired to 'Abd al-Muṭṭalib, and he sent one of his sons to aid her in the search; the little boy was discovered wandering in Upper Mecca, and restored to his mother.

Advantages to Moḥammad from residence among the Bedawīn

If we are right in regarding the attacks which alarmed Ḥalīma as fits of a nervous nature, they exhibit in the constitution of Moḥammad the normal marks of those excited states and ecstatic swoons which perhaps suggested to his own mind the idea of inspiration, as by his followers they were undoubtedly taken to be evidence of it. It is probable that, in other respects, the constitution of Moḥammad was rendered robust, and his character free and independent, by these five years among the Beni Sa'd. At any rate, his speech was thus formed upon one of the purest models of the beautiful language of the Peninsula; and it was his pride in after days to say: 'Verily, I am the most perfect Arab amongst you; my descent is from the Ḳoreish, and my tongue is the tongue of the Beni Sa'd.' When eloquence began to form an important element of success, a pure language and standard dialect were advantages to him of essential moment.

Grateful remembrance of Ḥalīma's nursing

Moḥammad ever retained a grateful impression of the kindness he had experienced as a child among the Beni Sa'd. Ḥalīma visited him at Mecca after his marriage with Khadīja. 'It was (the tradition runs) a year of drought, in which much cattle perished; and Moḥammad spoke to Khadīja and she gave to Ḥalīma a camel used to carry a litter, and forty sheep; so she returned to her people.' Upon another occasion he spread out his mantle for her to sit upon—a token of especial respect—and placed his hand upon her bosom in an affectionate and familiar way. Many years after, when, on the expedition against Aṭ-Ṭā'if, he attacked the Beni Hawāzin and took a multitude of them captive, they found ready access to his heart by reminding him of the days when he was nursed among them. About the same time a woman called Sheimà was brought in with some other prisoners to the camp. When they threatened her with their swords, she declared that she was the Prophet's foster-sister. Moḥammad inquired how he should know the truth of this, and she replied: 'Thou gavest me this bite upon my back, once upon a time when I carried thee on my hip.' The Prophet recognised the mark, spread his mantle over her, and made her to sit down by him. He gave her the option of remaining in honour and comfort with him, but she preferred to return with a present to her people.

In his sixth year his mother takes him to Medīna, A.D. 575-576

The sixth year of his life Moḥammad spent at Mecca under the care of his mother. She then planned a visit to Medīna, where she longed to show her boy to the maternal relatives of his father. So she departed with her slave-girl Um Aiman, who tended the child; and they rode upon two camels. Arrived in Medīna, she alighted at the house where her husband had died and was buried. The visit was of sufficient duration to imprint the scene and the society, notwithstanding his tender age, upon the memory of Moḥammad. He used in later days to call to recollection things that happened on this occasion. Seven-and-forty years afterwards, when he entered Medīna as a refugee, he recognised the place, and said: 'In this house I sported with Uneisa, a little girl of Medīna; and with my cousins, I used to put to flight the birds that alighted upon the roof.' As he gazed upon the mansion, he added: 'Here it was my mother lodged with me; in this place is the tomb of my father; and it was there, in that very pond, that I learnt to swim.'[1]

Reminiscences of the visit

Death of Āmina, and return to Mecca

After sojourning at Medīna about a month, Āmina bethought her of returning to Mecca, and set out in the same manner as she had come. But when about half way they had reached a spot called Al-Abwā, she fell sick and died; and she was buried there.[2] The little orphan was carried back to Mecca by Um Aiman, who, although then quite a girl, was a faithful nurse to the child, and continued to be his constant attendant.

Impression produced by his mother's death

The early loss of his mother no doubt imparted to the youthful Moḥammad something of that pensive and meditative character by which he was afterwards distinguished. In his seventh year he could appreciate the bereavement and feel the desolation of his orphan state. In the Ḳor'ān he has

[1] Ibn Sa'd, p. 73. [2] Ibn Hishām, p. 107; Ibn Sa'd, p. 73.

alluded touchingly to the subject. While reassuring his heart of the divine favour, he recounts the mercies of the Almighty; and amongst them the first is this: '*Did He not find thee an orphan, and furnished thee with a refuge?*'[1] On his pilgrimage from Medīna to Al-Ḥodeibiya he visited by the way his mother's tomb, and lifted up his voice and wept, and his followers likewise wept around him. When they asked him concerning it, he said: 'This is the grave of my mother: the Lord hath permitted me to visit it. And I sought leave to pray for her salvation, but it was not granted. So I called my mother to remembrance, and the tender memory of her overcame me, and I wept.'

Grief on visiting her tomb in after-life

'Abdal-Muṭṭalib undertakes charge of the orphan, A.D. 576

The charge of the orphan was now undertaken by 'Abd al-Muṭṭalib, who had by this time reached the patriarchal age of fourscore years. The child was treated by him with singular fondness. A rug used to be spread under the Ka'ba, and on it the aged chief reclined in shelter from the heat of the sun. Around the carpet, but at a respectful distance, sat his sons. The little Moḥammad was wont to run up close to the patriarch, and unceremoniously take possession of his rug; his sons seeking to drive him off, 'Abd al-Muṭṭalib would interpose, saying, 'Let my little son alone,' stroke him on the back, and delight to listen to his childish prattle. The boy was still under the care of his nurse; but he would ever and anon quit her, and run into the apartment of his grandfather even when he was alone or asleep.

'Abd al-Muṭṭalib dies A.D. 578

The guardianship of 'Abd al-Muṭṭalib lasted but two years, for he died eight years after the attack of Abraha.[2] The orphan child felt bitterly the loss of his indulgent grandfather; as he followed the bier he was seen to weep, and when he grew up, he retained a distinct remembrance of his death. The heart of Moḥammad in his tender years was thus again rudely wounded, and the fresh bereavement was rendered more poignant by the dependent position in which it left him. The nobility of his grandfather's descent, the deference paid to him throughout the vale of Mecca, and his splendid hospitality towards the pilgrims, in furnishing them with food and drink, were witnessed with satisfaction by

[1] Sūra, xciii. 6.

[2] Ibn Hishām, p. 108 ff.; Aṭ-Ṭabari, i. 1123; Ibn Sa'd, p. 74.

the thoughtful child. These things no doubt left behind them a proud remembrance, and formed the seed perhaps of many an ambitious thought and day-dream of power and domination.

Effect of death of 'Abd al-Muṭṭalib

The death of 'Abd al-Muṭṭalib left the children of Hāshim without any powerful head; while it enabled the other branch, descended from Omeiya, to gain ascendancy. Of the latter family the chief at this time was Ḥarb, who held the *Leadership* in war, and was followed by a numerous and powerful body of relations.

The sons of 'Abd al-Muṭṭalib

Of 'Abd al-Muṭṭalib's sons, Al-Ḥārith, the eldest, was now dead; the chief of those who survived were Az-Zubeir and Abu Ṭālib (both by the same mother as 'Abdallah), Abu Lahab, Al-'Abbās, and Ḥamza. The last two were still very young. Az-Zubeir was the oldest, and to him 'Abd al-Muṭṭalib bequeathed his dignity and offices. Az-Zubeir, again, left them to Abu Ṭālib, who, finding himself too poor to discharge the expensive and onerous task of providing for the pilgrims, waived the honour in favour of his younger brother Al-'Abbās. But the family of Hāshim had fallen from its high estate, and Al-'Abbās was able to retain only the giving of drink, while the furnishing of food passed into the hands of another branch. Al-'Abbās was rich, and his influential post, involving charge of the well Zemzem, was retained by him till the introduction of Islām, and then confirmed to his family by the Prophet; but he was not a man of strong character, and never attained to a commanding position at Mecca. Abu Ṭālib, on the other hand, possessed many noble qualities, and won greater respect; but, probably from poverty, he too remained in the background. It was thus that in the oscillations of phylarchical government, the prestige of the house of Hāshim had begun to wane, and nearly disappear; while the rival Omeiyad branch was rising to importance. This phase of the political state of Mecca began with the death of 'Abd al-Muṭṭalib, and continued until the conquest of the city by Moḥammad himself.

Abu Ṭālib and Al-'Abbās (margin note beside the preceding paragraph)

Abu Ṭālib becomes guardian of his orphan nephew

To Abu Ṭālib, the dying 'Abd al-Muṭṭalib consigned the guardianship of his orphan grandchild; and faithfully and kindly he discharged the trust. His fondness for the lad equalled that of 'Abd al-Muṭṭalib. He made him sleep by his bed, eat by his side, and go with him wherever he walked abroad. And this tender treatment was continued until his nephew emerged from the helplessness of childhood.

Mohammad at twelve years of age accompanies Abu Ṭālib to Syria, A.D. 582

It was during this period that Abu Ṭālib, accompanied by Moḥammad, undertook a mercantile journey to Syria. He intended to leave the lad behind; for now twelve years of age he was able to take care of himself. But when the caravan was ready to depart, and Abu Ṭālib about to mount, the child, overcome by the prospect of so long a separation, clung to his protector. Abu Ṭālib was moved, and carried him along with the party.[1] The expedition extended to Boṣra, perhaps farther. It lasted for several months, and afforded to the youthful Moḥammad opportunities of observation, which were not lost upon him. He passed near to Petra, Jerash, 'Ammān, and other remains of former mercantile grandeur; and the sight must have deeply imprinted upon his reflective mind the instability of earthly greatness.

Impression probably excited by this journey

The wild story of the valley of Al-Ḥijr, with its lonely deserted habitations hewn out of the rock, and the tale of divine vengeance descending on the cities of the plain over which now rolled the waves of the Dead Sea, would excite apprehension and awe; while such strange histories, rendered more startling and tragical by Jewish tradition and local legend, would win and charm the childish heart ever yearning after the marvellous. On this journey too, he passed through several Jewish settlements, and came in contact with the Christians of Syria. Hitherto he had witnessed, if at all, only an isolated and imperfect exhibition of their faith: now he saw its rites in full and regular performance by a whole community. The national and social customs founded upon Christianity; the churches with their crosses and images, their pictures and other symbols of the faith; the ringing of bells; the frequent assemblages for worship, were all forced on his attention. The reports, and possibly an actual glimpse, of the continually recurring ceremonial, effected (we may suppose) a deep impression upon him; and this impression would be rendered all the more practical and lasting by the sight of whole tribes, Arabs like himself, belonging to the same faith and practising the same observances. However fallen and materialised, the Christianity of Syria must have struck the

[1] Ibn Hishām, p. 115; Aṭ-Ṭabari, i. 1124 f.; Ibn Sa'd, p. 75 f.

thoughtful observer in strange contrast with the gross idolatry of Mecca. Once again, in mature life, Moḥammad visited Syria, and whatever reflections of this nature were then awakened would, no doubt, receive an augmented force and deeper colouring, from the vivid pictures and bright imagery which, upon the same ground, had been impressed on the imagination of his childhood.

No further incident of a special nature is related of Moḥammad, until he had advanced from childhood to youth.

CHAPTER II

FROM THE YOUTH OF MOḤAMMAD TO HIS FORTIETH YEAR[1]

A.D. 570-609

THE next passage in the life of Moḥammad brings us to events of a wider and more stirring interest.

'Sacrilegious War,' 580 to 590 A.D.

Between the years 580 and 590 A.D. the vale of Mecca and surrounding country were disturbed by one of those bloody feuds so frequently excited by the fiery pride, and prolonged by the revengeful temper, of the nation.

A fair held annually at 'Okāẓ

In Dhu'l-Ḳa'da, the sacred month preceding the annual pilgrimage, a fair was held at 'Okāẓ, where, within three days' journey east of Mecca, the shady palm and cool fountain offered a grateful resting-place to the merchant and traveller after their toilsome journey.

Chivalrous and poetical contests

Goods were bartered, vainglorious contests (those characteristic exhibitions of Bedawi chivalry) were held, and verses recited by bards of the various tribes. The successful poems produced at this national gathering were treated with distinguished honour. They were transcribed in illuminated characters, and thus styled *Golden;* or they were attached to the Ka'ba and honoured with the title *Suspended.*[2] The 'Seven suspended poems' still survive from a period anterior to Moḥammad, a wondrous specimen of artless eloquence. The beauty of their language and wild richness of their imagery are acknowledged by the European reader; but the subject is limited, and the beaten track seldom deviated from. The charms of his mistress, the envied spot marked by the

[1] Ibn Hishām, p. 117 ff.; Ibn Sa'd, p. 80 ff.

[2] [This explanation of the title Mo'allaḳāt is of late and doubtful authority. The meaning of the term is quite unknown.]

still fresh traces of her encampment, the solitude of her deserted haunts, his own generosity and prowess, the unrivalled glory of his tribe, the noble qualities of his camel;—these are the themes which, with little variation of treatment, and with no contrivance whatever of plot or story, occupied the Arab muse;—and some of them only added fuel to the besetting vices of the people, vainglory, envy, vindictiveness, and pride.

Origin of 'Sacrilegious War'

At the fair of 'Okāẓ, a rivalrous spirit had been about this period engendered between Ḳoreish and the Benī Hawāzin, a numerous tribe of kindred descent, which dwelt (and still dwells) in the country between Mecca and Aṭ-Ṭā'if. An arrogant poet, vaunting the superiority of his tribe, was struck by an indignant Hawāzinite; a maid of Hawāzin descent rudely treated by some Ḳoreishite youths; an importunate creditor insolently repulsed.[1] On each occasion the sword was unsheathed, blood flowed, and the conflict would have become general unless the leaders had interfered to calm the excited people. Such was the origin of the 'Sacrilegious War,' so called because it occurred within the sacred term, and was eventually carried within the sacred territory.

Precautions for peace

These incidents suggested the expediency of requiring all who frequented the fair to surrender, while it lasted, their arms, and to deposit them with 'Abdallah ibn Jud'ān, a chief of Mecca. By this precaution peace was preserved for several years, when a wanton murder supplied more serious cause of offence. The prince of Al-Ḥīra had despatched to the fair a caravan richly laden with perfumes and musk. It proceeded under the escort of an Hawāzin chieftain. Another chief, friend of Ḳoreish, jealous at being supplanted in charge of the convoy, watched his opportunity, and, falling upon the caravan, slew its leader, and fled with the booty. On his

Hostilities precipitated by a murder

[1] The incident affords a curious illustration of Arab manners. The dissatisfied creditor seated himself in a conspicuous place with a monkey by his side, and said: '*Who will give me another such ape, and I will give him in exchange my claim on such a one?*'—naming his debtor with his full pedigree from Kināna, an ancestor of Ḳoreish. This he kept vociferating to the intense annoyance of the Kināna tribe, one of whom drew his sword and cut off the monkey's head. In an instant the Hawāzin and Kināna tribes were embroiled in bitter strife. Ibn Ḳoteiba, p. 293.

flight he met a man of the Ḳoreish whom he charged to proceed with expedition to the fair then being held at 'Okāẓ, and communicate the intelligence to his confederate Ḥarb[1] and other Ḳoreishite chiefs. The message was promptly conveyed, and Ibn Jud'ān, thus privately informed of the murder, forthwith gave back to all their arms, and, feigning urgent business at Mecca, departed with his whole tribe. The news of the murder began rapidly to spread at 'Okāẓ, and as the sun went down it reached the ears of the Hawāzin chief, who at once, perceiving the cause of the precipitate departure of Ḳoreish, rallied his people and proceeded in hot pursuit. Ḳoreish had already entered the sacred limits, and so their enemy contented themselves with challenging them to a rencounter at the same period of the following year. The challenge was accepted, and both parties prepared for the struggle. Several battles were fought with various success, and hostilities, more or less formal, prolonged for four years, when a truce was called. The dead were numbered up, and as twenty had been killed of the Hawāzin more than of Ḳoreish, the latter consented to pay the price of their blood, and for this purpose delivered hostages. One of these was Abu Sufyān, the famous antagonist in after days of Moḥammad. In some of these conflicts, the whole of Ḳoreish and their allies were engaged. Each tribe was commanded by a chief of its own; and Ibn Jud'ān guided the general movements. The descendants of 'Abd Shams were headed by Ḥarb, son of Omeiya, and took a distinguished part in the warfare. The children of Hāshim were present also, under command of Az-Zubeir, eldest surviving son of 'Abd al-Muṭṭalib; but they occupied a less prominent position. In one of the battles Moḥammad attended upon his uncles; but, though now near twenty years of age, he had not acquired the love of arms. According to some, his efforts were confined to gathering up the arrows of the enemy as they fell, and handing them to his uncles. Others assign him a somewhat more active share; but the sentence in which even this is preserved does not imply much enthusiasm in the warfare; 'I remember,' said the Prophet, 'being present with my

A truce after four years' fighting

Omeiyad and Hāshimites both engaged in the struggle

Part taken by Moḥammad

[1] Ḥarb was the son of Omeiya and father of Moḥammad's opponent Abu Sufyān. As confederate of the murderer he was bound to take up his cause.

uncles in the Sacrilegious War; I discharged arrows at the enemy, and I do not regret it.' Physical courage, indeed, and martial daring, are characteristics which did not distinguish the Prophet at any period of his career.[1]

Probable influence upon Moḥammad of the fair at 'Okāẓ

The struggles for pre-eminence, indeed, and the contests of eloquence, at the annual fair, must have possessed for the youthful Moḥammad a more engrossing interest than the combat of arms. At these spectacles, while his patriotism was no doubt aroused and desire after personal distinction stimulated by the whole atmosphere of rivalry, he had rare opportunities of cultivating his genius, and learning from the greatest masters and most perfect models the art of poetry and power of rhetoric. But another and a nobler lesson might also be learned in the concourse at 'Okāẓ. The Christianity, as well as the chivalry, of Arabia had representatives there; and, if we may believe tradition, Moḥammad while a boy heard Ḳoss, bishop of Nejrān, preach a purer creed than that of Mecca, in accents which agitated and aroused his soul. And many at that fair, besides the venerable Ḳoss, though influenced it may be by a less catholic spirit, yet professed to believe in the same revelation from above, and preach the same good tidings. There too were Jews, serious and earnest men, surpassing the Christians in number, and equally with them appealing to an inspired Book. The scene thus annually witnessed by Moḥammad as he advanced into mature years, had, we cannot doubt, a deep influence upon him.

Lesson in poetry and rhetoric

Acquaintance with Christians and Jews

Possible germ of great catholic system

May there not have been here too the germ of his great catholic design; of that Faith round which the tribes of Arabia were all to rally? At the fair, religion clashed against religion in hopeless discord; and yet amid it all he might discern some common elements, a book, a name, to which all would reverently bow. With the Jews he was more familiar than the Christians, for as a child he had seen them at Medīna, heard of their synagogue and worship, and learned to respect them as men that feared God. Yet these glanced bitterly at the Christians, and, even when Ḳoss addressed them in language which approved itself to the heart of

[1] Among the chieftains in command of tribes, it is interesting to notice Khuweilid, father of Khadīja; Al-Khaṭṭāb, father of 'Omar 'Othmān and Zeid, two of the four '*Inquirers*' who will be noticed below besides other well-known names.

Moḥammad, they scorned his words, and railed at the meek and lowly Jesus of whom he spoke. Not less disdainfully did the Christians regard the Jews. And both Jews and Christians spurned the Arab tribes as heathens devoted to the wrath of an offended Deity. Yet if the inquirer sought to fathom the causes of this opposition, he would find that, notwithstanding the mutual enmity of Jews and Christians, there was a Revelation equally acknowledged by both to be divine; that both denounced idolatry as an unpardonable sin, and professed to worship One only true God; and (what would stir his inmost soul) that both repeated with profound veneration a common name,—the name of Abraham, the builder of the Ka'ba and author of the rites observed there by every Arab tribe. What, if there were truth in all these systems; —divine TRUTH, dimly glimmering through human prejudice, malevolence, and superstition? Would not that be a glorious mission to act the part of the Christian bishop, but on a still wider and more catholic stage; and, by removing the miserable partitions which hid and severed each sect and nation from its neighbour, to make way for the illumination of truth and love emanating from the great Father of all! Visions and speculations such as these were no doubt raised in the mind of Moḥammad by association with the Jews and Christians frequenting this great fair. Certain it is that, late in life, he referred with satisfaction to the memory of Ḳoss, the son of Sā'ida, and spoke of him as having preached there the 'true catholic faith.'

League amongst Ḳoreish for protecting the oppressed

A confederacy formed at Mecca shortly after the restoration of peace, for the suppression of violence and injustice, aroused an enthusiasm in the mind of Moḥammad which the martial exploits of the Sacrilegious War failed to kindle. The offices of State, and with them the powers of government, had (as we have seen) become divided among the various Ḳoreishite families. There was no one now to exercise an authority such as had been enjoyed by Ḳoṣai and Hāshim, or even by 'Abd al-Muṭṭalib. When any of the separate tribes neglected to punish its members for oppression and wrongdoing, no chief at Mecca was strong enough to stand up as champion of the injured. Right was not enforced: wrong remained unpunished. Certain glaring acts of tyranny suggested to the principal Ḳoreishite families the expedience of binding themselves by an oath to secure justice to the helpless.[1] The honour of originating the movement is ascribed to Az-Zubeir, eldest surviving son of 'Abd al-Muṭṭalib. The descendants of Hāshim and kindred families assembled in the house of Ibn Jud'ān, who prepared for them a feast; and they swore 'by the avenging Deity, that they would take the part of the oppressed, and see his claim fulfilled, so long as a drop of water remained in the ocean, or would satisfy it from their own resources.' The league was useful, both as a restraint against injustice, and on some occasions as a means of enforcing restitution. 'I would not,' Moḥammad used in after years to say, 'exchange for the choicest camel in all Arabia the remembrance of being present at the oath which we took in the house of 'Abdallah, when the Beni Hāshim, Zuhra ibn Kilāb and Teim ibn Murra swore that they would stand by the oppressed.'[2]

Moḥammad's occupation as a shepherd

The youth of Moḥammad passed away without any other incidents of interest. At one period he was employed, like other lads, in tending the sheep and goats of Mecca upon the neighbouring hills and valleys.[3] He used when at Medīna to refer to this employment and to say that it comported with his prophetic office, even as it did with that of Moses and David. On one occasion, as some people passed him carrying a load of *Arāk* berries, the Prophet said to his companions: 'Pick me out the blackest of them, for they are sweet;—even such was I wont to gather when I fed the flocks of Mecca at Ajyād. Verily there hath been no prophet raised up, who performed not the work of a Shepherd.' The hire received for this duty would contribute towards the support of his needy uncle, Abu Ṭālib, and the occupation itself was con-

[1] Ibn Hishām, p. 85 f.; Ibn Sa'd, p. 86.

[2] Zuhra was brother, and Teim the uncle, of Ḳoṣai. It is remarkable that only these three tribes joined the league. To the Beni Zuhra belonged Moḥammad's mother; and his friend Abu Bekr to the Beni Teim. That the league was only a partial one is probable from its name, the Oath of the Fuḍūl, *i.e.*, 'that which is unnecessary or supererogatory.' It seems to have been so called by the rest of Ḳoreish who did not join it. An instance is given in which after the death of Moḥammad the league was appealed to by Al-Ḥosein, son of 'Alī, against Mu'āwiya or his nephew.

[3] Ibn Sa'd, p. 79 f.

genial with his thoughtful and meditative character. While he watched the flocks, his attention would be riveted by the signs of an unseen Power spread all around him: the twinkling stars and bright constellations gliding through the dark blue sky silently along, would be charged to him with a special message; the loneliness of the desert would arm with a deeper conviction that speech which day everywhere utters unto day; while the still small voice, never unheard by the attentive listener, would swell into grander and more imperious tones when the tempest swept with its forked lightning and far-rolling thunder along the vast solitudes of the mountains about Mecca. Thus, we may presume, was cherished a deep and earnest faith in the Deity as an ever-present, all-directing Agent;—a faith which in after days the Prophet was wont to enforce from the memories, no doubt, of these early days, by eloquent and heart-stirring appeals to the sublime operations of Nature and the beneficent adaptations of an ever-present Providence.

Probable effect of shepherd life

Our authorities all agree in ascribing to the youth of Moḥammad a modesty of deportment and purity of manners rare among the people of Mecca. His virtue is said to have been miraculously preserved. 'I was engaged one night' (so he himself relates) 'feeding the flocks in company with a lad of Ḳoreish. And I said to him, If thou wilt look after my flock, I will go into Mecca and divert myself there, even as youths are wont by night to divert themselves.' But no sooner had he reached the precincts of the city, than a marriage feast engaged his attention, and he fell asleep. On another night, entering the town with the same intentions, he was arrested by heavenly strains of music, and, sitting down, slept till morning. Thus he escaped temptation. 'And after this,' said Moḥammad, 'I no more sought after vice; even until I had attained unto the prophetic office.' Making every allowance for the fond reverence which favoured the currency of such stories, it is quite in keeping with the character of Mohammad that he should have shrunk from the coarse and licentious practices of his youthful friends. Endowed with a refined mind and delicate taste, reserved and meditative, he lived much within himself, and the ponderings of his heart no doubt supplied occupation for leisure hours spent by others of a lower stamp in rude sports

Reserved and temperate youth of Moḥammad

and profligacy. The fair character and honourable bearing of the unobtrusive youth won the approbation of his fellow-citizens; and he received the title, by common consent, of AL-AMĪN, 'the Faithful.'

Abu Ṭālib suggests mercantile expedition. Ætat. 25

Thus respected and honoured, Moḥammad lived a quiet and retired life in the family of Abu Ṭālib, who (as we have seen) was prevented by limited means from occupying any prominent position in the society of Mecca. At last, finding his family increase faster than the ability to provide for them, Abu Ṭālib bethought him of setting his nephew, now of mature age, to earn a livelihood for himself. Moḥammad was never covetous of wealth, or at any period of his career energetic in the pursuit of riches for their own sake. If left to himself, he would probably have preferred the quiet and repose of his present life to the bustle and cares of a mercantile journey. He would not spontaneously have contemplated such an expedition. But when the proposal was made, his generous soul at once felt the necessity of doing all that was possible to relieve his uncle, and he cheerfully responded to the call. The story is as follows:[1]—When his nephew was now five-and-twenty years of age, Abu Ṭālib addressed him in these words: 'I am, as thou knowest, a man of small substance; and truly the times deal hardly with me. Now here is a caravan of thine own tribe about to start for Syria, and Khadīja, daughter of Khuweilid, needeth men of our tribe to send forth with her merchandise. If thou wert to offer thyself, she would readily accept thy services.' Moḥammad replied: 'Be it so as thou hast said.' Then Abu Ṭālib went to Khadīja, and inquired whether she wished to hire his nephew, but he added: 'We hear that thou hast engaged such an one for two camels, and we should not be content that my nephew's hire were less than four.' The matron discreetly answered: 'Hadst thou asked this thing for one of a distant or alien tribe, I would have granted it; how much rather now that thou askest it for a near relative and friend!' So the matter was settled, and Moḥammad prepared for the journey. When the caravan was about to set out, his uncle commended him to the men of the company. Meisara, servant of Khadīja, likewise travelled along with Moḥammad in charge of her property. The caravan took

Moḥammad accompanies a Syrian caravan in charge of Khadīja's venture

[1] Ibn Hishām, p. 119 f.; Aṭ-Ṭabari, i. 1127 f.; Ibn Sa'd, p. 82 f.

the usual route to Syria, the same which Moḥammad had traversed with his uncle thirteen years before. In due time they reached Boṣra, on the road to Damascus, about sixty miles to the east of the Jordan. The transactions of that busy mart, where the practised merchants of Syria sought to overreach the simple Arabs, were ill suited to the tastes and habits of Moḥammad; yet his natural sagacity and shrewdness carried him prosperously through the undertaking. He returned from the barter with a balance more than usually in his favour.

Reaches Boṣra, and barters to advantage

The reflective mind of Moḥammad, now arrived at the mature but still inquisitive period of early manhood, must have received deep and abiding impressions from all that he saw and heard upon the journey, and during his stay at Boṣra. Though the story of his interview with Nestorius (a monk who they say embraced him as 'the coming prophet'[1]) may be rejected as puerile, yet we may be certain that Moḥammad lost no opportunity of inquiring into the practices and tenets of the Syrian Christians or of conversing with the monks and clergy who fell in his way.[2] He probably experienced kindness, and perhaps hospitality, from them; for in his book he ever speaks of them with respect, and sometimes with praise.[3] But for their doctrines he had no sympathy. The picture of Christianity in the Ḳor'ān must have been, in some considerable degree, painted from the conceptions now formed. Had he witnessed a purer exhibition of its rites and doctrines, and seen more of its reforming and regenerating influences, we cannot doubt that, in the sincerity of his early search after truth, he might readily have embraced and faithfully adhered to the faith of Jesus. Lamentable, indeed, is the reflection that so small a

Impressions regarding Christianity

Distorted view presented by Syrian worship

[1] Thus Nestor, seeing Moḥammad as he sat under a tree below which none ever sat but a Prophet, immediately embraced him as such; he recognised him also by the redness of his eyes, &c.

[2] Arabic was spoken by the subjects of the Ghassānid dynasty, and Moḥammad would find little difficulty in effecting an interchange of ideas with those about him. Poets, merchants, and travellers from Medīna used to be guests at the Ghassānid court.

[3] Thus Sūra v. 85.—*Thou shalt surely find those amongst the people who profess Christianity to be the most inclined to the believers. This cometh to pass because there are priests and monks among them, and because they are not elated with pride.*

portion of the fair form of Christianity was disclosed by the ecclesiastics and monks of Syria to the earnest inquirer; and that little, how altered and distorted! Instead of the simple majesty of the gospel,—as a revelation of God reconciling mankind to himself through his Son,—the sacred dogma of the Trinity was forced upon the traveller with the misleading and offensive zeal of Eutychian and Jacobite partisanship, and the worship of Mary exhibited in so gross a form as to leave the impression upon the mind of Moḥammad that she was held to be a goddess, if not the third Person and consort of the Deity.[1] It must surely have been by such blasphemous extravagances that Moḥammad was repelled from the true doctrine of Jesus as 'the SON OF GOD,' and led to regard him only as 'Jesus, son of Mary,' the sole title by which he is spoken of in the Ḳor'ān. We may well mourn that the misnamed Catholicism of the Empire thus grievously misled the master mind of the age, and through him eventually so great a part of the eastern world.

Moḥammad reports to Khadīja the successful result

But to return. When Moḥammad had disposed of the merchandise and, according to her command, purchased for his mistress such things as she had need of, he retraced his steps in company with the caravan to his native valley.[2] The mildness of his manners and kind attention had won the heart of Meisara, and, as they drew near to Mecca, the

[1] Sura v. 116.—*And when* GOD *shall say: O Jesus son of Mary! Didst thou speak unto mankind, saying, 'Take me and my mother for two gods besides the Lord?' He shall answer, 'Praise be to thee! It is not for me to say that which I ought not,'* &c.

Moḥammad's knowledge of Christianity was unfortunately derived from the Orthodox party, who styled Mary 'Mother of God.' He may have heard of the Nestorians, and they are possibly referred to among the 'Sects' into which Jews and Christians are said in the Ḳor'ān to be divided. But, had he ever obtained a closer acquaintance with the Nestorian doctrine, at least in the earlier part of his career, it would (according to the analogy of his practice in other respects) have been more definitely mentioned in his revelation. The truth, however (as will be shown hereafter), is that Moḥammad's acquaintance with Christianity was at the best singularly dim and meagre.

[2] Though the *direct* route from Mecca to Boṣra would run a great way east of the Mediterranean, it seems possible that, either now or on the former journey, Moḥammad may have seen the Mediterranean Sea. Perhaps, the caravan visited Gaza, the favourite *entrepôt* of the Meccan merchants. His references in the Ḳor'ān to ships gliding majestically on the waters, *like mountains*, point to a larger class of vessels than he was

grateful servant persuaded Moḥammad to go in advance of the rest, and bear to his mistress first tidings of the successful traffic. Khadīja, surrounded by her maidens, was sitting upon the upper storey of her house,[1] on the watch for the earliest glimpse of the caravan, when a camel was seen rapidly to advance from the expected quarter, and as it approached she perceived that Moḥammad was the rider. He entered, recounted the prosperous issue of the adventure, and enumerated the various goods which agreeably to her commission he had purchased for her. She was delighted at all she heard; but there was a charm in the dark and pensive eye, in the noble features, and the graceful form of her assiduous agent as he stood before her, which pleased her even more than her good fortune. The comely widow was now forty years of age, she had been twice married, and had borne two sons and a daughter.[2] Yet she cast a fond eye upon the thoughtful youth of five-and-twenty; nor, when he departed, could she dismiss him from her thoughts.

She is charmed

Description of Khadīja,

Khadīja was a Ḳoreishite lady, distinguished by fortune as well as by birth. Her father, Khuweilid, was the grandson of Asad, and Asad was the grandson of Ḳoṣai. Khuweilid commanded in the Sacrilegious War a considerable section of Ḳoreish, and so did his nephew 'Othmān. Her substance, whether inherited, or acquired through her former marriages, was very considerable; and by means of hired agents she had increased it largely in mercantile speculation. To the blessing of affluence, she added the more important endowments of discretion, virtue, and an affectionate heart; and, though now mellowed by a more than middle age, she

likely to see on the Red Sea. The vivid pictures of sea-storms are among the finest sketches in the Ḳor'ān, and evidently drawn from nature: the waves and tempests may have been witnessed from the Arabian shore, but the 'mountain ships' more likely from the Syrian.

[1] Her house is still shown, a little to the north-east of the Ka'ba. It is called the birthplace of Fāṭima.

[2] There is no mention of these, as we should have expected from their relation to Moḥammad: they had probably already grown out of childhood. The only notice I find is that one of them, Hind, son of Abu Hāla al-Oseiyid, was killed fighting on 'Alī's side, in the battle of the Camel; *Ibn al-Athīr*, vol. iii. p. 217.

Khadīja's age is probably according to the intercalary year; in which case she might have been a year older by the lunar year.

retained a fair and attractive countenance. The chief men of Ḳoreish were not insensible to these charms, and many sought her in marriage; but choosing rather to live on in dignified and independent widowhood, she had rejected all their offers. The tender emotions, however, excited by the visit of Moḥammad overpowered her resolution. Meisara continued to sound in her not unwilling ears the praises of his fellow-traveller. At last her love became irresistible, and she resolved in a discreet and cautious way to make known her passion to its object. A sister (according to other accounts, a servant) was the agent deputed to sound his views. 'What is it, O Moḥammad,' said she, adroitly referring to the unusual circumstance of his being unmarried at so mature an age,—'what is it that hindereth thee from marriage?' 'I have nothing,' replied he, 'in my hands wherewithal I might marry.' 'But if haply that difficulty were removed, and thou wert invited to espouse a beautiful and wealthy lady of noble birth, who would place thee in affluence, wouldest thou not desire to have her?' 'And who,' said Moḥammad, startled at the novel thought, 'might that be?' 'It is Khadīja.' 'But how can I attain unto her?' 'Let that be my care,' returned the female. The mind of Moḥammad was at once made up, and he answered, 'I am ready.' The female departed and told Khadīja.

who sends to negotiate marriage with Moḥammad

Moḥammad is married to Khadīja

No sooner was she apprised of his willingness to marry her, than Khadīja despatched a messenger to Moḥammad or his uncle, appointing a time when they should meet. Meanwhile, as she dreaded the refusal of her father, she provided for him a feast; and when he had well drunk and was merry, she slaughtered for the company a cow, and casting over her father perfume of saffron or ambergris, dressed him in marriage raiment. While thus under the effects of wine, the old man united his daughter to Moḥammad in the presence of his uncle Ḥamza. But having recovered his senses, he began to look around with wonder, and inquire what meant these symptoms of a nuptial feast, the slaughtered cow, the perfumes and the marriage garment. So soon as he was made aware of what had happened—for they told him 'The nuptial dress was put upon thee by Moḥammad thy son-in-law'—he fell into a violent passion, and declared that he would never consent to give away to that poor youth a daughter courted by the great men of Ḳoreish. The friends of Moḥammad replied indignantly that the alliance had not originated in their wish, but was the act of no other than his own daughter. Weapons were drawn, and blood might have been shed, when the old man became pacified, and at last was reconciled.

The union fortunate and happy

Notwithstanding its stormy and inauspicious opening, the connubial state proved, both to Moḥammad and Khadīja, one of unusual tranquillity and happiness. Upon him the marriage conferred a faithful and affectionate companion, and, in spite of her age, a not unfruitful wife. Khadīja, on her part, fully appreciated the noble genius and commanding mind of Moḥammad, which his reserved and contemplative habit, while it veiled from others, could not conceal from her. She conducted as before the duties of her establishment, and left him to enjoy his leisure hours, undisturbed and free from care. Her house was thenceforward his home, and her bosom the safe receptacle of those doubts and longings after spiritual light which now began to agitate his soul.

Children of Moḥammad by Khadīja

Within the next ten or twelve years, Khadīja bore to Moḥammad two sons and four daughters. The firstborn was named Al-Ḳāsim; and after him, according to Arabian custom, Moḥammad received the title of ABU'L-ḲĀSIM, 'Father of Al-Ḳāsim.' This son died at the age of two years. Meanwhile, his eldest daughter Zeinab was born; and after her, at intervals of one or two years, three other daughters, Roḳeiya, Fāṭima, and Um Kulthūm. Last of all was born his second son, who died in infancy. Selma, maid of Ṣafīya Moḥammad's aunt, officiated as midwife on these occasions. Khadīja sacrificed at the birth of each boy two kids, and one at the birth of every girl. Her children she nursed herself. Many years after, Moḥammad used to look back to this period of his life with fond remembrance.

Mutual love of Moḥammad and Khadīja

Indeed so much did he dwell upon the mutual love of Khadīja and himself, that the envious 'Ā'isha declared herself more jealous of this rival whom she had never seen, than of all the other wives who contested with her the affection of the Prophet.

Person of Moḥammad described

No description of Moḥammad at this period has been attempted by traditionists.[1] But from the copious accounts

[1] *Cf.* Ibn Hishām, p. 266 f.

of his person in later life, an approximate outline may be traced of his appearance in the prime of manhood. Slightly above the middle size, his figure though spare was handsome and commanding; the chest broad and open; the bones and framework large, and the joints well knit together. His neck was long and finely moulded. His head, unusually large, gave space for a broad and noble brow. The hair, thick, jet black, and slightly curling, fell down over his ears. The eyebrows were arched and joined. The countenance thin, but ruddy. His large eyes, intensely black and piercing, received additional lustre from eyelashes long and dark. The nose was high and slightly acquiline, but fine, and at the end attenuated. The teeth were far apart. A long black bushy beard, reaching to the breast, added manliness and presence. His expression was pensive and contemplative. The face beamed with intelligence, though something of the sensuous might also be discerned. The skin was clear and soft; the only hair that met the eye was a fine thin line which ran down from the neck towards the navel. His broad back leaned slightly forward as he walked; and his step was hasty, yet sharp and decided, like that of one rapidly descending a declivity.[1]

His manner and conversation

There was something unsettled in his bloodshot eye, which refused to rest upon its object. When he turned towards you, it was never partially, but with the whole body. Taciturn and reserved,[2] he was yet in company distinguished by a graceful urbanity. His words were pregnant and laconic; but when it pleased him to unbend, his speech was often humorous and sometimes pungent. At such seasons he entered with zest into the diversion of the moment, and now and then would laugh immoderately.[3] But in

[1] This at Medīna degenerated into a stoop. Some say he walked like a man *ascending* a hill; others as if he were wrenching his foot from a stone. These descriptions imply *decision* of step. The hollows of his hands and feet were more than usually filled and level: a feature regarded by Orientals with interest.

[2] 'Moḥammad was sorrowful in temperament; continually meditating; he had no rest; he never spoke except from necessity; he used to be long silent; he expressed himself in pregnant sentences, using neither too few nor too many words.'

[3] When laughing immoderately, he showed his teeth and gums, and was at times so convulsed that he held his sides.

general he listened to the conversation rather than joined in it.

His emotions under control

He was the subject of strong passions, but they were so controlled by reason and discretion, that they rarely appeared upon the surface. When much excited, the vein between his eyebrows would mantle, and violently swell across his ample forehead; yet he was cautious and circumspect, and in action kept ever aloof from danger. Generous and considerate towards his friends, he knew, by well-timed favour and attention, how to gain over even the disaffected and rivet them to his service. His enemies, so long as they continued their opposition, were regarded by him with a vindictive and unrelenting hatred; yet he rarely pursued a foe after he had tendered timely submission. His commanding mien inspired the stranger with an undefined and indescribable awe; but on closer intimacy, apprehension and fear gave place to confidence and love.

Treatment of friends and enemies

Latent force of will

Behind his quiet retiring exterior lay hid a high resolve, a singleness of purpose, a strength and fixedness of will, a sublime determination, destined to achieve the marvellous work of bowing towards himself the heart of all Arabia as the heart of one man. Khadīja was the first to perceive the noble and commanding qualities of her husband, and with a child-like confidence surrendered to him her soul, her will, and faith.

Rebuilding of the Ka'ba, A.D. 605, *Ætat.* 35

The first incident which interrupted the even tenor of his married life was the rebuilding of the Ka'ba, when he was about five-and-thirty years of age.[1] One of those violent floods which at times sweep down the valley, had shattered the Holy House; its walls showed ominous rents, and they feared lest it should fall. The treasury was also insecure, owing to the absence of a roof; and thieves had lately clambered over and stolen some of the precious relics. These were recovered, but it was resolved that similar danger should for the future be avoided by raising the walls and covering in the roof. While Ḳoreish deliberated how this might best be done, a Grecian ship was driven by stress of weather not far off upon the Red Sea shore. The news reaching Mecca, the aged chief Al-Walīd, accompanied by a

[1] Ibn Hishām, p. 122 ff.; Aṭ-Ṭabari, i. 1138 f.; Ibn Sa'd, p. 93.

body of Koreish, proceeded to the wreck, purchased the timber of the broken ship, and engaged her captain, a Greek, by name Bākūm, skilled in architecture, to assist in the reconstruction of the Ka'ba.[1] The several tribes of Koreish were divided into four bodies, and to each was assigned the charge of one side. With such mysterious reverence was the Ka'ba regarded, that apprehensions were entertained lest the apparent sacrilege of dismantling the holy walls should expose even the pious restorers to divine wrath. At last Al-Walīd seized a pickaxe, and, invoking the Deity in a deprecatory prayer, detached and threw down a portion of the wall. They then retired and waited till the morning, when, finding that no mischief had befallen the adventurous chief, all joined in the demolition. They continued to dig till they reached a hard foundation of green stones which resisted the pickaxe stroke. From thence they began to build the wall. Stones of grey granite from the neighbouring hills were carried by the citizens upon their heads to the sacred enclosure. The whole body of Koreish assisted in the work, and all proceeded harmoniously until the structure rose four or five feet above the surface. At that stage it became necessary to build the Black Stone into the eastern corner, with its surface so exposed as readily to be kissed by pilgrims upon foot. This stone, which is semicircular, measures some six inches in height and eight in breadth; it is of a reddish-black colour, and notwithstanding the polish imparted by myriads of kisses, bears to the present day in its undulating surface marks of a volcanic origin.

The Black Stone

Rivalry for depositing the stone

The virtue of the edifice depending on this mysterious stone, each family of Koreish advanced pretensions to the exclusive right of placing it in its future receptacle. The contention became hot, and it was feared that bloodshed would ensue. For four or five days the building was suspended. At last Koreish again assembled on the spot amicably to decide the difficulty. Then the oldest citizen arose and said: 'O Koreish, hearken unto me! My advice is that the man who chanceth first to enter the court of the Ka'ba by yonder gate, he shall be chosen either to decide the difference amongst you, or himself to place the stone.' The

[1] Ibn Sa'd, p. 93. Ibn Ishāk does not mention the captain, and says a Copt carpenter rebuilt the House.—At-Tabari, i. 1135.

proposal was confirmed by acclamation, and they awaited the issue. Moḥammad, who was at the moment observed approaching, was the first to enter. Seeing him they all exclaimed: ‘Here comes the Faithful arbiter (*Al-Amīn*);

Front view of the Black Stone. Half actual size.

Side view

we are content to abide by his decision.’ Calm and self-possessed, Moḥammad received the commission, and at once resolved upon an expedient which should conciliate them all. Taking off his mantle and spreading it upon the ground, he

Moḥammad is chosen arbiter. His decision

placed the stone thereon, and said: 'Now let one from each of your four divisions come forward, and raise a corner of this mantle.' Four chiefs approached, and holding each a corner lifted thus the stone. When it had reached the proper height, Moḥammad, with his own hand, guided it to its place. The decision raised the character of Moḥammad for wisdom and judgment; while the singular and apparently providential call could hardly pass unnoticed by Moḥammad himself. His mind was given to auguries;

The Ka'ba, as at present, showing the curtain cut and adjusted; *a*, Black Stone.

and there was here a mysterious singling out of himself to be judge among his fellows in a sacred question, which might well have wrought upon a spirit less imaginative and enthusiastic than that of Moḥammad, and prompted the idea of his being chosen of God to be the prophet of his people.

The Ka'ba finished

The stone thus deposited in its proper place, Ḳoreish built on without interruption; and when the walls had risen to a considerable height they roofed them over with fifteen rafters resting upon six central pillars. A covering of cloth, thrown across the temple according to ancient custom, hung like a curtain round on every side.[1] The Ka'ba thus rebuilt was surrounded by a small enclosure, probably of not more

The Ka'ba, as it now stands, showing the curtain festooned at pilgrimage. *a*, The Black Stone; *b*, Emblazoned curtain of the door hung for display from the roof; *c*, Door; *d*, Spout.

than fifty yards in diameter. To the west stood the Hall of Council, with its door towards the Ka'ba. On the east was

[1] The custom of veiling the Ka'ba is of extremely remote date. Originally the cloth covered the whole building, including the top. Before a roof was built by Ḳoreish it must have constituted the only protection from the weather. The curtain is now attached only to the walls.

The covering in those days was of Yemen cloth. 'Omar renewed it yearly of Egyptian linen. Various materials, as striped Yemen stuff, red brocade, or black silk, have been at different times used; and it has been changed as often as six times a year. To supply the curtain came to be regarded as a sign of sovereignty.

It is now worked at Cairo, and renewed yearly at the season of pilgrimage. It 'is a coarse tissue of silk and cotton mixed.' A band of two feet, embroidered with texts, is inserted about a third from the top. 'It was of a brilliant black (says Burton), and the Hizam—the zone or golden band running round the upper portion of the building—as well as the Burka (face veil) were of dazzling brightness.' The Burka 'is the gold embroidered curtain covering the Ka'ba door.'—Vol. iii. p. 295.

the gateway of the Beni Sheiba, close by the sacred well Zemzem. At a respectful distance were built all round the houses of Ḳoreish. The great idol Hubal was placed in the centre of the Holy House; and outside were ranged various other images. The door for entering the Ka'ba was then, as now, near the Black Stone on the eastern side, and several feet above the ground,—a fact attributed by Moḥammad to the pride of Ḳoreish, and desire to retain in their own hands the power of admission. The building, though now substantial and secure, occupied somewhat less space than its dilapidated and roofless predecessor. The excluded area lay to the north-west, and is still without the sacred walls.[1]

Absence of any paramount authority

The circumstances which gave occasion for the decision of Moḥammad strikingly illustrate the absence of any paramount authority in Mecca, and the number of persons among whom the power of government was at this time divided. Each main branch of the Ḳoreishite stock was independent of the other; and the offices of state and

[1] The sill of the door is now about seven feet above the level of the ground, and a movable wooden staircase is used for ascending. It is distant six feet from the corner of the Black Stone. After the conquest of Mecca, Moḥammad is related to have said: 'Verily they have drawn back the foundations of the Ka'ba from their original limit; and if it were not that the inhabitants are fresh from idolatry, I would have restored to the building that which was excluded from the area thereof. But in case the people may again after my time need to renew the structure, come, and I will show thee what was left out.' So he showed a space in the *ḥijr* (or excluded area) of about seven yards.

This space at present lies to the north-west of the Ka'ba, about the distance pointed out by Moḥammad as the limit of the old building. It is now marked by a semicircular parapet of white marble, five feet high, facing the Ka'ba, and is still regarded as equally holy with the temple itself.

'Othmān A.H. 26, and Ibn az-Zubeir, A.H. 64, enlarged the square by purchasing and removing the adjoining houses of Ḳoreish, and enclosed it by a wall. Various similar changes and improvements were made by successive Caliphs till, in the third century of the Hijra, the quadrangle with its imposing colonnade assumed its present dimensions.

The Ka'ba, as it now stands, is an irregular cube, the sides of which vary from forty to fifty feet in length. The quadrangle, or court, corresponds loosely with the direction of its walls. 'Ka'ba' is probably the ancient idolatrous name; while 'Beit-ullah,' *The house of God* (used indifferently with the other in the time of Moḥammad), is the more modern title harmonising with Jewish phraseology.

religion created by Ḳoṣai with the view of securing undisputed command had, from their distribution among several independent families, lost their potency. It was a period in which the genius of a Ḳoṣai might have again dispensed with the prestige of place and birth, and asserted dominion by strength of will and inflexibility of purpose. But no such leader appeared, and the divided aristocracy moved on with feeble and distracted step. A curious story is related of an attempt made about this period to gain the rule at Mecca. The aspirant was 'Othmān, nephew of Khadīja's father. He was dissatisfied with the idolatrous system of Mecca, and travelled to the court of the Roman emperor, where he was honourably entertained, and admitted to Christian baptism.[1] Returning to Mecca, he laid claim, on the strength of an imperial grant, to the government of the city. But his claim was rejected, and he fled to Syria, where he found a refuge with the Ghassānid prince. He there revenged himself by using his influence for the imprisonment of the Ḳoreishite merchants who chanced to be at the Syrian court. But emissaries from Mecca, by offering gifts, counteracted his authority with the prince, and at last procured his death.

'Othmān ibn Al-Ḥuweirith attempts to seize the government

Notwithstanding the absence of a strong government, Mecca continued to flourish under the generally harmonious combination of the several independent phylarchies. Commerce was prosecuted towards Syria and Al-'Irāḳ with greater vigour than ever. About the year 606 A.D. we read of a mercantile expedition under Abu Sufyān, which for the first time penetrated to the capital of Persia, and reached even the presence of the Chosroes.

Commerce flourishes at Mecca

I proceed to notice some particulars of the domestic life of Moḥammad. The sister of Khadīja was married to Ar-Rabī', a descendant of 'Abd Shams, and had borne him a son called Abu'l-Aṣ, who in course of time had grown up, and was respected for his uprightness and mercantile success. Khadīja loved her nephew, and looked upon him as her own son. She prevailed upon Moḥammad to join him in marriage with their eldest daughter Zeinab, who had but just reached the age of womanhood. The union proved to be

Domestic life of Moḥammad. Marriage of three eldest daughters

[1] Ibn Hishām, p. 143 f.

one of real affection, though during the troubled rise of Islām it was chequered, as we shall see, by temporary severance, and by several romantic incidents. Somewhat later the two younger daughters, Roḳeiya and Ūm Kulthum, were given in marriage to 'Otba and 'Oteiba, sons of Abu Lahab, uncle of Moḥammad. Fāṭima, the youngest, was yet a child.

Adopts his cousin 'Alī

Shortly after the rebuilding of the Ka'ba, Moḥammad comforted himself for the loss of his infant son Al-Ḳāsim by adopting 'Alī, the child of his friend and former guardian Abu Ṭālib.[1] It fell out thus: a season of severe scarcity visited Mecca; and Abu Ṭālib, still poor, was put to shifts for the support of his numerous family. His difficulties were perceived by Moḥammad, who, prompted by his usual kindness and consideration, repaired to his rich uncle Al-'Abbās, and said: 'O 'Abbās! thy brother Abu Ṭālib hath a burdensome family, and thou seest what straits men are brought to. Let us go to him, and relieve him somewhat of the care of his children. I will take one son, if thou wilt take another. And we shall support them.' Al-'Abbās consenting, they proposed the thing to Abu Ṭālib; and he replied: 'Leave me 'Aḳīl and Ṭālib; and do ye with the others as it pleaseth you.' So Moḥammad took 'Alī, and Al-'Abbās took Ja'far. Alī, at this time not above five or six years of age, remained ever after with Moḥammad, and they exhibited towards each other the mutual attachment of parent and child.

Zeid, son of Ḥāritha, a Christian slave

The heart of Moḥammad was inclined to ardent and lasting friendships. About the period of 'Alī's adoption he admitted to his closest intimacy another person unconnected with him by family ties, but of more equal age. This was Zeid, son of Ḥāritha.[2] As he will be frequently alluded to, and his society must have had an important influence on the Prophet himself, it is important to trace his previous life. His father and mother belonged to Christian tribes in the south of Syria. Zeid was still a child when, journeying with his mother, the company was waylaid by a band of Arab marauders, who carried him away captive, and sold him into slavery. While yet a youth he fell into the hands of Ḥakīm, grandson of Khuweilid, who presented him to his aunt Khadīja shortly after her marriage with Moḥammad. He

[1] Aṭ-Ṭabari, i. 1163 f. [2] Ibn Ḳoteiba, p. 71.

was then about twenty years of age; and is described as small of stature, and dark in complexion, with a short and depressed nose. He was an active and useful servant; and Moḥammad soon conceiving a strong affection for him, Khadīja, to gratify her husband, made him a present of the slave. His father searched long in vain for Zeid; and his grief found vent in touching verses, some of which have been preserved to us by tradition. At last a party of the tribe when on a pilgrimage to Mecca recognised the youth, and communicated tidings of him to the disconsolate father, who immediately set out to fetch him home. Arrived at Mecca, Ḥāritha offered a large payment for his ransom. Moḥammad summoned Zeid, and left it in his option to go or stay. He chose to stay. 'I will not leave thee,' he said; 'thou art in the place to me of father and of mother.' Delighted by his faithfulness, Moḥammad took him straightway to the Black Stone of the Ka'ba and said: 'Bear testimony, all ye that are present. Zeid is my son; I will be his heir, and he shall be mine.' His father, contented with the declaration, returned home glad at heart; and his son, now a freed-man, was thenceforward called 'Zeid ibn Moḥammad,' *Zeid the son of Moḥammad.* By Moḥammad's desire he married his old attendant, Um Aiman. Though nearly double his age, she bore him a son called Osāma, who was the leader in the expedition to Syria at the time of Moḥammad's fatal illness.

Is also adopted by Moḥammad

Christianity prevailed in the tribes from which, both on the father's and mother's side, Zeid sprang;[2] and though severed from his home at too early an age to have acquired any extensive or thorough knowledge of its doctrines, he yet no doubt carried with him some impression of the teaching, and some fragments of the facts or legends, of the faith. These would form subjects of conversation between the youth and his adoptive father, whose mind was now feeling in all directions after religious truth. Among the relatives of Khadīja, too, there were persons who possessed a knowledge of Christianity, and observed perhaps something of its

Christian influence of Zeid;

[1] Zeid was probably about six years younger than Moḥammad. The difference of age between him and his bride was so great, that tradition tells us Moḥammad promised him *paradise* for marrying her.

[2] The Beni 'Odhra and Beni Ṭai'.

'Othmān ibn Al-Ḥuweirith; and Waraḳa

practice. Her cousin 'Othmān has been already noticed as having embraced Christianity at Constantinople, and made an unsuccessful attempt to gain the rule at Mecca. Waraḳa, another cousin, is said also to have become a convert to Christianity, to have been acquainted with the religious tenets and sacred Scriptures both of Jews and Christians, and to have even copied or translated some portion of the Gospels into Hebrew or Arabic.[1] In the following chapter it will be seen that this person had an acknowledged share in satisfying the mind of Moḥammad that his mission was divine.

The Four Inquirers

It is a fancy of tradition that, shortly before the appearance of Moḥammad, several inquirers were not only seeking after the true faith (or, as they style it, *the Religion of Abraham*), but, warned by prophecy and by the unguarded admissions of Jews and Christians, were in immediate expectation of the coming prophet.[2] Of such inquirers among Ḳoreish, Muslim biographies specify *four*. Two of these were *'Othmān* and *Waraḳa*, already mentioned. The third, *'Obeidallah* (by his mother a grandson of 'Abd al-Muṭṭalib) embraced Islām, emigrated with his brethren in the faith to Abyssinia, and there went over to Christianity.[3] The fourth was *Zeid*, cousin of 'Omar. Of him tradition says that he condemned the idolatrous sacrifices of the Ka'ba, reprobated the burying alive of infant daughters, and 'followed the religion of Abraham.' But not content with such assertions, the traditionists add that Zeid possessed distinct knowledge of the coming prophet and left his salutation to be delivered to him when he should appear. Nay, he described his person, stated that he would be of the family of 'Abd al-Muṭṭalib, and foretold that he would emigrate to Medīna! He died while the Ka'ba was rebuilding, and was buried at the foot of mount Ḥirā. Although such expectations of the coming Prophet must be rejected as mere fond imaginations, and the manifest tendency to invent anticipatory legends of this description makes it difficult to sever the real from the fictitious in the matter of these four Inquirers, yet it may be admitted as highly

'Obeidallah ibn Jaḥsh

Zeid ibn 'Amr

[1] Ibn Hishām, p. 143 f. [2] Ibn Ḳoteiba, p. 28 f.

[3] Aṭ-Ṭabari, i. 1772. He died in Abyssinia, and Moḥammad when in Medīna married his widow, Um Ḥabība, daughter of Abu Sufyān.

probable that a spirit of religious inquiry, the disposition to reject idolatry, and a perception of the superiority of Judaism and Christianity, did in some quarters about this time exist. With such inquirers Moḥammad would no doubt deeply sympathise, and hold converse on the gross idolatry of the Arabs, and need of a true and spiritual faith for their regeneration.

A spirit of inquiry probably abroad

Moḥammad was now approaching his fortieth year. Always pensive, he had of late become even more thoughtful and retiring. Contemplation and reflection engaged his mind. The debasement of his people pressed heavily on him; the dim and imperfect shadows of Judaism and Christianity excited doubts without satisfying them; and his soul was perplexed with uncertainty as to what was the true religion. Thus burdened, he frequently retired to seek relief in meditation amongst the solitary valleys and rocks near Mecca. His favourite spot was a cave in the declivities at the foot of mount Ḥirā,[1] a lofty conical hill two or three miles north of Mecca. Thither he would retire for days at a time; and his faithful wife sometimes accompanied him. The continued solitude, instead of stilling his anxiety, magnified into sterner and more impressive shapes the solemn realities which agitated his soul. Close by was the grave of the aged Zeid, who, after spending a lifetime in the same inquiries, had now passed into the state of certainty;—might he himself not reach the same assurance without crossing the gate of death?

Moḥammad seeks solitude

All around was bleak and rugged. To the east and south, the vision from the cave of Ḥirā is bounded by lofty mountain ranges, but to the north and west the weary prospect is thus described by Burckhardt:—'The country before us had a dreary aspect, not a single green spot being

Spiritual anxiety and groping after light

[1] Or Ḥarā, since called Jebel Nūr, or Mountain of Light, because Moḥammad is said to have received his first revelation there. The hill is so lofty as to be seen a long distance off. Burckhardt says: 'Passing the Sherīf's garden house on the road to Arafāt, a little further on, we enter a valley, which extends in a direction N.E. by N., and is terminated by the mountain, which is conical. . . . In the rocky floor of a small building ruined by the Wahabees, a cleft is shown about the size of a man in length and breadth. . . . A little below this place is a small cavern in the red granite rock, which forms the upper stratum of this mountain.' This valley was often trodden by Moḥammad on his way to and from the cleft and the cavern.

visible; barren, black, and grey hills, and white sandy valleys, were the only objects in sight.' There was harmony here between external nature, and the troubled world within. By degrees the impulsive and susceptible mind of Moḥammad was wrought up to the highest pitch of excitement; and he would give vent to his agitation in wild rhapsodical language, enforced often with incoherent oaths, the counterpart of inward struggling after truth. The following fragments belong probably to this period:—

Poetical fragments of this period.

Sūra ciii

By the declining day I swear!
Verily, man is in the way of ruin;
Excepting such as possess faith,
And do the things which are right,
And stir up one another unto truth and steadfastness.

And again—

Sūra c

By the rushing panting steeds!
Striking fire with flashing hoof,
That scour the land at early morn!
And, darkening it with dust,
Cleave thereby the Enemy!
Verily Man is to his Lord ungrateful,
And he himself is witness of it.
Verily he is keen after this world's good.
Ah! witteth he not that when what is in the graves shall be brought forth,
And that which is in men's breasts laid bare;—
Verily in that day shall the Lord be well informed of them.

Prayer for guidance

Nor was he wanting in prayer for guidance to the great Being who, he felt, alone could give it. The following petitions (though probably adapted subsequently to public worship) contain perhaps the germ of frequent prayer at this early period.

Sūra i

Praise be to God, the Lord of creation,
The most merciful, the most compassionate!
Ruler of the day of Reckoning!
Thee we worship, and invoke for help.
Lead us in the straight path;—
The path of those towards whom Thou hast been gracious;
Not of those against whom Thy wrath is kindled, or that walk in error.[1]

How such aspirations developed into the belief that the subject of them was divinely inspired, is a theme obscure and difficult, which I reserve for another chapter.

[1] The Fātiḥa, or opening Sūra of the Ḳor'ān, so often recited in public and private worship.

CHAPTER III

FIRST DREAMS OF INSPIRATION: ENDING IN THE CONVICTION THAT HE WAS THE PROPHET OF HIS PEOPLE

ÆTAT. 40-43. A.D. 609-612

Poetical fragments and rhapsodies

LIGHT struggled with the darkness in the soul of Moḥammad. Gradually certain grand verities took clear and definite shape before him :—God, the sole Creator, Ruler and Judge of men and angels; the hopeless wretchedness of his people sunk in heathenism and idolatry; heaven and hell; the resurrection, judgment, and recompense of good and evil in the world to come. The conflict waging within found vent in fragments of wild, impassioned poetry. These sometimes assume the character of soliloquies, full of melancholy reflection upon the state and prospects of mankind; sometimes fraught with burning words and imagery of terror, they seem intended for the warning or admonition of his fellow-citizens; sometimes they exhibit a mind intent upon itself, oppressed by perplexity and distress, and seeking for comfort and assurance by fleeing to its Maker. To aid in tracing the development of spiritual thought and religious belief in the mind of Moḥammad, extracts from these will now be laid before the reader.[1] Of the soliloquies, the following is a specimen :—

Specimens of these fragments

Sūra ci

> That which striketh! What is it which striketh?
> And what shall certify thee what THE STRIKING is?

[1] The earlier chapters of the Ḳor'ān are mostly composed each of a short piece delivered all at once; and the period of their appearance is thus more easily assigned than that of the later Sūras made up of fragments delivered on various occasions. The later Sūras also are much longer than the earlier; but in the Ḳor'ān, as finally arranged, the chapters are placed in an order precisely the opposite, the longest being first and the shortest last. The chronological sequence, in short, is reversed. Hence the casual reader of the Ḳor'ān forms no correct conception of the origin and development of Moḥammad's system.

The day on which mankind shall be like moths scattered abroad,
And the mountains like wool of divers colours carded.
Then as for him whose balances are heavy, he shall enter into Bliss;
And as for him whose balances are light, the Pit shall be his dwelling place.
And what shall certify thee what is the PIT? A raging FIRE!

These wild and incoherent rhapsodies are couched in words of rare force and beauty, with such flow and rhythm as the Arab loves, and which his noble tongue gives freest scope to. The Oracle sometimes begins now to come direct from the Deity, speaking as 'We,' and to Moḥammad as 'Thou.' The conviction, however, of being inspired, was not reached, as we shall see, till after a protracted time of mental throes. This fragment, for example, purports to come direct from heaven:—

Sūra xcv

I swear by the Fig tree and the Olive,
By mount Sinai, and by this land inviolate!
Verily WE made Man of the choicest creation,
Then WE rendered him the lowest of the low;—
Excepting such as believe and work righteousness;
Unto them shall be given a reward that fadeth not away.
Then, after this, what shall make thee deny the Day of reckoning?
What! is not God the justest of all Judges?

Warning and expostulation

The voice of expostulation and alarm was raised in accents such as these:—

Sūra civ

Woe unto the backbiter and the slanderer;—
Who heapeth up riches, and counteth them over!
He thinketh that his wealth shall remain with him for ever.
Nay! verily he shall be cast into the crushing fire;
And what shall cause thee to know what is the CRUSHING FIRE?
The fire of God kindled,
Which shall mount above the hearts;
Verily it shall rise above them as a curtain,
Stretched over lofty columns.

Arab and Jewish legend

Allusion is sometimes made, though in a form as yet brief and vague, both to Arab and Jewish legend. Thus in the 89th Sūra:—

Sūra lxxxix

What! hast thou not seen how thy Lord dealt with the children of 'Ad,—
The Iremites possessed of pillars,
The like whereof have not been builded in any city?—
And with the THAMŪDITES which hewed out the rock in the Valley;

And with PHARAOH that used the stakes![1]
  These all behaved insolently in the earth,
  And multiplied wickedness therein;
Wherefore thy Lord poured upon them the mingled cup of His wrath,
  Verily thy Lord is upon His watch-tower, &c.

Nor was there wanting special appeal to national mercies. The 105th Sūra, which recounts God's goodness in the overthrow of Abraha, 'Lord of the Elephant,' and preservation of the Holy City, belongs probably to this period.[2] And also the following:— Sūra cv

For the stirring up of ḲOREISH;— Sūra cvi
The stirring of them up unto the Winter and Summer caravans of merchandise;
  Let them worship the Lord of this House,
Who hath provided them food against Hunger,
And granted them immunity from Danger.[3]

In elucidation of Moḥammad's honest striving after Truth another passage may be quoted, in which are set forth the two paths of Virtue and Vice, and the difficulties of the Straight way:— 'The two Paths'

Verily I swear by this Territory, Sūra xc
(And thou art a resident thereof;)

---

[1] 'The stakes' to which the tyrant bound his victims. The Thamūdites are also mentioned in the 91st Sūra, which is quoted below as an early example of the rhyming style so frequent in the Ḳor'ān. Each verse ends with the syllable *ha* (pronoun, third person), as indicated by italics.

By the Sun and *his* rising splendour!
  By the Moon when she followeth *him!*
  By the Day when it showeth forth *his* glory!
  By the Night when it covereth *him* in darkness!
  By the Heavens and Him that made *them!*
  By the Earth and Him that spread *it* forth!
  By the Soul and Him that framed *it*,
  Inspiring in *it* wickedness and piety!
Verily he that purifieth *the same* is blessed;
And he is wretched that corrupteth *it*.
The Thamūdites in *their* impiety, accused their prophet (Ṣāliḥ) of imposture
  When the most abandoned among *them* arose (to slay the camel).
(Now the prophet of God had said unto them, 'It is the she-camel of the Lord;
  Give ye *her* to drink;)
But they rejected him, and slaughtered *her;*
Wherefore the Lord overthrew them for their crime and rendered unto them a recompense equal with *their Sin;*
And he feareth not the issue *thereof.*

[2] See *Introduction*, p. c. [3] *I.e.* inviolability of the sacred territory.

By the begetter, and by that which is begotten!
Surely WE have created man in trouble.
Ah! doth he think indeed that no one shall prevail over him?
He saith,—'I have wasted much wealth.'
Ah! doth he think that no one seeth him?
Have WE not made him two eyes, a tongue, and two lips;
And shown unto him the TWO HIGHWAYS.[1]
Yet he applieth himself not unto the ascent;—
And what shall teach thee what the ASCENT is?—
Freeing the captive,
Giving food in the day of want
To the orphan that is near of kin,
Or to the poor that lieth in the dust;—
Further, the Righteous are of those that believe, and stir up one another unto steadfastness and mercy.
These shall be the Companions of the Right hand;
But they that deny OUR signs, shall be Companions of the Left;
Around them the Fire shall close.

Moḥammad's early religious poetry

It seems probable that Moḥammad gave vent to his reveries in poetry of this kind for several years before he assumed the office of a divine teacher. The early Sūras, and no doubt other reflective and didactic pieces not preserved because not purporting to be inspired, would be recorded (as Moḥammad did not himself write) by the aged Waraḳa, by 'Alī, who was still a boy, possibly by Khadīja herself or by some of her relatives, who were inquirers more or less acquainted with Judaism and Christianity. The friends of Moḥammad no doubt listened with reverence to his admonitions, and sought to follow his injunctions as those of a faithful teacher guided haply by the spirit of God. Amongst these were certainly Khadīja herself, Zeid and Alī, his adopted sons, and perhaps Abu Bekr, his bosom friend, with Waraḳa, who saw in his teaching the counterpart of his own ideas. But without this little circle, superstition and the world held undisputed sway. Warning and expostulation were met by gross ignorance and repellant darkness. The kind and generous Abu Ṭālib smiled at the enthusiasm of his nephew. Abu Lahab, another uncle, mocked and insulted him. Abu Jahl and his party sneered. The great body of Ḳoreish were careless and indifferent. As Moḥammad passed by the knots that clustered about the Ka'ba discussing the events of the

His early followers

Makes no impression on his fellow-citizens

[1] *I.e.* Good and Evil.

day, they would point disdainfully at him as at a half-witted creature.

Necessity and likelihood of a divine commission

The more susceptible amongst the citizens listened, perhaps with attention at the first. But when pressed to throw in their lot with the Inquirers, they would answer: 'It is well enough for Jews and Christians to follow the purer faith thou speakest of. They, we know, had prophets with a message from heaven. If to us also, a prophet had been sent, we should doubtless have followed his directions, and been as devout and spiritual in our worship as the Jews and Christians. Let us therefore be content with the light given us, and remain as we are.'[1] Moḥammad felt the force of the reply, for it was in unison with thoughts hidden and undeveloped yet ever present in his heart. Would the Almighty be unmindful of the appeal thus made to Him for guidance? The appeal might itself be a divine intimation to furnish the direction so urgently needed and desired. And, again, whence the rush of inspiration regarding the unity of God, His power and providence, and a future recompense in heaven and hell? Whence the ecstatic moments, the flow of burning thoughts, the spontaneous burst of eloquence and heavenly speech, which gave form and substance to the long conceived yearnings of his heart, and transformed them as it were into the words of God himself? Could the prophets of old have had a more convincing test of inspiration? What if all this formed a supernatural call, a divine Mission? Why should he hesitate to take the name of God upon his lips, go forth boldly as his Legate, and trust that the same spirit

[1] There are many such passages in the Ḳor'ān, and the pretext thus explicitly put in the Sūra xxxv. 40 f., was probably the earliest of the kind he had to answer. It is as follows:—'The men of Mecca swore by the Lord with the most solemn oath that if a Prophet had come to them they would have followed his directions better than any of the other peoples; but now that a preacher (*i.e.* Moḥammad) is come unto them, it hath only increased their aversion from the truth, their arrogance in the earth, and their pursuit of evil.' See also Sūra vi. 156-158: 'And this book WE have sent down,—blessed; wherefore follow it and fear God that ye may find mercy. Lest ye should say: "Verily the Scripture hath been revealed to two Peoples before us, but we are unable to read in their language." Or lest ye should say: "If the Scripture had been revealed to us, we surely would have followed the direction better than they." And now verily hath a clear exposition come unto you from your Lord,—a direction and mercy,' &c.

which had guided Jewish and Christian prophets would put words into his mouth?

Mental depression and grounds of reassurance

While absorbed by such reflections, sometimes doubting, sometimes believing, Moḥammad at seasons suffered grievous mental distraction. To this period may be attributed such passages as the following, in which, after deep depression, he seeks to reassure his soul by remembering the past favours of the Almighty:—

Sūra xciii

By the rising sunshine!
By the night when it darkeneth!
Thy Lord hath not forsaken thee, neither hath He been displeased
The Future shall surely be better unto thee than the Past.
Thy Lord shall shortly dispense unto thee a gift; and thou shalt be satisfied.
What! Did He not find thee an Orphan, and give thee a home?
Found thee astray, and guided thee aright?
Now, therefore, as touching the Orphan, oppress him not!
And as touching him that asketh of thee, repulse him not;
And as touching the Favours of thy Lord, rehearse them.

And again:—

Sūra xciv

What! Have WE not opened for thee thy breast?
And eased thee of the burden,—
Which galled thy back;
And exalted the mention of thee?
Then truly with the difficulty, there shall be ease.
Verily with the difficulty there shall be ease.
And when thou hast finished,[1] then labour,
And towards thy Lord raise thy desire.

Seeks to commit suicide

Notwithstanding such consolations, his distress was sometimes insupportable; over and again he meditated suicide.[2] What if all this were but the simulation of divine impulse, the stirrings of the Evil one and his emissaries? Indeed, throughout the Ḳor'ān, no crime against the high majesty of Heaven is more fearful than to speak falsely in the name of

[1] *I.e.* finished *preaching* or *praying* (Beiḍāwi). Another early Sūra, of only three verses (cviii.), refers probably to the taunts of those who reproached him with the death of his sons as a mark of God's displeasure:—

Surely WE have given unto thee an abundance;
Wherefore pray unto thy Lord, and offer sacrifice.
Verily, he that hateth thee shall be childless.

[2] [*Cf.* Sūra xviii. 5; xxvi. 2.]

God. Rather than expose himself to a risk so terrible, he would anticipate the possibility by casting himself headlong from one of these wild cliffs. An invisible influence appeared to hold him back. Was it an influence divine; or might not this too be diabolical?

Belief in divine mission revives, mingled with ambition

At such seasons he found solace in the bosom of Khadīja, who, as tradition tells us, *tried* the Spirits, and assured him that his Visitants were not wicked, but innocent and virtuous. When thus comforted and re-established, the old hopes and aspirations would again revive in his heart stronger than ever. Bright visions of a united people abjuring their idolatry, would rise before him. Faith and piety should yet reign throughout Arabia:—

Sūra cx

When the help of the Lord shall come and victory,
And thou shalt see men entering into the faith of God in multitudes,
Then celebrate His praise, and ask pardon of Him, for He is forgiving.

'Moses led forth his people (he would say to himself), and so did other Jewish chieftains, to do battle for the Lord against the heathen. And why should not I, as the vicegerent of God, bring all Arabia in godly submission prostrate at His feet? Then, what vain superstition have I not seen in Syria; they have set up the Queen of Heaven, and burned incense to her! They have a Revelation, and profess to obey it. I will show to them from their own Book that they have corrupted and obscured the Truth. And Egypt, Persia, Abyssinia, Al-Ḥīra,—all around, why should I not dash to the ground the idols, and every thing that exalts itself against the true God;—if only my people will be convinced and rally around me to fight the battles of the Lord. The whole world, Jew and Christian, weary of strife and discord, yearns for a Prophet who shall restore unity and peace. Will not all, then, flock to my standard when I proclaim myself that which I surely feel myself to be,—the Prophet of the Lord?' Such conceptions were at this time, it may be, vague and undeveloped, but looking to the earliest fragments of his Revelation, there is little doubt that the germ of them existed in the mind of Moḥammad.

Moḥammad in expecta-

At this crisis, the future of Moḥammad and of Islām trembled in the balance. On the one hand, he was surrounded

tion of a divine commission

by a little knot of faithful and believing followers. Truth seemed to shine, clear and radiant as a sunbeam, into his heart; ecstatic trances impressed a seal, apparently divine, upon his convictions; he was conscious of a sincere desire, and fancied that he perceived a mission, to call forth his people from darkness into light. On the other hand, the ungodly laughed him to scorn; while solemn expostulation and warning were treated, even by the wise and sober, as the effusion of a fond enthusiast. Before the DIVINE COMMISSION all difficulties would vanish. He would wait, then, for the inspiring influence of the Holy Spirit to lead him as it had ofttimes led the prophets before him, in the right way. Gabriel,[1] perhaps, would visit him, as he visited Zacharias and Mary, to announce to him the advent of a new Dispensation.

Vision of Gabriel with commission to 'Recite in the name of God'

He was seated or wandering amidst the peaks of Ḥirā buried no doubt in reveries such as these, when suddenly an apparition rose before him. The heavenly Visitant stood clear and close beside him in a vision. It was no other than Gabriel, the Messenger of God, who now appeared in the sky, and, approaching within 'two bows' length,' brought from his Master this memorable behest:—

Sūra xcvi

RECITE in the name of the Lord who created,—
Created Man from nought but congealed blood;—
RECITE! For thy Lord is beneficent.
It is He who hath taught (to write) with the pen;—
Hath taught man that which he knoweth not. . . .
Hast thou not seen him that holdeth back
The Servant of God when he prayeth?
What thinkest thou? had he listened to right direction,
And commanded unto piety?
Dost thou not see that he hath rejected the Truth and turned his back?
What! Doth he not know that God seeth?
Nay, verily, if he forbear not, WE shall drag him by the forelock,—
The lying, sinful forelock!
Then let him call his company of friends, and WE shall call the guards of Hell;
Nay! submit not unto him; but worship, and draw nigh unto the Lord.

Moḥammad assumes authority

Thus was Moḥammad led,—by such process as we can only conjecture, but seemingly after a protracted period of doubt

[1] It is clear that at a later period at least, if not from the first, Moḥammad confounded *Gabriel* with the *Holy Ghost*.

and hesitancy,—to give forth his message as proceeding direct from the Almighty. Henceforth he spoke literally *in the name of the Lord.* And so scrupulous was he lest, in his words, there should be even the appearance of human influence, that every sentence of the Ḳor'ān is prefaced by the divine command, 'SPEAK' or 'SAY'; which, if not expressed is always to be understood.[1]

of God for his Revelations;

This commission pervaded now his whole career, and mingled with his every action. He was the servant, the prophet, the vicegerent of God; and however much the sphere of his mission might expand in ever widening circles, the principle on which it rested was the same. How far the two ideas, on the one hand of a resolution in his own mind involving spontaneous action, and on the other a supernatural inspiration objective and independent of his will, were at first consciously and simultaneously present, and in what respective degrees, it is difficult to conjecture. But it is certain that the conception of the Almighty as the immediate source of his inspiration and Author of his commission, soon took entire and undivided possession of his soul; and, however coloured by the events and inducements of the day, or mingled with apparently incongruous motives and desires, retained a paramount influence until the hour of his death. The above Sūra was, in fact, the starting point of Islām. Theologians and biographers generally hold it to be the first revealed Sūra; and Moḥammad himself used to refer to it as the commencement of his inspiration.[2]

and becomes his commissioned prophet

[1] Thus Sūra cxii. :—

SAY :—He is GOD alone : GOD the Eternal!
He begetteth not, and He is not begotten;
And there is not any like unto Him.

[2] Several years after he thus describes the same vision :—

By the Star when it riseth!
Your fellow erreth not, neither hath he gone astray.
Nor doth he speak of his own fancy.
Verily it is no other than a Revelation that hath been inspired :
One mighty and strong taught it him,—
One endued with wisdom. He stood
In the highest part of the horizon,
Then he drew near and approached,

The commission slighted by the people of Mecca

But the divine commission was unheeded at Mecca. Scorn and abuse gathered thicker than ever around him. He was taunted as a poet carried away by wild fancy; as a sorcerer given to magic, oaths and rhapsodies; or as one possessed by the Genii and demons. Grieved and dispirited, he fell back upon his commission. Was it a command to preach and call his stiff-necked and rebellious people to repentance; or not rather a simple message of the truth, for himself and his disciples? Wearied and perplexed, the Prophet stretched himself on his carpet, and wrapping his garments about him fell into a trance. The Angel was at hand, and Moḥammad was aroused from despondency to energy and action by this reanimating message:—

The vision and command to preach

Sūra lxxiv

Oh thou that art covered! Arise and preach![1] And magnify thy Lord.
Purify thy garments, and depart from all uncleanness.

* * * * * *

Leave ME and him whom I have created alone;
On whom I have bestowed abundant riches,
And sons dwelling before him;
And disposed his affairs prosperously;—
Yet he desireth that I should add thereto.
Nay! Because he is to OUR Signs an adversary,
I will afflict him with fierce calamity;
For he imagined and devised mischief in his heart,
May he be damned! how he devised!
Again may he be damned! how he devised!
Then he looked, and frowned and scowled;
Then he turned his back and looked contemptuously:—
And he said, '*Verily, this is nought but Magic to be wrought;*[2]
Verily, this is nothing but the speech of a mere mortal.'
Now, will I cast him into Hell-fire.
And what shall cause thee to know what HELL-FIRE is?
It leaveth not, neither doth it suffer to escape,
Candescent on the skin. . . .

Until he was at the distance of two bows' length, or yet nearer:
And he revealed unto his servant that which he revealed.
The heart did not belie that which he saw.
What! Will ye then dispute with him concerning that which he saw?'—Sūra liii.

Then he alludes to a *second* vision of Gabriel, which will be referred to hereafter.

[1] Preach in the sense of *warn*, or call to repentance.

[2] Alluding to the doctrine of the Resurrection; the revivification of dry bones and dust being laughed to scorn as mere magic.

Then, after an appeal to the former Scriptures :—

Nay, by the Moon !
By the night when it retireth !
By the morn when it reddeneth !
Verily this is one of the most weighty matters,—
A warning to mankind . . .
. . . The Companions of the Right hand, dwelling
In Gardens, shall inquire of the wicked ;—
'*What hath cast you into Hell?* And they shall reply,—
'*We were not of those that prayed; neither did we feed the poor;*
And we babbled vainly with the vain babblers;
And we were rejecters of the Day of Reckoning;
Until the conviction thereof overtook us.' . . .
Then what aileth them that they turn aside from this admonition ;—
As though they were affrighted asses fleeing from a lion?
Every man among them desireth that expanded Scrolls be given unto him.[1]
Nay ! they dread not the Life to come.
Nay ! this is a sufficient Warning ;
Whoso chooseth he shall be warned thereby.
But none shall be warned excepting as the Lord pleaseth.
He is to be feared, and HE is the Forgiver.

Traditional account

The steps by which Moḥammad was led to assume the office not only of an inspired Prophet, but also of a Leader commissioned to preach and summon his people to the faith of Islām, have now been traced from the various intimations gathered from the Ḳor'ān itself. To complete the view, I will farther give the corresponding narrative from the pen of the Biographers, premising only that on so mysterious a subject the imagination must, in the process of oral transmission, have had the fullest play.[2] The following is from Al-Wāḳidi :—

'First beginnings of inspiration,' as handed down by tradition

The first beginnings of Moḥammad's inspiration were *real visions.* Every vision that he saw was clear as the morning dawn. These again provoked the love of solitude. He would repair to a cave on mount Ḥirā, and there pass whole days and nights. Then, drawn by affection

[1] *I.e.* that the divine message recorded upon pages should be miraculously brought from heaven and placed in the objector's hands, in proof of Moḥammad's mission.

[2] Ibn Hishām, p. 157 ff. ; Aṭ-Ṭabari, i. 1142 ff. ; Ibn Sa'd, p. 112 ff. It must not be forgotten that Moḥammad at this period could not have been the object of much observation from without. Khadīja was almost the only witness of his earliest mental throes. 'Alī was but a boy ; and it is doubtful how far Zeid and Abu Bekr were yet on sufficiently close and intimate terms with him to be made the confidants of his most secret thoughts.

for Khadīja, he would return to his home. This went on till the truth burst upon him in the cave. It happened on this wise. Wandering in the hills around, an angel from the sky cried to him, '*O Moḥammad, I am Gabriel!*' He was terrified, for as often as he raised his head, there was the apparition of the angel. He hurried home to tell his wife. 'Oh, Khadīja,' he said, 'I have never abhorred anything as I do these idols and soothsayers; and now verily I fear lest I should become a soothsayer myself.' 'Never,' replied his faithful wife; 'the Lord will never suffer it thus to be,'—and she went on to speak of his many virtues, upon which she founded the assurance. Then she repaired to her cousin Waraḳa, and told him all. 'By the Lord,' cried the aged man, 'he speaketh truth! Doubtless it is the beginning of prophecy, and there shall come upon him the *Great Nāmūs*, like as it came upon Moses. Wherefore charge him that he think not aught but hopeful thoughts within his breast. If he be raised up a prophet while I am yet alive, surely I will stand by him.'

Moḥammad meditates suicide

Now the first Sūra revealed to Moḥammad was the 96th, verses 1-5, *Recite in the name of the Lord*, &c.; and that descended on him in the cave of Ḥirā. After this he waited some time without seeing Gabriel. And he became greatly downcast, so that he went out now to one mountain, and then to another, seeking to cast himself headlong thence. While thus intent on self-destruction, he was suddenly arrested by a voice from heaven. He looked up, and behold it was Gabriel upon a throne between the heavens and the earth, who said: '*O Moḥammad! thou art the Prophet of the Lord, in truth, and I am Gabriel.*' Then Moḥammad turned to go to his own house; and the Lord comforted him, and strengthened his heart. And thereafter revelations began to follow one upon another with frequency.[1]

Gabriel again appears and comforts him

[1] Al-Wāḳidi is here more succinct and natural than Ibn Hishām. Aṭ-Ṭabari again surpasses Ibn Hishām in miraculous statements, the number and variety of which illustrate the rapid fabrication and indiscriminate reception of such stories in the third century. Omitting such, the following is a brief outline from Ibn Hishām and Aṭ-Ṭabari of the first stirrings of inspiration :—

On the night whereon the Lord was minded to deal graciously with him, Gabriel came to Moḥammad as he slept with his family in the cave of Ḥirā. He held in his hand a piece of silk with writing thereon, and he said *Read!* Moḥammad replied, *I cannot read.* Whereupon the angel did so tightly gripe him that he thought death had come upon him. Then said Gabriel a second time *Read!* And Moḥammad, but only to escape the agony, replied, *What shall I read?* Gabriel proceeded :—*Read* (recite) *in the name of thy Lord*, &c.; repeating the 96th Sūra to the end of v. 5. When he had ended, the angel departed; and 'the words,' said Moḥammad, 'were as though they had been graven on my heart.' [This narrative seems to be a reminiscence of Isaiah xl. 6. The verb 'to read' means in Hebrew 'to cry.'] Suddenly the thought occurred to him that he was possessed of evil spirits, and he meditated suicide; but as he rushed forth with the intention of casting himself

Various accounts of stoppage of inspiration

The period succeeding the revelation of the 96th Sūra, during which inspiration was suspended, and Moḥammad in despondency contemplated suicide, is generally represented as of longer duration than in the above statement. The interval [which is called the *fetra*] is variously held to have lasted from six months to three years. At its close, the 74th and 93rd Sūras, containing assurance of mercy and command to preach, were delivered. The accounts, however, are throughout confused, and sometimes contradictory; and we can only gather with certainty that there was a time (corresponding with the deductions already drawn from the Ḳor'ān itself) during which the mind of Moḥammad hung in suspense, and doubted the reality of a heavenly mission.

Character of Moḥammad's ecstatic periods

It is not easy to say what was the outward manifestation of Moḥammad's ecstatic periods,—whether simply reveries of profound meditation, or swoons connected with a morbid excitability of mental or physical constitution, no doubt varied at different periods and under different circumstances. On a subject so closely allied to the supernatural, we must be on our guard against the tendency of a credulous and excited imagination to conjure up marvellous tales which would find ready currency and be eagerly handed by tradi-

down a precipice, he was arrested by the appearance again of Gabriel, and stood for a long time transfixed by the sight. At last, the vision disappearing, he returned to Khadīja who, alarmed at his absence, had sent messengers to Mecca in quest of him. In consternation he threw himself into her lap, and told her what had occurred. She reassured him, saying that he would surely be a prophet, and Waraḳa confirmed her in the belief. Ibn Hishām, p. 152 ff.; Aṭ-Ṭabari, i. 1147.

Another story is that Khadīja tested the character of the spirit by making Moḥammad sit first on her right knee, then on her left, in both of which positions the apparition continued before him. Then she took him in her lap, and removed her veil, or uncovered her garments, when the spirit disappeared,—thus proving that it was at any rate a modest and virtuous being. Whereupon Khadīja exclaimed: *Rejoice my cousin, for by the Lord! it is an angel, and no devil.*

On another occasion, being terrified, he entreated Khadīja to cover him up, on which was revealed the 74th Sūra beginning, *Oh thou covered!* Again, the Prophet receiving no visit from Gabriel for some time, Khadīja said to him: *Verily I fear that God is displeased with thee;* whereupon was revealed Sūra xciii.;—*Thy Lord hath not removed from thee, neither is He displeased*, &c. But such traditions appear simply to be attempts to explain or illustrate the several passages to which they relate.

tion. With this caution the following particulars may be read:[1]—

Traditional account

At the moment of inspiration, anxiety pressed upon the Prophet, and his countenance was troubled. He fell to the ground like an inebriate, or one overcome by sleep; and in the coldest day his forehead would be bedewed with large drops of perspiration. Even his she-camel, if he chanced to become inspired while mounted on her, would be affected by a wild excitement, sitting down and rising up, now planting her legs rigidly, then throwing them about as if they would be parted from her. To outward appearance inspiration descended unexpectedly, and without any previous warning to the Prophet.[2] When questioned on the subject he replied: 'Inspiration cometh in one of two ways; sometimes Gabriel communicateth the Revelation to me, as one man to another, and this is easy; at other times, it is like the ringing of a bell, penetrating my very heart, and rending me; and this it is which afflicteth me the most.' In the later period of life Moḥammad referred his grey hairs to the withering effect produced upon him by the '*terrific* Sūras.'[3]

Moḥammad's own account

Moḥammadan notions regarding devils and Genii

Before quitting the subject, it may be interesting to note what tradition says of the class of spirits called *Jinn* or Genii. Prior to the mission of the Prophet, the Genii, and devils or other spirits of the air, had access to the outskirts of heaven, and by assiduous eavesdropping secured some of

[1] Ibn Sa'd, p. 131 f.

[2] 'Abd ar-Raḥmān relates that on the return from Al-Ḥodeibiya (A.H. 6), he suddenly saw the people urging on their camels; and every one was inquiring of his neighbour the cause. They replied, *Inspiration hath descended on the Prophet.* So he too urged on his camel, and reached Moḥammad who, seeing that a sufficient number of people had gathered around him, began to recite the 40th Sūra. I remember no tradition which represents Moḥammad as beforehand aware that inspiration was about to come upon him.

[3] The 'terrific' Sūras, as specified in the numerous traditions on this subject, are, 'Sūra Hūd, and its Sisters';—the '*Sisters*' are variously given as Sūras xi., xxi., lvi., lxix., lxxvii., lxxviii., lxxxi., or ci.;—all revealed at Mecca, and some of them very early. We are told that while Abu Bekr and 'Omar sat in the Mosque at Medīna, Moḥammad suddenly came upon them from the door of one of his wives' houses (which opened into the mosque), stroking and lifting up his beard, and looking at it. Now his beard had in it many more white hairs than his head. And Abu Bekr said: 'Ah, thou, for whom I would sacrifice father and mother, white hairs are hastening upon thee!' The Prophet, raising his beard with his hand, gazed at it; and Abu Bekr's eyes filled with tears. 'Yes,' said Moḥammad, 'Hūd' (Sūra xi.) 'and its Sisters have hastened my white hairs.'—'And what,' asked Abu Bekr, 'are its Sisters?' 'The *Inevitable* (Sūra lvi.), and the *Striking* (Sūra ci.).'

the secrets of the upper world, which they communicated to soothsayers and diviners upon the earth. But on the advent of Moḥammad they were driven from the skies, and, whenever they dared to approach, flaming bolts were hurled at them, appearing to mankind like falling stars. Hence at this epoch the show of falling stars is said to have been brilliant and uninterrupted; and the Arabs were much alarmed at the portentous phenomenon.[1] Such a belief in the existence and history of the Genii, strange as it may appear, is clearly developed in the Ḳor'ān, and throws a mysterious light upon the inner recesses of the Prophet's mind.[2]

Conclusion as to Moḥammad's belief in his inspiration

The considerations bearing on the first conception by Moḥammad of a revelation from heaven, have now been given at length, both from tradition and from the Ḳor'ān itself; and, reaching us with such mysterious and strange surroundings, they leave on the mind no doubt of his sincere and earnest searching after truth at this period of his life. Revelations of the same nature, all shaped as messages or commands direct from God, continued to 'descend' upon the Prophet throughout his life, and as such are termed the *Ḳor'ān*, or Word of God.[3] As years advanced these began to lose the glow and fervour of the earlier rhapsodies. Ever and anon, indeed, even to the end, we meet with passages—those especially on the Being and Providence of God—grand, impassioned, and kindling with the early fire; but the ordinary style becomes tame and vapid. Moreover, when Moḥammad attained to temporal power, the Revelation was

[1] It is possible that at this period there may really have been an unusual display of falling stars, which at certain points of the earth's course are known to be specially abundant.

[2] In the Ḳor'ān the Genii are represented as conversing thus one with another:—'Verily we used to pry into the heavens, but we found them to be filled with a strong guard and with flaming darts. And we used to sit in some of the seats thereof to listen; but whoever listeneth now, findeth a flaming bolt in ambush. And we know not whether evil be hereby intended against those upon earth, or whether the Lord be minded to guide them into the right way.'—Sūra lxxii. 8-10. As we shall see below, many of the Genii, when they heard Moḥammad reciting his Revelation, are said to have been converted. The Ḳor'ān professes to have been revealed for the benefit and salvation *both of Men and Genii*. *Cf.* Sūra xv. 18; lxvii. 5; xxxvii. 6-10; xxvi. 210; lxxxi. 24.

[3] *Ḳor'ān*; that is, 'Scripture' or what is *read* or *recited*.

used as the means of reaching secular ends, and even, as we shall see, of ministering to lower objects. What could the source have been of 'Inspiration' ending thus? The answer can, at the best, be but conjecture. It will be for the reader, as he proceeds, himself to judge when and to what extent, consciously or unconsciously, material objects obscured for Moḥammad the spiritual vista;—whether, in fact, the eye being no longer single, the light that was in him, from whatever source, lost its ethereal virtue, and became dimmed by the turbid atmosphere of the world.

CHAPTER IV

FROM THE ASSUMPTION BY MOḤAMMAD OF THE PROPHETICAL OFFICE TO THE FIRST EMIGRATION TO ABYSSINIA

ÆTAT. 44-45. A.D. 613-614

Moḥammad in his forty-fourth year

THE weary region of uncertainty and speculation may now be left behind. Towards the forty-fourth year of his age we find Moḥammad, now emerged from doubt and obscurity, clearly and unequivocally asserting that he was ordained a prophet with a commission to the people of Arabia; reciting his warnings and exhortations as messages that emanated direct from God; and himself implicitly believing (to all outward appearance) his call and mission to be divine. We see him already surrounded by a little band of followers, all animated by ardent devotion to his person, and the belief that his guide and inspirer was God himself.

Earliest converts

It is strongly corroborative of Moḥammad's sincerity that the earliest converts to Islām were not only of upright character, but his own bosom friends and people of his household; who, intimately acquainted with his private life, could not fail otherwise to have detected those discrepancies which ever more or less exist between the professions of the hypocritical deceiver abroad and his actions at home. The faithful KHADĪJA is already known to the reader, as sharer in her husband's searchings of heart, and probably the first convert to his creed. 'So Khadīja believed' (runs the simple tradition), 'and attested the truth of that which came to him from God. Thus was the Lord minded to lighten the burden of his Prophet; for he heard nothing that grieved him touching his rejection by the people, but he had recourse unto her, and she comforted, reassured, and supported him.' ZEID, the adopted son and intimate friend of Moḥammad,

Khadīja

Zeid

who lived no doubt in close connection with the family, if not actually a member of it, was also one of the earliest believers.[1]

'Alī

'ALĪ, the Prophet's cousin, now thirteen or fourteen years of age, already gave tokens of the wisdom and judgment which distinguished him in after life.[2] Though possessed of indomitable courage, he was meditative and reserved, and lacked the stirring energy which would have rendered him an effective propagator of Islām. He grew up from a child in the faith of Moḥammad, and his earliest associations strengthened the convictions of maturer years. It is said that as Moḥammad was once engaged with him in prayer, in a glen near Mecca whither they had retired to avoid the jeers of their neighbours, Abu Ṭālib, his father, chanced to pass by, and said to Moḥammad, 'My nephew! what is this new faith I see thee following?' 'O my Uncle!' he replied, 'this is the religion of God, and of his angels, and of his prophets; the religion of Abraham. The Lord hath sent me an Apostle unto his servants; and thou, my Uncle, art the most worthy of all that I should address my invitation unto, and the most worthy to assist the Prophet of the Lord.' Abu Ṭālib answered: 'I am not able, my nephew, to separate from the religion and the customs of my forefathers, but I swear that so long as I live no one shall dare to trouble thee.' Then, turning to his son, who professed a similar faith and the resolution to follow Moḥammad, he said: 'Well, my son, he will not call thee to aught but that which is good; wherefore thou art free to cleave unto him.' To the family group it is hardly necessary to add WARAḲA, the aged cousin of Khadīja, whose profession of Christianity and support of Moḥammad have been already mentioned, because he had already died before Moḥammad had entered upon his public ministry.

Waraḳa

Abu Bekr

In the little circle there was one belonging to another branch of Ḳoreish, who, after Khadīja, may claim precedence in the profession of Islām. ABU BEKR had long been the familiar friend of Moḥammad, and with him no doubt had lamented the gross darkness of Mecca, and sought after a

[1] Ibn Hishām, p. 160 f.; Aṭ-Ṭabari, i. 1167 f.

[2] [Ibn Hishām (p. 158 f.) makes 'Alī the first male convert; Aṭ-Ṭabari, i. 1159 f.]

better faith.[1] He lived in the same quarter of the city as Khadīja. When Moḥammad removed thither the intimacy became closer, and the attachment of Abu Bekr was soon riveted by implicit faith in his friend as the apostle of God. 'Ā'isha, his daughter (born about this period, and destined while yet a girl to be the Prophet's bride), 'could not remember the time when both her parents were not true believers, and when Moḥammad did not daily visit her father's house morning and evening.' Of her father, the Prophet said: 'I never invited any one to the faith who displayed not hesitation and perplexity, excepting only Abu Bekr; who, when I had propounded unto him Islām, tarried not, neither was perplexed.' Abu Bekr was about two years younger than the Prophet; short in stature, and of small spare frame; the eyes deeply seated under a high projecting forehead. His complexion was fair, and face comely, but thin, so that you could see the veins upon it. Shrewd and intelligent, he yet wanted the originality of genius; his nature was mild and sympathetic, but not incapable of firm purpose when important interests required. Impulse and passion rarely prompted his actions; he was guided by reason and calm conviction. Faithful and unvarying in his attachment to the Prophet, he was known (and is to the present day familiar in the Muslim world) as AṢ-ṢIDDĪḲ, '*the True.*'[2] He was also styled 'the Sighing,' from his tender and compassionate heart. Abu Bekr was a diligent and successful merchant, and, being frugal and simple in his habits, possessed at his conversion about 40,000 silver pieces. His generosity was rare and his charity unwearying. The greater part of his fortune was now devoted to the purchase of such unfortunate slaves as were persecuted for their attachment to the new faith; so that but 5,000 pieces were left when, ten or twelve years after, he emigrated with the Prophet to Medīna. Abu Bekr was unusually familiar with the history of Ḳoreish, who often referred to him for genealogical information. His judgment was sound and impartial, his conversation agreeable, and his demeanour affable and engaging. His society

His appearance and character

His generosity and popularity

[1] Ibn Hishām, p. 161; Aṭ-Ṭabari, i. 1165, 1168.

[2] His proper name was 'Abdallah, son of 'Othmān Abu Ḳoḥāfa. It is not clear when he obtained the name of *Abu Bekr*, which means Father of the young Camel. See *The Caliphate*, p. 21.

and advice were therefore much sought after by Ḳoreish, and he was popular throughout the city.[1]

Abu Bekr gains five converts;

To have such a man a staunch adherent of his claims was for Moḥammad a most important step. Abu Bekr's influence was freely surrendered to the cause of Islām, and five of the earliest converts are attributed to his exertions and example.

Sa'd

Three were but striplings. *Sa'd*, the son of Abu Waḳḳāṣ, converted in his sixteenth or seventeenth year, was the

Az-Zubeir ibn al-'Auwām

nephew of Āmina, mother of the Prophet.[2] *Az-Zubeir*, probably still younger, was at once the nephew of Khadīja, and the son of Moḥammad's aunt Ṣafīya.[3] About the same

Ṭalḥa

age was *Ṭalḥa*, a relative of Abu Bekr and a renowned

'Othmān, son of 'Affān, and

warrior in after days. The fourth was *'Othmān*, son of 'Affān (successor of 'Omar in the Caliphate), who, though of the Omeiyad stock, was also, on his mother's side, grandson of 'Abd al-Muṭṭalib. Moḥammad's daughter Roḳeiya, being now, or shortly after, free from her connection with 'Otba (son of the hostile Abu Lahab), the Prophet gave her in marriage to 'Othmān, whose wife she continued until her death some ten or twelve years afterwards. 'Othmān was at this period between thirty and forty years of age. The fifth

'Abd ar-Raḥmān

was *'Abd ar-Raḥmān*, ten years younger than the Prophet, a man of wealth and character. 'Abd ar-Raḥmān, 'Othmān, and Ṭalḥa were, like Abu Bekr, merchants.

Four converts accompany 'Abd ar-Raḥmān

'Abd ar-Raḥmān was accompanied on his first visit to the house of Moḥammad by four companions, who at the same time embraced Islām: *'Obeida*, son of Moḥammad's uncle Al-Ḥārith; *Abu Selama*;[4] *Abu 'Obeida*, subsequently a warrior

[1] I agree with Sprenger in considering 'the faith of Abu Bekr the greatest guarantee of the sincerity of Moḥammad in the beginning of his career'—and, indeed, in a modified sense, throughout his life.

[2] Sa'd pursued the trade of manufacturing arrows, and is renowned as 'the first who shot an arrow' on the side of Islām.

[3] Az-Zubeir was the grandson of Khuweilid, Khadīja's father; and also the grandson of 'Abd al-Muṭṭalib by his daughter Ṣafīya. He was a butcher; and his father a grain merchant, or, as others have it, a tailor. He became a distinguished warrior, and bore a prominent part in the subsequent history. [For the trades followed by the first Muslims, *cf.* Ibn Ḳoteiba, *Kitāb al-Ma'ārif*, p. 283 f.]

[4] Abu Selama was ten years older than Moḥammad, and was present at Bedr. He emigrated twice to Abyssinia with his wife Um Selama. He died of wounds received at Oḥod, when Moḥammad married his widow.

of note; and *'Othmān*, son of Maẓ'ūn. The latter had already abandoned wine before his conversion, and was with difficulty persuaded by Moḥammad to renounce the asperities of an ascetic life. His family appears to have been well inclined to Islām, for we find two brothers, a son, and other relatives, in the list of early believers.[1]

Converted slaves, Bilāl and others

Of the slaves ransomed by Abu Bekr from persecution, the foremost is BILĀL, son of an Abyssinian slave-girl. He was tall, dark, and gaunt, with negro features and bushy hair. Moḥammad distinguished him as '*the first fruits of Abyssinia;*' and to this day he is known throughout the Muslim world as the Prophet's Muezzin, or crier to prayer. *'Āmir ibn Fuheira*, after being released from severe trial, was employed by Abu Bekr in tending his flocks.[2] *'Abdallah ibn Mas'ūd*, 'small in body, but weighty in faith,' the constant attendant who waited upon Moḥammad at Medīna;[3] and *Khabbāb*, a blacksmith, were also converted at this period.

Meccan slaves susceptible of religious impression

The slaves of Mecca were peculiarly accessible to the solicitations of the Prophet. As foreigners they were generally familiar either with Judaism or Christianity. Isolated from the influences of hostile partisanship, persecution had alienated them from Ḳoreish, and misfortune made their hearts susceptible of spiritual impressions.

Thirteen other early believers

In addition to the twenty persons now noticed as among the first confessors of the faith, tradition enumerates at least thirteen others as having believed '*before the entry of the Prophet into the house of Al-Arḳam;*'—by which expression (explained hereafter) the biographers mark the few earliest years of Islām. Among these thirteen we observe the youthful son *Sa'īd* and several relatives of the aged inquirer

[1] He wished to renounce the privileges of conjugal life; but Moḥammad forbade this, and recommended him to imitate his own practice in this respect, saying that the Lord had not sent his prophet with a monkish faith. The expressions attributed to Moḥammad on this occasion are strongly illustrative of his character; but the passage does not admit of further detail. [For the list of the first converts, *cf.* Ibn Hishām, p. 162 ff.]

[2] 'Āmir ibn Fuheira was a son (by a former owner) of Um Rūmān, Abu Bekr's wife, and mother of 'Ā'isha.

[3] 'Abdallah at Medīna was climbing up a date tree, and his companions were indulging in pleasantry at the expense of his spare legs, when Moḥammad used the expression here quoted.

Zeid, already some time dead, whose remarkable life has been already alluded to as possibly paving the way for Moḥammad. Sa'īd's wife, of the same family, and her brother, were likewise among the early converts. There were also among the number *'Obeidallah*, himself one of the 'Four inquirers,' and two of his brothers. On the persecution becoming hot, 'Obeidallah emigrated with his wife and others of his family, to Abyssinia, where he was converted to Christianity, and died in that faith.[1] It is interesting to note among the converts *Abu Ḥodheifa*,[2] son of 'Otba (father-in-law of Abu Sufyān), a family inveterately opposed to Moḥammad. We find also the name of *Al-Arḳam*, whose house will shortly be mentioned as memorable in the annals of Islām.

Several female converts

Beside this little group of three-and-thirty individuals, the wives and daughters of some of the converts are mentioned as also faithful and earnest professors of Islām. Religious movements in every age have found women to take a forward part, if not in direct and public assistance, yet in the encouragement and exhortation which are of even greater value; and Islām was no exception. On the other hand, as priority in the faith became in after years a ground of social distinction, we must not forget that, in estimating the number of early converts, their ranks have been unduly swelled by the traditions of those whose piety or ambition have imagined or invented such priority for their own ancestors or patrons. Weighing both considerations, we shall not greatly err if we conclude that, in the first three or four years after the assumption by Moḥammad of his prophetic office, the converts to his faith amounted to nearly forty souls.

Converts in first four years about forty

[1] Moḥammad (as we shall see) married his widow. 'Obeidallah was Moḥammad's cousin by his mother, a daughter of 'Abd al-Muṭṭalib. He was also brother of the famous Zeinab, who was married to Zeid (Moḥammad's freedman) and was afterwards divorced by him that the prophet might take her to wife. The whole of his tribe, the Beni Dūdān, resident at Mecca, were very favourable to Islām; at the Hijra they all emigrated to Medīna, men, women, and children, locking up their houses. It is remarkable that this tribe were *confederates* of Ḥarb and Abu Sufyān, leading opponents of Moḥammad;—the influence of Islām thus frequently overleaping and baffling the political combinations of Mecca.

[2] He challenged his father at the battle of Bedr to single combat. His sister Hind (wife of Abu Sufyān) retorted in satirical verses, taunting him with being squint-eyed, and with the barbarity of offering to fight his father. He was an ill-favoured man, with projecting teeth.

Steps by which this success was attained

By what degrees, under the influence of what motives or arguments, and at what precise periods, these individuals, one by one, gave in their adhesion to Moḥammad, we can scarcely determine further than in the general outline already before the reader. It is usual in tradition to assign to the Prophet three years of secret preaching and private solicitation, after which an open call was made to Ḳoreish at large. But we hardly find grounds for this theory in the Ḳor'ān. It is probable that the preliminary term of doubt and hesitancy (which we sought to trace in the preceding chapter) has been confounded by tradition with the actual assumption of the prophetic office. The facts we may conjecture to have been as follows: An interval of pious musing, and probably of expostulation with near relatives and friends, preceded the fortieth year of Moḥammad's life. About that time the resolution to 'recite in the name of the Lord' (in other words the *conviction of inspiration*) was fully formed. For some succeeding period his efforts would be naturally directed to individual persuasion and entreaty; but there is nothing to warrant the belief that the prophetic claim, once assumed, was ever confined as an esoteric creed within the limits of a narrow circle. It was after this that the Prophet received (as he imagined) the command to 'arise and preach;'[1] and forthwith his appeal was made to the whole community of Mecca. Gradually his followers increased, and the faith of each

[1] That is Sūra lxxiv. 1 ff. The biographers ordinarily quote another passage as the first command to preach:—

> 'And preach to (or warn) thy nearer kinsfolk.
> And lower thy wing to the believers that follow thee.
> And if they rebel against thee,' &c.—Sūra xxvi. 214 ff.

But the tradition that this passage was the first call to preach, appears erroneous. It is not only contained in a much later Sūra, but itself bears evidence of persecution, and of considerable progress. It was probably revealed while the Prophet with his relatives was shut up in the Quarter of Abu Ṭālib, as will be related in the next chapter, and while his preaching was necessarily confined to them. The stories also of the Prophet taking his stand upon mount Aṣ-Ṣafā, summoning his relatives, family by family, and addressing to them the divine message; of the contemptuous reply of Abu Lahab (see p. 107); of the miraculous dinner at which Moḥammad propounded his claim to his relatives, 'Alī alone standing forth as his champion and 'Vizier,' &c., are all apocryphal. At this dinner, food was prepared hardly sufficient for one person, but was so multiplied as to suffice for forty; and so forth.

(though only the reflection of his own convictions) was accepted by Moḥammad as new and independent evidence of his mission, emanating from Him who alone can turn the heart of man. Success made the sphere of Islām to expand before him; and that which was primarily intended for Mecca only, embraced at last in the ever-widening circle of its call, the whole Peninsula.

Persecution caused by attachment to national idolatry

An important change now occurred in the relations of Moḥammad with the citizens of Mecca. Hitherto they had treated his teaching as that of a harmless enthusiast. But now their hostility was aroused, and believers were subjected to indignity and molestation. The main ground of opposition was the deep-seated attachment of Ḳoreish to the worship of the Ka'ba. The same spirit was aroused in them as caused the multitude of old to shout 'Great is Diana of the Ephesians.' Their shrine, the glory of Mecca and the centre of pilgrimage from all Arabia, was in danger to be set at nought. The new doctrine must be crushed, and its followers forced to abandon it. By degrees the persecution grew hot. Those who were citizens for the most part escaped serious injury, being protected as a point of honour by their families; but the slaves, who had no such support, were exposed to much suffering.

Advantages of opposition to Moḥammad

Persecution, though it may sometimes have deterred the timid from joining his ranks, was eventually of unquestionable service to Moḥammad. It furnished in after years a plausible excuse for casting aside the garb of toleration; for opposing force to force against those who 'obstructed the ways of the Lord;' and last of all for the compulsory conversion of the unbelievers. Even before the Hijra it drove the adherents of the Prophet in self-defence into a closer union, and made them stand forth with a more resolute aim and bolder front. The severity and injustice of Ḳoreish, overshooting the mark, aroused at once personal and family sympathies; unbelievers sought to avert or to mitigate the sufferings of the followers of the Prophet; and in so doing they were themselves sometimes gained over to his side.

Period at which it commenced

It was not, however, till three or four years of his ministry had elapsed, that any general opposition to Moḥammad was organised. Even after he had begun publicly to summon his fellow-citizens to the faith, and his followers had multiplied, the people did not gainsay his doctrine. They would only point at him slightingly as he passed, and say: *There goeth the Fellow from among the children of 'Abd al-Muṭṭalib, to speak unto the people about the Heavens.* But (adds tradition) when the Prophet began to abuse their idols, and to assert the perdition of their ancestors who died in unbelief, then they became displeased and began to treat him with contumely. Hostility, once excited, soon showed itself in acts of violence. Sa'd, it is related, having retired for prayer with a group of believers to a valley near Mecca, some of his neighbours passed unexpectedly by. A sharp contention arose between them, followed by blows. Sa'd struck one of his opponents with a camel goad; and this was 'the first blood shed in Islām.'

Once formed, it grew rapidly

It was probably about this time that, in order to prosecute his mission peaceably and without interruption, Moḥammad took possession of the house of Al-Arḳam (a convert already noticed), situated a short distance from his own dwelling, upon the gentle rise of the Ṣafā.[1] Fronting the Ka'ba to the east, it was in a frequented position; and pilgrims, in the prescribed course, must needs pass often by it. Thither were conducted any who showed a leaning towards Islām, and there Moḥammad expounded to them his way more perfectly. Thus of one and another of the believers, it is recorded that 'he was converted after the entry into the house of Al-Arḳam, and the preaching there;'—or, that 'he was brought to Moḥammad in the house of Al-Arḳam, and the Prophet recited the Ḳor'ān unto him, and explained the doctrines of Islām, and he was converted and embraced the faith.' So famous was it as the birthplace of believers, that it was in after times styled *the House of Islām.*[2] Four

The house of Al-Arḳam, A.D. 613. *Ætat.* 44

Conversions there

[1] [This house is said to be still standing and is visited by pilgrims. It is not mentioned in Aṭ-Ṭabari apparently until the Caliphate of 'Othmān (35, A.H. i. 3055), nor in Ibn Hishām.]

[2] There is nothing to show on what footing Moḥammad occupied this building; whether with his family, or only as a meeting-house and place of safe retreat. From several incidental notices of converts remaining there concealed during the day, and slipping away in the evening, the latter appears to be the more probable view. 'Omar, converted at the close of the sixth year of the mission, was the last brought to this house; for his influence enabled Moḥammad then to dispense with secrecy.

Converts connected with 'Omar

brothers, confederates of Al-Khaṭṭāb, were the first to believe and '*swear allegiance to Moḥammad*'[1] in this house. Hence we may conclude that, although 'Omar, Al-Khaṭṭāb's son, was not yet converted, the leaven of the new doctrine was already spreading rapidly among his connections.

Story of Muṣ'ab

The story of *Muṣ'ab ibn 'Omeir*, will illustrate the obstacles at this time opposed to the progress of Islām. His wife was sister of 'Obeidallah (the Inquirer), and it was probably through the influence of her family that he visited the house of Al-Arḳam, listened to the exhortations of Moḥammad, and embraced his doctrine. But he feared publicly to confess the change; for his mother (who doted upon him and through whose fond attention he was known as the most handsomely dressed youth in Mecca), and the whole family, were inveterately opposed to Moḥammad. The conversion being at last noised abroad, his relatives seized and kept him in durance; but he escaped, and fled to Abyssinia with the first Muslim emigrants. When he returned, he looked so altered and wretched that his mother had not the heart to abuse him. At a later period, having been deputed by Moḥammad to teach the converts at Medīna, he revisited Mecca in company with them. His mother, apprised of it, sent to him saying: 'Ah, disobedient son! wilt thou enter a city in which thy mother dwelleth, and not first visit her?' 'Nay, verily,' he replied, 'I shall never visit the house of any one before the Prophet of God.' So, after he had greeted Moḥammad, he went to his mother, who thus accosted him: 'Well! I suppose thou art still a renegade?' He answered: 'I follow the Prophet of the Lord, and the true faith of Islām.' 'Art thou then well satisfied with the miserable way thou hast fared in the land of Abyssinia, and now again at Medīna?' Perceiving a design to seize him, he exclaimed: 'What! wilt thou *force* a man from his religion? If ye seek to confine me, I will assuredly slay the first person that layeth hands upon me.' His mother said: 'Then depart from my presence,' and she began to

[1] This remarkable expression is the same as that used for doing homage, or swearing fealty, to a leader or chief. The 'swearing allegiance to Moḥammad' was probably at this time only a general declaration of faith and submission to his teaching. Possibly it may be simply the loose anticipation of a phrase used at a later period.

weep. Muṣ'ab was moved, and said: 'Oh, my mother! I give thee affectionate counsel. Testify that there is no God but the Lord, and that Moḥammad is his servant and messenger.' She replied: 'By the sparkling stars! I shall never make of myself a fool by entering into thy religion. Begone! I wash my hands of thee and thy concerns, and cleave steadfastly unto mine own faith.[1]

Story of Ṭoleib

There were social causes, on the other hand, to aid the spread of the new doctrine. These may be exemplified by the conversion of Ṭoleib, a cousin of Moḥammad.[2] This young man, having been gained over in the house of Al-Arḳam, went to his mother, Arwa, a daughter of 'Abd al-Muṭṭalib, and told her that he now believed in the true God, and followed his Prophet. She replied that he did very right in assisting his cousin; 'And, by the Lord!' she added, 'if I had strength to do that which men do, I would myself defend and protect him.' 'But, my mother! what hindereth thee from believing and following him? And truly thy brother Ḥamza hath believed.' She replied: 'I wait to see what my sisters do, and will follow them.' 'But, I beseech thee, mother; wilt thou not go unto him and salute him, and testify thy faith?' And she did so; and thenceforward she assisted the cause of Moḥammad by word of mouth, and by stirring up her sons to aid him and fulfil his commands.

Story of the blind 'Abdallah Ibn Um Mektūm

The following tradition will illustrate at once the anxiety of Moḥammad to gain over the principal men of the Ḳoreish, and the readiness with which he turned to the poor and uninfluential citizens of Mecca. The Prophet was engaged in deep converse with the chief, Al-Walīd; for he greatly coveted his conversion. Just then the blind man 'Abdallah [or 'Amr] ibn Um Mektūm chanced to pass that way, and asked to hear the Ḳor'ān. Moḥammad, displeased at the interruption, spoke roughly to him. Others coming up still further occupied his attention; so he turned from the blind man frowningly and left him. But the heart of Moḥammad smote him, because he had thus slighted one whom God haply had chosen, and paid court to those whom God had reprobated. As usual, the vivid conception of the moment was framed into a divine revelation, which at once afforded relief

[1] Muṣ'ab distinguished himself at Bedr, and was killed at Oḥod.

[2] Ibn Sa'd, vol. iii. p. 87.

to his own mind, and ample amends to the neglected inquirer.

Sūra lxxx

> The Prophet frowned and turned aside,
> Because the blind man came to him.
> And what shall cause thee to know whether haply he may not be purified?
> Or whether he might not be admonished, and the admonition profit him?
> As for the Man that is rich,
> Him thou receivest graciously;
> And it is not thy concern that he is not purified.
> But he that cometh unto thee earnestly inquiring,
> And trembling anxiously,
> Him dost thou neglect.

This incident shows the tender and ready perception by Moḥammad of the slight he had offered, and the magnanimity with which he could confess his fault. 'Abdallah, though related to Khadīja, was at present but of little consideration. Yet he was not an ordinary man. He became remarkable for his knowledge of the Ḳor'ān, and at Medīna was repeatedly placed in positions of command.[1]

Further slave converts

Shortly after Moḥammad entered the house of Al-Arḳam, a further number of slaves professed themselves his converts. Of these, *Yesār* and *Jebr* are mentioned as among the persons accused by Ḳoreish of giving instruction to the Prophet. The latter was the Christian servant of a family from Ḥaḍramaut, and the Prophet is said to have much frequented his cell. The former, better known under the name of Abu Fukeiha, was subjected to great persecution. His daughter Fukeiha was married to Ḥaṭṭāb, a convert, whom we find with others of his family among the subsequent emigrants to Abyssinia. Both these slaves died probably before Moḥammad left Mecca.[2]

Yesār, or Abu Fukeiha

Soheib

A more important convert, styled by Moḥammad 'the first fruits of Greece,' was *Ṣoheib* son of Sinān.[3] His home was at Mosul or some neighbouring village in Mesopotamia. His father, or his uncle, had been the Persian governor of Obolla. A Grecian band having made a raid into Mesopotamia, carried him off while yet a boy to Syria, perhaps to Constantinople. Bought afterwards by a party of Bedawīn, he was sold at Mecca to the chief, Ibn Jud'ān, who gave him

[1] He was left in charge of the city at the battle of Oḥod.
[2] Ibn Hishām, p. 260. [3] *Ibid.* p. 265.

freedom and protection. A fair skin and ruddy complexion marked his northern birth, and broken Arabic betrayed a foreign education. By traffic he acquired considerable wealth at Mecca; but having embraced Islām, and being left by the death of his former master without a patron, he suffered much at the hands of the unbelieving Koreish. It is probable that Moḥammad gained some acquaintance with Christianity from him, and he may indeed be the person mentioned in the following verse as the source of his scriptural information;—*And indeed* WE *know that the Unbelievers say*, VERILY A CERTAIN MAN TEACHETH HIM. *But the tongue of him whom they intend is foreign, whereas this Revelation is in pure Arabic.*[1] At the general emigration to Medīna, the people of Mecca endeavoured to prevent Ṣoheib's departure; but he bargained to relinquish his whole property that they might let him go free. Moḥammad, when he heard of it, exclaimed: '*Ṣoheib, verily, hath trafficked to profit.*' Another freed slave, '*Ammār*, used to resort to the house of Al-Arḳam, and, simultaneously with Ṣoheib, embraced Islām.[2] His father, a stranger from the Yemen, his mother, and his brother, were also believers.

'Ammār

Persecution of converted slaves

As time went on, the jealousy and enmity of Ḳoreish were aggravated by the continued success of the new sect, which now numbered more than fifty followers. The brunt of their wrath fell upon the converted slaves and strangers, and the weak and poor of the lower classes who had no patron or protector. These were seized and imprisoned; or they were exposed on the scorching gravel of the valley to the intense glare of the mid-day sun. The torment was enhanced by intolerable thirst, until the wretched sufferers hardly knew what they said. If under this torture they reviled Moḥammad and acknowledged the idols of Mecca, they were refreshed by draughts of water, and then taken to their homes. Bilāl alone escaped the shame of recantation. In the depth of his anguish, the persecutors could force from him but one expression, AḤAD! AḤAD! 'ONE, ONE (only God)!' On such an occasion, Abu Bekr passed by, and secured liberty of conscience to the faithful slave by purchasing his freedom. Some of these confessors retained the scars

[1] Sūra xvi. 105. See also Sūra xxv. 5; and xliv. 13.
[2] Ibn Hishām, p. 165.

of sores and wounds now inflicted to the end of their lives. Khabbāb and 'Ammār used in after days to exhibit such marks of suffering and constancy to a wondering generation, in which fortune and glory had well-nigh effaced the very thought of persecution as a possible condition of Islām.

Converts permitted to dissemble.

Towards such as under these trying circumstances renounced their faith, Moḥammad showed much commiseration. He even permitted them to dissemble, in order that they might escape the torment. Happening to pass by 'Ammār, as he sobbed and wiped his eyes, Moḥammad inquired of him what was the matter. 'Evil; O Prophet! They would not let me go until I had abused thee, and spoken well of their gods.' '*But how dost thou find thine own heart?*' 'Secure and steadfast in the faith.' '*Then,*' replied Moḥammad, '*if they repeat their cruelty, repeat thou also thy words.*' A special exemption for such unwilling deniers of Islām is even provided in the Ḳor'ān.[1]

Moḥammad safe with Abu Ṭālib;

Moḥammad himself was safe under the shadow of the respected and now venerable Abu Ṭālib, who, although unconvinced by the Prophet, scrupulously acknowledged the claims of the kinsman, and withstood resolutely every approach of Ḳoreish to detach him from his guardianship. Abu Bekr, too, and those who could claim affinity with any powerful family of Mecca, though exposed perhaps to contumely and reproach, were generally secure from personal injury. The chivalry which makes common cause among the members and connections of an Arab family, and arouses fierce impetuosity against the injurers of a single member, deterred the enemies of Islām from open and violent persecution. Such immunity, however, depended in part on the goodwill of the convert's friends. Where the entire family or tribe was inimical to the new religion, there would always be the risk of insult and injury. Thus, when the Beni Makhzūm were minded to chastise the converts of their tribe, and among them Al-Walīd, son of their aged chief, they repaired to his brother Hishām, a violent opposer of the Prophet, and demanded his permission; this he readily gave, but added: '*Beware of killing*

and converts connected with influential families

[1] *Whoever denieth God after that he hath believed* (*excepting him who is forcibly compelled thereto, his heart remaining steadfast in the faith*) *on such resteth the wrath of God.*—Sūra xvi. 108.

him; for if ye do, verily I shall slay in his stead the chiefest among you.' [1]

First emigration to Abyssinia, A.D. 615

To escape these indignities, and the danger of perversion, Moḥammad now recommended such of his followers as were without protection, to seek an asylum in a foreign land.[2] '*Yonder*,' pointing to the west, '*lieth a country wherein no one is wronged:—a land of righteousness. Depart thither; and remain until it pleaseth the Lord to open your way before you.*' Abyssinia was well known at Mecca as a market for the goods of Arabia; and the Court of the Negus or *Najāshi* was the ordinary destination of a yearly caravan. In the seventh month of the 5th year of Moḥammad's mission, eleven men, some mounted, some on foot, and four of them accompanied by their wives, set out for the port of Sho'eiba;[3] where, finding two vessels about to sail, they embarked in haste, and were conveyed to Abyssinia for half a dinar apiece. Ḳoreish pursued them, but they had already left the port. Among the emigrants were 'Othmān, son of 'Affān, followed by his wife Roḳeiya the Prophet's daughter, and 'Abd ar-Raḥmān, both perhaps as merchants already acquainted with the country. The youths Az-Zubeir and Muṣ'ab were also of the number. The party was headed by 'Othmān, son of Maẓ'ūn, as its leader. They met with a kind reception from the Najāshi and his people, and the period of exile was passed in peace and in comfort.[4]

Bearing and advantages of this emigration

This is termed the *first* 'Hijra' or flight to Abyssinia, as distinguished from the later and more extensive emigration to the same quarter. On this occasion the emigrants were few, but the part they acted was of deep importance in the history of Islām. It convinced Ḳoreish of the sincerity and resolution of the converts, and proved their readiness to undergo any loss and any hardship rather than abjure the faith of Moḥammad. A bright example of self-denial was exhibited to the whole body of believers, who were led to regard peril and exile in 'the cause of God' as a privilege and distinction. It may also have suggested the idea that the hos-

[1] [Ibn Hishām, p. 207. Al-Walīd ibn al-Walīd was converted after the battle of Bedr.]

[2] Ibn Hishām, p. 208 ff.; Aṭ-Ṭabari, i. 1181 ff.; Ibn Sa'd, p. 136 f.

[3] The ancient port of Mecca, not far from Jidda.

[4] [Aṭ-Ṭabari, i. 1181 f.]

tile attitude of their fellow-citizens, combined with the merits of their creed, might secure for them within the limits of Arabia itself a sympathy and hospitality as cordial as that afforded by the Abyssinian king; and thus given birth to the idea of a greater 'Hijra,'—the emigration to Medīna. Finally, it turned the attention of Moḥammad more closely and more favourably to the Christian religion. If an Arab asylum had not at last offered itself at Medīna, the Prophet might haply himself have emigrated to Abyssinia, and Moḥammadanism have dwindled, like Montanism, into an ephemeral Christian heresy.

THE ḲOR'ĀN AS REVEALED DURING THE PERIOD OF THIS CHAPTER

Sūras of this period

To complete the view of the period just described, it is needful to examine the portions of the Revelation belonging to it; for their purport, and even their style, will throw an important light upon the inner, as well as the external, struggles of Moḥammad.

Change observable

To the two or three years intervening between the commission to preach and the first emigration to Abyssinia, may be assigned about twenty of the Sūras as they now stand in the Ḳor'ān. During even this short time a marked change may be traced, in form as well as sentiment. At first, like a mountain stream, the current dashes headlong, pure, wild, impetuous. Advancing, the language becomes calmer and more uniform; yet ever and anon, mingled with oaths and wild ejaculations, we come upon a tumultuous rhapsody, like the unexpected cataract, charged with thrilling words of conviction and fervid aspiration. Onward still, though the dancing stream sometimes sparkles and foam deceives the eye, we trace a rapid decline in the vivid energy of natural inspiration, and even the mingling with it of earth-born elements. There is yet, indeed, a wide difference from the prosaic, tame, and sluggish flow of later days; but the tendency cannot be mistaken. Decay of life is met by artificial expedient. Elaborate periods, and the measured cadence of rhyming prose, convey too often little more than simple truisms and antiquated fable. Although we still meet with powerful reasoning against idolatry and the burning words of a living faith, yet the chief substance begins to be of native legend

Gradual decline of life and spirit

expanded by the Prophet's imagination; pictures of heaven and hell, the resurrection and the judgment day; dramatic scenes in which the righteous and the wicked, angels, Genii and infernal spirits, converse in language framed adroitly as arguments in the cause of Moḥammad.

The Sūras become longer, and theory of inspiration further developed

The Sūras gradually extend in length. In the preceding stage a whole Sūra seldom exceeds the quarter of a page. Now it occupies one, and sometimes two pages.[1] The theory of inspiration becomes more fully developed. The Almighty, from whom revelation alone proceeds, is the sole authority also for its recitation and interpretation. On these points Moḥammad must wait for heavenly guidance. He must not be hasty in its repetition, for '*the Ḳor'ān is revealed by a gradual revelation*' (lxxvi. 23); and it is the prerogative of the Lord to prescribe what passages shall be remembered and what forgotten.[2] How much soever the Prophet may have sincerely believed that this regulating influence was exercised by the Deity, the doctrine offered the temptation to suit his revelations to the varying necessities of the hour. It led eventually to the teaching that

[1] It is interesting to watch the gradual lengthening of which Flügel's beautiful edition, each page having 22 lines, forms an excellent standard. The 22 Sūras first revealed contain an average of only five lines each. The next 20 (those of the present chapter) 16 lines. From this period to the Hijra, the average length of the 50 Sūras is about three-and-a-half pages; one being nearly twelve pages long. The average length of the twenty-one Medīna Sūras is five pages,—the Sūrat al-Baḳara having as many as 22 pages. As before noticed, the arrangement is directly the reverse of chronological, the longest and latest Sūras coming first, the shortest and earliest last. At first, the Sūras being shorter appear to have been produced at once, as we now find them. Subsequently it became the practice to throw together, according to their subject-matter, passages given forth at various times,—one reason why the latter Sūras are of such great length.

[2] 'We shall cause thee to rehearse (the Revelation), and thou shalt not forget excepting that which the Lord shall please; for He knoweth both that which is public and that which is hid; and We shall facilitate unto thee that which is easy.'—Sūra lxxxvii. 6. Again: 'And move not thy tongue in the repetition of the Ḳor'ān so that thou shouldest be hasty therewith. Verily upon Us devolveth the collection thereof, and the recitation thereof; and when We shall have recited it unto thee, then follow the recitation thereof. Further, upon Us devolveth the explanation thereof.'—Sūra lxxv. 17 f. So in a later Sūra: 'And be not hasty in reciting the Ḳor'ān, before that the revelation thereof hath been completed.'—Sūra xx. 113.

A heavenly original assigned to the Ḳor'ān

where two passages are opposed to one another, the earlier is *abrogated* by the later. Notwithstanding, we begin to trace the claim not only of divine inspiration, but of a heavenly original. So in Sūra lxxxv. 22: '*Truly it is the glorious Ḳor'ān*, IN THE PRESERVED TABLET;'[1] and the following:—

Sūra lxxx. 13, 14

> It is an admonition, in revered pages; exalted, pure;
> Written by scribes (angels) honourable and just.

Sūra xcvii

> Verily WE caused it to descend on the Night of power;
> And what shall make thee know what the Night of power is?
> The Night of power excelleth a thousand months:
> On that night, the Angels and the Spirit descend by their Lord's command upon every errand.
> It is peace until the breaking of the morn.[2]

The 'holy Spirit' came to signify Gabriel

It is not clear what ideas Moḥammad at first attached to 'the Spirit' here spoken of. They were perhaps indefinite. It was a phrase he had doubtless heard used, but with different meanings, both by Jews and Christians. That the 'Holy Ghost' (however understood) was intended by the term, appears probable from the recurrence in the Ḳor'ān of the expression—'*God strengthened Him* (Jesus) *by the holy Spirit*' (ii. 81, 254). But eventually there can be no doubt that the holy Spirit, in the acceptation of Moḥammad, came to signify the angel Gabriel. He had learned that Jesus was 'born of the Virgin Mary, by the power of the Holy Ghost;' and either knowingly rejecting the divinity of that blessed Person, or imperfectly informed as to His nature, confounded Gabriel announcing the conception, with the Holy Spirit that overshadowed Mary. And so the two expressions became, in the language of the Ḳor'ān, synonymous.

Visions of Gabriel

Gabriel, the 'Spirit,' was the messenger who communicated to Moḥammad the words of God, and appeared sometimes to him in a material form. The traditional account of the first vision of Gabriel has been already noticed; and it is perhaps

[1] *I.e.* 'The original of which is written on a tablet kept in heaven';—namely the Table of the divine decrees. See Sale *in loco;* also Prelim. Discourse, Sect. iii.

[2] Thus abruptly does the 97th Sūra, a fragment of five verses, open and close. What God is said to have sent down on this night may either signify (with Sale and the Commentators) the Ḳor'ān; or more probably the clear view of divine truth which on that night burst upon Moḥammad's mind. The 'Night of power' is the famous *Lailat al-Ḳadr*, of which so much has been made in after days.

to the same apparition that the Prophet alludes in an early Sūra of the present period :—

Sūra lxxxi. 15 ff.

I swear by the Star that is retrograde ;
By that which goeth forward, and that which disappeareth ;
By the Night when it closeth ; by the morn when it breaketh !
I swear that this verily is the word of an honoured Messenger ;
Powerful ; and, in the presence of the Lord of the Throne, of great dignity ; obeyed by all ; and faithful.
And your Companion is not mad ;
Truly he hath seen him in the clear Horizon ;
And he entertaineth not any suspicion regarding the Unseen ;
Neither is this the word of a rejected[1] Devil.
Whither then are ye going ?
Verily this is no other than an Admonition to all creatures,—
To him amongst you that willeth to walk uprightly.
But ye shall not will unless the Lord willeth—the Lord of Creation !

Doctrine of predestination

The concluding verses show that Moḥammad already contemplated his Revelation as a lesson for all mankind. But the vivid conviction of his heavenly commission contrasted strangely with the apathy and unbelief around him ; and hence is springing up the idea of election and reprobation, which alone could account for these spiritual phenomena :—*Ye shall not will unless the Lord willeth.* Again in the very strength of the asseveration that he was not deceived, and that his inspiration was not that of a 'rejected devil,' may we not trace symptoms of the old doubts and questionings ?

Teaching and precepts

The teaching of the Ḳor'ān is, up to this stage, very simple. The Unity of God, Moḥammad his messenger, the Resurrection of the dead, and Retribution of good and evil, are perhaps the sole doctrines insisted upon ; and the only duties, prayer,[2] and charity, honesty in weights and measures, truthfulness, chastity,[3] and the faithful observance of covenants.

[1] '*Driven away*,' and so unable to overhear the secrets of Heaven.

[2] The *times* of prayer are, up to this time, mentioned only generally as morning, evening, and night.

[3] Among other features of the Believer, his chastity is thus described, lxx. 29 f.:

'And they are continent,
Except as regardeth their Wives, and that which their right hands possess :—
For in respect of these they shall be blameless.
But he that lusteth after more than that, verily they are transgressors.'

Note that even at this early period Moḥammad admitted slave-girls to be lawful concubines, besides ordinary wives. Bond-women with whom

Renunciation of idolatry

It is doubtful whether, at this period, Moḥammad inculcated the rites of pilgrimage as of divine obligation. The absence of allusion to them inclines to the opinion that, though observed by himself and his followers, they formed no part of his positive teaching. There was at any rate a clear and conclusive renunciation of idolatry:—

Sūra cix

SAY, O ye unbelievers! I worship not that which ye worship,—
Nor do ye worship that which I worship.
Never shall I worship that which ye worship,
Neither will ye worship that which I worship.
To you be your Religion; to me mine.

This Sūra is said to have been revealed when the aged Al-Walīd pressed Moḥammad to consent to a compromise by which his God should be worshipped in conjunction with their deities, or alternately every other year.[1] Whatever the occasion, it breathes a spirit of uncompromising hostility to idolatry.

The Paradise of Moḥammad

The vivid pictures of Heaven and Hell, placed in close juxtaposition, are now painted in colours of material joy and torment; which, however strange to our conceptions, were well calculated to effect the wished-for impression on the simple Arab mind. Rest and passive enjoyment; verdant gardens watered by murmuring rivulets, wherein the believers, clothed in green silk brocades and silver ornaments, repose beneath the wide-spreading shade on couches well furnished with cushions and carpets, drink the sweet waters of the fountain, and quaff aromatic wine such as the Arab loved from goblets placed before them or handed round in silver

cohabitation is thus permitted are here specified by the same phrase as was afterwards used for female slaves taken captive in war, or obtained by purchase, viz. '*that which your right hands possess.*' The license, however, was not at this time used by Moḥammad himself, for he was now living continently with a single wife. Though, therefore, it was in after days taken advantage of both for his own indulgence, and as an inducement to fight in the hope of capturing females who would then be lawful concubines as 'that which their right hand possessed,' yet these were not the original motives for the rule. It was in fact the natural compromise by which Moḥammad fitted his system to the usages around him.

[1] Ibn Hishām, p. 239; Aṭ-Ṭabari, i. 1191 f.

cups resplendent as glass by beautiful youths;[1] while clusters of fruit hang close by inviting the hand to gather them;—such is the Paradise framed to captivate the inhabitant of the thirsty and sterile Mecca.

The Ḥūr of Paradise

Another element is soon added to complete the Paradise of the pleasure-loving Arab:—

Sūra lxxviii. 31 ff.

Verily for the Pious is a blissful abode;
Gardens and Vineyards,
And damsels with swelling bosoms, of an equal age,
And a full cup.

In the oft-described shady garden 'with fruits and meats, and beakers of wine causing not the head to ache, neither disturbing the reason,' these damsels of Paradise are introduced as '*lovely large-eyed girls resembling pearls hidden in their shells, a reward for that which the faithful have wrought. . . . Verily We have created them of a rare creation; We have made them virgins, fascinating, of an equal age.*'[2]

Further description of Paradise

The following passages will illustrate the artificial style into which the fire of early inspiration was now rapidly degenerating. The first is taken from a psalm with a fixed alternating versicle throughout, quaintly addressed in the dual number to men and Genii. To suit the rhyme the objects are introduced in pairs, excepting the damsels, whose number may not thus be limited.

Sūra lv. 43 ff.

* * * This is the Hell which the wicked deny;
They shall pass to and fro between the same and scalding water.
Which then of the Signs of your Lord will ye deny?
But to him that dreadeth the appearing of his Lord, there shall be two gardens,
Which then of the Signs of your Lord will ye deny?
Planted with shady trees, *Which then, &c.*
Through each of them shall two fountains flow, *Which then, &c.*
And in each shall there be of every fruit two kinds, *Which then, &c.*
They shall repose on brocaded carpets, the fruits of the two gardens hanging close by, *Which then, &c.*

---

[1] In one passage the wine is spoken of as sealed with musk and spiced with ginger. lxxxiii. 25 ff.; *cf.* lxxvi. 17.

[2] Sūra lii. 21 ff.; lvi. 11 ff. These Ḥūr come now first upon the stage. [*Ḥūr* means having the white of the eye intensely white and the black intensely black, or having eyes like a gazelle. For the fem. sing. *ḥūrīya* is used, whence the English 'houri.']

In them shall be modest damsels, refraining their looks, whom before
them no man shall have deflowered, neither any genius,
Which then of the Signs of your Lord will ye deny?
Like as if they were rubies or pearls.[1]

'Houris' revealed when Moḥammad had but one wife

It is remarkable that the notices in the Ḳor'ān of this voluptuous Paradise are *almost entirely confined* to a time when, whatever the tendency of his desires, Moḥammad was living a chaste and temperate life with a wife threescore years of age.[2] Gibbon characteristically observes that 'Moḥammad has not specified the male companions of the female elect, lest he should either alarm the jealousy of the former husbands, or disturb their felicity by the suspicion of an everlasting marriage.' The remark, made in raillery, is pregnant with meaning, and forms a sensible indictment against the paradise of Islām. Faithful women will renew their youth in heaven as well as faithful men; why should not their

[1] The above is the reward of the *highest* class of believers. Another set of gardens and females follows for the *common* faithful (v. 62 ff.)

And besides these, there shall be two other gardens,
Which then of the Signs of your Lord will ye deny?
Of a dark green, *Which then, &c.*
In each, two fountains of welling water. *Which then, &c.*
In each, fruits and the palm and the pomegranate. *Which then, &c.*
In them shall be women, amiable, lovely; *Which then, &c.*
Black-eyed damsels kept within pavilions; *Which then, &c.*
Whom no man shall have deflowered before them, nor any genius.
Which then, &c.
The Believers shall recline upon green rugs, and lovely carpets,
Which then of the Signs of your Lord will ye deny?

So at a somewhat later date: 'And close unto the believers shall be modest damsels refraining their looks, like unto ostrich eggs delicately covered over,' xxxvii. 47. In a passage of the same period, the faithful are said to be '*married*' to these 'black-eyed ones.' In other places of a later date, probably after Khadīja's death, the *Wives* of believers (their *proper* wives of this world apparently) are spoken of as entering into Paradise with their husbands. Did Moḥammad deem it possible that the earthly wives might still remain united to their husbands in Paradise, in spite of their black-eyed rivals?

[2] Note that in all the voluminous revelations of the ten years following the Hijra—women are only twice referred to as one of the rewards in Paradise; and on both occasions in these simple words,—*and to them there shall be therein pure wives.* Was it that satiety had then left no longings unfulfilled; or that closer contact with Judaism had repressed the picture of a sensual Paradise such as had been drawn at Mecca?

good works merit an equal and analogous reward? But Moḥammad shrank from the legitimate conclusion.

The Hell of the Ḳor'ān is no less material than its Heaven. The drink of the lost is described as boiling water and filthy corruption. When cast into the pit, they hear it roar wildly like the braying of an ass. 'Hell boileth over, it almost bursteth with fury: the smoke, rising in three columns, affordeth neither shade nor protection, but casteth forth great sparks like castles, or as it were yellow camels.' The Hell of the Ḳor'ān

* * And the companions of the Left hand, how miserable they! Sūra lvi. 40 ff.
In scorching blasts and scalding water,
And the shade of smoke,
That is neither cold nor is it grateful.
Verily before that, they lived in pleasure;
And they were bent upon great wickedness;
And used to say,
What! after we have died and become dust and bones, shall we be raised?
Or our Fathers that preceded us?
SAY, Yea, verily, both the former and the latter
Shall be gathered at the time of an appointed Day.
Then shall you, oh ye that err and reject the Truth,
Eat assuredly of the tree of ZAḲḲŪM,
Filling your bellies therewith,
And drinking with it boiling water,
As a thirsty camel drinketh.
This shall be your entertainment on the Day of reckoning!

The menace also of a nearer vengeance in this life begins to loom darkly forth, but as yet mingled mysteriously with the threats of the Judgment-day and Hell, thus:— Threats of temporal judgment

* * * The Day of separation! Sūra lxxvii. 14 ff.
And what shall teach thee what the *Day of separation* is?
Woe on that day unto the deniers of the Truth!
What! Have We not destroyed the former Nations?
Wherefore We shall cause the latter also to follow them.
Thus shall We deal with the wicked People!
Woe on that day unto the deniers of the Truth!

* * *

Verily, We warn you of a Punishment close at hand,— Sūra lxxviii.
The day whereon a man shall see that which his hands have wrought;
And the unbelievers shall say, *O would that I were dust!*

* * *

What! are ye secure that He who dwelleth in the Heavens will not cause the Earth to swallow you up, and she shall quake? Sūra lxvii 16 ff.

Or that He will not send upon an you overwhelming blast, then ye shall know my warning?
And verily the Nations that preceded thee, denied the Truth; and how awful was my vengeance!

Defiance of the Meccans

But the men of Mecca scoffed at the menace, and defied its execution:—

Sūra lxvii. 24 ff.

They say, *When shall this threatened vengeance be, if ye speak the truth?*
SAY, 'Nay, verily, the knowledge thereof is with God alone; as for me I am but a plain Warner.'
But when they see it, the countenance of those who disbelieved shall fall;
And it shall be said, *This is that which ye have been calling for.*
SAY, 'What think ye? whether the Lord destroy me and those that be with me, or have mercy upon us, who shall deliver the unbelievers from a dreadful punishment?'

Objections of the unbelievers

We begin also to find in the Ḳor'ān arguments used against the Prophet, and the mode in which he replied to them. The progress of incredulity can thus be followed, and some of the very expressions employed by either party traced. The Resurrection of the body was derided by his fellow-citizens as an idle imagination. When Moḥammad sought to illustrate the raising of the dead by the analogies of Nature, and the power of God in creation, he was scouted as a sorcerer or magician, who would pretend that a living body could be reproduced from dust and dead men's bones.

Resurrection derided

The Ḳor'ān impugned

The Ḳor'ān was denounced at times, as a bare-faced imposture,—as *Fables of the Ancients* borrowed from foreigners, and dressed up to suit the occasion; at others, as the effusion of a frenzied poet, or the incoherent drivelling of an insane madman.

Derision

Jeers and jests were the ordinary weapons by which the believers were assailed:—

Sūra lxxxiii. 29 ff.

Verily, the Sinners laugh the Faithful to scorn.
When they pass them by, they wink at one another.
And when they turn aside unto their own people, they turn aside jesting scurrilously.
And when they see them, they say, *Verily,* THESE *are the erring ones.*
But they are not sent to be keepers over them.
Wherefore one day the Faithful shall laugh the Unbelievers to scorn,
Lying upon couches, they shall behold them in Hell.

Patience and stead-

Amid the derision and the plots of Ḳoreish, patience is inculcated on the Prophet. His followers are exhorted to steadfastness and resignation, and in one passage reminded of the constancy of the Christian martyrs in Nejrān. fastness inculcated

Sūra lxxxv. 1 ff.

By the Heavens with their Zodiacal signs;
By the threatened Day!
By the Witness and the Witnessed!
Cursed be the *Diggers of the pits* filled with burning fuel, when they sat around the same.
They were witnesses of that which they did unto the Believers.
And they tormented them no otherwise than because they believed in God the Mighty and the Glorious.
Verily, they who persecute the Believers, male and female, and repent them not,
For such the torment of Hell is prepared, and a burning anguish, &c.[1]

Former Scriptures not referred to

There is at this period hardly any allusion to Jewish and Christian Scripture or legend. The Ḳor'ān did not as yet rest its claim on the evidence of previous revelation and its close correspondence therewith. But the peculiar phraseology of the new faith was already becoming fixed. The dispensation of Moḥammad was distinguished as ISLĀM, that is, Surrender of the soul to God; his followers as MUSLIMĪN (those who *surrender themselves*), or as Believers; his opponents as KĀFIRĪN, that is, *those who reject the divine message*, or as MUSHRIKĪN, such as *associate* companions with the Deity. Faith, Repentance, Heaven, Hell, Prayer, Almsgiving, and many other terms of the religion, soon acquired their stereotyped meaning. The naturalisation in Arabia of Judaism and Christianity (chiefly of the former) provided a large and ready fund of theological speech, which, if not already in current use, was at least widely known in a sense approaching that in which Moḥammad desired to use it.[2]

Language becoming fixed

[1] The 'diggers of the pits' were the Jewish persecutors of the Christians of Nejrān. See Introduction, Chap. II.

[2] See remarks on the prevalence of Jewish legends and expressions, in Introduction, Chapters II., III. It is difficult to overestimate the advantages which Moḥammad thus possessed in the tacit acquiescence of Ḳoreish in the truth of former Revelations, and in being able to appropriate apt and ready terms already current as expressive of the spiritual ideas he wished to attach to them, or at least of ideas closely allied.

Thus the phrase, 'the Merciful, the Compassionate,' affixed by Moḥammad to the name of God, though not actually in use, was known among the idolatrous tribes, as we shall see by the treaty of Al-Ḥodeibiya.

CHAPTER V

FROM THE FIFTH TO THE TENTH YEAR OF THE MISSION OF MOHAMMAD

ÆTAT. 45-50. A.D. 614-620

Return of the Abyssinian refugees, 615 A.D.

THREE months had hardly elapsed from the departure of the little band to Abyssinia, when, notwithstanding their secure retreat and hospitable reception at the Najāshi's Court, the refugees again appeared in Mecca.[1] Their return is linked with one of the strangest episodes in the life of the Prophet. Ibn Hishām contents himself with saying that they came back because tidings reached them of the conversion of Ḳoreish. But Al-Wāḳidi and Aṭ-Ṭabari narrate a story, of which the following is an outline.

Lapse of Moḥammad

Narrative by Al-Wāḳidi and Aṭ-Ṭabari

The aim of Moḥammad had been the regeneration of his people. But he had fallen miserably short of it. The conversion of forty or fifty souls ill compensated the bitter alienation of the whole community. His heart was vexed, and his spirit chafed, by the violent opposition of the most respected and influential chiefs. The prospect was dark; to the human eye, hopeless. Sad and dispirited, the Prophet longed for a reconciliation, and cast about how it could be effected. On a certain day the chief men of Mecca, gathered in a group beside the Ka'ba, discussed, as was their wont, the affairs of the city. Moḥammad appeared and seating himself near them in a friendly manner, began to recite in their hearing Sūra liii. The chapter opens with a description of Gabriel's first visit to Moḥammad (already known to the reader);[2] it then proceeds to unfold a second vision of that

[1] Ibn Hishām, p. 241; Aṭ-Ṭabari, i. 1194 f.; Ibn Sa'd, p. 137 f.

[2] See *ante*, p. 46; also p. 72.

angel, at which certain heavenly mysteries were revealed. The passage is as follows (v. 13 ff.):—

* * He also saw him (Gabriel) another time,
By the Lote-tree [1] at the furthest boundary,
Near to which is the Paradise of rest.
When the Lote-tree covered that which it covered,
His sight turned not aside, neither did it wander.
And verily he beheld some of the greatest Signs of his Lord.
What think ye of AL-LĀT and AL-OZZA,
And MANĀT the third beside?—

Satan suggests an idolatrous concession

When he had reached this verse, the devil suggested to Moḥammad (so we are told) thoughts which had long possessed his soul; and put into his mouth words of reconciliation and compromise such as he had been yearning that God might send unto his people, namely:—

These are exalted Females.
Whose intercession verily is to be sought after.

Koreish worship with him

Ḳoreish were astonished and delighted at this acknowledgment of their deities; and as Moḥammad wound up the Sūra with the closing words, *Wherefore bow down before God, and serve Him*, the whole assembly prostrated themselves with one accord on the ground and worshipped. Al-Walīd alone, unable from the infirmities of age to bow down, took a handful of earth and worshipped, pressing it to his forehead.

The people pleased

Thus all the people were pleased at that which Moḥammad had spoken, and they began to say: *Now we know that it is the Lord alone that giveth life and taketh it away, that createth and supporteth. And as for these our goddesses, they make intercession with Him for us; wherefore, as thou hast conceded unto them a portion, we are content to follow thee.* But their words disquieted Moḥammad, and he retired to his house. In the evening Gabriel visited him; and the Prophet (as was his wont) recited the Sūra to him; on which Gabriel said: *What is this that thou hast done? thou hast repeated before the people words that I never gave unto thee.* So Moḥammad grieved sore, and feared the Lord greatly; and he said, *I have spoken of God that which He hath not said.* But the Lord comforted his Prophet, and

Moḥammad disowns the whole proceeding

[1] The Lote is the wild plum tree, called in India the *Bēr*.

restored his confidence,[1] and cancelled the verse, and revealed the true reading thereof (as it now stands), namely—

> What think ye of AL-LĀT and AL-'OZZA,
> And MANĀT the third beside?
> What! shall there be male progeny unto you, and female unto Him?
> That were indeed an unjust partition!
> They are naught but names, which ye and your fathers have invented, &c.

Koreish more embittered

Now when Ḳoreish heard it, they spoke among themselves, saying: *Moḥammad hath repented his favourable mention of the rank of our goddesses with the Lord. He hath changed the same, and brought other words instead.* So the two Satanic verses were in the mouth of every one of the unbelievers, and they increased their malice, and stirred them up to persecute the faithful with still greater severity.[2]

The narrative founded on fact

Pious Mussulmans of after days, scandalised at the lapse of their Prophet into so flagrant a concession, would reject the whole story. But the authorities are too strong to be thus summarily dismissed. It is hardly possible to conceive how the tale, if not in some shape or other founded in truth, could ever have been invented. The stubborn fact remains, and is by all admitted, that the first refugees did return about this time from Abyssinia; and that they returned in consequence of a rumour that Mecca was converted. To this fact the narrative affords the only intelligible clue. At the same time it is by no means necessary to adopt in its entirety the exculpatory version of tradition; or seek, in a supernatural interposition, the explanation of actions to be equally accounted for by the natural workings of the Prophet's mind.

The concession not unpremeditated, nor immediately withdrawn

It may be assumed that the lapse was no sudden event. It was not a concession won by surprise, or an error of the

[1] Tradition tells us that Moḥammad was consoled by the following passage in Sūra xxii. 51, 52, which, however (from the reference to former apostles and prophets), must have been revealed at a somewhat later period: *And We have not sent before thee any Apostle, nor any Prophet, but when he longed, Satan cast suggestions into his longing. But God shall cancel that which Satan suggesteth. Then shall God establish His revelations (and God is knowing and wise);—that He may make what Satan hath suggested a trial unto those whose hearts are diseased and hardened, &c.*

[2] Ibn Sa'd, p. 137; Aṭ-Ṭabari, i. 1192 ff.

tongue committed unawares, and immediately withdrawn. The hostility of his people had long pressed upon the spirit of Moḥammad; and, in his inward musings, it is admitted even by orthodox tradition, that he had been meditating the very expression which, as is alleged, the Evil one prompted him to utter. Neither can we believe that the condition lasted but a day. To outward appearance the reconciliation must have been complete; and it must have continued at the least for some days, probably indeed longer, to allow of the report going forth and reaching the exiles in a shape sufficient to inspire them with confidence. We are warranted therefore in assuming a wider basis for the event than is admitted by tradition.

Moḥammad tempted by the hope of gaining over his people

The circumstances may be thus conceived. Up to this point Moḥammad's was a spiritual religion, of which faith, and prayer, and the inculcation of virtue, formed the prominent features. Though the Ka'ba and its ancient rites were held to have been founded by the patriarch Abraham, yet the worship of idols engrafted on it, and heretofore consistently rejected by Moḥammad, was an integral part of the existing system. To this superstition, with all its practices, the people were obstinately wedded; and, unless permission were given to join more or less the time-honoured institutions of Mecca with the true faith, there was little hope of a general conversion. How far would a strong expediency justify compromise with the prevailing system; and was it the will of God to approve it?

Considerations by which he may have been influenced

Was not the worship of the Ka'ba, after all, a *divine* institution? The temple was built at the command of God; the compassing of it symbolised the circling course of the heavenly bodies, and the obedience of all creation to the Deity. Pious devotion was nurtured by kissing the sacred corner-stone; the slaying of sacrifices, in commemoration of Abraham's readiness to offer up his son, signified a like submission; the pilgrimage to 'Arafāt, the shaving of the head, and other popular observances, were innocent, if not directly religious, in their tendency. But how shall he treat the idols, and the worship rendered to them? In their present mind Ḳoreish would never abandon these. If, however (as they now professed their readiness), they would acknowledge the one true God as the supreme Lord, and look to the idols only as symbolical of the angels, what harm would result from their bare continuance? Incredible as the concession may appear, and irreconcilable with his first principles of action, Moḥammad would seem to have acceded to it, and consented to maintain the heathen deities as representatives of heavenly beings 'whose intercession was to be hoped for with the Deity.' The imperfect and garbled notices of tradition give no further insight into the compromise. If Moḥammad stipulated for any safeguards against the abuses of idolatry, no trace of them can be now discovered. We are only told that the arrangements, of whatever nature, gave satisfaction to the chiefs and people, and produced a temporary union.

Error soon discovered; But Moḥammad was not long in perceiving the inconsistency into which he had been betrayed. The people still worshipped images, and not God. No reasoning on his part, no assurance from them, could dissemble the galling fact that and remedied by a complete disavowal idolatry was as gross and prevalent as ever. His only safety now lay in disowning the concession. Satan had deceived him. The words of compromise were no part of the divine faith received from God through his heavenly messenger. The lapse was thus atoned for. The heretical verses spoken under delusion were cancelled, and others revealed in their stead, denying the existence of female angels such as Al-Lāt and Al-'Ozza, and denouncing idolatry with a sentence of irrevocable condemnation. Henceforward the Prophet wages mortal strife with images in every shape. His system gathers itself up into a pure and stern theism; and the Ḳor'ān begins to breathe (though as yet only in the persons of Moses and Abraham) intimations of iconoclastic revenge.

Idols reprobated Ever after, the intercession of idols is scouted as futile and absurd. Angels dare not intercede with the Almighty; how much less idols, who

Sūra xxxv. 14 ff.

> Have no power over even the husk of a date stone;
> Upon whom if ye call, they hear not your calling,
> And if they heard they would not answer you;
> And in the Day of Resurrection, they shall themselves disclaim your deification of them.

And the government The following passage, produced shortly after his lapse, shows how Moḥammad refuted his adversaries, and adroitly turned against them the concession of the supreme divinity of God :— asserted to be God's only

> And if thou askest them who created the Heavens and the Earth, they will surely answer GOD. SAY, What think ye then? If the Lord be pleased to visit me with affliction, can those upon whom ye call besides God,—what! could *they* remove the visitation? Or if He visit me with mercy, could *they* withhold His mercy? SAY, God sufficeth for me; in Him alone let those that put their trust confide. Sūra xxxix. 39

However short his fall, Moḥammad retained a keen sense of its dishonour, and of the danger which lay in parleying with his adversaries;— The danger of compromise keenly felt

> And truly they had well-nigh tempted thee to swerve from what WE had revealed unto thee, that thou shouldest devise concerning US a different thing; and then would they have taken thee for their friend. Sūra xvii. 76 ff.
>
> And if it had not been that WE stablished thee, verily thou hadst nearly inclined unto them a little;
>
> Then verily WE had caused thee to taste both the punishment of Life and the punishment of Death;
>
> Then thou shouldest not have found against US any helper.

And now, ever and anon, the Prophet is cautioned in the Ḳor'ān to beware lest he should be induced to change the words of inspiration out of a desire to deal gently with his people; or be deluded, by the pomp and numbers of the idolaters, into following after them and deserting the straight and narrow path pointed out to him by God.

But although Moḥammad may have completely re-established his own convictions, and regained the confidence of his adherents, there is little doubt that the concession, followed by a recantation so sudden and peremptory, seriously weakened his position with the people at large. *They* would not readily credit the excuse, that words of error had been 'cast by Satan into his mouth.' Even supposing it to have been so, what faith could be placed in the revelations of a Prophet liable to such influences? The divine Author of a revelation must know beforehand all that he will at any subsequent period reveal. If the Ḳor'ān were in truth *His* oracle, Moḥammad would never be reduced to the petty shift of retracting as a mistake what had once been given forth as a message from heaven. And thus Ḳoreish laughed to scorn his futile endeavour to effect a compromise Moḥammad's position injured by the lapse

which should draw them away from idolatry. They addressed him ironically in such terms as these:—

Sūra xxv. 43 f.

And when they see thee, they receive thee no otherwise than scoffingly,—*Ah! is this he whom God hath sent as an Apostle? Verily he had nearly seduced us from our gods, unless we had patiently persevered therein.* But they shall know hereafter, when they see the torment, who had erred most from the right way.

He reiterates his own conviction

To the accusations thus cast upon him, Moḥammad could but oppose the reiteration of his own assurance:—

Sūra xvi. 103, 104

And when WE change one verse in place of another (and God best knoweth that which He revealeth) they say, *Verily thou plainly art a fabricator.* Nay! but the most of them understand not. SAY, The Holy Spirit hath brought it down from thy Lord in truth, to stablish them that believe.

Return of Abyssinian emigrants, A.D. 615

We have seen that the tidings of reconciliation with Ḳoreish induced the little band of emigrants, after residing but two months in Abyssinia, to set out on their return to Mecca. Approaching the city, they met a party of travellers who told them that Moḥammad had withdrawn his concessions, and that Ḳoreish had resumed their oppression. After consulting what should now be done, they resolved to go forward and visit their homes. If things came to the worst, they could but again escape to Abyssinia. So they entered Mecca, each under the protection of a relative or friend.[1]

Second emigration to Abyssinia, A.D. 615-616

The report brought by the emigrants of their kind reception by the Najāshi, following upon the late events, annoyed Ḳoreish, and the persecution became hotter than ever. Moḥammad, therefore, again recommended his followers to take refuge in Abyssinia. The first party of the new expedition set out about the 6th year of the mission; and thereafter at intervals small bodies of converts, accompanied sometimes by their wives and children, joined the exiles, until they reached (without calculating their little ones) the number of 101. Of these, 83 were men. Amongst the women, 11 were of Ḳoreish, and 7 belonged to other tribes. Thirty-three of the men and 8 women (including 'Othmān and his wife, Roḳeiya, the daughter of Moḥammad) again

[1] Ibn Hishām, 241 ff.

returned to Mecca, and eventually emigrated to Medīna. The rest of the refugees remained in Abyssinia for several years, and did not rejoin Moḥammad until his expedition to Kheibar, in the 7th year of the Hijra.

Endeavour to make Abu Ṭālib abandon Moḥammad

Although Moḥammad himself was not yet forced to quit his native city, he was nevertheless exposed to indignity and insult, while the threatening attitude of his adversaries gave ground for apprehension and anxiety. If, indeed, it had not been for the influence and steadfast protection of Abu Ṭālib, it is clear that the hostile intentions of Ḳoreish would have imperilled the liberty, perhaps the life, of Moḥammad. A body of Elders, we are told, repaired to the aged chief, and said: *This nephew of thine hath spoken opprobriously of our gods and our religion, and hath upbraided us as fools, and given out that our forefathers were all astray. Now, avenge us of our adversary; or (seeing that thou art in the same case with ourselves) leave him to us that we may take our satisfaction.* But Abu Ṭālib answered them softly and in courteous words; so they turned and went away. In process of time, as Moḥammad would not change his attitude, they went again to Abu Ṭālib in great exasperation; and, reminding him of their former demand that he would restrain his nephew from such offensive conduct, added: *And now verily we cannot have patience any longer with his abuse of us, our ancestors, and our gods: wherefore either do thou hold him back from us, or thyself take part with him that the matter may be decided between us.* Having thus spoken, they departed. While it appeared grievous to Abu Ṭālib to break with his people, and be at enmity with them, neither did it please him to desert and surrender his nephew. Thus being in straits, he sent for Moḥammad, and having communicated the saying of Ḳoreish, proceeded earnestly: *Therefore, save thyself and me also; and cast not upon me a burden heavier than I can bear.* Moḥammad was startled and alarmed. He imagined that his Uncle, finding himself unequal to the task, had resolved to abandon him. His high resolve did not fail him at this critical moment. *If they brought the sun on my right hand,* he said, *and the moon on my left, to force me from my undertaking, verily I would not desist therefrom until the Lord made manifest my cause, or I should perish in the attempt.* But the thought of desertion by his kind protector overcame him. He burst into tears, and turned to depart. The aged Chief was moved too. 'Son of my brother!' he cried, 'come back. And now depart in peace! and say whatsoever thou wilt. For, by the Lord of the Ka'ba, I will not, in any wise, give thee up for ever.'

Abu Ṭālib persists in his protection

Some add the following incident. The same day Moḥammad disappeared, and was nowhere to be found. Abu Ṭālib, apprehensive of foul play, forthwith made ready a band of Hāshimite youths each armed with a dirk, and set out for the Ka'ba. On the way he was stopped by the intelligence that Moḥammad was safe in a house at Aṣ-Ṣafā; so he returned with his people home. On the morrow the aged chief again made ready his party, and, taking Moḥammad with them, repaired to the Ka'ba. There standing before the assembly of Ḳoreish, he desired his young men to uncover that which they had with them; and each drew forth a sharp weapon. Then, turning to Ḳoreish, he exclaimed: *By the Lord! Had ye killed him, there had not remained one alive amongst you. Ye should have perished, or we had every one of us been slain.* The bold front of Abu Ṭālib awed Ḳoreish, and repressed their insolence.

Abu Ṭālib awes Ḳoreish at the Ka'ba

Personal indignities sustained by Moḥammad

Though the tendency of tradition is to magnify the insults of Ḳoreish, yet, apart from invective and abuse, we hardly read of any personal injury or suffering sustained by the Prophet himself. A few of the inveterate enemies of Islām (Abu Lahab among the number) who lived close by his house, used spitefully to throw unclean and offensive things at the Prophet, or upon his hearth as he cooked his food. Once they flung in the entrails of a goat, which Moḥammad, putting upon a stick, carried to the door, and called aloud! 'Ye children of 'Abd Menāf! What sort of good neighbourhood is this?" Then he cast forth the offensive stuff into the street. Two or three centuries afterwards, a little closet, a few feet square, was still shown at the entrance of Khadīja's house, within which, under the ledge of a projecting stone, the Prophet used to crouch when he retired for prayer, and shelter himself from the missiles of his neighbours. There is also a tradition (but ill sustained) of actual violence once offered to Moḥammad in public. As he passed through the court of the Ka'ba, he was suddenly surrounded by Ḳoreish, who 'leaped upon him as one man, and seized his mantle. But Abu Bekr stood manfully by him, and called out: 'Woe's me! Will ye slay a man because he saith that *God is my Lord?*' So they departed from him.[1]

In the sixth year of his mission, the cause of Moḥammad was strengthened by the accession of two powerful citizens, Ḥamza,[2] son of 'Abd al-Muṭṭalib's old age, and 'Omar. The details of their conversion will be interesting to the reader. The Prophet was one day seated on the rising ground of Aṣ-Ṣafā. Abu Jahl, coming up, accosted him with a shower of taunts and reproaches; while Moḥammad answered not a word. Both left the place, but a slave-girl had observed the scene. It chanced that, shortly after, Ḥamza returned that way from the chase, his bow hanging from his shoulder (for he was a hunter of renown); and the maid related to him with indignation the gross abuse of Abu Jahl. Ḥamza, though not much older than Moḥammad, was at once his uncle and his foster-brother. His pride was offended, his rage kindled. He hurried with rapid steps to the Ka'ba; and there, in the court of the Holy House, found Abu Jahl sitting with a company of Ḳoreish. Ḥamza rushed upon him, saying: *Ah! hast thou been abusing him, and I too follow his religion; there* (raising his bow and striking him violently), *return that if thou darest!* The kinsmen of Abu Jahl started to his succour; but Abu Jahl motioned them away, saying: 'Let him alone, for indeed I did revile his nephew shamefully.'[3] The profession of Islām, suddenly asserted by Ḥamza in the passion of the moment, was followed up by the deliberate pledging of himself to Moḥammad in the house of Al-Arḳam, and by a steady adherence ever after to his faith.

Conversion of Ḥamza, A.D. 615

The conversion of 'Omar took place shortly after.[4] He

[1] Ibn Hishām, p. 184; Aṭ-Ṭabari, i. 1186.

[2] Ibn Hishām, p. 184 f.; Aṭ-Ṭabari, i. 1187 f.

[3] Abu Jahl (so called by the Muslims as the 'father of ignorance' or folly) is the butt of tradition as the witless and obstinate opponent of Islām. He was a nephew of Al-Walīd, son of Al-Moghīra.

[4] Ibn Hishām, p. 224 ff.; Aṭ-Ṭabari, i. 1189. It occurred in Dhu'l-Hijra, the last month in the year. The Believers are said now to have amounted in all to 40 men and 10 women; or, by other accounts, to 45 men and 11 women. See *ante*, p. 63, *note*.

Conversion of 'Omar, A.D. 615-616

was notorious for his enmity to Islām, and the harshness and violence with which he treated its professors. His sister Fāṭima, and her husband Sa'īd, were both converts, but secretly, for fear of Ḳoreish.[1] While 'Omar was threatening certain believers, a friend suggested to him that he had better begin at home, and hinted the conversion of his sister and her husband. His wrath was aroused, and he proceeded forthwith to their house. They were listening to the 20th Sūra, which the slave Khabbāb recited to them from a manuscript. The persecutor drew near, and overheard the low murmur of the reading. At the noise of his steps Khabbāb retired into a closet. *What sound was that I heard just now?* exclaimed 'Omar, entering angrily. 'There was nothing,' they replied. '*Nay*,' said he, swearing fiercely, '*I hear that ye are renegades!*' 'But what, O 'Omar!' interposed his brother-in-law, 'may there not be truth in another religion than thine?' The question confirmed the suspicions of 'Omar, and he sprang exasperated upon Sa'īd and kicked him. His sister flew to the rescue. In the struggle her face was wounded, and began to bleed. Stung by the insult, she could no longer contain herself; and cried aloud: 'Yes, we are converted; we believe in God and in his Prophet; now do thy worst upon us.' When 'Omar saw her face covered with blood he was softened; and he asked to see the paper they had been reading. But his sister required that he should first cleanse himself; 'for none,' she said, 'but the pure may touch it.' So 'Omar arose and washed, and took the paper (for he could read), and when he had deciphered a part, he exclaimed: *How excellent is this discourse, and gracious!* Then Khabbāb came forth from his hiding-place, and said: 'O 'Omar! I trust that the Lord hath verily set thee apart for himself, in answer to his Prophet; it was but yesterday I heard him praying thus: '*Strengthen Islām, O God, by Abu Jahl, or by 'Omar!*' Then said 'Omar: 'Lead me unto Moḥammad, that I may make known unto him my conversion.' And he was directed to the house of Al-Arḳam. So 'Omar knocked at the door, and Ḥamza with others looked through a crevice, and started back, exclaiming that it was Omar. But Moḥammad bade them let him in, and, catching hold of his skirt and the sword-belt, said: 'How long, O

[1] [Ibn Isḥāḳ says for fear of 'Omar; Ibn Hishām, p. 225.]

'Omar, wilt thou not refrain from persecuting, even until the Lord send some calamity upon thee?' And 'Omar replied: '*Verily I testify that thou art the Prophet of God!*' Filled with delight, Moḥammad cried aloud, 'Allāhu Akbar! Great is the Lord.'[1]

Importance of these conversions

The gain of two such men was a real triumph to the cause. Ḥamza and 'Omar both possessed, with great bodily strength, an indomitable courage; which, added to their social position, secured an important influence at Mecca. The heroism of Ḥamza earned for him the title, familiar to the present day, of *the Lion of God;* but he was prematurely cut off on the field of Oḥod. 'Omar, now in the pride of early manhood, was robust in frame, ruddy in countenance, and of such commanding stature that he towered above his fellows as if he had been mounted. Bold and overbearing, impulsive and precipitate, endowed with a keen glance and steady purpose, he was always ready both in word and deed at the decisive moment. His anger was easily aroused, and Ḳoreish stood in awe of him, because of his uncertain and impetuous temper. 'Omar outlived Moḥammad and, succeeding Abu Bekr in the Caliphate, left the stamp of his dauntless spirit upon Islām. At the period of his conversion he was but six-and-twenty years of age, yet so great and instant was the effect of his accession upon Islām, that from this era is dated the commencement of its public and fearless profession at Mecca. From a cause of anxiety and alarm to Moḥammad, he was suddenly converted into a tower of strength. The house of Al-Arḳam was abandoned. The claims of the faith began to override the bonds of kinship, and members of the same family might be seen openly ranged on either side. Believers no longer concealed their worship within their own dwellings, but with conscious strength and defiant attitude assembled in companies about the Ka'ba, and there performed their rites of worship openly. Their courage rose. Dread and uneasiness seized Ḳoreish.

'Omar described

Position and fears of Ḳoreish

Ḳoreish, indeed, had cause for alarm. They were disquieted by the hospitable reception of the refugees at the Abyssinian Court. An embassy of two chief men from Mecca, laden with costly presents, had made a fruitless

[1] [According to another account, 'Omar heard Moḥammad praying in the Ka'ba one night, and was converted; Ibn Hishām, p. 228.]

attempt to obtain their surrender.[1] What if the Najāshi should support them with an armed force, and seek to establish a Christian or reformed faith at Mecca, as certain of his predecessors had done in the Yemen? Apart even from foreign aid, there was ground for apprehension at home. The Muslim body no longer consisted of oppressed and despised outcasts, struggling for a weak and miserable existence. Rather it was a powerful faction, adding daily to its strength by the accession of influential citizens. It challenged an open hostility. The victory of either party involved the downfall of the other.

[1] Ḳoreish despatched two envoys with presents of precious leather and other rare articles for the Najāshi. They gained over the courtiers, and then presented their gifts to the Christian Prince, saying, that 'certain fools amongst their own people had left their ancestral faith; they had not joined Christianity, but had set up a new religion of their own. They had therefore been deputed by Ḳoreish to fetch them back. The courtiers supported their prayer, but the king said he would inquire into the matter in presence of the accused. Now the refugees had agreed that they would not garble their doctrine, but, come what might, say nothing more nor less than the teaching of their Prophet. So on the morrow they were summoned into the royal presence, where also were the bishops with their books open before them. The king inquired of the refugees the cause of their secession. Ja'far (Moḥammad's cousin) answered, 'that they used to worship images, eat the dead, commit lewdness, disregard family ties and the duties of neighbourhood and hospitality, until Moḥammad arose a prophet;' he concluded by describing his system, and the persecutions which had forced them to flee to Abyssinia. On the king asking him to repeat some part of the Prophet's teaching, he recited Sūrat *Maryam* (regarding the births of John and Jesus, with notices of Abraham, Moses, &c.); whereupon the king wept, and the bishops also wept so that their tears ran down upon their books, saying: 'Verily, this revelation and that of Moses proceed from one and the same source.' Then the Najāshi said to the refugees: 'Depart in peace, for I will never give you up.' Next day the envoys endeavoured to entrap the refugees into a declaration depreciatory of Jesus, and therefore offensive to the king. But the king fully concurred in their doctrine that Jesus was nothing more than 'a servant of God, and his Apostle; his Spirit and his word, placed in the womb of Mary, the immaculate Virgin.' So the Ḳoreishite embassy departed in bad case.

The above story is, no doubt, a mere amplification of certain passages in the Ḳor'ān to the effect that the Jews and Christians wept for joy on hearing the Ḳor'ān because of its correspondence with their own Scriptures. A similar tale has been told of the bishops of Nejrān; and also regarding an embassy of Christians from Abyssinia, who are said to have visited

Communications cut off

Influenced by such fears, Ḳoreish fell upon a new device to check the dangerous opposition.[1] If Abu Ṭālib could not restrain his nephew, they would hold him responsible. Further they saw Moḥammad supported not only by his own disciples, but also, excepting Abu Lahab, by all the house of Hāshim, who, whether converts or not, held themselves bound to keep their kinsman safe. Accordingly they bound themselves in a new confederacy. Thus the religious struggle merged for a time into a civil feud [or boycott] between the Hāshimites and the rest of Ḳoreish; and (as we have seen) there were not wanting long-rooted associations to add bitterness to the strife. To secure their purpose, Ḳoreish entered into this league against the Hāshimites—*that they would not marry their women, nor give their own in marriage to them; that they would sell nothing to them, nor buy aught from them; in short, that dealings of every kind should cease.* The ban thus framed was committed to writing, and sealed with three seals. When all had thus bound themselves, the record was hung up in the Ka'ba, and religious sanction thus given to its provisions.

The Ban

The Shi'b or Quarter of Abu Ṭālib

Unable to withstand this hostile demonstration, the Hāshimites withdrew into the secluded quarter known as the *Shi'b* of Abu Ṭālib, a defile of the mountain, where the projecting rocks of Abu Ḳobeis pressed upon the eastern out-

Moḥammad at Mecca, so that not much reliance can be placed on the narrative.

When the Abyssinians rose up against their king on account of the favour he was showing to the Muslim doctrine, the Najāshi put into his pocket a scrap inscribed with the Moḥammadan creed, and on his people desiring him to say 'that Jesus was the Son of God,' he responded thus (putting his hand upon his pocket): 'Jesus never went beyond *this*' —apparently agreeing in what they said, but inwardly referring to the scrap!—a childish story. Moḥammad is said to have regarded him as a convert to Islām, and to have prayed for him as such at his death. A light is also related to have issued from his tomb.

There is probably a basis of truth for the general outline given in this note; but it would be difficult to draw a probable line between the real and the fictitious parts of it. Had the leaning towards Moḥammadan doctrine in Abyssinia been as great as is here represented, we should have heard more of its inhabitants in the troublous times immediately following Moḥammad's decease. Ibn Hishām, p. 217 ff.; Aṭ-Ṭabari, i. 1189.

[1] Ibn Hishām, p. 230 ff.; Aṭ-Ṭabari, i. 1189 f.; Ibn Sa'd, p. 139 f

skirts of the city. It was entered from the town by a narrow alley closed by a low gateway through which a camel could pass with difficulty. On all other sides it was detached by cliffs and buildings.[1]

Hāshimites with Moḥammad retire into the Shi'b, A.D. 616–617

On the first night of the first month of the seventh year of the mission, the Hāshimites, including the Prophet and his family, retired into the quarter of Abu Ṭālib; and with them followed also the descendants of Al-Muṭṭalib the brother of Hāshim. Abu Lahab alone, moved by hatred of the new religion, went forth to the other party. The ban of separation was put rigorously in force. The Hāshimites soon found themselves cut off from all supply of corn and other necessaries of life. They were not strong enough to send forth a caravan of their own; if foreign merchants came, they were made to withhold their commodities except at an exorbitant price; Ḳoreish themselves would sell them nothing; and a great scarcity ensued. No one ventured forth from the *Shi'b* except at the season of pilgrimage, when, all enmities being hushed, Moḥammad and his party were free to join securely in the ceremonies. For two or three years the attitude of both parties remained unaltered, and the failing stock of the Hāshimites, replenished only by occasional and surreptitious ventures, reduced them to want and distress.

Their distress

The citizens could hear the wailing of the famished children within the *Shi'b*. Many hearts were softened at the sight of such hardship, and mourned over the hostilities which gave them rise. Among these, and among the relatives of the isolated band, were found some who ventured, in spite of

[1] The several quarters of Mecca skirting the foot of Abu Ḳobeis are still distinguished by the name *Shi'b:* thus we have the *Shi'b al-Maulid* (quarter in which Moḥammad was born); and the *Shi'b 'Alī* which was probably comprised in the *Shi'b* of Abu Ṭālib. Burckhardt tells us: 'On the east side, towards the mountain, and partly on its declivity, stands the quarter called Shab Aly, adjoining the Shab eḷ Moled; here is shown the venerated place of Aly's nativity. Both these quarters are among the most ancient parts of the town where the Koreysh formerly lived; they are even now inhabited principally by Sherīfs, and do not contain any shops. The houses are spacious and in an airy situation.'—*Arabia*, i. 226. It was into one of these quarters of the city, situated in a defile having behind it the steep ascent of the hill, and so built about as to be inaccessible on all sides, except by a narrow entrance from the city, that the Hāshimites retired.

threats, to introduce from time to time provisions by stealth at night. Thus we read of one conducting a camel laden with corn cautiously into the *Shi'b*, and making over the burden to the hungry inmates. Ḥakīm, grandson of Khuweilid, used also, though the attempt was sometimes perilous, to carry supplies to his aunt Khadīja.

Unfavourable effect on the cause of Moḥammad

Though the sympathies of many were thus aroused by the sufferings of the Hāshimites, the cause of Islām itself did not advance during the period of this weary seclusion, which had its expected effect in cutting off the city from the personal influence of Moḥammad and his converts. The efforts of the Prophet were of necessity confined to the members of his own noble clan, who, though unbelievers in his mission, had resolved to defend his person; and to strengthening in the faith his previous converts. Accordingly we find in the portions of the Ḳor'ān delivered at this time directions to retire from the unbelievers, and confine his preaching to his kinsmen and to the faithful:—

Sūra li. 53 ff.

> Verily they are a rebellious people;
> Wherefore turn from them, and thou shalt not be blamed.
> And admonish; for admonition profiteth the believers.
> * * * * * * *

Sūra xxvi. 213 ff.

> Invoke with GOD no other god, lest thou be of those consigned to torment.
> And preach unto thy relatives, those that be of nearer kin.
> And conduct thyself gently[1] towards the believers that follow thee.
> If they disobey thee, SAY *I am free from that which ye do.*
> And put thy trust in Him that is glorious and merciful.

But closer union with the Hāshimites

The exemplary bearing of Moḥammad under these trying circumstances, and the spirit of clanship that knit together

[1] Literally, *Lower thy wings.* So in Sūra xv. 88 ff.; xvii. 25.

'Stretch not forth thine eyes unto the provision which We have given unto several of them, neither be covetous thereof.
But behave with gentleness (*lower thy wings*) towards the believers;
And say; Verily I am a plain preacher. . . .
And publish that which thou art commanded, and withdraw from the idolaters.
Verily, We shall suffice for thee against the scoffers, those that set up with GOD other gods; and they shall shortly know;
But do thou praise thy Lord with thanksgiving, and be among the worshippers:—
And serve thy Lord until death overtake thee.'

[So xvii. 25, 'lower to them the wing of humility.']

all who shut themselves up with him, must have secured in some degree the general countenance of the Hāshimites, and may perhaps have helped to add some few followers from their ranks. But the weary years of confinement dragged on with no important result. The time of pilgrimage alone afforded Moḥammad a wider field. That interval of universal amnesty was turned (as it had been before) to careful account in visiting and exhorting the various tribes that flocked to Mecca and the adjacent fairs. Thus the Prophet used to visit the great assemblages at 'Okāẓ and other places, as well as the pilgrim encampments at Mecca and Mina. On these occasions he warned his countrymen against idolatry; invited them to the worship and service of the true God; and promised them not only Paradise hereafter, but prosperity and dominion here on earth, if they would believe.[1] No one responded to his call. Abu Lahab would dog his steps crying aloud: *Believe him not, he is a lying renegade!*[2] And the strangers, too, would reply to Moḥammad in such taunting words as these: *Thine own kindred and people should know thee best; wherefore is it that they have cast thee off?* So the Prophet, dispirited and grieved, would look upwards and make complaint: *O Lord, if Thou willedst, it would not be thus!* But the prayer seemed to pass unheeded.

Moḥammad visits the fairs and assemblages of pilgrims

Is repulsed and dispirited

About this time Moḥammad must have found means of communicating with the Jews, or at least with some person acquainted with Jewish lore; for his revelation begins now to abound with narratives taken, often at great length, from

[1] Al-Waḳidi says that Moḥammad frequented the three great fairs in the neighbourhood *every* year. There is some foreshadowing of the victories of Islām in his supposed address, which rather throws doubt upon these traditions. This was the alleged drift: '*Ye people! Say,* THERE IS NO GOD BUT THE LORD. *Ye will be benefited thereby. Ye will gain the rule of all Arabia, and of Al-'Ajam* (foreign lands), *and when ye die ye will reign as kings in Paradise.*

There would be numerous Christians and Jews *at the fairs,* though they did not, of course, attend the Meccan pilgrimage.

[2] 'And behind him there followed a squint-eyed man, fat, having flowing locks on both sides, and clothed in raiment of fine Aden stuff. And when Moḥammad had finished his preaching, this man would begin to address them, saying: *This fellow's only object is to draw you away from your gods and Genii, to his fancied revelations; wherefore follow him not, neither listen unto him.* And who should this be but his uncle 'Abd al-'Ozza Abu Lahab.'—Ibn Hishām.

their Scriptures and legends, as will be seen from the following extracts.

THE ḲOR'ĀN AS REVEALED DURING THIS PERIOD

Analogies of God's power and of the Resurrection

About twenty Sūras belong to this period; they are considerably longer that the early ones, and occupy now each several pages. The style, though often enlivened by tales from native and (now also) from Jewish legend, has become as a rule still more flat and prosaic. The substance is little changed; but, mingled with instruction for believers, and denunciation of scoffers, we begin to have powerful illustrations from nature of the might and wisdom of the Deity, and of the reasonableness of the Resurrection from the dead. The following may be taken as a specimen:—

Sūra xxx. 45 ff.

> Of His signs it is one, that He sendeth the winds bearing good tidings, that He may cause you to taste of His mercy, and that the ships may sail by His command, and ye may seek to enrich yourselves of His bounty; peradventure ye may be thankful.
>
> And verily We have sent before thee, Apostles unto their nations, and they came unto them with clear proofs, and We took vengeance on the transgressors; and it behoved Us to assist the believers.
>
> It is God that sendeth the winds which raise up the clouds; then He spreadeth the same in the heavens as He pleaseth, and He disposeth them in layers, and thou mayest see the rain issuing from between them. And when He causeth the same to reach unto such of His servants as He chooseth, behold they are filled with joy; and before it was sent down unto them, they were already despairing.
>
> Wherefore survey the tokens of God's mercy, how He quickeneth the earth after it hath become dead; verily, the same will be the Quickener of those who have died; and He is over all things Mighty.
>
> And if We send a blasting wind, and they should see their fields withered, they would, after that, become ungrateful.
>
> Thou canst not make the dead to hear; neither canst thou make the deaf to hear thy calling, when they turn their backs upon thee. Nor canst thou guide the blind out of their error. Thou shalt make none to hear excepting such as believe in Our signs; for these are the true Muslims (*i.e.* those resigned unto God).

In language which though strange is full of meaning, Moḥammad repeatedly affirms that the universe was not made by chance or '*in play*,' but that God had in creation a sovereign purpose and design:—

Sūra xxi. 16ff.

> WE created not the heavens and the earth and that which is between them, by way of sport.

If WE had pleased to take diversion, verily WE had taken it in such wise as beseemeth Us, if WE had been bent thereon.

Nay, but WE will oppose the True to the False, and it shall confound the same; and, lo! it shall vanish away.

In another passage, but of later date, the doctrine of the responsibility of the human race and consequent liability to punishment, in contrast with those bodies which obey of necessity, is taught thus mystically:—

Sūra xxxiii. 72 f.

Verily WE offered FAITH unto the heavens and the earth and the mountains; but they refused to undertake the same, and were afraid thereof.

But man undertook it; for verily he is rash and foolish;—

That God should punish the evil-minded men, and the evil-minded women, and the idolaters and the idolatresses;

And that God may be turned graciously unto the believing men and believing women; for God is gracious and merciful.

Connection with Judaism, and appeal to Jewish Scriptures

A close connection is now springing up between Moḥammad and the Jews; and frequent reference to their books, and recital of their legends, begin to form a leading feature of the Ḳor'ān.[1] The Pentateuch is constantly mentioned as a revelation from God to Moses. The grand object of the Ḳor'ān at this stage is '*to attest*' the divine origin of the Taurāt and the succeeding Scriptures. The Jewish books are said to contain '*clear evidence*' of the truth of the Ḳor'ān, and of the mission of Moḥammad. Jewish witnesses are appealed to in proof that the dispensation of Islām is '*foretold*' in their sacred books, and that the Ḳor'ān is in close conformity therewith.[1]

Testimony of the Jews in favour of Moḥammad

The confidence with which Moḥammad thus refers to the testimony of the Jews and their Scriptures is very remarkable. It leaves no room to doubt that some amongst the Jews, acquainted perhaps but superficially with their own books and traditions, encouraged Moḥammad in the idea that he might be, or even affirmed that he was *that Prophet whom the Lord their God should raise up unto them of their brethren.* His profound veneration for the Jewish Scriptures would lull and draw the Israelites kindly towards him. 'If this man,' they would say, 'hold firmly by the Law and the Prophets,

[1] Sprenger has remarked that about this period the Ḳor'ān begins to mention a great number of 'prophets,' by the Jewish term *nabi;* the limited references before being to 'apostles,' or 'messengers,' from God (*rasūl*).

and seek the guidance of the GOD of our fathers, he will not go astray. Peradventure, the Lord will, through him, lead the heathen Arabs to the truth. Nay; what if we ourselves have erred in our interpretation as to the lineage of the coming prophet, and this prove the very Messiah sprung from the seed of Abraham? In anywise let us wait, watching the result; and meanwhile encourage him in the love of the Word of God, and the seeking of His face in prayer.' Every Jew must have exulted in the Jewish tendencies which had possessed his mind. We meet with frequent passages like the following (xiii. 36): 'Those unto whom We have given the Book *rejoice* for that which hath been revealed unto thee.' Some going further bore a direct and unequivocal testimony to his mission. Nothing short of such witness could be referred to by Moḥammad when he said: *They unto whom We have given the Scripture recognise the Prophet* (or the Ḳor'ān) *as they do their own children;* and— Sūra vi. 20

Verily this is a Revelation from the Lord of Creation; Sūra xxvi. 192 ff.
The faithful Spirit hath descended with it
Upon thy heart, that thou mightest be a Warner,
In the tongue of simple Arabic.
And verily it is borne witness to in the former Scriptures;
Hath it not been a Sign unto them that the learned among the Children of Israel recognised it;
And if We had revealed it to a Foreigner,
And he had recited it unto them, they had not believed.

SAY: What think ye, if this Revelation be from God, and ye reject it, and a Witness from amongst the children of Israel hath witnessed unto the like thereof (*that is, to its conformity with the Old Testament*), and hath believed therein, and ye turn away scornfully?—Verily, God doth not direct the erring folk. Sūra xlvi. 9

Whether this 'Witness,' and the other Jewish supporters of Moḥammad, were among his professed followers, slaves perhaps, at Mecca; or casual visitors there from the Israelitish tribes; or belonged to the Jewish residents of Medīna (with the inhabitants of which city the Prophet was on the point of establishing friendly relations), we can but conjecture. Whoever his Jewish friends may have been, it is evident that they had a knowledge—rude and imperfect, perhaps, but comprehensive—of the outlines of Jewish history and tradition. These, distorted by rabbinical fable, and embellished or travestied by the Prophet's fancy, supplied the material

Conjectures as to the 'Witness'

Materials for Ḳor'ān supplied by Jews

for the Scriptural stories which at this period form a chief portion of the Ḳor'ān. The mixture of truth and fiction, of graphic imagery and childish fancy, the repetition over and over of the same tales in stereotyped expression, and the elaborate effort to draw an analogy between the former prophets and himself, and between their opponents and Ḳoreish, by putting the speech of his own day into their lips, fatigue the patient reader of the Ḳor'ān. A bare enumeration of some of the topics will illustrate both the remarkable correspondence of the Ḳor'ān with the Jewish Scriptures, and the many strange and fanciful deviations from them. The fabulous turn of the stories can often be traced to rabbinical legend; thus to the facts of Abel's history, it is added that God, sending a raven to scratch the ground, thus instructed Cain that the corpse should be buried in the earth (v. 34). The narrative of the Creation is given by way of specimen below, from Sūra vii. For the rest it will suffice if we but allude to the stories of Abraham, who broke in pieces the idols of his people, and miraculously escaped the fire into which the tyrant cast him; of the angel's visit, when Sarah laughed at the promise of a son, and the patriarch, vainly pleading for Sodom, was told that Lot would be saved, but that his wife was predestined to destruction; of Abraham's hand being stayed from the sacrifice of his son, who was ransomed by 'a noble victim;' of Joseph, in envy of whose beauty the Egyptian women cut their hands with knives; of Jacob, who, when the garment of Joseph was cast over him by the messengers from Egypt, recovered his long-lost sight; of mount Sinai held above the heads of the terrified Israelites to force their acceptance of the law; of the Seventy who, when struck dead upon the same mount, were quickened to life again; of David, whom the mountains joined in singing the praises of God; and of Solomon, on whose gigantic works the Genii and devils were forced to labour at his bidding; of the Genii, who brought the throne of the Queen of Sheba to Solomon in 'the twinkling of an eye,' and of the lapwing that flew to her with the royal summons; of the Jews, who broke the sabbath, and were changed into apes; of Ezekiel, who quickened a great multitude of the dead; and of Ezra, who with his ass was raised to life after being dead a hundred years. The follow-

Illustrations

ing passage may be taken as a fair specimen of the half-Scriptural, half-legendary style of these stories:—

Sūra vii. 10 ff.

And verily WE created you, then fashioned you, and then said unto the Angels, 'Fall down and worship Adam;' and they all worshipped, excepting Iblīs who was not one of the worshippers;—

God said, 'What hindereth thee that thou worshippest not when I command thee?' He answered, 'I am better than he: Thou createdst me of fire, and thou createdst him of clay.'

God said, 'Get thee down from Heaven; it shall not be given thee to behave arrogantly therein; get thee hence; verily, thou shalt be amongst the despicable.'

He said, 'Respite me unto the day of Resurrection.'

God said, 'Verily, thou art of the number respited.'

The Devil said, 'Now, for that Thou hast caused me to fall, I will lie in wait for them in thy straight path;—

Then I will fall upon them from before and from behind, and from their right hand and from their left; and Thou shalt not find the most part of them thankful.'

God said, 'Depart from hence, despised and driven away; verily, whosoever of them shall follow thee, I will surely fill hell with you together.

And thou, Adam, dwell thou and thy wife in Paradise, and eat of its fruit wherever ye will; but approach not this tree, lest ye become of the number of the transgressors!'

And the Devil tempted them both, that he might discover that which was hidden from them of their nakedness.

And he said, 'Your Lord hath only forbidden you this tree, lest ye should become Angels, or become immortal.'

And he sware unto them, 'Verily, I am unto you as one that counselleth good.'

And he caused them to fall through guile; and when they had tasted of the tree, their nakedness appeared unto them, and they began to join the leaves of Paradise, to cover themselves withal.

And their Lord called unto them, 'What! did I not forbid you this tree, and say unto you that Satan was your manifest enemy?'

They said, 'Oh, our Lord! We have injured our own souls, and if Thou forgivest us not, and are not merciful unto us, we shall be numbered with the lost.'

God said, 'Get ye down, the one of you an enemy to the other; and there shall be unto you on the earth an habitation and a provision for a season:'—

He said, moreover, 'Therein shall ye live, and therein shall ye die, and from thence shall ye be taken forth.'

Certain favourite passages from the Old Testament are the subject of special amplification and repetition, some as often as a dozen times. Such are the history of Moses, the catastrophe of the Flood, and the overthrow of Sodom, through which the Arabian prophet, with a wearisome reiteration, seeks to deal forth exhortation and warning to the citizens of Mecca. An adequate conception of these curious recitals can be gained only from a perusal of the Ḳor'ān itself; if the reader have patience and interest let him peruse, for an example, the history of Moses in the 20th and 28th Sūras.

Time spent in study and composition

To acquire so minute a knowledge of considerable portions of Jewish Scripture and legend, to assimilate these to his former materials, and to work them up into elaborate and rhythmical Sūras, was a work that no doubt required much time and patience. The revelation is seldom now the spontaneous eloquence of a warm imagination; it is rather the tame and laboured result of ordinary composition. For this end many a midnight hour must have been stolen from sleep. Such employment is probably referred to in passages like the following:—

Sūra lxxiii. 1 ff.

> Oh thou that art wrapped up!
> Arise during the night, excepting a small portion thereof:—
> A half thereof; or diminish the same a little,
> Or add thereto. And recite the Ḳor'ān with well measured recitation.
> Verily, WE shall inspire thee with weighty words.
> Verily, the hours of night are the best for fervent devotion, and distinct utterance;
> For truly by day thou hast a protracted labour.
> And commemorate the name of thy Lord, and consecrate thyself wholly unto Him.

Idea of study and inspiration possibly blended together

It is possible that the convictions of Moḥammad may have become so blended with his grand object and course of action, that the study and repetition of the Ḳor'ān were regarded as his best seasons of devotion. But the way in which he now made use of Jewish information and produced the result *as evidence of inspiration*, points to the beginning of an active, though it may have been unconscious, course of unacknowledged appropriation;[1]—a weak point on which his enemies were not slow to seize. They accused him of

[1] Thus, in the story of Man's creation and the fall of Satan, Moḥammad is desired to say: '*I had no knowledge regarding the Heavenly Chiefs when they disputed; verily, it hath been revealed unto me for no other purpose than* (to prove) *that I am a public Preacher.*'

fabrication, and of being assisted therein by others: 'They are fables,' they said, 'of the ancients which he hath had written down; they are dictated unto him every morning and evening.' To these imputations Moḥammad could only answer: 'He hath revealed it who knoweth that which is hidden in heaven and in earth: He is forgiving and merciful.'

Imputations of his enemies

Sūra xxv. 5-7

Up to this period there is little mention of the Christian Scriptures, the available sources of information being probably as yet imperfect.

Christian Scriptures little mentioned

—Sūra xxxviii. 69 f. So regarding Moses at Mount Sinai, Sūra xxviii. And again, after relating the history of Joseph, it is added: '*This is one of the secret histories which We have revealed unto thee; thou wast not present with them*,' &c.—Sūra xii. 103.

CHAPTER VI

VISIT TO AṬ-ṬĀ'IF. ISLĀM PLANTED AT MEDĪNA

A.D. 620-621

Moḥammad and his party under the ban from 617-619 A.D.

IN the tenth year of his ministry, the fiftieth of his life, Moḥammad and his kinsmen were still shut up in the isolated quarter of Abu Ṭālib; the only interval of freedom and relief being at the annual pilgrimage. Between them and the rest of Ḳoreish the intercourse of social life was totally suspended. The Hāshimites were thus virtually blockaded for the space of two or three years. At last the sympathies of many were aroused. They saw in the persecution of Moḥammad something more than a conscientious struggle against an impostor. The justice of extending the ban to the whole Hāshimite stock was doubtful, and many, especially those related to the clan, grieved at the rupture.

Sympathy of their opponents

Abu Ṭālib upbraids Ḳoreish; deed eaten by insects

It was discovered by some friend of the Prophet that the parchment in the Ka'ba, on which the ban was engrossed, had been defaced by ants. The important news was told to Moḥammad; and Abu Ṭālib resolved to found thereon an effort for the dissolution of the league. The venerable chief, now more than fourscore years of age, issued forth from his defile and proceeded, with a band of followers, to the Ka'ba. Addressing the chief men of Ḳoreish assembled there, he said: 'Intelligence hath reached me that your parchment is eaten up of insects. If my words be true, desist from your evil designs; if false, I will deliver up my brother's son unto you that ye may do with him as ye list.' The company agreed that it should be so, and sent for the document. When they had opened it out, they saw that it was even as Abu Ṭālib had said; a great part had been devoured by white ants and was no longer legible. Abu Ṭālib, perceiving their confusion, bitterly upbraided their inhumanity and breach of social obligations. He then advanced with his band to the Ka'ba, and, withdrawing behind the curtain that shrouded the Holy House, prayed for deliverance from their machinations. This done, he straightway retired to his secluded abode.

Ban removed, A.D. 619

The murmurs of the sympathisers now found utterance. The partisans of the Prophet were emboldened. Ḳoreish had scarce recovered from surprise at the sudden appearance and as sudden departure of Abu Ṭālib, when five chief men (possibly on a preconcerted plan) rose up from their midst, and, declaring themselves opposed to the league, put on their armour and proceeded to the defile of Abu Ṭālib. Standing by its entrance, they commanded all that had taken refuge there to go forth to their respective homes in security and peace. So they went forth. Ḳoreish, confounded by the boldness of the stroke, offered no opposition. They perceived that a strong party had grown up who would resent by arms any attempt to lay violent hands upon the Muslims.

Domestic trials

Repose and liberty followed the breaking up of the hostile league; but they were not long to be enjoyed without alloy by Moḥammad. In a few months he was visited by trials more severe than any that had yet befallen him. The tenth year (third before the Hijra) had not yet passed when Khadīja died; and five weeks later he lost his protector Abu Ṭālib.[1] The death of his wife was a grievous affliction. For five-and-twenty years she had been his counsellor and support; and now his heart and home were desolate. His family, however, no longer needed maternal care. The daughters had all left him for their husbands' homes, excepting the youngest, Fāṭima, who was approaching womanhood, and between whom and her cousin 'Alī an attachment was perhaps already forming. Though Khadīja (at her death threescore-and-five years old) must long ago have lost the charms of youth, and though the custom of the country allowed polygamy, yet Moḥammad was during her lifetime restrained from other marriages by affection and gratitude, perhaps also by the wish to secure the influence

Death of Khadīja, December, A.D. 619

[1] Ibn Hishām, p. 276 ff.; Aṭ-Ṭabari, i. 1199.

of her family more entirely for his cause. His grief at her death at first was inconsolable, liable as he was to violent and deep emotion; but its effects were transient. The place of Khadīja could be filled, though her devotion might not be rivalled, by her many successors. The virtues of this noble lady are still held in veneration; and her tomb, in the valley just above the city, is visited to the present day by Muslim pilgrims.[1]

Death of Abu Ṭālib, January, A.D. 620

The loss of Abu Ṭālib, who died as he had lived, an unbeliever, was, if possible, a still severer bereavement. We may dismiss the legend that on his deathbed he declared, in reply to the Prophet's earnest appeal, that he was prevented from assenting to the creed of Islām only lest Ḳoreish should set it down to fear at the approach of death. Whatever he may have said to comfort Moḥammad, his life belies the accusation that apprehended contempt of Ḳoreish restrained him from avowing his convictions. The sacrifices to which Abu Ṭālib exposed himself and his family for the sake of his nephew, while yet incredulous of his mission, stamp his character as singularly noble and unselfish. They afford at the same time strong proof of the sincerity of Moḥammad. Abu Ṭālib would not have acted thus for an interested deceiver; and he had ample means of scrutiny.

The loss of Abu Ṭālib severely felt

When the patriarch felt that life was ebbing, he summoned his brethren, the sons of 'Abd al-Muṭṭalib, around his bed; commended his nephew to their protection; and, relieved of the trust, died in peace, and was buried near Khadīja's grave. Moḥammad wept as he followed the bier, and not without reason. For forty years Abu Ṭālib had been his faithful friend,—the prop of his childhood, the guardian of his youth, and in later life a very tower of defence. His unbelief only made his influence the stronger. So long as he survived, Moḥammad needed not to fear violence or attack. But there was no strong hand now to protect him from his foes. A second Khadīja might be found, but not a second Abu Ṭālib.

Grieved and dispirited by these bereavements following

[1] Sprenger thinks that, but for Khadīja, Moḥammad would never have been a prophet, and that by her death Islām lost in purity and the Ḳor'ān in dignity. Moḥammad is said occasionally to have slaughtered a sheep and distributed it among the poor in remembrance of her.

Abu Lahab protects Moḥammad for a little

so closely one upon the other, and dreading the now unchecked insolence of Ḳoreish, Moḥammad seldom went abroad. The dying behest of Abu Ṭālib had now an unexpected effect; for Abu Lahab, heretofore the avowed enemy of Moḥammad, was softened by his despondency and distress, and spontaneously became his guardian. '*Do*,' he said, '*as thou hast been in the habit of doing while Abu Ṭālib was yet alive. By Al-Lāt! no one shall hurt thee while I live.*' But the pledge was not long observed, for Abu Lahab was soon gained back again by Ḳoreish, and became his enemy more determined than before. At first, indeed, he was rather praised by Ḳoreish for his attempt to 'bind up family differences.' But, bid by Abu Jahl to ask where 'Abd al-Muṭṭalib now was, and on the Prophet confessing that he was in the place of the lost, Abu Lahab left him in indignation, saying, 'I will not cease to be thine enemy for ever;' and so he did remain.[1] The embittered relations between Abu Lahab and his nephew, notwithstanding that two of his sons had married daughters of Moḥammad, may be gathered from a memorable passage in the Ḳor'ān. The Prophet, we are told, called his relatives together to hear his message. When he had delivered it, 'Blast the fellow!' cried Abu Lahab; 'is that all that he hath called us for together?' To chide the blasphemer, and also to curse his wife, who had strewn thorns in his path, this drastic Sūra, containing a savage play upon the name, was promulgated:—

Bitter relations resumed

> Blasted be the hands of Abu Lahab! and let himself be blasted!
> His riches shall not profit him, nor that which he hath gained.
> He shall be cast into the broiling *Flame;*
> His wife also, laden with fuel,
> A halter of palm-coir round her neck.—Sūra cxi.[2]

The indignities he suffered at this time evince the hostile attitude of the city. On one occasion the populace cast dirt upon his head; returning home in this plight, one of his

[1] Ibn Sa'd, p. 141.

[2] It is uncertain when this incident occurred. From the short and impulsive style of the Sūra, it may probably have belonged to an earlier period; but anyhow it illustrates the Prophet's feelings towards his hostile uncle. The play is on the name *Lahab*, 'flame.' Ibn Hishām, p. 233; Aṭ-Ṭabari, i. 1170 f.

daughters rose to wipe it off, and as she did so, wept. Moḥammad seeing it, comforted her and said: '*My daughter, weep not! for verily the Lord will be thy father's helper.*'[1] It is added that he suffered no such indignity as that while Abu Ṭālib lived. His position indeed was now becoming critical. He must either gain the ascendancy at Mecca, abandon his prophetical claims, or else perish in the struggle. Islām must destroy idolatry, or idolatry destroy Islām. Things could not remain as they were. His followers, though devotedly attached, and numbering some once influential citizens, were but a handful against a host; besides, the greater part of them were now in Abyssinia. Open hostilities, notwithstanding every endeavour to prevent them, might any day precipitate the struggle, and irretrievably ruin his cause. The new faith had not recently been gaining ground at Mecca. There had been no conversions, none at least of any note, since those of 'Omar and Ḥamza three or four years before. A few more years of similar discouragement, and his chance of success was gone.

Critical position of Moḥammad

He resolves to make trial of Aṭ-Ṭā'if

Urged by such reflections, Moḥammad began to look around. Mecca knew not the day of its visitation, and its doom was well-nigh sealed. It might perchance be the will of the Lord that succour should come from some other quarter. Aṭ-Ṭā'if (sixty or seventy miles east of Mecca) was the nearest city of importance. God might turn the hearts of its inhabitants, the idolatrous Thaḳīf, use them as instruments to chastise the reprobate men of Mecca, and establish the true religion on the earth. To them, accordingly, he would now deliver his message.[2]

His journey thither, January, A.D. 620

Abu Ṭālib had been buried hardly a fortnight when the Prophet, followed only by the faithful Zeid, set out, Jonah-like, to summon Aṭ-Ṭā'if to repentance. His road as far as 'Arafāt was the pilgrim route, and then lay over dismal rocks through barren defiles for about forty miles, when it emerged

[1] Ibn Hishām, p. 277. [Ibn Hishām says (p. 184): 'The worst of what the Apostle met with from Ḳoreish was that he went out one day, and not one of the people looked at him or spoke to him or injured him, either freeman or slave. So the Apostle returned to his dwelling and wrapped himself up for the violence of his calamity.' Then God sent down (Sūra lxxiv.): 'O thou wrapt up, arise and warn,' &c.]

[2] Ibn Hishām, p. 279 ff.; Aṭ-Ṭabari, i. 1199 f.; Ibn Sa'd, p. 141 f.

on the crowning heights of Jebel Kora. Thence, descending through fertile valleys, the smiling fruits and flowers of which suggested perhaps the bright picture of the conversion of the Thakīfites, he advanced to their city. Though connected by frequent intermarriage, the inhabitants of Aṭ-Ṭā'if were jealous of the Koreish. They had a *Lāt*, or chief idol, of their own. It might be possible, by appealing to their tribal pride as well as conscience, to enlist them on the side of Islām against the people of Mecca. Moḥammad went first to the three principal men of the city, brothers; and having explained his mission, invited them to the honour of sustaining the new faith, and supporting him in the face of his hostile tribe. But he failed in producing conviction. They cast in his teeth the common objections of his own people, and advised him to seek protection in some other quarter.

Is ignominiously expelled the city.

Moḥammad remained in Aṭ-Ṭā'if for about ten days; but, though many influential men came at his call, no hopeful impression was made. Thus repulsed, he solicited only one favour; that they would not divulge the object of his visit, for he feared on his return the taunts and aggravated hostility of Koreish. But this, even if it had been possible, the men of Aṭ-Ṭā'if were little likely to concede. For the first few days, perhaps, the common people regarded with awe the prophet who had turned Mecca upside down, and whose preaching probably most of them had heard at some of the neighbouring fairs or at the yearly pilgrimage. But the neglect manifested by their chiefs, and the disproportion to outward eye between the magnitude of the prophet's claims and his present solitary helpless condition, turned fear into contempt. Stirred up to hasten the departure of the unwelcome visitor, the people hooted him through the streets, pelted him with stones, and at last obliged him to flee the city pursued by a relentless rabble. Blood flowed from both his legs; and Zeid, endeavouring to shield him, was wounded in the head. The mob did not desist until they had chased him two or three miles across the sandy plain to the foot of the surrounding hills. There, wearied and mortified, he took refuge in one of the numerous orchards, and rested under a vine. In this the day of his humiliation, little did even his unwavering faith anticipate that in little more than ten years he should stand upon the same spot at the head of a conquering army; and that the great idol of Aṭ-Ṭā'if, despite the entreaties of its votaries, would be demolished at his command.

Rests at a garden in the outskirts of Aṭ-Ṭā'if

Hard by was a vineyard belonging to two Ḳoreish, 'Otba and Sheiba; for the wealthy citizens of Mecca had gardens (as they still have) in the vale of Aṭ-Ṭā'if. They watched the flight of Moḥammad; and, moved with compassion, sent 'Addās their servant with a tray of grapes for his refreshment. The servant, a Christian slave from Nineveh, marvelled at the pious invocation with which the fruit was received by the weary traveller 'in the name of the Lord;' and a conversation ensued in which Moḥammad, learning from whence he came, made mention of 'the righteous Jonas, son of Mattai of Nineveh,—a brother prophet like himself.' Thereupon 'Addās did homage to Moḥammad, who, we may believe, was solaced more by the humble devotion of the slave than by the welcome fruit and grateful shade.[1] After a little, composed and reassured, he betook himself to prayer, and the following touching petitions are still preserved as those in which his burdened soul gave vent to its distress:—

His prayer

O Lord! I make my complaint unto thee of my helplessness and frailty, and my insignificance before mankind. But thou art the Lord of the poor and feeble, and thou art my Lord. Into whose hands wilt thou abandon me? Into the hands of strangers that beset me round about? or of the enemy thou hast given at home the mastery over me? If thy wrath be not upon me, I have no concern; but rather thy favour is the more wide unto me. I seek for refuge in the light of thy countenance. It is thine to chase away the darkness, and to give peace both for this world and the next; let not thy wrath light upon me, nor thine indignation. It is thine to show anger until thou art pleased; and there is none other power nor any resource but in thee.[2]

And reassured thus he again set out on his return to Mecca.

Audience of the Genii at Nakhla

Half way lay the vale of Nakhla, with an idol fane and shady grove. Dreading the reception at home which, after his sorry mission to the rival city, might await him, he halted there. And, as he arose at night to prayer, or perhaps in a dream or trance, his excited imagination pictured

[1] We are told that 'Addās fell to kissing the head, hands, and feet of Moḥammad, to the astonishment of his masters looking on from a distance; and that he influenced them afterwards in favour of Islām.' Ibn Hishām, p. 280 f.

[2] Aṭ-Ṭabari, i. 1201.

crowds of Genii pressing forward to hear his exhortations, and ardent to embrace Islām. The romantic scene is thus pictured in the Ḳor'ān:—

And do thou call to mind when WE caused a company of the Genii to turn aside unto thee, listening to the Ḳor'ān. When they were present at its recitation they said one to the other, *Give ear*. And when it was ended, they returned unto their people, preaching. They said,—Oh our People! verily we have been listening to a Book which hath been sent down since the days of Moses, and which attesteth the truth of the preceding Scripture. It guideth unto the truth, and into the straight path. Oh our People! obey the preacher of God, and believe in him, that he may forgive you your sins, and save you from a fearful doom. Sūra xlvi. 28 ff.

And again:—

SAY: It hath been revealed unto me that a company of Genii listened, and they said,—'Verily we have heard a marvellous discourse; Sūra lxxii. 1 ff.
It guideth toward the right faith;
Wherefore we believed therein, and we will not henceforth associate any with our Lord;
And as to Him (may his Majesty be exalted!)
He hath taken no spouse, neither hath He any offspring.'

And so on, at considerable length, the Genii in this curious passage speaking the language of true believers.[1]

[1] The passage is so curious, and the scene so grotesque, that I give the continuation below:—

'But verily the foolish people amongst us have spoken of God that which is unjust;
And we verily thought that no one amongst Men or Genii would have uttered a lie against God.
And truly there are people amongst men who have sought for refuge amongst the Genii, but they only multiplied their folly.
And they fancied, as ye do, that God would not raise any from the dead.
And we tried the Heavens, but found them filled with a powerful guard, and with flaming darts;
And we sat on some of the Stations to listen, but whoever listeneth now findeth an ambush of flaming darts. * * *
And verily we thought that no one could frustrate God on earth, neither could we escape from him by flight;
Wherefore when we heard the right direction, we believed therein'—(*and so on, the Genii speaking as Muslims*). * * *
And verily when the servant of God (Moḥammad) stood up to call upon Him, they (the Genii) were near jostling him by their numbers,' &c.

Notwithstanding the *crowds* of Genii here spoken of as *jostling* the Prophet, Ibn Hishām (whose authorities had a wonderful acquaintance with their habits and haunts) states (p. 281) that there were but *seven*

Moḥammad returns to Mecca

After spending some days at Nakhla, he again went on towards Mecca. But before entering the city, which he feared to do (now that the object of his visit to Aṭ-Ṭā'if could not be kept secret) without a protector, he turned aside by a northward path to his ancient haunts on mount Ḥirā. From thence he sent twice to solicit the guardianship of certain influential chiefs; but without success. At last he bethought him of Al-Muṭ'im (one of those who had helped to procure the removal of the ban); and sent word beseeching that he would bring him into the city under his protection. The chief assented; and, having summoned his sons, bade them buckle on their armour and take their stand by the Ka'ba. Assured of his guarantee, Moḥammad and Zeid re-entered Mecca.[1] When they had reached the Ka'ba, Al-Muṭ'im stood upright on his camel and called aloud: 'O ye Ḳoreish! verily I have given the pledge of protection unto Moḥammad; wherefore, let not any one amongst you molest him.' Then Moḥammad went forward, kissed the corner-stone, and returned to his house guarded by Al-Muṭ'im and his party. The generosity and faithfulness of this chief have been perpetuated by Ḥassān ibn Thābit, the poet of Medīna and the Prophet's friend.[2]

Mission to Aṭ-Ṭā'if memorable

There is something lofty and heroic in this journey of Moḥammad to Aṭ-Ṭā'if; a solitary man, despised and rejected by his own people, going boldly forth in the name of God, like Jonah to Nineveh, and summoning an idolatrous city to

Genii belonging to Nisibin, who, happening to pass that way, were arrested by hearing Moḥammad reciting the Ḳor'ān; others that there were *nine*, and that they came from the Yemen, or from Nineveh, and professed the Jewish religion!

[1] Ibn Hishām, p. 251; Aṭ-Ṭabari, i. 1203.

[2] The following are the lines. They show how valuable contemporary poetry may be as an auxiliary to tradition:—

Weep, O my eyes! for the chief of men; let tears gush forth; and when they run dry, then pour forth blood!
If greatness had caused any to survive for ever amongst mankind, then greatness had preserved Al-Muṭ'im unto this day.
Thou gavest the pledge of protection to the Prophet of God from Ḳoreish; and they became thy servants so long as a pilgrim shall shout 'Labbeik!' or assume the pilgrim garb.

Al-Muṭ'im was a chief descended from Naufal, brother of Hāshim (great-grandfather of Moḥammad); and, along with Ḥarb, commanded his tribe in the Sacrilegious War, A.D. 586.

repent and support his mission. It sheds a strong light on the intensity of his belief in the divine origin of his calling.

Marries Sauda and is betrothed to 'Ā'isha; *ætat.* 51

The outlook was dark. If help should not come from elsewhere, there was little hope of success at Mecca. Meanwhile, amid trial and discouragement, Moḥammad sought solace in fresh nuptials. Sauda, the lady on whom he now set his affections, was of mature age, widow of Sakrān. Of Ḳoreishite blood (but of a stock remote from Moḥammad), they both became early converts to Islām, and emigrated to Abyssinia. Sakrān had recently died on their return to Mecca. Moḥammad now made suit to Sauda, and the marriage was celebrated within two or three months from the death of Khadīja.[1] About the same time he betrothed himself to 'Ā'isha, the daughter of Abu Bekr; an alliance mainly designed to cement the attachment of his bosom friend. The yet undeveloped charms of 'Ā'isha could hardly have swayed the Prophet's heart. He was now fifty, she but six or seven. years of age. Still there may have been something more than ordinarily precocious about the child, for the marriage took place about three years afterwards.

His private means

We are not told of the terms on which Moḥammad continued to live with the family of Khadīja, and whether he retained any part of the property that belonged to her. During the troublous years he had lately encountered, and especially under the ban, it is probable that her wealth had much diminished. Perhaps he shared it with the poorer brethren. It is certain that during the remaining stay at Mecca he had not much at his disposal; and there are even indications (as we shall see) of straitened means. He still continued to live, at least occasionally in the quarter, if not in the house, of Abu Ṭālib.

Moḥammad meets pilgrim party from Medīna, March, A.D. 620;

Repulsed from Aṭ-Ṭā'if, and despairing of success at home, the fortunes of Moḥammad were enveloped in thick

[1] On the conquest of Kheibar, eight years after, Sauda had her portion assigned her from its revenues with the Prophet's other wives. In the following year it is said somewhat obscurely that either on account of her age, or some doubt of her fidelity, Moḥammad wished to put her away, but was afterwards reconciled. She is also said to have given up 'her turn' to 'Ā'isha. She survived Moḥammad ten years. She had by Sakrān a son who was killed in the wars under 'Omar.

gloom, when a gleam of hope shot across his path from an unexpected quarter. The season of pilgrimage was at hand; and, as his custom was, the Prophet plied the crowds of devotees wherever he saw a likely audience. The rites were nearly over, and the multitudes about to disperse, when, wandering through the busy scene in the narrow valley of Mina, he was attracted by a little group of six or seven men, whom he recognised as strangers from Medīna.[1] '*Of what tribe are ye?*' said he, coming up and kindly accosting them. 'Of the tribe of Al-Khazraj,' they replied. '*Ah! confederates of the Jews?*' 'We are.' '*Then, why not sit ye down for a little, and I will speak with you?*' The offer was accepted willingly, for the fame of Moḥammad had been noised abroad in Medīna, and the strangers were curious to see more of the man who had created such turmoil in Mecca. So he expounded to them his doctrine, asserted the warrant of a divine mission, and, after setting forth the difficulties of his position at home, asked whether they would receive and protect him at Medīna. 'Thy teaching we commend,' they said; 'but as for protecting thee, our tribes have been long at deadly feud among ourselves and have fought great battles. If thou comest to us thus, we may be unable to rally round thee. Let us, we pray thee, return unto our people, if haply the Lord will create peace amongst us; and we will come back again to thee at this set time next year.' So they returned to their homes, and invited their people to the faith; and many believed, so that there remained hardly a family in Medīna in which mention was not made of the Prophet.[2]

who believe and spread his cause in Medīna

Settlement of the Jews at Medīna

As the interest of our story will now in great measure centre in Medīna, an account must here be given of its inhabitants and the state of parties there. Arab legend peoples northern Arabia in ancient days with Amalekites, probably Abrahamic races of other than Israelitish descent. From time to time, these were supplanted by inroads of the Jews. The sack of Jerusalem by Nebuchadnezzar, the attack of Pompey 64 years before the Christian era, with that of Titus 70 years after it, and the bloody retribution inflicted by Hadrian on Judea, A.D. 136, are some of the later causes

[1] Ibn Hishām, p. 286 f.; Aṭ-Ṭabari, i. 1208 ff.

[2] See Introduction, p. civ ff.

which dispersed the Jews and drove large numbers into Arabia. Such may have been the three tribes, An-Naḍīr, Ḳoreiẓa, and Ḳainuḳā', who, finding Medīna (the ancient *Yathrib*) weakly peopled, took possession of the city, formed settlements in its neighbourhood, and built for themselves strong castellated houses capable of resisting armed attack.

Supplanted by the Aus and Khazraj

In the beginning of the 4th century, a branch of those numerous Arab tribes, which (as we have seen) had been migrating from the Yemen northwards and settling on the Syrian border, gained a footing at Medīna. They were divided into two clans, the Aus and the Khazraj. These soon encroached upon the Jews; and enmity sprang up between them. Aided by their Syrian brethren, and having treacherously massacred the leading Jews assembled at a banquet, they became masters of Medīna, and took possession of the richest lands around it. Thus established, it was not long before the Aus and the Khazraj fell out among themselves; and in the beginning of the 6th century we find them in a state of chronic enmity, if not actual warfare with each other. Four or five years previous to the period of our history, hostilities had reached a crisis between them. Each was reinforced by allies from other Arab tribes;[1] the Jews were divided, the Beni Ḳoreiẓa and An-Naḍīr siding with the Aus, Ḳainuḳā' with the Khazraj. In the year 616 A.D. there was fought the great battle of Bo'āth. At first the Aus were worsted and fled; but their chief, in indignation, pierced himself and fell; and at the sight, stung by shame, they returned to the charge and fought so bravely that they dispersed the Khazraj with great slaughter. They burned the date groves of their enemy, and were scarce restrained from razing their fortified houses to the ground.

Discord between the two clans

Abdallah ibn Obei

The Khazraj were humbled but not reconciled. No open engagement after this took place, but numerous assassinations gave token from time to time of hardly suppressed ill-blood. Wearied with the protracted discord, both parties

[1] Thus a deputation from the Aus sought aid from Ḳoreish; but they declined to fight against the Khazraj, with whom some (as Moḥammad's own family) were allied by marriage. The Prophet is said to have addressed this embassy, and pressed the claims of his mission upon them, but without success.

were about to take 'Abdallah ibn Obei, a distinguished citizen of the Khazraj, as their chief. This man had resented the treacherous murder by his own tribe of certain Jewish hostages; he had taken no part in the field of Bo'āth; and he was respected by both factions. But his bright prospects were destined to be eclipsed by the rising fortunes of the stranger driven from Mecca.

Medīna prepared for Islām

From this review it will be clear that the success at Medīna of Islām, though unexpected, was not without perceptible cause. There was, first, the vague expectation, derived from the Jews, of a coming prophet. When the Jews, dividing their allegiance between the Aus and Khazraj clans, used to fight on either side, they would say: *A prophet is about to arise; his time draweth nigh. Him shall we follow; and then we shall slay you with the slaughter of the ungodly nations of old.* So when Moḥammad addressed the pilgrims of Medīna at Mina, they spoke one with another: *Know surely that this is the prophet with whom the Jews are ever threatening us; wherefore let us make haste and be the first to join him.* Such is the Muslim tradition, and there is truth, no doubt, though exaggerated and distorted, in it. In their close and constant intercourse with the Arabs of Medīna, the expectation of a Messiah must in some form or other have been communicated by the Jews to their heathen neighbours. Nor could the people live in daily contact with a race professing the pure theism and stern morality of the Old Testament without realising its practical protest against the errors of heathenism, and its contrast with the worship of the one true God. Moreover, Medīna was only half the distance of Mecca from the Christian tribes of Syria; the poet Ḥassān ibn Thābit, and men of his stamp from Medīna, used to frequent the Christian court of the Ghassānid king; and thus Christianity as well as Judaism had probably wrought a more powerful effect upon the social condition of Medīna than upon any other part of the Peninsula. Again, the city had been long torn by internal war. The recent sanguinary conflict of Bo'āth had weakened and humiliated one of the factions without materially strengthening the other. Assassination succeeded open strife. No one yet appeared bold enough to seize the reins of government; the citizens, both Arab and Jewish, lived in uncertainty and suspense. With such varied

Internal strife neutralised fear of foreign influence

distractions, the advent of a stranger would excite but little jealousy and apprehension.

Medīna prepared to accept Moḥammad

Such was the position of Medīna. Its people addicted to the superstition of Mecca, yet well acquainted with a purer faith, were in the best state of preparation to join one who aimed at reforming the worship of the Ka'ba. Impressed with the Jewish anticipation of a Messiah, they might be ready to recognise in Moḥammad the coming prophet. A city wearied with faction and strife would cheerfully admit him to their hospitality as a refugee, if not welcome him to their counsels as a chief. And lastly, the politics of Mecca and the ministry of the Prophet were well known at Medīna. Syrian caravans of Ḳoreish not unfrequently halted there. Occasional intermarriages took place between the inhabitants of the two cities. Moreover, through the marriage of Hāshim with a lady of Medīna, Moḥammad himself had the blood of the Khazraj in his veins; and a favourable interest, among that tribe at least, was thus secured. Abu Ḳeis, a famous poet of Medīna, had some time before addressed Ḳoreish in verses intended to dissuade them from interference with Moḥammad and the new religion. The Jews were already acquainted with the Prophet as a zealous supporter of their Scriptures. Parties from Medīna went up yearly to the solemnities of the Ka'ba. Many had thus come under the direct influence of his preaching, and all were familiar with the general tenour of his claims. To this was now to be superadded the advocacy of actual converts.[1]

Its inhabitants familiar with his claims

[1] We find notices of conversion among the citizens of Medīna at an earlier period, but none well substantiated. Thus, before the battle of Bo'āth, when a deputation visited Mecca seeking for auxiliaries, we are told that 'they listened to Moḥammad, and a youth of their number declared that this new doctrine was far better than the errand they had come upon; but their chief cast dust upon him, saying that they had another business than to hear such things.' The youth, killed shortly after in the struggles at Medīna, died a true Muslim. Similarly, Suweid, a Medīna poet, repeated to the Prophet at Mecca the Persian tale of Loḳmān. Moḥammad, saying he had something better than that, recited the Ḳor'ān to him. The poet was delighted with it; 'he was not far from Islām, and some said that he died a Muslim.'

And again: 'The first that believed at Medīna were As'ad and Dhakwān, who set out for Mecca to contend in rivalry with 'Otba son of Rabī'a. On their arrival, 'Otba said: *That praying fellow who fancieth himself to be a prophet, hath occupied us to the exclusion of every other*

A time of anxiety and suspense, A.D. 620

To return to Mecca, the year A.D. 620 was to Moḥammad one of expectation and anxiety. Would the handful of Medīna converts remain steady to the cause? Would they succeed in winning adherents from amongst their fellow-citizens? If they should prove unfaithful, or fail of success, what then? He might be forced to flee to Syria or Abyssinia; and seek refuge at some Christian court, or with the Ethiopian Negus, or amongst the tribes of the northern desert. Such are the doubts that must have exercised his soul, during this long year of waiting.

First pledge of the 'Aḳaba by men of Medīna, April, A.D. 621

The days of pilgrimage at last came round, and Moḥammad sought the appointed spot, in a narrow sheltered glen near Mina.[1] His apprehensions were at once dispelled; a band of twelve faithful disciples were there ready to acknowledge him their prophet. Ten were of the Khazraj, and two of the Aus, tribe. They plighted their faith to Moḥammad thus: '*We will not worship any but the one God; we will not steal, neither will we commit adultery, nor kill our children; we will not slander in anywise; nor will we disobey the Prophet in anything that is right.*' This was afterwards called the Pledge of Women, because, as not embracing any stipulation to *defend* the Prophet, it was the only oath required of the female sex. When the twelve had taken this engagement, Moḥammad replied: '*If ye fulfil the pledge, Paradise shall be your reward. He that shall fail in any part thereof, to God belongeth his concern either to punish or to forgive.*' The memorable proceeding is known in the annals of Islām as THE FIRST PLEDGE OF THE 'AḲABA, for that was the name of the little eminence or defile whither Moḥammad with the twelve retired. A Mosque still marks the spot hard by the pilgrim road.

Spread of Islām at Medīna, A.D. 621

The twelve were now committed to the cause of Moḥammad. They returned to Medīna missionaries of Islām, again to report their success at the following

business. Now As'ad used to converse with a friend at Medīna about the unity of God. When Dhakwān, therefore, heard this saying of 'Otba, he exclaimed: *Listen, O As'ad! this must be thy religion.* So they went straight to Moḥammad, who expounded to them Islām, and they both believed. On their return to Medīna, As'ad related to his friend what had passed, and he said: *I too am a believer with thee.*' Ibn Sa'd, p. 146.

[1] Ibn Hishām, p. 288 f.; Aṭ-Ṭabari, i. 1211 f.; Ibn Sa'd, p. 147 f.

pilgrimage. So prepared was the ground, and so zealous the propagation, that the new faith spread rapidly from house to house and from tribe to tribe. The Jews looked on in amazement. The people whom for generations they had vainly endeavoured to convince of the errors of heathenism were now of their own accord casting their idols to the moles and to the bats, and professing belief in the one true God. The secret lay in the adaptation of the instrument. Judaism, foreign in its birth, touched no Arab sympathies; Islām, engrafted on the faith and superstition, the customs and the nationality of the Peninsula, found ready access to the heart.

Muṣ'ab deputed to instruct converts at Medīna

The leaders in the movement soon found themselves unable to keep pace with its rapid spread. So they wrote to Moḥammad for a teacher, able to recite the Ḳor'ān, and instruct inquirers in the faith. The young disciple Muṣ'ab, who had lately returned from exile in Abyssinia, was deputed for that purpose. He lodged at Medīna with As'ad ibn Zurāra, who had been already in the habit of gathering the converts together for prayer and reading of the Ḳor'ān.[1]

[1] Muṣ'ab will be remembered as the youth whose pathetic interview with his mother has been before described. In course of time others were sent for the same purpose, and among them the blind 'Abdallah ibn Um Mektūm, see *ante*, p. 65.

The following narrative (though of doubtful authority) will illustrate the manner in which Islām was propagated at Medīna: 'As'ad and Muṣ'ab visited the quarter of the Aus, and, entering one of their gardens, sat down by a well, where a company of believers gathered round them. Now Sa'd ibn Mo'ādh and Oseid, chief men of the tribe, heard of the gathering at the well, and Sa'd unwilling himself to interfere (being related to As'ad) bade Oseid go and disperse them. Oseid seized his weapons, and hurrying to the spot, abused them. *What brings you two here amongst us*, he said, *to mislead our youths and silly folk? Begone, if ye have any care for your lives.* Muṣ'ab disarmed his wrath by courteously inviting him to sit down and listen. Then Oseid stuck his spear into the ground and seated himself; and as he listened, he was charmed with what he heard and forthwith embraced Islām. And he said: "there is another beside me, even Sa'd ibn Mo'ādh, whom I will send to you; if you can gain him over, there will not be one in his tribe left unconverted." So he departed and sent Sa'd, and Muṣ'ab persuaded him in like manner. So Sa'd returned to his tribe and swore that he would not speak to man or woman who did not acknowledge Moḥammad. So great was his influence that *by the evening every one of his clan was converted.*' Ibn Hishām, p 291.

There is a story of an aged chief who, like others at Medīna, had an

The devotions of the Aus and the Khazraj tribes were now conducted together by the earnest missionary; for even in such a matter the rival clans were impatient of a common leader from amongst themselves. So speedily, without let or hindrance, did Islām grow and take firm root at Medīna, and thus unexpectedly were the people prepared for a greater demonstration at the next time of pilgrimage.[1]

image in his house. This image the young converts used to cast every night into a filthy well, and the old man as regularly cleansed it; till, one day, they tied it to a dead dog and cast it into the well; whereupon he abandoned his image and believed.

[1] Ibn Sa'd, p. 148; Ibn Hishām, p. 289. [Ibn Isḥāḳ says Moḥammad sent Muṣ'ab of his own accord.]

CHAPTER VII

SPREAD OF ISLĀM AT MEDĪNA. THE HIJRA, OR FLIGHT TO THAT CITY

ÆTAT. 52-53 A.D. 621-622

The midnight journey to Jerusalem and Heaven

THE hopes of Moḥammad were now fixed upon Medīna. Visions of the north flitted before his imagination and carried him onwards to the Holy Land. It was thus that the famous romance of the heavenly journey was enacted in this expectant period. Jerusalem had been long regarded by the Prophet with the utmost veneration; and, indeed, until his breach with the Jews at Medīna, the Temple remained his *Ḳibla*, or place towards which at each stated genuflexion he turned to pray. Now, even in his dreams his thoughts were veering northward. The musings of the day reappeared in the slumbers of the night. He dreamed that he was swiftly carried by Gabriel on a winged steed past Medīna to the temple at Jerusalem, where a conclave of the ancient Prophets met to welcome him. His excited spirit conjured up a still more transcendent scene. From Jerusalem he mounted upwards, ascending from one heaven to another, till at last, reaching the seventh, he found himself in the awful presence of his Maker, and was dismissed with the behest that his people were to prostrate themselves in prayer five times in the day. When he awoke next morning in the house of Abu Ṭālib, the vision was still before him with all the freshness of reality; and he exclaimed to the daughter of Abu Ṭālib that during the night he had performed his devotions in the temple of Jerusalem.[1] He was going forth to make the vision known, when she seized him by the mantle, and conjured him not thus to expose

[1] Ibn Hishām, p. 263 ff.; Ibn Sa'd, 142 ff.

himself to the derision of the unbelievers. But he persisted. As the story spread abroad, unbelievers scoffed, and believers were staggered; some are even said to have gone back. But Abu Bekr, who supported the Prophet, declared his implicit belief in the journey as a simple matter of fact; and in the end the cause suffered no material harm. Tradition decks out the tale in gorgeous drapery; and, upon the rock over which the Mosque of 'Omar in Jerusalem stands, there is still shown the print of the Prophet's foot as he vaulted from it upon his winged steed. It is, indeed, a congenial theme for which tradition has given loose rein to pious and excited imagination. But the only mention of the journey in the Ḳor'ān is in the following verse:—

The vision embellished by tradition

Only notice of it in the Ḳor'ān

Sūra xvii 1

> Praise be to Him who by night carried His servant from the sacred Temple at Mecca to the farther Temple the environs of which WE have blessed, that WE might show him some of Our signs. Verily HE it is that heareth and seeth.

Moḥammad watches struggle between Persia and Roman empire

The political events in the north had long engaged the attention of Moḥammad. The prospect of finding a home in Medīna, and moving closer to the Syrian border, quickened his interest in the fortunes of the Byzantine empire. For several years the arms of Persia had been turned successfully against the Grecian frontier. The Bedawi tribes, who used to oscillate between one dominion and the other according to the fortune of war, were the first to fall into the hands of Persia. Syria was ravaged; Jerusalem sacked; Egypt and Asia Minor overrun. The enemy advanced upon the Bosphorus, and a Persian camp was pitched above ten years almost within sight of Constantinople. About the time of the first Pledge of the 'Aḳaba, A.D. 621, when the fortunes of Byzantium were at their lowest ebb, Heraclius was roused from his ignoble slumber, and after several years of arduous conflict, rolled back the invasion, and totally discomfited the Persians.

His sympathies with Heraclius; foretells victory of Greeks

In this struggle, the sympathies and hopes of Moḥammad were on the Kaiser's side. Christianity was a divine faith which might coalesce with Islām; but the fire-worship and superstitions of Persia were repugnant to his views It was while the career of Persian conquest was yet unchecked, that Moḥammad, in the 30th Sūra, uttered this sagacious augury:—

Sūra xxx. 1 ff.

The GREEKS have been smitten
In the neighbouring coasts;
But, after their defeat, they shall again be victorious,
In a few years. To GOD belongeth the matter from before, and after; and, in that day, the Believers shall rejoice
In the aid of GOD.
He aideth whom He chooseth; the GLORIOUS, the MERCIFUL.
It is the promise of GOD, who changeth not His promise; but the greater part of mankind know it not.[1]

And the prophecy, as we have seen, was justified by the event.

Relations with Christianity

About this period, with his increasing interest in the Roman empire, Moḥammad must have gained, either from Christian slaves at Mecca,[2] the neighbouring fairs, or from fragments of the Gospels copied by Waraḳa or others, some acquaintance with the outlines of our Saviour's life. As will appear in the Sūras cited in this chapter, he never showed the same interest in the Christian as in the Jewish faith, nor indeed had he the same means of learning its history and doctrines. His treatment of Christianity is mainly confined to the narration, often in the very words of the Evangelist, but in the ordinary legendary style, of a few passages connected with the birth and life of Jesus, whom he acknowledged as the last and greatest of the Jewish prophets, but whose Sonship he strenuously denied. At the same time, his attitude towards Christianity was just as favourable as it was towards Judaism; nor was his intercourse with its professors at any period embittered by such causes as afterwards led to hostilities with the Jews. But, on the other hand, his relations with the Christian faith never advanced materially beyond the point at which we find them now stated in the Ḳor'ān; and, in point of fact, if we except one or two campaigns against distant Christian tribes, and the reception of embassies from them, he came throughout his life into little personal contact with the professors of the faith of Jesus.

[1] The word 'few,' used here, ordinarily signifies from 3 to 10. The commentators add a very apt story in illustration. Abu Bekr, on this passage appearing, laid a wager of ten camels with Obei ibn Khalaf, that the Persians would be beaten within *three* years. Moḥammad desired him to extend the period to *nine* years, and to raise the stake. This Abu Bekr did, and in due time won one hundred camels from Obei's heirs. Al-Beiḍāwi, *loc. cit.*

[2] As Ṣoheib; see above p. 66.

A lull at Mecca

There was now a lull at Mecca. Moḥammad despaired, by the simple influence of preaching and persuasion, of further progress there. His eye was fixed upon Medīna, and he waited patiently until succour should come from thence. Meanwhile, Islām was for the present no longer to be aggressive. And Ḳoreish, congratulating themselves that their enemy had tried his worst and now was harmless, relaxed their vigilance and opposition. For this new course divine authority was at hand :—

Sūra vi. 106 ff.

Follow that which hath been revealed unto thee from thy Lord ;—there is no God but he ;—and retire from the idolaters.
If God had so desired, they had not followed idolatry ; and We have not made thee a keeper over them, neither art thou unto them a guardian.
Revile not those whom they invoke besides God, lest they revile God in enmity, from lack of knowledge.
Thus have WE rendered attractive unto every people their own doings ; then unto the Lord
Shall be their return, and He shall declare unto them that which they have wrought.[1]

Moḥammad's continued assurance of success

But with this cessation of aggressive measures there was no wavering of principle, nor any distrust of eventual success. A calm and lofty front was maintained of superiority, and even of defiance. Eventual success, in spite of present discouragement, was clear and assured. The whole tenour of the Revelation at this period is marked by quietness and confidence, and therein for the present lay the Prophet's strength. To all his apostles of old the Lord had given the victory, and he would give the same to Moḥammad :—

Sūra xxi. 18, 41, 42

We shall hurl the Truth against that which is false and it shall shiver it, and lo, the False shall vanish ;—Woe unto you for that which ye imagine ! * * *
Vengeance shall fall suddenly upon them. It shall confound them. They shall not be able to oppose it, neither shall they be respited.
Verily, Apostles before thee have been mocked ; but they that laughed them to scorn were encompassed by the vengeance which they mocked at. * * *

[1] The Opposition begin to be termed 'the Confederates' (Sūra xi.), and they are thus contrasted with the Muslims : 'The likeness of the two Parties is as the blind and the deaf, compared with him that hath both sight and hearing. What ! are these equal in resemblance ? Ah ! do ye not comprehend ?'

The unbelieving people said unto their Apostles—*We will surely expel you from our land, or ye shall return to our religion.* Then their Lord spake by revelation unto them, saying;—*Verily WE shall destroy the unjust.* Sūra xiv. 16 ff., 47, 48

And WE shall cause you to inherit the land after them;—this shall be for him that feareth My appearing and feareth My threatening.

So they asked assistance of the Lord, and every tyrant and rebellious one was destroyed. * * *

Verily, they have devised evil devices; but their devices are in the hands of God, even if their devices could cause the mountains to pass away.

Wherefore think not thou that God will work at variance with his promise which He made unto his Apostles. Verily the Lord is mighty, and a God of vengeance.

A dearth fell upon Mecca;—it was a punishment from God because the people had rejected his Messenger. Relief at length came; it was intended to try whether the goodness of God would not lead them to repentance. If they still hardened their hearts, a more fearful fate was denounced.[1] That tenfold vengeance would overtake the people if they continued to reject the truth, Moḥammad believed surely.

Judgments threatened against Mecca;

Which Moḥammad might or might not behold

[1] There are no very distinct traditions regarding this visitation; but the notices of it in the Ḳor'ān are so clear and distinct as to allow no doubt that some affliction of the kind did occur, and was attributed by Moḥammad to the divine vengeance:—

> And if WE have mercy upon them and withdraw the affliction that befell them, then they plunge into their wickedness, wandering wildly. Sūra xxiii. 77-79
>
> And verily WE visited them with affliction, and they humbled not themselves before their Lord, nor made supplication:—
>
> Until, when WE open unto them a door of severe punishment, lo! they are in despair thereat.

This punishment the commentators refer to the discomfiture at Bedr, but that would be an anachronism. Again:—

> And when WE made the people to taste mercy, after affliction befell them, lo! they devise deceit against Our Signs. SAY, God is more swift in stratagem than ye; Verily Our Messengers write down that which ye devise. Sūra x. 22-24
>
> It is He that maketh you travel by land and by water, so that when ye are in ships and sail in them with a fair breeze, they rejoice thereat.
>
> A fierce storm overtaketh them, and the waves come upon them from every side, and they think that verily they are closed in thereby; then they call upon God, rendering unto Him pure service, and saying, *If Thou savest us from this, we shall verily be amongst the grateful.*
>
> But when He hath saved them, behold! they work evil in the earth unrighteously. Oh ye people, verily your evil working is against your own souls, &c.

He might not live to see it; but the decree of God was unchangeable:—

Sūra xliii. 39-41

What! canst thou make the deaf to hear, or guide the blind, or him that is wandering widely?

Wherefore, whether WE take thee away, verily WE will pour our vengeance upon them,—

Or, whether WE cause thee to see that which WE have threatened them with, verily WE are all powerful over them.

Therefore hold fast that which hath been revealed unto thee, for thou art in the straight path.[1]

Sublime spectacle presented by Moḥammad

Moḥammad thus holding his people at bay; waiting in the still expectation of victory; to outward appearance defenceless, and with his little band as it were in the lion's mouth; yet trusting in His almighty power whose Messenger he believed himself to be, resolute and unmoved; presents a spectacle of sublimity paralleled only by such scenes in the Sacred Records as that of the prophet of Israel when he complained to his Master, 'I, even I only, am left.' Nay, the spectacle is in one point of view even more amazing; for the prophets of old were upheld (as we may suppose) by the prevailing consciousness of a divine inspiration, and strengthened by the palpable demonstrations of miraculous power; while with the Arabian, his recollection of former doubts, and confessed inability to work any miracle, may at times have cast across him a shadow of uncertainty. It is this which brings if possible into still bolder prominence the marvellous self-possession and enthusiasm which sustained Moḥammad on his course. 'Say unto the Unbelievers,' such was the reiterated
Sūra xi. 122 message from on high, '*Work ye in your place. Wait in expectation;* WE *too in expectancy are waiting.*' And again:
Sūra xx. 135 'Say, *Each of us awaiteth the issue; wait therefore. Hereafter ye shall surely know who they are that have chosen the straight path, and who hath been guided aright.*'

Authority assumed over followers

Moḥammad's bearing towards his followers, no less than towards his opponents, exhibits the assurance of being the vicegerent of God and the exponent of His will. His name is now associated with the Deity in the symbol of

[1] There are many other passages in the Sūras of this period to the same effect; thus: 'Wherefore persevere patiently, for the promise of God is true, whether We cause thee to see some part of that wherewith We have threatened them, or cause thee first to die; and unto Us shall they return.'—Sūra xl. 77.

faith;[1] and obedience to *God and his Apostle* becomes the watchword of Islām. 'Whosoever disobeyeth GOD AND HIS PROPHET, for him is prepared the fire of Hell; they shall remain therein for ever!'[2]

Oaths that his revelation is not fabricated

The confidence in his inspiration is sometimes expressed with imprecations, which one cannot read without a shudder:—

Sūra lxix. 38 ff.

I swear by that which ye see,
And by that which ye see not,
That this is verily the speech of an honourable Apostle!
It is not the speech of a Poet; little is it ye believe!
Neither is it the speech of a Soothsayer; little is it ye reflect!
It is a Revelation from the Lord of creation.
And if he (Moḥammad) had said concerning Us any sayings of his own,
Verily WE had caught him by the right hand;
Then had WE cut asunder the artery of his neck,[3]
Neither had there been among you any to hinder therefrom.
But verily it is an Admonition to the pious,
And truly WE know that there are amongst you those who belie the same;
But it shall only cause sighing unto the Unbelievers,
For it is the TRUTH;—the CERTAIN!
Therefore praise the name of thy Lord,—the GLORIOUS!

---

[1] 'There is no God but the Lord, and Moḥammad is His Prophet.' There is nothing, however, to show when the creed assumed this precise form.

[2] Sūra lxxii. v. 24. The sequel is singular; God sends a guard to attend his Prophet to see that the message is duly delivered, as if there were reason to doubt his fidelity in this respect:—

When they see the vengeance they were threatened with, then they shall know who were the weaker in succour, and the fewer in number.
SAY I know not whether that which ye are threatened with be near, or whether my Lord shall appoint for it a set term.
He knoweth the secrets of the future, and He unveileth not His secrets unto any,—
Except it be to an Apostle that pleaseth Him; and He maketh a guard to march before him, and behind him;
That He may know that they have delivered the messages of their Lord.

In further illustration of the text, see Sūra lxiv. v. 8: 'Wherefore believe in GOD AND HIS APOSTLE, and the light which WE have sent down.' And again: 'And obey *God and obey the Apostle;*—but if ye turn back, verily our Apostle hath only to deliver his message.' Thenceforward the expression becomes common.

[3] Commentators observe that the allusion is to the mode of execution still practised in the East; the executioner seizes the victim by the right hand, while with a sharp sword he aims a blow at the back of the neck, and detaches the head at a stroke.

Straitened means

It would seem as if the difficulties of the Prophet were at this period aggravated by straitened means. Though supported, no doubt, by help from his relatives and followers, there was yet ground for misgiving and anxiety. The divine promise reassures him in such terms as these:—

Sūra xx. v. 131 f.

> And cast not thine eyes on the provision WE have made for divers among them, the show of this present life, that WE may prove them thereby; for the provision of the Lord is better and more lasting.
>
> And command thy Family to observe prayer, and persevere therein: WE ask thee not to labour for a provision; WE will provide for thee, and a prosperous issue shall attend on piety.

Preparations for Second Pledge of Al-'Aḳaba, March, A.D. 622

Thus another year passed away in comparative tranquillity, and the month of pilgrimage, when the Medīna converts were again to rally around the Prophet, drew nigh.[1] Messages and reports of the amazing success of Islām had no doubt reached Moḥammad; but he could hardly have been prepared for the enthusiastic numbers ready to crowd to his standard, and swear allegiance to him as prophet and master. But the occasion was critical, and it was necessary to proceed with caution. Ḳoreish, if aware of the hostile confederacy—hostile because pledged to support a faction in their community—would have good ground for umbrage; the sword might prematurely be unsheathed, and the cause of Islām endangered. The movement, therefore, was conducted with the utmost secrecy. Even the great body of Medīna pilgrims, in whose company the converts travelled, were unaware of their object.

Muṣ'ab reports success to Moḥammad

Muṣ'ab, the teacher sent to Medīna, who accompanied the pilgrim party, immediately on his arrival repaired to Moḥammad and related all that happened at his new scene of labour. The Prophet rejoiced greatly when he heard of the numbers of the converts, and their eagerness in the service of Islām.

Arrangements for meeting by night at close of pilgrimage

To elude the scrutiny of the citizens the meeting between Moḥammad and his new adherents was to be by night; and that the strangers, in case suspicion were aroused, might be as soon as possible beyond reach of their enemies, the time was deferred to the close of the pilgrimage when, the ceremonies and sacrifices being finished, the multitude would on the following morning disperse to their homes. The spot was to

[1] Ibn Hishām, p. 293 ff.; Aṭ-Ṭabari, i. 1217 ff.; Ibn Sa'd, p. 148 f.

be the same secluded glen of Al-'Aḳaba, outside Mina, where the men of Medīna had met Moḥammad before. They were to move thither cautiously, after all had retired to rest;—'waking not the sleeper, nor tarrying for the absent.'

Moḥammad and Al-'Abbās proceed at midnight to the spot

An hour or two before midnight, Moḥammad, attended only by his uncle Al-'Abbās, repaired to the rendezvous, the first of the party. To secure the greater secrecy, the intended meeting had been kept profoundly hidden even from his own followers at Mecca.[1] Al-'Abbās, the wealthiest of the sons of 'Abd al-Muṭṭalib, was weak in character, and ordinarily sailed with wind and tide. He was not a convert; but near relationship, and the close community of interest created by three years' confinement with Moḥammad and his followers in the isolated quarter of Abu Ṭālib, rendered him sufficiently trustworthy on the present occasion.

Joined by the Medīna converts

They had not long to wait. Soon the converts from Medīna, singly and by twos and threes, were descried through the moonlight moving stealthily along the stony valley and barren rocks towards the spot. They were 73 in all (62 of the Khazraj, 11 of the Aus) with two women, and included the twelve converts who had before met the Prophet there. When all were seated, Al-'Abbās, in a low voice, broke silence by a speech something to this effect:—Ye men of the KHAZRAJ![2] This my kinsman dwelleth amongst us in honour and in safety. His clan will defend him—both those that are converts, and those that still hold to their ancestral faith; defend him to the last. But he preferreth to seek protection from you. Wherefore, ye Khazrajites, consider the matter well, and count the cost. If ye be resolved, and are able to defend him, then give the pledge. But if you doubt your ability, at once abandon the design.'

Speech of Al-'Abbās;

and of Al-Barā

Then spoke Al-Barā, an aged chief: 'We have listened to thy words. Our resolution is unshaken. Our lives are at the Prophet's service. It is now for *him* to speak.'

Address of Moḥammad

Moḥammad began, as was his wont, by reciting passages

[1] Or if they were admitted to the secret, they were instructed not to be present, the less to excite suspicion. Even Muṣ'ab appears not to have accompanied the Medīna converts; for we are told that 'there was no one with Moḥammad besides Al-'Abbās.'

[2] The people of Medīna, both of the Aus and Khazraj tribes, used to be addressed collectively as Al-Khazraj.

from the Ḳor'ān; he invited all present to the service of God, and dwelt upon the claims and blessings of Islām; then coming to the business of the night, he ended by saying that he should be content if the strangers pledged themselves to defend him as they would defend their wives and children. At once, from every quarter, arose a confused, tumultuous noise; it was the eager voices of the 'Seventy' testifying their readiness to take the pledge, and protesting that they would receive and defend the Prophet even at the cost of life and property. Then Al-'Abbās, holding his nephew's hand, called aloud: 'Hush! There may be spies abroad. Let your men of years stand forth, and speak on your behalf. Of a truth, we are fearful for your safety if our people should discover us. Then when you have plighted your faith depart silently to your camp.' So their chief men stood forth. Then said Al-Barā: 'Stretch out thy hand, O Moḥammad!' He stretched it out; and Al-Barā struck his hand thereon, as the manner was in taking oath of fealty. The Seventy came forward one by one, and did the same.[1] Then Moḥammad named twelve of the chief men, and said: *Moses chose from amongst his people twelve leaders. Thus shall ye be the leaders and sureties for the rest, even as the apostles of Jesus were; and I am the surety for my people.* They answered, 'Be it so.'[2]

Second pledge of Al-'Aḳaba

At this moment the voice of one crying aloud, a straggler perchance, searching for his company, was heard at hand. Excited fancy conjured up a Ḳoreishite if not an infernal spy.[3] Moḥammad gave command, and the assembly dispers-

[1] The women repeated only the words of the pledge taken by the Twelve in the former year. Moḥammad never took women by the hand on such an occasion; they used to step forward and recite the prescribed words, and then he would say, 'Go: you have pledged yourselves.'

Al-Barā, who bore here so conspicuous a part, died the following month. He was the first over whose grave Moḥammad prayed in the formula usual afterwards: *O Lord, pardon Him! Be merciful unto him! Be reconciled unto him! and verily thou art reconciled.*

[2] *Naḳīb*, 'Leader,' is the term which ever after honourably marked the Twelve. Four were of the number who had met Moḥammad here before. Three were of the Aus tribes; the rest, Khazrajites. Several are mentioned as able to *write* Arabic, and as *Kāmil* (perfect), *i.e.* expert in writing, archery, and swimming.

[3] We are told that when the ceremony was ended, the devil called out with a loud voice: *Ye people of Mecca! Have ye no concern for Moḥammad and his renegades? They have counselled war against you.*

ing hurried back to their several halting places. And so ended the memorable night of the SECOND PLEDGE OF THE 'AḲABA.[1]

Koreish challenge the Medīna chiefs

So large a gathering could not be held close by Mina without rumours reaching the Ḳoreish enough to rouse suspicion. It was notorious that great numbers at Medīna had begun to embrace the doctrines of Moḥammad. The clandestine meeting must have been on his behalf; and as such, an unwarrantable interference in the domestic affairs of Mecca; it was virtually a hostile movement. Accordingly, next morning the chief men of the Ḳoreish repaired to the Medīna encampment, stated their suspicions, and complained of unfriendly conduct at the hand of a tribe with whom, of all tribes in Arabia, it would grieve them most to be at war. The converts glanced at each other, and held their peace.[2] The rest of the pilgrims from Medīna, ignorant of their comrades' proceedings, protested that the people of Mecca had been misinformed, and that the report was without foundation. Their chief, 'Abdallah ibn Obei, assured the visitors that none of his people would have ventured on such a step without consulting him. Ḳoreish were satisfied, and took their leave.

And again, 'When we had pledged ourselves to the Prophet, Satan called out with a piercing cry, such as I never heard before: *Oh ye that are encamped round about! Have ye no care for* MUDHAMMAM' (the 'blamed,' the antithesis of Moḥammad the 'praised') '*and the renegades that are with him? They have resolved on war with you.* Then said Moḥammad: "That is the demon of Al-'Aḳaba; the son of the devil. Hearest thou not, enemy of God? Verily I will ease me of thee!"' So also, at the battle of Oḥod, the voice which cried 'Moḥammad is fallen' was that of 'the demon of Al-'Aḳaba, namely, the devil.'

[1] Ibn Hishām, pp. 196-200.

[2] A story is told by Ka'b, one of the Seventy, that at this moment, to divert attention, he pointed to a new pair of shoes which a Ḳoreishite chief, had on, and said to one of his friends, 'Why couldst not thou, *our* chief, wear a pair of new shoes like this Ḳoreishite chief?' The latter, taking off the shoes, threw them at Ka'b, saying: 'Put them on thyself.' His friend said: 'Tush! give back the shoes.' Ka'b refused; the Ḳoreishite chief then tried to snatch them from him. A commotion ensued, which was just what Ka'b desired, as it served to cover the awkward situation of the Medīna converts. Such tales of service to the cause of Islām were plentifully fabricated in the earliest times, and, though deserving little credit, are sometimes useful as illustrating the course of events.

They pursue the Medīna caravan,

Shortly after, the vast concourse at Mina broke up. The numerous caravans prepared for their journey, and took each its homeward course. The Medīna party had already set out, when the Ḳoreish having inquired into the midnight assembly (which Moḥammad hardly cared to keep secret now) found, to their confusion, that not only had it really taken place, but that far larger numbers than they suspected had pledged themselves to the defence of Moḥammad. Foiled and exasperated, they pursued the Medīna caravan in the hope that they might lay hands on some of the delinquents; but, though they scoured the roads leading to Medīna, they fell in with only two. Of these one escaped. The other, Sa'd ibn 'Obāda, they seized and, tying his hands behind his back, dragged him by his long hair back to Mecca. There he would, no doubt, have suffered further maltreatment, had he not been able to claim protection from certain Ḳoreishite chiefs to whom at Medīna he had rendered service. He was released, and rejoined the caravan just as his friends were about to return in search of him.

and maltreat one of the converts

Ḳoreish, enraged, recommence persecution;

It soon became evident that, in consequence of the Pledge of the 'Aḳaba, Moḥammad and his followers contemplated an early flight. The prospect of such a movement, which would remove their opponents entirely out of reach, and plant them in an asylum where they might securely work out their machinations and as opportunity offered take an ample revenge, at first kindled the wrath of Ḳoreish. They renewed their persecution; and, wherever they had the power, sought either to force the confessors to recant, or by confinement prevent their escape.[1] Such severities, or the dread of them (for the Muslims were conscious that they had now seriously compromised their loyalty as citizens of Mecca), hastened the crisis. And, indeed, when Moḥammad had

and thus precipitate departure of converts

[1] The two things would react on one another; the persecution hastening the departure of the converts, and each fresh departure irritating Ḳoreish to greater cruelty. Aṭ-Ṭabari says: 'There were two occasions on which persecution raged the hottest; *first*, the period preceding the emigration to Abyssinia; *second*, that following the second pledge of the 'Aḳaba.' There is reason, however, to suspect that, had the persecution been as bad as is spoken of, we should have had more frequent notices of it. Yet, excepting the imprisonment or surveillance of a few waverers, we have no detail of any injuries or sufferings inflicted on this occasion by Ḳoreish.

once resolved upon a general emigration, there was no advantage from a protracted residence among his enemies. It was therefore but a few days after the 'Second pledge of the 'Aḳaba,' that Moḥammad gave command to his followers, saying: *Depart unto Medīna; for the Lord hath verily given unto you brethren in that city, and a home in which ye may find refuge.*[1] So they made preparation, chose companions for the journey, and set out in parties secretly. Such as had the means rode two and two upon camels; the rest walked on foot.

Moḥammad gives command to emigrate to Medīna

Persecution and artifice caused a few to fall away from the faith. An example will suffice. 'Omar had arranged a rendezvous with 'Aiyāsh, son of Abu Rabī'a, and a friend, at a spot in the environs of Mecca whence they were to set out for Medīna. The friend was held back by his family, and relapsed for a time into idolatry. 'Thus I, and 'Aiyāsh,' says 'Omar, 'started alone, and journeyed to Ḳobā, a suburb of Medīna, where we alighted, and were hospitably received at the house of Rifā'a. But his half-brothers Abu Jahl and Al-Ḥārith[2] followed 'Aiyāsh to Medīna, and told him that his mother had vowed she would retire beneath no shade, nor suffer a comb or any oil to touch her hair, until she saw his face again. Then I cautioned him (continues 'Omar), saying: "By the Lord! they only desire to tempt thee from thy faith. Thy mother will soon relax her vow. Beware, 'Aiyāsh! return not nigh to Mecca." But he replied: "Nay, I will not recant. But I have property at Mecca. I will go and fetch it, and it will strengthen me. And I will also release my mother from her vow." Seeing that he was not to be diverted from his purpose, I gave him a swift camel and bade him, if he suspected treachery, to save himself thereon. So when the party alighted at a certain place, his companions

Some fall away

Story of 'Aiyāṣh

[1] Moḥammad, we are told, saw in a dream the place of emigration, 'a saline plain, with palm trees, between two hills.' He waited some days, uncertain where this might be, and then went forth joyously to his followers, saying: 'Now have I been made acquainted with the place appointed for your emigration. It is *Yathrib.* Whoso desireth let him emigrate thither.' Ibn Sa'd, p. 152. Long before this, however, he had made up his mind where he was going. The story probably grew out of the idea that Moḥammad must have had a special and divine command for so important a step as that of emigration to Medīna.

[2] They were all three sons of Asmā of Temīm.

seized him suddenly, and bound him with cords; and, as they carried him into Mecca in broad daylight, they exclaimed: *Even thus, ye men of Mecca, should ye treat your foolish ones!* Then they kept him in durance.'[1]

The emigration, April A.D. 622, continues for two months

Two or three weeks after the Pledge of the 'Aḳaba, that is, about the beginning of Moḥarram, the emigration commenced. Medīna lies some 180 miles north of Mecca, and the journey is accomplished by the pilgrim caravans in eleven days, or if pressed for time, in ten.[2] Within two months nearly all the followers of Moḥammad, excepting the few detained in confinement or unable to escape from slavery, had migrated with their families to their new abode. They numbered between one and two hundred souls.[3] They were welcomed with cordial and even eager hospitality by their brethren at Medīna, who vied with one another for the honour of receiving them into their homes, and supplying their domestic wants.

Ḳoreish paralysed by the sudden movement

Ḳoreish were paralysed by a movement so carefully planned, and put into such speedy execution. They looked on in amazement, as families silently disappeared, and house after house was abandoned. One or two quarters of the city were entirely deserted, and the doors of the dwelling-houses

[1] Ibn Hishām, p. 319 f. 'Aiyāsh under such treatment relapsed into idolatry. 'Omar says that until Sūra xxxix. 54 was revealed, it was thought that no apostate could be saved. When that passage appeared, he copied it out and sent it to 'Aiyāsh at Mecca; 'Aiyāsh on this took courage, and forthwith mounted his camel for Medīna. The verse is as follows: 'Say;—O my servants who have transgressed against your own souls, despair not of the mercy of God; for God forgiveth sins wholly: verily He is gracious and merciful.'—Ibn Hishām, p. 320.

[2] *Burckhardt.* The *Ṭaiyāra* or 'Flying Caravan' goes in less time. 'It is a dromedary caravan, in which each person carries only his saddle bags. It usually descends (from Medīna) by the road called El Khabṭ, and makes Mecca on the *fifth* day.' The stages by the Nejd, or eastern route, travelled by Burton, are given as eleven, and the distance estimated at 248 miles.

[3] We have no exact statement of the numbers of those who emigrated before Moḥammad himself left Mecca. Eighteen months later, at the battle of Bedr (when every emigrant but a very few unavoidably detained was present), Moḥammad had 314 fighting-men, of whom *eighty-three* were emigrants from Mecca. A few of these may have joined Moḥammad after he reached Medīna; and we shall probably not err in making the whole number who emigrated *at first*, including women and children, about 150.

left locked.[1] There was here a determination and self-sacrifice on which Ḳoreish had hardly calculated. But even if they had foreseen and resolved to oppose the emigration, it would have been difficult to prevent it. The number of independent clans and powerful families stood in the way of combined action. Here and there a slave or helpless dependent might be intimidated or held back; but in no other case was there the right to interfere with private choice or family counsel; and the least show of violence might have roused a host of champions to avenge the insulted honour of their tribe.

Moḥammad, Abu Bekr, and 'Alī left behind

At last Moḥammad and Abu Bekr with their families, including 'Alī, now a youth of about twenty years of age, were the only believers left (excepting those unwillingly detained) at Mecca. Abu Bekr was ambitious of being the companion of the Prophet in his flight; and daily urged him to depart. But Moḥammad told him that 'his time was not yet come: the Lord had not as yet given him the command to emigrate.' Perhaps he was deferring his departure until he could receive assurance from Medīna that the arrangements for his reception were secure, and that his adherents there were not only ready, but able in the face of any opposition, to execute their engagement for his defence.[2] Or, there may have been the more generous desire to see all his followers safely away from Mecca before he himself fled for refuge to Medīna. Might he even be waiting with the vague surmise

[1] 'The Beni Ghanam emigrated in a body, men, women, and children, and left their houses locked: not a soul was to be seen in the quarters of the Beni Ghanam, Abu'l-Bukeir, and Maẓ'ūn.'

''Otba, Al-'Abbās, and Abu Jahl passed by the dwelling-place of the Beni Jaḥsh, and the doors were locked, and the houses deserted. 'Otba sighed heavily, and said: "Every house, even if its peace be lengthened, at the last a bitter wind will reach it. The quarter of the Beni Jaḥsh is left without an inhabitant! This is the work of our pestilent Nephew, who hath dispersed our assemblies, ruined our affairs, and made a split amongst us."'—Ibn Hishām, p. 317.

[2] During the two months elapsing between the Pledge of the 'Aḳaba and Moḥammad's departure, he was kept informed of what was going on at Medīna. During this interval, some of the Medīna converts revisited Mecca, with the view, no doubt, of making further arrangements with Moḥammad. These Medīna converts had thus the merit of being not only 'Anṣār,' *i.e. Helpers* at Medīna, but also *Refugees*, as having in a sense also emigrated from Mecca when they returned to Medīna.

that divine retribution, as already threatened, was about to descend on the unbelieving city, in which peradventure even ten righteous men could not now be found? Meanwhile Abu Bekr made preparations for the journey. In anticipation of the emergency, he had already purchased for 800 pieces two swift camels, which were now tied up and highly fed in the yard of his house. A guide, accustomed to the devious tracks and byways of the Medīna route, was hired, and the camels were committed to his custody.[1]

Preparations of Abu Bekr

Council of Ḳoreish

Ḳoreish were perplexed at the course Moḥammad was taking. They had expected him to emigrate with his people; and perhaps half rejoiced at the prospect of being rid of their enemy. By remaining almost solitary behind, he seemed by his very loneliness to challenge and defy attack. What might the motive be for this strange procedure? The chief men assembled to deliberate on what might be their wisest course. Should they imprison him? his followers would come to his rescue. Should they forcibly expel him? he might agitate his cause among the tribes of Arabia, and readily lure adherents by the prospect of supremacy at Mecca. Should they assassinate him? the Beni Hāshim would exact an unrelenting penalty for their kinsman's life. But what if representatives from every house, including that of Hāshim, were each to plunge his sword into the Prophet—would the Hāshimites dare to wage a mortal feud with the whole body of Ḳoreish thus implicated in the murder? Even then there would remain the followers at Medīna, whose revenge on account of their Master's blood would surely be fierce and ruthless. Assassination by an unknown hand on the road to Medīna might prove the safest course; but there the chances of escape would preponderate. At last they resolved that a deputation should proceed to the house of Moḥammad.

Their deliberations

[1] Aṭ-Ṭabari, i. 1227 ff.; Ibn Hishām, p. 323. The guide was 'Abdallah ibn Arḳaṭ [or Al-Oreiḳiṭ]. His mother was a Ḳoreishite; his father was from a tribe affiliated to Ḳoreish. He was still an idolater; and Al-Wāḳidi (anticipating the era when war was waged against all idolaters) adds, 'but Moḥammad and Abu Bekr had given him quarter, or pledge of protection'; as if he had required any protection from the fugitives whom he was guiding! The expression illustrates the proleptic way in which subsequent principles and events were anticipated, insensibly throwing back their light and colour upon the tissue of tradition.

What was the decision as to their future course of action, what the object even of the present deputation, it is impossible amid the marvels of tradition to conclude. There is little reason to believe that it was assassination, although we are told that such was determined upon at the instigation of Abu Jahl, supported by Satan, who, in the person of an old man from Nejd shrouded in a mantle, joined the council.[1] Moḥammad himself refers in the Ḳor'ān to the designs of his enemies in these indecisive terms: *And call to mind when the Unbelievers plotted against thee, that they might detain thee, or slay thee, or expel thee. Yea, they plotted; but God plotted likewise. And God is the best of plotters.* Assuredly had assassination been the sentence, and its immediate execution ordered by the council, Moḥammad would not have been slow to indicate the fact in clearer language than these alternative expressions. A resolution so fatal would unquestionably have been dwelt upon at length both in the Ḳor'ān and in tradition, and have been produced in justifica-

Chiefs deputed to visit Moḥammad

Sūra viii. 30

[1] The following is the narrative:—Ḳoreish, irritated at the warm reception of the converts at Medīna, held a council. Satan, in the shape of an old man shrouded in a cloak, stood at the door saying that he was a Sheikh from Nejd, who had heard of their weighty consultation, and had come if haply he might help them to a right decision; so they invited him to enter. One proposed to imprison, another to expel, Moḥammad. The old man from Nejd warmly opposed both suggestions. Then said Abu Jahl: 'Let us choose one courageous man from every family of Ḳoreish, and place in the hands of each a sharp sword, then let the whole slay him with the stroke of one man; so his blood will be divided amongst all our families, and the relatives of Moḥammad will not know how to avenge it.' The old man of Nejd applauded the scheme, saying: 'May God reward this man; this is the right advice and none other.' So they separated, having agreed upon it. Gabriel forthwith apprised Moḥammad of the design, who arose and made 'Alī lie down upon his bed. The murderous party came at dusk, and lay in wait about the house. Moḥammad went forth, and casting a handful of dust at them, recited the first eight verses of Sūra xxxvi., ending with the words, *and We have covered them so that they shall not see.* Thus he departed without their knowing what passed; and they continued to watch, some say till morning, thinking that the figure on the bed was Moḥammad. As light dawned, they found out their mistake and saw that it was 'Alī. Others say they watched till some one passed and told them that Moḥammad had left, when they arose in confusion and shook from their heads the dust which Moḥammad had cast upon them.—Ibn Hishām, p. 324 f.

tion of subsequent hostilities. Had such been the decision, it *must* sooner or later have reached the ears of Moḥammad, and so have found its way into the Ḳor'ān.

Moḥammad and Abu Bekr escape to the cave Thaur

Whatever the object of the visit, Moḥammad received previous notice of it, and anticipated the danger by stealing away from his house.[1] There he left 'Alī; around whom, that the suspicions of neighbours might not be aroused, he threw his own red mantle, and left him lying thus upon his bed. He himself went straightway to the house of Abu Bekr, and after a short consultation matured the plan for immediate flight. Abu Bekr shed tears of joy; the hour for emigration had at last arrived, and he was to be the companion of the Prophet's journey. After a few hasty preparations, among which Abu Bekr did not forget to secure his remaining funds, they crept in the shade of evening through a back window, and escaped unobserved from the southern suburb. Pursuing their way south, and clambering in the dark up the bare and rugged ascent, they reached at last the lofty peak of mount Thaur, distant about an hour and a half from the city, and took refuge in a cavern near its summit.[2] Here they rested in security, for the attention of their adversaries would first be fixed upon the pathways north of Mecca on the Medīna route.

The cave referred to in the Ḳor'ān

Several years after, Moḥammad thus alludes in the

1 Ibn Sa'd, p. 153 ff.

2 Ibn Hishām, p. 328 f.; Aṭ-Ṭabari, i. 1236. The following is from Burckhardt:—'JEBEL THOR. About an hour and a half south of Mecca, to the left of the road to the village of Hosseynye, is a lofty mountain of this name, higher it is said than Djebel Nur. On the summit of it is a cavern, in which Moḥammad and his friend Abu Bekr took refuge from the Mekkawys before he fled to Medīna.' But he did not visit the spot, nor did 'Alī Bey.

In the Begum of Bhopal's *Pilgrimage to Mecca* (1870) the mountain is described. The pathway from Mecca is 'excessively rugged and difficult,' the pilgrim being obliged sometimes to crawl over the great rocks on his hands and knees. The entrance to the cave is still preserved, in what is believed to be its original state; and the pilgrim acquires merit by forcing himself with difficulty, as the Prophet must have done, through the aperture, which is, 'not more than 1½ span in breadth'; but a wide passage has been opened out at the other end of the cave. The hills are wild and bare; huge masses of rock lie scattered about; and nothing green is in sight, save occasionally wild thorny bushes, such as the Indian 'gookru'

Ḳor'ān to the position of himself and his friend in the cave of mount Thaur :—

If ye will not assist the Prophet, verily GOD assisted him aforetime when the Unbelievers cast him forth, in the company of a Second only; when they two were in the cave alone, when the Prophet said unto his companion, *Be not cast down, for verily God is with us.* And God caused to descend tranquillity[1] upon him, and strengthened him with hosts which ye saw not, and made the word of the Unbelievers to be abased; and the word of the Lord, that is exalted, for GOD is mighty and wise. Sūra ix. 40

Abu Bekr 'the Second of the two'

The 'sole companion,' or in Arabic phraseology *The Second of the Two*, became one of Abu Bekr's most honoured titles. Ḥassān, the contemporary poet of Medīna, thus sings of him :—

And the Second of the two in the glorious Cave, while the foes were searching around, and they two had ascended the mountain;
And the Prophet of the Lord, they well knew, loved him,—more than all the world; he held no one equal unto him.[2]

Legends regarding cave

Legends cluster around the cave. A spider wove its web across the entrance. Branches sprouted, covering it in on every side. Wild pigeons settled on the trees to divert attention, and so forth. Whatever may have been the real peril, Moḥammad and his companion felt it, no doubt, to be a time of jeopardy. Glancing upwards at a crevice through which the morning light began to break, Abu Bekr whispered: 'What if one were to look through the chink, and see us underneath his very feet.' '*Think not thus, Abu Bekr!*' said the Prophet; 'WE ARE TWO, BUT GOD IS IN THE MIDST A THIRD.'[3]

Moḥammad's trust

[1] *Sekīnah*, the 'Shekinah' of the Jews; frequently used in the Ḳor'ān in this sense.

[2] On Moḥammad asking Ḥassān whether he had composed any poetry regarding Abu Bekr, the poet answered that he had, and at Moḥammad's request repeated the lines in the text. Moḥammad was amused, and laughed so heartily as even to show his back teeth. 'Thou hast spoken truly, O Ḥassān,' he said. 'It is just as thou hast said.'

[3] The crowd of miracles that cluster about the cave are so well known as hardly to need repetition here. It is interesting, however, to note how far they are related by our early authorities. Al-Wāḳidi says that after Moḥammad and Abu Bekr entered, a spider came and wove her webs over the mouth of the cave. Ḳoreish hotly searched after Moḥammad in all directions, till they came up to the entrance. When they looked, they said: *Spiders' webs are over it from the birth of Moḥammad;* and

Food and intelligence conveyed to them

'Amir ibn Fuheira, while in company with other shepherds of Mecca tending his master Abu Bekr's flock, stole away unobserved every evening with a few goats to the cave and furnished its inmates with a plentiful supply of milk. 'Abdallah, Abu Bekr's son, in the same manner at night brought them food cooked by his sister Asmā. It was his business also to watch by day the progress of events and of opinion at Mecca, and to report the result at night.

Search after Moḥammad

The city was in a ferment when the disappearance of Moḥammad was first noised abroad. The chief men of Ḳoreish went to his house, and finding 'Alī there, asked where his cousin was. 'I have no knowledge of him,' replied 'Alī; 'am I his keeper? Ye bade him go, and he hath gone.' Then they repaired to Abu Bekr's house and questioned his daughter Asmā.[1] Failing to elicit from her any information, they sent scouts in all directions, with the view of gaining a clue to the track and destination of the Prophet, if not with less innocent instructions. But the precautions of Moḥammad and Abu Bekr rendered it a fruitless search. One by one the emissaries returned with no trace of the fugitives; and at last it was believed that, having gained a fair start, they had outstripped pursuit. The people soon reconciled themselves to the idea. They even breathed more freely now that their troubler was gone. The city again was still.

Moḥammad and Abu Bekr resolve to quit the cave

On the third night, the report of 'Abdallah satisfied the

so they turned back. Again: 'God commanded a tree and a spider to cover the Prophet, and two wild pigeons to perch at the entrance of the cave. When a company of two men from each clan of Ḳoreish, armed with swords, pursuing the Prophet, were now close to him, the foremost saw the pigeons, and returned to his companions, saying that he was sure from this that nobody was in the cave. The Prophet, hearing his words, blessed the pigeons, and made them sacred ever after in the Holy territory, where it is sacrilege to harm them.

There are other miraculous stories, but of somewhat later growth, regarding Abu Bekr putting his hand into the crevices of the cave to remove the snakes that might be lurking there, and being unharmed by their venomous bites.

[1] Asmā relates that, after the Prophet had gone, a company of Ḳoreish, with Abu Jahl, came to her house. As they stood at the door, she went forth to them. 'Where is thy father?' said they. 'Truly I know not where he is,' she replied. Upon which Abu Jahl, who was a bad and impudent man, slapped her on the face with such force that one of her ear-rings dropped.'—Ibn Hishām, p. 329.

refugees that search had ceased, and busy curiosity relaxed. The opportunity was come. They could slip away unobserved now, and the sooner the better. Longer delay might excite suspicion, and the visits of 'Abdallah and Ibn Fuheira attract attention to the cave. The roads were clear; they might leave at once fearless of pursuit, and travel without apprehension of arrow or dagger from the wayside enemy. 'Abdallah therefore received commission to have all things ready for the following evening. The guide was instructed to wander about with the two camels near the summit of mount Thaur. Asmā prepared food for the journey, and in the dusk brought it in a wallet to the cave. In the hurry of the moment, she had forgotten the thong for fastening it. So, tearing her girdle in two, with one strip she closed the wallet, and with the other bound it to the camel's saddle. From this incident Asmā is honourably known in Islām as 'She of the two shreds.'[1] Abu Bekr, not forgetful of his money, had safely secreted among his other property a purse of between five and six thousand pieces.

Preparations for the journey

The camels were now ready. Moḥammad mounted the swifter of the two, Al-Ḳaṣwā, thenceforward his favourite, with the guide; and Abu Bekr having taken his servant Ibn Fuheira behind him on the other, they started. Descending mount Thaur, and leaving the lower quarter of Mecca a little to the right, they struck off by a track considerably to the left of the common road; and, hurrying westward, soon gained the vicinity of the seashore nearly opposite 'Osfān. The day of the flight was the 4th Rabī'I. of the first year of the Hijra,[2] or, by the calculations of M. Caussin de

They start for Medīna June 20, A.D. 622;

[1] There is a curious tradition that Abu Bekr's father, Abu Ḳohāfa, now so old that he could hardly see, visited his grand-daughters (Asmā and 'Ā'isha) after Abu Bekr as he thought had departed, to condole with them on being left without means, and bringing money with him to help them. To comfort the old man, Asmā placed pebbles in a recess and, covering them with a cloth, put his hands upon them to make him believe that it was his son's money which he had left for their support; so the old man went away happy.—Ibn Hishām, p. 230 f.

Asmā was the mother of Ibn az-Zubeir, and lived to be over 100. See the touching scene with her son before he was killed in battle, A.H. 73.—*The Caliphate*, p. 340.

[2] *Hijra*, 'emigration.' Though referring *par excellence* to the flight of the Prophet, it is also applicable to all his followers who emigrated to Medīna *prior to the capture of Mecca;* and they are hence called

Perceval, June 20, A.D. 622; and the 53rd year of the Prophet's life.

And safely escape pursuit

By daybreak they reached a Bedawi encampment, where an Arab widow sat at her tent-door with viands spread out for any chance traveller that might pass that way. Fatigued and thirsty, for it was now the hottest season of the year, they refreshed themselves with the food and draughts of milk offered by the lady. During the heat of the day, they rested at Ḳodeid. In the evening, being now as they deemed at a safe enough distance, they fell into the common road. But they had not gone far when they met one of the mounted scouts returning from his search. Surāḳa (for that was his name), seeing that he had small chance single-handed of success against his four opponents, offered no opposition. but on the contrary pledged his word that, if permitted to depart in peace, he would not reveal that he had met them. The party proceeded. The Prophet of Arabia was safe.[1]

Tidings reach Mecca of their flight

The first tidings that reached Mecca of the course actually taken by Moḥammad were brought, two or three days after his flight, by a traveller from the Bedawi camp at which he had rested. It was now certain, from his passing there, that he was bound for Medīna.

'Alī quits for Medīna

'Alī remained three days at Mecca after the departure of Moḥammad, appearing every day in public, for the purpose of restoring the property placed by various persons in the Prophet's trust. He met with no opposition or annoyance, and then leisurely took his departure for Medīna.

Families of Moḥammad and Abu Bekr unmolested at Mecca

The families of Moḥammad and of Abu Bekr were equally unmolested. Zeinab continued for a time to dwell at Mecca with her unconverted husband. Roḳeiya had already gone with 'Othmān to Medīna. The Prophet's other two daughters, Um Kulthūm and Fāṭima, with his wife Sauda, were for some weeks left behind at Mecca.[2] 'Ā'isha his bride, yet

Muhājirīn, *i.e.* the Emigrants, or Refugees. We have seen that they commenced to emigrate from the beginning of Moḥarram (the first month of the Era as subsequently settled in 'Omar's Caliphate) two months before.

[1] Ibn Hishām, p. 231 f.

[2] Um Kulthūm had been married to one of the sons of Abu Lahab, but was now living in her father's house. Zeinab's husband, Abu'l-'Āṣ, was still an unbeliever, and is said to have kept her back at Mecca in confinement. But subsequent events show that there was a strong mutual attachment.

a child, with the rest of Abu Bekr's family and several other women, likewise remained in Mecca for a time.

Forbearance of Ḳoreish

Moḥammad and Abu Bekr trusted their respective clans to protect their families from insult. But no insult or annoyance was offered by Ḳoreish, nor was any attempt made to detain them; although it was not unreasonable that they should have been detained as hostages against any offensive movement from Medīna. Hence we may, perhaps, be led to doubt the intensity of the hatred and cruelty which the strong colouring of tradition at this period attributes to Ḳoreish.

Thus ends the first great stage of the Prophet's life. The next scene opens at Medīna.

Relation of Islām to Christianity. Teaching of Moḥammad during the last three Years at Mecca. Effect produced by his Preaching

Sūras revealed during last three years at Mecca

During the last three years of Moḥammad's residence at Mecca about thirty new Sūras appeared. Some of these are very long, extending over as many as fifteen to twenty pages; and, being in part composite, contain many later passages subsequently added to them at Medīna. Before proceeding to a brief description of these Sūras and the teaching they contain, I propose to pause for a little and describe the relation of Islām to Christianity.

Relation of Islām to Christianity

It has been already said that in the chapters revealed before the tenth year of the Prophet's ministry we find few notices of the Gospels and the Christian faith. In the Sūras, however, of the following three years, frequent mention of Christianity begins to appear. Indeed, the approach now made by Moḥammad never afterwards became closer, nor did his acquaintance with it enlarge, or his views materially alter. It may, therefore, be not inappropriate here to review, from first to last, the relation of Islām to Christianity.

Notices of Christianity in Ḳor'ān few and scattered

Though Christians and the Messiah are frequently referred to throughout the Ḳor'ān by name, yet there are but few sketches at any length either of the substance or doctrines of their Scriptures; so few, indeed, that it will be possible (and I doubt not to the reader interesting) to enumerate them all and give extracts of their strange and

Earliest account of the Gospel narrative

often fabulous details. The following, which is the fullest and earliest account of the Gospel narrative, was given by Moḥammad shortly after his return from Aṭ-Ṭā'if. From its subject the Sūra is entitled *Maryam* or MARY, and opens thus:—

Sura xix. 1 ff.

A Commemoration of the mercy of the Lord to his servant ZACHARIAS;—
When he called upon his Lord with a secret invocation,
He said;—O Lord! as for me, my bones are decrepit, and my head white with hoar hair.
And I have never prayed unto thee, O Lord! unheard.
Verily, I fear my kinsmen after me; and my wife is barren.
Wherefore grant unto me from thyself a successor;
Who shall be my heir, and an heir of the family of Jacob; and make him, O Lord! well pleasing.
O ZACHARIAS! We bring thee good tidings of a son, whose name shall be John;
WE have not made any to be called by that name before.
He said;—O Lord! whence shall there be a son unto me, since my wife is barren, and I truly have reached the imbecility of old age?
The Angel said:—So shall it be. Thus saith thy Lord,—It is easy unto me; for verily I created thee heretofore when thou wast nothing.
He said;—Lord! give me a sign. The Angel said;—This is thy sign; thou shalt not speak unto any for three nights, though sound in health.
And he went forth unto his people from the chamber, and he motioned unto them that they should praise God morning and evening.
O John! Take the Book (of the Law) with power; and WE gave him wisdom as a child,
And compassion from us, and purity; and he was virtuous, and dutiful unto his parents; he was not overbearing nor rebellious.
Peace be on him the day he was born, and the day he shall die, and the day he shall be raised to life!
And in the Book make mention of Mary, when she withdrew from her people into an eastern place;
And took a curtain withal to hide herself from them.
And WE sent unto her OUR SPIRIT, and he appeared unto her a perfect man,
She said;—I seek refuge in the Merciful from thee, if thou fearest God!
He said;—Nay, verily, I am a messenger of thy Lord sent to give unto thee a virtuous son.
She said;—How shall there be to me a son, and a man hath not touched me, and I am not unchaste.
He said;—So shall it be. Thus saith thy Lord;—It is easy with me; and we shall make him a sign unto mankind, and a mercy from us, for it is a thing decreed.
And she conceived him, and withdrew with him (*in the womb*) unto a distant place.

And the pains of labour came upon her by the trunk of a palm tree;
She said,—Would that I had died before this, and been forgotten out of mind!
And there cried one from below her;—Grieve not!—verily thy Lord hath provided beneath thee a fountain:—
And shake unto thee the root of the palm tree; it will drop upon thee ripe dates, ready plucked.
Wherefore eat and drink, and be comforted; and if thou seest any man,
Say,—Verily I have vowed unto the Merciful a fast, and I will not speak to any man this day.
And she came with the child unto her people, carrying him. They said; O MARY! verily thou hast done a strange thing:
O sister of Aaron! thy father was not a wicked man, nor was thy mother unchaste.
And she motioned to the child. They said;—How shall we speak with him that is an infant in the cradle?
He (*the child*) said; Verily I am the servant of God; He hath given me the Book, and made me a Prophet;
And made me blessed wheresoever I may be, and hath commanded me (*to observe*) prayer and almsgiving while I remain alive;
And made me dutiful to my mother, and not overbearing nor wretched:—
Peace be on me the day I was born, and the day I shall die, and the day I shall be raised alive!
This is JESUS, the Word of truth, concerning whom they are in doubt.
It is not for God to take unto Him a Son:—glory be to Him!
When He hath decreed a matter, He only saith unto it BE, and it shall be.

The births of John and of Jesus are once again related, as well as the birth of the Virgin Mary, in a passage (Sūra iii. 31 ff.) delivered at Medīna only a few years before the death of Moḥammad, on the occasion of an embassy from the Christian tribe of Nejrān.

Another detailed account of Christ's birth

Of the *life* of Christ the statements are altogether poor and scant. The object of His mission to the Jews was to confirm their Scriptures, to modify and lighten some of the burdens of the Mosaical law, and to recall them to the service of God. His miracles are thus described:—

Statements regarding the life of Christ

God shall say;—O JESUS! Son of Mary! call to mind my grace given to thee and to thy MOTHER, when I strengthened thee with the HOLY SPIRIT, that thou shouldest speak with men in the cradle, and in after life;—and when I taught thee the Scripture and Wisdom, and the Law and the Gospel;—and when thou formedst of clay like unto the figure of a bird by My permission;—and thou blewest thereupon and it became a bird by My permission; and thou didst heal the blind and the leper by My permission;—and when thou didst raise the dead by My

Sūra v. 109 ff.

permission;[1] and when I held back the children of Israel from thee at the time thou shewedst unto them evident signs, and the unbelievers among them said, Verily this is nought but manifest sorcery. . . .

When the Apostles of JESUS said,—O JESUS, Son of MARY! is thy Lord able to cause a Table to descend upon us from Heaven? He said,—Fear God; if ye be faithful. They said,—We desire that we may eat therefrom, and that our hearts be set at ease, and that we may know that thou verily hast spoken unto us the truth, and that we may be witnesses thereof. Then spake JESUS, Son of MARY,—O God our Lord! send down unto us a Table from Heaven, that it may be unto us a Feast day[2] unto the first of us and unto the last of us, and a sign from Thee; and nourish us, for Thou art the best of nourishers. And God said,—Verily I will send it down unto you; and whoever after that shall disbelieve amongst you; surely I will torment him with a torment, the like of which I shall not torment any other creature with.

And when God shall say,—O JESUS, Son of MARY! didst thou speak unto mankind saying,—Take me and my mother for two Gods besides the Lord? He shall say,—Glory be to Thee! it is not for me to say that which I know to be not the Truth; if I had said that, verily Thou wouldest have known it. Thou knowest that which is in me, but I know not what is in Thee; verily Thou art the Knower of secrets. I spake not unto them aught but what Thou commandedst me, saying—Worship God, my Lord and your Lord. . . .

Allusion to the Lord's Supper

This passage is remarkable as affording in the supernatural table which descended from heaven, a possible allusion, the only one traceable in the Ḳor'ān, to the Lord's Supper. The tale is probably founded on some misapprehended tradition regarding 'the *Table* of the Lord.'[3] It only remains to add that Jesus escaped the machinations of his enemies, and was taken up alive to heaven. In a passage aimed at his Jewish enemies, Moḥammad thus upbraids their rebellious forefathers:—

Jesus not crucified, but ascended to Heaven

Sūra iv. 155 ff.

. . . For their unbelief; and for that they have spoken against Mary a grievous calumny; and have said,—*Verily we have slain the Messiah,*

[1] These miracles are repeated in Sūra iii. 43, where Jesus is represented as adding: 'And I will tell unto you what ye eat, and that which ye store in your houses,' *i.e.* as a proof of his knowledge of the invisible.

[2] Or '*'īd*,' *i.e.* a religious festival recurring periodically, referring apparently to the institution of the Lord's Supper as a feast to be perpetually observed.

[3] The prolific fancy of the Traditionists and Commentators has created a host of miraculous accompaniments to this table:—fruit from the trees of Paradise, bread, meat, with fish which, though broiled, were still alive, and which for the convenience of the guests threw aside their scales and bones! The poor, the lame, and the wretched, were invited to the feast, which lasted forty days. The commentators probably confused the Lord's Supper with the feeding by Jesus of the multitudes.

JESUS, Son of MARY, the Apostle of God. And they slew him not, neither did they crucify him, but he was simulated (in the person of another) unto them. And verily they that have differed about him, are in doubt concerning this thing. They have no knowledge regarding it, but follow only a conjecture. And they slew him not, certainly. But God raised him up unto Himself; and God is the GLORIOUS, the WISE! And of the People of the Book shall every one believe in him before his death, and in the day of Judgment he will be a witness against them.[1]

If Jesus was worshipped, why not deities of Mecca?

In addressing the idolaters of Mecca, Moḥammad appealed to the ministry and preaching of Jesus and His rejection by His people, as he was wont to appeal to the history of other prophets, in support of his mission. His adversaries retorted that, if Jesus, who appeared in human form, was worshipped by his followers, there could be nothing absurd in their praying through images, the representatives of heavenly powers, to God. The reply was revealed thus:—

Moḥammad's reply that Jesus was but a servant. Sūra xliii. 57 ff.

When JESUS, Son of MARY, was proposed as an example, lo, thy people shouted at thee,
And said, What! Are our own gods better, or he?
They have proposed this unto thee only as a cause of dispute;
Yea, they are a contentious people!
Verily he was no other than a servant, to whom WE were gracious, and made him an example unto the children of Israel:—
(And if WE pleased WE could make from amongst yourselves Angels to succeed you upon earth:)
And verily he shall be for a sign of the last hour. Wherefore doubt not thereof, and follow Me; this is the right way.
And let not Satan mislead you, for he is your manifest enemy.

Denies divine Sonship of Jesus; and Trinity denied

This was in fact the only position which Moḥammad could consistently fall back upon. Some terms of veneration, in use among Christians, are indeed applied to Jesus, as 'the WORD of God,' and 'His SPIRIT which he breathed into Mary.' But the divine Sonship is steadfastly denied. The worship of Jesus by the Christians is placed in the same category as the supposed worship of Ezra by the Jews; and, in one place, the doctrine of the Trinity is expressly reprobated. It is a Medīna Sūra:—

Sūra iv. 169 f.

Ye people of the Book! Commit not extravagances in your religion; and speak not of God aught but the truth. For verily the Messiah,

[1] 'The People of the Book,' *i.e.* Jews as well as Christians. There is a passage (Sūra iii. 52) which would seem to imply the death of Jesus when on earth, but it is generally explained otherwise by the commentators. *Cf.* also Sūra xix. 34 above, p. 145.

JESUS, Son of MARY, is an Apostle of God, and His WORD which he placed in Mary, and a Spirit from him. Wherefore believe in God, and in the Apostles; and say not, *There are Three.* Refrain: it will be better for you. Verily the Lord is one God. Glory be to Him! far be it from Him, that there should be to Him a Son. To Him belongeth whatsoever is in the Heavens and in the earth; and He is a sufficient patron. The Messiah disdaineth not to be a servant of God; neither the Cherubim that draw nigh unto Him.

Sources of Christian information imperfect and defective

It may well be doubted whether Moḥammad ever had the means of knowing the real doctrines of Christianity. The few passing observations regarding our faith to be found in the Ḳor'ān commenced at a period when his system was already, in great part, matured; and they were founded on information meagre, fabulous, and crude. The whole of his historical knowledge[1] (for whatever he knew it was his practice to embody in his Revelation) is contained in the few extracts now before the reader; and this, apocryphal and scanty in itself—especially so when compared with his familiar knowledge of Jewish Scripture and tradition—shows that the sources from which he derived his Christian information were singularly barren and defective. The rite of baptism is not even alluded to; and, if there be an allusion to the Eucharist, we have seen it to be disfigured, and well nigh lost in fable. The doctrine of redemption through the death of Christ was apparently unknown (for if it had been known and rejected, it would doubtless, like other alleged errors, have been combated in the Ḳor'ān), and his very crucifixion denied. We do not find a single ceremony or doctrine of Islām in any degree moulded, or even tinged, by the peculiar tenets of Christianity; while, on the contrary, Judaism has given its colour to the whole system, and lent to it the shape and type, if not the actual substance, of many ordinances. But although Christianity is thus so remote from Islām as to have had practically no

Christianity had little real influence on Islām;

Yet theoretically stood equal if not superior to Judaism

1 The only trace of acquaintance with the period subsequent to the Ascension and the spread of Christianity is the story (Sūra xxxvi. 12 ff.) of the three Apostles (one of whom is supposed to have been Peter) who went to Antioch, and of a convert suffering martyrdom there. The tale of the seven Sleepers, who, with their dog, slumbered 309 years, and then awakening found to their astonishment the whole idolatrous world become Christian, can hardly come under this head. It will be found, with abundance of childish romance, in Sūra xviii. Both Sūras belong to the late Meccan period.

influence in the formation of its creed and ritual, yet in the *theory* of Moḥammad's system it occupies a place equal, if not superior, to that of Judaism. To understand this we must take a brief review of the development of the system itself.

Growth of Moḥammad's teaching

At the outset of his ministry Moḥammad professed no distinct relation with any previous religion, except perhaps with the purer element of Arabian worship said to have been derived from Abraham, though now grievously overlaid with idolatry and superstition. His mission was to recall the Arabs to the service of the true God and belief in 'the day of reckoning.'

Ḳor'ān at first held to be simply the auxiliary of previous Scriptures

As time went on, he gained some scant acquaintance with the Scriptures of the Jews and Christians, and the religion founded thereon. The new revelation for Arabia was now announced as concurrent with the previous 'Books.' The Ḳor'ān was described as being mainly an attestation, in the Arabic tongue and intended for the people of Mecca and its neighbourhood, of the preceding Scriptures. It was strictly auxiliary in its object and local in its action. From the attacks of his opponents, Moḥammad took shelter under the authority of the sacred writings of the Jews and Christians—an authority admitted in some measure even by his adversaries. When his own work was condemned as a 'forgery' or 'antiquated tale,' the most common and most effective retort was:—'Nay, but it is a confirmation of the preceding Revelation, and a warning in simple Arabic to the people of the land.' The number and the solemnity of such asservations secured the confidence or at least the neutrality, of both Jews and Christians (xlvi. 11, etc.).

But gradually acquires a superior and superseding character

But the teaching of Moḥammad could not stop here. Was he not an Apostle, equally inspired with his predecessors? Was he not foretold as the last of the prophets, by Moses in the Pentateuch, and in the Gospel by Jesus? and if so, would not the catholic faith as now moulded by him remain permanent to the end of time? These conclusions were fast ripening in the mind of Moḥammad; and their effect was to make the Ḳor'ān rise superior in authority over both the Old Testament and the New. Not that he ever held it to be superior *in kind* to either. All three—the Ḳor'ān, the Law, and the Gospel—are spoken of indifferently as 'the Word of God,' and the belief in them inculcated

As the latest revelation of God's will

equally on pain of everlasting punishment.[1] But the Ḳor'ān was the *latest* revelation; and, in so far as it pleased the Almighty to modify His preceding commands, it must be paramount.

I. Old Testament and Gospel enjoined on Jews and Christians respectively

In this latter phase again there are two stages. Moḥammad did not at once substitute his own Revelation for the previous Scriptures. The Jew was still to follow the Law; and in addition he was to believe also in the New Testament and in the mission of Jesus. The Christian was to hold fast by his Gospel. But both Jew and Christian were to admit, as co-ordinate with their own Prophets and Scriptures, the apostleship of Moḥammad and the authority of the Ḳor'ān. The necessity, indeed, of conforming to their respective Revelations is urged upon Jews and Christians in the strongest terms. The Jews of Medīna are repeatedly summoned 'to judge by the Book,' that is by the Old Testament; and are warned against the danger of accepting a part only of God's Word, and rejecting a part. The following passages inculcate a similar duty on both Jews and Christians:—

Sūra v. 72

SAY, Oh, ye people of the Book! ye do not stand upon any sure ground until ye set up both the Law[2] and the Gospel, as well as that which hath been (now) sent down unto you from your Lord (*i.e.* the Ḳor'ān).

Sūra v. 47 ff.

And how will they (the Jews of Medīna) make thee their judge, since they have already by them the Law, wherein is the command of God, and have not obeyed it! They will surely turn their backs after that; and they are not believers.

Verily WE have sent down the Old Testament, wherein are direction

---

[1] The New Testament is called in the Ḳor'ān *Injīl* (Evangelium), and described as a revelation *given by God to Jesus.* It is evident that by 'the Gospel' Moḥammad meant the sacred Scriptures in common use amongst the Christians of the day. He may have supposed that these Scriptures were 'given' to Jesus; or intended only that the doctrines of the Gospel were revealed by God to Jesus, and by him taught to the Apostles who afterwards recorded them. However this may be, the fact is in nowise affected, that Moḥammad, when he speaks of 'the Gospel' and 'the Book,' means the canon of Scripture at the time in use among the people of the Book, the perusal and observance of which is strictly and unconditionally enjoined upon the Christians of the day.

[2] 'The Taurāt,' which, as used in the Ḳor'ān, means either the Pentateuch or the entire Scriptures of the Old Testament. According to the context here, the latter is intended.

and light. The Prophets that professed the true faith judged the Jews thereby: and the Doctors and Priests did likewise, in accordance with the Book of God committed to their charge; and they were witnesses thereof. Wherefore fear not men, but fear me; and sell not the signs of God for a small price. AND WHOSOEVER DOTH NOT JUDGE BY THAT WHICH GOD HATH REVEALED, VERILY THEY ARE THE UNBELIEVERS (*Kāfirīn*). And WE have written therein for them;—Verily life for life, and eye for eye, and nose for nose, and ear for ear, tooth for tooth, and for wounding retaliation: and he that remitteth the same as alms, it is an atonement for him. AND WHOSOEVER JUDGETH NOT BY THAT WHICH GOD HATH REVEALED, THEY ARE THE TRANSGRESSORS.

And WE caused JESUS, the Son of MARY, to follow in their footsteps, attesting the Scripture, viz., the Law which preceded him. And We gave him the Gospel wherein are guidance and light, attesting the Law given before it, a direction and an admonition to the pious:—and that the people of the Gospel (Christians) might judge according to that which God hath revealed therein. AND WHOSOEVER DOTH NOT JUDGE ACCORDING TO THAT WHICH GOD HATH REVEALED, THEY ARE THE WICKED ONES.

And WE have revealed unto thee the Book of the Ḳor'ān in truth, attesting the Scripture which precedeth it; and a custodian (*or* witness) thereof. Wherefore judge between them in accordance with what God hath revealed, and follow not their vain desires away from that which hath been given unto thee.

To every one have WE given a law and a way. And if God had pleased, He had made you all one People. But (*He hath done otherwise*) that he might try you in that which He hath severally given unto you. Wherefore press forward in good works. Unto God shall ye all return, and He will declare unto you that concerning which ye disagree.

Judge therefore between them according to what God hath revealed, and follow not their desires, and beware of them lest they tempt thee aside from a part of that which God hath revealed unto thee.

Thus the former revelations were to be believed in collectively as the Word of God by all the faithful of whatever sect. The Old and New Testaments were further to be followed implicitly, the former by the Jews, the latter by the Christians, and both were to be observed by Moḥammad himself when determining their respective disputes. In contested and doubtful points, the Ḳor'ān was to be the conclusive oracle.

Grand catholic faith;—the faith of Abraham

In conformity with this expansive system, we find that at a period long anterior to the Hijra, Moḥammad propounded in the Ḳorān the doctrine that to every people a prophet had been sent, so that a grand catholic faith had pervaded all ages and revelations,—a faith which, in its purest form, had been held by the patriarch Abraham. This primitive religion, varying at each dispensation only in accidental rites, comprised, as its essential features, belief in the one true God, rejection of idolatry and of the worship of mediators as 'sharers' in the power and glory of the Deity, and implicit surrender of the will to God. Such surrender is termed 'Islām'; and hence Abraham is called 'the first of Muslims.' This grand fact it was now the mission of Moḥammad to reaffirm. Each successive dispensation had been abused by its votaries, who in the course of time had turned aside from its catholic groundwork. They had magnified or misinterpreted rites intended to be but ancillary and external; by perverting doctrines, they had turned the gift into a curse. Amidst the contending factions, truth might be discovered by the earnest inquirer, but by steps now difficult and uncertain. The Jew denounced the Christian, and the Christian the Jew. Some worshipped not only Jesus but his mother also; others held both to be mere creatures. From the labyrinth of confusion and error it pleased the Almighty once again to deliver mankind. Moḥammad was the Apostle of this grand and final mission, and, amid the clash of opposing authorities, his judgment was to be heard unquestioned and supreme. Thus in a passage revealed at Mecca:—

Perverted in the course of ages

Moḥammad the final Restorer

Sūra xlii. 11 ff.

> He hath ordained unto you the religion which he commanded unto Noah; and which WE have revealed unto thee, and which WE commanded Abraham and Moses and Jesus; saying, Set up the faith and fall not into dissension. . . .
>
> And they fell not into dissension until after the knowledge (of divine revelation) had come unto them, out of enmity among themselves; and if the Word from thy Lord had not gone forth (respiting them) unto a set time, the matter had been decided between them. And verily they that have inherited the Scriptures after them are in a perplexing doubt regarding the same.
>
> Wherefore call them thereto (*i.e.* unto the catholic Faith) and be steadfast as thou hast been commanded, and follow not their desires; and say,—I believe in all the Scriptures which God hath revealed; and I am commanded to do justice between you. God is our Lord and your Lord. To us will be reckoned our works, and to you your works. There is no ground of difference or contention between us and you.

Thus in the growth of Moḥammad's opinions there was a preliminary stage in which previous religions were on an equal footing with Islām, if only purged of their perversions. But in the final development of his creed, Moḥammad makes the Ḳor'ān rise triumphant over both the Law and the Gospel, and casts them unheeded into the shade. This, however, was not the result of any express teaching, but rather the necessary though tacit outcome of his system. The impression which would attribute to Moḥammad either formal cancelment of the Jewish and Christian Scriptures, or imputations against their genuineness and authority, is without foundation. No expression regarding either the Jewish or Christian Scriptures ever escaped the lips of Moḥammad other than of implicit reverence.[1] It was the opposition of the Jews, and the martial supremacy of Islām, that imperceptibly led to the exclusive authority of Moḥammad and the Ḳor'ān. The change by which the Prophet dispensed with previous Revelations was made in silence. In the concluding, as in the earliest days of his mission, Moḥammad hardly ever refers to the former Scriptures, whether Jewish or Christian. His scheme was now complete, and rested upon other pillars. The steps by which he had ascended were left far beneath, forgotten and uncared for. In his later years Islām diverged rapidly from all sympathy with the Bible. An appeal to previous Revelation would now have proved embarrassing, and silence was natural. Whatever effect the doctrines of Christianity properly understood might have had on Moḥammad while yet inquiring and moulding for himself a creed, it is evident that long before the final settlement of Islām his system had become crystallised into a form which it was impossible for any new influences materially to alter. Argument now was out of place. Moḥammad was the Prophet of God, and his word was law. Opposing doctrine must vanish before the divine command. The exclusive and intolerant position finally assumed by Islām is sufficiently manifest in the ban

II. Ḳor'ān entirely supersedes previous Revelation;

Which towards the close of his career is hardly alluded to

Islām eventually diverges from the Bible

Jewish and Christian religions allowed only on sufferance

[1] In a treatise by the Author, entitled *The Testimony borne by the Coran to the Jewish and Christian Scriptures* (published by the S.P.C.K.) it is shown that unequivocal testimony is borne by the Ḳor'ān to the Jewish and Christian Scriptures as current in the time of Moḥammad; that the evidence extends equally to their genuineness and authority; and that there is not a hint anywhere throughout the Ḳor'ān of their cancelment or interpolation. [But *cf.* iv. 48 and parallel passages.]

issued at the Farewell pilgrimage against Jews and Christians, who were for ever debarred the sacred rites and holy precincts of the Ka'ba; and by the divine command to war against them until, in confession of the supremacy of Islām, they should consent to the payment of tribute.

Knowledge whence derived?

From whence, we may now inquire, did Moḥammad gain such a meagre and deceptive view of Christianity?

Misleading teaching as to crucifixion

A significant feature in the teaching of the Ḳor'ān is that Jesus was not crucified; but one resembling Jesus, and mistaken by the Jews for him. This is alleged not in contradiction of the Christians, but *in opposition to the Jews*, who gloried in the assertion that Jesus had been put to death by them. Hence it would almost seem that Moḥammad believed his teaching on this head to accord with that of the Church; and that he was ignorant of the fundamental doctrine of the Christian faith, the death of Christ, and redemption through it.

Connection of Moḥammad's teaching with Gnosticism

The singular correspondence between the allusions to the crucifixion in the Ḳor'ān and the wild speculations of certain early heretics has led some to conjecture that Moḥammad derived his notions from a Gnostic source. But Gnosticism had disappeared from Egypt before the sixth century, and there is no reason for supposing that it had at any time gained a footing in Arabia. Besides, there is no affinity between the supernaturalism of the Gnostics and Docetæ, and the rationalism of the Ḳor'ān. According to the former, the Deity must be removed far from the gross contact of evil matter: and the æon Christ, which alighted upon Jesus at his baptism, must ascend to its native regions before the crucifixion. With Moḥammad (apart from some passages implying a higher origin), Jesus Christ was a mere man, wonderfully born indeed, but still an ordinary man; a servant of the Almighty, as others had been before him. But although there is no ground for believing that Gnostic doctrines were taught to Moḥammad, yet some of the strange fancies of those heretics preserved in Syrian tradition may have come to the ears of his Jewish converts, and have been by them adopted as a likely and convenient mode of reconciling both Jews and Christians to the new religion. The Israelite would have less antipathy to the catholic faith of Islām and the recognition of the mission of

Jesus, if allowed to believe that Christians as well as Jews had been in error; that his people had not, in fact, put Jesus the promised Moḥammad to a shameful death; but that, like Enoch and Elijah, he had been received up into the heaven. 'Christ *crucified*' was still, as in the days of Paul, 'a stumbling-block' to the Jews. But thus the stumbling-block might be removed; and, without offence to his national pride, the Jew might confess his belief in a weak and mutilated Gospel. It was a compromise that might readily approve itself to a Jewish mind already unsettled by the prophetic claims of Moḥammad.

Denial of crucifixion a compromise between Jews and Christians

By some again it has been attempted to trace the Christian element in the Ḳor'ān to certain apocryphal gospels supposed to have been within the reach of Moḥammad. But, though some few of its details do coincide with these spurious writings, its statements as a rule in no wise correspond.[1] Whereas had there been a ready access to such books, we cannot doubt that Moḥammad would (as in the case of Jewish history and legend) have borrowed largely from them. Others believed that Moḥammad acquired his knowledge from no written source, but from Christian tradition in the peninsula. As his sole source of information, however, the indigenous tradition of Arabia was altogether insufficient for the purpose. There is no ground for believing that either at Mecca or Medīna there existed anything of the kind from which could have been framed a narrative agreeing, as that of the Ḳor'ān does in many particulars and even in some of its expressions, with the Gospels both genuine and apocryphal, while in others it follows if not outstrips the popular legend.

Apocryphal gospels not accessible to Moḥammad

Christian tradition in Arabia insufficient

But tradition, quite sufficient for this end, survived in the southern confines of Syria, and from thence no doubt reached Moḥammad through some Jewish medium. The general outline of Christian story, as we find it in the Ḳor'ān, having

Syrian tradition likeliest source of Moḥammad's knowledge

[1] The 'Gospel of Barnabas' is of course excepted, because it is the modern work of a Christian convert to Islām. [An English translation of this Gospel accompanied by the Italian text has been published by L. and L. Ragg, Oxford, 1907. This undertaking was due to the representations of Dr J. W. Youngson, a missionary to Moḥammadans in India. An Arabic version has also appeared in Egypt in 1907, for the use of Muslims. Cf. *Expository Times*, vol. xix., p. 263 ff.]

a few salient points in accordance with the Gospel and the rest filled up with fabulous matter, is just such as we may expect an inquiring Jew to learn from the traditions current amongst the lower classes in the Holy Land. Something may have been learned from the Christian slaves of Mecca; but these had generally been carried off in boyhood, and would remember little more than a few Scriptural histories with perhaps some fragments of their creed. Either the Jew, or the Christian may also have heard the opening of the Gospel of Luke, and communicated to Moḥammad the story of the births of John and Jesus, as we find them in the Ḳor'ān. It is also possible that some one may have repeated to Moḥammad from memory, or read to him from a manuscript, the narrative in the Gospel containing these details;—but this is mere conjecture.[1]

Trinity of the Ḳor'ān; and the Virgin Mary

It is not very apparent, from the few indistinct notices in the Ḳor'ān, what Moḥammad believed the Christian doctrine of the Trinity to be. In a passage already quoted, Christians are reprobated for 'taking Jesus and his Mother for two Gods besides the Lord.' It is hence concluded that the Trinity of the Ḳor'ān is that of the Father, Mary, and Jesus. Such may have been the case, but it is not certain. The service of Mary had long been carried to the pitch nearly of divine worship; the 'Orthodox' party persecuted those who would not accord her the title 'Mother of God'; and Moḥammad may have censured the Christians for thus virtually taking 'Jesus and his Mother for two Gods,' possibly without any advertence to the Trinity. On the other hand, the assertion that Moḥammad believed Mary to be held by the Christians as divine is supported by the absence of any recognition of the Holy Ghost as a person in the Trinity. The only passage in which the Trinity is specifically mentioned makes no allusion whatever to the Holy Ghost; nor are the expressions 'the Spirit,' and 'the Holy Spirit,' which occur frequently in the Ḳor'ān, used by Moḥammad as if in the Christian creed they signified a divine person; for, as already shown, they usually mean Gabriel, the messenger of God's revelations to Moḥammad. A confusion of Gabriel with the Holy Spirit

Holy Ghost unknown to Moḥammad as person in the Trinity

[1] It is very doubtful whether an Arabic translation of the Scriptures, or any part of them, was ever within Moḥammad's reach, notwithstanding the traditions regarding Waraḳa having copied from them.

may possibly have arisen in the Prophet's mind from Gabriel having been the medium of the Annunciation, while Christians at the same time hold that Jesus was conceived by the power of the Holy Ghost. The phrase is also repeatedly used in a more general sense as signifying *the Spirit that gives life and inspiration.* It was the divine 'Spirit' breathed into the clay which imparted life to Adam; and Jesus, who like Adam had no earthly father, is also spoken of as 'the SPIRIT FROM GOD' breathed into Mary. So also when it is said that God '*strengthened Jesus with the Holy Spirit,*' we may perhaps trace the use of current Christian speech, not inconsistent with Jewish ideas.[1]

Jewish and Christian prophecies and expectations

The assurance with which Moḥammad appeals to Jews and Christians as both in expectation of a promised prophet whom, if they would put aside their prejudices, they must at once recognise in himself 'even as they recognised their own sons,' is very singular, and must surely have been countenanced by converts from both religions. Two different and indeed incompatible expectations were adroitly combined into a cumulative proof of his own mission. The Jewish anticipation of their Messiah, and the perfectly distinct anticipation by the Christians of the second advent of Christ, were thus fused into a common argument for a coming prophet expected by both Jews and Christians and foretold in all the Scriptures;—which expected personage was the Prophet himself. That the promise of the Paraclete was capable of perversion we see in the heresy of Montanus; and it is probable that a garbled version of the same promise communicated to Moḥammad may have given rise to the following passage:—

Promise of the Paraclete;

And call to mind when JESUS, Son of MARY, said:—Oh Children of Israel; Verily, I am an apostle of God unto you, attesting the Book of the Law revealed before me, and giving good tidings of a prophet that shall come after me, whose name is AḤMED.[2]

Sūra lxi. 6

And of the Messiah perverted

The prophecy of Moses to the Israelites, that 'God will raise up unto thee a prophet from the midst of thee, *of thy brethren*, like unto me,' may also plausibly have been adduced

[1] Compare Psalm li. 12: 'Uphold me with thy free spirit.'

[2] *Aḥmed* is from the same root as *Moḥammad*, signifying 'the Praised. See John xvi. 7, where παράκλητος may in some imperfect or garbled translation have been rendered by the equivalent of περικλυτός.

by some perverted Jew in favour of the Arabian prophet, and other predictions referring to the Messiah were doubtless forced into a similar service. That he was the Prophet promised to both Jews and Christians lay indeed at the root of the catholic system so strongly inculcated by Moḥammad in the middle stage of his course. He persuaded himself that it was so: and the assumption, once admitted, retained possession of his mind.

Moḥammad the Prophet looked for by both people

Meccans taunt him with being prompted by others

From these remarks we may conclude that, while some information regarding Christianity may have been drawn from Christian slaves or Arabs, Moḥammad gained his chief knowledge of Christianity from Syria, through the same Jewish medium which, at an earlier period, furnished the more copious details of Jewish history. His adversaries at Mecca did not conceal their suspicion that the prompting from which the Scriptural and legendary tales proceeded was not solely that of a supernatural inspiration. They imputed to him the aid of strangers:—

Sūra xliv. 12 ff.

From whence shall there be an Admonition for them; for, verily, there hath come unto them an evident Apostle;—
Then they turn from him and say,—*One taught by others, a Madman!*
And the Unbelievers say; *Verily this is a fraud which he hath fabricated, and other people have assisted him therein.* But they say that which is unjust and false. * * *

Sūra xxv. 6 f.

They say; *These are Fables of the ancients which he hath had written down; which are dictated unto him morning and evening.*
SAY: He hath revealed it who knoweth that which is hidden in Heaven and in Earth. He is forgiving and merciful. * * *

Sūra xvi. 105

And again: Verily WE know that they say,—*Surely a certain man teacheth him.* But the tongue of him whom they hint at is foreign, while this Revelation is in the tongue of simple Arabic.

Promptings of ignorant Jews transformed into 'divine Ḳor'ān'

Whatever the rough material, its passage through the alembic of 'simple Arabic' converted it, to the Muslim eye, into a gem of unearthly water. The recitations of some credulous and ill-informed Jew reappeared as the inspirations of the Almighty dictated by Gabriel, the noblest of his heavenly messengers. The wild legend and the garbled Scripture story of yesterday comes forth on the morrow as a portion of the divine and eternal Ḳor'ān.

Style of Ḳor'ān

Teaching of Moḥammad during his last three years at Mecca.—The Ḳor'ān continues during the last three years of

Moḥammad's residence at Mecca to be made up, as before, of arguments in refutation of the errors and cavillings of his fellow-citizens; of the proofs of God's omnipotence, omniscience, and unity; of vivid picturings of the judgment day and of heaven and hell; and of legendary and Spiritual stories. The later Sūras contain repeated allusions to the approaching emigration. The great verities of a minute and over-ruling providence and final retribution are sometimes illustrated by passages of grand imagery and true poetry. The bold impersonation of THUNDER in the following quotation may be taken as a sample:— during this period

Verily God changeth not his dealings with a People, until they change that which is in their souls. And when God willeth evil unto a People, there is none that can turn it away, nor have they any protector besides Him. Sūra xiii. 12 ff.

It is He that showeth you the Lightning to inspire fear and hope, and raiseth the heavy clouds. The THUNDER doth celebrate His praise; and the Angels also, from awe of Him. And He sendeth forth His bolts; and shivereth therewith whom He pleaseth, while they are wrangling about God:—for He is terrible in might!

He alone is rightly invoked. And those whom they invoke beside Him, they answer them not at all, otherwise than as one stretching forth both hands unto the water that it may reach his mouth, and it reacheth it not. So is the invocation of the unbelievers founded only in error. And to God boweth down in worship whatsoever is in the Heavens, and in the Earth, voluntarily or by force; and their shadows likewise in the morning and in the evening.[1]

SAY:—Who is the Lord of the Heavens and of the earth? Say—GOD. SAY:—Wherefore, then, do ye take besides Him guardians who have no power to do even their ownselves a benefit nor an injury? Say:—What! Are the blind and the seeing equal! What! is the darkness equal with the light? Or do they give unto God partners that create like unto His creation, so that the creation (of both) should appear alike in their eyes? Say:—GOD is the Creator of all things. He is the ONE; the AVENGER!

He bringeth down from on high the rain, and the valleys flow, each according to its measure; and the flood beareth the swelling froth. And from that which men melt in the furnace to make ornaments or vessels withal, there ariseth a scum, the like thereof. Thus doth God compare the truth with falsehood. As for the scum it passeth away like the froth: but that which benefiteth mankind remaineth on the Earth.

Thus doth God put forth similitudes.

---

[1] A conceit Moḥammad was fond of. The shadows perform obeisance to God, being long and prostrate in the morning, upright during the day, and again elongated in prostration in the evening.

Positive precepts

The positive precepts of this period are still very limited. The five times of prayer are said to have been enjoined by God at the period of the Prophet's ascent to heaven one or two years before the Hijra. The flesh of animals was permitted for food *if killed 'in the name of the Lord,'*[1] but the blood, and that which dieth of itself, and the flesh of swine, were strictly prohibited.[2] While some superstitions were denounced, and the practice of compassing the Ka'ba naked was proscribed as a device of Satan,[3] the rites of pilgrimage were now enjoined as of divine authority and in themselves propitious to piety. It is probable that the Jews strongly objected to this new feature of the reformed faith, and we accordingly find a laboured defence of it :—

Superstitions denounced

But Meccan pilgrimage and rites maintained

Sūra xxii. 27 ff.

And call to remembrance when WE gave unto Abraham the site of the Temple (at Mecca); saying,—Associate not in worship anything with ME, and purify My house for them that compass it, and for them that stand up and bow down to pray.

And proclaim unto Mankind a pilgrimage, that they may come unto thee on foot, and upon every lean camel,[4] flocking from every distant road :—that they may testify to the benefits they have received, and commemorate the name of God, on the appointed days, over the brute beasts which WE have given them for a provision :—Wherefore eat thereof and feed the needy and the poor. Then let them stop the neglect of their persons,[5] fulfil their vows, and compass the ancient House.

This do. And he that honoureth the sacred ordinances of God it is well for him with his Lord. The flesh of cattle is lawful unto you excepting that which hath been read unto you. Wherefore abstain from the pollutions of idols, and abstain from false speech, following the catholic faith respecting God, not associating any with Him ; for he that associateth any with God is like that which falleth from the heavens,

---

[1] The reason was the same as that which led to the Apostolical admonition to abstain from 'pollutions of idols,' and 'meats offered to idols,' and points to the Arab practice of slaying their animals as a sacrifice to, or in the name of, their deities.

[2] The influence of Jewish habit and precept is here manifest. It is possible that some of the pieces quoted above as Meccan may have been in reality of later date ; they may have been given forth at Medīna after the emigration, and relegated to passages of corresponding tenor in Meccan Sūras.

[3] Sūra vii. 29. This was connected with the *Ḥoms :* see Introduction, p. cxviii.

[4] Lean and famished from the long journey.

[5] *I.e.* they might now again pare their nails, shave their heads, &c., and resume their ordinary dress. See Introduction, p. ci.

and the birds snatch it away, or the wind bloweth it into a distant place.

Hearken:—whosoever honoureth the Sacrifices of God, verily they proceed from piety of the heart. From them (the victims) ye derive benefits until the appointed time: then they are brought for sacrifice unto the ancient House.

And unto every People have WE appointed rites, that they may commemorate the name of GOD over the brute beasts with which He hath provided them. And your GOD is ONE GOD; wherefore submit thyself unto him and bear good tidings unto the humble:—Unto those whose hearts, when God is mentioned, tremble thereat;—and unto those that patiently bear what befalleth them and observe prayer, and spend in alms of that WE have provided them with.

And the Victims have WE made unto you as ordinances of God. From them ye receive benefit. Commemorate therefore the name of God over them as they stand disposed in a line, and when they fall slain upon their sides, eat thereof, and give unto the poor, both to him that is silent and him that beggeth. Thus have WE given thee dominion over them that ye may be thankful. Their flesh is not accepted of God, nor yet their blood: but your piety is accepted of Him.

Effect produced by teaching of Moḥammad

Few and simple as were the precepts of Moḥammad up to this time, his teaching had wrought a marvellous and a mighty work. Never since the days when primitive Christianity startled the world from its sleep and waged mortal combat with heathenism, had men seen the like arousing of spiritual life, and faith that suffered sacrifice and took joyfully the spoiling of goods for conscience' sake.

Previous dark and torpid state of Mecca and Arabia

From time beyond memory, Mecca and the whole peninsula had been steeped in spiritual torpor. The slight and transient influences of Judaism, Christianity, or philosophical inquiry, upon the Arab mind had been but as the ruffling here and there of the surface of a quiet lake; all remained still and motionless below. The people were sunk in superstition, cruelty, and vice. It was a common practice for the eldest son to take to wife his father's widows, whom he inherited with the rest of the estate. Pride and poverty had introduced among them (as they have among the Hindoos) the crime of female infanticide.[1] Their religion was a gross idolatry; and their faith the dark superstitious dread of unseen beings whose goodwill they sought to propitiate and whose displeasure to avert, rather than the belief in an over-ruling

[1] It is stringently proscribed in the Ḳor'ān (lxxxi. 8, &c.), and disappeared with the progress of Islām.

Providence. The Life to come and Retribution of good and evil as motives of action were practically unknown.

Effect produced on converts by Moḥammad's ministry at Mecca

Thirteen years before the Hijra, Mecca lay lifeless in this debased state. What a change had those thirteen years now produced! A band of several hundred persons had rejected idolatry, adopted the worship of One God, and surrendered themselves implicitly to the guidance of what they believed a Revelation from Him; praying to the Almighty with frequency and fervour, looking for pardon through His mercy, and striving to follow after good works, almsgiving, purity, and justice. They now lived under a constant sense of the omnipotent power of God, and of His providential care over the minutest of their concerns. In all the gifts of nature, in every relation of life, at each turn of their affairs, individual or public, they saw His hand. And, above all, the new existence in which they exulted was regarded as the mark of His especial grace; while the unbelief of their blinded fellow-citizens was the hardening stamp of reprobation. Moḥammad was the minister of life to them, the source under God of their new-born hopes; and to him they yielded an implicit submission.

Their sacrifices and abandonment of home

In so short a period Mecca had, from this wonderful movement, been rent into two factions which, unmindful of the old landmarks of tribe and family, arrayed themselves in deadly opposition one against the other. The Believers bore persecution with a patient and tolerant spirit. And though it was their wisdom so to do, the credit of a magnanimous forbearance may be freely accorded. One hundred men and women, rather than abjure their precious faith, had abandoned home and sought refuge, till the storm should be overpast, in Abyssinian exile. And now again a still larger number, with the Prophet himself, were emigrating from their fondly loved city with its sacred Temple, to them the holiest spot on earth, and fleeing to Medīna. There, the same marvellous charm had within two or three years been preparing for them a brotherhood ready to defend the Prophet and his followers with their blood. Jewish truth had long sounded in the ears of the men of Medīna; but it was not until they heard the spirit-stirring strains of the Arabian prophet that they too awoke from their slumber, and sprang suddenly into a new and earnest life.

The virtues of his people may be described in the words of Moḥammad himself:—

Description of his followers by Moḥammad

Sūra xxv. 64 ff.

The servants of the Merciful are they that walk upon the earth softly; and, when the ignorant speak unto them, they reply, PEACE!

They that spend the night worshipping their Lord, prostrate and standing;—

And who say,—'O our Lord! turn away from us the torment of hell; verily, from the torment thereof there is no release. Surely it is an evil abode and resting place!'

Those that when they spend are neither profuse nor niggardly, but take a middle course;—

Those that invoke not with God any other god; and slay not a soul that God hath forbidden, otherwise than by right; and commit not fornication;

(For he who doeth this is involved in sin,—his torment shall be doubled unto him in the day of judgment; therein ignominiously shall he remain for ever,—Excepting him that shall repent and believe and perform righteous works; as for them God shall change their evil things into good things; and God is forgiving and merciful. And whoever repenteth and doeth good works, verily, he turneth unto God with a true repentance):—

They who bear not witness to that which is false; and when they pass by vain sport, they pass it by with dignity:—

They who, when admonished by the Revelations of the Lord, fall not down as if deaf and blind;—

Who say, 'O our Lord. Grant us of our wives and children such as shall be a comfort unto us, and make us examples unto the pious!'

These shall be rewarded hereafter with lofty mansions, for that they persevered; and they shall be accosted therein with welcome and salutation:—

For ever therein:—a fair abode and resting place!

PART SECOND

MOḤAMMAD AT MEDĪNA

CHAPTER VIII

ARRIVAL AT MEDĪNA. BUILDING OF THE MOSQUE

A.H. I.—*June* A.D. 622 *to January* A.D. 623

Flight of Moḥammad and Abu Bekr

AT the close of last chapter we left Moḥammad and Abu Bekr, on the second day of their escape from the cave, already beyond the reach of pursuit, and rapidly wending their way towards Medīna. Leaving devious paths, they had now taken the common road to Syria which runs near the shore of the Red Sea. On the morning of the third day a small caravan was observed in the distance. The apprehensions of the fugitives were soon allayed, for Abu Bekr recognised at the head of the caravan his cousin Ṭalḥa returning from the north. Warm was the greeting, and loud the congratulations. Ṭalḥa opened his stores, and, producing two changes of fine white Syrian raiment, bestowed them on the Prophet and on his kinsman also. The present was welcome to the soiled and weary travellers; yet more welcome was the assurance that Ṭalḥa had left the Muslims at Medīna in eager expectation of their Prophet. So Moḥammad and Abu Bekr proceeded on their journey with lighter hearts and quickened pace; while the merchant resumed his way to Mecca. There Ṭalḥa disposed of his venture; and so little were Ḳoreish even now disposed to molest the believers, that, after quietly adjusting his affairs, he set out unopposed some little time afterwards for Medīna, with the families of Moḥammad and Abu Bekr.

They meet Ṭalḥa by the way

After travelling some way farther by the common road, Moḥammad and his companion struck off at Bedr to the

Progress towards Medīna

right, thus taking the eastern route, which passes through Medīna to the north. The valleys which they crossed, the defiles and steeps they ascended, and the spots on which the fugitive Prophet performed his devotions, have all been preserved in tradition by the pious zeal of his followers.[1] When now within two days of Medīna, one of the camels, worn out by the rapid travelling, was unable to proceed. A chief of the tribe residing in the neighbourhood supplied a fresh camel in its stead, and also furnished a guide.

They approach the city

At length, on the morning of Monday, eight days after quitting Mecca, the little party crossed the valley of the 'Aḳīḳ in the mountain tract some five miles S.W. of Medīna.[2] The heat was intense; for the summer sun, now approaching the meridian, beat fiercely on the bare ridges and stony defiles, the desolation hardly relieved by an occasional clump of wild acacia. Climbing the opposite ascent, they reached the crest of the mountain. Here a scene opened on them which contrasted strangely with the dark frowning peaks and naked rocks, in the midst of which for hours they had been toiling. It was the ancient Yathrib, *Al*-Medīna—'*the* city,' as by pre-eminence it was now to be called—surrounded by verdant gardens and groves of the graceful palm. What thoughts must have crowded on the mind of the Prophet and

Medīna and its environs

[1] Ibn Hishām, p. 332 f.; Ibn Sa'd, p. 157.

[2] The Wādi al-'Aḳīḳ has a north-westerly direction, and discharges its waters into Al-Ghāba, the basin in which collects the drainage of the Medīna plain. Burton describes the mountains on this side as you approach Medīna, as composed of 'inhospitable rocks, pinnacle-shaped, of granite below, and in the upper parts, fine limestone'; but about the Wādi al-'Aḳīḳ the surface is 'black scoriaceous basalt.' According to Burckhardt, 'all the rocky places' about Medīna, 'as well as the lower ridge of the northern mountainous chain, are covered by a layer of volcanic rock; it is of a bluish-black colour, very porous, yet heavy and hard, not glazed like Schlacken, and contains frequently small white substances in its pores of the size of a pin's head, which I never found crystallised. The plain has a completely black colour from this rock, and the pieces with which it is overspread. I met with no lava, although the nature of the ground seemed strongly to indicate the neighbourhood of a volcano.' Burckhardt adds that lava from a volcanic outburst, A.D. 654, passed not far from Medīna, on the east; but he attributes the volcanic substances about the town and the valley 'Aḳīḳ to some earlier eruption.

Medīna is due north of Mecca, but, as the shore bends somewhat to the west, it is by so much further from the sea—about 100 miles.

his faithful friend as they gazed on the prospect below them! Widespread is the view from the heights on which they stood, and well fitted to stir the heart of any traveller. The vast plain of Nejd stretches away towards the south-east as far as the eye can reach; while the eastern horizon is bounded by a low line of dark hills. To the north the prospect is arrested, at the distance of a few miles, by the granite masses of Oḥod, a spur of the great central chain. A well-defined watercourse, flowing from the south-east under the nearest side of Medīna, is lost among the north-eastern hills, the cliffs of which approach and even touch the city on the north. To the right, Jebel 'Ā'ir, a range nearly corresponding in distance and height with that of Oḥod, projects into the plain and bounds it on the south-west. Closely embracing the city and in contrast with the rugged rocks on which our travellers stand, are the orchards of palm-trees for which from time immemorial Medīna has been famous. One sheet of gardens, the loveliest and most verdant spot in all the plain, extends uninterruptedly to Ḳobā, a suburb little more than two miles to the south. Around the city in every direction date-trees and green fields meet the eye, interspersed here and there with the substantial houses and fortified hamlets of the Jewish tribes, and the suburban residences of the Beni Aus and Khazraj. The tender reminiscence of childhood, when he visited Medīna with his mother, was perhaps the first thought to cross the mind of Moḥammad. But more pressing considerations were now at hand. How would he be received? Were his adherents powerful enough to secure for him an harmonious welcome? Or would either of the contending factions, by whom that peaceful plain had been so often stained with blood, be roused against him? Before putting the friendship of the city to the test, it would be prudent to retire to one of the suburbs, and Ḳobā lay invitingly before them. 'Lead us,' said Moḥammad to the guide, 'straight to the Beni 'Amr at Ḳobā, and draw not yet nigh unto Medīna.' So, leaving the path to Medīna on the left, they descended at once into the plain and made for Ḳobā.[1]

Moḥammad makes for Ḳobā

For several days the city had been in expectation of its illustrious visitor. Tidings had been received of Moḥammad's disappearance from Mecca; but no one knew of his

People of Medīna watch for his coming

[1] Aṭ-Ṭabari, i. 1242.

three days' withdrawal to the cave. He ought before now to have arrived, even with the delay of a devious route. Every morning a company of Medīna converts and refugees from Mecca had for some days gone forth a mile or two on the Mecca road, and posted themselves on the first rocky ridge to the west. There they watched till the heat of the ascending sun drove them from the unsheltered spot to their homes. On this day they had gone out as usual and after a fruitless watch had retired to the city, when a Jew, catching a glimpse of the three travellers wending their way to Ḳobā, shouted from the top of his house: 'Ho! ye Beni Ḳeila![1] he has come! he whom ye have been looking for has come!' Every one now hurried forth from the city to Ḳobā. A shout of joy arose from the Beni 'Amr (the Ausite tribe inhabiting Ḳobā) when they found that Moḥammad had come amongst them. The wearied travellers, amidst the greeting of old friends and smile of strange faces, alighted and sat down under the shadow of a tree.[2] It was Monday, June 28, A.D. 622. The journey had been accomplished in eight days. The ordinary time is eleven.[3]

He arrives 12th Rabī' I. A.H. I. June 28, A.D. 622

Is joyfully received

The joyful news spread speedily over the city. The very children in the streets cried out with delight: 'Here is the Prophet! He is come! He is come!' The converts from all quarters flocked to Moḥammad and made obeisance to him. He received them courteously, and said: 'Ye People! show your joy by giving your neighbours the salutation of peace; send portions to the poor; bind close the ties of kinsmanship; and offer up your prayers whilst others sleep. Thus shall ye enter Paradise in peace.' It was shortly arranged that Moḥammad should for the present lodge at

Lodges with Kulthūm at Ḳobā

[1] Ḳeila, mother of the two patriarchs of the Beni Aus and Khazraj.

[2] This quarter was called *'Alīya*, or upper Medīna, from its more elevated position, and included Ḳobā and some other hamlets with the Jewish settlements of the Beni Ḳoreiẓa and the Naḍir. When Moḥammad was seated on Abu Bekr's camel, few knew which was the Prophet, till the sun's rays fell upon him, and then Abu Bekr rose to place him in the shade. Out of this, probably, has grown the tradition that the people of Medīna recognised the Prophet from his body *casting no shadow*. Abu Bekr was known to some of the citizens, as he used to pass through Medīna on his mercantile trips to Syria. Ibn Hishām, p. 334; Aṭ-Ṭabari, i. 1243.

[3] It *can* be travelled by swift dromedaries in five.

Ḳobā with Kulthūm, a hospitable chief, who had already received many of the emigrants on their first arrival. A great part of every day was also spent in the house of Sa'd, son of Khaithama, one of the Ausite 'Leaders.' There Moḥammad received such persons as wished to see him, and conferred with his friends on the state of feeling in Medīna.[1] Abu Bekr was entertained by Khārija, another chief, in the adjoining suburb of the Sunḥ. He showed his gratitude by marrying the daughter of his host, and permanently took up his residence with the family.[2]

Abu Bekr lodges at the Sunḥ

A day or two after, 'Alī, who, as we have seen, remained only three days at Mecca after the disappearance of Moḥammad, reached Medīna and was accommodated by Kulthūm in the same house with the Prophet. It was soon determined that Moḥammad might with safety enter Medīna. The welcome he had already received was warm, and to all appearance unanimous and sincere. Elements of disaffection might be slumbering among the Jews and other unconverted citizens; but they were unnoticed amid the universal joy and the first impulses of generous hospitality. Moḥammad, therefore, stopped only four days at Ḳobā, from Monday till Friday. During this period, he laid the foundations of a mosque at Ḳobā, which at a later period was honoured in the Ḳor'ān with the name of the 'Mosque of godly fear.'[3]

'Alī joins Moḥammad

Moḥammad remains four days at Ḳobā

On the morning of Friday, Moḥammad mounted his favourite camel Al-Ḳaṣwā, with Abu Bekr seated behind him, and surrounded by a crowd of followers proceeded towards the city. He halted at a place of prayer in the vale of the Beni Sālim, a Khazrajite tribe, and there performed his first Friday service with about a hundred

Departure for Medīna

Performs public service by the way

[1] Sa'd being a bachelor, the unmarried refugees were accommodated in great numbers in his house, so that it went by the name of the 'bachelors' hostelry.' Aṭ-Ṭabari, i. 1243.

[2] That is to say, his wife remained at her father's house, and he used to visit her there when it was her turn to enjoy his society, for he had other wives. Khārija was joined in *brotherhood* (a practice explained below, p. 174) to Abu Bekr.

[3] Sūra ix. 109. Moḥammad enlarged it after the Ḳibla was changed, and advanced its foundations and walls 'to their present position.' With his followers he aided in the pious work by carrying the materials. He used to visit it every Saturday, and attached to the saying of prayers therein the merit of the *'Omra* or Lesser pilgrimage; *cf.* p. 447 *n*

Muslims; the spot is still shown to pilgrims, and is marked by a building called in memory of the event the *Masjid al-jum'a*, or 'the Friday mosque.'[1] On this occasion he added an address composed chiefly of religious exhortation and eulogy of the new faith. Friday was thenceforward set apart for the weekly celebration of public worship.

Entry into the city

When the service was finished, Moḥammad resumed his progress. He had sent a message to the Beni an-Najjār, his relatives through Selma, mother of Abd al-Muṭṭalib, to escort him into the city. But there was no need of special invitation. The tribes and families of Medīna came streaming forth, and vied one with another in showing honour to their noble visitor. It was indeed a triumphal procession. Around the camels of Moḥammad and his immediate followers, rode the chief men of the city clad in their best raiment and in glittering armour. The cavalcade pursued its way through the gardens and palm-groves of the southern suburb; and as it now threaded the streets of the city, the heart of Moḥammad was gladdened by the incessant call from one and another as they flocked around: 'Alight here, O Prophet! We have abundance with us, means of defence and weapons and room. Abide with us.' So urgent was the appeal that sometimes they seized hold of Al-Ḳaṣwā's halter. Moḥammad answered them courteously and kindly: 'The decision,' he said, 'rests with the camel; make way for her; let her go free.' It was a stroke of policy. His residence would be hallowed in the eyes of the people as selected supernaturally; while the jealousy which otherwise might arise from the quarter of one tribe being preferred to that of another would thus receive decisive check.

His camel halts at an open yard

Onwards Al-Ḳaṣwā moved, with slackened halter; and, leaving the larger portion of the city to the left, entered the eastern quarter inhabited by the Beni an-Najjār. There finding a large and open courtyard with a few date-trees, she halted and sat down.[2] The house of Abu Eiyūb was

[1] Ibn Hishām, p. 335.

[2] To invest the incident with a supernatural air, it is added that Moḥammad having left the halter quite loose, Al-Ḳaṣwā got up again and went a little way forward; perceiving her error, she returned straightway to the selfsame spot, knelt down, and, placing her head and neck on the ground, refused to stir.

close at hand. Moḥammad and Abu Bekr, alighting, inquired who the owner was. Abu Eiyūb stepped forward and invited them to enter. Moḥammad became his guest, and occupied the lower storey of his house for seven months, until the Mosque and his own apartments were ready. Abu Eiyūb offered to resign the upper storey in which his family lived, but Moḥammad preferred the lower as being more accessible to his visitors.[1]

Moḥammad occupies Abu Eiyūb's house;

When Moḥammad had alighted, Abu Eiyūb lost no time in carrying into his house the saddle and other property of the travellers; while As'ad ibn Zurāra, a neighbour, seized Al-Ḳaṣwā's halter and conducted her to his courtyard, where he kept her for the Prophet. Dishes of choice viands, bread and meat, butter and milk, presently arrived from various houses; and this hospitality was kept up daily so long as the Prophet resided in the house.

And is treated hospitably

The first concern of Moḥammad was to secure the plot of land on which Al-Ḳaṣwā halted. It was a neglected spot: on one side was a scanty grove of date-trees; the other, covered here and there with thorny shrubs, had been used partly as a burial-ground and partly as a yard for tying camels up. It belonged to two orphan boys under the guardianship of As'ad, who had rudely constructed a place of worship there, and had already held service within its roofless walls. The Prophet called the two lads before him, and desired to purchase this piece of ground from them that he might build a mosque upon it. They replied: 'Nay, but we will make a free gift of it to thee.' Moḥammad would not accept the land in gift; and so the price was fixed at ten golden pieces, which Abu Bekr by desire of Moḥammad paid over to the orphans.

Purchases the yard

Arrangements for the construction of a great Mosque upon the spot, with two houses adjoining—one for his wife Sauda, the other for his intended bride, the precocious maiden 'Ā'isha—were forthwith set on foot. The date-trees

Prepares to build Mosque and habitation

[1] Ibn Hishām, p. 335 f.; Aṭ-Ṭabari, i. 1258 f. Abu Eiyūb used to tell that he and his wife accidentally broke a water-pot in the upper storey, and, having wiped up the water as best they could with their clothes, hurried down to Moḥammad's apartment in alarm lest any of it should have dropped on him. Ibn Hishām, p. 338 Abu Eiyūb was killed at Constantinople, A.H. 52

and thorny bushes were cut down. The graves were dug up, and the bones elsewhere deposited. The uneven ground was carefully levelled, and the rubbish cleared away. A spring, oozing in the vicinity, rendered the site damp; it was blocked up and drained, and at length quite disappeared. Bricks were prepared, and other materials collected.[1]

Is joined by his family from Mecca;

Having taken up his residence in Abu Eiyūb's house, Moḥammad bethought him of his family, and despatched his adopted son Zeid with a slave named Abu Rāfi'[2] on two camels, with a purse of 500 dirhems, to fetch them from Mecca. They met with no difficulty or opposition, and returned with Sauda, the Prophet's wife, and his daughters Fāṭima and Um Kulthūm. The latter had been married into the family of Abu Lahab, but, being separated from her husband, had for some time been living in her father's house. Zeinab, the eldest daughter, remained at Mecca with her husband Abu'l-'Aṣ. Roḳeiya, the second, had already emigrated to Medīna with her husband 'Othmān. Zeid brought with him his own wife Um Aiman (Baraka) and their son Osāma. Accompanying the party were 'Ā'isha and her mother, Um Rūmān, with other members of the family of Abu Bekr, who had no doubt supplied the purse to Zeid. They were conducted by Abu Bekr's son and Ṭalḥa.[3] The family of Abu Bekr, including 'Ā'isha, was accommodated in a neighbouring house. Sauda must have lived with Moḥammad in the house of Abu Eiyūb; from the time of her marriage with Moḥammad, shortly after the death of Khadīja, she had been for three or four years his only wife.[4]

And by Abu Bekr's family

Sauda, Moḥammad's wife

[1] The courtyard in the time of Ibn Jubeir contained fifteen date-trees; they are now (according to Burton) reduced to a dozen in a railed-in and watered space, called 'Fāṭima's garden'; it also contains the remains of a venerable lote-tree. The 'Prophet's well' is hard by.

[2] Ibn Ḳoteiba, p. 71. He had been the servant of Moḥammad's uncle Al-'Abbās, and was given by him to Moḥammad, who freed him on his bringing tidings of the conversion of Al-'Abbās.

[3] Ṭalḥa, as we have seen, met the Prophet on his way to Medīna. He married Um Kulthum, daughter of his cousin Abu Bekr; and with him he always seems to have been on terms of close intimacy.

[4] Fāṭima probably lived with Sauda. Eighteen months afterwards she was married to 'Alī.

The climate of Medīna contrasts strongly with that of Mecca. In summer, the days are intensely hot (a more endurable and less sultry heat, however, than that of Mecca); but the nights are cool and often chilly. The cold in winter is for the latitude severe, especially after rain, which falls heavily in occasional but not long-continued showers; and even in summer these are not infrequent. Continuous rain always deluges the adjacent country. The drainage is sluggish, and after a storm the water forms a widespread lake in the open space between the city and the southern suburb. The humid exhalations from this and other stagnant pools, and perhaps also the luxuriant vegetation in the neighbourhood, render the stranger liable to attacks of intermittent fever, which is often followed by swellings and tumours in the legs and stomach, and is sometimes fatal. The climate is altogether unfavourable.[1]

Unwholesome climate of Medīna

Accustomed to the dry air and parched soil of Mecca, the Refugees were sorely tried by the dampness of the Medīna summer and the rigour of its winter. Moḥammad himself escaped, but most of his followers were prostrated by fever. Abu Bekr and his household suffered greatly. 'Ā'isha once related to Moḥammad how they all wandered in their speech when struck down by the fever, and how they longed to return to their home at Mecca; on which Moḥammad, looking upwards, prayed: 'O Lord! make Medīna dear unto us, even as Mecca, or

Refugees suffer from Medīna fever

[1] The cold in winter is severe; ice and snow are not unknown in the adjoining hills. This is natural if, as Burton says, the city be 6,000 feet above the sea; but this estimate is surely exaggerated. The height, however, must be great, as the rise of the mountains is rapid and continuous from the seashore on the western side, and the descent insignificant on the eastern. The city is much exposed to storms. We learn from Burton that 'chilly and violent winds from the eastern deserts are much dreaded; and though Oḥod screens the town on the N. and N.E., a gap in the mountains to the N.W. fills the air at times with rain and comfortless blasts. The rains begin in October, and last with considerable intervals through the winter; the clouds, gathered by the hill tops and the trees near the town, discharge themselves with violence; and at the equinoxes, thunderstorms are common. At such times the Barr el Munākhah, or the open space between the town and the suburbs, is a sheet of water, and the land about the S. and S.E. wall of the faubourg a lake.'—ii. 172

even dearer. Bless its produce, and banish far from it the pestilence!'[1]

'*Brotherhood*' between Refugees and Citizens

To raise the spirits of his followers thus home-sick and suffering, and draw them into nearer relations with the Medīna converts, Moḥammad established a new fraternity between the Refugees and Citizens. 'Become brethren every two and two of you,' he said; and he set the example by taking 'Alī, or as others say 'Othmān, for his brother. Accordingly each of the Refugees selected one of the Citizens as his brother. The bond was of the closest description, and involved not only a special devotion to each other's interests in the persons thus associated, but in case of death the 'brother' inherited the property of the deceased. From forty to fifty Refugees were thus united to as many Citizens of Medīna. This peculiar custom lasted for about a year and a half, when Moḥammad, finding it after the victory of Bedr to be no longer necessary for the encouragement of his followers, and probably attended with some inconvenience and unpopularity as overriding the ties of nature, abolished the bond and suffered inheritance to take its usual course.[2]

'Abd ar-Raḥmān and Sa'd

The following incident shows at once the familiar and friendly footing on which the strangers were received by the Citizens, and something also of their manner of life. 'Abd ar-Raḥmān, on his first reaching Medīna, was lodged by Sa'd ibn ar-Rabī', a convert of Medīna, to whom Moḥammad had united him in brotherhood. As they sat at meat S'ad thus addressed his guest: 'My brother! I have abundance of wealth; I will divide with thee a portion. And behold my two wives! choose which of them thou likest best, and I will divorce her that thou mayest take her to thyself to wife.' And 'Abd ar-Raḥmān replied: 'The Lord bless thee, my brother, in thy family and in thy property!' So he married one of the wives of Sa'd. Moḥammad, meeting him with the nuptial attire of saffron upon him, said: 'How is this?' 'Abd ar-Raḥmān replied: 'I have married me a wife from amongst the people of Medīna.' 'For what

[1] So prevalent was the fever that at one time Moḥammad was almost the only person at prayers able to stand up; but he said, 'the prayer of one who sits is worth only half the prayer of him that stands'; so they all made efforts to stand.

[2] Ibn Hishām, p. 344 ff.

dower?' 'For a small gold piece the size of a date stone.' 'And why,' replied Moḥammad, 'not a goat?'[1]

Building of the Mosque;

During the first half-year of Moḥammad's residence at Medīna his own attention and that of his followers was mainly occupied by the construction of the Mosque and of houses for themselves.[2] In the erection of the Mosque all united with enthusiasm. Their zeal was stimulated by the Prophet, who himself took an active share in the work, and joined in the song which the labourers chanted with loud and cheerful voice, as they bore along their burdens:—

> O Lord! there is no joy but the joy of Futurity.
> O Lord! have mercy upon the Citizens and the Refugees![3]

The site (on the southern portion of the ground which he had just purchased) is the same as that now occupied by the great Mosque and its spacious court; but the style and dimensions were naturally less ambitious. It was built four-square, each side being one hundred cubits or somewhat less in length.[4] The foundations to three cubits above the ground were of stone, the rest of the wall of brick. The roof was

[1] The story is meant to illustrate the poverty of 'Abd ar-Raḥmān when he reached Medīna, as contrasted with his vast wealth in after days. 'At his death he left gold in such quantities that it was cut with hatchets till the people's hands bled.' He had 1,000 camels, 3,000 sheep, and 100 horses. He had issue by sixteen wives, besides children by concubines. Each of his four widows inherited 100,000 dinars.

The Prophet warned him once against his penuriousness: 'Oh son of 'Auf! Verily thou art amongst the rich, and thou shalt not enter Paradise but with great difficulty. Lend therefore to thy Lord, so that He may loosen thy steps.' And he departed by Moḥammad's advice to give away all his property. But the Prophet sent for him again, and told him by Gabriel's desire that it would suffice if he used hospitality and gave alms.

[2] Ibn Hishām, p. 337 ff.

[3] The couplet ran thus:

> Allāhumma lā 'aisha illā 'aisha 'l-ākhira,
> Allāḥumma 'rhami'l-Anṣār w'l-Muhājira.

Moḥammad joining in the chorus would transpose the last words into *al-Muhājira w'al-Anṣār*, thus losing the rhyme. Having been taunted at Mecca with being a mere rhapsodist, he affected to have no ear for poetry, and tradition gives this as an instance. The fine rhythm of the Ḳor'ān was thus held to be all the stronger evidence of divine origin.

[4] According to some authorities the breadth was only sixty or seventy cubits.

supported by trunks of palm-trees and covered over with branches and rafters of the same material. The Ḳibla, or quarter whither the faithful directed their faces when they prayed, was towards Jerusalem. While leading the public prayers Moḥammad tood close to the northern wall looking in that direction; his back was thus turned upon the congregation, who facing similarly fell into rows behind him. When the prayers were ended, he turned himself round to the people, and, if there was occasion for an address, made it then. To the south, opposite the Ḳibla, was a doorway for general entrance.[1] Another opened on the west, called *Bāb Raḥma*, the Gate of Mercy, a name it still retains. A third gate, on the eastern side, was reserved for the use of Moḥammad; south of this entrance, and forming part of the eastern wall of the Mosque itself, were the apartments destined for the Prophet's wives. The house of 'Ā'isha was at the extreme S.E. corner, the road into the Mosque passing behind it. That of Sauda was next; and beyond it were the apartments of Roḳeiya and her husband 'Othmān, and of the two other daughters of Moḥammad. In later years, as Moḥammad added to the number of his wives, he provided each with a room or house, on the same side of the Mosque. From these he had private entrances into the Mosque, used only by himself. The eastern gate still bears in its name *Bāb an-Nisā* (' *Women's* porch ') the memory of these arrangements. To the north of the Mosque the ground was open, and on that side a place was appropriated for the poorer followers of Moḥammad who had no other home. They slept in the Mosque, and had within its courts a sheltered bench or pavement. Moḥammad used to send them portions from his table; and others followed his example. But in a few years victory and the spoil of war caused poverty and distress to disappear, and 'the men of the bench' survived in memory alone. To be near the Prophet, his chief Companions by degrees erected houses for themselves in the vicinity, some of which adjoined upon its court and had doors opening directly on it.

And apartments for Prophet's wives

The Mosque, how used

It is to the north of the Mosque, as thus erected by

[1] This was probably closed when the Ḳibla was turned towards the south. It corresponded with the doorway afterwards opened out to the north.

Moḥammad, that subsequent additions have been mainly made. The present magnificent buildings occupy probably three or four times the area of the primitive temple. Asked why he did not build a more substantial roof to the House of Prayer, he made answer thus: 'The thatching is as the thatching of Moses, rafters and branches; verily man's estate is more fleeting even than this.' But though rude in material, and insignificant in dimensions, the Mosque of Moḥammad is glorious in the history of Islām. Here the Prophet and his Companions spent most of their time: here the daily service, with its oft-recurring prayers was first publicly established: and here the great congregation assembled every Friday, listening with reverence and awe to messages from Heaven. Here the Prophet planned his victories; here he received embassies from vanquished and contrite tribes; and from hence issued edicts which struck terror amongst the rebellious to the very outskirts of the Peninsula. Hard by, in the apartment of 'Ā'isha, he yielded up the ghost; and there, side by side with his first two Successors, he lies entombed.

Type of Saracenic architecture

The simple building, with its slender arches and tapering supports, laid the type for Saracen architecture. It is the model after which buildings for prayer throughout the Muslim world (finding their ideal at Agra in the exquisite Motee Masjid) have been everywhere constructed. The graceful minaret and dome, such as we find them in the Taj Mehal, may perhaps be traced to the same original. Certainly, if these are the legitimate developments of the Medīna mosque, Art owes some of its most signal triumphs to this humble germ.[1]

Houses of Sauda and 'Ā'isha

The Mosque and its adjoining houses were finished within seven months from Moḥammad's arrival, and by the winter Sauda was established in her new abode. Shortly after the Prophet celebrated his marriage with 'Ā'isha at her father's house in the suburb of the Sunḥ, and then brought her to the bridal home, alongside that of her 'sister' Sauda. 'Ā'isha was Moḥammad's only virgin bride; all his other wives had been married before they came to him; and 'Ā'isha, though

Marriage with 'Ā'isha

[1] The idea is Sprenger's. He thinks it probable that only the inner part of the temple (that namely next the northern wall, and which formed the 'bachelors' bench,' or hostelry), was originally roofed over; and that the rest, or about two-thirds of the area, as in modern mosques, was open to the heavens.

three years affianced, was still a girl only ten years of age. But her accomplishments both of body and mind must have developed rapidly. Slim and graceful, her ready wit and arch vivacity set off attractions of no ordinary charm.

Change wrought in Moḥammad's domestic life

Thus, at the age of fifty-three, a new phase commenced in the life of Moḥammad. Hitherto, limiting himself to a single wife, he had shunned the indulgences, with the cares and discord, of polygamy. The unity of his family was now broken, never again to be restored. Thenceforward his love was to be shared by a plurality of wives, and his days spent alternately between their several houses; for Moḥammad had no separate apartment of his own.

'Ā'isha's influence over him

For some time we may suppose that the girl of ten or eleven years would require at the hands of Moḥammad the solicitude of a father, rather than the devotion of a husband. He conformed to the childish ideas of his bride, who carried her playthings with her to her new abode; and at times even joined in her nursery games. As time went on she enthralled the heart of Moḥammad; and, though exposed while still a girl to the rivalry of many beautiful women, she maintained her supremacy in the Prophet's harem to the end.

Polygamy creates divergence from Christianity

By uniting himself to a second wife Moḥammad made a serious movement away from Christianity, by the tenets and practice of which he must have known that polygamy was forbidden. Christianity, however, had little influence over his life; and the step was not repugnant to Judaism, the authority of which he still recognised, and which in the example of many illustrious kings and prophets would afford powerful support to his procedure. But, whatever the bearing of this second marriage, it was planned by Moḥammad in a cool and unimpassioned moment three years before at Mecca. And it may be doubted whether the propriety of interfering with the license of Arabian practice, and enforcing between the sexes the stringent limitations of Christianity, was at any time even debated in his mind.

CHAPTER IX

STATE OF PARTIES AT MEDĪNA. FIRST TWO YEARS OF MOḤAMMAD'S RESIDENCE THERE

A.H. II.—A.D. 623

Parties at Medīna

AS the enthusiasm of the Citizens gradually subsided, various sentiments began to be entertained towards their visitor by different sections of the community; and there arose in consequence a new disposition of parties in the city. Let us glance for a moment at each of these.

I. *Muhājirīn*, or 'Refugees'

The disciples of Moḥammad who forsaking house and home had preceded or now followed him into exile, were called by the title, soon to become illustrious, of MUHĀJIRĪN, or Refugees. They are already known to the reader as a devoted band, forward to acknowledge Moḥammad not only as their prophet but now also as their chief and leader. Upon them he could depend to the uttermost.[1]

II. *Anṣār*, or converts of Medīna

Next come the converts of Medīna. Bound to Moḥammad by fewer ties of blood or fellowship, they did not yield to the Refugees in loyalty to his person, or in enthusiasm for the faith. They had made less outward sacrifice; but their pledge at the 'Aḳaba had involved them in serious risks, as

[1] *Muhājir* (participle of the same root as *hijra*) signifies one who has emigrated, or fled from his home, for the faith. Among the 'Refugees' are reckoned not only those who having quitted Mecca were now at Medīna, but also all who subsequently joined Moḥammad (whether from Mecca, Abyssinia, or elsewhere) up to the conquest of Mecca A.H. VIII. The roll of the Refugees then closed; for Mecca itself being converted, the merit of emigrating from it ceased.

well at home, should their fellow-citizens resent or disown the engagement, as from the men of Mecca. In short, they had compromised themselves almost as deeply as the Refugees. Bound by their oath only to defend Moḥammad in case of attack, they soon practically identified themselves with the Refugees in offensive measures against his enemies at Mecca. Hence they were styled ANṢĀR, 'Helpers' or 'Allies.' But as in process of time Medīna was entirely converted, and as Moḥammad found other auxiliaries amongst the Arab tribes, it will be more convenient to speak of them simply as Citizens or men of Medīna.[1]

Enmity of the Aus and Khazraj suppressed by Islām

The ancient feuds of the Aus and Khazraj were almost forgotten among the converts from those tribes. Acceptance of the faith required that as Muslims they should acknowledge not only the spiritual but also the temporal authority of Moḥammad, and, holding subordinate every distinction of race and kindred, regard each other as brethren. Having surrendered to his will and government, little room was left for tribal rivalry. Still, the memory of long-standing jealousy and strife was not always suppressed by the lessons of religion; and believer was sometimes arrayed against believer in unseemly if not dangerous contention. We have no precise data for calculating the proportion of the inhabitants thus actively ranged on the side of Moḥammad. The 75 adherents who pledged themselves at the 'Aḳaba were but the representatives of a larger body even then existing at Medīna; and the cause of Islām had since that time been daily gaining ground. We may conclude that the professed converts at this time numbered several hundreds.

Converts at Medīna numerous

Abu 'Āmir and followers go off to Mecca

There was at Medīna one Abu 'Āmir, who had travelled in Syria and other countries, and from his secluded habits was called the *hermit.* This man professed to be a teacher in religion; and he challenged Moḥammad with having superadded doctrines of his own to the 'Faith of Abraham.' Offended at the popularity of the new religion and sympathising rather with the people who had cast forth the upstart Prophet, Abu 'Āmir, with about twenty

[1] Before Moḥammad's death, the two terms *Anṣār* and *Citizens* became convertible; that is to say, all the citizens of Medīna were ostensibly converted and so became *Anṣār.*

followers, retired to Mecca.[1] Eventually he died an exile in Syria.[2]

Moḥammad's authority recognised over his own adherents

The body of unconverted inhabitants were at the first neutral, or at least outwardly passive. There was no active opposition, nor, as at Mecca, any open denial of Moḥammad's supernatural claims; neither was his temporal authority over his adherents questioned. The constitution of society enabled him to exercise absolute and unquestioned control over his own people, without for the present arrogating jurisdiction over others. But although there was nowhere apparent hostility, and the whole body of the citizens, unbelievers as well as converts, held themselves bound in honour to fulfil the pledge of protecting the Exile, yet it was not long before an undercurrent of jealousy and discontent amongst a large and influential part of the community set in against him. We have seen that 'Abdallah ibn Obei, chief of the Khazrajites and the most powerful citizen in Medīna, was already aspiring to the sovereign power when his hopes were blighted by the arrival of Moḥammad.[3] Around

Idolatry and scepticism suppressed

[1] When Moḥammad denied his imputations against Islām, Abu 'Āmir abused him as 'a poor solitary outcast.' 'Nay,' replied the Prophet, 'that will be thine own fate, thou liar!' He took a prominent part with fifty followers against Moḥammad in the battle of Oḥod, in which his own son Ḥanẓala, a devoted Muslim, was killed fighting on the other side. After the conquest of Mecca, he retired to Aṭ-Ṭā'if. When Aṭ-Ṭā'if gave in its adhesion to Moḥammad, he proceeded to Syria; and there died (in fulfilment of the Prophet's curse) 'a solitary wretched outcast.' He seems to have been an ascetic, and is described by Sprenger as the leader of a party who adhered to the Jews as Proselytes of the Gate.

[2] Aṭ-Ṭabari, i. 1399; Ibn Hishām, pp. 411, 561.

[3] *Vide* p. 115 f. The following incident is related of him: One day Moḥammad saddled his ass and went forth to inquire after Sa'd ibn 'Obāda, who was sick. By the way he passed 'Abdallah sitting with a circle of his followers under the shade of his house. Moḥammad's courtesy would not permit him to pass without speaking; so he alighted, and saluted him and sat a little while beside him reciting some portion of the Ḳor'ān, and inviting him to the faith. 'Abdallah listened quietly till he ended; then he said: 'Nothing could be better than this discourse of thine, if it were true. Now, therefore, do thou sit at home in thine own house, and whosoever cometh to thee preach thus unto him, and he that cometh not unto thee refrain from troubling him with that which he dislikes.' Moḥammad went on his way to the house of Sa'd, downcast at what 'Abdallah, the enemy of God, had said unto him. Sa'd, perceiving him dispirited, inquired the cause. Moḥammad told

'Abdallah rallied a numerous party sceptical of the Prophet's claims and unfriendly to the extension of his rule; but these were unable to check the mysterious influence of the Stranger, or stem the tide of his popularity. The circle of his adherents steadily expanded, and soon embraced nominally the whole city. Idolatry disappeared, and scepticism, overmatched, was forced to hide its head.

III. The *Disaffected*

Real belief in Moḥammad was not, however, always of such rapid growth. Doubts and jealousies possessed the hearts of many; and in private, and at convenient distance, found free expression. They had foolishly espoused an Exile's cause which would make them run the gauntlet of all Arabia; and for what return? Only to lose their liberties, and bring themselves under bondage to a foreign usurper! The class which cherished these sentiments are named Hypocrites in the Ḳor'ān. But *hypocrisy* and *disaffection* are, in its vocabulary, nearly synonymous; and, as the views of this party developed into political rather than into religious antagonism, it will be more correct to call them the DISAFFECTED. Such outward conformity, cloaking an opposition ill concealed, was more dangerous than open animosity. The class soon became peculiarly obnoxious to Moḥammad; he established through his adherents a close and searching watch over both their words and actions; and in due time followed up his espionage by acts which struck dismay into the hearts of the disaffected.[1]

him what 'Abdallah had said. Then Sa'd replied: 'Treat him gently, for I swear that when God sent thee unto us, we had already strung pearls to crown him, and he seeth that thou hast snatched the kingdom out of his grasp.' Ibn Hishām, p. 411 ff.

[1] Ibn Isḥāḳ thus describes them: 'When the Jewish doctors were filled with hatred and envy of Moḥammad, because God had chosen a prophet from amongst the Arabs, there joined them certain men of the Aus and Khazraj, who were in reality little removed from heathenism and unbelief, only that Islām had by its prevalence overpowered them. So they took the faith outwardly as a shield unto them from death; but in secret they were traitors, and their hearts were with the Jews in their rejection of the Prophet.' Ibn Hishām, p. 351.

Tradition delights to hold up this class to scorn, in stories such as this:—'Julās, the hypocrite, said privately of Moḥammad's teaching: "Verily, if this man speak the truth, we are all worse than asses." 'Omeir, his ward, a believer, overheard the saying and told it to Moḥammad; Julās went also to Moḥammad, and swore by the day of

IV. The *Jews*

On an entirely different footing were the three JEWISH TRIBES established in their settlements without the city. Moḥammad had acknowledged the divine authority of their religion, and had even rested his claim, in an important degree, upon the evidence of their Scriptures and the testimony of their learned men. One of the objects nearest his heart was a federal union with the Jews. His feasts, his fasts and ceremonies were, up to this time, framed in close correspondence with Jewish custom. His very Ḳibla, the Holy of holies to which he and his people turned five times a day while they prostrated themselves in prayer, was Jerusalem. No concession, in fact, short of the abandonment of his claim to the prophetic office, was too great to gain the Jews over to his cause.

Treaty of Medīna with the Jews

It was natural that Moḥammad, holding these sentiments, should desire to enter into a close and binding union with the Jews, and this he did in a formal manner shortly after reaching Medīna. He associated them with himself by a treaty of mutual obligation drawn up in writing, which bound his followers on the one hand, and the Jews on the other, and confirmed the latter among other things in the practice of their religion and the secure possession of their property. The main provisions are the following :—

'IN THE NAME OF GOD, THE COMPASSIONATE, THE MERCIFUL!

'THE CHARTER of Moḥammad the Prophet, in behoof of the Believers, and whosoever else joineth himself unto them and striveth with them for the faith. The Refugees shall defray the price of blood shed among themselves, and shall ransom honourably their prisoners. The Believers of the various tribes of Medīna (named in detail) shall do the same. Whosoever is rebellious, or seeketh to spread enmity and sedition, the hand of every man shall be against him, even if he be a son. No Believer shall be put to death for the blood of an infidel; neither shall any infidel be supported against a Believer. Whosoever of the Jews followeth us shall have aid and succour; they shall not be injured, nor shall any enemy be aided against them. No unbeliever shall grant protection to the people of Mecca, either in person or property, nor inter-

judgment that 'Omeir lied. Whereupon a passage of the Ḳor'ān (vii. 75), convicting Julās of falsehood, was revealed.' There are also tales of the 'disaffected' being ignominiously expelled from the Mosque, and even from the clubs or social circles of the citizens; but all such tales are to be received with caution, owing to the natural bias against this class. Ibn Hishām, p. 355 ff.

pose between the Believers and them.[1] Whosoever killeth a Believer wrongfully the Muslims shall join as one man against him.

'The Jews shall contribute with the Muslims, while at war with a common enemy. The Jewish clans in alliance with the several tribes of Medīna are one people with the Believers.[2] The Jews will profess their religion, the Muslims theirs. As with the Jews, so with their adherents. No one shall go forth to war excepting with the permission of Moḥammad; but this shall not hinder any from seeking lawful revenge. The Jews shall be responsible for their expenditure, the Muslims for theirs; but, if attacked, each shall come to the assistance of the other. Medīna shall be sacred and inviolable for all that join this treaty. Strangers, under protection, shall be treated as their protectors are; but no female shall be so received save with consent of her kindred. Controversies and disputes shall be referred to the decision of God and His prophet. None shall join the men of Mecca or their allies; for verily the engaging parties are bound together against every one that shall threaten Medīna. War and Peace shall be made in common. He that goeth forth shall be secure; and he that sitteth at home shall be secure; —saving him that transgresseth and committeth wrong. And verily God is the protector of the righteous and the godly; and Moḥammad is His Prophet.'[3]

Ill-will grows up between Moḥammad and Jews

We are not told when this treaty was entered into, but it probably was not long after the arrival of Moḥammad at Medīna. For a short time the Jews remained on terms of cordiality with their new ally; but it soon became evident that Judaism could not go hand in hand with Islām. The position of Moḥammad was no longer negative: his religion was not a mere protest against error and superstition. It was daily becoming more positive, exclusive, and exacting in its terms. The Prophet rested his claims on the predictions of the Jewish Scriptures; yet he did not profess to be the

[1] *Unbeliever* here refers apparently to that portion of the population of Medīna which had not yet submitted to Moḥammad's claims, and who are thus brought indirectly within the covenant.

[2] Said to refer to Jewish proselytes from the Aus and Khazraj; but the expression may also mean Jews who had simply attached themselves to those tribes.

[3] Ibn Hishām, p. 341 ff. The translation is in an abridged form. There is throughout frequent reiteration that upright and honest dealing shall be observed, and whoever transgresses shall do so at his own risk, &c. There are some references to the hostility of Mecca and also anticipatory allusions to religious wars—additions made apparently at a later time. As there is no reason to believe that the original or any copy was preserved, we can only regard the treaty as transmitted by memory, and this will account for spurious clauses and loose expression.

Messiah of the Jews;—the Messiah had already appeared in the person of Jesus, and had been rejected by their forefathers. He was another, and a greater Prophet, also foretold in their Book. The Jews knew this well. They recognised in him the promised Prophet, 'even as they recognised their own sons'; yet, out of jealousy, and wilful blindness, they rejected him, in like manner as they had rejected their own Messiah. This was the position Mohammad now held, and to concede it was simply to abandon Judaism. Thus Judaism and Islām came rapidly into antagonism. In short, a Jew, in joining Mohammad, of necessity now abandoned his ancestral faith, and went over to another. With few exceptions, however, the Jews remained steadfast, and fearlessly testified that their Scriptures contained no warrant for the assumptions of the Ishmaelite;—the prophet that was to come —their long-looked for Messiah—should be not of Arabian, but of Jewish blood, and of the lineage of David. The cherished and now disappointed hope of the Jews, that they would find in Mohammad a supporter of their faith, soon changed into bitter hostility. What availed his oft-repeated professions of respect for their ancient prophets and of allegiance to their Scriptures, when he now so openly contradicted their clearest testimony?

They are inveighed against as blind and stiff-necked

The few faithless Jews, whom Mohammad was able (by what inducements we shall see by-and-by) to gain over, were of the utmost service to his cause. They are constantly referred to as his 'Witnesses.' They bore evidence that the person and character of Mohammad agreed in every particular with the prophetic description in their Books. Their brethren, jealous that the gift of prophecy should pass from them to another people, had hid the proofs of the Prophet's mission, or, by 'dislocating' them from the context, had misinterpreted the clear prediction. Of the believing few alone, the eyes were open. Judicial blindness had seized the rest; a 'thick covering' enveloped their hearts, and rendered them seared and callous. They followed in the footsteps of their forefathers. What but unbelief and rebellion should be looked for from the descendants of those who murmured against Moses, killed their prophets, and rejected the Messiah?

Such was the plausible reasoning by which Mohammad

The Jews a standing cause of annoyance to Moḥammad

succeeded with his own followers in setting aside the adverse testimony of the Jews. Yet the Jews were a constant cause of trouble and anxiety. They plied him with questions of which the point was often difficult to turn aside. The very people to whose testimony he had so long appealed in the Ḳor'ān, proved now a stubborn and standing witness against him.[1] The Jewish tribes were also allied each with some one or other of the Medīna clans; they had stood by them in trouble, and repeatedly shed blood in their defence. Sympathy in such a direction, especially amongst the doubting and disaffected Citizens, was dangerous to Moḥammad. He resolved to rid him of the risk and trouble; and he was not long in finding means to gain his end.

Notices of them in Ḳor'ān

Meanwhile, the portions of the Ḳor'ān given forth at this period teem with invectives against the Israelites. The tales of their forefathers' disobedience, folly, and idolatry are reiterated at wearisome length; and the conclusion is continually drawn that the descendants of so flagitious and incorrigible a race must themselves be equally incorrigible and flagitious. All this led, as will be explained in the following chapter, to the early and decisive secession of Moḥammad from the Jews, his abandonment of their customs and institutions, and the widening of the breach between the two.[2]

[1] Tradition gives a great variety of tales in illustration, but they are all cast in a mould of ridicule and contempt of the Jew, who is represented as always coming off the worst, humbled and abased. We may be allowed to doubt whether the scales did not oftener turn on the other side. Moḥammad evidently smarted at this period under the attacks of the Jews.

[2] We find, for example, such injunctions as the following in the Sūras of this period: 'Neither the Jews nor the Christians will rest satisfied with thee, until thou followest their religions. SAY,—Verily, God is the Guide, if thou followest their desires, thou shalt not have God for thy Master nor thy Helper.'—Sūra ii. 114.

CHAPTER X

RELIGIOUS INSTITUTIONS, AND MISCELLANEOUS EVENTS DURING THE FIRST AND SECOND YEARS OF THE HIJRA[1]

A.H. I. & II.—A.D. 623

The five times of daily prayer

THE new faith touched the outer life of its votaries at every step. Five times a day, as commanded in the Heavenly journey,[2] the Believer, however occupied, must turn aside to prayer. The rite remains to the present day the same, and consists in repeating a few petitions or short passages, with fixed ceremonial of genuflexion and prostration. The prayers by day were ordinarily said in the Mosque by the Prophet and such as dwelt in the vicinity. They might with equal merit be offered anywhere, at home or by the way, singly or in companies, but ever at the stated times. The service was invariably led by Moḥammad himself, when present; in his absence, by the chief person in the assembly, or by any one else charged by the Prophet with the duty. The nightly prayers were generally said at home.[3]

Lustration preliminary to prayer

Lustration had by this time become the necessary preliminary to prayer. When prescribed is uncertain. It may have been at Mecca; but, however that may be, it was evidently borrowed from the Jews, with whose teaching the

[1] Ibn Hishām, p. 346 f. [2] See p. 121.

[3] When the fast of Ramaḍān was appointed, the people in their zeal gathered in the Mosque at a late hour for the nightly prayer; and, fancying that the Prophet had fallen asleep, coughed at his door as a sign for him to issue forth. He came out, and said: 'I have observed for some days your coming for the nightly prayer into the Mosque, until I feared that it would grow by custom into a binding ordinance; and, verily, if it were so commanded, my people could not fulfil the command. Wherefore, pray ye at eventide in your own houses. Truly, the best prayer is that which a man offers up in his own house, excepting only the prayers which are commanded to be offered up in the Mosque.'

ordinances established by Moḥammad respecting ceremonial impurity and ablutions very closely correspond.

Daily round of prayer

The Believer's life has thus from the first been a daily round of religious observance. At dawn he begins the day with lustration, preliminary to the matin prayer; at mid-day he must for the moment leave his employment for the same duty; in the afternoon, and again when the sun has set, the ceremony is repeated; and the day is closed when darkness has set in by the same rite with which it opened. With this duty nothing may interfere. Saints and sinners join in the stereotyped form; no engagement, good or bad, however inappropriate to the occasion, may interfere with the performance of these devotions; and the neglect to observe them is an abnegation of the faith and insult to the majesty of Islām which demands interposition of the temporal arm.

Friday, or public service

The daily prayers are not necessarily congregational. They may be offered up by the worshippers singly or in companies, in the mosque, at home, or by the way. But at mid-day of Friday, the service took a more public form, at which the Believers as a body, unless detained by sufficient cause, were expected to attend. The usual prayers were on this occasion followed by an address or sermon pronounced by Moḥammad. This weekly oration was usefully adapted to the circumstances of the day and feelings of the audience. It allowed full scope for the Prophet's eloquence, and by its frequent recurrence helped to confirm his influence and rivet the claims of Islām. No religious antagonism is to be supposed in the selection of Friday for the public service, because, when he fixed upon it, Moḥammad was still on friendly terms with the Jews, and inclined to adopt their institutions. In the Christian Sunday he had a precedent for change, and he may have desired in a similar manner to distinguish the sacred day of Islām from the Jewish Sabbath.[1]

Sermon

[1] There is, moreover, no close analogy between the Jewish Sabbath and the Muslim Friday. In the latter there is no *hallowing* of the day as one meant for rest or religious worship. After the public service, the people were encouraged to return to their ordinary work. [Wellhausen holds the contrary opinion, that the sacred symbols of Islām were intended to cut it off from both Christianity and Judaism; Friday instead of Sunday and Sabbath, the call to prayer instead of bells and trumpets, Ramaḍān instead of Lent and the day of atonement.—*Das arabische Reich und sein Sturz*, p. 12.]

Perhaps also he hoped by the choice of another day to secure the attendance of the Jews at his public service, which was composed, like theirs, of prayer, reading of the Scripture, and a sermon. As a Jew (according to the doctrine of Moḥammad at this time) might follow all the precepts of Moses and yet be a perfect Muslim, it is by no means improbable that some Jews may at the first have attended both the synagogue and the mosque. There are instances of Rabbins being present at the service in the Mosque, as, indeed, there also are of the Synagogue being visited by Moḥammad himself, and by his followers.

Jerusalem the first Ḳibla

But in the second year, a change took place, which rendered it impossible for faithful Jews any longer to join in the Muslim service. Jerusalem was the first *Ḳibla* of Moḥammad; that is to say, after the fashion of the Jews, he and his followers prayed with their faces turned towards the Temple of Solomon. When no longer any hope remained of gaining over the Jews, or of fusing into one religion Judaism and Islām, then the ceremony lost its value. Rather it opened a vulnerable point: 'This Prophet of yours,' said the Jews tauntingly, 'knew not where to find his Ḳibla, till we pointed it out to him.' He might now avoid the charge by transferring the homage of his people from Jerusalem, and concentrating it upon the Ka'ba. His system would receive a fresh accession of strength and local influence if he were thus to magnify the Holy House and make it the Ḳibla of his people.

The Ḳibla changed to the Ka'ba. A.H. II. Nov. A.D. 623

Moḥammad, we are told, and also some of his followers, greatly desired the change. How it was effected is told us with the usual supernatural colouring. Sixteen or seventeen months after his arrival, the Prophet thus addressed his guardian angel: 'O Gabriel! would that the Lord might change the direction of my face at prayer away from the Ḳibla of the Jews!' 'I am but a servant,' replied Gabriel; 'address thy prayer to God.' So Moḥammad made his petition to the Lord. And it came to pass that on a certain day, as he was praying towards the Temple of Jerusalem, and raising his face upwards in that direction, the following divine revelation came unexpectedly to him: '*Verily We have seen thee turning about thy face towards the Heavens; wherefore We shall cause thee to turn towards a Ḳibla that shall please thee. Turn therefore thy face toward the holy Temple of Mecca. Wheresoever ye be, when ye pray, turn toward the same.*'[1] The Prophet had already performed two prostrations with his face towards Jerusalem, when, receiving this behest, he turned suddenly round, and with him all the worshippers in the Mosque, and finished thus the service looking to the south. Thenceforward Jerusalem was abandoned for the Ka'ba as the Ḳibla of Islām.[2] The incident significantly marked a change of policy. The tide, rising rapidly towards Judaism, now stayed and turned. The Jews, knowing full well the motives for the change, were mortified and estranged. Moḥammad had broken, as it were, the last outward link that bound him to their creed. They charged him with fickleness, and worshipping towards an idolatrous Temple, charges which he endeavoured in the Ḳor'ān to meet.[3] But it required the victory at Bedr, and

[1] Sūra ii. 139. [For the date when the change took place, *cf.* Aṭ-Ṭabari, i. 1279 f.]

[2] About three miles to the N.W. lies a mosque called the 'Mosque of the *double Ḳibla*,' where some say the change took place. Others give the title also to the mosque at Ḳobā. The change of the Ḳibla has elicited a great mass of discrepant tradition. Many spots are mentioned as the scene of its occurrence, and many different companies claim the honour of being its witnesses. Tradition delights to tell how, as the rumour spread abroad, one and another was startled by the strange intelligence. The most probable account gives the Great mosque as the scene, and the time that of mid-day prayer.

[3] The passage is instructive :—

Sūra ii. 136 ff. 'The Fools from amongst the people will say, *What hath turned them from their Ḳibla, towards which they used to pray?* SAY, Unto God belongeth the East and the West: He guideth whom He chooseth into the right way. Thus have We made you an intermediate People, that ye should be Witnesses for mankind; and the Prophet shall be Witness for you. We appointed the Ḳibla towards which thou usedst to pray, only that We might know him who followeth the Apostle from him that turneth back on his heels, although it be a stumbling block, excepting unto those whom God hath directed.' [*Here follows the verse quoted in the text; after which the passage proceeds:*] 'And verily, if thou wert to show unto those who have received the Scriptures every kind of sign, they would not follow thy Ḳibla; and thou shalt not follow their Ḳibla. Neither doth one part of them follow the Ḳibla of the other part.* And if thou wert to follow their desires after the knowledge that hath reached thee, then verily thou shouldest be amongst the Transgressors. They to

* Christians turn towards the East, and Jews towards Jerusalem: whence Moḥammad would argue a propriety in having a distinctive Ḳibla for Islām.

hostilities against the Jews themselves, to silence their objections. From this time forward Islām cast aside the trammels of the Mosaic law, and bound itself up with the worship of the Ka'ba.

The rite of circumcision is hardly to be mentioned as an institution of Islām. It was current among the Arabs as an Abrahamic ceremony, and so continued (without any command in the Ḳor'ān) [in which it is not mentioned or referred to] to be practised by the followers of Moḥammad.[1]

Circumcision

A few months after his arrival in Medīna, Moḥammad saw the Jews keeping the great Fast of the Atonement;[2] and he readily adopted it for his own people. Prior to this,

Fast of Atonement, A.H. II. Sept. A.D. 622

whom We have given the Scriptures know this,* even as they know their own children; but verily, a party amongst them hideth the truth designedly. . . . And every (people) hath a direction to which it turneth (in prayer). . . . Now, therefore, from whatsoever place thou comest forth, turn thy face towards the Holy Temple; for it is the truth from thy Lord, and God is not regardless of that which ye are doing. . . . Fear them not therefore; but fear Me, that I may fulfil My grace upon you, and that ye may be rightly directed.'

Shortly after comes the following passage (addressed probably also to the Jews) in justification of the pilgrim ceremony at the *Ṣafā* and *Merwa*, alleged to be, or to have been, the sites where two idols stood: 'Verily the *Ṣafā* and *Merwa* are of the monuments of God. Whosoever, therefore, performeth the Greater pilgrimage, of the Holy house, or the Lesser, it shall be no crime in him if he perform the circuit of them both. And whosoever performeth that which is good of a willing heart, verily God is grateful and knowing.' Sūra ii. 153. Ibn Hishām, p. 381 f.

[1] The practice is incumbent on Muslims as a part of the *Sunna* (custom or example of the Prophet), but it is curious that we have no authentic account of Moḥammad's own circumcision.

[2] '*Ashōr*, or the 'Fast of the Tenth,' *i.e.* tenth day of the seventh month.—*Lev.* xxiii. 27. It was a day of affliction and atonement; but popular tradition at Medīna assigned to it another origin. 'When Moḥammad asked the Jews what was the origin of the Fast, they said that it was in memory of the delivery of Moses out of the hands of Pharaoh, and the destruction of the tyrant in the Red Sea: "*We* have a greater right in Moses than they," said Moḥammad; so he fasted like the Jews, and commanded his people to fast also. Afterwards, when the Muslim Fast of Ramaḍān was imposed, Moḥammad did not command the Fast of 'Ashōr (*i.e.* of the tenth) to be observed, neither did he forbid it;' *i.e.* he left it optional to keep up the one as well as the other. Aṭ-Ṭabari, i. 1281. 'Āshūrā is the tenth (or ninth) day of the first month, Moḥarram.

* Either the change, or Moḥammad himself.

Fast of Ramaḍān substituted. A.H. II. Dec. A.D. 623

fasting does not appear to have been a prescribed ordinance of Islām. It was established at a period when it was the object of Moḥammad to bring his religion into harmony with the Jewish rites and ceremonies. But when he had cast off Judaism and its customs, this fast was to be superseded by another. Accordingly about a year and a half later, the divine command was promulgated that the following month of Ramaḍān (or Ramzan) was to be observed thenceforward as an annual fast. Although the new ordinance was expressly ordained as similar in principle to that of the Jews, yet its term and the mode of its observance were entirely different. At first the Muslims (following the Jews, who fasted for four-and-twenty hours from sunset to sunset) thought themselves bound to abstain from all enjoyments night and day throughout the month. Moḥammad checked this ascetic spirit. His followers were to fast rigorously by day, but from sunset till dawn they might eat and drink and indulge in all pleasures that were otherwise lawful.[1]

Its unequal pressure and rigour

It was winter when this fast was ordained, and Moḥammad probably then contemplated its being always

Sūra ii. 180 ff.

[1] 'O ye that believe! A Fast is ordained for you, as it was ordained for those before you, that haply ye may follow Piety,—

'For the computed number of days. The sick amongst you, and the traveller (shall fast), an equal number of other days; but he that is able to keep it (and neglecteth) shall make amends by the feeding of a poor man. And whoever performeth that which is good, of a willing heart, it shall be well for him. And if ye fast it shall be well for you, if ye comprehend,—

'In the month of Ramaḍān; wherein the Ḳor'ān was sent down . . . Wherefore let him that is present in this month fast during the same; but he that is sick, or on a journey, shall fast an equal number of other days God willeth that which is easy for you: He willeth not for you that which is difficult. . . . It is lawful unto you, during the nights of the Fast, to consort with your wives. They are a garment unto you, and ye are a garment unto them. God knoweth that ye are defrauding yourselves, wherefore He hath turned unto you, and forgiven you. Now, therefore, sleep with them, and earnestly desire that which God hath ordained for you; and eat and drink until ye can distinguish a white thread from a black thread, by the daybreak. Then keep the fast again until night, and consort not with them during the day; but be in attendance in the places of worship. These are the limits prescribed by God: wherefore draw not near unto them. Thus God declareth His signs unto mankind, that they may follow Piety.'

kept at the same season, in which case the prohibition to eat or drink during the day would not, even for a month, have involved any extreme hardship.[1] In the course of time, however, by the introduction of the lunar year, Ramaḍān gradually shifted till it reached the summer season; and then the prohibition to taste water from morning till evening became a burden heavy to bear. The strictness of the fast, as thus instituted, has nevertheless been maintained unrelaxed at whatever season it may fall; and to this day, in the parched plains of the East, for the whole month, however burning the sun and scorching the wind, the follower of Moḥammad may not suffer a drop of water, during the long summer day, to pass his lips; and he looks forward with indescribable longing for the sunset when, without compromising his faith, he may slake his thirst and refresh with food his drooping frame. For the sick and for travellers a dispensation is given; but, with this exception, a penalty is imposed on every breach. The trial, though thus unequally severe in different climes and at different terms of the cycle, is no doubt a wholesome exercise of faith and self-denial; but its limitation to the daytime must defeat the lesson of self-control, so far, at least, as certain classes of indulgence are concerned.

‘Īd al-Fiṭr, or Festival of ‘breaking the fast.’ A.H. II. Feb. A.D. 624

As soon as the new moon of the following month was seen (and it is still eagerly looked for every year throughout the Muslim world) the restriction was to cease, the next day being celebrated as a festival, called the ‘Īd al-Fiṭr, or ‘Breaking of the fast.’ A day or two previously, Moḥammad assembled the people, and instructed them in the ceremonies to be observed on the occasion. Early in the morning, they were to bring together their offerings for the poor; each one, young or old, bond or free, male or female, a measure of dates, of barley, or of raisins, or a smaller measure of wheat.[2] ‘See,’ said he, ‘that ye give plenty to the poor this day, so

[1] The Jewish intercalary year, which was probably in use at this time, would have prevented any change of season for a long series of years (see *ante*, p. cii). But when Moḥammad introduced the lunar year, that which might have been ‘easy’ at the first, came by the change of seasons to be often a grievous burden to his followers.

[2] This was before the imposition of regular almsgiving, or Zakāt, which will be noticed hereafter.

that they need not to go about and beg.' Having thus presented their alms, all went forth with the Prophet, who was clad in festive garments, to the *Muṣalla*, or place or prayer, outside the city on the road to Mecca.[1] A short spear or iron-shod staff (brought by Az-Zubeir from Abyssinia) was carried before him by Bilāl and planted on the spot. Taking his stand there, the Prophet recited certain prayers appropriate to the occasion, and then addressed the assembled multitude. The service over, they returned to their homes, after which Moḥammad, having made a feast at the Mosque, distributed the alms of his followers amongst the poor.[2]

'Īd al-Aḍha combined with Fast of Atonement. Dhu'l-Ḥijja, A.H. I. March, A.D. 623

Another great festival was established shortly after;—the 'ĪD 'AL-AḌHA, or 'Day of sacrifice.' At the annual pilgrimage of Mecca (as we have seen) victims have from time immemorial been slain at the close of the ceremonies in the vale of Mina. For the first year at Medīna the occasion passed unnoticed. But, Jewish rites being still in favour, Moḥammad kept the great Day of Atonement with its sacrifice of victims in its stead; and had he continued on a friendly footing with the Jews, he would, no doubt, have maintained the practice. In the following year, however, it was in keeping with his altered relations to abandon altogether the Jewish ritual of sacrifice, and to substitute for it another somewhat similar in character, but grounded on the ceremonies of the Ka'ba and held simultaneously with them. It was after having waged war against one of the Jewish tribes settled in the suburbs of Medīna, and having expatriated them from the country, that Moḥammad resolved upon the change. Accordingly at the moment while the votaries of the Ka'ba were engaged in the closing solemnities of the pilgrimage at Mina, Moḥammad, preceded by Bilāl carrying the Abyssinian staff, and followed by the people, went forth to the place of prayer without the city. After a

But subsequently shifted to correspond with Meccan pilgrimage. A.H II. April, A.D. 624

[1] Speaking of 'Moḥammad's mosque in the Munākha' (or open space between the city and its western suburb), Burton writes: 'Others believed it to be founded upon the Musalla el Nabi, a place where the Prophet recited the first Festival prayers after his arrival at El Medinah, and used frequently to pray, and to address those of his followers who lived far from the Harem' (or Great mosque).—ii. 192.

[2] At-Ṭabari, i. 1281.

service resembling that of the breaking of the Fast, two fatted sucking kids, with budding horns, were placed before him. Seizing a knife, he sacrificed the first, saying: 'O Lord! I offer this for my people, those that bear testimony to thy Unity and to my Mission.' Then he called for the other, and, slaying it likewise, said:—'O Lord! this is for Moḥammad, and for the family of Moḥammad.' Of the latter kid both he and his family partook, and that which was over he gave to the poor. The double sacrifice seems in its main features to have been founded on the practice of the Jewish high-priest at the Day of the Atonement, when he sacrificed 'first for his own sins, and then for the people's.'[1] The ceremony was repeated by Moḥammad every year when present at Medīna, and it is still observed throughout the Muslim world at the time when the sacrificial rite is being performed at Mina which closes the Greater pilgrimage.[2]

The Azān, or call to prayer

The summons to prayer was at first the simple cry, 'To public prayer!' After the Ḳibla was changed, Moḥammad bethought himself of a more formal call. Some suggested the Jewish trumpet, others the Christian bell; but neither was grateful to the Prophet's ear.[3] The AZĀN, or call to prayer, was then established. Tradition claims for it a supernatural origin;—'While the matter was under discussion, a citizen dreamed that he met a man clad in green raiment carrying a bell, and he sought to buy it, saying that it would do well for assembling the faithful to prayer. "I will show thee," replied the stranger, "a better way than that; let a crier call aloud, GREAT IS THE LORD! GREAT IS THE LORD! *I bear witness that there is no God but the Lord: I bear witness that Moḥammad is the Prophet of God. Come*

[1] Heb. vii. 27; Lev. xvi. Aaron offered a sacrifice 'for himself and for his house,' besides 'the goat of the sin-offering that is for the people.'

[2] Aṭ-Ṭabari, i. 1362. The short staff or lance, used at the two Festivals by the Prophet, was still in the keeping of the Muezzin at Medīna in the 2nd or 3rd century, and used to be carried in state before the Governor of Medīna when he went forth to celebrate these Festivals.

[3] Ibn Hishām says that he had actually given orders for a trumpet to be made, which was probable enough during his first relations with the Jews. Afterwards disliking the idea, he ordered a wooden bell or 'gong' to be constructed; and it was already hewn out, when this dream settled the question in favour of the *Azān*.

unto Prayer: Come unto Salvation. God is Great! God is Great! There is no God but the Lord!" Awaking from sleep, he went straightway to Moḥammad, and told him the dream; when, perceiving that it was a vision from the Lord, the Prophet forthwith commanded Bilāl, his negro servant, to carry out the divine behest.' Ascending the top of a lofty house beside the Mosque while it was yet dark, Bilāl watched for the break of day, and on the first glimmer of light, with his far-sounding voice, aroused all around from their slumbers, adding to the divinely-appointed call these words, 'Prayer is better than Sleep! Prayer is better than Sleep!' Every day, at the five appointed times, the well-known cry summoned the people to their devotions. For twelve centuries the same call has continually sounded forth from a myriad minarets; and the traveller in the East is still startled in his sleep at early dawn by Muezzins crying aloud from their various mosques the self-same words used by Bilāl.[1]

Call used for convening a general assembly

The old cry, 'To public prayer,' was still retained for secular occasions, as when an assembly was summoned for the announcement of a victory, or for the proclamation of a general order, such as the going forth to war. The people hurried to the Mosque at the call, but it had no longer any connection with their devotions.

The pulpit

On the spot where Moḥammad used to stand in the Great Mosque at public prayers, the branch of a date-tree was planted as a post for him to hold by. When the Ḳibla was changed, the post was taken up from the northern end and fixed near the southern wall. In process of time Moḥammad, now beyond the prime of life, began to feel

[1] Ibn Hishām, p. 347 f. After crying the Azān, Bilāl used to come to the door of Moḥammad and rouse him thus: 'To prayer, oh Apostle of God! to Salvation!' Then Bilāl would take his stand in the front row of the worshippers, who used strictly to follow his example in the prayers and genuflexions. There were two other Muezzins employed by Moḥammad, but they acted only in case of Bilāl's absence. As the Prophet's treasurer, Bilāl also kept the money and the gifts presented to Moḥammad. He was held in much esteem by the Muslims; and by his influence obtained a free-born Arab wife for his negro brother. Bilāl, like many other Muslim warriors, was granted landed property at Damascus, where he died A.H. 20, aged sixty, and where his tomb is still shown. *Caliphate*, p. 238.

fatigue at standing throughout the long Friday service. So he consulted with his followers; and one said: 'Shall I make for thee a pulpit such as I have seen in the churches of Syria?' The thing pleased Moḥammad, both as a relief to himself, and with the view of being better seen and heard at public worship. Accordingly one or two tamarisk trees were felled and fashioned into a pulpit, having a place to sit on, and three steps leading up to it. It was erected near the southern wall on the spot which the pulpit of the Great mosque occupies to the present day.

Manner of daily prayer

Moḥammad ascended the pulpit for the first time on a Friday. As he mounted the steps, he turned towards the Ka'ba, and uttering a loud *Tekbīr*, 'God is most great!' the whole assembly from behind burst forth into the same exclamation. Then he bowed himself in prayer, still standing in the pulpit with his face to the south, and his back to the people; after which he descended, stepping backwards, and at the foot of the pulpit prostrated himself towards the Ka'ba. This he did twice, using appropriate verses and ejaculations. Then, the prayers being ended, he turned round to the assembly and told them he had done all this that they might know and imitate his manner of worship. Such was the form of daily prayer; and, handed down from generation to generation, such to the minutest point it has continued ever since. Worshippers drawn up now as then by rows in the mosques, the wayfarer who overtaken at the hour spreads his carpet for prayer by the roadside, high and low, rich and poor, prince and peasant, all follow with exactest scrupulosity the example of their Prophet in his forms of obeisance and prostration.[1]

And of the Friday service

The order of the Friday service, which all were expected to attend, is thus described. On entering the place of worship the Prophet mounted the pulpit and gave the assembly the salutation of peace. Then he sat down, while Bilāl sounded forth the call to prayer. When this was over he descended, and, turning towards the Ka'ba, performed

[1] A series of two obeisances followed by prostration, with appropriate ejaculations and prayers, is called a *Rak'a*. It is said that Moḥammad, a month after his arrival at Medīna, prescribed two such Rak'as for each time of prayer, but subsequently increased them to four, excepting for persons on a journey.

the prayers as at other times. After this, he usually ascended the pulpit again, and delivered one or more addresses, sitting down between each. He would on such occasions gesticulate in earnest discourse, with outstretched arm and pointed finger. The people, with faces raised, would hang upon his words, and at the close join in a loud *Amen.* As he discoursed he leant upon a staff. On Fridays and Festivals he was clad in a mantle of striped Yemen stuff thrown over his shoulders, with a girdle of fine cloth from 'Omān, bound about his waist. At the conclusion of the service, these robes were folded up and carefully put away. At other times he ministered in his ordinary dress.

Extraordinary sanctity of the pulpit

The pulpit was invested with a special sanctity. Oaths regarding disputed rights were taken close beside it. Any one who should swear falsely by it, 'even if the subject were as insignificant as a toothpick,' was doomed to hell. The Prophet used to speak of the space between the pulpit and his door 'as one of the gardens of paradise.' The figurative words were soon taken literally, and the fond conceit we find perpetuated to the present day by flowery carpeting on the floor, and festoons to correspond, upon the walls. 'It is a space,' says Burton, 'of about eighty feet in length, tawdrily decorated, so as to resemble a garden. The carpets are flowered, and the pediments of the columns are cased with bright green tiles, and adorned to the height of a man with gaudy and unnatural vegetation in arabesque.'[1]

The moaning post

When Moḥammad took possession of the pulpit, he expressed in feeling terms his sorrow at parting with the post by side of which he had so long prayed, and commanded it to be buried beneath the pulpit. Tradition adds the romantic story that the post moaned loudly at its desertion, and would not cease until the Prophet, placing his hand upon it, soothed its grief.[2]

[1] Similarly, Moḥammad said that his pulpit was 'over one of the Fountains of Paradise';—as a church might be called 'the gate of Heaven.' The sanctity of the pulpit was so great that, at times other than the public assembly, worshippers used to come, and, catching the knob of the pulpit, pray, holding it with their hands.

[2] It is a congenial subject for tradition. The people were terrified at the noise, for the groanings of the post were 'like those of a she-camel ten months gone with young'; and it ceased not till the Prophet fondly stroked it with his hand. It was then buried under the pulpit, or, as

During the first year of his residence Moḥammad lost two of his chief adherents among the men of Medīna. Kulthūm, with whom he had lodged at Ḳobā, died shortly after his arrival. And the Mosque was hardly completed, when As'ad, son of Zurāra, one of the earliest converts, was seized with a virulent sore-throat. He belonged to the famous Six who first met Moḥammad at Mina. Elected 'Leader' of the Beni an-Najjār when they pledged their faith to the Prophet at the 'Second 'Aḳaba,' he had ever since taken a prominent part in the spread of Islām. Muṣ'ab, when sent from Mecca to instruct the inquirers at Medīna, lodged with him, and together they had openly established prayers in the city His house was hard by the Great Mosque, where, as we have seen, he welcomed Moḥammad on his arrival, and took charge of his favourite camel. The Prophet was deeply grieved at his illness; but most of all was he troubled by the insinuations of the Jews and disaffected citizens. 'If this man were a prophet,' they said, 'could he not have warded off sickness from his friend?' 'And yet,' said Moḥammad, 'I have no power from my Lord over even mine own life, or over that of any of my followers. The Lord destroy the Jews that speak thus!' He visited his sick friend frequently, and twice caused his neck to be cauterised all round. But the remedies were of no avail; he sank rapidly and died. Moḥammad preceded the funeral procession to the spot which had been selected for a burial-ground. It was a large enclosure, studded with thorny shrubs, without the city, to the east, called *Baḳī' al-Gharḳad.*[1] As'ad was the first of the illustrious band of early heroes buried in the cemetery, whose tombs are still visited by the pilgrim.[2]

Death of Kulthūm and As'ad ibn Zurāra

For many months after their arrival, it so happened that no children were born to the Muslim women; and the rumour began to spread abroad that their barrenness was due to the sorcery and enchantments of the Jews. More than a year of the Hijra had elapsed when the first infant was born to the Refugees—the wife of Az-Zubeir presenting

Barrenness of the Muslim women

others say, placed among the rafters of the roof. According to another tradition, Moḥammad *embraced* the post, and then it stopped moaning; on which the Prophet said, that 'had he not done so, it would not have ceased to moan till the Day of Judgment.'

[1] So called from the thorns that covered it. [2] Aṭ-Ṭabari, i. 1260 f.

him with a son; and shortly after, the same good fortune happened to one of the Citizens. These births, dispelling their apprehensions, caused great joy among the Believers. It may possibly have been with reference to such supposed enchantments that Moḥammad composed one or other of the two short Sūras which now stand at the close of the Ḳor'ān and which are used as spells to counteract mischievous designs. A later occasion (hereafter mentioned) is, however, assigned them by tradition.[1]

Moḥammad's nervous temperament

The Prophet was of a highly strung and nervous temperament. So afraid was he of darkness, that, on entering a room at night, he would not sit down till a lamp had been lighted for him; and Al-Wāḳidi adds that he had such a repugnance to the form of the cross that he broke everything brought into the house with the figure upon it. When cupped, he would have the operation performed an *odd* number of times, believing that the virtue was greater than with an even number. He also fancied that cupping on any Tuesday which fell on the 17th of the Month was peculiarly efficacious, a remedy even for all the disorders of the coming year. If the heavens were overcast with heavy clouds, he would change colour, and betray a mysterious apprehension till they cleared away; and he was also strangely anxious about the effect of the winds.[2] Such traditions, which, from their number and agreement, must be more or less founded on fact, illustrate the nervous sensibility, and apprehension of unseen and supernatural influences for good or for evil, which were liable to affect his mind.

[1] *Op. cit.* i. 1263 f.

[2] 'When the wind blew ('Ā'isha tells us) the Prophet would say: "O Lord! verily I supplicate Thee for good from this wind, and good from its nature, and good for that thing for which it is sent; and I seek protection with Thee from the bad effects of this wind, and its baneful influence, and the harm which it was sent to do." And when black clouds loured, he used to change colour; and he would come out, go in, walk forwards and backwards; and when they rained, and passed away without doing harm, his alarm would cease. On 'Ā'isha asking him the reason, he said: "O 'Ā'isha! peradventure these clouds and winds might be like those which are mentioned in the history of the tribe of 'Ād. For when they saw a cloud overshadowing the heavens, they said, *This is a cloud bringing rain for us;* but it was not so, but a punishment because they had called for rain impatiently; and there was in it a destroying wind."'

Simplicity of Moḥammad's life

Moḥammad lived a simple life. His wives' apartments, in which he dwelt by turns, were homely in appearance, built of unburnt brick and thatched with palm-branches, in dimension but twelve or fourteen feet square, and so low that the roof might be reached by the hand. The doorway was protected by a screen of goat and camel hair; but 'Ā'isha's apartment had a wooden door. Some had an outer room or verandah formed by a second wall, in others by a mere partition of palm-twigs daubed with mud. At the door of 'Ā'isha's chamber was a closet, where in the evening or at night Moḥammad used to retire for his devotions. The furnishings were in keeping. A leathern mattress stuffed with palm-coir was spread for repose upon the floor, with pillows of the same material. The Prophet himself sometimes used a cot of teak-wood strung with coarse cords of the palm;[1] but ordinarily the mattresses sufficed. In place of garniture the walls were hung with skins such as are used in the East to hold water, milk, or honey, and when empty are blown out and so suspended.

'Abdallah, the attendant of Moḥammad

The constant attendant of Moḥammad was 'Abdallah ibn Mas'ūd, whose mother, once like her son a slave, performed the same menial office for the Prophet's wives. Both were now free. 'Abdallah was secretary to Moḥammad as well as body-servant, and attended him in his campaigns. He took charge of his bed, his shoes or sandals, his toothpicks, and his washing gear. When bathing he screened him; when sleeping he watched him; and he accompanied him abroad. If the Prophet went forth upon a visit, 'Abdallah would bring his shoes for him to put on, and taking charge of his staff precede him on the way. Reaching his destination, 'Abdallah again took charge of his shoes and gave the staff into his hand; returning home, he did as before, re-entering in advance. He resided close by the Mosque, and was always ready at the call of Moḥammad. From 'Abdallah much of the tradition regarding the life and habits of the Prophet has been gathered; and his known intelligence and veracity have secured for his narrations special weight.[2]

[1] The cot is said to have been a gift from As'ad. After the Prophet's death it was used as a bier at funerals, and was eventually sold for a great price.

[2] If one may judge by the style of his traditions, he was particularly careful and conscientious in the statement of his recollections; though,

Anas also attended the Prophet, and above a dozen other persons are named as having served him at various times: but 'Abdallah was his favourite.[1]

Contrast between Moḥammad's simple life and the luxury of his followers

Comparing the sumptuous luxury which rapidly sprang up throughout the Muslim world with the homeliness of Moḥammad's life, tradition would draw for his degenerate followers a lesson of frugality and self-denial, and even imply that the Prophet suffered want and hardship. But meanness and discomfort lay only in contrast with the pomp and splendour of a Caliph's court. Bred in the simplicity of Arab life, artificial comforts, soon regarded by his followers as necessaries of life, would to him have been irksome and weary. The Prophet was happier with his wives each in her small and rudely furnished cabin, than he would have been surrounded with all the delicacies and grandeur of a palatial residence.

In this, and the preceding chapter, the history has been somewhat anticipated in order to trace the development of several of the social and religious institutions that followed close upon the Hijra. Our story will now lead us to more stirring scenes.

like the other Companions of the Prophet, he used to be surrounded by crowds of curious inquirers, and thus had every temptation to exaggerate. He was settled by 'Omar at Al-Kūfa with great distinction, and survived Moḥammad twenty years.

[1] Anas, or Anis, must now have been young, for some seventy-five years after we find him seized by the tyrant Al-Hajjâj, but liberated with honour by the Caliph, 'as one who had faithfully waited on the Prophet for ten years.' See *Caliphate*, p. 345.

CHAPTER XI

HOSTILITIES BETWEEN MEDĪNA AND MECCA

A.H. I. & II.—A.D. 623

Repose at Medīna for the first six months

THE first six months of Moḥammad's residence at Medīna were disturbed neither by alarms from without nor by hostile councils at home. Vindictive thoughts died out of Mecca. He who had for so many years kept the city in excitement, broken up old parties, and introduced a new faction of his own, was now with all his adherents gone, and his absence gave immediate relief. The current of society, long troubled and diverted by his designs, now returned to flow peaceably for a while in its ancient channel.

Hostilities contemplated by Moḥammad from the first;

The thoughts of Moḥammad, on the other hand, from the day of his flight, were not thoughts of peace. In his Revelation vengeance was threatened against his enemies — a vengeance not postponed to a future life, but immediate and overwhelming even now. Sheltered in his present refuge, he might become the agent for executing the divine sentence, and at the same time triumphantly impose the true religion on those who had rejected it. Hostility to Ḳoreish lay as a seed germinating in his heart; it wanted but a favourable opportunity to spring up.

But deferred from motives of policy

The opportunity did not at once present itself. The people of Medīna were pledged only to defend the Prophet from attack, not to join in aggressive steps against enemies. He must take time to gain their affections, and secure co-operation in offensive measures against those who had cast him out. His followers from Mecca were too few to measure arms alone with Ḳoreish. They were also, like himself, at present occupied by the duty of providing dwelling-places for their families. In fulfilling this domestic obligation, in establishing friendly relations with the citizens of Medīna and at the first also with the Jewish tribes, in organising civil and religious institutions for his followers now fast assuming the position of an independent body, and in riveting the hold of his theocratic government upon them, the autumn of the first year passed away. From midsummer to winter was passed in peace.

Extent and value of the caravan trade of Mecca with Syria

But in their caravan traffic with the north (the beaten path of which passed between Medīna and the seacoast), the Ḳoreish offered a point for attack too vulnerable, and prospect of booty too tempting, for this inaction long to last. The trade of Mecca was large and profitable. From thence, and from its sister city Aṭ-Ṭā'if, caravans proceeded in the autumn to the Yemen and Abyssinia, and in spring to Syria. Leather, gums, frankincense, the precious metals, and other products of Arabia, formed the staples of export. The leather of Mecca, Aṭ-Ṭā'if, and the Yemen was in much request both in Syria and Persia, and fetched a high price. Piece-goods, silk, and articles of luxury were received in exchange at Gaza and other Syrian marts, and carried back to Mecca. We read of at least six such expeditions during the year following the Flight, and there were, no doubt, several more. Some of these caravans were very large and very rich. One consisted of 2,000 camels, whose freight was valued at 50,000 dīnārs. The annual export trade of Mecca has been estimated by Sprenger at not less than 250,000 dīnārs, and the return merchandise at the same amount.[1] The ordinary profit being 50 per cent., it is easy to see how lucrative was the traffic, and how greatly the merchants of Mecca must have been dismayed at any contingency that

[1] These figures can only be taken as conjectural; but as each camel carried about 2 cwt. of costly goods, the value must, no doubt, have been very considerable. The dīnār (or *mithḳāl*) was a golden coin corresponding with the Byzantine *aureus;* the dirhem (drachma) a silver coin. Sprenger, by elaborate calculation, estimates the dīnār at about 15 francs,—or say about two-thirds of a pound sterling. The silver dirhem he rates at 72 centimes, say *6d.* to *8d.* Considering the high value in that age of the precious metals, the caravans at the figures mentioned in the text must have been rich indeed. By the Byzantine system, gold stood to silver in the ratio of 14⅖ to 1; among the Muslims, strange to say, the ratio was as low as 8 or 9, and even 7, to 1; at which rate the legal demands were commuted; subsequently the ratio rose to 10 or 12. Gold was the currency in the Byzantine provinces, as Syria and Western Mesopotamia; silver in Persia and Babylonia.

might threaten its safety. Moreover, the whole city of Mecca was devoted to the trade. While the leading merchants embarked great sums in these expeditions, almost every citizen who could spare a dīnār or two invested in them his little capital. A caravan was ordinarily under the conduct of the one or two chief men who owned the bulk of the merchandise; but these for a consideration of half the profit, readily took charge also of the smaller ventures, as commissions to be accounted for on their return. It thus happened that in some of the larger caravans, almost every citizen, man and woman, having any means at command, owned a share however small; and when such a caravan was threatened the whole city was thrown into alarm.

The whole city devoted to the traffic

The caravans, indeed, had always been subject to a certain risk from the attack of Arab bandits. Halting by day and travelling by night, the long strings of camels, with but a slender escort, were at once thrown into confusion, especially in defiles and narrow passes, by the onset of a few determined brigands, who in the turmoil could secure their plunder and effect an easy retreat. The danger from such desultory attack was ordinarily met by extreme caution on the part of the leader, whose scouts gave timely notice of any risk, and who was able accordingly, either by retiring or by a hurried movement forward, to avoid it. But Ḳoreish were not slow to perceive that their position must be very different now with an enemy on the watch, who, like an eagle from his eyrie, was ever ready to swoop down unawares upon their caravans. During the first six months, however, it was not the period for traffic northwards, and Moḥammad was otherwise engaged at home. But the season was now approaching; and Ḳoreish watched with anxiety the attitude of the Prophet and his exiled band towards the first caravans which they were now despatching to Syria.

This trade a vulnerable point of attack from Medīna

The earliest acts of hostility were of a petty and marauding character; but still sufficiently indicative of the impending struggle.[1] In the winter, about seven months after his arrival,[2] Moḥammad despatched his uncle Ḥamza, at the head of some 30 Refugees, to surprise a caravan returning

Expeditions against Ḳoreishite caravans

[1] Ibn Sa'd, p. 2 ff.; Al-Wāḳidi, p. 33 f.

[2] I follow the chronology of M. C. de Perceval. Sprenger makes the date fall about two and a half months later.

First: Ḥamza, Ramadān. A.H. I. Dec. A.D. 622

from Syria under the guidance of Abu Jahl.[1] Guarded by 300 Koreish, it was overtaken near the seashore, when a chief of the Beni Juheina, confederate of both, interposed between the parties already drawn up for an encounter; Ḥamza upon this retired to Medīna, and Abu Jahl proceeded on his journey. About a month later a body, double the strength of the first, was sent by Moḥammad under command of his cousin 'Obeida, in pursuit of another caravan protected by Abu Sufyān with 200 men.[2] Ḳoreish were surprised while their camels were grazing by a fountain in the valley of Rābigh; but the Muslims found the escort too strong for them, and, beyond the discharge of arrows from a distance, no hostilities were attempted. 'Obeida is distinguished in tradition as he who, on this occasion, 'shot the first arrow for Islām.' In the convoy there were two Believers who, finding an opportunity, fled from the caravan and joined the party of 'Obeida. After the lapse of another month, a third expedition started, under the youthful Sa'd with 20 followers, in the same direction.[3] He was to proceed as far as a certain valley on the road to Mecca, and there lie in wait for a caravan expected to pass that way. Like most of the subsequent parties intended to effect a surprise, they marched by night and lay in concealment during the day. Notwithstanding this precaution, when they reached their destination on the fifth morning, they found that the caravan had passed a day before, and so they returned empty-handed to Medīna.

Second: 'Obeida ibn al-Ḥārith. A.H. I. Jan. A.D. 623

Third: Sa'd ibn abi Waḳḳāṣ

A standard presented by Moḥammad to each leader

These excursions occurred in the winter and spring of the year. On each occasion, Moḥammad mounted a white banner on a staff or lance, and presented it to the leader on his departure. In these and all other expeditions of any importance the names of the leaders, and also of those who carried the standard, are carefully recorded by tradition.[4]

Three expeditions conducted by Moḥammad himself:— Al-Abwā Safar, A.H. II. June, A.D. 623

In the summer and autumn of the same year, Moḥammad led in person three somewhat larger, though equally unsuccessful, expeditions. The first set out in midsummer, nearly twelve months after his arrival, and was directed to Al-Abwā

[1] Ibn Hishām, p. 419 f.; Aṭ-Ṭabari, i. 1265 f.
[2] Ibn Hishām, p. 416 f.; Aṭ-Ṭabari, i. 1267
[3] *Op. cit.* p. 422 f., and i. 1265 f.
[4] A small night attack is called *sarīya;* a larger expedition, especially one in which Moḥammad himself took part, *ghazwa*—a term still in use.

(the spot where his mother was buried) in pursuit of a Koreishite caravan.[1] The prey was missed; but something was gained in a friendly treaty concluded with a tribe hitherto connected with Mecca, but now detached from its alliance. The treaty was committed to writing, the first that Moḥammad entered into with any outside body. He returned, after fifteen days' absence, to Medīna. Next month, the Prophet again marched, at the head of 200 followers, including a large number of the Citizens,[2] to Bowāṭ on the caravan route south-west of Medīna. A rich burden laden on 2,500 camels, under the escort of one of Moḥammad's chief opponents, Omeiya ibn Khalaf, with 100 armed men, was to proceed that way. But it eluded pursuit, and passed on safely. The presence of so many Citizens shows the advancing influence of Moḥammad; they were, no doubt, tempted by the hope of so great a prize; but whether or no, they had now crossed the Rubicon and identified themselves with Moḥammad in hostilities against Ḳoreish. Shortly after their return, some of the camels and flocks of Medīna, while feeding in a plain a few miles from the city, were fallen upon by Kurz ibn Jābir, a marauding Bedawi chieftain, and carried off.[3] Moḥammad pursued him nearly to Bedr, but he made good his escape. We find him not long afterwards converted to Islām, and leading a Muslim expedition against a Bedawi robber like himself.

Bowāṭ: A.H. II. July, A.D. 623

(Kurz ibn Jābir makes a raid near Medīna)

Two or three months elapsed before Moḥammad set out on his third expedition.[4] Volunteers were invited, and from 150 to 200 followers joined the party. They had between them only thirty camels, on which they rode by turns. At 'Osheira, distant nine marches on the way to Yenbo', they expected to waylay a rich caravan which Abu Sufyān was conducting towards Syria, and of the departure of which from Mecca tidings had been received. But it had passed several days before. It is the same caravan which, on its

'Osheira: A.H. II. Oct. A.D. 623

[1] Ibn Hishām, p. 415 f.; Aṭ-Ṭabari, i. 1270.

[2] Ibn Hishām, p. 421; Aṭ-Ṭabari, i. 1268. More than half must have been Medīna men: for at the battle of Bedr, when every exile from Mecca was mustered, there were but 83 Refugees present.

[3] Ibn Hishām, p. 423. [This raid is sometimes called 'the first Bedr.'] Aṭ-Ṭabari, i. 1269 f.

[4] [According to Ibn Hishām (p. 421 f.) and Aṭ-Ṭabari (i. 1269 f.) a few days before.]

return from Syria, gave occasion to the famous action of Bedr. In this excursion the Prophet entered into an alliance with several tribes inhabiting the vicinity of 'Osheira. He was thus gradually extending his influence along the sea-shore, and so still further hedging the passage of the Meccan caravans. An instance of the pleasantry in which the Prophet sometimes indulged is here recorded. 'Alī had fallen asleep on the dusty ground under the shade of a palm-grove. Moḥammad espied him lying thus, all soiled with the dust, and, pushing him with his foot, called out, 'Ho! Abu Torāb! (*Father of dust*) is it thou? Abu Torāb, sit up!' 'Alī, half-ashamed, sat up; and the sobriquet ever after clung to him.[1] On each of these expeditions Moḥammad appointed a standard-bearer to carry his white banner. Ḥamza, Sa'd, and 'Alī successively had this honour.

Moḥammad concludes alliance with tribes by the way

Moḥammad calls 'Alī Abu Torāb

His standard-bearers

Moḥammad leaves representative at Medīna

Whenever the Prophet left Medīna to proceed to any distance, he named a representative to exercise authority over those who were left behind, and to lead the public prayers during his absence. The first person selected for the office was one of the twelve 'Leaders,' Sa'd ibn 'Obāda, of the Beni'l-Khazraj. The next who received this token of confidence was Sa'd ibn Mo'ādh, of the Beni'l-Aus, so carefully was Moḥammad minded to distribute his favours between these two jealous tribes. On the third occasion his friend Zeid was honoured with the post.

Affair of Nakhla. Rajab: A.H. II. Nov. A.D. 623

In November and December, Moḥammad did not himself quit Medīna; but he sent forth 'Abdallah ibn Jaḥsh, with seven other Refugees, on an expedition attended with more serious results than any of the preceding.[2] As he bade farewell to 'Abdallah, the Prophet placed in his hands a closed packet, and charged him not to open it till he entered a certain valley two days' march toward Mecca. On reaching the spot, 'Abdallah broke open the letter, and read it aloud to his comrades as follows: *Go forward to Nakhla, in the name of the Lord, and with His blessing! Yet force not any of thy followers against his inclination. Proceed with those that accompany thee willingly; and when thou hast arrived at the valley of Nakhla, lie there in wait for the caravans of*

[1] Aṭ-Ṭabari, i. 1272 f.

[2] Ibn Hishām, p. 423 ff.; Aṭ-Ṭabari, i. 1275 ff.; Al-Wāḳidi, p. 34 f.; Ibn Sa'd, p. 5.

Ḳoreish. Nakhla has been already noticed as lying to the east of Mecca, about half-way to At-Ṭā'if; and the trade with South Arabia all passed that way. Watched and pursued in their commerce with Syria, traffic would be all the more securely and busily prosecuted towards the South by the merchants of Mecca; for the route lay far removed from the outlook of their enemy. Moḥammad had, no doubt, intimation of some rich venture, shortly expected at Mecca by this route, and by his sealed instructions effectually provided against intelligence of his design being conveyed to Ḳoreish.

A Ḳoreishite killed, and caravan plundered

Having read the order, 'Abdallah told his comrades that any who wished was at liberty to go back: 'As for myself,' he said, 'I will go forward and fulfil the command of the Prophet.' All joined in the same determination, and proceeded onwards; but two fell behind in search of their camel, which had strayed, and lost the party.[1] The remaining six, having reached Nakhla, waited there. In a short time the expected caravan, laden with wine, raisins, and leather from the South, came up. It was guarded by four Ḳoreish, who, seeing the strangers, were alarmed and halted. With the view of disarming their apprehensions, one of 'Abdallah's party shaved his head, thus making the convoy believe that they had just returned from the Lesser pilgrimage; for this was one of the months in which that ceremony was ordinarily performed. The men of the caravan seeing his shaven head were reassured, and, turning the camels adrift to pasture, began to cook their food. Meanwhile, 'Abdallah and his comrades debated what to do. It was the last day of Rajab, in which it was forbidden to fight; and so they said to one another: 'If we defer the attack this night, they will surely move off, and find asylum in the Holy territory; and if we fight against them now, it will be a transgression of the Sacred month.' They were thus fixed on the horns of a dilemma. At last they overcame their scruples. One of their number advanced covertly, and, discharging an arrow, killed a man of the convoy, 'Amr ibn al-Ḥaḍrami, on the spot. All then rushed upon the caravan, and securing two, 'Othmān ibn 'Abdallah ibn al-

[1] By some accounts they took advantage of the option to go back, and turned aside. The straying of the camel may have been invented to cover what in after days must have appeared discreditable lukewarmness.

Moghīra and Al-Ḥakam ibn Keisān, carried them off prisoners, with the spoil, to Medīna. Naufal, brother of 'Othmān, leaped on his horse and escaped to Mecca; but too late to give alarm for the pursuit.

Moḥammad at first disclaims responsibility

On 'Abdallah reaching Medīna, he acquainted Moḥammad with what had passed. The Prophet, who had probably not expected the party to reach Nakhla till after the close of Rajab, appeared displeased, and said: 'I never commanded thee to fight in the Sacred month.' So he put the booty aside, pending further orders, and kept the prisoners in bonds. 'Abdallah and his comrades were crestfallen, and the people reproached them. But Moḥammad was unwilling to discourage his followers; and, soon after, a revelation appeared, justifying warfare even in the sacred months as a lesser evil than hostility to Islām:—

Then promulgates an approving revelation

Sūra ii. 214

They will ask thee concerning the Sacred months, whether they may war therein. SAY:—Warring therein is grievous; but to obstruct the way of God and to deny Him, to hinder men from the Holy temple, and to expel His people thence, that is more grievous with God. Tempting (to idolatry) is more grievous than slaughter.[1]

Having promulgated this dispensation, Moḥammad made the booty over to the captors, who (anticipating the subsequent practice) presented a fifth to Moḥammad, and divided the remainder among themselves.

Prisoners ransomed

The relatives of the two prisoners now sent a deputation from Mecca for their ransom. Sa'd and 'Otba, the two who had wandered from 'Abdallah's party, were not yet returned. Moḥammad, apprehensive for their safety, refused to ransom the captives till he was assured that no foul play had been used towards them: 'If ye have killed my two men,' he said, 'verily, I will put yours also to death.' But, soon after, they made their appearance, and Moḥammad accepted the proffered ransom, forty ounces of silver, for each.[1] Al-Ḥakam, however, continued at Medīna, and eventually embraced Islām.

Importance of this expedition

Arabian writers rightly attach much importance to this expedition. 'This,' says Ibn Hishām, 'was the first booty which the Muslims obtained, the first captives they seized, and the first life they took.' 'Abdallah is said to have been called in this expedition *Amīr al-Mu'minīn*—an appellation,

[1] The silver *ūḳīya*, or ounce, was equal to forty dirhems. For the value of the dirhem see note *ante*, p. 204.

'Commander of the Faithful,' assumed in after days by the Caliphs, and first by 'Omar.

Growing hostility towards Ḳoreish

It was now a year and a half since Moḥammad and his followers had fled for refuge to Medīna. Their attitude towards Mecca was becoming daily more hostile. Latterly, no opportunity had been lost of threatening the numerous caravans passing through the Ḥijāz. On the regular and uninterrupted march of these to Syria depended the prosperity of Mecca, for the traffic with the Yemen and Abyssinia was of greatly less importance; and even for it, as now appeared, their enemy would allow them no security. The last attack had also shown that Moḥammad and his followers, in the combat on which they were entering, would respect neither life nor the inviolability of the Sacred months. Blood had been shed—treacherously and sacrilegiously shed—and was yet unavenged. Still Mecca made no hostile response. Though followers of the Prophet were in the city, no cruelties were perpetrated on them, nor any reprisals attempted. But the breach was widening, and the enmity becoming deeper seated: blood could be washed out by blood alone.

Forbearance of Ḳoreish

Command to fight against Ḳoreish

At Medīna, on the other hand, the prospect of mortal conflict with their enemies was steadily contemplated, and openly spoken of by Moḥammad and his adherents. At what period the divine command to fight against the Unbelievers was promulgated, is uncertain. Repeated attacks on the caravans of Ḳoreish had been gradually paving the way; and at last, when given forth, the heavenly behest appeared but as the embodiment of a long-formed resolution for revenge. The following are the earliest passages on the subject:—

Sūra xxii. 38 ff.

Bear good tidings unto the Righteous! Truly the Lord will keep back the Enemy from those who believe, for God loveth not the perfidious Unbeliever. Permission is given to bear arms against those that have wronged them, and verily the Lord is mighty for the assistance of such as have been driven from their homes for no other cause than that they said, *God is our Lord.* And truly if it were not that God holdeth back mankind, one part by means of another part, Monasteries and Churches and Places of prayer and worship, wherein the name of the Lord is frequently commemorated, would be demolished. God will surely assist them that assist Him. For God is Mighty and Glorious.

Sūra ii. 186 ff., 212 f.

Fight in the way of God with them that fight against you: but transgress not, for God loveth not the Transgressors. Kill them wheresoever ye find them; and expel them from whence they have expelled you: for temptation (to idolatry) is more grievous than killing. Yet fight not against them beside the Holy temple, until they fight with you thereat. * * * Fight, therefore, until temptation to idolatry cease, and the Religion be God's. And if they leave off, then let there be no hostility, excepting against the Oppressors.

War is ordained for you, even if it be irksome unto you. Perchance ye may dislike that which is good for you, and love that which is evil for you. But God knoweth, and ye know not.

Fighting prescribed on religious grounds

Thus war, upon grounds professedly religious, was established as an ordinance of Islām. Hostilities, indeed, were justified by the 'expulsion' of the Believers from Mecca. But the main and undisguised issue which Mohammad in this warfare set before him was the victory of Islām. They were to fight '*until the religion became the Lord's alone.*'

The fearful reproved

Although the general bearing of his followers was, like that of their Prophet, defiant and daring, yet there were timorous men amongst them, who needed encouragement and reproof:—

Sura xlvii. 22 f.

The Believers say,—*If a Sūra were revealed* (*commanding war*) *we would fight;* yet now when a plain Sūra is revealed, and fighting mentioned therein, thou seest those in whose heart is an infirmity, looking towards thee with the look of one overshadowed with death. But obedience had been better for them, and propriety of speech. Wherefore, when the command is established, if they give credit unto God, it shall be well for them.

For such as might fall in battle, the promise of Paradise is given:—

Paradise promised to the slain

Sūra xxii. 57 f.

They who have gone into exile for the cause of God, and then have been slain, or have died, We shall certainly nourish these with an excellent provision, for God is the best Provider. He will surely grant unto them an entrance such as they will approve. For God is knowing and gracious.

The cause not dependent on their efforts

Yet the Believer was not to imagine the success of Islām dependent on his feeble efforts. God could accomplish the work equally without him. Thus after a fierce exhortation to 'strike off the heads of the Unbelievers, to make great slaughter amongst them, and bind them fast in bonds, the command runs thus:—

Sūra xlvii. 5 f.

This do. If the Lord willed, He could surely Himself take vengeance on them: but (He hath ordained fighting) in order that He may prove some of you by others. They that are slain in the way of God, He will not suffer their works to perish. He will guide them, and dispose their hearts aright. He will lead them into the Paradise whereof He hath told them.

Furthermore, the true Believer was not only to fight: he was to contribute also of his substance towards the charges of war:—

Believers to contribute towards war expenditure

> What hath befallen you that ye contribute not of your substance in the cause of God? and to God belongeth the inheritance of the Heavens and of the Earth. Those of you that contribute before the victory,[1] and fight, shall not be placed on the same level, but shall have a rank superior over those who contribute after it and fight. Who is he that lendeth unto the Lord a goodly loan? He shall double the same, and he shall have an honourable recompense.

Sura lvii. 10 f.

> The Lord asketh you not for (all) your substance. Had He asked you for (the whole of) it, and importunately pressed you, ye had become grudging, and it had stirred up your ill-will. But ye are they who are called on to contribute part of the same in the cause of God, and there be some of you that grudge; but whosoever grudgeth, he verily grudgeth against his own soul. God needeth nothing, but ye are needy. If ye turn back, He will substitute in your room a people other than you, and they shall not be like unto you.

Sūra xlvii. 38 ff.

And somewhat later:—

> Prepare against them what force ye can, and troops of horse of your ability, that ye may thereby strike terror into the enemy of God and your enemy, and into others beside them; ye know them not, but God knoweth them. And what thing soever ye contribute in the cause of God, it shall be made good unto you, and ye shall not be treated unjustly.

Sūra viii. 62

Such passages were promulgated within two or three years after Moḥammad's arrival in Medīna. They are no longer addressed to the Refugees only, but to all Believers, including the Citizens. We have seen that some of these latter had already joined in expeditions against the caravans of Mecca: but the first occasion on which they came forward in any considerable number to the aid of Moḥammad, was on the field of Bedr;—and there, probably more from the hope of sharing in the spoil of a richly-laden caravan, than with any idea of fighting for the faith, and avenging the exiles' wrongs. But the effect was equally important to Moḥammad. It pledged them to his cause.

These commands addressed to the Citizens as well as Refugees

[1] *Al-Fatḥ;* the victory of God and of Islām over the idolaters. The term came subsequently to be applied *par excellence* to the taking of Mecca—the great crisis, prior to which there was a peculiar merit in fighting for and supporting Islām. But the word had of course at this moment no such distinct and anticipative sense.

CHAPTER XII

BATTLE OF BEDR[1]

Ramaḍān, A.H. II.—*January*, A.D. 624

Great detail with which campaign of Bedr is related

WITH the battle of Bedr opens a new era in Islām. The biographers of Moḥammad have shown their sense of the influence it exercised on his future fortunes, by the extraordinary space allotted to this chapter of their story. The minutest circumstances and most trifling details, even to the name of each person engaged in it, have been carefully treasured up. From this vast mass of undigested tradition it will be my endeavour to frame a brief and consistent narrative.

Scouts for news of Abu Sufyān's caravan. A.H. II. Jan. A.D. 624

The caravan of Abu Sufyān, which, on its passage through the Ḥijāz, had escaped pursuit in the autumn, would now, in ordinary course, after two or three months, be returning to Mecca. Moḥammad was resolved that it should not this time elude his grasp. His first step was to secure the neutrality, if not co-operation, of the tribes upon the way. In the beginning of January he despatched two scouts to Al-Ḥaurā, a caravan station on the seashore west of Medīna, for early intelligence of the approach of Abu Sufyān. They were hospitably lodged and concealed by an aged chief of the Juheina tribe, whose family was subsequently rewarded by the grant of Yenbo'. When the caravan appeared, they were to hasten back and apprise Moḥammad of its approach.

Abu Sufyān, warned; sends for succour

The Prophet had not yet learned to mask his movements. His intention of attacking the caravan was noised abroad. The rumour reached Abu Sufyān while yet on the confines of Syria. He was warned, perhaps by the treachery of some

[1] Aṭ-Ṭabari, i. 1281 ff.; Ibn Hishām, p. 427 ff.; Al-Wāḳidi, p. 37 ff.; Ibn Sa'd, p. 6 ff.

disaffected Citizen, to be on his guard as Moḥammad had entered into confederacy with the tribes upon the road to surprise the caravan. Greatly alarmed, he forthwith despatched a messenger, named Ḍamḍam, to Mecca, bidding Ḳoreish hasten with an army to his rescue. The caravan then moved with quickened pace, and yet with caution, along the route which lay close by the shore of the Red Sea.

Moḥammad gives command for the campaign

Moḥammad, becoming impatient, and apprehensive lest the caravan should, as on previous occasions, be beforehand with him, resolved not to wait for the spies' return. He called upon his followers at once to make ready, with this command;—'See! here cometh a caravan of Ḳoreish in which they have embarked much wealth. Come! let us go forth; peradventure the Lord will enrich us with the same.' The love of booty and of adventure, so passionate in the Arab, induced not only all the Refugees, but a large body of the Citizens also, to respond with alacrity to the call. Of the former, 'Othmān alone remained behind to tend the sick-bed of his wife Roḳeiya, the Prophet's daughter.'[1]

[1] The motive which prompted most of Moḥammad's followers to accompany the force, as well as tempted many to join Islām itself, is illustrated by the following anecdote, which bears the stamp at least of verisimilitude. Two Citizens of Medīna, still heathens, were noticed by Moḥammad among the troops. He called them near his camel, and asked them what had brought them there. 'Thou art our kinsman,' they replied, 'to whom our city hath given protection; and we go forth with our people in the hope of plunder.' 'None shall go forth with me,' said Moḥammad, 'but he who is of our Faith.' They tried to pass, saying that they were great warriors, and would fight bravely by his side, requiring nothing beyond their share of plunder; but Moḥammad was firm. 'Ye shall not go thus. *Believe and fight!*' Seeing no alternative they 'believed,' and confessed that Moḥammad was the Prophet of God. 'Now,' said Moḥammad, 'go forth and fight!' So they accompanied the army, and became noted spoilers both at Bedr and in other expeditions. On Moḥammad's return to Medīna, one of the Citizens exclaimed: 'Would that I had gone forth with the Prophet! Then I had surely secured large booty!'

Eight persons who remained behind are popularly counted in the number of the veterans of Bedr—the future nobility of Islām; *three* Refugees, viz. 'Othmān and the two spies; and *five* Citizens, viz. the two left in command of the City and of Upper Medīna, a messenger sent back to the Beni 'Amr ibn 'Auf at Ḳobā, and two men, who, having received a hurt on the road, were left behind. The names of the famous Three hundred and five were recorded in a Register at Medīna, called *Ṣadr al-Kitāb.*

Marches from Medīna, Ramaḍān, A.H. II. Jan. 8, A.D. 623

On Sunday, the 12th of Ramaḍān, Moḥammad set out upon his march. He left Abu Lubāba, one of the Citizens, in charge of Medīna; and, for some special reason, appointed another over Ḳobā and Upper Medīna.[1] At a short distance from the city on the Mecca road, he halted to review his little army, and sent back the striplings unfit for action. The number that remained, with which he proceeded onwards, was 305. Eighty were Refugees; of the remainder, about one-fourth belonged to the Aus, and the rest to the Khazraj. They had but two horses; and there were 70 camels, on which by turns they rode.

Spies sent forward by Moḥammad to Bedr

For two or three days they travelled by the direct road to Mecca, but, on reaching Aṣ-Ṣafrā, turned to the west by a pathway leading to Bedr, a halting-place on the route to Syria. While on the march, Moḥammad despatched two spies thither, to find out whether any preparations were making for the reception of Abu Sufyān; for it was at Bedr that he hoped to waylay the caravan.[2] At the fountain there, the spies overheard some women who had come to draw water talking among themselves 'of the caravan expected on the morrow or the day after,' and they returned in haste with the intelligence to Moḥammad.

Abu Sufyān, discovering traces of the scouts, hastens forward and escapes

Let us now turn to Abu Sufyān. As he approached Bedr, his apprehensions were quickened by the dangerous vicinity, and he hastened in advance to reconnoitre the spot. Reaching Bedr, he was told by a chief of the Beni Juheina that no strangers had been seen, excepting two men, who, after resting their camels for a little by the well, and drinking water, went off again. Proceeding to the spot, he carefully scrutinised it all around. 'Camels from Yathrib!' he exclaimed, as among their litter he spied out the small stone peculiar to the dates of Medīna;—'these be the scouts of Moḥammad!' With such words, he hurried back to the

[1] It is said that he did this because he heard something suspicious regarding the Beni 'Amr ibn 'Auf, who lived there. He also sent back Al-Ḥārith from his camp with a message to the same tribe. The two persons left in charge, as well as this messenger, belonged to the Beni Aus.

[2] This was probably on the Monday. It is somewhat difficult to find time for all the events that crowd in between Sunday and Thursday evening. The spies were of the Juheina tribe which dwelt on the sea-shore; they were acquainted with the vicinity, and better fitted than either Refugees or Citizens to gain the information Moḥammad required.

caravan; and striking to the right, so as to keep close by the seashore, pressed forward, halting neither day nor night, till he was soon beyond the reach of danger. Then hearing that an army had marched from Mecca to his aid, he despatched a courier to them saying that all was safe, and that they should now return.

Alarm at Mecca

Koreish resolve to rescue caravan

Ten or twelve days before this, Mecca had been thrown into great alarm by the sudden appearance of Ḍamḍam, the first messenger of Abu Sufyān. Urging his camel at full speed along the valley and up the main street of Mecca, he made it kneel down in the open space before the Ka'ba, hastily reversed its saddle, cut off its ears and nose, and rent his shirt before and behind. Having signified thus the alarming import of his mission, he cried at the pitch of his voice to the crowd around him:—'Ḳoreish! Ḳoreish! your caravan is pursued by Moḥammad. Help! O help!' Immediately the city was in a stir; for the caravan was the chief one of the year, in which every Ḳoreishite of any substance had a venture; and the value of the whole was 50,000 golden pieces. It was at once determined to march in force, repel the marauding troops, and rescue the caravan. 'Doth Moḥammad, indeed, imagine,' said they among themselves, 'that it will be this time as in the affair of the Ḥaḍramite!' alluding to the treacherous surprise at Nakhla where, two months before, 'Amr ibn al-Ḥaḍrami had been slain. 'Never! He shall know it otherwise.'

Meccan army meets Abu Sufyān's messenger

Preparations were hurried forward on every side. The resolve, at any sacrifice, to chastise and crush the Muslims was universal. Every man of consequence prepared to join the army. A few, unable themselves to go, sent substitutes; among these was Moḥammad's uncle, Abu Lahab.[1] One

[1] Some say that Abu Lahab neither went himself nor sent a substitute; others that he sent in his stead Al-Āṣ, a grandson of Al-Moghīra, in consideration of the remission of a debt of 400 dirhems; others that he refused to accompany the army in consequence of a dream of his sister 'Ātika. I have omitted any allusion to this dream, as well as to other dreams and prodigies seen by Ḳoreish, anticipatory of the disasters at Bedr, because I believe them all to be fictitious. The tinge of horror in after days reflected back on the 'sacrilegious' battle, the anxiety to excuse certain families, and the wish to invest others with a species of merit in having, even while unbelievers, served Islām by dreams or prophecies, combined to give them rise.

fear there was that Mecca might, during their absence, be surprised by the Beni Bekr, an adjacent tribe, with which there was a present feud. But this was obviated by the guarantee of a powerful chief allied to both tribes. So great was the alacrity, that in two or three days after the alarm by Ḍamḍam, and about the very time that Moḥammad was marching from Medīna, the army was in motion. They then despatched a messenger to apprise Abu Sufyān of their approach, but he missed the caravan, which (as we have seen) had left the ordinary route. The army marched in haste, but not without some rude display; for singing women, with their tabrets, followed and sang by the fountains at which they halted. At Al-Joḥfa, the second courier of Abu Sufyān (who himself, with his caravan, passed unnoticed by a route closer to the sea) reached the army with intelligence of his safety, and the message that now they should go back.

Ḳoreishite army debates whether to return or go forward

On receiving this welcome intimation, the question of going forward or of turning back was warmly debated by the leading chiefs. On the one hand, it was argued that, their object being now secured, they might at once retrace their steps; and further, that, being all so closely related to the army of Moḥammad, they should abstain from fatal extremities. 'When we have fought, and spilled the blood of our brethren and our kinsmen,' said the advocates of peace, 'of what use will life be to us any longer? Let us now go back, and we will be responsible for the blood-money of 'Amr, killed at Nakhla.' Many persons, and among them 'Otba ibn Rabī'a and Ḥakīm, the nephew of Khadīja (he who supplied food to Moḥammad's party when shut up with Abu Ṭālib), were urgent with this advice. Others, and Abu Jahl at their head, demanded that the army should advance. 'If we turn back,' they said, it will surely be imputed to our cowardice. Let us go forward to Bedr; and there, by the fountain, spend three days eating and making merry. All Arabia will hear of it, and ever after stand in awe of us.' The affair of Nakhla, and the slaughter of the Ḥaḍrami still rankled in the heart of Ḳoreish, and they listened willingly to the warlike counsel. Two tribes alone, the Beni Zuhra and 'Adī, returned to Mecca.[1]

They resolve to advance on Bedr

[1] The reason is not given; the Beni Zuhra (of whom 100 men were present) was the tribe of Moḥammad's mother; the Beni 'Adī, that of 'Omar. [Ibn Isḥāḳ says (p. 438) that none of the latter tribe left Mecca.]

The rest marched onwards.[1] Leaving Medīna to the right, they kept straight along the Syrian road, and made for Bedr.

Mohammad receives intelligence of Koreish-ite army. Thursday

We now return to Moḥammad. He, too, was advancing rapidly on Bedr; for there he expected, from the report of his spies, to find the caravan. On Tuesday night he reached Ar-Rūḥā; as he drank from the well there, he blessed the valley in terms of which the pious traveller is reminded to the present day. On Wednesday he proceeded onwards. Next day, while on the last march to Bedr, the startling news was brought by some wayfarers that the enemy was in full march upon him. This was the first intimation that Ḳoreish, having heard of the danger to the caravan, were on their way to defend it. A council of war was summoned, and the chief men invited to offer their advice. There was but one opinion, and each delivered it more enthusiastically than another. Abu Bekr and 'Omar advised an immediate advance. The Prophet turned to the men of Medīna, for their pledge did not bind them to offensive action, or even to fight in his defence when away from their city. Sa'd ibn Mo'ādh, their spokesman, replied: 'Prophet of the Lord! march whither thou listest: encamp wheresoever thou mayest choose: make war or conclude peace with whom thou wilt. For I swear by Him who hath sent thee with the Truth, that if thou wert to march till our camels fell down dead, we should go forward with thee to the world's end. Not one of us would be left behind.' Then said Moḥammad: 'Go forward, with the blessing of God! For, verily, He hath promised one of the two—the army or the caravan—that He will deliver it into my

Council of war decides on onward march

[1] But they sent back the singing girls. The messenger, who carried the intelligence to Abu Sufyān that Ḳoreish refused to turn back, reached him near Mecca; and Abu Sufyān is represented as lamenting the folly of his countrymen. All this seems apocryphal. Till viewed in the light of its disastrous issue, the advance on Bedr must have appeared a politic and reasonable measure. It was not *an attack on Medīna*, for Bedr was on the road to Syria, so that Ḳoreish left Medīna far on their right. If therefore they should meet any enemy at Bedr, it could only be because they had come forth gratuitously to attack the Mecca caravan—a fair and sufficient *casus belli;* for what security could there any longer be if the men of Medīna were allowed thus with impunity to attack the convoys, and plunder the caravans of Mecca?

hands.[1] By the Lord! methinks I even now see the battle-field strewn with dead.'[2]

Muslims more implacable than Ḳoreish

It is remarkable, when comparing this council with that of Ḳoreish at Al-Joḥfa, to find that in the minds of Moḥammad and his followers there was no trace whatever of compunction at the prospect of a mortal combat with their kinsmen. Ḳoreish, goaded as they had been by oft-repeated attacks upon their caravans and the blood shed at Nakhla, were yet staggered by the prospect of an internecine war, and nearly persuaded by their better feelings to turn back. The Muslims, though the aggressors, were hardened by memory of former injuries, by the dogma that their faith had severed all earthly ties without the pale of Islām, and by a fierce fanaticism for the Prophet's cause. At one of the stages, where he halted to lead the public devotions, Moḥammad, after rising from his knees, thus called down the curse of God upon the infidels, and prayed: 'O Lord! Let not Abu Jahl escape, the Pharaoh of his people! Lord! let not Zama'a escape; rather let the eyes of his father run sore for him with weeping, and become blind!' The Prophet's hate, indeed, was unrelenting against his chief opponents, and his followers imbibed from him the same inexorable spirit.

Moḥammad learns strength of enemy

In the afternoon of Thursday, on nearing Bedr, Moḥammad sent forward 'Alī, with a few others, to reconnoitre the rising ground about the springs. There they surprised three water-carriers filling their skins at the wells. One escaped to Ḳoreish; the other two were captured and taken to the Muslim army. The chiefs questioned them about the cara-

[1] This point is alluded to in the Ḳor'ān, which henceforth becomes often the vehicle of the 'general orders' of Moḥammad, as of a military commander. 'And when the Lord promised one of the two parties that it should be given over unto you: and ye desired that it should be the party unarmed for war (*i.e.* that ye should meet the caravan, and not the Ḳoreishite army), whereas the Lord willed to establish the Truth by His words, and to cut away the foundation from the Unbelievers;—that He might establish the Truth, and abolish Falsehood, even though the transgressors be averse thereto.'—Sūra viii. 7, 8.

[2] The latter clause may be apocryphal. In later traditions it is worked out to a fabulous extent. Moḥammad, for example, points out what was to be the death spot, as seen in the vision, of each of his chief opponents; 'and,' it is added, 'the people were by this apprised for the first time that it was the Ḳoreishite army they were about to encounter and not the caravan.'

van, imagining that they belonged to it; and, receiving no satisfactory answer, had begun to beat them, when Moḥammad, coming up, soon discovered the proximity of his enemy. The camp, they replied to his inquiries, lay just beyond the sandhills skirting the western side of the valley. As they could not tell the strength of the force, the Prophet asked how many camels they slaughtered for their daily food. 'Nine,' they answered, 'one day, and ten the next, alternately.' 'Then,' said Moḥammad, 'they are between 900 and 1,000 strong.' The estimate was correct. There were 950 men;—more than threefold the number of the Muslim force. They were mounted on 700 camels and 100 horses, the horsemen all clad in mail.[1]

Escape of caravan a benefit to Moḥammad

The followers of Moḥammad were chagrined at finding their expectation of an easy prey thus changed into the prospect of a bloody battle. They seemed to have advanced even to the field of action with the hope that they might still, as conquerors, pursue and seize the caravan. But it was, in truth, a fortunate event that it had already passed, for the continuing jeopardy of the caravan would have nerved the enemy and united them by a bond which the knowledge of its safety had already dissipated. The prize of victory on the field of Bedr was of incomparably greater consequence to Moḥammad than any spoil, however costly.

Moḥammad's position at Bedr

The valley of Bedr consists of a plain, with steep hills to the north and east; on the south is a low rocky range; and on the west a succession of sandy hillocks. A tiny rivulet from the eastern hills ran through the valley, breaking out here and there into springs, which at various spots were dug for the use of travellers into cisterns. At the nearest of these springs, the army of Moḥammad halted. Al-Ḥobāb, a Citizen acquainted with the ground, advised him to proceed onwards: 'Let us go,' he said, 'to the farthest spring on the side of the enemy. I know a never-failing fountain of sweet water there; make that our reservoir, and destroy all other wells.' The advice was good. It was at once adopted, and the command of water thus secured.

Moḥammad sleeps in a hut of palm branches

The night was drawing on. So, near the well, they hastily ran up a hut of palm branches, in which Moḥammad and Abu

[1] Weil would make their number 600, but apparently on insufficient grounds.—*Einleitung*, p. 20.

Bekr passed the night. Sa'd ibn Mo'ādh kept watch by the entrance with his drawn sword. It rained during the night, but more heavily towards the camp of Ḳoreish.[1] The Muslim army, wearied with its long march, enjoyed sound and refreshing sleep—a mark of the Divine favour, we are told. The dreams of Moḥammad turned upon his enemies, and they were pictured to his imagination as a weak and contemptible force.[2] In the morning rising betimes he drew up his little army, and, pointing with an arrow which he held in his hand, arranged thus the ranks. The previous day, he had placed the chief banner, that of the Refugees, in the hands of Muṣ'ab, who nobly proved his right to the command. The Khazrajite ensign was committed to Al-Ḥobāb; that of the Aus, to Sa'd ibn Mo'ādh.[3]

Moḥammad draws up his army

Ḳoreish, after further dissensions, move forward

Meanwhile dissension again broke out in the camp of Ḳoreish on the policy of fighting with their kinsmen. Sheiba and 'Otba, two chiefs of rank, influenced by their slave, 'Addās (the same who comforted the Prophet on his flight from Aṭ-Ṭā'if), strongly urged that the attack should be abandoned. Just then, 'Omeir, a diviner by arrows, having ridden hastily round the valley, returned to report the result of his reconnaissance. 'Ye Ḳoreish,' he said, after telling the enemy's number, 'calamities approach you, fraught with destruction. Their numbers are small, but death is astride upon the camels of Yathrib. Their only refuge is the sword; dumb as the grave, their tongues they put forth with the serpent's deadly aim. Not a man of them shall fall but in his stead one of ourselves will be slain; and when there shall

[1] The rain is thus alluded to in the Ḳor'ān: 'When He overshadowed you with a deep sleep, as a security, from Himself; and caused to descend upon you Rain from the heavens, that He might purify you therewith, and take from you the uncleanness of Satan; and that He might strengthen your hearts, and establish your steps thereby.'—Sūra viii. 11. As a foil to this picture, Ḳoreish are represented as being apprehensive and restless till morning broke.

[2] 'And when God caused them to appear before thee in thy sleep, few in number; and if He had caused them to appear unto thee a great multitude, ye would have been affrighted, and have disputed in the matter (of their attack). But truly God preserved thee, for He knoweth the heart of man.'—viii. 45.

[3] The name given is *Liwā*, a white ensign. The *Rāya*, Moḥammad's black banner, is said to have been first unfurled five years later on the expedition to Kheibar.

have been slaughtered amongst us a number equal unto them, of what avail will life be to us after that!' The words began to tell, when Abu Jahl taunted his comrades with cowardice, and, turning to 'Āmir ibn al-Ḥaḍrami, bade him to call his brother-blood to mind. The flame burst forth again. 'Āmir threw off his clothes, cast dust upon his body and began frantically to cry aloud his brother's name. The deceased had been a confederate of the family of Sheiba and 'Otba themselves, and their honour was affected; thoughts of peace must now be scattered to the winds; and their name vindicated from the imputation of cowardice cast on it by Abu Jahl. The army was at once drawn up in line. The three standards, for the centre and wings, were borne, according to ancient privilege, by members of the house of 'Abd ed-Dār. They moved forward slowly over the sandy hillocks which separated them from the enemy, and which the rain had made heavy and fatiguing. The same rain, acting with less intensity, had rendered the ground in front of Moḥammad lighter and more firm to walk upon. Ḳoreish laboured under another disadvantage; facing eastwards, the rising sun was in their eyes, a serious drawback that told in favour of the Muslim side.

Moḥammad's earnest prayer

Moḥammad had barely arrayed his line of battle, when the advanced column of the enemy was discerned over the rising sands in front. Their greatly superior numbers were concealed by the fall of the ground behind; and this imparted confidence to the Muslims.[1] But Moḥammad knew the dis-

[1] Represented in the Ḳor'ān (Sūra viii.) as the result of divine interposition. After mentioning Moḥammad's dream, the passage proceeds: 'And when He caused them to appear in your eyes, at the time ye met, to be few in number, and diminished you in their eyes, that God might accomplish the thing that was to be;' *i.e.* by this ocular deception his followers were encouraged in their advance to victory, and Ḳoreish lured on to their fate. So again: 'When ye were on the hither side, and they on the farther side (of the valley), and the caravan below you;* and if ye had made a mutual appointment to fight, ye would surely have declined the appointment; but (the Lord ordered otherwise) that he might bring to pass the thing that was to be—that He who perisheth might perish by a manifest interposition, and he that liveth might live by a manifest interposition;'—that is, each army advanced to the field of battle, without knowing of the approach of the other; an unseen hand led them on.

In a later passage (iii. 11), the interposition of God is represented as

* *I.e.* on the plain, by the seashore, passing on towards Mecca.

parity of his little army; and, alive to the issue that hung upon the day, retired for a moment with Abu Bekr to his hut; and, there raising his hands aloft, he thus poured forth his soul: 'O Lord! I beseech thee, forget not Thy promise of assistance and of victory. O Lord! if this little band be vanquished, Idolatry will prevail, and the pure worship of Thee cease from off the earth!' 'The Lord,' rejoined his friend, 'will surely come to thine aid, and will lighten thy countenance with the joy of victory.[1]

Fierce combat by the reservoir

The time for action had arrived. Moḥammad again came forth. The enemy was already close; but the army of Medīna remained still. Moḥammad had no cavalry to cover an advance; and before superior numbers he must keep close his ranks. Accordingly his followers were strictly forbidden to stir till he should order an advance; only if their flank were threatened by the Ḳoreishite cavalry, they were to check the movement by a discharge of archery. The cistern was guarded as their palladium. Some desperate warriors of Ḳoreish swore that they would drink water from it, destroy it, or perish in the attempt. But they were met with equal daring and hardly one escaped alive the fatal enterprise. With signal gallantry, Al-Aswad advanced close to the brink, when a blow from Ḥamza's sword fell upon his leg and nearly severed it from his body. Still defending himself he crawled onwards and made good his vow; for he drank of the water, and with his remaining leg demolished part of the cistern before the sword of Ḥamza put an end to his life.

Three Ḳoreish challenge Muslims to single combat

Already, after Arab fashion, single combats had been fought at various points, when the two brothers Sheiba and 'Otba, and Al-Walīd the son of 'Otba, still smarting from the taunts of Abu Jahl, advanced into the space between the armies, and defied three champions from the enemy to meet them singly. Three Citizens stepped forward; but Moḥammad, unwilling that the glory or the burden of the

doubling the army of Medīna in the eyes of Ḳoreish. The discrepancy is thus explained by the commentators: Ḳoreish were at first drawn on by fancying Moḥammad's army to be a mere handful; when they had actually closed in battle, they were terrified by the exaggerated appearance of the Muslims, who now seemed a great multitude.

[1] Sprenger (iii. 122) says that outside the hut a swift dromedary was tied up to carry Moḥammad off in case of defeat; but I do not remember seeing this in any early authority.

opening conflict should rest with his allies, called them back;[1] and, turning to his kinsmen: 'Ye sons of Hashim!' he cried, 'arise and fight, according to your right.' Then Ḥamza, 'Obeida and 'Alī, uncle and cousins of the Prophet, went forth. Ḥamza wore an ostrich feather in his breast, and 'Alī a white plume in his helmet. But their features were hid by their armour. 'Otba, therefore, not knowing who his opponents might be, cried aloud: 'Speak, that we may recognise you! If ye be equals, we shall fight with you.' Ḥamza answered: 'I am the son of 'Abd al-Muṭṭalib, *the Lion of God, and the Lion of his Prophet*.' 'A worthy foe,' exclaimed 'Otba; 'but who are these others with thee?' Ḥamza repeated their names. 'Meet foes, every one!' replied 'Otba.

Koreishite champions slain

Then 'Otba called to his son Al-Walīd, 'Arise and fight!' So Al-Walīd stepped forth and 'Alī went out against him. They were the youngest of the six. The combat was short and sharp; Al-Walīd fell mortally wounded by the sword of 'Alī. Eager to avenge his son's death, 'Otba hastened forward, and Ḥamza advanced to meet him. The swords gleamed quick, and again the Ḳoreishite warrior was slain by the Muslim lion. Sheiba alone remained of the three champions of Mecca; and 'Obeida, the veteran of the Muslims, threescore years and five, now drew near to fight with him. Both well advanced in years, the conflict was less decisive than before. But at the last, Sheiba dealt a blow which severed the tendon of 'Obeida's leg and brought him to the ground. At this, Ḥamza and 'Alī rushed on Sheiba and despatched him with their swords. 'Obeida survived but for a few days, and was buried on the march back at Aṣ-Ṣafrā.

The armies close

The fate of their champions was ominous for Ḳoreish, and their spirits sank. The ranks began to close, with the battle-cry on the Muslim side of *Ya manṣūr amit*, 'Ye conquerors, strike!' and the fighting became general. But there were still many of those scenes of individual bravery which characterise the irregular warfare of Asiatic armies, and impart an Homeric interest to the page. Prodigies of valour were exhibited on both sides; but the army of the Faithful

[1] [Ibn Isḥāḳ (p. 443) states that the Ḳoreish champions declined to fight with them (their quarrel being only with their own tribesmen), and called upon Moḥammad to send them champions from Ḳoreish.]

was borne forward by an enthusiasm which the half-hearted warriors opposite were unable to withstand. What part Moḥammad himself took in the battle is not clear. Some traditions represent him as moving along the ranks with a drawn sword. It is more likely, according to others, that he contented himself with inciting his followers by the promise of divine assistance, and by holding out the prospect of Paradise to those who fell. Tradition revels in details of gallantry. Thus we read that the spirit of 'Omeir, a stripling of sixteen, was kindled within him as he listened to the Prophet's words. Throwing away a handful of dates which he was eating—'Is it these,' he cried, 'that hold me back from Paradise? Verily I will taste no more of them until I meet my Lord!' And so, rushing on the enemy, he obtained the fate he coveted.

Moḥammad incites his followers

Muslims put Ḳoreish to flight

It was a stormy day. A piercing blast swept across the valley. *That*, said Moḥammad, *is Gabriel with a thousand angels charging down upon the foe.* Another, and yet another blast:—it was Michael and Seraphil, each with a like angelic troop. The battle raged. The Prophet stooped, and lifting a handful of gravel, cast it at the enemy, shouting—*Confusion seize their faces!* The action was well timed. Before the onset of the brave Three hundred, they began to waver. Their movements were impeded by the heavy sands on which they stood; and, when the ranks gave way, their numbers added but confusion. The Muslims followed eagerly their retreating steps, slaying or taking captive all that fell within their reach. Retreat soon turned into ignominious rout; and the flying host, casting away their armour, abandoned beasts of burden, camp, and equipage. Forty-nine were killed and a like number taken prisoners. Moḥammad lost only fourteen, of whom eight were Citizens and six Refugees.

Slaughter of Moḥammad's chief opponents. Abu Jahl

Many of the principal men of Mecca, and some of Moḥammad's bitterest opponents, were amongst the slain. Chief of these was Abu Jahl. Mo'ādh brought him to the ground by a blow which cut his leg in two. Mo'ādh, in his turn, was attacked by 'Ikrima, the son of Abu Jahl, and his arm nearly severed from his shoulder. As the mutilated limb hanging by the skin impeded his action, Mo'ādh put his foot upon it, pulled it off, and went on his way fighting. Such were the heroes of Bedr. Abu Jahl was yet breathing when 'Abdallah ran up, and, cutting off his head, brought it to his master. 'The head of the enemy of God!' exclaimed Moḥammad; 'God! there is none other God but he!' 'There is no other!' responded 'Abdallah, as he cast it gory at the Prophet's feet. 'It is more acceptable to me,' cried Moḥammad, 'than the choicest camel in all Arabia.'

Abu'l-Bakhtari

But there were others whose death caused no gratification to Moḥammad. Abu'l-Bakhtari had shown him special kindness at the time when he was shut up in the quarter of Abu Ṭālib; Moḥammad, mindful of this favour, had commanded that he should not be harmed. Abu'l-Bakhtari had a companion seated on his camel behind him. A warrior, riding up, told him of the quarter given by Moḥammad; but added, 'I cannot spare the man behind thee.' 'The women of Mecca,' Abu'l-Bakhtari exclaimed, 'shall never say that I abandoned my comrade through love of life. Do thy work upon us.' So they were killed, both he and his companion.

Cruel slaughter of some of the prisoners

After the battle was over, some of the prisoners were cruelly put to death. Omeiya ibn Khalaf and his son, unable to escape with the fugitive Ḳoreish, and seeing 'Abd ar-Raḥmān pass, implored that he would make them his prisoners. 'Abd ar-Raḥmān, mindful of ancient friendship, cast away the plunder he was carrying, and, taking charge of both, was proceeding with them to the Muslim camp. As the party passed, Bilāl espied his old enemy, for Omeiya had used to persecute him when a slave; and he screamed aloud, 'Slay him. This man is the head of the Unbelievers. I am lost, if he lives, I am lost!' From all sides the infuriated comrades, hearing Bilāl's appeal, poured in upon the wretched captives; and 'Abd ar-Raḥmān, finding resistance impossible, bade them save their lives as best they could. Defence was vain; and the two prisoners were immediately cut in pieces. Such was the savage spirit already characteristic of the faith.[1]

[1] Two other prisoners were slaughtered in cold blood. The first was Naufal, for whose death 'Alī overheard Moḥammad praying; so, when he saw him being led off a prisoner, he fell upon him and killed him. Moḥammad uttered a *tekbīr* of joy when told of it, and said that it had happened in answer to his prayer. The other was Ma'bad. 'Omar met one of his comrades carrying him off, and taunted him: 'Well, ye are beaten now!' 'Nay, by Al-Lāt and Al-'Ozza!' said the prisoner. 'Is that the manner of speech for a captive Infidel towards a Believer? cried 'Omar, as he cut off the wretched man's head by one blow of his scimitar.

Enemy's dead cast into a pit

When the enemy had disappeared, the army of Medīna spent some time in gathering the spoil. Then as the sun declined, they hastily dug a pit on the battle-field, and cast the enemy's dead into it. Moḥammad looked on. Abu Bekr too stood by, and, examining their features, called aloud their names. ''Otba!—Sheiba!—Omeiya!—Abu Jahl!' exclaimed Moḥammad, as one by one the corpses were, without ceremony, thrown into the common grave. 'Have ye now found true that which your Lord did promise you? What my Lord promised me, that verily have I found to be true. Woe unto this people! Ye have rejected me, your Prophet! Ye cast me forth, and others gave me refuge; ye fought against me, and others came to my help!' 'O Prophet!' said the bystanders, 'dost thou speak unto the dead?' 'Yea, verily,' replied Moḥammad, 'for now they well know that the promise of their Lord hath fully come to pass. At the moment when the corpse of 'Otba was tossed into the pit, a look of distress overcast the countenance of his son, Abu Ḥodheifa. Moḥammad turned kindly to him, and said: 'Perhaps thou art distressed for thy father's fate?' 'Not so, O Prophet of the Lord! I do not doubt the justice of my father's fate; but I knew well his wise and generous heart, and I had trusted that the Lord would have led him to the faith. But now that I see him slain, and my hope destroyed, it is for that I grieve.' So the Prophet comforted Abu Ḥodheifa, and blessed him; and said, 'It is well.'[1]

Colloquy of Moḥammad with the dead

Abu Ḥodheifa's grief for his father

The booty is collected

On the way home from Bedr, the day after the battle, the booty was divided. Every man was allowed to retain the plunder of such as had been slain by his own hand. The rest was thrown into a common stock. The booty consisted of 115 camels, 14 horses, an endless store of vestments and carpets, articles of fine leather, with much equipage and armour. A diversity of opinion arose about the distribution. Those who had hotly pursued the enemy and exposed their lives in securing the spoil, claimed the whole, or at least a

[1] On the other hand, we are told that when 'Otba came forth to challenge the Muslim army, Abu Ḥodheifa arose to combat with his father, but Moḥammad bade him sit down. It is said that he aided Ḥamza in giving his father the *coup de grâce*. Tradition gloats over such savage passages; and it is all the more pleasing to light upon the outburst of natural affection in the text.

superior portion; while such as had remained behind upon the field of battle for the safety of the Prophet and of the camp, urged that they had equally with the others fulfilled the part assigned to them, and that, restrained by duty from the pursuit, they were entitled to an equal share. The contention was so sharp that Moḥammad interposed with a message from Heaven, and assumed possession of the whole. It was God who had given the victory, and to God the spoil belonged: 'They will ask thee concerning the prey. Say, the prey is God's and his Prophet's. Wherefore, fear God, and dispose of the matter rightly among yourselves; and be obedient unto God and his Prophet, if ye be true Believers;' and so on in the same strain. Shortly afterwards, the following ordinance, the law of prize to the present day, was given forth:

Contention about its division decided by revelation

Sūra viii. 1

> And know that whatsoever thing ye plunder, verily one Fifth thereof is for God and the Prophet, and for him that is of kin (unto the Prophet), and for the Orphans, and the Poor, and the Wayfarer,—if ye be they that believe in God, and in that which WE sent down to our Servant on the day of Discrimination, the day on which the two armies met: and God is over all things powerful.—Sūra viii. 42.

In accordance with this command, the booty gathered on the field was placed under a Citizen who acted the part of prize agent for the army. It was then divided, as they encamped at Aṣ-Ṣafrā, in equal allotments, among the whole army, after the Prophet's Fifth had been set apart.[1] All shared alike, excepting that each horseman received two extra portions for his horse. To the lot of every man fell a camel, with its gear; or two camels unaccoutred; or a leathern couch, or some such equivalent. Moḥammad obtained the camel of Abu Jahl, and the famous sword known as Dhu'l-Fiḳār.[2] This sword was selected by him beyond his share; for, in virtue of the prophetic dignity, he was privileged to choose from the booty, before division, whatever thing might please him most.

Spoil divided near Aṣ-Ṣafrā

The army of Medīna, leading their captives handcuffed and carrying their dead and wounded, retired in the evening

A prisoner put to death by Moḥammad

[1] Weil supposes the distribution to have been equal all round; and that the passage ordaining the Fifth was subsequently revealed. *Einleitung*, p. 21.

[2] We find notices of this sword at Medīna, A.H. 145, and again at Baghdad, A.H. 320. *Caliphate*, pp. 452, 561.

to the valley of Al-Otheil, several miles from Bedr; and there Moḥammad passed the night. On the morrow, the prisoners were brought up before him. As he scrutinised each, his eye fell fiercely on An-Naḍr, made captive by Miḳdād. 'There was death in that glance,' whispered An-Naḍr trembling to a bystander. 'Not so,' replied the other; 'it is but thine imagination.' The unfortunate prisoner thought otherwise, and besought Muṣ'ab to intercede for him; on which Muṣ'ab reminded him that he had denied the faith and persecuted Believers. 'Ah!' said An-Naḍr, 'had Ḳoreish made thee a prisoner, they would never have put thee to death!' 'Even were it so,' replied Muṣ'ab scornfully, 'I am not as thou art; Islām hath rent all bonds asunder.' Miḳdād, the captor, fearing lest his prisoner, and with him the chance of a rich ransom, was about to slip from his hands, cried out: 'The prisoner is mine!' At this moment, the command to 'strike off his head!'[1] was interposed by Moḥammad, who had been watching what passed. 'And, O Lord!' he added, 'do thou of Thy bounty grant unto Miḳdād a better prey than this.' An-Naḍr was forthwith beheaded by 'Alī.

'Okba, another prisoner, executed

Two days afterwards, about half-way to Medīna, 'Oḳba, another prisoner, was ordered out for execution. He ventured to expostulate, and demand why he should be treated more rigorously than the other captives. 'Because of thine enmity to God and his Prophet,' replied Moḥammad. '*And my little girl!*' cried 'Oḳba, in the bitterness of his soul—'*who will take care of her?*' 'Hell-fire!' exclaimed the Prophet; and on the instant the victim was hewn to the ground. 'Wretch that thou wast!' he continued, 'and persecutor! unbeliever in God, in his Prophet, and in his Book! I give thanks unto the Lord that hath slain thee, and comforted mine eyes thereby.'[2]

[1] The phrase, *Strike his neck*, used for beheading. The executioner, by a dexterous stroke of the sword on the back of the neck can sever the head at one blow. It is still the mode of capital punishment in Moḥammadan countries. [The scene of An-Naḍr's execution was Aṣ-Ṣafrā, according to Ibn Isḥāḳ.—Ibn Hishām, p. 458.]

[2] The incident was made plentiful use of in the factious days ending in 'Othmān's death; for Um Kulthūm, daughter of 'Oḳba, was foster-sister to that unfortunate Caliph; as was Ibn abi Sarḥ (noticed at the taking of Mecca) his foster-brother. See Ibn al-Athīr, iii. 56.

Mohammad said to have been reprimanded for saving prisoners alive

We are even told that it had been in contemplation to put the whole of the prisoners, some 50 in number, to death. Indeed, Moḥammad is represented as himself directing this course.[1] Abu Bekr, always on the lenient side, pleaded for mercy. 'Omar, the personification of stern justice, urged Moḥammad vehemently to put them to death. At this juncture Gabriel brought a message from heaven, leaving it at the Prophet's option either to slay the captives or demand a ransom; with the condition, however, that, for every captive spared, a Believer would be hereafter slain in battle the ensuing year.[2] Moḥammad consulted his followers; and they said:—'Let us save the prisoners alive, and take their ransom; hereafter, they that are killed in lieu thereof will inherit Paradise and the crown of martyrdom;'—which counsel was adopted. These traditions embody the popular belief on the subject. But the only mention of the matter in the Ḳor'ān is the following verse, which, though produced by Moḥammad rather to justify the slaughter of the few prisoners put to death by himself and his followers, and to gain the character of having, against the divine commission, erred on the side of mercy, has, no doubt, given rise to this mass of fiction:—

Teaching of Ḳor'ān on the subject

Sūra viii. 68 ff.

> It is not for a prophet to take prisoners until he hath inflicted a grievous wound upon his enemies on the Earth. Ye seek after the good things of this Life: but God seeketh after the Life to come. . . . Unless a revelation from the Lord had interposed, surely a grievous punishment had overtaken you for (the ransom) which ye took. Now, therefore, enjoy of that which ye have gained, whatever is lawful and good; and fear God, for God is gracious and merciful.

---

[1] Thus Moḥammad said: 'Tell not Sa'd of his brother Ma'bad's death' (see *ante*, p. 227 note); 'but kill ye every man his prisoner.' Again: 'Take not any man his brother prisoner, but rather kill him.' I would not, however, lay much stress on these traditions. I am inclined rather to view them as called into existence by the passage quoted from the Ḳor'ān. Moḥammad (they say) likened Abu Bekr to Michael, Abraham, and Jesus, all advocates of mercy; and 'Omar to Gabriel, Noah, and Moses, the ministers of Justice. He added that if the sin of Bedr in sparing the prisoners had been punished rigorously, none would have escaped but 'Omar and Sa'd ibn Mo'ādh (another sanguinary Believer, as we shall have full proof hereafter), who both urged the slaughter of all the prisoners. [Ibn Isḥāḳ says Moḥammad gave orders before the battle not to kill any of the house of Hāshim.—Ibn Hishām, p. 446 f.]

[2] 'Which thing' (tradition adds) 'came to pass at Oḥod.'

'O thou Prophet! speak thus unto thy prisoners:—If God should know anything in your hearts which is good He will give unto you better than that which hath been taken from you; and He will forgive you, for the Lord is forgiving and merciful. But if they seek to act unfaithfully towards thee—verily they have acted unfaithfully towards the Lord already, and God is knowing and wise.'

It will be seen from this quotation that Moḥammad already contemplated the possibility of converting the prisoners to his cause; and in some instances, as we shall see, he was successful.[1]

Tidings of victory reach Medīna

From Al-Otheil, shortly after the battle, Moḥammad had despatched Zeid and 'Abdallah the poet, to make known his victory at Medīna. At the valley of Al-'Aḳīḳ, 'Abdallah struck off to the right, and spread the good tidings throughout Ḳobā and Upper Medīna. Zeid, mounted on Al-Ḳaṣwā proceeded straightway to the city. The disaffected Citizens had buoyed themselves with the hope of Moḥammad's defeat; and now, seeing his favourite camel approach without her master, they prognosticated that he had been slain. But they were soon undeceived and crestfallen; for Zeid, taking his stand at the entrance of the city, proclaimed the overthrow of Ḳoreish and named the chief men slain or taken prisoner. The joy of the Prophet's adherents was unbounded; and, as the news ran from door to door, even the little children made the streets resound with the cry, *Abu Jahl, the sinner, is slain!*

Moḥammad's return; death of his daughter Roḳeiya

The next day, Moḥammad himself arrived. His gladness was damped by finding that his daughter Roḳeiya had died during his absence. They had just smoothed the earth over her tomb in the graveyard of the Baḳī', as Zeid entered Medīna. 'Othmān had watched tenderly over her death-bed; and Moḥammad sought to solace him by uniting him, a few months later, to his remaining single daughter, Um Kulthūm. Like Roḳeiya, she had been married to one of Abu Lahab's sons, but had for some time been separated from him. She died a year or two before Moḥammad, who used, after her death, to say he so dearly loved 'Othmān, that, had there been a third daughter, he would have given her in marriage to him also.

[1] [One of the prisoners was his uncle Al-'Abbās, who redeemed himself and his two nephews 'Aḳīl and Naufal.—Aṭ-Ṭabari, i. 1345.]

In the evening, the prisoners were brought in. Sauda, the Prophet's wife, had gone out to join in lamentation with the family of a Citizen who had lost two sons at Bedr. On her return, she found, standing by her house, Suheil, one of the prisoners, with his hands tied behind his neck.[1] Surprised at the sight, she, without thinking, offered to loose his hands, when she was startled by the voice of Moḥammad, calling loudly from within: 'By the Lord and his Prophet! O Sauda, what art thou doing?' She replied that she had addressed Suheil from an involuntary impulse. Yet Moḥammad was far from intending to treat the prisoners whose lives he had spared, with harshness. He rather hoped, by kind and friendly demeanour, to win their affections and draw them over to the Faith. Thus, when Um Selama was engaged mourning at the same house with Sauda, news was brought that some of the prisoners had been quartered at her home. She went at once to Moḥammad, whom she found with 'Ā'isha, and thus addressed him:—'O Prophet! my uncle's sons desire that I should entertain certain of the prisoners, anoint their heads, and comb their dishevelled hair; but I did not venture to do so until I had first obtained thine orders.' Moḥammad replied that he did not at all object to these marks of hospitality, and desired her to do to them as she was minded.[2]

Prisoners brought into Medīna

In pursuance of Moḥammad's command, and in accord with the passage already quoted, the Citizens, and such of the Refugees as had houses of their own, received the prisoners with kindness and consideration. 'Blessings on the men of Medīna!' said one of these in later days: 'they made us ride, while they themselves walked afoot; they gave us wheaten bread to eat when there was little of it, contenting

Prisoners treated kindly;

[1] Perhaps greater stringency was used in his restraint, as he had nearly escaped on the road. Moḥammad gave orders to chase and kill him. Coming up with him, he spared his life, but bound his hands behind his neck, and tied him with a rope to his camel. Osāma met Moḥammad entering Medīna with Suheil following in this condition, and exclaimed: 'What! Abu Yazīd!' (Suheil's cognomen). 'Yes,' said Moḥammad, 'it is the same; the Chief who used to feed the people with bread at Mecca.'

[2] A year or two afterwards, on her husband's death, Moḥammad married this lady.

themselves with dates.' It is not surprising, therefore, that some of the captives, yielding to these influences, declared themselves Believers, and to such their liberty was at once granted. The rest were kept for ransom. But it was long before Ḳoreish could humble themselves to visit Medīna for the purpose. The kindly treatment was thus prolonged, and left a favourable impression on the minds even of those who did not at once go over to Islām. Eventually the army of Bedr was enriched by the large payments given. The captives were redeemed according to their several means—some paying a thousand, and others as much as four thousand pieces. Such as had nothing to give were liberated without payment; but a service was required which shows how far Mecca was in advance of Medīna in learning. To each were allotted ten boys, to be taught the art of writing; and the teaching was accepted as a ransom.

And ransomed from Mecca

Importance of the victory, and rank assigned to those engaged in it

The importance of Bedr is marked, as already said, by the marvellous labour with which every incident relating to it has been treasured up, so that the narrative far exceeds in profusion of detail that of probably any other of the great battles that have shaped the destinies of the world. Its significance is also stamped by the exalted rank assigned to the famous Three Hundred. Their names were enrolled in the first rank of the 'Register of 'Omar,' as entitled to the highest of all the princely dotations there recorded.[1] They were, in fact, the peerage of Islām. 'Bring me hither the garment in which I went forth to Bedr; for this end have I kept it laid up unto this day.' So spake Sa'd, the youthful convert of Mecca, now about to die at fourscore years. Crowned with renown as the conqueror of Persia, the founder of Al-Kūfa, and the Viceroy of Al-'Irāḳ', his honours were cast into the shade by the glory of having been one of the heroes of Bedr. In his eyes the 'garment of Bedr' was the highest badge of nobility, and in it would he be carried to his grave.[2]

The victory a divine declaration in favour of Islām

The battle of Bedr was indeed a critical point in the career of Moḥammad. However skilful in turning every in-

[1] See *Caliphate*, p. 157.

[2] He had amassed great wealth in his various commands, and, avoiding the civil wars which followed the death of the Caliph 'Othmān, had retired to his castle at Al-'Aḳīḳ near Medīna, where he died A.H. 55.

cident into proof of the divine interposition for the furtherance of Islām, he would have found it difficult to maintain his position at Medīna in the face of a reverse. The victory now supplied him with new and cogent arguments. He did not hesitate to ascribe his success to the miraculous assistance of God; and this was the easier in consequence of the superior numbers of Ḳoreish. Passages have already been quoted to this effect, and the following are equally conclusive. An Angelic host, a thousand strong, was present on his side:— Angelic auxiliaries

When ye sought assistance from your Lord; and He answered, *Verily, I will assist you with a thousand Angels, in squadrons following one upon another*:—This the Lord did as good tidings for you, and to confirm your hearts thereby. As for victory, it is from none other than from God: for God is glorious and wise. Sūra viii. 9 f.

Verily there hath been given unto you a Sign in the two armies which fought. One army fought in the way of God. The other was unbelieving, and saw their enemy double of themselves by the sight of the eye. And God strengtheneth with His aid whom He pleaseth. Verily, therein is a lesson unto the discerning people. Sūra iii. 11

And ye slew them not, but God slew them. Neither was it thou, O Prophet, that didst cast the gravel; but God did cast it; that He might prove the Believers by a gracious probation from Himself. Verily, God heareth and knoweth. It was even so. And God weakeneth the devices of the Infidels. Sūra viii. 17 ff.

If ye (the unbelievers) desire a decision, now verily the decision hath already come unto you. If ye hold back, it will be better for you; but if ye return, WE also shall return. And your troops will not avail you anything, even though they be many in number, for surely God is with the Believers.

Furthermore, not only was divine aid afforded to the army of Medīna, but the help which Satan had designed for the army of Mecca was signally frustrated:— Satan forced to abandon Ḳoreish

Be not like unto those who went forth from their habitations vaingloriously to be seen of men, and who turned aside from the way of God: and God compasseth about that which they do. Sūra viii. 49 f.

Remember, when Satan bedecked their works unto the Enemy, and said,—*None shall prevail this day against you; for I verily am your confederate*. But when the armies came within sight one of the other, he turned back upon his heels, and said,—*Verily I am clear of you. Truly I see that which ye see not. I fear God, for God is terrible in vengeance.*[1]

---

[1] As may be imagined, these passages have given rise to endless legends. The Devil appeared in the favourite form of Ibn Surāḳa. This

Mohammad now stands or falls by success in the field

The cause of Moḥammad, it was distinctly admitted, must stand or fall by the result of the armed struggle with his native city on which he had now fairly entered: difficult and dangerous ground, no doubt, for a fallible mortal to stand upon; but the die was cast, and the battle must be fought out to the death. The scabbard cast away, little additional risk was incurred when success in arms became the criterion of his prophetical claim. However strong his position otherwise, it could not be maintained in the face of an armed defeat; however otherwise weak, the sword would establish it triumphantly.

Chief Koreish killed at Bedr

There was much in the battle of Bedr which Moḥammad could plausibly represent as a special interposition of the Deity in his behalf. Not only was a most decisive victory gained over a force three times his own in number, but the slain on the enemy's side included in a remarkable manner many of his most influential opponents. In addition to the chief men killed or made prisoners, Abu Lahab, who was not present in the battle, died a few days after the return of the fugitive army—as if the decree marking out the enemies of the Prophet was inevitable.[1]

Consternation and thirst for revenge at Mecca

At Mecca, the news of the defeat was received with consternation. Burning shame and thirst for revenge stifled for a time all outward expression of grief. 'Weep not for your slain,' was the counsel of Abu Sufyān, 'mourn not their loss, neither let the bard bewail their fate. If ye lament with elegies, it will ease your wrath and diminish your enmity

man was seen running away from the field of battle, and was taxed with it by Ḳoreish—while all the time it was the Devil! We have gravely given to us the circumstantial evidence of a witness regarding the Devil's words and behaviour on this occasion, his jumping into the sea, &c. As to the angels, we have pages filled with accounts of them:—such as that one of the enemy suddenly perceived a tall white figure in the air, mounted on a piebald horse; it was an angel who had bound his comrade, and left him on the spot a prisoner, and this was the cause of his conversion. But it would be endless and unprofitable to multiply such tales. See p. 262, *n.* 2.

[1] 'Abbāsid traditions add that his death was caused by malignant and infectious ulcers; that he remained two days unburied, as no one would approach the offensive corpse; that he was not washed, but that water was cast from a distance on his body, which was then carried forth and thrown into a well in Upper Mecca, and stones heaped over the well. The bias is palpable.

towards Moḥammad and his fellows. And, should that reach their ears, and they laugh at us, will not their scorn be worse than all? Haply the turn may come, and ye may yet obtain your revenge. As for me, I will touch no oil, neither approach my wife, until I shall have gone forth again to fight with Moḥammad.' It was this savage pride which so long prevented their sending to Medīna for the ransom of their captive kinsmen.[1]

Wailing for the dead at Mecca

A month elapsed thus; and then they could refrain no longer. The wild cry of long-stifled grief burst forth at last from the whole city. In almost every house there were tears and wailings for the captive or the dead. And this lasted an entire month.[2] One house alone was silent: 'Why sheddest thou no tears,' said they to Hind, the wife of Abu Sufyān; 'why weep not for thy father 'Otba, thine uncle also, and thy brother?' 'Nay,' replied Hind, 'I will not weep until ye again wage war with Moḥammad and his fellows. If tears could wipe the grief from off my heart, I too would weep as ye; but it is not thus with Hind.' To mark her sullen sorrow, she forswore to use oil for her hair, or to go near the bed of Abu Sufyān, until an army should march forth against Medīna.

[1] Abu Sufyān declared that he would not send to ransom his own son, even if Moḥammad kept him a whole year. His son was eventually exchanged for a Muslim who incautiously visited Mecca for the Lesser pilgrimage.

[2] A plaintive illustration of the force of pent-up grief is given by Al-Wāḳidi with all the pathos of Arab feeling. The blind and aged Aswad had lost two sons and a grandson in the battle. Like the rest of Ḳoreish, he sternly repressed his grief; but as days rolled on he longed to give vent to his feelings. One night he heard the wild notes of a female wailing, and he said to his servant; 'Go see! it may be that Ḳoreish have begun to wail for their dead: perchance I, too, may wail for Zam'a, my son; for grief consumeth me within.' The servant returned, saying, that it was but the voice of a woman lamenting for her strayed camel. On this the old man gave way to a burst of beautiful and impassioned poetry. 'Doth she weep for her camel, and for it banish sleep from her eyes? Nay, if ye will weep, let us weep over Bedr:—Weep for 'Oḳeil, and for Al-Ḥārith the lion of lions!' &c. Ibn Hisham, p. 462.

CHAPTER XIII

THE YEAR FOLLOWING THE BATTLE OF BEDR

Ramaḍān, A.H. II., *to Sha'bān*, A.H. III.—A.D. 624

ÆTAT. 56

Important effect of victory on Moḥammad's position at Medīna

THE triumph of Bedr was not less important in its effect upon the inhabitants of Medīna than it was upon Ḳoreish at Mecca. It was, indeed, more important. It consolidated the power of Moḥammad over the wavering, and struck alarm into the hearts of the Disaffected. The issue had been put not on political, but upon religious grounds. It was for their unbelief Ḳoreish were overthrown. The victory, the 'Decision,' was vouchsafed by God to vindicate the Faith. The Lord had 'frustrated the devices of the Infidels; for surely God is with the believers.' The conclusion applied with equal force to the Unbelievers of Medīna. 'Verily,' said the Prophet in his Revelation, 'herein is a lesson unto the discerning people'; and the citizens were not slow to learn it. 'Abdallah ibn Obei still possessed great influence; he was the head of all who had not gone over to the new faith or tendered allegiance to the Stranger. Moḥammad on his first arrival had been counselled to deal tenderly with this Chief, and he had followed the advice. 'Abdallah saw no opportunity for a successful rupture; his own position was too insecure, and the attitude of his people too weak and wavering, for an open conflict with the enthusiasm of Moḥammad's followers. The stranger's power was daily undermining his authority and rising on its ruins.

Disaffected Jews a thorn in Moḥammad's side

Still there were clans as well as individuals who declined to go over to the new faith, and there were the Jewish tribes, and their adherents, whom, on account of their religion, Moḥammad was obliged at first to respect. All these were a thorn in his side. They spoke covertly against him, and ridiculed him in satires which passed readily into the mouths of the Disaffected, but they had not calculated on the policy of Moḥammad and his power to crush them. The unquestioning devotion of his followers made them ready instruments not only of an all-pervading espionage from which no family was secure, but also for ridding him of those whose opposition was dangerous to his cause. Even secret conversations were reported to the Prophet, and on such information he countenanced proceedings that were sometimes both cruel and unscrupulous. It was the strength gained at Bedr which enabled him fearlessly to enter on this course.

Assassination of 'Aṣmā, Ramaḍān, A.H. II. January, A.D. 624;

The first blood shed at Medīna with the countenance of Moḥammad was a woman's. 'Aṣmā, daughter of Merwān, belonged to a disaffected tribe, the Aus, and to a family which had not as yet thrown off their ancestral faith.[1] She made no secret of her dislike to Islām; and, being a poetess, composed some couplets, after the battle of Bedr, on the folly of receiving and trusting a Stranger, who had risen against his own people, and slain the chief of them in battle. The verses quickly spread from mouth to mouth (one of the few means of giving expression to public opinion), and at last reached the ears of the Muslims. They were offended; and 'Omeir, a blind man of the same tribe (and according to some a former husband of 'Aṣmā) vowed that he would kill the author. It was but a few days after the return of Moḥammad from Bedr, that this man, in the dead of night, crept into the apartment where 'Aṣmā with her little ones lay asleep. Feeling stealthily, he removed her suckling babe, and plunged his sword into her breast with such force that it transfixed her to the couch. Next morning, in the Mosque at prayer, Moḥammad, who was aware of the bloody design, said to 'Omeir: 'Hast thou slain the daughter of Merwān?' 'Yes,' he answered; 'but tell me now, is there cause of apprehension?' 'None,' said Moḥammad; 'a couple of goats will hardly knock their heads together for it.' Then turning to the people assembled in the Mosque, he said: 'If ye desire to see a man that hath assisted the Lord and his Prophet, look ye here!' 'What!' cried 'Omar, 'the blind 'Omeir!' 'Nay,' replied the Prophet, 'call him not blind; call him

[1] Al-Wāḳidi, p. 90 f.; Ibn Sa'd, p. 18. [The event comes later in Ibn Hishām (p. 995 f.); not mentioned by Aṭ-Ṭabari.]

rather *'Omeir the Seeing.'* As the assassin returned to his home in Upper Medīna, he passed the sons of 'Aṣmā burying their mother; they accused him of the murder, which without compunction he avowed, and added that if they dared to repeat things such as she had uttered he would slay the whole clan of them. The bloody threat had the desired effect. Those of the family who had secretly espoused the cause of Moḥammad now openly professed their faith, and the whole tribe soon succumbed before the fierce determination and growing influence of the Prophet's followers. In short, as Sprenger remarks, the only alternative to a hopeless blood-feud was the adoption of Islām.

And of Abu 'Afak, A.H. II. February, A.D. 624

Many weeks did not elapse before another murder was committed by expressed authority of Moḥammad.[1] The victim was an aged Jewish proselyte, Abu 'Afak, whose offence was similar to that of 'Aṣmā. He belonged to the Beni 'Amr, whose doubtful loyalty, it will be remembered, is marked by the message sent them by the Prophet on his march to Bedr. Notwithstanding his change of faith, Abu 'Afak still lived with his tribe in Upper Medīna; and, though (as is said) above a hundred years of age, was active in his opposition to the new religion. He, too, had composed some stinging and disloyal verses which annoyed the Muslims. 'Who will rid me of this pestilent fellow?' said Moḥammad to those about him; and not long after a convert from the same tribe watched his opportunity, and falling unawares upon the aged man, as he slept in the courtyard outside his house, despatched him with his sword. The death shriek drew his neighbours to the spot; but though they vowed vengeance against the murderer, he escaped unrecognised.

Alarm of Jews

These lawless and sanguinary acts alarmed all that party at Medīna which still regarded the strangers and the new faith with suspicion and dislike. And above all, terror crept over the hearts of the Jews. There was good reason for it.

Beni Ḳainuḳā' threatened by Moḥammad

The Beni Ḳainuḳā', who followed the goldsmith's craft in their stronghold outside the city, were the first of the three Jewish tribes to bear the brunt of the Prophet's displeasure.[2]

[1] Ibn Hishām, p. 994 f.; Al-Wāḳidi, p. 91; Ibn Sa'd, p. 19; [not in Aṭ-Ṭabari].

[2] Ibn Hishām, p. 545 f.; Aṭ-Ṭabari, i. 1360 ff.; Al-Wāḳidi, p. 92 f.; Ibn Sa'd, p. 19.

It is asserted that they rebelled and broke their treaty. How the breach first occurred is not altogether certain. Moḥammad, we are told, went to their chief place of resort, shortly after his return from Bedr; and, having assembled the chief men, summoned them to acknowledge him as their Prophet. 'By the Lord!' he said, 'ye know full well that I am the Apostle of God. Believe, therefore, before that happen to you which has befallen Ḳoreish!' They refused, and defied him to do his worst. An incident soon occurred which afforded the pretext for attack. A Muslim maiden visited their market-place, and at a goldsmith's shop, waiting for some ornaments, sat down. A silly neighbour, unperceived, pinned her skirt behind to the upper dress. When she arose, the awkward exposure excited laughter, and she screamed with shame. A Muslim, apprised of the affront, slew the offending Jew; the brethren of the Jew, in their turn, fell upon the Muslim and killed him. The family of the murdered Muslim appealed to the converts of Medīna, who espoused their cause. Though bound by a friendly treaty, Moḥammad made no attempt to compose the quarrel, or single out the guilty. Forthwith he marshalled his followers, and, placing the great white banner, which had waved over the field of Bedr but a month before, in the hands of Ḥamza, marched forth to attack the offending tribe. Their settlement, sufficiently fortified to resist assault, was invested, and a strict blockade maintained. This happened within one month from the battle of Bedr.

Quarrel between Jews and citizens of Medīna

Beni Ḳainuḳā' are besieged. A.H. II. February, A.D. 624

The beleaguered garrison expected that 'Abdallah ibn Obei and the Khazraj, with whom they had long been in alliance, would have interfered in their behalf; but no one dared to stir. For fifteen days they were closely besieged; and at last, despairing of the looked-for aid, they surrendered at discretion. As, one by one, they issued from the stronghold, their hands were tied behind their backs, and preparations made for execution. But 'Abdallah, fallen as he was from his high estate, could not endure to see his faithful allies led thus away to be massacred in cold blood. Approaching Moḥammad, he begged for mercy; but Moḥammad turned his face away. 'Abdallah persisted in his suit, and seizing the Prophet by the arm, as he stood armed in his coat of mail, reiterated the petition. 'Let me

Surrender at discretion, and are sent into exile

alone!' cried Moḥammad; but 'Abdallah did not relax his hold. The marks of anger mantled in the Prophet's face, and again he exclaimed loudly: 'Wretch, let me go!' 'Nay!' said 'Abdallah, 'I will not let thee go until thou hast compassion on my friends; 300 soldiers armed in mail, and 400 unequipped—they defended me on the fields of Ḥadāiḳ and Bo'āth from every foe.[1] Wilt thou cut them down in one day, O Moḥammad? As for me, I am one verily that feareth the vicissitudes of fortune.' 'Abdallah was yet too strong for Moḥammad with safety to neglect the appeal so urgently preferred. 'Let them go!' the Prophet said, reluctantly; 'the Lord curse them, and him too!' So Moḥammad released them, but commanded that they should be sent into exile. They were led forth some distance by 'Obāda, one of the Khazrajite 'leaders'; thence they proceeded to the Jewish settlement of Wādi al-Ḳora, and, being assisted there with carriage, reached Adhri'āt, on the confines of Syria. The spoil consisted mainly of armour and goldsmiths' tools, for that was the chief occupation of the tribe: they possessed no agricultural property, nor any fields. Moḥammad took his choice of the arms—three bows, three swords, and two coats of mail. The royal Fifth was then set aside, and the rest distributed amongst the army.

The spoil

Effect on the Jews and disaffected Citizens

The Jews might now see clearly the designs of Moḥammad. It was no petty question of an affronted female. Blood had, no doubt, been shed in the quarrel; but it was shed equally on both sides. And had there not been relentless enmity, and predetermination to root out the Israelites, the difference might easily have been composed. Moreover, Moḥammad was bound by treaty to deal justly and amicably with the tribe: the murderer alone was 'liable to retaliation.'[2] Indeed, of such minor importance was the quarrel, that some biographers do not mention it at all, but justify the attack by a heavenly message revealing Jewish treachery. The violent treatment of the tribe widened also to some extent the breach between the Believers and the disaffected Citizens. 'Abdallah thus upbraided 'Obāda (both were principals in the confederacy with the Ḳainuḳā') for the part he had taken in abandoning their allies, and aiding in their exile: 'What! art thou free

[1] See *ante*, p. 115.

[2] See *ante*, p. 183.

from the oath,' he said, 'with which we ratified their alliance? Hast thou forgotten how they stood by us, and shed for us their blood, on such and such a field?'—and he began enumerating the engagements in which they had fought together. 'Obāda cut him short: 'Hearts have changed,' he said, 'Islām hath blotted all treaties out.'

Affair of the *Mealbags*, petty attack by Abu Sufyān. A.H. II. April, A.D. 624

After the expulsion of the Beni Ḳainuḳā', Medīna enjoyed a month of repose. It was then thrown into alarm by a petty inroad of Ḳoreish.[1] Abu Sufyān, smarting under the defeat at Bedr, and still bound by his oath of abstinence, resolved, by way of revenge, to beard his enemies at their very doors. Setting out with 200 mounted followers, he took the eastern road skirting the tableland of Nejd, and arrived by night at the settlement of the Beni an-Naḍīr, one of the Jewish tribes living close to Medīna. Refused admittance by their chief Ḥuyei, Abu Sufyān repaired to another leading man of the same tribe, who furnished him with intelligence regarding Medīna, and hospitably entertained his party during the night. When the dawn was about to break, the party moved stealthily forward, and fell upon the corn-fields and palm-gardens two or three miles north-east of the city. Some of these, with their farm-houses, they burned to the ground, and killed two of the cultivators. Then, holding his vow fulfilled, Abu Sufyān hurried back to Mecca. Meanwhile, the alarm was raised in Medīna, and Moḥammad hastened, at the head of the Citizens, in pursuit. To accelerate their flight, Ḳoreish cast away their wallets filled with meal (whence the name of the expedition), which were picked up by the pursuers. After an absence of five days, Moḥammad returned from the fruitless chase. And shortly after, he celebrated the first festival of the '*Īd al-Aḍḥa*, already described.

Expedition to Ḳarḳarat al-Ḳudr, against the Ghaṭafān and Suleim. A.H. III. May, A.D. 624

During the summer and autumn, two or three expeditions were undertaken against the tribes inhabiting the plain east of Medīna.[2] These were of minor interest in their immediate results, but are significant of the widening circle of the struggle. The Juheina and other tribes on the sea-

[1] Ibn Hishām, p. 543; Aṭ-Ṭabari, i. 1364; Al-Wāḳidi, p. 94; Ibn Sa'd, p. 20.

[2] Ibn Hishām, p. 543; Aṭ-Ṭabari, i. 1363; Al-Wāḳidi, p. 95; Ibn Sa'd, p. 21.

coast being already in the interest of Moḥammad, the Syrian trade by that route was now absolutely barred. There remained the eastern route to Babylonia. This passed through the territories of two powerful nomad tribes, Suleim and Ghaṭafān, both allied to Ḳoreish and employed by them as carriers. They inhabited part of the great plain of Nejd, in the centre of the Peninsula. There the Beni Suleim had their headquarters in a fruitful plain, the seventh station from Mecca on the caravan route which crosses the table-land to the head of the Persian Gulf. Ḳoreish now turned their eyes towards this territory, and entered into closer bonds with the tribes inhabiting it. Henceforth the attitude of the Suleim and Ghaṭafān, especially of the former, became actively hostile towards Moḥammad. Incited by Ḳoreish, and by the example of Abu Sufyān, they now projected a plundering attack upon Medīna, a task in itself congenial with their predatory habits. Timely intelligence reached Medīna that they had begun to assemble at Ḳarḳarat al-Kudr; Moḥammad, anticipating their design, hastened to surprise them, at the head of 200 men. On reaching the spot he found it deserted; but a herd of 500 camels, securely feeding under charge of a single boy, fell into his hands, and was divided as spoil of war. The boy was made captive, but afterwards, on professing faith in Moḥammad, released.

Second expedition against the Ghaṭafān, to Dhu Amar. June

A month later, the Beni Ghaṭafān were reported to be again collecting troops in Nejd. Heading a strong force of 450 men, some mounted on horses, Moḥammad himself proceeded to disperse them. In three or four marches he reached the spot; but the enemy, having notice of his approach, had retired to the hills, and secured in fastnesses their families and cattle. One of them, who was met on the road, and employed as a guide, embraced Islām and was spared. In effecting this demonstration Moḥammad was absent eleven days. In the autumn he led another attack, at the head of three hundred followers, against the Beni Suleim, who still maintained a threatening attitude. Arrived at their rendezvous, he found that the force had broken up. So, after staying unavailingly for some time to watch the autumn caravans of Ḳoreish proceeding northwards, he returned without meeting the enemy.[1]

And against the Suleim, to Baḥrān. August

[1] Ibn Hishām, p. 544; Aṭ-Ṭabari, i. 1367 f.; Al-Wāḳidi, p. 100; Ibn Sa'd, p. 23 f.

The following month was marked by a more successful affair.[1] Ḳoreish, finding the seashore closely watched by Moḥammad, dared not expose their merchandise to the perils of that route. They were reduced to great straits. 'If we sit still at home,' they said, 'we shall be eating up our capital; how can we live, unless we keep up the winter and the summer caravans? We are shut out from the coast; let us try the eastern road by Al-'Irāḳ.' Water is scarce upon this route, but the summer was now past, and, moreover, a sufficient supply could be carried on camels between the distant wells. Accordingly, they equipped a caravan to traverse the tableland of the central desert. It was headed by Ṣafwān, and Ḳoreish sent much property with him for barter, chiefly in vessels and bars of silver. An Arab guide promised to lead them by a way unknown to the followers of Moḥammad; but intelligence of the rich venture, and of the road which it was to take, reached the Prophet through an Arab who chanced to visit the Jews at Medīna; whereupon Zeid was immediately despatched in pursuit, with a hundred picked and well-mounted men. He came up with the caravan, and fell suddenly upon it. The leaders of Ḳoreish fled, the rest were overpowered, and all the merchandise and silver were carried off, with one or two prisoners, to Medīna. The booty was valued at 100,000 pieces; so that, after appropriation of the Prophet's Fifth, 800 pieces fell to the lot of each soldier. The guide was brought to Moḥammad, who promised him liberty if he would believe. He embraced Islām, and was set free. This was the first occasion on which the Muslims secured the rich plunder of a caravan. Zeid obtained great distinction in consequence, and thenceforward became a favourite commander.

Zeid plunders caravan at Al-Ḳarada. September

No further expedition took place this year; but I must not omit to notice another of those dastardly acts of cruelty which darken the pages of the Prophet's life.[2] Ka'b ibn al-Ashraf was the son of a Jewess of the Beni an-Naḍīr, and with that tribe appears to have identified himself. He was

Assassination of Ka'b son of Al-Ashraf. A.H. III. July, A.D. 624

[1] Ibn Hishām, p. 547; Aṭ-Ṭabari, i. 1373 f.; Al-Wāḳidi, p. 100 f.; Ibn Sa'd, p. 24.

[2] Ibn Hishām, p. 548; Aṭ-Ṭabari, 1368 f.; Al-Wāḳidi, p. 95 f. : Ibn Sa'd, p. 21.

a 'proselyte of the gate,' and is said to have followed Moḥammad till he abandoned Jerusalem as his Ḳibla. The victory of Bedr deeply mortified him, in common with other ill-wishers of the Prophet. He made no attempt to conceal his discontent; and soon after proceeded to Mecca, where, being a poet, he stirred up Ḳoreish to avenge their heroes buried in the pit of Bedr, by elegies lamenting their hard fate. On his return to Medīna he was further accused of disquieting the Muslims by the publication of amatory sonnets addressed to certain of their women—a curious and favourite mode of annoyance amongst the Arabs.[1] Moḥammad, apprehensive that the free expression of hostile feeling by persons of such influence would sap his authority at Medīna, made no secret of his animosity towards Ka'b. He prayed aloud: '*O Lord, deliver me from the son of Al-Ashraf, in whatsoever way it seemeth good unto Thee, because of his open sedition and his verses.*' But instead of adopting a straightforward course, he prompted his followers, as on previous occasions, to take his life, by saying to them: 'Who will ease me of the son of Al-Ashraf? for he troubleth me.' Moḥammad, son of Maslama, replied: 'Here am I;—I will slay him.' Moḥammad, signifying his approval, desired him to take counsel with Sa'd ibn Mo'ādh, chief of his tribe, the Aus. By the advice of Sa'd, the conspirator chose four other men from the same clan as accomplices, and, taking them to Moḥammad, obtained his sanction to their plan of

[1] The following couplets are quoted in support of the accusation:—

Alas my heart! Wilt thou pass on? Wilt thou not tarry to praise her? Wilt thou leave Um al-Faḍl deserted?

Of saffron colour is she: so full of charms, that if thou wert to clasp her, there would be pressed forth Wine, Henna, and Katam; *

So slim that her figure, from ankle to shoulder, bends as she desires to stand upright, and cannot.

When we met she caused me to forget (my own wife) Um Halīm, although the cord that bindeth me to her is not to be broken.

Sprung of the Beni 'Āmir my heart is mad with the love of her; and if she chose she could cure Ka'b of his sickness.

She is the Princess of women; and her father the Prince of his tribe, the Entertainer of strangers, the Fulfiller of promises.

I never saw the sun appear by night, except on one dark evening when she came forth unto me in all her splendour.†

* The elements of beauty; red, yellow, and black. † Aṭ-Ṭabari, i. 1369.

throwing the victim off his guard by fair words and pretence of unfriendliness to the Prophet's rule. Abu Nā'ila, foster-brother of Ka'b, being deputed to pave the way, complained to him of the calamities and poverty which the advent of Moḥammad had brought upon them, and begged that he would advance corn and dates for the sustenance of himself and a party like-minded with him. Ka'b, taken in the snare, demanded security; Abu Nā'ila agreed that they should pledge their arms, and appointed a late hour of meeting at the house of Ka'b, when the bargain would be completed. Towards evening the conspirators assembled at the house of Moḥammad. It was a bright moonlight night, and the Prophet accompanied them to the outskirts of the town. As they emerged from the low shrubs of the Muslim burying-ground, he bade them god-speed: 'Go!' said he; 'the blessing of God be with you, and assistance from on High!' The house of Ka'b was near one of the Jewish suburbs, two or three miles from the city. When they reached it he had retired to rest. Abu Nā'ila called aloud for him to come down, and Ka'b started from his couch. His bride (for he had been lately married, and the biographers omit nothing that adds to the heartlessness of the affair) caught him by the skirt, and warned him not to go. 'It is but my brother Abu Nā'ila,' he said; and, as he pulled the garment from her, gaily added the verse: 'Shall a warrior be challenged and not respond?' Descending, he was not alarmed to find the party armed, as the weapons were to be left with him in pledge. They wandered along, conversing on the misfortunes of Medīna, till they reached a waterfall, and upon its bank they proposed to pass some part of the moonlight night. Meanwhile, his foster-brother, having thrown his arm around Ka'b, was familiarly drawing his hand through his long locks, and praising their sweet scent, which Ka'b said was that of his bride. Suddenly the traitor seized his hair, and dragging him to the ground, shouted! '*Slay him! Slay the enemy of God!*' Drawing their swords, they fell upon the victim. The wretched man clung so close to his foster-brother that he was with difficulty put to death. As he received the fatal wound he uttered a fearful scream, which resounded far and near amongst the strongholds of the Jews, and lights were seen at the windows of the affrighted inhabitants. The assassins, fearful of pursuit, retired in haste, carrying in their arms one of their number who had received two sword-cuts aimed at Ka'b. As they regained the burying-ground, they shouted the well-known *tekbīr*, 'Great is the Lord'; which Moḥammad hearing knew that their work had been successfully accomplished. At the gate of the Mosque he met them, saying: 'Welcome; for your countenances beam of victory.' 'And thine also, O Prophet,' they exclaimed, as they cast the ghastly head of their victim at his feet. Then Moḥammad praised God for what had been done, and comforted the wounded man.

Reflections on Ka'b's assassination

I have been thus minute in the details of the murder of Ka'b, as it faithfully illustrates the ruthless fanaticism into which the teaching of the Prophet was fast drifting. It was a spirit too congenial with the passions of the Arabs not to be immediately caught up by his followers. The strong religious impulse under which they acted hurried them into excesses of barbarous treachery, and justified that treachery by the interests of Islām and approval of the Deity. I am far from asserting that every detail in the foregoing narrative, either of instigation by Moḥammad, or of deception by the assassin, is beyond question. The actors, indeed, in such scenes were not slow to magnify and embellish their own services at the expense of their imagination. There may also have been the desire to justify an act of perfidy that startled even the loose morality of the day, by casting the burden of it on the infallible Prophet. But, after due weight given to both considerations, enough remains to prove some of the worst features of assassination, and the presumption that these were countenanced, if not in some instances directly prompted, by Moḥammad himself.[1]

[1] There can be little doubt that some Muslims were at times scandalised by crimes like this; though it is not in the nature of tradition to preserve the record of what they said. The present is one of the few occasions on which such murmurs have come to light. When Merwān was Governor of Medīna, he one day asked Benjamin, a convert from Ka'b's tribe, in what manner Ka'b met his death. 'By guile and perfidy,' said Benjamin. Now Moḥammad, son of Maslama (the assassin), by this time a very aged man, was sitting by. He exclaimed: 'What, O Merwān! could the Prophet of the Lord, thinkest thou, be guilty of perfidy? By the Lord! we did not kill him but by command of the

Murder of Ibn Suneina, a Jew,

On the morning after the murder of Ka'b, Moḥammad, exasperated at the opposition (or, as tradition puts it, the treachery) of the Jews, accorded a general permission to his followers to slay them wherever met. Accordingly, Muḥeiṣa, having encountered Ibn Suneina, a Jewish merchant, slew him, though a confederate of his tribe.[1] The occurrence is alluded to by the biographers rather for the purpose of explaining the sudden conversion of the assassin's brother Ḥuweiṣa, than to record the murder of a petty Jewish trader. When Ḥuweiṣa upbraided his brother for killing the confederate Jew, and appropriating his wealth;—'By the Lord!' replied Muḥeiṣa, 'if he that commanded me to kill him had commanded to kill thee also, I would have done it.' 'What!' Ḥuweiṣa cried; 'wouldst thou have slain thine own brother at Moḥammad's bidding?' 'Even so,' answered the fanatic. 'Strange indeed!' Ḥuweiṣa responded; 'hath the new religion reached to this? Verily, it is a wonderful faith.' And Ḥuweiṣa was converted from that very hour. The progress of Islām begins to stand out in unenviable contrast with that of early Christianity. Converts were gained to the faith of Jesus by witnessing the constancy with which its confessors suffered death; they were gained to Islām by the spectacle of the readiness with which its adherents inflicted death. In the one case conversion imperilled the believer's life; in the other, it was the only means of saving it.

Causes conversion of the murderer's brother

New treaty with the Jews

The Jews were now in extreme alarm. None ventured abroad. Every family lived in fear of a night attack; every individual dreaded the fate of Ka'b and Ibn Suneina. A deputation of their principal men waited upon Moḥammad and complained that he had treacherously cut off one of their chiefs without fault or apparent cause. 'Had Ka'b

Prophet. I swear that no roof, save that of the Mosque, shall hereafter cover thee and me.' Then, turning to Benjamin, he swore that if he had had a sword in his hand, he would have cut off his head. The unfortunate Benjamin could not thenceforward quit his house without first sending a messenger to see that Moḥammad was out of the way; but one day he was caught at a funeral by Moḥammad, who seized a bundle of date branches from a woman passing by, and broke them every one over the face and back of Benjamin. Thus were murmurers against such acts silenced in the early days of Islām.

[1] Ibn Hishām, p. 553 f.; Aṭ-Ṭabari, i. 1372; Al-Wāḳidi, p. 97 f.

conducted himself,' replied Moḥammad, 'as ye have done, he would not have been cut off. But he offended me by his seditious speeches and his evil poetry. And if any one amongst you,' he added, 'doth the same, verily the sword shall be again unsheathed.' At the same time he invited them to enter into a fresh compact with him, such as he might deem sufficient for the interests of Islām. So a new treaty was written out and deposited with 'Alī. Nevertheless, adds Al-Wāḳidi, the Jews thenceforward lived (as well they might) in a state of depression and disquietude.

Moḥammad marries Ḥafṣa, A.H. III. November, A.D. 624

Towards the close of the year 624 the Prophet took to himself a third wife, Ḥafṣa, the daughter of 'Omar, then about twenty years of age. She was the widow of Khoneis, an early convert, who had died six or seven months previously. By this marriage Moḥammad not only gratified the passion for fresh espousals, a leading feature of his advancing years, but bound himself closer in friendship to her father 'Omar. Abu Bekr and 'Omar were now connected equally with the Prophet, and through their daughters had access to his ear. There was much rivalry between 'Ā'isha and Ḥafṣa; but youth, vivacity, and beauty maintained the supremacy of 'Ā'isha.

Marriage of Fāṭima with 'Alī, A.D. 624; birth of Al-Hasan and Al-Ḥosein

The marriages contracted by Moḥammad at Medīna were all unfruitful. But meanwhile his house was built up in the female line of Khadīja's progeny. We hear of no issue, certainly of none that survived, by his daughters Zeinab and Um Kulthūm, though the name of the latter would imply maternity. Roḳeiya bore 'Othmān a son, two or three years before the Flight, but his eyes were pecked out at Medīna by a fowl, and he died still a child. It was through Fāṭima alone that the Prophet's race, the famous *Seiyids* or nobility of Islām, was to be perpetuated. 'Alī was now five-and-twenty years of age. Though not above middle stature, he was broad and powerful in make, with a ruddy complexion, and a thick and comely beard. He had already given proof of daring gallantry and prowess on the field of Bedr. Endowed with a clear intellect, warm in affection, and confiding in friendship, he was from boyhood devoted heart and soul to the Prophet. Simple, quiet, and unambitious, when in after days he obtained the rule of half the Muslim world, it was rather thrust upon him than sought. Shortly after the field of Bedr (some authorities say before it) Moḥammad gave him the hand of Fāṭima his youngest daughter, now seventeen or eighteen years of age, in marriage. Within the next twelve months she gave birth to Al-Ḥasan, the first grandson born to Moḥammad that survived, and the year after to Al-Ḥosein;—names famous in Islām.

CHAPTER XIV

THE BATTLE OF OḤOD[1]

Shauwāl, A.H. III.—*January*, A.D. 625

ÆTAT. 56

Ḳoreish resolve to avenge defeat at Bedr

THE third year of Moḥammad's life at Medīna had nearly closed, and the winter had again set in, when a storm clouded the horizon. Twelve months had elapsed since the battle of Bedr. The cry of revenge had ever since resounded in the valley of Mecca; and the long-suspended threat was now put into execution.

Moḥammad receives intimation from Al-'Abbās

Rumours of a threatened attack had for some time been reaching Moḥammad; but the first authentic notice of impending invasion with a sealed letter placed in his hands, while at the Mosque in Ḳobā, by a messenger from Mecca. It was from his uncle Al-'Abbās, who, as usual holding with both sides, had engaged the courier, by a high reward, to deliver it in three days. The letter, read aloud on the spot, contained the startling intelligence that Ḳoreish, 3,000 strong, were on the point of marching. Moḥammad enjoined secrecy; but the tidings could not be suppressed. The Prophet communicated the news privately to Sa'd, the Khazraji 'Leader,' and his wife overheard it. Whether thus, or otherwise, the coming attack was soon noised abroad, and caused great excitement, especially among the Jews and those who sympathised with them.

Ḳoreish march from Mecca. A.H. III. January, A.D. 625

The movement did, indeed, justify alarm. Ḳoreish had unanimously agreed to devote the profits of the caravan, whose precious freight was still retained in the Council-Ḥall as it were in bond, and for which so much blood had been

[1] Ibn Hishām, p. 555 ff.; Aṭ-Ṭabari, i. 1383 ff.; Al-Wāḳidi, p. 101 ff.; Ibn Sa'd, p. 25 ff.

shed at Bedr, towards avenging their defeat. These profits amply sufficed for the equipment and provisioning of a great army. Emissaries were despatched throughout the Bedawī tribes, connected with Ḳoreish by alliance or descent, inviting them to join the enterprise. At length, in the month of January, they commenced their march, 3,000 strong; 700 were mailed warriors, and 200 well-mounted cavalry; the remainder rode on camels. The Beni Zuhra (who had, on the previous occasion, retired before reaching Bedr) alone remained behind; but the army was reinforced by 100 men from Aṭ-Ṭā'if. The chiefs of Ḳoreish all joined the force. After a sharp discussion, women were allowed to accompany them; and fifteen, including two wives of Abu Sufyān, availed themselves of the permission. Taking timbrels in their hands, they sang to their wild cadence songs of vengeance for kinsmen slain at Bedr. Foremost, Hind, the wife of Abu Sufyān, thirsting for the blood of Ḥamza who slew her father in that field, had engaged an Ethiopian, with his deadly javelin, to make sure of her victim. There was also with the army a band of Medīna citizens under Abu 'Āmir, 'the Monk,' who, it will be remembered, went over to Mecca in disgust at the enthusiastic reception of Moḥammad, and now boasted that his simple presence with the army would produce an immediate reaction amongst his former fellow-citizens.

And encamp near Medīna. Thursday

The army took the ordinary route by the seashore, and, after ten days, reached Dhu'l-Ḥuleifa, in the valley of Al-'Aḳīḳ, about five miles west of Medīna. It was Thursday morning; and the same day, fetching a circuit to the left, and then marching northward for a few miles, they encamped in the fertile plain beneath the hill of Oḥod. The corn was cut down as forage for the horses; and the camels, set loose to graze, trampled the rich fields around. Friday was passed inactively. Between the city and the plain were several rocky ridges, which rendered it secure from direct attack on that side; but the Syrian highway, sweeping eastward under Oḥod, and then south, reached the northern suburb by an easy circuit. Ḳoreish feared to advance by this route, as the houses upon it afforded their adversaries a position of dangerous offence. They hoped rather to draw them to the outskirts, and overpower them there by superior numbers upon

Friday

equal ground. Perhaps, also, they expected by delay to create some dangerous diversion in the city.

Proceedings in Medīna. Thursday

Meanwhile Moḥammad, by his spies, was kept apprised of the enemy's movements. Al-Ḥobāb reconnoitred their camp and brought back an alarming estimate of its strength, which the Prophet desired him to keep secret. The farmers, with their cattle and their stuff, had affected a timely retreat; but the destruction of their fields was a trial sore to bear. Still, there was no ebullition of feeling against Moḥammad as the cause of their misfortune. Indeed, so great was the hold he had already gained, that, the elements of disaffection notwithstanding, he was at once recognised throughout the city as the leader and director in its defence. Several chief men, with an armed band of Citizens, posted themselves at the great Mosque, and kept watch throughout the night by his door. The sleep of Moḥammad was troubled. He dreamed that, securely clad in mail, he rode upon a ram, when suddenly his sword was broken at its point, and a steer was slaughtered in his sight.

Resolution to remain within the city.

Friday

The next day, Friday, the people came together, and Moḥammad discussed with them the course to be pursued. He told them of his dream. 'The fracture in my sword portendeth an injury to myself,' he said; 'the slaughter of the steer, some damage to the people; riding upon the ram signifieth carnage amongst the enemy; and the impenetrable coat of mail is Medīna fortified and safe. Within the city we are secure: without it there is risk and danger.' In this opinion the men of years and wisdom, both Citizens and Refugees, agreed. 'Abdallah ibn Obei, who, notwithstanding his jealousy of Moḥammad, was equally concerned in the defence, strongly supported the views of Moḥammad: 'O Prophet! Our city,' he said, 'is a virgin inviolate. Quitting it, we have ever suffered loss: remaining, we have beaten back attack. Leave Ḳoreish alone. If they remain, it will be in evil case. At length, frustrated in their designs, they will retire.' It was resolved accordingly to bring all outlying inhabitants within the walls, and, if Ḳoreish should venture near, to drive them back by a galling discharge of arrows and stones from the walls and house-tops.

The decision was displeasing to the younger and more impetuous Citizens. 'Shall we sit quietly here,' they asked indignantly, 'a laughing-stock to all Arabia, and look on in patience while our possessions are ravaged all around? Disgrace will cleave to us ever after, and the enemy, emboldened, will repeat the insult. Nay, we will go forth and smite our foes, even as we did at Bedr.'[1] There were not wanting men even among the Refugees who sided with this party, and their ardour was so great that Moḥammad against his better judgment at last gave way, and announced his readiness to offer battle. Ascending the pulpit for the weekly service (the day was Friday) he stirred up the people, in his discourse, to fight courageously: 'If ye be steadfast,' he said, 'the Lord will grant you victory.' Then he commanded to make ready for the battle. The most part rejoiced greatly, but some were grieved that the first decision had been set aside.

Set aside by ardour of younger converts

By the time the afternoon prayer was ended, the people had assembled in the court of the Mosque, armed for battle. Moḥammad then retired with Abu Bekr and 'Omar, to make ready. In a little while he issued from his chamber clad in

Moḥammad puts on his armour;

[1] As usual, we are overwhelmed with anecdotes of believers bent on martyrdom, and dreams and pious anticipations of rewards to be enjoyed in Paradise. These are the growth of after years; the halo pictured by tradition around the martyr's head. There were nevertheless worldly motives enough to justify this party in their desire to go forth. The Citizens were grieved at the occupation of their fields; the barley crops were being destroyed, and the season for sowing was passing away. Even Ḥamza joined them on political considerations. 'We fear,' he said, 'lest Ḳoreish should attribute our backwardness to cowardice, and that it will embolden them ever after. We were but few at Bedr, and we are many now. Verily, this is the day we have longed and prayed to the Lord for; and now He hath driven the enemy as a prey into our very midst.'

Some specimens of the martyr spirit may interest the reader. One said to Moḥammad: 'The slaughtered steer thou sawest was an emblem of the dead amongst thy followers, and verily I shall be of the number; wherefore, hinder me not from Paradise. Let us go forth; surely, by the one God! I shall quickly enter therein.' Again, Khaithama told Moḥammad that his son, whom he had lost at Bedr, appeared to him in his sleep;—'A goodly appearance truly he had; he described to me the blessedness of Paradise; all is true that our Lord hath promised; and he besought me to come quickly, and be his companion there. And now, verily, I am old, and long for the meeting with my Lord. Pray, therefore, that God would grant me martyrdom, and reunite me with my son.' So Moḥammad prayed; and Khaithama was slain at Oḥod. Such are the tales which tradition delights to embellish or haply to create.

mail and helmet, his sword hanging from a leathern girdle,[1] and shield slung over his shoulder. The Citizens, seeing him thus accoutred, repented of their rash remonstrance, and prayed that he would even now do as seemed good to him. But it was too late. 'I invited you to this,' he said, 'and ye would not. It becometh not a prophet, when once he hath girded himself to the battle, to lay his armour down again until the Lord hath decided betwixt him and his enemies. Wait, therefore, on the Lord. Only be steadfast, and He will send you victory.'

Marches from Medīna, and halts. Friday night

So saying, he called for three lances, and fixed banners upon them. One for the Refugees he gave to Muṣ'ab, the second and third to the leaders of the Aus and Khazraj. 'Abdallah ibn Um Mektūm (the blind man of whom we read at Mecca) was appointed to command the city, and lead the public prayers. Just then the bier of a Citizen was brought into the Mosque. Moḥammad pronounced over it the usual service; then mounting his horse, and surrounded by his followers, he took the road to Oḥod. There was but one other horse with the Muslim army. Arrived at an eminence, the Prophet turned round and saw following, amid the palm plantations on the right, a rude and disorderly band of men, and being told that they were the Jewish confederates of 'Abdallah ibn Obei, he commanded that they should go back; 'for,' said he, 'ye shall not seek the aid of Unbelievers to fight against the unbelieving.' He then passed onwards to Esh-Sheikhain, half-way to Oḥod,[2] and having reviewed the force, and sent back some striplings unequal to the fight, there halted for the night. 'Abdallah ibn Obei, with his followers, encamped near at hand; but, displeased at the rejection of his advice, and also at the unfriendly treatment of his Jewish friends, kept sullenly aloof. Moḥammad passed the night with the Beni an-Najjār, and a guard of faithful followers was stationed over him. Moḥammad, son of Maslama, patrolled the camp with fifty

[1] This girdle was preserved and handed down in the family of Abu Rāfi', Moḥammad's servant.

[2] Burckhardt notices it as 'a ruined edifice of stones or bricks,' a mile from the town, 'where Moḥammad put on his coat of mail'; *i.e.* on the following morning. 'Farther on,' he tells us, there is a stone where the Prophet 'leaned for a few minutes on his way to Oḥod.'

men. A similar duty was performed for Ḳoreish by 'Ikrima with a troop of horse; these approached close enough to alarm the Muslims by their neighing, but did not venture over the ridge which still separated the two armies.

Mohoammad advances to Oḥod, and draws up line of battle. Saturday, A.H. III. January, A.D. 624

At early dawn the army of Medīna, 1,000 strong, was in motion. In the dim morning light they marched, by the nearest path, through the intervening fields and gardens,[1] and emerged upon the sandy plain beneath the peaks of Oḥod. The vicinity owes its verdure to a watercourse, which carries off the drainage of the country lying to the south and east. The hill of Oḥod, three miles distant from Medīna, is a rugged and almost insulated offshoot of the mountain range, projecting eastward for three or four miles into the plain. The torrent, sometimes swollen so as quite to inundate the adjacent tract, sweeps along its southern and western face, and discharges its flood into the *Ghāba*, or low basin lying beyond. Now dry, its course was marked only by deep sand and scattered stones. On the farther bank, upon a slightly sloping plain, bare and stony, over which, as Burton tells us, 'the seared and jagged flanks of Ohod rise like masses of iron,' Moḥammad halted his army. By this time it was daylight, and, although the columns of the enemy were in sight, the cry for morning prayers was raised by Bilāl, and the whole army, led by the Prophet, prostrated itself in worship. 'Abdallah ibn Obei at this moment wheeled suddenly round, and, deserting the army with his 300 followers, took the road back to the city. Moḥammad was thus left with but 700 followers, of whom only a hundred were clad in mail; but they were all true men, and, fighting in what they believed to be the cause of God, they boldly faced a well-appointed enemy four times their number. Advancing, they occupied the rising ground in front; their

[1] As he passed through one of these gardens, its owner, a blind man, murmured at the injury to his property, and cast dust at Moḥammad. One of the Aus sprang up and beat him. A chief of the Khazraj resented the affront, and a fierce contention arose. It was ended by a savage threat from Oseid, the Ausite 'Leader,' who said that had he not known that it would be displeasing to Moḥammad, he would have cut the blind man's head off. There must, no doubt, have been difficulty in keeping down these intestine quarrels and jealousies, though, in the hands of a skilful administrator like Moḥammad, they were really elements of power.

rear was thus protected by the frowning heights of Oḥod, excepting on the left, where the rocks, receding, afforded the enemy a dangerous opening, suited to the movements of the Ḳoreishite horse. Moḥammad, therefore, posted on an adjoining eminence the flower of his archery, and gave their leader stringent orders on no possible contingency to quit the spot, but steadily to check any attempts which Ḳoreish might make to turn his flank: 'Guard our rear,' he said, 'and stir not from this spot: if ye see us pursuing and plundering the enemy, join not with us: if we be pursued and even worsted, do not venture to our aid.' Then he drew out his line, facing towards Medīna;—Muṣ'ab, with the Refugee standard, being in the centre, and the Aus and Khazraj clans forming either wing. He forbade his followers to engage the enemy till he gave command; for he knew that the strength of his position would be sacrificed by a premature advance. Having thus disposed his force, he put on a second coat of mail, and calmly awaited the enemy's approach.

Army of Mecca advances

Meanwhile Abu Sufyān, as hereditary leader, brought up the Meccan army; and, facing Oḥod, marshalled it in front of the Muslim line. The banner, which had been duly mounted on its standard in the Council-Hall at Mecca, was borne by Ṭalḥa, grandson of 'Abd al-'Ozza.[1] The right wing was commanded by Khālid; the left by 'Ikrima, son of Abu Jahl. 'Amr ibn al-'Āṣ (the famous 'Amr) was over the Ḳoreishite horse. The women at first kept to the front, and beat their timbrels to shrill martial song; but as the line advanced, they fell to the rear.

Battle opens with single combats

The battle opened by the inglorious advance of the exile Abu 'Āmir, who vainly expected his fellow-citizens of Medīna

[1] This Ṭalḥa is to be distinguished from Ṭalḥa, son of 'Obeidallah, who stood by Moḥammad in the battle. The Ṭalḥa in the text was of the family of 'Abd ed-Dār, which retained the right of carrying the Ḳoreishite standard (*vide* p. xcvi.). Abu Sufyān desired not only to lead the army, but to carry the standard, or at least to raise a second banner; but the descendants of 'Abd ed-Dār would hear of no encroachment on their ancestral privilege. There is a tradition that, as the enemy drew near, Moḥammad inquired who bore their standard. On being told that it was one of the house of 'Abd ed-Dār, he exclaimed: 'Our side is more worthy of the honour;' and, calling for Muṣ'ab (who was of the same lineage), he placed the standard in his hands.

to fraternise with him. He was received with a shower of stones, and forced with his band of followers to retire; Ṭalḥa crying out indignantly:—'Get to the rear, ye slaves! Guard the camp,—a fitting employment for you!' Then, flourishing the Ḳoreishite banner, Ṭalḥa advanced alone, and challenged the enemy to single combat, shouting these words:—

> The standard-bearer hath the right
> To dye its shaft in blood,
> Till it be broken in his hand.

'Alī stepped forth, and, rushing on him, with one blow of his sword brought him to the ground.[1] Moḥammad, who had intently watched the rapid combat, exclaimed with loud voice, *Great is the Lord!* and the cry, taken up all round, arose in an overwhelming shout from the whole Muslim army. Ṭalḥa's brother, 'Othmān, who was in charge of the women, then ran forward and seized the banner which lay by the lifeless body. The women beat their timbrels loudly, as they sang:—

> Daughters of the brave are we,
> On carpets step we delicately;
> Boldly advance, and we embrace you!
> Turn your backs and we will shun you,—
> Shun you with disdain.

Ḥamza responded to 'Othmān's challenge, and, after a brief encounter, brought him also lifeless to the ground. Then striding proudly back to the Muslim ranks, he shouted: 'I am the son of him that gave the pilgrims drink,'—meaning of 'Abd al-Muṭṭalib, who had held that office. One after another, the family of Ṭalḥa, two brothers and three sons, seized the standard; one after another, they fell in single combat.[2]

[1] Moḥammad declared that thus was fulfilled that part of his vision in which he appeared to ride upon a ram. Ṭalḥa was the ram.

[2] One of the sons was wounded by an arrow, shot by 'Āṣim. The wounded lad was carried to his mother Sulāfa, at the rear. She asked him, as he was breathing his last, who killed him. He said that as his foe shot the arrow, he heard him cry: 'Take that from me, the son [that is, grandson] of Al-Aḳlaḥ!' 'By the Lord!' Sulāfa said, 'it was 'Āṣim, one of our own kin'; and she vowed she would yet drink wine out of 'Āṣim's skull. The savage vow was nearly being fulfilled, as we shall see hereafter.

Ḳoreish are pressed, and waver

This Arab custom of single combat put the two armies on an equality for the time. So long as it went on, the Ḳoreish derived no advantage from their superior numbers; and the rapid destruction of their standard-bearers carried dismay into their ranks. A general engagement ensued; and, pressed by the fierce ardour of the Muslims, the Meccan army began to waver. Their horse sought repeatedly to turn the left flank of Moḥammad; but they were each time forced back by the galling archery of the little band which Moḥammad had posted there. The same daring contempt of danger was displayed as at Bedr. The Meccan ranks might be seen to quiver as Abu Dujāna, distinguished by a red kerchief round his helmet, swept along the enemy's ranks, and, with a sword given him by Moḥammad, dealt death on every hand.[1] Ḥamza, conspicuous from his waving ostrich feather; 'Alī, known by his long white plume, and Az-Zubeir, by his bright yellow turban, like heroes of the Iliad,—carried confusion wherever they appeared. Such were the scenes in which were reared the great leaders of the Muslim conquests.[2]

Day changed by charge of Khālid, and army of Medīna routed

But now the Muslims pressed too hotly their success. Their line lost form and order; and a portion, piercing the enemy's ranks, fell to plundering his camp. The archers, who had hitherto held the Meccan horse in check, saw from their height the tempting opportunity, and, casting the Prophet's strict injunction to the winds, as well as the earnest expostulation of their leader, hurried to the spoil. The ready eye of Khālid saw the chance, and he hastened to retrieve the day. Wheeling his cavalry round the enemy's left, and

[1] There is a mass of tradition about Abu Dujāna's prodigies of valour. At the commencement of the action Moḥammad held up his sword, and said: 'Who will take this sword, and give to it its due?' 'Omar, Az-Zubeir, &c., one after another, came forward and were rejected; last of all Abu Dujāna offered, and Moḥammad gave it to him; 'And he clave therewith the heads of the Unbelievers.'

After the battle, 'Alī, giving his bloody sword to Fāṭima to wash, said: 'Take this sword, for it is not to be despised,' alluding to his own acts of prowess that day. Moḥammad added: 'If thou hast done well, O 'Alī! verily Al-Ḥārith and Abu Dujāna have done well also.' Ibn Hishām, p. 588.

[2] For example, in this battle we have Sa'd and Abu 'Obeida on the side of Moḥammad, and Khālid and 'Amr on the side of Ḳoreish; all famous in after days.

sweeping from the rising ground the few remaining archers, he suddenly appeared in rear of the Muslims and charged into their ranks. The surprise was fatal, and the discomfiture complete. Muṣ'ab was slain, and his banner disappeared.[1] Hind's wild negro, Waḥshi, who had been watching for Ḥamza, now singled out his victim, and swinging his javelin with unerring aim, brought him lifeless to the ground. Ḳoreish now raised their war cry of *Yā lal-'Ozza! Yā la-Hubal!* and advanced with rapid step. The Muslims broke at every point, and fled for refuge to the heights of Oḥod.

Moḥammad wounded

It was a moment of peril for Moḥammad. He was still in the rear watching from a rising ground the first success, when he narrowly escaped the sweeping charge of Khālid's horse. Marvellous tales are given of his prowess, as well as of repeated signal escapes. With the staff of followers who surrounded him, he joined in discharging arrows till his bow was broken; and then he betook himself to casting stones. He is even said to have inflicted a deadly wound on one of Ḳoreish, who pressed madly forward to cut him down. When the Muslim ranks were broken and forced back, he tried to stay their flight, crying aloud: *Whither away? Come back! I am the Apostle of God! Return!* But still they fled. The enemy soon bore down upon the Prophet himself; and if a party of devoted followers (seven Citizens and seven Refugees) had not rallied round the spot, he surely had been slain. Ḳoreish scoured the field in special quest of their arch enemy. Suddenly, Ibn Ḳami'a, the hero who had just slain Muṣ'ab, and others, came upon the little group. Stones and arrows flew thick around. A missile wounded the Prophet's under lip and broke one of his front teeth.[2] Another blow drove the rings of his helmet deep into his cheek, and made a gash in his forehead. The sword of Ibn Ḳami'a was barely warded off his head by the naked hand of Ṭalḥa, son of 'Obeidallah, whose fingers were thereby for life disabled.

[1] Tradition tells it was seized by an angel. 'The angels,' it is added, 'though present, did not fight that day; but had the Believers stood fast they would have fought.'

[2] The spot of Moḥammad's misfortunes is marked by a Cupola, *Ḳubbat eth-Thenāyā*, the dome of the teeth, 'nearer the foot of the mountain' than the graves of Ḥamza, &c. The print of a tooth is still shown there.

Moḥammad fell to the ground, and Ibn Ḳami'a returned to his comrades exclaiming that he had killed him. The cry was taken up all round, and resounded from the rocks of Oḥod.[1] It spread consternation among his followers;—'Where now,' they cried, 'the promise of his Lord?' At the same time, however, the rumour checked the ardour of the enemy's pursuit. Their controversy was with Moḥammad rather than Medīna. If he were killed, their object was accomplished, their revenge fulfilled.

Cry that Moḥammad is slain

Moḥammad takes refuge behind rocks of Oḥod

But Moḥammad was only stunned. The cliffs of Oḥod were close behind. Ṭalḥa (himself in several places wounded) raised him gently, and, with one or two others affording support, helped him to climb the rocks where the greater part of his army had already found secure retreat. The joy of his followers was unbounded at finding their Prophet still alive. Ka'b ibn Mālik met him on the way, and began to call aloud the good news; but Moḥammad, feeling that he was not yet beyond the reach of danger, motioned him to be silent. When they had found shelter in a cave,[2] the first care of his followers was to remove the helmet from his head. Two of its rings were so firmly imbedded in his cheek that Abu 'Obeida lost two teeth in the endeavour to extract them. The blood flowed copiously from the Prophet's wounds. 'Alī ran to a hollow in the rock, and brought some water in his shield. Moḥammad could not drink of it, but only rinsed his mouth. As the blood was being washed off his face, he cried out: *How shall a people prosper that treat thus their Prophet who calleth them unto the Lord! Let the wrath of God burn against the men that have besprinkled the face of His Apostle with his own blood!*[3] He then put on the yellow

[1] As usual, it is the Devil who is accused of this piece of malice. In the shape of Ibn Surāḳa (see *ante*, p. 235 note), he screamed aloud that Moḥammad was dead. [This idea of Satan as Ju'āl ibn Surāḳa is, of course, not found in either Ibn Hishām or Aṭ-Ṭabari, but is common in Al-Wāḳidi.]

[2] It is still shown to the pilgrims. Burton, ii. 248. There are some stories of Moḥammad's party having been pursued up the hill. Also that they were in danger of being shot upon by their own people, who mistook them for the enemy. But they seem embellishments.

[3] 'He cursed those that inflicted the wounds, saying: *Let not the year pass over them alive;* and it came to pass that not one of those that shot at the Prophet survived beyond the year.' Compare Luke xxiii. 34.

helmet of Ka'b in place of his own broken one; and, joining the rest of his followers, watched thus the movements of Ḳoreish in the plain below. Many of the Muslim warriors, wearied with the struggle, fell asleep. And so mid-day passed away.

Colloquy between Abu Sufyān and 'Omar. Ḳoreish retire

The leaders of Ḳoreish were now busy on the field of battle. They sought for the body of Moḥammad, and, not finding it, began to doubt his death. Many acts of barbarous mutilation were committed on the slain. Hind gloated over the body of her victim Ḥamza. Tearing out his liver, she chewed it, fulfilling thus a savage vow, and she strung his nails and pieces of his skin together to bedeck her arms and legs.[1] When Ḳoreish had spent some time thus, and had leisurely disposed of their own dead, Abu Sufyān drew near to the foot of the hill, and, raising his voice, called aloud the names successively of *Moḥammad*, *Abu Bekr*, *'Omar*. Receiving no reply (for the Prophet enjoined silence) he cried again: 'Then all are slain, and ye are rid of them!' 'Omar could contain himself no longer. 'Thou liest!' he exclaimed; 'they are all alive, thou enemy of God, and will requite thee, yet.' 'Then,' rejoined Abu Sufyān, 'This day shall be a return for Bedr. Fortune alternates, even as the bucket. Hearken! ye will find mutilated ones upon the field: this was not by my desire, but neither am I displeased thereat. Glory to AL-'OZZA! Glory to HUBAL! AL-'OZZA is ours; not yours!'[2] At the bidding of Moḥammad, 'Omar replied: *The Lord is ours; He is not yours.*' Abu Sufyān said: 'We shall meet after a year again at Bedr.' 'Be it so,' answered 'Omar. With these words Abu Sufyān turned to go, and the Meccan army began its homeward march.

Number of slain

As soon as the enemy was out of sight, Moḥammad and his followers descended from their retreat. The full extent of the overthrow was now apparent. Seventy-four corpses were strewn upon the plain,—four were Refugees,[3] and

[1] But tradition delights to abuse Hind, as it did Abu Jahl; and we must beware of the patent tendency to exaggerate.

[2] A play on the word, which signifies *glory* as well as the idol of the goddess Al-'Ozza.

[3] One Refugee, being mortally wounded, was carried to Upper Medīna, where he died; but his body, by desire of Moḥammad, was carried back to Oḥod, and buried there. The tombs of the four Refugees are still shown to pilgrims and maintained in repair.

seventy citizens of Medīna. Indeed, it was evident that the destruction of the whole force was only averted by the foresight of Moḥammad in keeping a secure place of refuge in his rear. On the enemy's side the loss was but twenty.

The news reaches Medīna

The news of the discomfiture reached Medīna, with rumours of the death of Moḥammad; and the road was soon covered with men and women hastening to nurse the wounded or search for the dead. The disaffected citizens did not conceal their satisfaction, and some even talked of an embassy to Abu Sufyān.

Dressing of Moḥammad's wounds

Arrived at the field of battle, Fāṭima dressed the gash on her father's temple, staunching the blood with the ash of some burned matting. This added to the ghastly appearance of the wound, which was deep, and did not fully heal for above a month.

Ṣafīya mourns over her brother Ḥamza

Ṣafīyā, the Prophet's aunt, was fondly attached to her brother Ḥamza; and Moḥammad, fearful of the effect which the sight of his mangled remains might have upon her, had desired her son Az-Zubeir to keep her aside till the body was buried; but she was not to be kept back. 'Where is my brother?' she eagerly inquired of Moḥammad. 'Among the people,' he replied. 'I will not go back,' she cried, 'until I see him.' So he led her to the spot, saying: 'Leave her to her grief alone.' She sat down with Fāṭima by the body, and both sobbed aloud. Moḥammad wept also. His spirit was stirred within him at Ṣafīya's anguish and the disfigured remains of the noble dead. Seizing his beard and pulling it angrily, as when grieved and agitated he was wont to do, he swore that he would mutilate the bodies of thirty of Ḳoreish in Ḥamza's stead.[1] To comfort Ṣafīya, he told her that her brother's name was already enrolled in Paradise as the *Lion of God and of his Apostle.* He spoke comfortingly also to the women of Medīna, who were wailing over their dead. The graves being now ready, and the bodies laid out in order, he prayed over them, and commanded that they should be buried by twos and threes in each

[1] But he afterwards thought better, and forbade the savage practice. The passage is at the end of Sūra xvi., which, however, is a Meccan one, and does not bear very plainly on the occasion here referred to. However this may be, there is no doubt that Moḥammad abolished the practice of mutilation, and it is to the credit of his humanity that he did so.

grave.[1] The obsequies ended, he mounted his horse, and the whole company, turning sadly from Oḥod, took the homeward road.

Moḥammad returns to Medīna

The Meccan army, though withdrawn from the field of battle, might still have fallen upon Medīna, uncovered as it was by the absence of the Muslim army. Moḥammad and his followers trembled for the safety of their families. On descending from the heights, the Prophet had despatched Sa'd, son of Abu Waḳḳāṣ, to watch the movements of the enemy. When they reached the valley of Al-'Aḳīḳ, Koreish paused there awhile. Their counsels were divided. Some urged to follow up their success by a blow on the defenceless city. Others pointed to the danger of entanglement and loss in the outskirts and narrow streets, and contended that they should rest content with their signal victory. The opinions of the latter prevailed; mounting their camels, and leading their horses,[2] they slowly wended their way through the defiles that led back to Mecca. Sa'd, hurrying at once to Moḥammad, cried aloud the joyful news. 'Gently,' said Moḥammad; 'let us not appear before the people to rejoice at the departure of the enemy!' The intelligence, nevertheless, brought intense relief both to Mohammad and his people; for the crestfallen, crippled army of Medīna could ill have ventured on a second struggle.

Ḳoreish, after hesitation, take route to Mecca

As Moḥammad and his followers reached the foot of the intervening ridge, the whole company, at his command, fell into two lines, with the women ranged behind, and there offered up prayer to God. As they entered the city, the voice was heard all round of women wailing for their dead: 'And Ḥamza!' cried Moḥammad, 'alas for Ḥamza! who is there to wail for him!' The wounded here received permis-

Night of distress and insecurity at Medīna

[1] They were not washed. 'Wind them,' said the Prophet, 'as they are, in their wounds and in their blood. I will be surety for them;' alluding to the necessity for legal ablution. Hence the angels are said to have washed Ḥamza and Ḥanẓala. Some of the traditions, to the effect that the latter was in a state of legal impurity, can hardly be quoted.

[2] This was the sign given by Moḥammad to Sa'd: 'If they mount their horses,' said he, 'and lead their camels, then they meditate an advance on Medīna; if they mount the camels, and lead the horses, then they are going home.' The camel was their working animal. Ibn Hishām, p. 583.

sion to go to their homes. The rest followed Moḥammad to the Mosque, which they reached in time for the sunset prayer. It was a night of mourning. A sense of insecurity still prevailed, for Ḳoreish might even yet return, and so the chief men again kept watch at the Prophet's door. Some of the wounded were laid near the Mosque, and the fires kindled for them cast a fitful and lurid light around its courts. Moḥammad slept heavily, and did not answer the call of Bilāl for eventide prayer. Shortly afterwards he awoke, and, rising, asked who it was that wailed so loudly near the Mosque. It was the wailing of the women, who had heard his plaintive words regarding Ḥamza, and came there to mourn for him. Moḥammad blessed them, and sent them to their homes. And so it grew to be a custom at Medīna for the women, when they mourned for their dead, first to wail for Ḥamza.

Moḥammad makes demonstration in pursuit of Ḳoreish

On the morrow, Moḥammad commanded Bilāl to proclaim through the city that he was about to start in pursuit of Ḳoreish, but that none should accompany him excepting those who had been present at the battle of Oḥod. It was intended thus to raise the spirits of his followers, remove the impression of defeat, and show Ḳoreish that an attack upon the city would have been vigorously repelled. As the warriors assembled at the Mosque, Ṭalḥa came up: 'What thinkest thou,' inquired Moḥammad of him; 'how far have Ḳoreish by this time reached on their journey homewards?' 'To the valley of Seiyāla,' he answered, one long march from Medīna. 'So was I thinking also,' rejoined Moḥammad; 'but, Ṭalḥa! they will never again inflict upon us such a disaster as we suffered yesterday,—no, not till we wrest Mecca from them.' The white flag of the Refugees was not recovered from the field of battle; but one of the other banners stood in the Mosque yet unfurled, and the Prophet placed it in the hands of Abu Bekr.[1] Stiff and disfigured as he was, he mounted his horse, and set out on the Meccan road. Two scouts, whom he sent in advance, fell into the enemy's hands, and were put to death; their bodies were found at Ḥamrā al-Asad, a little way short of Aṣ-Ṣafrā, which Moḥammad reached the day after it was evacuated by

[1] Ibn Hishām, p. 588 f.; Aṭ-Ṭabari, i. 1427 f.; Al-Wāḳidi, p. 149 f.; Ibn Sa'd, p. 34.

Ḳoreish. At this spot the force spent three days, and regaled themselves with fresh dates, a plentiful harvest of which had just been gathered. Having kindled five hundred fires on the adjoining heights, to make Ḳoreish believe that the pursuing force was very large, Moḥammad, contenting himself with this demonstration, returned to Medīna, after an absence of five or six days.

Abu 'Azza, a prisoner, put to death

At Ḥamrā al-Asad Moḥammad made prisoner one of the enemy, the poet Abu 'Azza, who had loitered behind the rest. He had been taken prisoner at Bedr, and, having five daughters dependent on him, had been freely released on the promise that he would not again bear arms in the war against the Prophet. He now sought for mercy: 'O Moḥammad!' he prayed, 'forgive me of thy clemency!' 'Nay, verily,' said the Prophet, 'a Believer may not twice be bitten from the same hole. Thou shalt never return to Mecca; stroke thy beard, and say, *I have again deceived Moḥammad.* Lead him forth to execution!' So saying, he motioned to a bystander, who with his sword struck off the captive's head.

Another, after three days' truce, pursued and killed

Another Ḳoreishite, Mu'āwiya, son of Al-Moghīra, perished by too great confidence in the generosity of his enemy. When quitting Oḥod, he missed his way, and passed the night near Medīna. Next morning he ventured to the house of 'Othmān, the Prophet's son-in-law, who procured for him a three days' truce, and, having found him a camel and provisions for the way, joined Moḥammad on his march to Hamrā al-Asad. The Ḳoreishite incautiously lingered at Medīna till the last day of his term of grace, when he set out for Mecca. In the endeavour to avoid the returning Muslim force, he again lost his way; and Moḥammad, hearing of his delay, sent men upon his track, who came up with him, and killed him.

Halo of glory around the Martyrs of Oḥod

The field of Oḥod came before long to be invested with a special interest. A flood of glory crowns the memory of the dead. Moḥammad used to visit the scene once a year, and bless the martyrs buried there. '*Peace be on you!*' he would say, '*for that which ye endured,—and a blessed Futurity above!*' The citizens, as they passed to and fro, visiting their fields at Al-Ghāba, would invoke blessing on the souls of the warriors buried by the way; and, to the invocation 'Peace be upon you,' would conjure up the audible response, 'And on you be peace!' We are also told that, half a century after, a great flood having ploughed up the banks of the torrent and uncovered many graves, the bodies of the martyrs were seen reclining in the attitude of sleep, fresh as the day of their interment, and blood still trickling from their wounds.

But Moḥammad's prestige affected at the time

Thus a halo, in course of time, settled on the 'Martyrs of Oḥod' and glorified their memory. But at the present moment humiliation and not glory overshadowed the battle-field. Murmurs at the inglorious retreat were rife throughout the city. Tradition passes lightly over the uncongenial subject, and dwells complacently on the ignominious manner in which 'Abdallah ibn Obei, and the Jews who hazarded remarks disparaging to the Prophet, were treated, and on the boastful threats of 'Omar against them. But the Ḳor'ān tells a different story. We there find that even the adherents of Moḥammad were staggered by the reverse. It was natural that they should be. The success at Bedr had been assumed as proof of divine support: and, by parity of reasoning, the defeat at Oḥod was subversive of the prophetic claim. The Jews broadly advanced this stubborn argument.[1] It required all the address of Moḥammad to avert the dangerous imputation, sustain the credit of his cause, and reanimate his followers. This was done by a message from Heaven, forming now the latter half of the third Sūra.[2] A lofty tone of assurance pervades the studied explanation and remonstrance of the Prophet. Stress is laid on the marvellous interposition which brought victory at Bedr. But the reverse at Oḥod was necessary to sift true Believers from such as were Hypocrites at heart. The light afflictions of the day were a meet prelude to the eternal glories of Paradise. The faithful, coveting the blessed state of the martyrs at Bedr, had longed for the same fortune; and now, when death presented itself, they fled before its terrors! The slaughter, anywise,

Line of argument by which Moḥammad obviated its ill effect

[1] 'How can Moḥammad pretend now,' they asked, 'to be anything more than an aspirant to the *kingly* office? No true claimant of the *prophetic* dignity hath ever been beaten in the field, or suffered loss in his own person and that of his followers, as Moḥammad hath.'—Al-Wāḳidi.

[2] The third Sūra is a collection of passages belonging to various periods. We have in it portions revealed shortly after Bedr, A.H. II.; after Oḥod, A.H. III.; after the second Bedr A.H. IV.; also after an interview with the Nejrān Christians, A.H. IX.

could not have been averted by following the counsels of those who stayed at home; for the hour of death is fixed for every one, and is inevitable. Future success was largely promised, if Believers would but remain steadfast and courageous. The Lord had already at Oḥod placed victory within their reach, when by cowardice and disobedience they drew defeat upon themselves. Even if Moḥammad had been killed in battle, what then? he was but the Messenger of God, like other Apostles who had died before him. The cause itself was immortal and divine. Such is the line of argument, mingled with comfort, reproof, and exhortation. Whatever the Disaffected might say of the Prophet's reasoning, it served to reassure his loyal followers, and while these were with him heart and soul, his position at Medīna was secure.

Passages from Sūra iii. on the subject

The style and tenor of this remarkable chapter so fully and curiously illustrate the present situation of Moḥammad that the reader will not, I think, object to a somewhat lengthy extract:—

> Remember when thou wentest forth from thy family in the early morning to secure for the Faithful an encampment for the battle; . . . And when two companies of you[1] became anxious, so that ye lost heart; and God is the Patron of both, and in God let the Believers put their trust. And, truly, God helped you at Bedr, when ye were fewer in number . . . When thou saidst to the Believers: *What! doth it not suffice you that your Lord should aid you with* 3,000 *Angels sent down?* Nay, if ye persevere, and fear God, and this Enemy were to come suddenly upon you, your Lord would help you with five thousand Angels attired for battle;—And God made this promise none otherwise than as glad tidings for you, and that your hearts might be stayed. Victory cometh from God alone, the Glorious, the Wise, that He may cut off the uttermost part of the unbelievers. * * * * * v. 117 ff.
>
> Be not cast down, neither be ye grieved. Ye shall be yet victorious if ye are true Believers. If a wound hath befallen you, verily a wound like unto it hath befallen your enemy. This various success WE cause to alternate among men, that God may know those that believe, and may have witnesses amongst you . . . that God might prove them that believe, and annihilate the Infidels. What! did ye think to enter Paradise, while as yet God knew not those that fight for Him, and knew not the persevering ones amongst you? And truly ye were longing for death before ye faced it. And verily ye saw it and looked on. v. 133 ff.

[1] Meaning apparently both *Refugees* and *Citizens;* though the commentators refer it to the two wings the *Aus* and the *Khazraj*, in whose minds an ill impression had arisen by the desertion of 'Abdallah ibn Obei.

Sūra iii. Battle of Oḥod

Moḥammad is no more than an Apostle, as other Apostles that have gone before him. What! if he were to die or be killed, must ye needs turn back upon your heels? He that turneth back upon his heels injureth not God in the least degree; but God will reward the thankful. Furthermore, no soul dieth but by the permission of God, as it is written and predestined. * * * How many Prophets have fought against those that had multitudes on their side. And they were not cast down at that which befell them fighting in the way of God, neither did they become weak, nor make themselves abject; and God loveth the persevering. * * * * *

v. 144 ff. WE will surely cast terror into the hearts of the Infidels, because they have associated with God that which He hath nowise authorised. Their resting-place shall be the Fire: wretched is the abode of the transgressors! And truly the Lord had already made good unto you His promise at what time ye were, by His permission, cutting them to pieces;—until ye lost heart and fell to variance in the matter, and disobeyed.[1] Amongst you were those that desired the present Life, and amongst you those that desired the Life to come. Then He caused you to flee from before them, that He might prove you (but now He hath pardoned you, for God is gracious unto the Believers), when ye made for the mountain (Oḥod), and looked not back on any one, though the Apostle was calling unto you,—even unto those of you that were behind. Wherefore He caused grief to overtake you upon grief, that ye may not be afflicted hereafter at that which ye lose, nor at that which shall befall you: for God knoweth what ye do. Then He caused to descend upon you after the grief, Security, even slumber which covered a part of you;[2] and a part of you were troubled in your own souls,—questioning about God that which is not the truth,—a questioning of ignorance;—In that ye said, *What! Is there any reality in this matter unto us?*[3] SAY:—Verily the matter belongeth wholly unto God. They concealed in their hearts that which they did not open unto thee. They say,—*Had there been any reality in the matter, we had not been slain here.* Say,—If ye had been in your own houses, verily those would have gone forth for whom fighting was decreed, unto the places of their death;—and (so it came to pass) that the Lord might prove what is in your hearts, for God knoweth the breast of Man. Verily they amongst you who turned their backs on the day when the two armies met, Satan caused them to slip for some part of that which they had wrought: but God hath forgiven them, for God is Forgiving and Merciful.

Blessedness of the Martyrs. Sūra iii. 163 f.

The blessed state of the Martyrs is thus described:—

Think not in anywise of those killed in the way of the Lord, as if they were dead. Yea, they are alive, and are nourished with their Lord,—

---

[1] The disobedience of the archers who quitted their post.

[2] Those who fell asleep on finding refuge on the mountain.

[3] *I.e.* questioning the truth of Moḥammad's mission, and his promise of divine interposition and victory.

exulting in that which God hath given them of His favour, and rejoicing on behalf of those who have not yet joined them, but are following after. No terror afflicteth them, neither are they grieved.[1]

Moḥammad addressing people in Mosque

The reader may picture to himself the now venerable Prophet delivering, as the spokesman of the Almighty, these pregnant messages. He is about to issue from one of the apartments which, built for his increasing ḥarīm, form the eastern side of the Mosque. Under its rude but spacious roof of palm-branches, the Citizens and Refugees assemble at mid-day for the weekly service, throng around the pulpit, and occupy the long space in front of it. As Moḥammad appears, the hum and bustle cease (for it was the hall of business and politics, as well as the house of worship), and the whole congregation fall into the ranks for prayer. Moḥammad advances to the foot of the pulpit, and with his face turned toward the holy temple of Mecca, and his back to the people, goes through the stated ritual. The assembly, arrayed in rows behind, follow every motion of their leader, as a Muslim congregation at the present day follow the genuflexions and prostrations of their Imām. The prayers ended, the Prophet, with grave step, ascends the slightly elevated pulpit, and in a solemn voice, and accents suited to the measured cadence of the revelation, delivers to the audience the message which he says that he has received from Heaven. Fear creeps over the heart. It is as if the Deity were present by some visible token, like the cloud overshadowing the Tabernacle. The

[1] To secure the crown of martyrdom, it sufficed to make at the very last moment the simplest and most formal profession of faith in God and Moḥammad. Thus 'Amr ibn Thābit had, up to the day of Oḥod, been an open unbeliever. He accompanied the Muslim army and was mortally wounded on the field. His comrades asked him regarding his creed; with his dying breath he whispered in reply that it was for Islām he had fought, and that he believed in God and in his Prophet. When this was told to Moḥammad, he blessed his memory, and said that he was already an inheritor of Paradise. On the other hand, any amount of bravery without such formal profession was of no avail. Thus, a Jew named Ḳozmān, who was numbered among the Disaffected, showed incredible valour at Oḥod, killing with his own hands seven or eight of Ḳoreish. When expiring on the field, and being congratulated on the prospect of Paradise, he said, with his last breath, that he had been fighting not for the faith, but for his people, and in defence of his native city. Moḥammad, when told of it, declared that in spite of his services he was 'a child of hell-fire.'—Ibn Hishām, p. 578.

Disaffected may scoff elsewhere, and the Jew in his own assembly curse the upstart Prophet; but at this moment, disaffection and treason vanish, for the dread sense of immediate communication with the Almighty overwhelms all other feelings. And now the rhetoric of Moḥammad comes into play. In his oration are mingled rebuke, exhortation, encouragement, in pure and nervous eloquence, such as no Arab could hear without emotion. Hell, with its flaming gates, and the gardens and joys of Paradise, are conjured up as vivid and close realities before the hearer; for the hour, the present life fades into insignificance, excepting as the means of escaping the one, and of winning the other. Thus did Moḥammad wield at will the awe-stricken assembly, and wind his enchantments in inextricable folds around them. Thus he moulded to his purpose the various elements about him, and even under adversity and misfortune maintained his influence supreme.

Execution of Al-Ḥārith for the murder of Al-Mujedhdhar

In close connection with the field of Oḥod was the execution of a stern judicial sentence.[1] Al-Mujedhdhar, a confederate of the Aus party, had a few years previously in the pre-Islāmite disputes, slain Suweid, a chief of the Khazraj. The battle of Bo'āth ensued; but the blood there shed did not efface the memory of the murder. Al-Ḥārith, son of Suweid, had long sought to avenge his father's death; at last, he found his opportunity at Oḥod. In the confusion of that reverse, he treacherously drew near to Al-Mujedhdhar, and killed him. A comrade, who was witness of the deed, reported it to Moḥammad. An investigation was held, and the crime brought home to Al-Ḥārith. Shortly after his return from Ḥamrā al-Asad, the Prophet called for his ass, and rode forth to Ḳobā. It was not one of the days (Saturday and Monday) on which he ordinarily repaired to that suburb, and the men of Upper Medīna boded no good from his visit. He entered their mosque and received the salutation of the chief inhabitants of the vicinity. At length the culprit himself, clothed in a yellow dress, and little anticipating the event, came up. Perceiving him approach, Moḥammad called aloud to 'Oweim, chief of the Aus to which the murdered man belonged: *Take Al-Ḥārith son of Suweid unto the gate of the mosque, and there strike off his head,*

[1] Ibn Hishām, p. 579 (not in Aṭ-Ṭabari); Al-Wāḳidi, p. 140.

because of al-Mujedhdhar whom he slew on the day of Oḥod. 'Oweim prepared to obey, when Al-Ḥārith desired leave to speak, and hastening towards Moḥammad laid hold of his stirrup as he was about to mount his ass. He begged for mercy, and promised to expiate the crime by any sacrifice the Prophet might direct. Moḥammad turned from him, and reiterated the order of execution. Seeing the decree to be irrevocable, 'Oweim dragged Al-Ḥārith back to the gate, and there beheaded him, in the presence of Moḥammad, the sons of Al-Mujedhdhar, and the assembled chiefs. The assumption of supreme authority was unquestioned, and is evidence of the absolute command now exercised by the Prophet over the whole city.

Widow of Sa'd entertains Moḥammad at a feast

Another scene which occurred shortly after the battle of Oḥod illustrates the manner in which the oracles of Moḥammad were given forth, and the incidental way in which the political and social code that still rules the Muslim world grew up. Among the slain was Sa'd, son of Ar-Rabī',[1] who left a widow and two daughters, but whose brother, according to the practice of the times, took possession of the whole inheritance. The widow was grieved at this; and, being a discreet and prudent person, pondered how she might obtain redress. She invited Moḥammad to a feast, with some twenty of his chief companions. He agreed to go. A retired spot among the palm-trees of her garden was sprinkled with water, and the repast there spread. Moḥammad arrived and with his followers seated himself upon the carpets prepared for them. He spoke kindly to the widow of her husband's memory, so that the women wept, and the eyes of the Prophet also filled with tears. The supper was then eaten, and a feast of fresh dates followed. When the repast was over, the widow arose, and thus disclosed her grief: 'Sa'd, as thou well knowest, was slain at Oḥod. His brother hath seized the inheritance. There is nothing left for the two daughters; and how shall they be married without a portion?' Moḥammad, moved by the simple tale, replied: 'The Lord shall decide regarding the inheritance; for no command hath been yet revealed to me in this matter. Come again unto me when I shall have returned home.' So he

Origin of the law of female inheritance

[1] Al-Wāḳidi, p. 146 f. The same who allowed 'Abd ar-Raḥmān, when he lodged with him on his arrival, to choose one of his two wives.

departed. Shortly after, as he sat at his door surrounded by companions, symptoms of inspiration came upon him;—he was oppressed, and drops of sweat fell like pearls from his forehead. Then he commanded that the widow of Sa‘d and his brother should be summoned, and when they came, he thus addressed the latter: ‘Restore unto the daughters of Sa‘d two-thirds of that which he hath left behind him, and one-eighth part unto his widow: the remainder is for thee.’ The widow, overjoyed, uttered the *Tekbīr:* ‘God is most great.’ Such was the origin of one of the main provisions of the Moḥammadan law of inheritance.[1]

[1] See Sūra iv. 8 ff. Supplementary rules are added at the close of the Sūra.

CHAPTER XV

FROM THE BATTLE OF OḤOD TO THE EXPULSION OF THE BENI AN-NAḌĪR.

A.H. IV.—A.D. 625

ÆTAT. 57

Satisfaction of Koreish at the victory of Oḥod

ḲOREISH were satisfied with the punishment they had inflicted upon Moḥammad. Abu Sufyān, on his return home, went straight to the Ka'ba, where he rendered thanks to HUBAL for the victory, shaved his head, and returned to his home absolved from his vows of abstinence. Medīna enjoyed a long respite from the designs of Ḳoreish. But the prestige of Moḥammad had been seriously shaken among the Arab tribes; and these, emboldened by his late defeat, or it may be instigated by Ḳoreish, gave, from time to time, fresh trouble and anxiety. The early intelligence, however, which he secured by means of an effective espionage, enabled him to anticipate these movements, and generally to disperse the gatherings without serious loss. But there were exceptions.

Beni Asad dispersed. A.H. IV. April, A.D. 625

The first two months after the battle were passed in tranquillity; but with the opening of the fourth year of the Hijra, rumours reached Moḥammad from various quarters of gatherings being organised against him, and he hastened to take the initiative. The Beni Asad, a powerful tribe, confederates of Ḳoreish, ranged over an extensive territory in the central desert. Intelligence was received that their chief, Ṭoleiḥa, had assembled a force of cavalry and rapid camel-riders to make a raid upon Medīna. Moḥammad forthwith despatched 150 men, Citizens and Refugees indifferently, under Abu Selama, with instructions to march at night by an unfrequented route, and conceal themselves by day, so as to take the hostile camp by surprise.[1] They were so far successful as to fall unexpectedly upon a large herd of camels, which, with three of the herdsmen, they captured, and, having ravaged the country far and wide, returned after eleven days with their booty to Medīna. The usual share of the plunder, with one of the captives, having been set apart for Moḥammad, the remainder was divided amongst the soldiers. The Beni Asad were effectually dispersed for the present; but they reserved their hostility for a future occasion. This Ṭoleiḥa is the same who at a later period set himself up as a prophet in antagonism to Moḥammad. Abu Selama had signalised himself at Bedr, and there received a deep wound. It broke out afresh on this expedition, and in the end proved fatal, as we shall see.

Chief of Liḥyān assassinated. A.H. IV. April, A.D. 625

Another gathering took place at 'Orana [or Nakhla], a spot between Mecca and Aṭ-Ṭā'if.[2] The Liḥyān, a branch of the Hudheil (which inhabited, as they still do, a territory two days east of Mecca), and other neighbouring tribes, rallied round Sufyān ibn Khālid, their chief, with the avowed intention of following up the late victory at Oḥod. Moḥammad, knowing that their movements depended solely upon Sufyān ibn Khālid, despatched 'Abdallah ibn Oneis, with instructions to assassinate him. 'Abdallah joined Sufyān ibn Khālid as a volunteer, fell upon him unawares while no one was near, and, having cut off his head, carried it away with him. He eluded pursuit, and, reaching Medīna in safety, presented himself before Moḥammad in the Mosque. The Prophet welcomed him, and asked the issue of his adventure. 'Abdallah replied by displaying the head of his victim. Moḥammad, in token of his gratification, presented 'Abdallah with his staff: '*This,*' said he, '*shall be a token betwixt thee and me on the day of resurrection. Verily, few on that day shall have wherewithal to lean upon.*' 'Abdallah joined the precious memorial to his sword, and wore it by his side till the day of his death, when it was buried with him. The murder of Sufyān ibn Khālid broke up the assemblage at

[1] Ibn Hishām, p. 975; Aṭ-Ṭabari, i. 1759 (under the year X. A.H.); Al-Wāḳidi, p. 151 f.; Ibn Sa'd, p. 35.

[2] Ibn Hishām, p. 981; Aṭ-Ṭabari, i. 1760 [in both which the chief is called Khālid ibn Sufyān]; Al-Wāḳidi, p. 224 f. [in the year VI.]; Ibn Sa'd, p. 35.

'Orana; and probably, from the laxity of Arab morals, the outrage did not much affect the reputation of the Prophet; but Moḥammad had no right to complain when he shortly afterwards paid the penalty in the loss of several of his followers by an act no worse than 'Abdallah's.

Mishap at Ar-Rajī'. A.H. IV. May, A.D. 625

In the following month, Moḥammad despatched six of his followers in the direction of Mecca. The object is variously stated. The most likely is that they were simply spies sent to gain information of the intentions of Ḳoreish. But the tradition most generally received is, that they were deputed for the instruction of two small tribes, which, at the instigation of the Beni Liḥyān, pretended a desire to embrace Islām.[1] The party were, with one exception, Citizens. When they had journeyed as far as Ar-Rajī', a stage or two from Mecca, they were treacherously surrounded and overpowered by an armed band of the Liḥyān, who thirsted to avenge the assassination of their chief. Three died fighting bravely:[2] the other three were seized and bound as prisoners to be sold at Mecca. One succeeded in loosening his bands and had nearly escaped when he was crushed by pieces of rock hurled down upon him; his tomb is preserved and visited to the present day at Marr aẓ-Ẓahrān. The only survivors, Zeid and Khobeib, were purchased by the heirs of two chiefs of Ḳoreish slain at Bedr. They were kept till the sacred month of Ṣafar had expired; and then taken to At-Tan'īm, beyond the limits of the holy territory, where, in presence of a large concourse from Mecca, they were put to death. The scene is memorable. The two 'martyrs,' for such to the cause of Islām they really were, refused their liberty at the price of recantation. The curse of Khobeib was not easily forgotten by the witnesses of the spectacle. After praying briefly, while they bound him to the stake, he called out with a loud voice: '*O Lord! number these men one by one, and destroy them utterly. Let not one escape!*' At this imprecation, the

Martyrdom of Zeid and Khobeib

[1] Ibn Hishām, p. 638 f.; Aṭ-Ṭabari, i. 1431 ff.; Al-Wāḳidi, p. 156 f.; Ibn Sa'd, p. 39 f.

[2] One of these was 'Āṣim, out of whose skull Sulāfa, whose two sons he had slain at Oḥod, swore that she would drink wine. See *ante*, p. 259 *n*. The Beni Liḥyān were about to cut off the head of 'Āṣim and carry it to Sulāfa, but a swarm of bees interposed, and when the people went to seek for it afterwards, the Lord had swept it away with a flood, and thus frustrated the vow of Sulāfa.

multitude, thinking to avoid its potency, fell with their children flat upon the ground. Then, with daggers put into the hands of children whose fathers had fallen at Bedr,[1] they stabbed the bodies of their victims. And thus ended the wretched tragedy.[2]

Muslim party cut to pieces at Bi'r Ma'ūna. A.H. IV. May, A.D. 625

In the same month another and more serious catastrophe took place.[3] The Beni 'Āmir, and their neighbours the Beni Suleim, belonged to the great Hawāzin tribe in Nejd, which some time before had fought against Ḳoreish. They were under the leadership of two chiefs, Abu Berā and 'Āmir ibn aṭ-Ṭofail. The former, from great age relieved from active command, paid a friendly visit to Moḥammad about this time.[4] He came with a present of two horses and two riding-camels. These the Prophet refused to receive, unless Abu Berā would embrace Islām. This he declined; but

[1] To keep up the fiction that it was *the children* who slew the victims in retaliation for their parents' death.

[2] I see no reason to doubt the main facts of the story, although in the details much of the marvellous has been superadded. Thus Khobeib, when in confinement, was supplied by supernatural visitants with large bunches of grapes, not a single grape being at the season to be had elsewhere. At his execution he bade his salutation to be sent to Moḥammad, and there being none to take it, Gabriel himself carried it to the Prophet, who returned the salutation in the hearing of his companions. When imprisoned, the only requests he made were to be furnished with sweet water, to have no food that had been offered to idols, and to be told beforehand of the time of his execution. The day before he was put to death, he desired a razor to shave himself with, which a female attendant sent by her little boy. He asked the child whether he did not fear that he would kill him with it, out of revenge. The mother was alarmed, and then Khobeib said: 'Nay, fear not. I would never kill your son; for treachery is not allowable in our religion.' When they had bound him to the stake, they said: 'Now abjure Islām, and we will let thee go.' 'Not so,' he said; 'I would not abjure Islām if it were to get me the whole world in return.' 'Wouldst thou not that Moḥammad were in thy place, and thou sitting in security at home?' 'I would not,' he replied, 'that I should have deliverance, and Moḥammad suffer the pain even of a thorn.' Similar stories are told of Zeid. They embraced each other when they came to the place of execution.

[3] Ibn Hishām, p. 648 f.; Aṭ-Ṭabari, i. 1441 f.; Al-Wāḳidi, p. 153 f.; Ibn Sa'd, p. 36.

[4] Abu Berā (called also 'Āmir ibn Mālik) at a later period consulted Moḥammad regarding an internal disease from which, in his old age, he was suffering. It is possible that this visit also may have had a similar object.

said: 'If thou wilt send a company of thy followers to my people, the Beni 'Āmir, I have hopes that they will accept thy call.' Moḥammad replied, that he feared for the safety of his people among the treacherous tribes of Nejd, some of whom were in immediate alliance with Ḳoreish. But Abu Berā declared that he would himself be responsible for their safety. Trusting to this pledge, Moḥammad despatched forty (by some accounts seventy) of his followers, mostly Citizens of Medīna, with a letter to the Beni 'Āmir.[1] After four days, they reached a fountain called Bi'r Ma'ūna, lying between the Beni 'Āmir and Suleim. Here they halted, and despatched a messenger with the letter to 'Āmir ibn aṭ-Ṭofail. This chief, without reading the letter, put the messenger to death, and called upon his tribe to attack the rest of the party; but they refused to break the pledge of Abu Berā. 'Āmir then sought the aid of the Beni Suleim, who, having lost some of their kinsmen at Bedr, were bitterly hostile to Moḥammad. Joined by a large body of these, he proceeded to Bi'r Ma'ūna and fell upon the party still waiting the return of their messenger. They were all cut to pieces, excepting two men, one who was left for dead on the field, and another 'Amr ibn Omeiya, who, having been absent with the camels at the time of the slaughter, was spared on his return by the chief, in fulfilment of a vow made at his mother's grave.[2]

Moḥammad's grief and comminatory prayer

The news of this disaster, following immediately on that

[1] They are described as chiefly Citizens who spent the day in hewing wood and drawing water for Moḥammad's family, and at night slept in the Mosque. But there were several Refugees; and among them 'Āmir ibn Fuheira, the freedman of Abu Bekr, who accompanied his master and the Prophet in their flight from Mecca. The number *seventy* is a favourite one; Al-Wāḳidi remarks that seventy men of Medīna were killed at Oḥod; seventy at Bi'r Ma'ūna; seventy at Al-Yemāma; and seventy at Jisr Abi 'Obeid, or the battle of the Bridge.

[2] Al-Mundhir, the leader, escaped the massacre and was offered quarter, which he refused. Moḥammad, on hearing this, declared that *he embraced death;* which expression has been magnified into meaning that he proceeded on the expedition with a sure presentiment of his end. When 'Āmir ibn aṭ-Ṭofail went over the field, he asked his prisoner to identify the dead bodies. This he did, but the corpse of 'Āmir ibn Fuheira was nowhere to be seen; whereupon one of the tribe declared that when Ibn Fuheira was stabbed he heard him call out, '*I have gained Paradise*,' and saw him straightway ascend in the air to heaven. There is a multitude of such traditions.

of Ar-Rajī', greatly afflicted Moḥammad. Next day, when concluding the morning prayer, he invoked the Divine vengeance on the perpetrators of both these massacres, saying: '*O Lord! in thine indignation trample under foot the Beni Liḥyān, Beni Ri'l, Beni Dhakwān*' (and so on, naming the several tribes in succession); '*make their years like unto the years of Joseph,*[1] *for that they have rebelled against God and rebelled against His Prophet!*' This commination was offered up with the daily prayers in public for a month. The Prophet professed also to have received through Gabriel the following message from the martyrs of Ma'ūna: 'Acquaint our People that we have met our Lord. He is well pleased with us, and we are well pleased with Him.'[2]

Moḥammad pays blood-money for two men, wrongly killed as reprisals

'Amir ibn Omeiya, on his way home from the disaster, fell in with two men belonging to a branch of the Beni 'Āmir, and slew them while asleep as a reprisal for the massacre at Bi'r Ma'ūna. But it turned out that these men were returning from Moḥammad, with whom they had just entered into terms. When 'Amir, therefore, reported what he had done, instead of being praised, he was rebuked by Moḥammad, who declared his intention of paying blood-money for the two murdered men. The act, indeed, being a breach of truce, was so contrary to the international code of the Arabs, that 'Āmir ibn aṭ-Ṭofail himself sent a despatch to Moḥammad, complaining of it. Accordingly, full compensation for both was transmitted to the tribe, together with the booty taken from them.

[1] Alluding to the seven bad years in Pharaoh's dream. The tribes named after the Beni Liḥyān were the clans of the Beni Suleim who joined in the attack.

[2] This formed a verse of the Ḳor'ān; but, for some reason not apparent, it was 'cancelled' and removed. On receiving the message, Moḥammad prayed: 'O Lord! guide the Beni 'Āmir to the truth. I seek unto thee for protection from 'Āmir ibn aṭ-Ṭofail!' The visit of Abu Berā, and what immediately follows, show that there had been some friendly communication between the parties. Perhaps there were divided opinions in the tribe. The mode in which tradition treats the massacre, and Moḥammad's having almost immediately after entered into communication with 'Āmir ibn aṭ-Ṭofail on the subject of a claim for blood-money, look as if the attack was not so gratuitous as might appear. Moḥammad at first attributed it to Abu Berā; but Abu Berā cleared himself. His son attacked 'Āmir with a spear, to show that his father disowned the transaction.

Beni an-Naḍīr ordered into exile. A.H. IV. June, A.D. 625

The tragedy of Bi'r Ma'ūna involved a still graver issue.[1] The Beni an-Naḍīr, one of the Jewish tribes in the vicinity, were confederate with the Beni 'Āmir. Moḥammad thought it right, perhaps on account of the ill-treatment he had received from their allies, that they should aid in defraying the blood-money for the two men murdered by 'Amir. Attended by a few followers, he visited their settlement, distant two or three miles from Ḳobā, and laid his request before their chiefs. They answered courteously, promised assistance, and invited him to sit down while they made ready a repast. After sitting thus for a little while, he arose abruptly and walked out of the assembly. His followers waited long, expecting his return. But they waited in vain; at length they got up, and went back to Medīna. To their surprise, they found that Moḥammad had returned straightway to the Mosque, and given out that his hasty departure was due to a divine monition that the chiefs of the Naḍīr had formed a plot to ascend the roof, and roll down great stones upon him. But as he makes no mention of this in the Ḳor'ān (which dwells at some length on the siege), and there had been nothing to excite the suspicion of his companions, the story is somewhat doubtful. However this may be, Moḥammad resolved that the tribe should no longer remain in the neighbourhood of Medīna. Moḥammad, son of Maslama (the assassin of Ka'b), was immediately commissioned to deliver this command: '*Thus saith the Prophet of the Lord, Ye shall go forth out of my land within the space of ten days: whosoever after that remaineth behind shall be put to death.*' Startled and alarmed, 'Oh Moḥammad!' they said, 'we did not think that thou, our friend, or any other of the Aus, would ever have consented to be the bearer of a message such as this.' '*Hearts are changed now,*' was his only reply, as he turned and left them in dismay.

They refuse, and are besieged

They hesitated. At first they began their preparations to depart. But it was a grievous prospect to be exiled from the home of their fathers, from their fertile fields and choice date-groves. 'Abdallah ibn Obei, and others who had not yet forgotten the close and ancient obligations which bound them to the Jews, were displeased at the order for their

[1] Ibn Hishām, p. 652 f.; Aṭ-Ṭabari, i. 1448 ff.; Al-Wāḳidi, p. 160 ff.; Ibn Sa'd, p. 40 f.

banishment. 'Abdallah at first strove to bring about a reconciliation.[1] Failing in this, he accused Moḥammad of having invented the charge of treachery against the Jews, and promised himself to stand by them with his own people and with allies from Nejd. Reassured by this hope, and trusting to the strength of their fortress, they resolved to hold fast. So they sent to Moḥammad, saying: 'We shall not depart from our possessions; do what thou wilt against us.' '*Allah Akbar!*' cried the Prophet, when he heard it, unable to conceal his delight: '*The Jews are going to fight! Great is the Lord!*' and the cry, taken up by his companions, re-echoed through the courts of the Mosque. Arming at once, they marched forth, 'Alī carrying the standard, to invest the stronghold of the rebellious tribe. The besiegers were kept at a distance by arrows and stones; but the Naḍīr looked in vain for succour either from Medīna or from the tribes of Nejd. The Beni Ḳoreiẓa, the only remaining Jewish tribe, either swayed by ancient jealousies or fearful of incurring the Prophet's wrath, pretended that they could not break their treaty with him, and held aloof. It would have been better for them now to have perished on the field than to have had to rue the day two years later on. Notwithstanding these disappointments, the Naḍīr held bravely out, and gallantly defied all the attempts of their enemy. Moḥammad became impatient, and at last, to hasten their departure, had recourse to an expedient, unusual, if not unwarranted, by the laws of Arab warfare. He cut down the surrounding clumps of palm-trees, and burned the choicest of them to the roots with fire. The Jews remonstrated against this proceeding as not only barbarous in itself but specially forbidden by the law of Moses; and Moḥammad, sensible of the reproach, had to justify the act by divine command.[2]

Their date-trees are burned

[1] That 'Abdallah really broke faith with the Jews in promising them aid, and then holding back, is questionable, for tradition delights to cast contempt and abuse upon 'Abdallah as the impersonation of disaffection and hypocrisy. The accusation, however, appears in the Ḳor'ān, as will be seen below. The position of 'Abdallah was trying. The new faith had penetrated into every branch of the Medīna tribes, and rendered any combined opposition to Moḥammad impossible. He probably found it impracticable to fulfil his promise.

[2] The Beni Naḍīr, on their palm-trees being cut down, called out from their ramparts: 'O Moḥammad! thou wert heretofore wont to

They submit to expatriation

When the siege had now lasted for two or three weeks, the unfortunate Jews, seeing no prospect of relief, sent to say that they were now ready to lay down their arms and abandon the lands which had already lost to them their special value. Moḥammad was glad to accede to the offer; for the siege might still have been indefinitely prolonged, and there were dangerous elements around him. They submitted, moreover, to the stipulation that they should leave their weapons behind them. Upon this, the besieging force retired; and the Naḍīr, having laden their property, even to their doors and lintels, upon camels, set out, with tabrets and music, on the road to Syria. Some of them, with their chiefs Ḥuyei and Kināna, turned aside at Kheibar. The rest went on to Jericho and the highlands south of Syria. Two only of their number abandoned their ancestral faith, and, having embraced Islām, were maintained in the possession of their fields and property. Thus early were temporal inducements brought to bear on the aggrandisement of Islām.

Two renegades

Fields of the Beni an-Nadīr divided among Refugees

The spoil consisted of fifty coats of mail, fifty stand of armour, and three hundred and forty swords. But of greater importance was the fertile tract now at the disposal of Moḥammad. This, by a special revelation, was exempted from the usual law of distribution, because it had been gained without actual fighting; and he divided it at his discretion. A portion of the confiscated lands was kept for the support of his own family and for the relief of the poor. Two indigent Citizens who had distinguished themselves in the field also received grants, but with this exception the remainder was given entirely to the Refugees, who were now enabled to dispense with the bounty of their neighbours, and promoted to a position of independence and affluence. Abu Bekr, 'Omar, Az-Zubeir, and other chief Companions, are named among the persons endowed thus with valuable estates.

Importance of victory over the Beni an-Naḍīr

The expulsion of the Naḍīr was a material triumph for Moḥammad. One by one he was breaking up the Jewish settlements, and weakening the cause of disaffection; for a combination at any time, between the Jews and the other enemies of Islām, would have proved critical to his safety at

forbid injustice on the earth, and to rebuke him that committed it. Wherefore, then, hast thou cut down our palm-trees, and burned them with fire?'—Ibn Hishām, p. 653. The prohibition is in Deut. xx. 19.

Notices of it in Ḳor'ān

Medīna. An entire Sūra is devoted to the victory now achieved, which is ascribed to the terror struck by the Almighty into the Jewish heart. The following are extracts:—

Sūra lix. 1 f.

All that is in the Heavens and in the Earth praiseth God—the Mighty and the Wise. He it is that hath driven forth the unbelieving Jews from their habitations to join the former exiles. Ye thought not that they would go forth; and they themselves thought that their Strongholds would defend them against God. But God visited them from a quarter on which they counted not, and cast terror into their hearts. They destroyed their houses with their own hands, and with the hands of the Believers. Take warning, therefore, ye that have eyes. And if God had not decreed against them expatriation, He had verily punished them otherwise in this World; and in the World to come there is prepared for them the punishment of Fire. This because they set themselves up against God and his Prophet; and whosoever setteth himself up against God,—verily God is strong in Vengeance. That which thou didst cut down of the Date-trees, or left of them standing upon their roots, it was by the command of God,—that He might abase the evildoers. And that which God gave unto his Prophet as booty from them;—ye did not march horses or camels against them; but God giveth unto His Prophet dominion over whom He pleaseth; and God is over all things Powerful. That which God hath given unto His Prophet from the inhabitants of the Villages (thus surrendering), is for God and the Prophet, and his Kindred, and the Orphan and the Destitute, and the Wayfarer, that the turn (of booty) be not confined unto the Rich amongst you. That therefore which the Prophet giveth unto you, receive it: and that which he withholdeth from you, withhold yourselves from the same; and fear God, for God is strong in vengeance. It is for the poor of the Refugees,—those who have been driven forth from their homes and from their properties, desiring the grace of God and His favour, and assisting God and His Apostle. These are the sincere ones. They that were before them in possession of the City (Medīna) and the faith, love those that have taken refuge with them, and find not in their breasts any want of the spoil:[1] they prefer (their Guests) before themselves, even if they themselves be destitute. * * * *

v. 11 ff.

Hast thou not observed the Disaffected?[2] They say unto their Brethren,—the unbelieving People of the Book: '*If ye be driven forth, we will surely go forth with you. We will never submit concerning you unto any one: and if ye be attacked we shall certainly aid you.*' But God is witness that they are liars. If such are driven forth, these will not go forth with them; and if they be attacked, they will not assist them; and if they were to assist them, they would surely turn their backs, and then they would be bereft of aid. Verily ye are the stronger, because of the terror cast into their breasts from God;—this, because

---

[1] That is, the Citizens of Medīna had no grudge against the Refugees because the booty was appropriated to them.

[2] Referring to 'Abdallah's promise of assistance.

they are a People devoid of understanding. They shall never fight against you unitedly, excepting in fenced towns, or from behind walls. Their warlike strength is mighty among themselves; ye think they are united, but their hearts are divided, because they are a people that doth not comprehend.

They are like unto those that shortly preceded them (*i.e.* the Beni v. 16 ff
Ḳainuḳā'); they have tasted the grievous punishment of their undertaking. They are like unto Satan when he said unto Man: '*Become an Infidel;*' and when he had become an Infidel, the Tempter said: '*Verily, I am clear of thee! Verily, I fear the Lord of all Worlds.*' Wherefore the end of them both is that they are cast into the Fire, dwelling for ever therein! That is the reward of the transgressors.

Peroration on the Deity

The Sūra, catching (as the oracle every here and there still does) something of its early fire, closes with a splendid peroration:—

He is the Lord. Beside Him there is no God. It is He that knoweth v. 23 ff.
both the Seen and the Unseen. The Merciful, the Compassionate. There is no God but He; the King, the Holy, the Giver of Peace, the Faithful, the Guardian, the Glorious, the Almighty, the Most High. Far exalted is the Lord above that which they associate Him with,—God, the Creator, the Maker, the Framer. Most goodly are His names. All that is in the heavens and in the earth praiseth Him. He is the Glorious, the Wise.

Zeid qualifies himself as secretary by learning Hebrew and Syriac

Moḥammad had hitherto trusted Jewish amanuenses with the transcription of such despatches as were needed in the Hebrew or Syriac tongues. But his relations were gradually expanding northwards, and he could no longer trust documents of political importance in the hands of any one belonging to a people whom he had so deeply injured. About this time, therefore, he desired a youth of Medīna, Zeid, the son of Thābit, to learn the Hebrew and Syriac languages. He had already been taught to write Arabic by one of the prisoners of Bedr. Moḥammad now made use of him as secretary, both for his vernacular and his foreign despatches. It is the same Zeid who was afterwards employed by Abu Bekr in collecting the scattered Sūras and fragments of the Ḳor'ān into one volume; and was also appointed controller of the syndicate charged with its recension in the Caliphate of 'Othmān.[1]

[1] He was eleven years old when Moḥammad arrived in Medīna, and was now therefore fifteen or sixteen. He learned Hebrew (or Syriac) in *half a month*, it is said. Moḥammad used to tell him to stick his pen behind his ear, 'for this will bring to remembrance that which the distracted mind is seeking after.'

CHAPTER XVI

THE FOURTH AND FIFTH YEARS OF THE HIJRA;

OR, FROM THE MIDDLE OF A.D. 625 TO THE END OF A.D. 626

ÆTAT. 57, 58

Bedr the Second. Moḥammad marches to Bedr. Ḳoreish remain at home. A.H. IV. February, March, A.D. 625

FOR about a year and a half after the expulsion of the Beni Naḍīr, Medīna was little disturbed by the hostile sound of arms at home. The summer and autumn of the fourth year of the Hijra passed in peace. But at last the winter came round when, by appointment, the forces of Mecca and Medīna were again to meet at Bedr.[1] The year being one of drought, Abu Sufyān was desirous that the expedition should be deferred to a more plentiful season. Accordingly, Ḳoreish engaged No'eim, of a neutral tribe, to repair to Medīna, and there give forth an exaggerated account of the preparations at Mecca, in the hope that, with the field of Oḥod yet fresh in memory, the Muslims might be deterred from setting out. Ḳoreish eventually marched from Mecca with 2,000 foot and 50 horse; but after one or two days, the scarcity of provender forced them to retrace their steps. The report of No'eim alarmed the inhabitants of Medīna, and a disinclination appeared in some quarters again to meet the enemy. But Moḥammad, indignant at this cowardly spirit, or it may be better informed of the real counsels of Ḳoreish, declared with an oath that he would go forth to Bedr, even if he went alone. His bold front inspired such confidence that 1,500 men, a force double the number he had as yet commanded, rallied round his standard; and they carried with them a great store of wares and merchandise for the annual fair. They maintained a standing camp at

[1] Ibn Hishām, p. 666; Aṭ-Ṭabari, i. 1457 ff.; Al-Wāḳidi, p. 167 ff.; Ibn Sa'd, p. 42.

Bedr for eight days in defiance of Ḳoreish, and, having bartered their goods to advantage, returned to Medīna. Moḥammad was much pleased at the result of the campaign, which is named the Second Bedr, and the divine approbation was signified in a special revelation:—

Moḥammad gratified at the result

Sūra iii. 166 ff.

Those that responded to the call of God and His Prophet, after the wound which they had received—to such of them as are virtuous and fear God, there shall be a great reward. Certain men said unto them, '*Verily the people have gathered themselves against you; wherefore be afraid of them.*' But it increased their faith, and they said,—'*God sufficeth for us: He is the best Patron.*' Therefore they returned with a blessing from God, and favour. No evil touched them. They followed after that which is well pleasing unto God: and God is possessed of boundless grace.

Verily this devil[1] would cause you to fear his friends; but fear Me if ye be Believers.

Ḳoreish mortified

Ḳoreish, mortified at this triumph, projected another grand attack against Moḥammad. But a year elapsed before the design was carried into execution: meanwhile Medīna enjoyed a respite.

Expedition to Dhāt ar-Riḳā'. A.H. V. May, A.D 626

In the beginning of the fifth year, a party of 400 men, commanded by Moḥammad himself, set out to disperse certain tribes of the Beni Ghatafān, assembled with suspicious purpose at Dhāt ar-Riḳā'.[2] They fled to the mountains at his approach. Moḥammad advanced unexpectedly upon their habitations, and carried off some of their women. After an absence of fifteen days the party returned to Medīna.[3] It was in this short campaign that the 'Service of

'Service of danger'

[1] Applied by some to Abu Sufyān; by others, with more likelihood, to No'eim.

[2] Ibn Hishām, p. 661 ff.; Aṭ-Ṭabari, i. 1454 ff.; Al-Wāḳidi, p. 172 f.; Ibn Sa'd, p. 43 f.

[3] A story illustrative of the kind and unbending manner by which Moḥammad engaged the affections of his followers may be briefly recounted here, as it relates to the present expedition. Jābir, a poor Citizen, son of a man slain at Oḥod, was mounted on a wretched camel, which Moḥammad (after miraculously transforming it from a slow into a very rapid walker) said he would buy from him. He spoke to Jābir kindly concerning his father, and five-and-twenty times invoked mercy on him. Then in a livelier strain: 'Hast thou married lately?' Jābir replied, 'Yes.' 'A maiden, or one that had before been married?' 'The latter,' said Jābir. 'And why not a young damsel, who would have sported with thee, and thou with her?' 'My father,' he explained, 'left seven daughters, so I married a woman of experience, able to guide

Danger' was introduced. Fearing that the enemy, who held the fastnesses above the Muslim army, might attempt a surprise to rescue their women, a part of the force was kept constantly under arms. The public prayers were therefore repeated twice,—one division watching while the other prayed. The revelation sanctioning this practice is quoted less for its own interest, than to illustrate the tendency of the revelation to become the vehicle of military commands. In the Ḳor'ān, victories are announced, success promised, actions recounted; failure is explained, bravery applauded, cowardice or disobedience chided; military or political movements are directed;—and all this as an immediate communication from the Deity. The passage resembles what one might expect to find in the 'General Orders' of some Puritan leader, or Commander of a crusade in the Holy Land:—

Ḳor'ān, a vehicle for 'general orders'

Sūra iv. 102 f.

When ye march abroad in the earth, it shall be no crime unto you that ye shorten your prayers, if ye fear that the Unbelievers may attack you; for the Unbelievers are an open enemy unto you. And when thou art amongst them, and leadest their prayers, let one Division of them arise to prayer with thee, taking their weapons with them, and when they have worshipped, let them remove behind you. Then let the other Division come up that hath not prayed, and let them pray with thee, and let them take their due precaution and their weapons. The Unbelievers would that ye should neglect your weapons and your baggage; then would they fall upon you with one onset. It shall be no crime unto you, if ye be incommoded by rain, or if ye be sick, that ye lay down your weapons; but take your due precaution. Verily God hath prepared for the Unbelievers an ignominious punishment.

Campaign to Dūmat al-Jandal. A.H. V. July, A.D. 626

During the summer, another campaign was undertaken by Moḥammad.[1] It was in the direction of Dūma, an Oasis and *entrepôt* on the borders of Syria midway between the Red Sea and the Gulf of Persia, where marauding bands, driven to violence by the prevailing famine, were plundering

them.' 'Thou hast done well,' rejoined Moḥammad; (he might here himself have learned a lesson from his humble follower)—'Now when we reach thy home, we shall kill a camel and rest there, and thy wife will hear of it and will spread carpets for us.' 'But, O Prophet! I have not any carpets.' 'We shall get them for thee: do therefore as I have said.' On Moḥammad's returning home, Jābir took his camel to Moḥammad, who not only gave him its full price, but also returned to him the camel itself. Jābir, thus set up in life, prospered greatly. Al-Wāḳidi, p. 173 [not in Ibn Hishām nor Aṭ-Ṭabari].

[1] Ibn Hishām, p. 668; Aṭ-Ṭabari, i. 1462; Al-Wāḳidi, p. 174 f.; Ibn Sa'd, p. 44.

travellers, and even threatened a raid upon Medīna. Moḥammad stopped short a march or two from Dūma, and contented himself with capturing the herds which grazed in the neighbourhood. The robbers fled without offering any opposition. This expedition is touched upon very lightly in a brief notice of two or three lines; but it was in reality most important. Moḥammad, followed by a thousand men, had reached the confines of Syria; distant tribes learned the terror of his name; the political horizon was extended; the lust of plunder in the hearts of the Muslims acquired a wider range, and they were inured, at the hottest season of the year, to long and fatiguing marches. The army was absent for nearly a month. On his way back Moḥammad entered into a treaty with 'Oyeina, chieftain of the Fezāra, for the right to graze on certain tracts of tableland to the east of Medīna, where, notwithstanding the drought, forage was still procurable.[1]

Moḥammad marries a fourth wife, *Zeinab bint Khozeima.* A.H. IV. January, 626

We now turn to what was passing within the home of Moḥammad. Since his marriage with Ḥafṣa—that is for above a year—Moḥammad had been content with the three inmates of his ḥarīm. He now added to the number two other wives. The first was Zeinab, daughter of Khozeima, widow of his cousin 'Obeida, killed at Bedr. Noted for her charity, she gained the title of *Mother of the Poor.* She survived but a year or two, being the only one of the Prophet's wives (excepting Khadīja) who died before him.[2]

And a fifth, Um Selama. A.H. IV. February, 626

Within a month of this marriage, he sought the hand of a fifth wife. Um Selama was the widow of Abu Selama, to whom she had borne several children. Both had been exiles to Abyssinia, from whence they returned to Medīna. At Ohod, Abu Selama was wounded; but he had so far recovered as to take the command against the Beni Asad, when the wound broke out afresh. Moḥammad visited his death-bed. He was breathing his last, and the women wailed loudly. 'Hush!' said the Prophet as he entered. 'Invoke not on yourselves aught but what is good; for verily the angels are present with the dying man, and say *Amen* to that which ye pray. *O Lord! give unto him width and*

Prayer at death-bed of her previous husband

[1] Aṭ-Ṭabari, i. 1463; Ibn Sa'd, p. 45.

[2] Aṭ-Ṭabari, i. 1441 and 1460, &c. Reiḥāna, the Jewess, also died a year before him; but it is doubtful whether she was ever more than his concubine.

comfort in his grave: Lighten his darkness: Pardon his sins: Raise him to Paradise: Exalt his rank among the Blessed; and raise up faithful followers from his seed! Ye indeed are looking at the fixed eyes, but the sight itself hath already followed the dead.' So saying he drew the palm of his hand over the eyes of his departed friend, and closed them. It was eight months after being wounded at Oḥod that Abu Selama died; and four months afterwards Moḥammad made proposals of marriage to his widow, who though not young was very beautiful. She at first excused herself on the score of her age and rising family; but the Prophet removed her objection by saying that he too was well advanced in years, and that her children should be his care. After the marriage he tarried three days with his bride—a precedent followed by Muslim husbands when adding fresh inmates to their ḥarīms. Her son 'Omar was brought up by Moḥammad.

Moḥammad marries *Zeinab bint Jahsh*, divorced by his adopted son, Zeid. A.H. V. June, A.D. 626

Moḥammad was now near threescore years of age; but weakness for the sex seemed but to grow with age; and the attractions of his increasing *ḥarīm* instead of satisfying appear rather to have stimulated desire after new and varied charms.[1] Happening one day to visit his adopted son Zeid, he found him absent. As he knocked, Zeinab his wife, now over thirty years of age, but fair to look upon, invited him to enter; and, starting up in her loose and scanty dress, made haste to array herself for his reception. But the beauties of her figure through the half-opened door had already unveiled themselves too freely before the admiring gaze of Moḥammad. He was smitten by the sight: '*Gracious Lord!*' he exclaimed; '*Good Heavens! how Thou dost turn the hearts of men!*' The rapturous words, repeated in a low voice as he turned to go, were overheard by Zeinab, who perceived the flame she had kindled, and, proud of her conquest, was nothing loth to tell her husband of it. Zeid went straightway to Moḥammad, and declared his readiness to divorce Zeinab for him. This Moḥammad declined: 'Keep thy wife to thyself,' he said, 'and fear God.' But Zeid saw probably that the admonition proceeded from unwilling lips, and that the Prophet had still a longing eye for Zeinab. Perhaps he did not care to keep her, when he found that she desired to leave him, and was ambitious of the new and distinguished alliance. And so he

[1] Aṭ-Ṭabari, i. 1460 ff.

formally divorced her. Moḥammad still hesitated. There might be little scandal according to Arab morals in seeking the hand of a married woman whose husband had no wish to keep her; but the husband in the present case was Moḥammad's adopted son, and even in Arabia such a union was unlawful. The flame, however, would not be stifled; and so, casting his scruples to the winds, he resolved at last to have her. Sitting by 'Ā'isha, the prophetic ecstasy appeared to come over him. As he recovered, he smiled joyfully and said: 'Who will go and congratulate Zeinab, and say that the Lord hath joined her unto me in marriage?' His maid Selma made haste to carry the glad news to Zeinab, who showed her delight by bestowing on the messenger all the jewels she had upon her person. Moḥammad made no delay, but hastened to fulfil the divine behest; and, having made a great feast in the court of the Mosque, took thus a second Zeinab to be his wife.[1]

And supports the marriage by divine command

The marriage caused no small obloquy, and, to save his reputation, Moḥammad had to fall back upon the Oracle. A revelation appeared, in which a divine warrant is given for the union, the objections on the score of adoptive affinity are disallowed, and the Prophet is even reprehended for his hesitation and fear of men:—

Sūra xxxiii. 4 f.

God hath not given to a man two hearts within him. * * * Nor hath He made your adopted sons your (real) sons. This your speech

---

[1] Zeid, her previous husband, was short and not well favoured, having a pug-nose; but he was ten years younger than the Prophet.

Zeinab was industrious, and could tan leather and make shoes. What she made in this way, even after her marriage with the Prophet, was given away to the poor. She survived Moḥammad ten or eleven years.

Aṭ-Ṭabari is the fullest of the earliest authorities on this passage, and in the text I have followed him closely. He gives a second narrative, differing only in this, that, as Moḥammad waited at Zeid's door, the wind blew aside the curtain of Zeinab's chamber and disclosed her in a scanty undress. After Zeid had divorced her, Moḥammad asked him whether he had ever seen anything to dislike in her. 'Nothing,' he replied, 'only good.' 'Ā'isha relates that strange misgivings arose in her heart when she heard the divine message commanding the marriage, and, mindful of the beauty of Zeinab, feared lest she should glory over the other wives of Moḥammad as his divinely appointed bride. We learn from tradition that Zeinab did thus vaunt herself, saying that *God had given her in marriage to His Prophet, whereas his other wives were given to him by their relatives.*

Sūra xxxiii. proceedeth from your mouths; but God speaketh the Truth; and He directeth in the right way. Let your adopted sons go by their own fathers' names. This is more just with God. * * *

v. 37 f. And when thou saidst to him on whom God hath bestowed favours, and upon whom thou too hast bestowed favours:[1] '*Keep thy wife to thyself and fear God;*' and thou didst conceal in thy breast that which God was minded to make known, and thou fearedst man—whereas God is more worthy to be feared. And when Zeid had fulfilled her divorce, WE joined thee with her in marriage, that there might hereafter be no offence to Believers in marrying the Wives of their adopted sons, when they have fulfilled their divorce; and the command of God is to be
v. 40. fulfilled. . . . Moḥammad is not the father of any man amongst you. Rather he is the Apostle of God, and the Seal of the Prophets; and God knoweth all things.

Scandal of the transaction thus removed

Strange to say, the scandal was removed by this revelation, and Zeid was thenceforward called not 'the son of Moḥammad,' as heretofore, but by his proper name, 'Zeid, the son of Ḥāritha.' We hear of no doubts or questionings, and can only attribute the confiding spirit of his followers to the absolute ascendancy of his powerful mind over all who came within its influence.

Veil and other restrictions imposed on Moḥammad's wives

The seclusion of the *Veil* or curtain was at this time enjoined upon the wives of Moḥammad. Himself well stricken in years, surrounded by six wives, some of them sprightly, young, and beautiful, and with a continual concourse of courtiers, visitors, and suitors, such a restriction was not unneeded. Indeed, he had himself proved in the case of Zeinab the danger that might arise from the too free admission of friends or strangers; and his followers could hardly expect to be freer from temptation than the Prophet himself. No one unless bidden was to enter his wives' apartments; they were not to be spoken to but from behind a curtain; and to slake the last embers of jealousy (or uneasiness as it is euphemistically called), an interdict is declared against their ever marrying again, even after his death. Henceforward they were known as '*the Mothers of the Faithful.*' Here is the passage. How has the fine gold become dim!—

Sūra xxxiii. 53. O ye Believers! Enter not the apartments of the Prophet, except ye be called to sup with him, without waiting his convenient time. When

[1] Meaning Zeid, whom Moḥammad, after freeing, had adopted. In the following verse he is mentioned *by name*, a singular instance, for no other follower is named in the Ḳor'ān.

ye are bidden, then enter; and when ye have eaten, then disperse. And stay not for familiar converse;—for verily that giveth uneasiness to the Prophet. It shameth him to say this unto you: but God is not ashamed of the Truth. And when ye ask anything of the Prophet's wives, ask it of them from behind a curtain; this will be more pure for your hearts and for their hearts. It is not fitting that ye should give uneasiness to the Apostle of God, nor that ye should marry his Wives after him for ever. Verily that would be a grievous thing in the sight of God. * * *
The Prophet is nearer unto the Believers than their own souls, and his Wives are their Mothers. v. 6.

Muslim women to be partly veiled when walking abroad

Certain restrictions, but of a less stringent nature, were about the same time placed upon the dress and demeanour of all believing women. These were exposed in their walks abroad to the rude remarks of disaffected and licentious Citizens; they were therefore commanded to throw their garments around them so as partially to veil their persons, and conceal their ornaments. The men who thus troubled the Muslim females were threatened with expulsion and with a general slaughter, thus:—

O Prophet! Speak unto thy wives and thy daughters, and the wives of the Believers, that they throw around them a part of their mantles. This will be more seemly, that they may be known (as women of reputation) and may not be subject to annoyance; for God is gracious and merciful. And truly, if the Disaffected, and they in whose hearts is disease (of incontinency), and the propagators of falsehoods in the city, hold not back, We shall surely stir thee up against them. Then they shall not be permitted to live near unto thee therein but for a little. Accursed! wherever they are found, they shall be taken and killed with a great slaughter. This is the wont of God concerning those that have gone before. And these shall not find in the wont of God any variation. Sura xxxiii. 59 ff.

And elsewhere:—

Speak unto the Believing women that they restrain their eyes, and preserve their modesty; and display not their ornaments, except what appeareth thereof; and let them throw their veils over their bosoms; and let them not display their ornaments except to their husbands, fathers (and so on, enumerating a number of relations, and ending with slaves, eunuchs, and children). And let them not shake their feet that their hidden ornaments be discovered. Sūra xxiv. 31

Rules for entering houses, &c., of neighbours

Rules and precautions were also prescribed to regulate the visits of strangers to their neighbours' houses, and to prevent the privacy of Believers being intruded upon without due warning.[1]

[1] Believers are forbidden to enter any house but their own (even if there be no one inside) until they have first asked leave and saluted the

Restrictions rendered necessary by loose code of Ḳor'ān

Out of these commands have grown the stringent usages of the Ḥarīm and Zenana, which, with more or less seclusion, prevail throughout the Muslim world. However degrading and austere these usages may appear, yet with the loose code of polygamy and divorce some restraints of the kind are almost indispensable in Islām, if only for the maintenance of decency and social order.[1]

A goodly row of modest dwellings, one for each of the 'Mothers of the Faithful,' now formed the Eastern side of the Mosque and of its court. Moḥammad shared his attentions equally amongst his wives, spending thus a day and night in the chamber of each successively. Thus their turn was

family. During three periods of the day—*i.e.* before morning prayer, at the time of the siesta, and after evening prayer—even slaves and young children (who are otherwise excepted) must ask permission before entering an apartment. Women past child-bearing may alone dispense with the outer garment. The sick, and certain near relatives, are also exempted from the prohibition of dining familiarly in each other's inner apartments.—Sūra xxiv. 62, 53 f.

[1] European manners and customs in this respect would be altogether unsuited to Moḥammadan society. The tendency of the *system* without its present checks would certainly be unfavourable to morality. Let the laxity of manners be conceived, if with unrestricted social intercourse there existed also under the sanction of divine revelation the practice of polygamy, divorce, and remarriage; if the marriage bond were simply at the discretion of the husband to hold or to break; if any man might look upon any married woman (relatives excepted) as within his reach by marriage; and if every married woman felt like Zeinab, that she might become the lawful wife of any other man who could persuade her husband to pronounce a divorce! The foundations of society would be broken up.

Burckhardt tells us of an Arab, forty-five years old, who had had fifty wives. And as regards the sacred city itself, we have the evidence of a keen observer, the late reigning Begum of Bhopal, herself an orthodox follower of the Prophet. After performing the pilgrimage a few years ago, her Highness tells us: 'The women frequently contract as many as ten marriages, and those who have been only married twice are few in number. If a woman sees her husband growing old, or if she happen to admire any one else, she goes to the Sherīf, and, after having settled the matter with him, she puts away her husband, and takes to herself another, who is perhaps young, good-looking, and rich. In this way, a marriage seldom lasts more than a year or two.' It may be remarked that the *wife* (excepting under a few rare conditions) has not legally the power of divorce; but the impression on the Begum's mind from personal intercourse with the upper society of Mecca sufficiently proves the laxity of morals prevailing there.

known as 'the day of Sauda, the day of Zeinab,' and so on. Yet 'Ā'isha maintained her pre-eminence; and, however much there may have been the formal circuit reducing nominally her portion to one day in six, still hers was the most frequented of all the houses, and best deserved the name of *home*. The irregularity of his attentions at length provoked a natural discontent; and Moḥammad was by a divine dispensation released from the obligation of consorting with his wives equally and in undeviating order:—

> Postpone the turn of such as thou mayest please; and admit unto thyself her whom thou choosest, as well as her whom thou mayest desire of those whom thou hadst put aside; it will be no offence in thee. This will be easier, that they may be satisfied, and not repine, but be all content with that thou givest unto them.[1]

Sūra xxxiii. 51.

The command was incorporated in the Ḳor'ān (whether Moḥammad intended that it should be so, we have no means of judging); and to this day it is recited in its course, as part of the Word of God, in every Mosque throughout Islām.

Moḥammad attacks and takes captive the Beni 'l-Muṣṭaliḳ. A.H. V. December, A.D. 626

We gladly turn to other matters. Some months after his return from Dūma, rumours reached the Prophet of new projects against him in the neighbourhood of Mecca.[2] The Beni'l-Muṣṭaliḳ, a branch of the Khozā'a hitherto friendly to his cause, were now raising forces with the view of joining Ḳoreish in their long-talked-of attack on Medīna. Having inquired into these reports through a Bedawi spy who ingratiated himself with the hostile chief, Moḥammad at once resolved by a bold inroad to anticipate their design. Besides

[1] A passage follows probably of a later stage, for in this Sūra are collected a great variety of precepts, of different periods, relating to the treatment of women: 'No more Women are lawful unto thee after this: nor that thou shouldest exchange any of thy wives for others, even though their beauty fascinate thee, excepting such (slaves) as thy right hand may possess, and God observeth all things.' Some commentators think that this prohibition was abrogated by a preceding verse, which makes lawful to the Prophet in marriage any of his maternal or paternal cousins, and 'any believing woman who might willingly give herself to him in case he desired to take her to wife.' Others say that the passage was revealed after his number of nine wives was completed. In the latter case, it is to be noted that cohabitation with slaves as concubines, in addition to his regular wives, is still permitted.

[2] Ibn Hishām, p. 725; Aṭ-Ṭabari, i. 1511 ff.; Al-Wāḳidi, p. 175 ff.; Ibn Sa'd, p. 45 f.

his own adherents, many of the Citizens hitherto lukewarm towards Islām, with 'Abdallah ibn Obei at their head, desirous to maintain a friendly appearance, or allured by the hope or plunder, joined his standard. Moḥammad could now muster thirty well-appointed horse.[1] After eight days he encamped by the seashore at the wells of Al-Moraisī', some marches short of Mecca. Here he had a tent of leather pitched for himself and for 'Ā'isha and Um Selama, his companions in the campaign. The tidings of his approach struck terror into the Beni'l-Muṣṭaliḳ, and caused their allies to fall away. The force advanced, and, after a brisk discharge of archery, closed so rapidly on the tribe, that they were all surrounded and taken prisoners with their families, herds, and flocks. Of the enemy ten were killed, while Moḥammad lost but one man, and that from an erring shot by a Muslim. Two hundred families, 2,000 camels, and 5,000 sheep and goats, besides much household goods, formed the booty. It was divided in the usual manner.[2]

Altercation between the Citizens and Refugees

The army having encamped for several days at the wells of Al-Moraisī', an altercation sprang up between a Citizen and 'Omar's servant, a Refugee. The latter struck the Citizen a blow, and the men of Medīna rushing in to avenge their comrade's insult, the Refugee cried loudly on his fellows for aid. High words passed on both sides, swords were drawn, and the result might have been serious, had not the Citizen been induced to withdraw his complaint and forgive the injury. During the quarrel, the disaffected party gave free expression to their disloyal feelings:—'This,' said 'Abdallah ibn Obei openly, 'ye have brought upon yourselves, by inviting these strangers to come amongst us. Wait till we return to Medīna; then the Mightier shall surely expel the Meaner!'

Moḥammad orders immediate march

Moḥammad no sooner heard of the strife, and of the violent language of 'Abdallah, than he gave orders for an

[1] Of the thirty horse, twenty belonged to citizens and ten to Refugees. The standard of the Refugees was held by Abu Bekr, that of the Citizens by Sa'd ibn 'Obāda.

[2] The household stuff was sold to the highest bidder. In the division a camel was reckoned equal to ten sheep or goats. Each horseman had three times the share of a footman, two being reckoned for the horse. Moḥammad desired by this rule to encourage the development of cavalry in his army.

immediate march. The discontent of the Citizens and momentary antagonism betwixt them and the Refugees, if allowed to spread, would have been dangerous; indeed, it was the one thing he had to dread as fatal to his cause. By breaking up the camp, and at once ordering a long and wearisome march, he would divert attention from the events of the morning and make the quarrel to die away. Therefore, though the hour was early and unseasonable, and amity had apparently been re-established, Moḥammad started without delay, and kept the army marching the whole of that day and night and the following day, till the sun was high. Then he halted, and the force, overpowered with fatigue, was soon asleep. From thence they proceeded home by regular marches.

'Abdallah and disaffected Citizens reprimanded in Ḳor'ān

Before the army moved, 'Abdallah protested that he had not made use of the expressions attributed to him; and Moḥammad, although some of his followers counselled severe and decisive measures, received with civility his excuse. When 'Abdallah was being hardly handled by his own fanatical son, who tried to extort from him the confession that *he* was the *Meaner*, and Moḥammad the *Mightier*,[1] the Prophet, chancing to pass by, interfered and said! 'Leave him alone! For, by my life! so long as he remaineth with us, we shall make our companionship pleasant unto him.' Still, when he returned to Medīna, and found himself again firmly fixed in the affections of the Citizens, the Prophet deemed it necessary to administer to 'Abdallah and his followers a public reprimand. The heavenly message contains

[1] There are worse speeches than this attributed to 'Abdallah's son. He offered to bring his father's head, if Moḥammad desired it; saying: 'If he is to be killed, I will do it myself. If any other man commits the deed, the Devil will tempt me to avenge my father's blood: and by killing a Believer for an Unbeliever, I shall go to hell. Suffer me to kill him myself!'

'Omar also is said to have counselled Moḥammad at Al-Moraisī' to put 'Abdallah to death. But Moḥammad replied: ''Omar! How will it be if men should say that Moḥammad killeth his own followers? nay, but let us give orders for an immediate march.' In after days when 'Abdallah's authority waned, and he was treated without reverence even by his own people, Moḥammad reminded 'Omar of his advice on this occasion, and asked whether it was not far better to have reserved him for this fate, than to have put him to death. 'Omar confessed the wisdom of the Prophet.

a curse against the insincere and disaffected professors of Islām; while the quotation of 'Abdallah's very words points the rebuke, notwithstanding his denial, against him.[1]

Moḥammad marries the captive *Juweiriya*, his seventh wife

The captives of the Beni'l-Muṣṭaliḳ having been carried to Medīna with the rest of the booty, men from their tribe soon arrived to make terms for their release. One of them was Juweiriya, a damsel of birth and beauty, about twenty years of age, and married to one of the chiefs of the tribe. She fell to the lot of a citizen, who, taking advantage of her rank and comeliness, fixed the ransom at nine ounces of gold.[2] Despairing to raise so large a sum, she ventured into the presence of the Prophet while seated in the apartment of 'Ā'isha, and pleaded for some remission. A qualm passed over 'Ā'isha, as she saw the Prophet listening to the fair and winning suppliant, and soon perceived that the conqueror had become the captive of his prisoner. 'Wilt thou hearken,' he said, 'to something that may be better than what thou askest of me?' Marvelling at his gentle accents, she asked what that might be. 'Even that I should pay thy ransom, and take thee for myself!' The maiden was nothing loth. And so the ransom was paid. Moḥammad, taking her at once to wife, built a seventh house for her reception. As soon as the marriage was noised abroad, the people said that, the Beni'l-Muṣṭaliḳ having now become their relatives, they

[1] The following is the passage:—When the Disaffected come before thee, they say: *We testify that thou art the Prophet of God:* and God knoweth that thou art his Prophet, and God testifieth that the Disaffected are liars. This because they believed, and afterwards disbelieved; Wherefore, their hearts are sealed, and they understand not. When thou seest them, thou admirest their outward man; but when they speak, thou listenest to their words, as if of logs set up (against the wall); they fancy every cry is against themselves. Beware of them! God curse them! How are they turned unto lies!' And when it is said unto them: *Come! let the Prophet of God ask pardon for you*, they avert their heads, and ye see them turn aside, puffed up with pride. . . . These are they which say: *Withhold your Wealth from those that are with the Prophet of God, and so they will disperse*:—Whereas unto God belong the treasures of the Heavens and of the Earth: But the Disaffected understand not. They say: *When we return unto Medīna, verily the Mightier shall expel from thence the Meaner*:—Whereas Might belongeth to God and His Prophet, and to the Believers: but the Disaffected do not comprehend.'—Sūra lxiii. 1 ff., 7 f.

[2] The ordinary ransom of a woman or child was ten camels.

would let the rest of the prisoners go free as Juweiriya's dower; 'and so,' 'Ā'isha used in after days to say, 'no woman was ever a greater blessing to her people than this Juweiriya.'

'Ā'isha's misadventure with Ṣafwān

But a severer trial than the advent of a new rival was at that moment hanging over 'Ā'isha.[1] Her virtue was about to be called in question. The wives of Moḥammad, when they marched with him, travelled each in a camel litter which, since the order for the veil, was carefully shrouded from the public gaze. At the hour of marching, the litter was brought up and placed close to the door of the lady's tent; at her convenience she would enter and close the curtain, when the servants would approach, and, lifting the litter, fasten it upon the camel's back. When alighting the same privacy was observed. When the army returned to Medīna from the expedition against the Beni'l-Muṣṭaliḳ, the litter of 'Ā'isha was set down at the door of her house near the Mosque; but when opened it was found to be empty. Some little time after, Ṣafwān, one of the Refugees, appeared leading his camel, with 'Ā'isha seated upon it. Her explanation of the misadventure was this. On the previous night, just before the hour to march, she had occasion to go to some little distance from her tent, when she dropped her necklace of Yemen beads. On returning to enter her litter, she missed the necklace, and went back to seek for it. Meanwhile the bearers came up, and, imagining 'Ā'isha to be within the litter (for she was of light and slender figure), lifted it into its place, and so led the camel away. On her return, 'Ā'isha was astonished to find the litter and tent both gone, and no one left anywhere in sight.[2] So, expecting that the mistake would be discovered, and the litter brought back for her, she wrapped her clothes around her, sat patiently on the ground and fell fast asleep. Towards morning, Ṣafwān, who had been also accidentally detained, passed by, and, recognising 'Ā'isha, expressed surprise at finding one of the Prophet's wives in this predicament. She did not answer him. No other words (so 'Ā'isha declared) passed between them, excepting this, that Ṣafwān brought his camel near her, and turning his face away so as not even

[1] Ibn Hishām, p. 731 ff.; Aṭ-Ṭabari, i. 1517 ff.

[2] The tent, being small and light, was easily taken down and carried off immediately she was supposed to have entered the litter.

to see her, desired her to mount. Then he approached, and, holding the halter, led the camel towards Medīna. Though he made every haste, he could not overtake the army; and thus, some time after the others had alighted and pitched their camp, 'Ā'isha, led by Ṣafwān, entered the city before the gaze of all.

Moḥammad's estrangement from 'Ā'isha

The scandal-loving Arabs were not slow in drawing sinister conclusions from the inopportune affair, and spreading them abroad. These, reaching the ears of Moḥammad, caused him much uneasiness. 'Ā'isha felt his change of manner towards her, and (though professing ignorance till some time after of the cause) it preyed upon her mind. She fell sick; and learning at length from a friend the rumours affecting her character, obtained permission to return to her father's house. The estrangement of Moḥammad from his favourite wife strengthened the grounds of defamation. Her fall was gloried over by those who bore no love to the Prophet, and became a topic of malicious conversation even among some of his staunch adherents. At the head of the former was 'Abdallah ibn Obei; and foremost among the latter were Misṭaḥ (a relative and dependent of Abu Bekr), the poet Ḥassān, and Ḥamna, daughter of Jaḥsh, who rejoiced over the dishonour of her sister Zeinab's rival.[1]

Scandal occasioned in Medīna

Moḥammad chides his followers for meddling in the matter

When matters had gone on thus from bad to worse for several weeks, Moḥammad resolved to put an end to the scandal. He mounted the pulpit, and sharply upbraided his followers:—'O ye people!' he said, 'what concern is it of others that they should disquiet me in affairs touching my family, and unjustly blame them! Whereas, I myself know naught but that which is good concerning them. And moreover ye have traduced Ṣafwān, a man regarding whom likewise I know not ought but what is good.' Then Oseid, a leader of the Aus, arose and swore that he would punish the delinquents, even to the death, if Moḥammad would but give command. On this an altercation sprang up between him and the Khazraj, to whom the chief offenders amongst

[1] 'Ā'isha says: 'Now Ḥamna took up the scandal, because she was sister of Zeinab, daughter of Jaḥsh (the former wife of Zeid); and there was none that dared to put herself in competition with me but Zeinab only. She herself said nothing bad; but her sister did so, envying me because of my superiority to Zeinab.'

the Citizens belonged. The quarrel was with some difficulty appeased by Moḥammad, who then left the Mosque and proceeded to the house of Abu Bekr. There, having called to him Osāma [1] and 'Alī, he asked counsel of them. Osāma, declared his utter disbelief of the slanderous report. 'Alī, with greater caution, recommended the examination of 'Ā'isha's maid; and the maid when called could only give testimony which, if anything, was in her mistress's favour.[2]

He consults Osāma and 'Alī

Moḥammad then went to the chamber where 'Ā'isha herself was sitting. From the time she had first learned the imputation on her character, she abandoned herself to excessive grief. Her mother used to exhort her to patience: 'Assuage thy sorrow, my daughter!' she would say; 'it is seldom that a beautiful woman is married to one who loves her and has other wives besides, but these multiply scandal against her; and so do men likewise.' But she ever refused to be comforted, and continued to pine away. When Moḥammad now entered, with her father and mother, he sat down beside her, and said: 'Ā'isha! thou hearest what men have spoken of thee. Fear God. If indeed thou art guilty, then repent toward God, for the Lord accepteth the repentance of His servants.' She held her peace, expecting (as she tells us) that her parents would reply for her;—but they too were silent. At last she burst into a passionate flood of tears, and exclaimed: 'By the Lord! I say that I will never repent towards God of that which ye speak of. I am helpless. If I confess, God knoweth that I am not guilty. If I deny, no one believeth me. All I can say is that which Joseph's father said,—*Patience becometh me, and the Lord is my helper!*'[3] Then, as all sat silent, Moḥammad appeared to

'Ā'isha cleared by revelation from heaven

[1] Son of the Prophet's nurse Baraka (Um Aiman) and her husband Zeid.

[2] 'Alī answered Moḥammad: 'O Prophet! there is no lack of women, and thou canst without difficulty supply her place. Ask this servant girl about her, perchance she may tell the truth.' So Moḥammad called the maid. 'Alī arose and struck her, saying: 'Tell the truth unto the Prophet.' 'I know nothing,' said she, 'of 'Ā'isha but what is good:—excepting this, indeed, that one day I was kneading corn, and I asked her to watch it, and she went asleep, and the goats came and ate thereof.' We must not forget, however, that all this is from 'Ā'isha herself, who had a strong antipathy to 'Alī.

[3] 'Ā'isha says that the name of *Jacob* having gone out of her head at the moment, she substituted the words *Joseph's father*.

fall into a trance. They covered him over, and placed a pillow under his head. Thus he lay seemingly unconscious. 'Ā'isha assures us that her mind was perfectly tranquil at the moment, confident that her innocence would be vindicated from heaven. In a little while he recovered, cast off the clothes, and sat up. Wiping away the great drops of sweat from his forehead, he exclaimed: *'Ā'isha! rejoice! Verily the Lord hath declared thine innocence.'* 'Embrace thy husband!' cried her mother. But 'Ā'isha could do no more than ejaculate, '*Praise be to the Lord!*'

Passages revealed on the occasion

Then Moḥammad went forth to the people, and recited before them the commands he had received in this matter, which form the law of adultery to the present day. The 24th Sūra opens with declaring one hundred stripes[1] the punishment for harlotry, and proceeds thus:—

Sūra xxiv. 4 f.

They that slander married women, and thereafter do not bring forward four witnesses, scourge them with four-score stripes: and ye shall never again receive their testimony; for they are infamous,—Unless they repent after that, and amend, for God is forgiving and merciful.[2]

v. 11 ff.

* * * Verily as for them,—a party amongst you,—that have fabricated lies, think it not to be an evil unto you. To every man amongst them shall be dealt out punishment according to the crime which he hath wrought; and he that hath been forward amongst them in aggravating the same, his punishment shall be grievous.[3] Wherefore, when they heard it, did not the faithful men and women imagine good in their hearts, and say,—*This is a manifest falsehood?* Have they brought four witnesses thereof? Wherefore, since they have not produced the witnesses, they are liars, these men, in the sight of God. If it were not for the favour of God upon you, and His mercy in this world and in the next, verily for that which ye have spread abroad, a grievous punishment

[1] Sūra xii. 18. This penalty is made by the Muslim divines to apply to fornication only, and not to adultery. For the latter no punishment is mentioned *in the Ḳor'ān*, but the Sunna awards death by stoning for it.

[2] Here intervenes the ordinance prescribed for a husband charging his wife with adultery. If he have no witnesses, the charge, sworn to by himself four times, with a fifth oath imprecating the wrath of God if swearing falsely, is accepted without witnesses. The wife may avert the punishment by similar oaths and a similar imprecation. No corresponding privilege is conceded to the wife who accuses her husband of adultery.

[3] The expression here is so strong that some take it to mean hell, and apply it to 'Abdallah. Others refer it to Ḥassān, who shortly after became blind. But the natural meaning is the punishment of stripes, severe enough certainly for the honourable class on whom it was inflicted.

had overtaken you;—when ye published it with your tongues, and said with your mouths that of which ye had no knowledge: and ye counted it light, but with God it is weighty. Why, when ye heard it, did ye not say: *It belongeth not to us that we should speak of this;—Gracious God! It is a monstrous calumny!*

God admonisheth you that ye return not to the like again for ever. . . . Verily, they who love that infamy should be published regarding the Believers: to them shall be a grievous torment in this world and in the next. And if it had not been for the grace of God upon you, and His mercy,—Verily, God is merciful and forgiving. v. 18 f.

Calumniators of 'Ā'isha scourged

After some further denunciations and threats of punishment, both in this life and the next, against the publishers of scandal and traducers of innocent females, Moḥammad stopped short; and, in accordance with the divine command, ordered the prescribed punishment to be inflicted on the calumniators of 'Ā'isha. Misṭaḥ and Ḥassān received each four-score stripes; and even Ḥamna, the sister of the favourite Zeinab, did not escape. Against 'Abdallah alone, Moḥammad did not venture to enforce the sentence. It was fortunate that he refrained from doing so, for a time of trial was at hand when the alienation of this powerful Citizen and his adherents might have proved dangerous to his cause.

Ḥassān conciliated by present of an estate

Satisfied with such emphatic vindication of his favourite wife, Moḥammad dropped the grudge, and sought now rather to conciliate her calumniators. Ṣafwān (the hero of the misadventure), smarting from the imputations veiled under the satires of the poet Ḥassān, drew his sword upon him and inflicted a deep wound. Ḥassān and his friends seized and bound Ṣafwān, and carried him before Moḥammad. The Prophet first rebuked Ḥassān for troubling the Citizens with his lampoons; and then, having composed the difference, more than compensated the Poet for his wound and the disgrace of the stripes, by conferring on him a valuable estate and mansion in the vicinity of Medīna. He also commanded Abu Bekr not to withdraw from Misṭaḥ, his indigent relative, the support he had hitherto given him.[1]

[1] This was not thought too small a matter for a special injunction; see Sūra xxiv. 22. Of Ḥassān, we learn that, though by far the first poet in Medīna, his character was not such as to inspire respect. He was foul-mouthed and cowardly, and never went into battle. Combing his hair over his forehead and eyes, and dyeing his moustache a bright red while the rest of his hair was black, he affected often the wild appearance of a wolf.

Ḥassān reconciles 'Ā'isha by an ode

'A'isha resumed her place, more secure than ever, as the queen of the Prophet's heart and home. Ḥassān, changing his muse, sang in glowing verse of her purity, elegance, and wit, and (what she piqued herself the most upon) her slender, graceful figure.[1] The flattering compliment reconciled her to the Poet; but she never forgave 'Alī for his doubting.

Guilt or innocence of 'Ā'isha

Little remark is needed regarding the character of 'Ā'isha and the revelation to which it gave occasion. The reason assigned for her innocence and the punishment of her slanderers, namely, the absence of four witnesses, is inconclusive; but her life both before and after must lead us to believe her innocent of the charge. It might have been necessary that Moḥammad should caution his followers, and even punish them, for lightly or maliciously damaging a reputation hitherto untarnished; but to prohibit, on pain of stripes, all comment on suspicious morality unless attested by four witnesses, is to cast a veil over conduct which the interests of society might imperatively require to be canvassed and held up to reprobation. The direct evidence of four eye-witnesses is still needed to prove the charge of adultery, so that the draconic penalty of stoning is practically inoperative.[2] But the law itself is a fair example of the way in which the Code of Islām grew out of the circumstances of the day, concrete rather than based on abstract considerations.

Law of slander established by Moḥammad

Moḥammad cautions his wives against immodesty

Although admitting so decisively the innocence of 'Ā'isha, Moḥammad did not deem the character of his wives above the necessity of caution, and the threat of a double punishment if they erred. They were not as other women; far more than others they were bound to abstain from every word and action that might encourage those 'whose hearts are diseased.' The passage enjoining this is too curious to be curtailed, even at the risk of the reader's patience.

Sūra xxxiii. 28 ff.

O Prophet, say unto thy Wives,—*If ye seek after this present Life and the fashion thereof, come, I will make provision for you and dismiss you with a fair dismission.* But if ye seek after God and His Apostle, and the

---

[1] *Dīwān*, No. cxlvi. When he came to the passage referring to her *slimness*, she archly interrupted him by a piece of raillery at his own corpulence.

[2] *Vide* p. 302, note 1. It is true that an exception is made in favour of the husband, whose oath five times repeated may be substituted, as above noted (page 302, note 2)

Life to come, then verily God hath prepared for the excellent amongst you a great reward. O ye Wives of the Prophet! if any amongst you should be guilty of incontinence, the punishment shall be doubled unto her two-fold; and that were easy with God. But she that amongst you devoteth herself to God and His Apostle, and worketh righteousness, WE shall give unto her her reward twice told, and WE have prepared for her a gracious maintenance.

O ye Wives of the Prophet! Ye are not as other women. If ye fear the Lord, be not bland in your speech lest he indulge desire in whose heart is disease. Yet speak the speech that is suitable. And abide within your houses; and array not yourselves as ye used to do in the bygone days of Ignorance. And observe the times of Prayer; and give Alms: and obey God and His Apostle. Verily the Lord desireth only to purge away from you impurity, ye that are of (his) household, and to purify you wholly. And keep in memory that which is recited in your houses, of the Word of God, and Wisdom: for God pierceth that which is hidden, and is acquainted with all things.

CHAPTER XVII

SIEGE OF MEDĪNA,[1] AND MASSACRE OF THE BENI ĶOREIẒA

Dhu'l-Ka'da, A.H. V.—*February, March*, A.D. 627

Stirring scenes open upon Moḥammad

WHILE Moḥammad thus busied himself with the cares of his increasing ḥarīm, and, by messages addressed from heaven, enjoined upon its inmates virtue and propriety of life, more stirring scenes awaited him. A storm was gathering in the south.

Ķoreish, joined by Bedawīn tribes, march against Medīna

The winter season was again come round, at which it had become the wont of Ķoreish to arm themselves against Medīna. Their preparations now exceeded those of any previous year. Ḥuyei, and other exiled Jewish chiefs, undertook to rouse the Bedawīn tribes bound by alliance or sympathy in the same cause. Among these were several clans of the Ghaṭafān family, between whom and Moḥammad there had already been some warlike passages. Ashja' and Murra each brought 400 warriors; and the Beni Fezāra a large force, with 1,000 camels, under 'Oyeina; the Suleim, who had been concerned in the massacre at Bi'r Ma'ūna, joined the army on the way, with 700 men. The Beni Sa'd and Asad also swelled the force, the latter still smarting from the attack made on them by Moḥammad about two years before. Ķoreish themselves brought into the field 4,000 soldiers, including 300 horse, and 1,500 riders upon camels. The banner was mounted in the Hall of Council and delivered to 'Othmān, son of Ṭalḥa the standard-bearer killed at Oḥod. The entire force was estimated at 10,000 men. They marched in three separate camps; all were under the general leadership of Abu Sufyān, but, when the time for action

[1] Ibn Hishām, p. 668 ff.; Aṭ-Ṭabari, i. 1463 ff.; Al-Wāķidi, p. 190 ff.; Ibn Sa'd, p. 47 ff.

came, the several chiefs each for a day commanded in succession.

Moḥammad defends Medīna by a trench. A.H. V. February, A.D. 627

Moḥammad was apprised of the danger by a friendly message from the Khozā'a, but barely in time to prepare. Alarm overspread Medīna. The defeat at Oḥod by numbers much inferior put it out of the question to offer battle; and the only anxiety now was how successfully to defend the city. By advice of Salmān 'the Persian'—who, taken captive in Mesopotamia, was familiar with warlike tactics practised there—it was resolved to entrench Medīna, a stratagem as yet unknown to the Arabs.[1] The outer line of houses was built together so compactly that, for a considerable length, they presented a high stone wall, of itself a solid defence against the enemy. But it was necessary to connect this barrier on one hand with the rocks which on the north-west approach the city,[2] and on the other to carry it round the open and unsheltered quarter on the south and east. The work, consisting of a deep ditch and rude earthen dyke, was portioned out amongst the various clans. Shovels, pickaxes, and baskets were borrowed from the Beni Ḳoreiẓa. Moḥammad stimulated the enthusiasm of his followers by himself carrying basket-loads of the excavated earth, and joining in their song, as at the building of the Mosque:—

> O Lord! there is no happiness but that of Futurity.
> O Lord! have mercy on the Citizens and the Refugees!

He also frequently repeated the following verses, covered as he was, like the rest, with earth and dust:—

> O Lord! without Thee, we had not been guided!
> We should neither have given alms, nor yet have prayed!
> Send down upon us tranquillity, and in battle stablish our steps!
> For they have risen up against us, and sought to pervert us, but we refused!—Yea, WE REFUSED.

And as he repeated the last two words, he raised his voice high and loud.

[1] He is said to have been a Christian captive of Mesopotamia, bought by a Jew from the Beni Kelb, and ransomed on his profession of Islām. This is the first occasion on which he comes to notice. See Ibn Hishām, p. 136 ff.

[2] The fortress or castle of Medīna is now built on this 'out-cropping mass of rock.'—*Burton.* Burckhardt calls it a small rocky elevation. Speaking of the great mountain chain, he also says: 'The last undula-

Army of Medīna posted within trench. A.H. V. March 2, A.D. 626

In six days the trench was dug, deep and wide throughout almost the whole length of the defence; and well-sized stones were piled along its inner bank to be used against the enemy. The dwellings outside the town were evacuated, and the women and children bidden to stay at the top of the double-storied houses within the entrenchment. These things were barely done when the enemy was reported to be advancing, as before, by the hill of Oḥod. The army of Medīna, 3,000 strong, marched out at once into the open space between the city and the trench. It commanded the road leading to Oḥod, its rear resting upon the north-eastern quarter of the city and the eminence of Sal'. The northern face was the most vulnerable point, the approaches from the east being covered by walls and palm enclosures. A tent of red leather was pitched for Moḥammad on the ground, in which 'Ā'isha, Um Selama, and Zeinab visited him by turns.

Ḳoreish encamp opposite them,

Ḳoreish, with their Bedawi hordes, and multitudes of camels and horses, encamped at first upon their old ground, under the hill of Oḥod. Then, finding the country deserted, they swept rapidly round by the scene of their former victory, and, still advancing unopposed, were brought to a stand by the trench. Closely guarded all along by pickets on the city side, it formed a barrier which they could not pass. They were astonished and disconcerted at the new tactics of Moḥammad. Unable to come to close quarters, they pitched their camps on the plain beyond, and contented themselves for some time with a distant discharge of archery.

And detach Beni Ḳoreiẓa from allegiance to Moḥammad

Meanwhile, Abu Sufyān succeeded in detaching the Beni Ḳoreiẓa, now the only remaining Jewish tribe, from their allegiance to Moḥammad. Ḥuyei, the exiled Jew and ally of the Ḳoreish, sent by him to their fortress, was at first refused admittance. But, persevering in his solicitations, dwelling upon the ill-concealed enmity of Moḥammad towards the Jews at large, and representing the overwhelming numbers of the confederate army as 'a surging sea,' he at

tions of these mountains touch the town on the north side.' This is apparently what, in tradition, is called *Sal'*, though Burckhardt gives that name, 'Jebel Sila,' to the *Monākh* (or encamping ground) lying immediately to the south. I gather that the part of modern Medīna immediately to the east of the fort was in ancient times open and unbuilt upon.

last persuaded Ka'b their chief to relent. It was agreed that the Beni Ḳoreiẓa would assist Ḳoreish, and that Ḥuyei should retire into their fortress in case the allies marched back without inflicting a fatal blow upon Medīna. Rumours of this defection reaching Moḥammad, he sent the two Sa'ds, chiefs of the Aus and Khazraj, to ascertain the truth; and strictly charged them, if the result should prove unfavourable, to divulge it to none other but himself. They found the Beni Ḳoreiẓa in a sullen mood. 'Who is Moḥammad,' said they, 'and who is the Apostle of God, that we should obey him? There is no bond or compact betwixt us and him.' After high words and threats, the messengers took their leave, and reported to Moḥammad that the temper of the Jews was worse even than he had feared.[1]

[1] It is not easy to say exactly what campact did at this time exist between Moḥammad and the Beni Ḳoreiẓa, and what part the Beni Ḳoreiẓa actually took in assisting the Allies. The evidence is altogether *ex parte*, and naturally adverse to the Beni Ḳoreiẓa. The Ḳor'ān, our surest guide, says simply that they 'assisted' the Allies; and the best traditions confine themselves to this general expression. Had they entered on active hostilities, no doubt it would have been more distinctly specified in the Ḳor'ān. On the other hand, a tradition from 'Ā'isha states that, when the Allies broke up, the Beni Ḳoreiẓa, 'returned' to their fort; and some traditions, though not of much weight, speak of them as part of the besieging force *before Medīna*. There is also a weak tradition that Ḥodheifa, sent by Moḥammad as a spy to the enemy's camp, overheard Abu Sufyān telling his comrades the good news that the Beni Ḳoreiẓa had agreed to join him, *after ten days' preparation*, provided he sent seventy warriors to hold their fortress while they were absent in the field; and that Ḥodheifa's report was the first intelligence Moḥammad had of the defection.

On the whole, my impression is that the Beni Ḳoreiẓa entered into some kind of league with the Jewish exile Ḥuyei, making common cause with him, and promising to take part in following up any success on the part of Ḳoreish—a promise which they were in the best position to fulfil—their fortress being, though at some distance from the city, on its undefended side. But, before opportunity offered, they saw the likelihood of the siege failing, and then distrust of Ḳoreish broke out, and so their promise never was fulfilled. The compact existing betwixt them and Moḥammad is described by Al-Wāḳidi as a '*slight*' one. Al-Jauhari says that this term means a treaty entered into without forecast or design, or 'infirm.' 'Fœdus vel pactum forte initum, vel haud firmum.'

Sprenger notes these alternatives;—*First*, that, as at Oḥod, the Beni Ḳoreiẓa were forbidden by Moḥammad to take part with him in the fight; *second*, that of their own free-will they remained neutral. He

Danger to Medīna from this defection, and measures for its safety

The news alarmed Moḥammad and disturbed the city. The Jews, whom the previous treatment of their brethren might now drive to desperate measures, had still a powerful party in their favour; and the defences, moreover, were weakest on that side. Disaffection lurked everywhere, and some began even to talk of deserting to the enemy. To protect the town in the quarter most exposed, and guard against surprise or treachery, Moḥammad was obliged to detach from his force, already barely adequate to man the trench, two parties under Zeid and a Citizen respectively, which night and day patrolled the streets. A strong guard was also posted over the Prophet's tent.

Attack on trench repulsed

The vigilance of the Muslim pickets kept at bay the Confederate host, who proclaimed the trench to be an unworthy subterfuge. 'Truly this ditch,' they cried in their chagrin, 'is the artifice of strangers, a shift to which no Arab yet has ever stooped.' But it was, nevertheless, the safety of Medīna. The Confederate host resolved if possible to storm the trench, and, having discovered a narrow and ill-guarded part, a general attack was made upon it. Spurring their horses, a few of them, led by 'Ikrima, son of Abu Jahl, cleared the ditch, and galloped vauntingly before the Muslim line. No sooner was this perceived, than 'Alī with a guard of picked men moved out against them. These, by a rapid manœuvre, gained the rear of 'Ikrima, and, occupying the narrow point which he had crossed, cut off his retreat. At this moment 'Amr, an aged chief in the train of 'Ikrima, challenged his adversaries to single combat. 'Alī forthwith accepted the challenge, and the two stood man to man in the open plain. 'Amr, dismounting, maimed his horse, in token of his resolve to conquer or to die. They closed, and for a short time were hidden in a cloud of dust. But it was not long before the loud *Tekbīr*, 'Great is the Lord!' from 'Alī's lips, made known that he was the victor.[1] The rest, taking

decides in favour of the first;—that they resisted the temptation and remained faithful, and that even the Jews of Kheibar kept aloof from Ḳoreish for fear of compromising their brethren at Medīna.

The question is important as bearing on the sentence executed against the Beni Ḳoreiẓa after Ḳoreish retired.

[1] Ḳoreish, it is said, offered a great sum for the body; but Moḥammad returned the 'worthless carcase' (as he termed it) free.

advantage of the diversion, again spurred their horses across the trench, and escaped, all excepting Naufal, who, failing in the leap, was despatched by Az-Zubeir [or according to another account by 'Alī].[1]

General attack successfully repelled

Nothing further was attempted that day. But great preparations were made during the night; and next morning, Moḥammad found the whole allied forces drawn out against him. It required unceasing vigilance to frustrate their manœuvres. Now they would threaten a general assault; now breaking up into divisions they would attack various posts in rapid and distracting succession; and at last, watching their opportunity, they would mass their troops together on the least protected point, and, under cover of galling archery, attempt to force the trench. Once and again a gallant dash was made at the city by such leaders of renown as Khālid and 'Amr, and the tent of Moḥammad himself was at one moment in peril; but the brave Muslim front, and showers of arrows, drove the assailants back. This continued throughout the day; and, as the army of Moḥammad was but just sufficient to guard the line, there could be no relief. Even at night Khālid's troop kept up the alarm, and rendered outposts at frequent intervals necessary But the endeavours of the enemy were all without effect. The trench was never crossed in force; and during the whole affair Moḥammad lost only five men. Sa'd ibn Mo'ādh, chief of the Aus, was wounded severely by an arrow in the shoulder; the archer crying aloud:—'There, take that from the son of Al-'Araḳa.[2] Whereupon Moḥammad exclaimed, with a bitter play upon the name: 'The Lord cause thy face to sweat ('arraḳa) in hell fire!' The Confederates had but three men killed.

Prayers repeated in the evening for those omitted during day

No prayers had been said that day: the duty at the trench was too heavy and incessant. When it was dark, therefore, and the greater part of the enemy had retired, the Muslim troops assembled, and a separate service was held for each omitted prayer. On this occasion Moḥammad cursed the allied army thus:—'They have kept us from our daily prayers: God fill their bellies and their graves with fire!'

Distress at Medīna

Though the loss of life had been trifling, yet the army

[1] Aṭ-Ṭabari, i. 1475 f.; Al-Wāḳidi, p. 210.

[2] [He is not mentioned by Ibn Hishām or Aṭ-Ṭabari.]

of Medīna was harassed and wearied with unceasing watch and duty night and day. They were, moreover, dispirited by finding themselves hemmed in, and seeing no prospect of the siege being raised. Moḥammad himself was in constant alarm lest the trench should be forced, or his rear be threatened by the Jews or disaffected Citizens. Many followers, whose possessions lay outside the city, afraid lest they should be plundered, begged leave to go and protect them. Moḥammad was to outward look weak and helpless. 'Where,' it was asked, 'were now the Prophet's hopes, and where his promises of Heaven's assistance?' It was a day of rebuke, when (as we read in the vivid language of the Ḳor'ān) '*the enemy came upon them from above and from beneath, and the sight became confused; and hearts reached to the throat; and the people imagined of God strange imaginations; for there were the Faithful tried, and made to tremble violently.*' In this state of alarm, when the siege had now lasted ten or twelve days, Moḥammad bethought him of buying off the Bedawīn as the least hostile portion of his foe. He sent therefore to 'Oyeina, chief of the Beni Fezāra, and sounded him as to whether he would engage to withdraw the Ghaṭafān tribes, on condition of receiving one-third of the produce of the date-trees of Medīna. 'Oyeina signified his readiness, if one-half were guaranteed. But Moḥammad had over-estimated his authority. On sending for the two Sa'ds, as representatives of the Aus and of the Khazraj, they spurned the compromise; but, still maintaining their subordination to the Prophet, added: 'If thou hast received a command from heaven for this, then do thou act according to the same.' 'Nay,' said Moḥammad, 'If I had received a bidding from the Lord, I had not consulted you; I but ask your advice as to that thing which is the most expedient.' 'Then,' said the chiefs, 'our counsel is to give nothing unto them but the Sword.' And so the project dropped.

Sūra xxxiii. 10 f.

Secret negotiation to buy off Beni Ghaṭafān

Mutual distrust sown between Ḳoreish and Jews by emissary from Moḥammad

Another and more artful device was now tried. There was a man of the allied army, who possessed the ear of both sides—the same No'eim who had been employed by Ḳoreish in the previous year to prevent Moḥammad from advancing upon Bedr, by exaggerated accounts of the preparations at Mecca. He is here represented as an exemplary believer, but secretly for fear of his tribe. His services now offered were gladly accepted. 'See now,' said Moḥammad to him, 'whether thou canst not break up this confederacy: for War after all is but a game of deception.' No'eim went first to the Beni Ḳoreiẓa and, representing himself as their friend, artfully insinuated that the interests of the allied army were diverse from theirs; before they compromised themselves irretrievably by joining in the renewed attack on Medīna, they ought to demand from Ḳoreish hostages, as a guarantee against being in the last resort deserted and left in the power of Moḥammad.[1] Suspecting no harm, they agreed to act on his advice. Next he went to the allied chiefs and cautioned them against the Jews: 'I have heard,' said he, 'that the Beni Ḳoreiẓa intend asking for hostages; beware how ye give them, for they have already repented of their compact with you, and promised Moḥammad to give him up the hostages to be slain, and then join in the battle against you.' The insidious plot immediately took effect. When Ḳoreish sent to demand of the Beni Ḳoreiẓa the fulfilment of their engagement to join in a general attack on the following day, they pleaded their Sabbath as a pretext against fighting on the morrow, and their fear of being deserted as a ground for demanding hostages. The Allies, regarding this as a confirmation of No'eim's intelligence, were so fully persuaded of the treachery of the Beni Ḳoreiẓa that they began even to fear an attack upon themselves from that quarter.

The Confederate chiefs were already disheartened. After the first two days of vigorous fighting, they had not again attempted any general assault.[2] The hopes entertained from another engagement, during which the Beni Ḳoreiẓa were to have fallen upon the city in the rear of Moḥammad, were now changed into the fear of hostilities from the Beni Ḳoreiẓa themselves. Forage was obtained with the utmost difficulty; provisions were running short, and the camels and horses

[1] The tenor of No'eim's advice, as given uniformly by tradition, is opposed to the supposition that the Beni Ḳoreiẓa had as yet joined in active hostilities against Moḥammad, or committed any such overt act as would have prevented them rejoining his cause. Sprenger says that, at this stage, Ḥuyei made a last attempt to persuade the Beni Ḳoreiẓa to fall upon the rear of the Muslims at the time of a general attack, but did not succeed.

[2] Perhaps the system by which the chiefs commanded each on successive days may have paralysed their energies.

A tempest: Abu Sufyān orders allied force to break up

dying daily in great numbers. Wearied and damped in spirit, the night set in upon them cold and tempestuous. Wind and rain beat mercilessly on the unprotected camp. The storm rose to a hurricane. Fires were extinguished, tents blown down, cooking vessels and other equipage overthrown. Cold and comfortless, Abu Sufyān suddenly resolved on an immediate march. Hastily summoning the chiefs, he made known his decision: 'Break up the camp,' he said, 'and march; as for myself, I am gone.' With these words he leaped on his camel (so great, we are told, was his impatience) while its fore leg was yet untied, and led the way. Khālid with 200 horse brought up the rear, as a guard against pursuit. Ḳoreish took the road by Oḥod for Mecca, and the Beni Ghaṭafān retired to their desert haunts.

Enemy retires

Moḥammad attributes relief to divine interposition

The grateful intelligence soon reached Moḥammad, who had sent a follower in the dark to spy out the enemy's movements. In the morning not one of them was left in sight. This happy issue was an answer, the Prophet said, to the earnest prayer he had for some days been offering up: '*O Lord! Revealer of the Book, thou that art swift in taking account! turn to flight the confederate Host! Turn them to flight, O Lord, and make them to quake!*' The Lord, in answer, had sent the tempestuous wind, he said; the armies of heaven had been fighting for them; terror had been struck into the heart of the enemy. And now they were gone.

Muslim army breaks up,

The army of Medīna, thus unexpectedly relieved, joyfully broke up their camp, in which they had been besieged now for fifteen days, and returned to their homes. Moḥammad had no thoughts of a pursuit: it would have been affording Ḳoreish that which perhaps they still desired—an action in the open country. His thought was of a surer and more important blow nearer home.[1]

But immediately reformed to chastise Beni Ḳoreiẓa

He was still cleansing himself from the dust of the field, when suddenly Gabriel brought him command to proceed against the Jews. 'What!' said the heavenly visitant reproaching him, 'hast thou laid aside thine armour, while as yet the Angels have not laid theirs aside! Arise! go up against the Beni Ḳoreiẓa. Behold I go before thee to shake

[1] Ibn Hishām, p. 684 ff.; Aṭ-Ṭabari, i. 1485 ff.; Al-Wāḳidi, p. 210 ff.; Ibn Sa'd, p. 53 f.

Siege of Beni Ḳoreiẓa fortress. A.H. V. March, A.D. 626

the foundations of their stronghold.'[1] Instantly Bilāl made proclamation throughout the town;—immediate march was ordered; all were to be present at evening prayer in the camp pitched before the fortress, two or three miles south-east of Medīna. The great banner, standing yet unfurled in the Mosque, was placed in the hands of 'Alī. Moḥammad mounted his ass, and the army (as before 3,000 strong, with 36 horse) followed. The fortress was at once invested, and a discharge of archery kept up steadily, but without effect. One man, approaching incautiously near, was killed by a Jewess casting down a millstone from the walls. The improvident Jews, whom the fate of their brethren should have taught to better purpose, had not calculated on the chances and necessities of a siege. Soon reduced to great distress, they sought to capitulate on condition of quitting the neighbourhood even empty-handed. But Moḥammad, having no longer other Jewish neighbours to alarm or aleniate, was bent on severer measures, and refused. In this extremity, the Beni Ḳoreiẓa appealed to their ancient friendship with the Aus, and the services rendered to them in bygone days. They begged that Abu Lubāba, an ally belonging to that tribe, might be allowed to visit them. He came, and, overcome by the wailing of the children and the cries of the women, had no heart to speak; but, symbolically drawing his hand across his throat, intimated that they must fight to the last, as death was all they had to hope for. On retiring, he felt that he had been too plain and honest in his advice; for 'War,' as the Prophet had said, 'was a game of deception.' Therefore he went to Moḥammad, and, confessing his guilt, said: 'I repent; for verily I have dealt treacherously with the Lord, and with his Prophet.' Mohammad vouchsafed no

Abu Lubāba visits Beni Ḳoreiẓa

[1] Tradition abounds with stories of Gabriel on this occasion. He was seen to go before the Muslim army in the appearance of Diḥya the Kelbite, who 'resembled Gabriel in his beard and face.' Again, Moḥammad desired to postpone the campaign a few days as his people were fatigued; but Gabriel would not admit of a moment's delay, and galloped off with his troop of angels, raising a great dust. Gabriel's dress is particularised: he rode on a mule with a silken saddle, a silken turban, &c. Moḥammad had washed the right cheek and was beginning to wash the left, when Gabriel appeared and gave him the order to march to the siege of the Beni Ḳoreiẓa; so, leaving thus his face half washed he obeyed at once!

reply; and Abu Lubāba, the more strongly to mark his contrition, went straightway to the Mosque and bound himself to one of its posts. In this position he remained for several days, till at last Moḥammad relented, and sent to pardon and release him. The 'Pillar of repentance' is still pointed out to the pious pilgrim.

They surrender at the discretion of the Aus

At last the wretched Jews, brought now to the last verge of starvation, offered to surrender, on condition that their fate should be decided by their allies the Aus. To this Moḥammad agreed; and, after a siege of two or three weeks, the whole tribe, men, women, and children, over 2,000 souls, came forth from their stronghold. The men, their hands tied behind their backs, were kept apart, under Moḥammad, the assassin of Ka'b. The women and children, torn from their protectors, were placed under charge of a renegade Jew. As they passed before the conqueror, his eye marked the lovely features of Reiḥāna, and he destined her for himself. The spoil, consisting of household stuff, clothes and armour,[1] camels and flocks, were all brought forth to await the arbiter's award. The store of wine and fermented liquors was poured forth, as now forbidden to Believers.

Sa'd ibn Mo'ādh appointed arbiter of their fate

The Aus, with whom the judgment lay, were urgent with the Prophet that their ancient allies should be spared. 'These are *our* confederates,' they cried importunately; 'show them at least the same pity as, at the suit of the Khazraj, thou didst show to *their* allies the Beni an-Naḍīr.' 'Are ye then content,' replied Moḥammad, 'that they be judged by one of yourselves?' They answered, 'Yes,' and Moḥammad forthwith nominated Sa'd ibn Mo'ādh to be the judge.

Bloody judgment of Sa'd

Sa'd still suffered from the injury inflicted by the arrow at the trench. From the field of battle he had been carried to a tent pitched by Moḥammad, in the courtyard of the Mosque, where the sick were waited on by Rufeida, an experienced nurse. His wound had begun apparently to heal. But the sense of the injury still rankled in his heart; and Moḥammad, no doubt, knew the bitter hate into which his former friendship had been turned by the treachery of the

[1] There were 1,500 swords, 1,000 lances, 500 shields, and 300 coats of mail.

Beni Koreiẓa.[1] He was now summoned. Large and corpulent, he was mounted with some difficulty on a well-padded ass, and, amidst appeals for mercy from his tribesmen crowding round him, was conducted to the camp. He answered not a word till he approached the scene, and then replied: 'Verily, to Sa'd hath this grace been given, that he careth not, in the cause of God, for any blame the Blamers may cast upon him.' As he drew near, Moḥammad called aloud to those around him: 'Stand up to meet your Master, and assist him to alight.'[2] Then he commanded that Sa'd should pronounce his judgment. It was a scene well worthy the pencil of a painter. In the background, the army of Medīna watch with deep interest this show of justice, regarding eagerly the booty, the household stuff and armour, the camels and flocks, the date-groves, and the deserted town, all, by the expected decree of confiscation, about to become their own. On the right, with hands pinioned behind their backs, are the captive men, seven or eight hundred in number, dejection and despair at the ominous rigour of their treatment stamped upon their faces. On the left, are the women and the little children, pale with terror, or frantic with grief and alarm for themselves and for their husbands and fathers, from whom they have been just now so rudely dragged. In front is Mohammad, with his chief Companions by his side, and a crowd of followers thronging behind. Before him stands Sa'd, supported by his friends, weak and jaded with the journey, yet distinguished above all around by his portly and commanding figure. 'Proceed with thy judgment!' repeated the Prophet. Sa'd turned himself to his people, who were still urging mercy upon him, and said: 'Will ye, then, bind yourselves by the covenant of God that whatsoever I shall decide, ye will accept?' There was a murmur of assent. '*Then*,' proceeded Sa'd, '*my judgment is that the men shall be put to death, the women and children sold*

[1] On his being wounded, Sa'd is said to have cursed the Beni Ḳoreiẓa and prayed: 'O Lord! suffer me not to die until my heart hath had its revenge against them.'

[2] The Refugees held with much pertinacity that this order was only addressed to the Citizens of Medīna, as Sa'd was their chief. The Citizens, on the contrary, regarded the words as addressed to all then present, including the Refugees, and as significant of the honourable and commanding post of judge, assigned to Sa'd.

into slavery, and the spoil divided amongst the army.' Many a heart quailed, besides the hearts of the wretched prisoners, at this bloody decree. But all questionings were forthwith stopped by Moḥammad, who sternly adopted the verdict as his own, nay, declared it to be the solemn judgment of the Almighty. '*Truly,*' he said, '*the judgment of Sa'd is the judgment of God pronounced on high from beyond the seventh heaven.*'

Butchery of the Beni Ḳoreiẓa

No sooner was the sentence passed and ratified than the camp broke up, and the people wended their way back to Medīna. The captives, still under charge of Moḥammad, were dragged roughly along; one alone was treated with tenderness and care,—it was Reiḥāna the beautiful Jewess, set apart for Moḥammad. The men were shut up in a yard, separate from the women and children; they were supplied with dates and spent in prayer the hours of darkness, repeating passages from their Scriptures and exhorting one another to faith and constancy. During the night trenches sufficient to contain the dead bodies of the men were dug across the market-place of the city. In the morning, Moḥammad, himself a spectator of the tragedy, commanded the male captives to be brought forth in companies of five or six at a time. Each company as it came up was made to sit down in a row on the brink of the trench destined for its grave, there beheaded, and the bodies cast therein. And so with company after company, till all were slain.[1] One woman alone was put to death; it was she who threw the millstone from the battlements. When she heard that her husband had been slain, she loudly avowed what she had done, and demanded of Moḥammad that she might share her husband's fate;—a petition which, perhaps in more mercy than was meant, he granted; and she met her death with a cheerful countenance. This heroine's smile, as she stepped fearless to her death, 'Ā'isha tells us, haunted her ever after. For Az-Zabīr, an aged Jew, who had saved some of the Aus in the

[1] As the messenger went to bring up each successive party, the miserable prisoners, not conceiving a wholesale butchery possible, asked what was about to be done with them. 'What! will ye never understand?' said the hard-hearted keeper; 'will ye always remain blind? See ye not that each company goeth and returneth not hither again? What is this but death?'

battle of Bo'āth, Thābit ibn Ḳeis interceded and procured a pardon, including the freedom of his family and restoration of his property. 'But what hath become of all our chiefs,—of Ka'b, of Ḥuyei, of 'Azzāl the son of Samuel?' asked the old man. As one after another he named the leading chiefs of his tribe, he received the same reply;—they had all been put to death already. 'Then of what use is life to me any longer? Leave me not in the tyrant's power who hath slain all that are dear to me. Slay me also, I entreat thee, that I may join them in their home. Here, take my sword, it is sharp; strike high and hard.' Thābit refused, and gave him over to another who, under 'Alī's orders, beheaded the aged man, but attended to his last request in obtaining freedom for his family. When told of his dying words, Moḥammad answered: '*Yea, he shall join them in their home,—the fire of Hell!*'

Moḥammad takes the captive Reiḥāna for his concubine

The butchery, begun in the morning, lasted all day, and continued by torchlight till the evening. Having thus drenched the market-place with the blood of seven or eight hundred victims,[1] and having given command for the earth to be smoothed over their remains, Moḥammad returned from the horrid spectacle to solace himself with the charms of Reiḥāna, whose husband and all her male relatives had just perished in the massacre. He invited her to be his wife; but she declined, and chose to remain (as indeed, having refused marriage, she had no alternative) his slave or concubine.[2] She also declined the summons to conversion, and continued in the Jewish faith, at which the Prophet was much

[1] The numbers are variously given as six hundred, seven hundred, eight hundred, and even nine hundred. If the number of arms enumerated among the spoil in a former note be correct, nine hundred would seem to be a moderate calculation for the adult males; but I have taken eight hundred as the number more commonly given.

[2] She is represented as saying, when he offered her marriage and the same privileges as his other wives: 'Nay, O Prophet! But let me remain as thy slave; this will be easier both for me and for thee.' By this is probably meant that she would have felt the strict seclusion as a married wife irksome to her. That she refused to abandon the faith of her fathers shows a more than usual independence of mind; and there may have been scenes of sorrow and aversion in her poor widowed heart, which tradition is too one-sided to hand down, or which indeed tradition may have never known. She died A.H. 632, a year before Mohammad himself.

concerned. It is said, however, that she afterwards embraced Islām. She did not many years survive her unhappy fate.

The women and children sold as slaves in Nejd

The booty was divided into four classes—lands, chattels, cattle, and slaves; and Moḥammad took a fifth of each. There were (besides the little children who counted with their mothers) a thousand captives; from his share of these, Moḥammad made certain presents to his friends of slave girls and female servants. The rest of the women and children he sent to be sold among the Bedawi tribes of Nejd, in exchange for horses and arms in the service of the State; for he kept steadily in view the advantage of raising a body of efficient cavalry. The remaining property was divided amongst the 3,000 soldiers of Medīna, to the highest bidders among whom the women were also sold.[1]

Notice of these events in Ḳor'ān

We are told that three or four men of the doomed tribe saved their lives, their families, and property by embracing Islām, probably before the siege began. No doubt the whole tribe might have, on the same terms, bought their safety. But they remained firm, and may be counted as martyrs to their faith.

The siege of Medīna, and the massacre of the Beni Ḳoreiẓa, are noticed, and the Disaffected bitterly reproached for their cowardice before the besieging army, in a passage revealed shortly after, and recited by Moḥammad, as was customary, from the pulpit;—

Sūra xxxiii. 9 ff.

O ye that believe! Call to mind the favour of God unto you, when Hosts came against you, and WE sent upon them a tempest and Hosts which ye saw not; and God beholdeth that which ye do;—when they came at you from above you, and from beneath, and when the sight was confused, and the hearts reached to the throat, and ye imagined of God strange imaginations. There were the Faithful tried and made to tremble violently. And when the Disaffected said, and they in whose hearts is a disease said, *God and His Prophet have promised only a delusion*:—And when a Party amongst them said:—*O men of Yathrib*

[1] Moḥammad (Ka'b's assassin) said that, being mounted, his share was three females with their children, worth forty-five golden pieces; the whole booty at the prize valuation would thus be 40,000 dīnārs. Moḥammad sold a number of the State slaves to 'Othmān and 'Abd ar-Raḥmān, who made a good speculation therefrom. They divided them into old and young. 'Othmān took the old, and found as he expected much money on their persons. Large sums were obtained from the Jews of Kheibar and other places for the ransom of such of the women and children as they were interested in.

there is no security for you, wherefore retire; and a part of them asked
leave of the Prophet to depart, saying, *Our houses are without protection;*
and they were not without protection, but they desired only to escape :—
And if an entrance had been effected amongst them (by the enemy) from
some adjacent quarter, and they had been invited to desert, they had
surely consented thereto; then they had not remained in the same, but
for a little. And verily they had heretofore covenanted with God, that
they would not turn their backs. Say,—Flight will not profit you, were
ye to flee from death and slaughter; and if ye did, ye would enjoy this
life but for a little. . . . Verily God knoweth those amongst you that v. 18
turn others aside, and such as say to their brethren,—*Come hither to us;*
and they go not to the battle excepting for a little. Covetous are they
towards you. But when fear cometh, thou mayest see them looking
towards thee, their eyes rolling, like unto one that is overshadowed with
death. Then, when the fear hath gone, they attack thee with sharp
tongues, covetous of the choicest of the spoil. They thought that the
Confederates[1] would not depart. And if the Confederates should come
(again), they would wish themselves away amongst the Bedawīn, asking
tidings of you. And if they were amongst you, they would not fight,
excepting a little. . . . And when the Believers saw the Confederates, v. 22
they said,—*This is what God and His Apostle promised us, and God and*
His Apostle have spoken the Truth. And it only increased their faith v. 24
and submission. . . . Verily God is forgiving and merciful. And God
drave back the heathen in their rage. They obtained no advantage.
And God sufficeth for the Believers in battle. He is strong and mighty.

And He hath caused to descend from their strongholds the Jews that assisted them. And he struck terror into their hearts. A part ye slaughtered, and a part ye took into captivity. And He hath made you to inherit their land, and their habitations, and their wealth, and a land which ye had not trodden upon; and God is over all things powerful.

Moḥammads' position greatly improved

In reviewing these transactions, it is evident that the position of Moḥammad was now greatly improved in strength and influence. The whole weight of Ḳoreish and of the Bedawi tribes, with all their mighty preparations, had been successfully repelled, and that with hardly any loss. The entire defence of Medīna, by tacit consent, had been conducted by Moḥammad as its Chief; and notwithstanding the ill-concealed disaffection of some of the inhabitants, he was now the acknowledged Ruler, as well as Prophet, of the city. The negotiation with 'Oyeina was, no doubt, a proof of weakness at the moment, and distrust in his own cause; but, fortunately for him, it was hardly entered upon when, by the firmness of the two Sa'ds, it was broken off; and the episode was lost sight of afterwards in the signal success of the defence.

[1] Ḳoreish and their allies.

Effect of massacre of the Beni Ḳoreiẓa on Moḥammad's position

The fate of the Beni Ḳoreiẓa removed the last remnant of open opposition, political or religious, from the immediate neighbourhood of Medīna; and though the bloody deed did not at the time escape hostile criticism, yet it struck so great a terror into the hearts of all, and the authority of the Prophet was already invested with so mysterious and supernatural a sanction, that no one dared openly impugn it. The ostensible grounds upon which he proceeded were political, for as yet he did not profess to *force* men to join Islām, or to punish them for not embracing it. It may be admitted that a sufficient *casus belli* had arisen. The compact with the Beni Ḳoreiẓa indeed was weak and precarious. Moḥammad's policy towards the Jews, from a period shortly after his arrival at Medīna, had been severe and oppressive; he had attacked and expatriated the other two tribes on very doubtful grounds; he had caused the assassination of several Jews in such a manner as to create universal distrust and alarm; after the murder of Ka'b and the incautious permission at the moment given to slaughter the Jews indiscriminately, he himself felt that the existing treaty had been practically set aside, and, to restore confidence, he had entered into a new compact.[1] All these circumstances must plead against the strength of obligation which bound the Beni Ḳoreiẓa to his cause. They had, moreover, stood by the second contract at a time when they might fairly have set it aside and joined the Beni an-Naḍīr. That they now hearkened to the overtures of Ḳoreish, through a singular want of prudence and foresight, was no more than Moḥammad might have expected. Still the Beni Ḳoreiẓa had joined his enemies at a critical period, and he had now a sufficient cause for warring against them. He had, furthermore, fair grounds of political necessity for requiring them perhaps to quit altogether a vicinity where they must have continued a dangerous nucleus of disaffection, and possibly an encouragement for renewed attack. We might even concede that the conduct of their leaders amounted to treason against the city, and warranted a severe retribution. But the indiscriminate slaughter of eight hundred men, and the subjugation of the women and children of the whole tribe to slavery, cannot be recognised otherwise than as an act of monstrous cruelty. The plea of divine

[1] See p. 249 f.

ratification or command may allay the scruples of the Muslim; but it will be summarily rejected by those who call to mind that the same authority was now habitually produced for personal ends, and for the justification even of questionable actions. In short, the butchery of the Beni Ḳoreiẓa casts an indelible blot upon the life of Moḥammad.

Death-bed of Sa'd ibn Mo'ādh

Before closing this chapter, I will follow to its end the career of Sa'd ibn Mo'ādh.[1] After delivering himself of the bloody decree, he was conducted back upon his ass to Rufeida's tent. But the excitement was fatal to him; the wound burst forth anew. Moḥammad hastened to the side of his bed; embracing him, he placed the dying man's head upon his knee and prayed thus: *O Lord! Verily Sa'd hath laboured in thy service. He hath believed in thy Prophet, and hath fulfilled his covenant. Wherefore do thou, O Lord, receive his spirit with the best reception wherewith thou receivest a departing soul!'* Sa'd heard the words, and in faltering accents whispered: 'Peace be on thee, O Apostle of God!—Verily I testify that thou art the Prophet of the Lord.' When he had breathed his last, they carried to his home the corpse.[2] After the forenoon prayer, Moḥammad proceeded to join the burial. He reached the house as they were washing the body. The mother of Sa'd, weeping loudly, gave vent to her grief in plaintive Arab verse. They chid her for reciting poetry on such an occasion; but Moḥammad interposed, saying: 'Leave her thus alone; all other poets lie but she.' The bier was then carried forth, and Moḥammad helped to bear it for the first thirty or forty yards. Notwithstanding

His burial

[1] Ibn Hishām, p. 697 f.; Al-Wāḳidi, p. 221 ff.

[2] The tale of Sa'd is surrounded with supernatural associations. For instance, when Moḥammad went to be present at the washing of the body, he walked so rapidly that the people could scarcely keep up with him; 'you would have thought the thongs of their sandals would have broken, and their mantles fallen from their shoulders, they hurried so fast.' When they asked why he hastened so, he replied: 'Verily, I feared lest the Angels should have reached the house before us, as they came before us to Ḥanẓala;'—alluding to the burial of the latter, and the supposed washing of his corpse by the angels (p. 265). Then there are numerous legends about the angels crowding into the room where the corpse was laid out, and one of them spreading out his wing for Moḥammad to sit upon. These traditions have grown out of the reply of Moḥammad to the Disaffected, viz., that the bier was light, *because supported by a crowd of Angels.*

that Sa'd was so large and corpulent, the bier was reported to be marvellously light. The Disaffected said: 'We have never heard of a corpse lighter in the bier than that of Sa'd: know ye why this is? It is because of his judgment against the Beni Ḳoreiẓa.'[1] Moḥammad, hearing the rash remark, turned aside its point by a mysterious explanation which was eagerly caught up by his followers: 'The angels are carrying the bier,' he said, 'therefore it is light in your hands. Verily the throne on high doth vibrate for Sa'd, and the portals of heaven are opened, and he is attended by seventy thousand angels that never trod the earth before.' The long procession, with Moḥammad at its head, wended its way slowly to the burial-ground. When they reached the spot, four men descended into the grave, and lowered the body into its place. Just then Moḥammad changed colour, and his countenance betrayed strong emotion. But he immediately recovered himself, and gave praise to God. Then he three times uttered the *Tekbīr*, 'Great is the Lord!' and the whole concourse, which filled the burial-ground to overflowing, took up the words, until the place re-echoed with the shout. Some of the people asked him concerning his change of colour, and he explained it thus:—'At that moment the grave became strait for your comrade, and the sides thereof closed in upon him. Verily, if any one could have escaped the straitening of the tomb it had been Sa'd. Then the Lord gave him expansion therein.' The mother of Sa'd drew near, desiring to look into the grave, and they forbade her. But Moḥammad said: 'Suffer her to look.' So she looked in, before the body was covered over. As she gazed on the remains of her son, she said: 'I commit thee unto the Lord'; and Moḥammad

[1] The death of Sa'd followed so immediately on his sanguinary judgment, that the Disaffected coupled the two together. To avert this inference, tradition tells us that Sa'd had prayed thus: 'O Lord! If thou hast in store any further fighting with Ḳoreisḥ, then preserve me to take part in it: but if thou hast put an end to their warring against thy Prophet, then take me unto thyself!' which when he prayed, he was to all appearance well; the wound presenting only a cicatrised ring. But shortly after he was carried to the tent, and died. Although, in fact, there was hardly any more fighting with Ḳoreish after this date, yet the prayer is evidently an afterthought. For at the time it was quite uncertain whether Medīna might not again be besieged by Ḳoreish, in proof of which see Sūra xxxiii. 20.

comforted her. Then he went aside and sat down near the grave, while they built it over with bricks, and filled in the earth. When the whole was levelled, and the tomb sprinkled with water, the Prophet again drew near, and, standing over the grave, prayed once more for the departed chief. Then he turned, and retired to his home.

SŪRAS REVEALED DURING THE FIRST FIVE YEARS OF MOḤAMMAD'S RESIDENCE AT MEDĪNA

We have now reached a stage at which it may be useful once more to pause, review the Revelations given forth by Moḥammad during the early years of the Hijra, and consider the points in which they illustrate his life and the principles of Islām. **Review of portions of Ḳor'ān revealed at Medīna**

The people most prominently addressed in the first Medīna Sūras are the Jews. Like the closing Sūras at Mecca, these abound in Jewish fable and legend, based upon the Old Testament and rabbinical tradition. The marvellous interpositions of the Almighty in behalf of His people of old are recounted with the object of stirring up the neighbouring Jewish tribes to gratitude, and of inciting them to publish unreservedly the evidence which their Scriptures contained in substantiation of his claims. They are appealed to in language such as this:— **Moḥammad calls on Jews to bear evidence in his favour**

> Ye children of Israel! Remember my favour wherewith I have favoured you, and have preferred you above all the world. And fear the day whereon no soul shall at all make satisfaction for another soul; nor shall intercession be accepted therefrom: neither shall compensation be received from it,—and they shall not be helped. * * * O children of Israel! Fulfil my Covenant: so will I fulfil your Covenant. And believe in that (*i.e.* the Ḳor'ān) which I reveal attesting the Revelation which is with you; and be not the first unbelievers therein; and sell not my signs for a small price: and let Me be your fear. And clothe not the Truth with falsehood; neither conceal the Truth while ye know it. Set ye up prayer, and give alms; and bow down (in prayer) with them that bow themselves down. What! will ye command men to do justice, and forget your own selves, while yet ye read the Scripture? What! do ye not understand? **Sūra ii. 44 f., also 116 f.** **v. 38 f.**

But, excepting a few, the Jews, as we have seen, refused to acknowledge the Arabian prophet; he had none of the signs of the Messiah, who was to come of the seed of Jacob

On their refusal he changes style of address to rebuke and reproach

and David, and not from amongst a strange people the progeny of Ishmael. They did not object to enter into a treaty with him of amity and good neighbourhood, but they scorned to bow to his spiritual pretensions. Their refusal was set down to envy and malice. The Jews could not brook that the prophetic dignity should pass from themselves to another people; they well knew the prophecies regarding Islām; but they stifled their convictions, suppressed the plain declarations of their Scriptures, and perverted their meaning by 'dislocating' the context, or producing false glosses of the Rabbins. Their hearts were hardened, and every avenue to conviction closed. It was in vain to seek for their conversion to Islām, for they had already shown themselves proof against the Word of God as revealed in the Old Testament. They were following in the steps of their stiff-necked forefathers who slew the prophets, departed from the true God, and sought out inventions of their own creation. As an example of such passages which abound at this period, take the following:—

Sūra ii. 81 And verily WE gave Moses the Scriptures, and WE made Apostles to
follow after him; and WE gave JESUS son of Mary evident miracles, and
WE strengthened him with the Holy Spirit. Wherefore is it that so
often as an Apostle cometh unto you with that which ye desire not, ye
are puffed up; and some ye reject as liars, and some ye put to death?
v 83 * * * And when a Book (*i.e.* the Ḳor'ān) cometh unto them from God,
attesting that Scripture which is with them,—and truly they had aforetime been praying for assistance against the Unbelievers,[1]—yet when there came unto them that which they recognised, they disbelieved the same. Wherefore the curse of God is on the Unbelievers. Evil is that for which they have sold themselves, to reject what God hath revealed, out of rebellion against God for sending down a portion of His favour upon such of His servants as He pleaseth.[2] Wherefore they have incurred wrath upon wrath; and for the Unbelievers there is prepared an ignominious punishment. And when it is said unto them, *Believe in that which is sent down*, they say, *We believe in that which God hath sent down to us;* and they disbelieve in that which came after it, although it be the Truth attesting that Scripture which is with them. Say,—Why, therefore, have ye killed the Prophets of God aforetime, if ye are Believers? And verily Moses came with evident Signs; then ye took the Calf thereupon, and became transgressors, &c.

---

[1] That is, when oppressed by the Aus and Khazraj they used to pray for the coming of Messiah to vanquish them.

[2] *I.e.* envious at the gift of prophecy being shared by an Arab people.

This denunciation of the Jews' malice, unbelief, and perversion of the truth, naturally aroused their hatred. They no longer put faith in the assertion of Moḥammad that he was come to 'attest their Scripture,' and re-establish the divine doctrines it contained. The hope, once fondly cherished, that, through their holy Oracles which he professed to revere and follow, he would be guided towards the Truth, they now saw to be fallacious. Political inferiority, indeed, compelled them to disguise their hatred; but their real feelings transpired in various ways, and among others in expressions of double meaning, which greatly displeased and affronted Moḥammad:— Jews thus stirred up to hatred of Moḥammad

Of the Jews there are that pervert words from their places, saying, *We have heard and disobeyed*, and *Hear without hearing*, and (RĀ'INA) *Look upon us*, twisting their tongues and reviling the Faith.[1] But if they had said, *We have heard and obeyed*, and *Hearken*, and (UNẒURNA) *Look upon us*, it had been better for them; but God hath cursed them for their Unbelief; wherefore they shall not believe, excepting a few. O ye to whom the Scripture hath been given, believe in What we have sent down, attesting that (*i.e.* the Old Testament) which is with you,—before We deface your countenances, turning the face backwards; or curse them as We cursed those that broke the Sabbath. Sūra iv. 48 f.

And two or three years later:—

O ye that believe! Take not as your friends those who make a laughing-stock and a sport of your Religion, from amongst the people of the former Scripture and the Infidels: and fear God, if ye be Believers. . . . Say,—Ye people of the Book! Do ye keep aloof from us otherwise than because we believe in God, and in that which hath been sent down to us, and in that which hath been sent down before, and because the greater part of you are evil? Say,—Shall I announce unto you what is worse than that, as to the reward which is with God? He whom God hath cursed, and against whom He is wroth, and hath made of them Apes and Swine,[2] these, and the worshippers of Idols, are in an evil case. Sūra v. 62 ff.
* * * Thou shalt see multitudes of them running greedily after wicked- v. 67
ness and injustice, and eating what is forbidden. Alas for that which they work! Wherefore do their Rabbins and their Priests restrain them not from uttering wickedness, and eating that which is forbidden. Alas for that which they commit! The Jews say, *The hand of God is tied up.*

---

[1] Terms of contumely in Hebrew, but so pronounced as to appear innocent in Arabic. [There seems to be a reference to the word Raca in Matt. v. 22.]

[2] Alluding to the legendary punishment inflicted on the Israelites who broke the Sabbath day, in turning their faces backwards, and making monkeys and swine of them.

Nay, their own hands are tied up, and they are cursed for what they say. But His hands are both stretched out. That which hath been revealed to thee from thy Lord shall but increase rebellion and impiety in many of them. We have cast among them enmity and hatred, until the day of Judgment. So often as they shall kindle the fire of war, God shall extinguish the same; and they shall set themselves to do wickedness in the Earth. And God loveth not the wicked doers.

Jews accused of encouraging idolatry at Mecca

In another passage the Jews are even accused of encouraging Ḳoreish to continue in idolatry by representing that it was preferable to the doctrine of Moḥammad:—

Sūra iv. 47 ff.

Hast thou not seen those to whom a portion of the Scripture hath been given? They believe in false gods and idols. They say to the Unbelievers,—*These are better directed in the right way than those that believe.* These are they whom God hath cursed; and for him that God curseth, thou shalt find no helper. Shall *they*, indeed, have any portion in the Kingdom, since, if they had, they would not part unto men with the least iota thereof? Do they envy men that which God hath given them of His bounty? And Verily WE gave unto the house of Abraham the Scripture, and Wisdom; and WE gave them a great Kingdom. And there is amongst them such as believe in him (Moḥammad); and there is that turneth aside from him. But the raging fire of hell will suffice for such. Verily, they that reject our Signs, WE will surely cast them into the fire. So often as their skins are burned, WE will change for them other skins, that they may fully taste the torment. For God is mighty and wise. They that believe and do good works, We shall introduce them into gardens with rivers running beneath them; they shall abide therein for ever. And there shall they have pure Wives; and WE shall lead them into grateful shades.

Removal of Jews from the scene

Eventually, as we have seen, Moḥammad did not confine his communications with the Jewish tribes of Medīna to simple threats of divine wrath, but himself inflicted condign punishment upon them, till by exile and slaughter they were all removed from the scene. Such was fast becoming the spirit of Islām. Judaism would not yield to its pretensions. And Moḥammad, notwithstanding his respect for other creeds, the still reiterated assurance that 'he was only a public preacher, and his guarantee that 'there should be no constraint in Religion,' could not brook the profession of any tenets opposed to his claims. The first step had now been taken for sweeping from the Peninsula every creed but that of the Ḳor'ān.

The disappearance of the Jews is followed by a corresponding change in the material of the Ḳor'ān. The Revelations of Moḥammad formed in no respect an abstract and systematic compilation. The Ḳor'ān is purely concrete in its origin and progress. It grew up and formed itself, both as regards its dogmas and its social code, out of the circumstances and sentiments of the day. Hence, the necessity for referring to Jewish Scripture and history having passed away with the disappearance of the Jews themselves, we have no longer in the later Sūras those allusions to the Old Testament and repetition of Biblical stories and legends which so teemed throughout the Oracle's middle stage. The few notices which hereafter occur bear as much upon the Christian as upon the Jewish record. Both are still spoken of, though with extreme infrequency, yet with veneration and respect. And, as already stated, there is nowhere to be found throughout the Ḳor'ān any imputation whatever against either the authority or the genuineness of the one or of the other. The occasion for their mention having died out, they pass into oblivion.

Followed by discontinuance in Ḳor'ān of Jewish legends and reference to Scriptures

But Scriptures still referred to with reverence

I have drawn attention to the Ḳor'ān as a medium for the publication of what we might call *general orders*, such as passages which touch on victory or defeat, rebuke backwardness and cowardice, or applaud constancy and courage. But it was not merely in respect of military affairs, as the reader will have observed, that the Revelation contains comments and commands. Scattered throughout its Sūras, we have, to some extent, the archives of a theocratic government in all its departments. The conduct of the Disaffected, the treatment of Allies, the formation of treaties, the acceptance of terms, and other political matters, not infrequently find a place among the heavenly messages. Liberality in contributing towards the expenses of war, the only object as yet requiring a public purse, is continually inculcated. The elements also of a code both civil and criminal are introduced. Punishments are specified, and legislation laid down for the tutelage of orphans, marriage, divorce, sales, bargains, wills, evidence, usury, and other similar concerns. Further, there are copious instructions for the guidance of the Believer in his private life; and special provisions, some of which I have quoted at length, regulating the intercourse of Moḥammad with his people, and with his own family. These all partake of the essential character of the Ḳor'ān, being in the form of a Revelation; and they ordinarily end with some such phrase

Ḳor'ān contains orders in all departments of theocratic government

as, 'God is knowing and wise'—'God is forgiving and merciful'—'Evil is the fate of the Transgressors,' &c., thus completing the rhythm, and investing the record with an inspired and oracular character. Throughout this, which may be styled the *administrative* portion of the Ḳor'ān, are interspersed as heretofore passages inculcating piety and virtue, denouncing infidelity and vice, and containing directions for social duties and religious ceremonies. In the exhortations and denunciations, the main change is that at first the Jews, and subsequently the Disaffected, now usurp almost entirely the place before occupied by the Idolaters of Mecca.

Though simple in habits, Moḥammad assumed regal power and dignity

The advancing power and dignity of Moḥammad may be traced in the reverence and submission prescribed in the Ḳor'ān as due to him. A kingly court was not in accord with the customs of the people, nor with the tastes and habits of Moḥammad himself. The artless life and simple dress and surroundings of an Arab chieftain were not departed from at Medīna; and it is this which, in vivid contrast with the state and luxury of his Successors, has induced tradition to cast around the Prophet's life an air of hardship and privation.[1]

[1] For example, we have stories such as the following. Moḥammad having hurt his hand, they carried him into his house, and placed him on a bed plaited with ropes of palm-fibre, and put under his head a pillow of leather stuffed with the same material. 'Omar, seeing the marks of the corded bedding on his side, wept aloud. On Moḥammad asking why he wept, he replied: 'Verily, I called to mind how the Chosroes and the Kaiser sit upon thrones of gold, and wear garments of silk and brocade; and thou art in this sad condition!' 'What 'Omar!' said the Prophet, art thou not content that *we* should have the portion of Futurity, and *they* the portion of this Life?' On another occasion, Moḥammad having risen from sleep with the marks of the matting on his side, 'Abdallah, his attendant, rubbed the place, and said: 'Let me, I pray thee, spread a soft covering for thee over this mat.' 'Not so,' replied Moḥammad; 'What have I to do with the comforts of this life? The world and I, what connection is there between us? Verily, the world is no otherwise than as a tree unto me; when the traveller hath rested under its shade, he passeth on.'

Notwithstanding anecdotes like these, exaggerated by strong contrast with the subsequent luxury of the Muslims, it is evident that Moḥammad had everything in abundance which he really desired, and which wealth or authority could procure. He would give a large price for his clothes: once he exchanged nineteen (others say seventeen) camels for a single dress, and he bought a mantle for eight golden pieces. He had a collyrium box, from which at bedtime he used to apply antimony to his

The misconception is manifest; for Moḥammad and his Companions enjoyed all that the resources of the land and plunder of their enemies could yield; and if they maintained plain and frugal habits, it was not from necessity, but because magnificence and pomp were foreign and distasteful. A row of modest houses, built of sun-dried brick, and covered in with rough palm-branches, the inner walls hung about with water-bags of leather for domestic use, formed a habitation for the Prophet and his wives far more desirable than the most splendid seraglio 'ceiled with cedar and painted with vermilion.' A mattress of date-fibre covered with leather was a luxury to the Arab incomparably greater than any stately 'bed of the wood of Lebanon, decked with tapestry.' The trappings of a royal camp would have ill comported with the grave simplicity of Moḥammad, while an ordinary nomad tent afforded him ample accommodation; and his bag, with ivory comb, toothpick, oil for his hair and antimony for his eyes, supplied all the comforts within the compass of an Arab's imagination. The luxurious and pampered courtiers of Damascus and Baghdad marvelled at the tales of their Prophet having mended his sandals, and of 'Omar having tended his own flock of goats, not reflecting that a more artificial state would have been at variance with everything around, and that the habits of threescore years had become a second life.

Honour and reverence paid to Moḥammad

His prerogatives

Nevertheless, in whatever constitutes real dignity and power, Moḥammad was not behind the most absolute Dictator, or pompous Sovereign. To him every dispute must be referred, and his word was law. On his appearance the assembly rose, and gave place to him and his chief Companions; the people were required to approach him reverently, to speak softly in his presence, and not to crowd around or

eyelids, saying that it made the sight more piercing, and caused the hair to grow. The Governor of Egypt sent him a crystal goblet; and either this, or another jug from which he drank, was set in silver. He had also a copper vase, which he used in bathing. He was very fond of perfumes, and indulged, as 'Ā'isha tells us, in 'men's scents,' *i.e.* in musk and ambergris; he used also to burn camphor on odoriferous wood, and enjoy the fragrant smell. Anas, his servant, says: 'We always used to know when Moḥammad had issued forth from his chamber by the sweet perfume that filled the air.'

Such were perhaps the only luxuries which, from his simple habits, he was able to appreciate.

throng him. They were not to visit his house unasked; and even when invited they must not linger long, or indulge familiarly in discourse with him. 'The calling of the Apostle was not to be as the calling of one Believer to the other;' it was to be implicitly heard and promptly obeyed. Those in attendance were not to leave without permission first received. His wives were withdrawn from the vulgar gaze; none might communicate directly or familiarly with them excepting their near relatives and domestic servants. The Prophet was the favourite of Heaven; the true Believer but followed the example of the heavenly hosts, and of God himself, when he invoked blessings upon him:—

Sūra xxxiii. 56 f.

Verily, God and His angels invoke blessings upon the Prophet. O ye that believe! do ye also invoke blessings upon him, and salute him with a reverential salutation. Verily, they that trouble God and His Apostle, God hath cursed them in this world, and in that which is to come: He hath prepared for them an ignominious punishment.

Special prerogatives; but no supernatural character asserted

The idea that he was *the Favourite of Heaven* may be the key to the peculiar privileges which he claimed, especially in his conjugal relations. Still, no supernatural character was assumed by Moḥammad. He did not differ from the former Prophets. Like other men he was mortal; and equally with them needed to pray to God for the pardon of his sins.

Irreverent manner in which weekly service at first observed

I have before observed that Moḥammad did not consecrate any day, like the Seventh, to religious Worship. On Friday, the day appointed for public prayer, business and merchandise might, after its conclusion, be transacted as much as on any other day. The weekly service, indeed, appears at first to have been treated with little respect. On a certain Friday, while Moḥammad discoursed from the Pulpit to a crowded assembly in the Mosque, the sound of drums announced the arrival of a Syrian caravan, when the greater part of his audience hurried forth to meet it, and left Moḥammad standing in the Pulpit nearly alone. Hence this passage:—

Sūra lxii. 9 f.

O ye that believe! When the call to Prayer is raised on the day of Assembly, then hasten to the commemoration of God, and leave off trafficking—that will be better for you, if ye knew it. And when the Prayers are ended, then disperse abroad, and seek (gain) from the favour of God, and make frequent mention of God, that ye may prosper When they see Merchandising or Sport, they break away, flocking thereto, and leaving thee standing; say, That which is with God is better than sport or merchandise; and God is the best Supporter.

Drunkenness common, till wine was forbidden

Elsewhere we find Moḥammad forbidding his followers to be present at prayer in a state of drunkenness: 'O ye that believe; draw not nigh unto Prayers, while ye are drunken, until ye can understand that which ye say.' This injunction, being connected with another of a general nature,[1] may be viewed as additional evidence of the lax manner in which the devotions of the Muslims were at the first performed, as well as of the prevalence of intemperance. In a previous passage the use of Wine had been discouraged, though not prohibited, on the ground that it was productive of greater injury than good:—

Sūra ii. 216.

> They will ask thee concerning Wine, and Casting of lots. Say,—In both there is great evil, and also advantages, to Mankind; but the evil of them is greater than the advantages of them.

But Moḥammad at last perceived that the sanctions of Islām were too weak to enforce a middle course, and that the imposition of entire abstinence was the only means by which he could check intemperance. The command against the use of wine was issued in the fourth year of the Hijra, during the siege (it is said) of the Beni an-Naḍīr, and is as follows:—

Sūra v. 93 f.

> O ye that believe! Verily Wine, and the Casting of lots, and Images, and Divining-arrows, are an abomination from amongst the works of Satan: Shun them, therefore, that ye may prosper. Verily, Satan seeketh that he may cast amongst you enmity and hatred through Wine and Games of chance, and hinder you from the remembrance of God and from Prayer. Will ye not, then, refrain? Obey God, and obey the Apostle; and beware! For if ye turn back,—Verily, our Apostle's duty is but to deliver his Message publicly.

Influence of Judaism still maintained in moulding institutions

Jewish influence may still be traced in moulding the institutions of Moḥammad. Usury is forbidden. The criminal code follows largely the Law of retaliation. Ceremonial purification before prayer is enjoined, and in the absence of water sand may be used as a substitute. An oath something resembling the curse of jealousy is permitted to a wife suspected by her husband of infidelity. And generally in the relations established between the sexes, a considerable degree of similarity may be traced to the injunctions of the Pentateuch.

As in other matters, so in those referring to Marriage and Divorce, instead of general principles, we have particular and

[1] *I.e.* ceremonial ablution.

Rules regarding marriage, divorce, and sexual relations

detailed instruction. Apart altogether from the tenor of these precepts, the language in which they are expressed is offensive to the European ear. Making every allowance for the rudeness of speech and sentiment current in Arabia, much remains that cannot be so excused. Further, the legislation of the Ḳor'ān on relations between the sexes has given birth to endless volumes, by Jurists and Theologians, of interpretation, illustration, construction, corollary, supplement, which cannot but have a deteriorating effect upon Moḥammadan students of the law. To define the line between the forbidden and the lawful, ingenuity and labour have been expended lavishly in describing and solving cases the very mention of which is repugnant to modesty, in drawing elaborate distinctions and demonstrating points of casuistry within a domain of thought which cannot even be approached without moral injury and contamination. The Arabic language, as moulded by the system which grew out of the precepts of Islām, is itself evidence of this evil,[1] for which, at the first remove, the Ḳor'ān itself is responsible.

Evil engendered thereby in Muslim literat

Four wives allowed, and any number of slave-girls

The number of lawful wives is restricted to four; but these may at any moment be divorced at the caprice and by the simple word of the husband, and others substituted in their stead. As regards female slaves with whom (irrespective of his four wives) a Muslim may, without antecedent ceremony or any guarantee of continuance, cohabit, there is no limit. Female slavery, being a condition necessary to the legality of this indulgence, will hardly ever be put down, without alien pressure, by any Muslim community. As a general rule slaves are in Muslim families maintained in comfort; but this is by indulgence, and not of right.[2] They are liable to be treated as an inferior and degraded class. Under the same restrictions as married wives, the female slave is expressly excluded from any title to conjugal privilege. She is the toy of her master, sported with at his pleasure, or cast

[1] This will be painfully evident from a glance into some of our Arabic dictionaries. As to the 'Ḥadīth,' I altogether fail to understand how any translator can justify himself in rendering into English much that is contained in the Sections on marriage, purification, divorce, and female slavery.

[2] At the Farewell pilgrimage, as we shall see, Moḥammad enjoined that slaves should be fed and clothed as their masters; and if they misbehave, they are to be sold and not tormented.

unheeded aside. The one redeeming feature is that, when once a slave-girl has borne a child to her master, she cannot be sold, and at his death obtains her freedom.[1] The child of the slave is also as legitimate as that of her married sister.[2]

Unmarried women, how affected by this system

It has been asserted that the institutions of Moḥammad have tended to elevate and improve the state of Woman. Yet, excepting in so far as she necessarily shares in the general elevation and improvement introduced by a purer religion and more spiritual worship,[3] it is very doubtful whether, in married life, her position has not been rendered more dependent than in Arab life it was before. I do not speak of unmarried and widowed females; for, if we put aside the Veil and the depressing influence which the constraint and thraldom of the married state has exercised upon *the sex at large*, the unmarried free woman has nothing to complain of. And, in one particular, viz. the inheritance by the son of his father's wives, she was delivered by Moḥammad from a gross and intolerable abuse. No free woman can be forced, under the code of Islām, to marry against her will; and, so long as single, she is mistress of her actions.

Married women and female slaves occupy inferior position

But in respect of the married state (which in the East embraces practically the whole sex during the greater part of their lives), the condition of woman is that of a dependent,

[1] This is not provided for in the Ḳor'ān, but rests on the precedent of Moḥammad, who freed his own slave-girl Mary, on her bearing a son to him. Such a slave is called *Um el-Weled*, or 'Mother of the child.'

[2] On the laxity of morals in connection with female slavery, I quote again from the Moḥammadan Princess who lately visited Mecca. Speaking of the great numbers of African and Georgian slaves, the Begum of Bhopal wrote: 'Some of the women are taken in marriage, and after that on being sold again, they receive from their masters a divorce, and are sold in their houses; that is to say, they are sent to the purchaser from their master's house on receipt of payment, and are not exposed for sale in the Dakkah (slave market); they are only *married* when purchased for the first time. * * * When the poorer people buy slaves, they keep them for themselves, and change them every year as one would replace old things by new.'—(*Pilgrimage to Mecca*. Translated by Mrs W. Osborne, 1870.) Such, according to a shrewd observer, are the results of female slavery in the holiest city of Islām.

[3] The notion that the female sex is overlooked in the rewards of the future life arose, apparently, from their not having been provided with indulgences similar to those promised to the other sex. Not only is the idea of their exclusion from Paradise at variance with the whole tenor of the Ḳor'ān, but it is contradicted by express passages.

destined for the service of her lord, liable to be cast off without the assignment of any reason and without the notice of a single hour. While the husband possesses the power of divorce, absolute, immediate, unquestioned, no privilege of a corresponding nature has been reserved for the Wife.[1] She hangs on, however unwilling, neglected or superseded, the slave of her lord,—if such be his will. When divorced, she can, indeed, claim her dower,—her *hire*, as in too plain language it is called; this, however, is but a poor security against capricious taste, and in the case of female slaves, even that is wanting. The power of divorce is not the only power that may be arbitrarily exercised by the tyrannical husband: authority to confine and to beat his wives is vested in his discretion:—

Sūra iv. 38

Men stand above Women, because of the superiority which God hath conferred on one of them over the other, and because of that which they expend of their wealth. Wherefore let the good Women be obedient, preserving their purity in secret, in that wherein God preserveth them. But such as ye may fear disobedience or provocation from, rebuke them, and put them away in separate apartments, and chastise them. But, if they be obedient unto you, seek not against them an excuse for severity; verily God is lofty and great.

Position of married women impaired by Islām

The 'exchanging of one wife for another' (that is, the divorcing of one in order to marry another) is recognised in the Ḳor'ān, with only this caution, that the dower stipulated at marriage be given in full to her that is put away.[2] Thus restrained and secluded, liable at the caprice or passion of the moment to be turned adrift, it would be hard to say that the position of a wife was improved by the code of Moḥammad. Indeed, it may be doubted whether she was not possessed of more freedom, and exercised a healthier, and more legiti-

[1] The Ḳor'ān does not contemplate anywhere the contingency of divorce being claimed by the wife. The idea of any independent right of the kind was foreign to Moḥammad's notions of the position of the sex. The Moḥammadan doctors have, indeed, determined that under a few rare contingencies divorce may be demanded; but they are so exceptional as hardly to deserve notice.

[2] 'And if ye be desirous to exchange one wife in place of another wife, and ye have given one of them a talent, then take not away anything therefrom. What! will ye take it away falsely, and commit an open sin: And how can ye take it away, seeing that one of you hath gone in unto the other, and they have received from you a firm covenant?'—Sūra iv. 24 f.

mate influence, under the pre-existing institutions of Arabia.

Divorce thrice repeated irrevocable. Revolting condition on which alone original marriage can be reverted to

In the conditions of Divorce, there is one which (much as I might desire) cannot be passed over in silence. A husband may twice divorce his wife, and each time receive her back again. But when it has been thrice repeated, the divorce is, with a hateful exception, irreversible. However unjust or injurious the action, how much soever the result of passion or caprice, however it may affect the interests not only of an innocent wife, but also of her innocent children, however desirous the husband may be of undoing the wrong,—the decision cannot be recalled; the divorced wife can return to her husband but on one condition, and that is that she shall first be married to another, and after cohabitation be again divorced.[1] The tone of Moḥammadan manners may be imagined from the functions of the *temporary* husband hired to legalise re-marriage with a thrice-divorced wife, having passed into a proverb.[2] Such flagrant breach of decency,

[1] 'And if he (a third time) divorce her, she shall not be lawful unto him after that, until she shall have married a husband other than he; and if the latter divorce her, then there shall be no sin in the two that they again return to each other, if they think that they can observe the limits appointed by God. These are the ordinances of God, which He manifesteth to people that understand.'—Sūra ii. 230.

[2] I quote from Burckhardt:—'*A thousand lovers, rather than one mostahel.* Many lovers or gallants cause less shame to a woman than one Mostahel (*i.e.* husband procured for the occasion). According to the Muslim law, a person who has (thrice) divorced his wife cannot re-marry her until she has been married to some other man, who becomes her legitimate husband, cohabits with her for one night, and divorces her next morning; after which the first husband may again possess her as his wife. Such cases are of frequent occurrence—as men in the haste of anger often divorce their wives by the simple expression (*I divorce thee*), which (thrice repeated) cannot be retracted. In order to regain his wife a man hires (at no inconsiderable rate) some peasant, whom he chooses from the ugliest that can be found in the streets. A temporary husband of this kind is called Mostahel, and is generally most disgusting to the wife.'—(*Arabic Proverbs*, p. 21.) Some commentators hold the practice to be illegal; whether legal or not, I gladly believe that it is far from being so frequent as here represented. But its existence is undoubted; and it has existed, in a more or less revolting form, ever since the verse was revealed. A case is mentioned by tradition in which Moḥammad himself insisted on cohabitation with another husband, before married life could be returned to, and that in language which, one may hope, prurient tradition has fabricated for him. Tradition and

such cruel violation of the modesty of an unoffending wife, may be an abuse the full extent of which was not at the time contemplated by Moḥammad; but it is not the less an abuse for which, as a direct result of the unnatural and revolting provision framed by him, Moḥammad is responsible.[1]

Warlike spirit of Ḳor'ān

The warlike spirit of the Sūras of this period has been perhaps sufficiently illustrated in the preceding chapters. I may here just refer to one passage which is peculiarly demonstrative of the lust of plunder which had been stirred up, and which (so natural was it to the Arab) the Prophet soon found it difficult to restrain within expedient bounds. Only those could be lawfully slain and plundered who were *disbelievers* in his mission; but so insatiable had the thirst for spoil become, that cases now occurred of Muslims slaying others who had made profession of the Moḥammadan faith, on pretext that they were insincere Believers. Stringent prohibition was required to guard against this abuse. Whoever trifled with the life of any one professing Islām, did so at the peril of his soul. After prescribing the penalty or penance for killing a Muslim unintentionally, the ordinance proceeds:—

Sūra iv. 95 f.

But whosoever killeth a Believer wilfully, his reward shall be Hell,—for ever therein. God shall be wroth with him, and shall curse him; He hath prepared for him a great punishment. O ye that believe! When ye go forth fighting in the way of God, rightly discriminate, and say not to him that saluteth you,[2] *Thou art not a Believer*,—seeking the

---

law books abound with fetid commentaries illustrative of this subject, and with checks against the intermediate marriage and cohabitation being merely nominal.

It must not be forgotten that all the immorality of speech and action connected with this shameful institution, and the outrage done to female virtue (not necessarily for any fault of the wretched wife, but the passion and thoughtlessness of the husband himself), has arisen solely out of the verse quoted above. It is a sorry excuse that Moḥammad wished thereby to check inconsiderate divorce: a good object is not to be sought for by such evil means.

[1] See Deut. xxiv. 4: 'Her former husband, which sent her away, may not take her again to be his wife after that she is defiled; *for that is an abomination before the Lord.*'

[2] *I.e.* with the salutation peculiar to Islām (*as-salamu 'aleikum*), which was held equivalent to professing oneself a Muslim. Abu Bekr, in sending forth expeditions against the rebel tribes, on the same principle, made it a strict injunction that wherever the Azān for prayer was heard, attack was to be suspended.—*Caliphate*, p. 17.

transitory things of this present life,—whilst with God there is great spoil. And such were ye yourselves aforetime, but God had favour towards you. Wherefore carefully discriminate, for God is attentive to that which ye do.

Though Mecca with its heathen inhabitants has now faded in the distance, and Ḳoreish are hardly ever referred to but for their hostile inroads, still we find occasional passages, after the old Meccan style, in reprobation of Idolatry, and menace of the city 'which had cast out its Prophet.' Polytheism and Idolatry are denounced as the only unpardonable sins. The tone of defiance becomes bolder and at times exulting. Moḥammad and his people are 'to fight till opposition shall cease, and the Religion becometh God's alone.' Until this glorious consummation, 'they are not to faint, neither invite to peace.' A complete and speedy victory is promised. God is the stronger, and will prevail: Islām shall shortly be established triumphantly. Such as withdraw from Mecca, and rally around the standard of Moḥammad while the struggle yet impends, shall have a merit superior far to the merit of those who join it after opposition shall have been beaten down. The waverers, who, though persuaded of the truth, cannot make up their minds to abandon Mecca, are told that their excuse of inability will not be accepted of God;—'their habitation shall be Hell, an evil journey thither!' But a word of comfort is added for 'the weak,' withheld by real helplessness from leaving Mecca. The rescue of such from their unhappy position is adduced as a powerful motive why their more fortunate brethren at Medīna should fight bravely in the cause:—

References to Ḳoreish and to idolatry

Waverers threatened

Weak believers at Mecca comforted

Sūra iv. 76 f.

Fight in the way of God, ye that sell the present Life for that which is to come. Whosoever fighteth in the way of God, whether he be slain or be victorious, We shall surely give him a great Reward. And what aileth you that ye fight not in the way of God, and for the Weak amongst the men and women and children, who say, 'O Lord! Deliver us out of this City, whose people are oppressors; and grant us from thyself a Protector, and grant us from thyself a Defender.'

From these numerous quotations (so numerous, I fear, as to have been irksome to the reader) it will be evident that the style of the Ḳor'ān, though varying greatly in force and vigour, has for the most part lost the stamp of vivid imagination and poetic fire which marks the earlier Sūras. It

Style tame, but with occasional touches of poetic fire

becomes, as a rule, tame and ordinary both in thought and language. Occasionally, indeed, we still find traces of the former spirit. Here for instance the Deity is described in a passage [called the Throne verse] of which the followers of Moḥammad are justly proud :—

Sūra ii. 256 God! There is no God but He: the Living, the Eternal. Slumber doth not overtake Him, neither Sleep. To Him belongeth all that is in the Heavens and in the Earth. Who is he that shall intercede before Him, excepting by His permission? He knoweth that which is before them, and that which is behind them, and they shall not comprehend anything of His knowledge, saving in so far as He pleaseth. His throne stretcheth over Heaven and Earth, and the protection of them both is no burden unto Him. He is the Lofty and the Great.

In the following extract, the verses in which Infidelity is compared to a tempestuous Sea, of which the crested waves below mingle with the lowering clouds above,—a scene of impenetrable darkness and despair, are to my apprehension amongst the grandest and most powerful in the whole Ḳor'ān. The Sūra belongs to the Fifth year of the Hijra; but part of it is in the best style of the Meccan period.

Sūra xxiv. 35 God is the Light of the Heavens and the Earth. The likeness of
His light is as the niche wherein is a Lamp inclosed in glass;—the glass
is as a refulgent Star. It is lighted from a blessed tree, an Olive neither
of the East nor of the Wẹst. Its Oil is near unto giving light, even if
the fire did not touch it; light upon light. God directeth towards His
light whom He pleaseth. (Here follows a description of the worship
v. 39 and good works of Believers.) And those that disbelieve;—their works
are as the *Serāb* in the plain; the thirsty man thinketh it to be water,
until, when he cometh thereto, he doth not find it anything; but he
findeth God to be about him, and He will fulfil unto him his account;
for God is swift in taking account:—

Or as the Darkness in a bottomless Sea, covered by wave riding upon wave. Above them are clouds. Darkness of one kind over another kind. When one stretcheth forth his hand, he hardly seeth it. And to whomsoever God doth not grant light, he shall have no light.

What! seest thou not that unto God giveth praise everything that is
in the Heavens and in the Earth, and the Birds with expanded wing.
Truly every one knoweth his prayer and his hymn of praise; and God
v. 43 knoweth whatsoever they do. . . . Seest thou not that God driveth the
clouds along, then gathereth them together, then setteth them in layers;
and thou seest the rain issuing forth from between them. And he sendeth
down from the heavens as it were mountains wherein is hail. He striketh
therewith whom He pleaseth, and averteth the same from whom He
pleaseth. The brightness of His lightning well-nigh taketh the sight away.

CHAPTER XVIII

SIXTH YEAR OF THE HIJRA

A.D. 627, 628

ÆTAT. 59

THE Sixth year of the Hijra was one of considerable activity at Medīna. No important battle indeed was fought, nor any great expedition undertaken. But small parties were constantly in motion, either for the chastisement of hostile tribes, for the capture of caravans, or for the repulse of robbers and marauders. We read of as many as seventeen such affairs during the year. They generally resulted in the dispersion of the enemy and the capture of flocks and herds, which enriched the Prophet's followers, and stimulated their zeal for active service; they also served to spread terror of his name. But few of them were otherwise attended with marked results; and it will not therefore be necessary to narrate them all.[1]

Numerous minor expeditions in Sixth year of the Hijra

Two of the expeditions were led by Moḥammad himself. One was against the Beni Liḥyān,[2] whom he had long been desirous of chastising for their treacherous attack, two years before, on the little band of his followers at Ar-Rajī'. During the summer he set out with a selected body of two hundred men on camels, and twenty horse. That he might the more

Expedition by Moḥammad against Beni Liḥyān. A.H. VI. June, A.D. 627

[1] Weil regards the comparative insignificance of these expeditions, and especially the smallness of Moḥammad's following on the pilgrimage to Al-Ḥodeibiya, as a proof how low his authority had sunk. But there was no object on these occasions for any great exertion or extensive following. The authority of Moḥammad, which had been materially increased by his successful resistance to the grand confederation at the siege of Medīna, was steadily advancing.

[2] Ibn Hishām, p. 718 f.; Aṭ-Ṭabari, i. 1500 f.; Al-Wāḳidi, p. 226 f.; Ibn Sa'd, p. 56 f.

surely fall upon his enemy unawares, he first took the road N.W. towards Syria. After two or three marches, he suddenly turned south, and travelled rapidly along the seashore by the way to Mecca. But the stratagem was of no avail, for the Beni Liḥyān had notice of his approach, and, taking their cattle with them, retired to heights where they were safe from attack. At the spot where his followers had been slaughtered, he halted, and invoked pardon and mercy on them. Small parties were sent to scour the vicinity, but no traces of the tribe were anywhere to be found. Being now within two marches of Mecca, he advanced to 'Osfān with the view of alarming Ḳoreish. From thence Abu Bekr was sent with ten horsemen, as it were the vanguard, to approach still nearer. Satisfied with this demonstration, the force retraced its steps to Medīna. On his way back from this fruitless journey, the Prophet, who had been greatly incommoded by the heat, is said to have prayed thus: '*Returning and repentant, yet if it please the Lord, praising His name and serving Him, I seek refuge in God from the troubles of the way, the vexation of return, and the evil eye which affecteth family and wealth.*'

Pursuit of 'Oyeina, who attacked camels at Al-Ghāba. A.H. VI. July, A.D. 627

Not many days after, Medīna was early one morning startled by a cry of alarm from the adjoining height of Sal'.[1] The chieftain 'Oyeina, with a troop of Fezāra horse, came down upon the plain of Al-Ghāba, within a few miles of Medīna, fell upon the milch camels of Moḥammad which were grazing there, drove off the whole herd, and having killed the keeper carried off his wife. A Citizen, early on his way to the pasture lands, saw the marauding band and gave the alarm. The call to arms was ordered by Moḥammad. A troop of horse was shortly at the gate of the Mosque.[2] A flag was mounted for them, and they were despatched at once in pursuit, Moḥammad himself with some 600 men following shortly after. Sa'd ibn 'Obāda, with 300 armed

[1] Ibn Hishām, p. 719 ff.; Aṭ-Ṭabari, i. 1502 ff.; Al-Wāḳidi, p. 227 ff.; Ibn Sa'd, p. 58 ff.

[2] Al-Miḳdād being the first to come up, Moḥammad mounted the flag on his spear, which occasioned some to say that he was the leader of the expedition, while that honour belonged in reality to Sa'd ibn Zeid. There is a curious anecdote on this point, which shows that Ḥassān's poetry sometimes originated errors in tradition. In his piece on this expedition, the poet speaks of *the horsemen of Al-Miḳdād*, as if he had been

followers, remained behind, to guard the city. The advanced party hung daringly upon the rear of the marauders, slew several of them, and recovered half of the plundered camels. On the side of the Muslims only one man was killed. Moḥammad, with the main body, marched onwards as far as Dhu Ḳarad, in the direction of Kheibar; but by this time the robbers were safe away in the desert. The captive female effected her escape on one of the plundered camels which she vowed on reaching her home in safety to offer up as a sacrifice of thanksgiving. On acquainting Moḥammad with her vow, he rallied her on the ingratitude of seeking to slay the animal which had saved her life, and which moreover was not hers to offer up. He bade her go to her home in peace. Finding that hostile tribes were gathering around them in dangerous numbers, the force returned, having been five days absent from Medīna.

Affair at Dhu'l-Ḳaṣṣa: party of Muslims cut up. A.H. VI. August, A.D. 627

Scarcity still prevailing in Nejd, and rain having fallen plentifully towards Medīna, the Ghaṭafān tribes were tempted in their search for pasture to advance beyond their usual limits.[1] The herds of camels belonging to the Muslims, greatly increased by the plunder of late years, had been sent out to graze in the same direction. They offered a tempting prize for a foray, and the neighbouring tribes were suspected to be gathering for the purpose. Moḥammad ibn Maslama was deputed with ten followers to visit the locality and ascertain how matters stood. At Dhu'l-Ḳaṣṣa, two or three days' distance, he was surrounded in the night-time by overpowering numbers. After a short resistance, his men were all slain, and he himself left on the field as dead. A friend, happening to pass that way, assisted him on his journey back to Medīna. A body of forty well-mounted soldiers under Abu 'Obeida was despatched to chastise the offenders; but they had dispersed among the neighbouring heights, and, excepting the plunder of some flocks and household stuff, no reprisals were effected.

the leader. On hearing the poetry recited, Sa'd repaired in great wrath to Ḥassān, and required amends for the misrepresentation. The poet quietly replied that his name did not suit the rhythm so well as Al-Miḳdād's. And yet, says Al-Wāḳidi the verses remained in circulation and gave rise to the erroneous tradition that Al-Miḳdād was leader.

[1] Aṭ-Tabari, i. 1554; Al-Wāḳidi, p. 233; Ibn Sa'd, p. 61 f.

A Meccan caravan plundered at Al-'Īṣ. A.H. VI. September, A.D. 627

During the autumn an interesting episode occurred. A well-freighted caravan from Mecca, venturing to resume the seashore route to Syria, was overpowered at Al-'Īṣ, and carried into Medīna with a large store of silver and some of those who guarded it as prisoners.[1] Among these was Abu'l-'Āṣ, son-in-law of Moḥammad. His romantic story deserves recital, as well for its own interest, as for the share which the Prophet himself bore therein. The reader will remember that Moḥammad, at Khadīja's desire, gave his daughter Zeinab in marriage to her nephew Abu'l-'Āṣ, a prosperous trader in Mecca. While declining to embrace Islām, Abu'l-Āṣ equally resisted the bidding of Ḳoreish to abandon Zeinab and choose one of their own daughters in her stead. 'I will not separate from my wife,' he said; 'neither do I desire any other woman from amongst your daughters.' Moḥammad was much pleased at the faithfulness of Abu'l-'Āṣ to his daughter. The attachment was mutual, for when the family emigrated to Medīna, Zeinab remained behind at Mecca with her husband.

Abu'l-'Āṣ and Zeinab Moḥammad's daughter

Abu'l-'Āṣ, when taken at Bedr, had been freed on condition of sending Zeinab to Medīna

In the battle of Bedr, Abu'l-'Āṣ had been amongst the captives; and when Ḳoreish deputed men to ransom their prisoners, Zeinab sent by their hands such property as she had for her husband's freedom.[2] Among other things was a necklace, which Khadīja had given her on her marriage. The Prophet, seeing this touching memorial of his former wife, was overcome, and said to the people: 'If it seem right in your eyes, let my daughter's husband go free, and send these trinkets back.' All agreed; but as the condition of his freedom, Moḥammad required of Abu'l-'Āṣ that he should at once send Zeinab to Medīna. Accordingly, on his return to Mecca, he sent her away mounted on a camel-litter, under charge of his brother Kināna. Certain of the baser sort, however, from amongst Ḳoreish went in pursuit, determined to bring her back. The first that appeared was Habbār, who struck the camel with his spear, and so affrighted Zeinab as to bring on a miscarriage. Kināna at once made the camel sit down, and by the mere sight of his bow and well-filled quiver, kept the pursuers at bay. Just then Abu Sufyān

[1] Ibn Hishām, p. 464 f.; Aṭ-Ṭabari, i. 1555; Al-Wāḳidi, p. 233 f; Ibn Sa'd, p. 63.

[2] Ibn Hishām, p. 464 ff.; Aṭ-Ṭabari, i. 1347 ff.

came up and held parley with Kināna: 'Ye should not,' he said, 'have gone forth thus publicly, knowing the disaster we have so lately sustained at the hands of Moḥammad. The open departure of his daughter would be regarded as proof of our weakness and humiliation. But it is no object of ours to keep back this woman from her father, or to retaliate our wrongs upon her. Return, therefore, for a little while to Mecca, and when this excitement shall have died away, then set out secretly.' They followed his advice, and some days after, Zeinab, escorted by Zeid, who had been sent to fetch her, reached Moḥammad in safety.

Abu'l-'Āṣ taken prisoner, is converted. A.H. VI.

It was three or four years after this that Abu'l-'Āṣ was now again made prisoner with the caravan at Al-'Īṣ. As the party carrying him captive approached Medīna, he contrived by night to have an interview with Zeinab, who gave him the guarantee of her protection, on which he rejoined the other prisoners. At morning prayer she called aloud from her apartment that she had passed her word to Abu'l-'Āṣ. When prayers were ended, Moḥammad thus addressed the assembly: 'Ye have heard, as I have, the voice of my daughter. I swear by Him in whose hands is my life, that I knew nothing of her guarantee until this moment. But the pledge even of the least of my followers must needs be kept.' Thus saying, he retired to his daughter, and desired her to treat Abu'l-'Āṣ with honour, as a guest, but not recognise him as her husband. Then sending for the captors of the caravan, he reminded them of his connection with Abu'l-'Āṣ, and said: 'If ye treat him well, and return his property unto him, it would be pleasing to me; but if not, the booty is yours which the Lord hath given into your hands, and it is your right to keep it.' They all with one consent agreed to let the prisoner go free, and return to him his property. This generosity, and the continued attachment of Zeinab, so wrought on Abu'l-'Āṣ, that when he had adjusted his affairs at Mecca, he made profession of Islām and rejoined her at Medīna. Their domestic happiness, however, was not of long continuance; for Zeinab died the following year from the illness caused by the attack of Habbār at Mecca.[1] The treatment of his daughter on that

[1] They had a daughter, whom 'Alī married after the death of Fāṭima. It is satisfactory to find that at Mecca, the cruelty of Habbār was

Moḥammad commands that his daughter's pursuers be put to death

occasion had greatly incensed Moḥammad. Once, when a party was setting out on an expedition towards Mecca, he commanded that if Habbār, and another who had joined him in the pursuit of Zeinab, fell into their hands, they should both be burned alive; but the same night he countermanded it in these words; 'It is not fitting for any of His creatures to punish by fire but God only. Wherefore if ye seize them put them to death simply by the sword.'

Beni Judhām chastised for robbing Diḥya, sent by Moḥammad on an embassy to Syria. A.H. VI. October, A.D. 627

About this time we read of Moḥammad's first communication with the Roman Empire. One of his followers, named Diḥya, was sent on a mission to the Emperor, or rather perhaps to one of the Governors of Syria.[1] He was graciously received, and presented with a dress of honour. On his way home, he was plundered of everything near Wādi al-Ḳora, by the tribe of Judhām. A neighbouring tribe, however, under treaty with Moḥammad, attacked the robbers, recovered the spoil, and restored his property to Diḥya. On the robbery reaching the ears of Moḥammad, he despatched Zeid (now a favourite commander) with 500 men, to chastise the delinquents. Marching by night, and concealing themselves by day, they fell unexpectedly on Judhām, killed their leader and several others, and carried off one hundred women and children, with all their herds and flocks. Unfortunately, the branch thus punished had just tendered submission to Moḥammad. The chief therefore hastened to Medīna and appealed against these proceedings. He produced the letter of terms which the Prophet had made with his people, and demanded justice. 'But,' said Moḥammad, 'how can I compensate thee for those that have been slain?' 'Release to us the living,' was the reply; 'as for the dead, they are beneath our feet.' Moḥammad acknowledged the justice of his demand and despatched 'Alī to order restoration. He met Zeid returning to Medīna, and the prisoners and booty were immediately surrendered to the chief.

scouted as unmanly. Even Hind, wife of Abu Sufyān, gave vent to her indignation; meeting the party as it returned, she extemporised some severe verses against them: 'Ah! in time of peace ye are very brave and fierce against the weak and unprotected, but in battle ye are like women with gentle speeches,' &c.

[1] Ibn Hishām, p. 975 f.; Aṭ-Ṭabari, i. 1555 f.; Al-Wāḳidi, p. 234 f.; Ibn Sa'd, p. 63 f.

Second expedition to Dūmat. A.H. V. November, 627

Soon after, 'Abd ar-Raḥmān set out with 700 men, on a second expedition to Dūmat al-Jandal.[1] Moḥammad bound a black turban, in token of command, about his head. He was first to gain over, if possible, the people of Dūmat al-Jandal, and fight only in the last resort:—'but in no case,' said the Prophet, 'shalt thou use deceit or perfidy, or kill any child.' On reaching Dūmat al-Jandal, 'Abd ar-Raḥmān summoned the tribes around to embrace Islām, and allowed them three days' grace. Within that period, Al-Asbagh, a Christian chief of the Beni Kelb, gave in his adhesion, and many followed his example. Others preferred to be tributaries, with the condition of being allowed to retain profession of the Christian faith. 'Abd ar-Raḥmān sent tidings of this success to Moḥammad, who, in reply, desired him to marry Tomāḍir, daughter of the chief. 'Abd ar-Raḥmān accordingly brought this lady with him to Medīna, where she bore him Abu Selama (the famous jurisconsult of after days) and, amid many rivals, maintained her position as one of his wives, till her husband's death.[2]

Beni Fezāra chastised. A.H. VI. December, A.D. 627

Zeid having set out upon a mercantile expedition to Syria, with ventures from many of the Citizens, was waylaid near Wādi al-Ḳora, and maltreated and plundered by the Beni Fezāra.[3] This occasioned much exasperation at Medīna. When he was sufficiently recovered from the injuries inflicted by the robbers, Zeid was deputed with a strong force to execute vengeance upon them. Approaching stealthily, he surprised and captured the marauders' stronghold. Um Ḳirfa, aunt of 'Oyeina, a lady who had gained celebrity as mistress of this nest of robbers, was taken prisoner with her daughter. Neither the sex, nor great age of Um Ḳirfa, saved her from a death of extreme barbarity. Her legs were tied each to a separate camel. The camels were driven asunder, and thus she was torn in pieces. Two young brothers were also put to death. Zeid, on his return, hastened to Moḥammad, who

Barbarous execution of Um Ḳirfa

[1] Ibn Hishām, p. 991; Aṭ-Ṭabari, i. 1556; Al-Wāḳidi, p. 236.; Ibn Sa'd, p. 64 f.

[2] For some account of 'Abd ar-Raḥmān's conjugal relations, see *ante*, p. 174. Besides slave-girls, he had issue by sixteen wives. There were several unimportant raids this year hardly requiring mention; but I must not omit one for the cruel deed that closed it.

[3] Ibn Hishām, p. 979 f.; Aṭ-Ṭabari, i. 1557 f.; Al-Wāḳidi, p. 236: Ibn Sa'd, p. 64.

hurried forth to meet him with dress ungirded: and, learning the success of the expedition, embraced and kissed him. We do not read of disapprobation at the inhuman treatment of the aged female. The daughter was given to 'Ā'isha as her waiting-maid; but the brigand spirit survived in her, and a few years after we find her slain in a similar encounter with Khālid.[1]

Assassination of Abu Rāfi', a Jewish chief. A.H. VI. December, A.D. 627

His old enemies, the Jews, were still the cause of annoyance. A party of the Beni an-Naḍīr, after their exile, settled down among their brethren at Kheibar. Abu Rāfi', their chief, having taken a prominent part in the Confederate force which besieged Medīna, was now suspected of encouraging certain Bedawi tribes in their depredations. An expedition was therefore undertaken by 'Alī against the Jews of Kheibar, but besides the capture of their camels and flocks, it produced no other result. As a surer means of stopping these attacks, Moḥammad resolved on ridding himself of their supposed author, the Jewish chief.[2] The Khazraj, emulous of the distinction which their brethren gained some years before by the assassination of Ka'b, had long offered themselves for like service. Moḥammad therefore, having chosen five, gave them command to make away with Abu Rāfi'. On approaching Kheibar, they concealed themselves till nightfall, when they repaired to their victim's house. The leader, who was familiar with the tribe and with their language, called out at the door to the chief's wife, and thus gained admittance on a false pretext. When she perceived that his companions were armed, she screamed aloud; but they pointed their weapons at her, and forced her to be silent. Then, rushing in, they despatched Abu Rāfi' with their swords; and hastily retiring, hid themselves in an adjacent cave till the pursuit was over. Moḥammad, meeting them as they returned, exclaimed: 'Success attend you!' 'And thee, O Prophet!' they replied. They recounted to him all that had happened; and, as each

[1] Al-Wāḳidi says she was given by Moḥammad to one of his followers. But we find in the Caliphate of Abu Bekr, A.H. XI., that a daughter of Um Ḳirfa, called Um Ziml, who had waited on 'Ā'isha as her maid, afterwards having escaped, raised a rebellion, and like her mother was slain in battle by Khālid. I presume it must have been the same. See the *Caliphate*, p. 23. Aṭ-Ṭabari, i. 1901 f.

[2] (Ibn Hishām, p. 351); At-Ṭabari, i. 1375 ff. (A.H. III.); Al-Wāḳidi, p. 170 f. (A.H. IV.); Ibn Sa'd, p. 66.

one claimed the honour of the deed, Moḥammad examined their weapons, and, from the marks on the sword of 'Abdallah ibn Oneis, who has already been mentioned as the assassin of Sufyān, chieftain of the Beni Liḥyān, assigned to him the merit of the fatal blow.

Oseir and party of Jews slain. A.H. VI. January, A.D. 628

The assassination of Abu Rāfi' did not relieve Moḥammad of his apprehensions from the Jews of Kheibar; for Oseir, or Yuseir, elected in his room, maintained the same relations with the Ghaṭafān, and was even reported to be designing fresh movements against Medīna.[1] Moḥammad deputed a Citizen, Ibn Rawāḥa, to Kheibar, with three followers, to make inquiries as to how Oseir also might be taken unawares. But he found the Jews too much on the alert to admit of a second successful attempt. On his return, therefore, a new plan was devised. Ibn Rawāḥa was now sent openly with thirty men to persuade Oseir to visit Medīna. They assured him that Moḥammad would make him ruler over Kheibar and treat him with distinction; and gave him a solemn guarantee of safety. Oseir consented, and set out with thirty followers, each Muslim taking one of the Jewish party behind him on his camel. The unfortunate chief was mounted on the camel of 'Abdallah ibn Oneis, who relates that, after they had travelled some distance, he perceived Oseir stretching out his hand towards his sword. Urging forward his camel till he was well beyond the rest of the party, 'Abdallah called out: 'Enemy of the Lord! Treachery! Twice hath he done this thing.' As he spoke, he leaped from the camel, and aimed a deadly blow at Oseir, which took effect on the hip joint. The chief fell mortally wounded to the ground, but in his descent succeeded in wounding 'Abdallah's head with the camel staff, the only weapon within his reach. Upon this, each of the Muslims turned upon his man, and they were all murdered, excepting one who eluded pursuit. The party continued their journey to Medīna, and reported the tragedy to Moḥammad, who gave thanks and said: 'Verily, the Lord hath delivered you from an unrighteous people.'[2]

[1] Ibn Hishām, p. 980 f.; Aṭ-Ṭabari, i. 1759 f.; Al-Wāḳidi, p. 239; Ibn Sa'd, p. 66 f.

[2] The reader will judge for himself on which side treachery is likeliest to have occurred, on that of the unarmed Oseir, or of Ibn Oneis, already known as an assassin. But I have given the narrative as I find it.

Certain robbers executed barbarously, for plunder and murder

A party of eight Bedawi Arabs had some time previously visited Medīna and embraced Islām. The damp of the climate affected their spleen, and for a cure Moḥammad bade them join his herd of milch camels grazing in the plain south of Ḳobā, and drink of their milk.[1] Following his advice they soon recovered; but with returning strength they revived also the lust of plunder. They drove off the herd, and attempted to escape. The herdsman pursued the plunderers, but was seized and barbarously handled; his hands and legs were cut off, and thorny spikes thrust into his tongue and eyes, till he died. When tidings of this outrage reached Moḥammad, he despatched twenty horsemen in pursuit.[2] They surrounded and seized the robbers, and recovered the camels excepting one, which had been slaughtered by them. The captives were conducted to Moḥammad, who was justly exasperated at their ingratitude and savage treatment of his servant. They had merited death; but the mode in which he inflicted it was unworthy of Islām. Their arms and legs were cut off, and their eyes put out. The mutilated sightless trunks were then impaled upon the plain of Al-Ghāba (where Moḥammad chanced himself to be), until life was extinct. But, on reflection, Moḥammad felt that the punishment exceeded the bounds of humanity. He accordingly promulgated a law by which capital sentence is limited to simple death or crucifixion. Amputation of the hands and feet is, however, sanctioned as a penal measure; and amputation of the hands even enjoined as the proper penalty for theft. Such is the cruel law throughout Islām to the present day, as sanctioned by the following passage:—

Mutilation recognised as a legal punishment

Sūra v. 37

Verily the recompense of those that fight against God and his Prophet, and haste to commit wickedness in the land, is that they shall be slain or crucified; or that their hands and feet of the opposite sides be

---

[1] Ibn Hishām, p. 998 f.; Aṭ-Ṭabari, i. 1559; Al-Wāḳidi, p. 240 f.; Ibn Sa'd, p. 67 f.

[2] They were commanded by Kurz ibn Jābir, whom we have seen, *ante*, p. 207, as engaged in one of the first raids against Medīna. At what period he was converted and came to Medīna is not mentioned. [He was one of the Muslims killed at the taking of Mecca. Ibn Hishām, p. 817.]

cut off; or that they be banished from the land. That shall be their punishment in this life, and in the life to come they shall have great torment. * * *

As regards the robber, male and female, cut off the hands of both.[1] v. 42

Attempt to assassinate Abu Sufyān

Al-Wāķidi assigns to this period an attempt, under the orders of Moḥammad, to assassinate Abu Sufyān.[2] As its cause, we are told that a Bedawi had been commissioned by Abu Sufyān on a similar errand against Moḥammad; but that the emissary was discovered, and confessed the object of his mission. According to Ibn Hishām (who makes no mention of this latter circumstance), the attempted assassination was ordered by Moḥammad in the *fourth* year of the Hijra, in revenge for the execution of the two captives taken at Ar-Rajī'. Whatever the inciting cause, there seems no reasonable doubt that a commission was given by the Prophet to 'Amr ibn Omeiya to proceed to Mecca, and compass the death of Abu Sufyān. 'Amr was recognised as he lurked near the Ka'ba before he could carry his design into effect, and was obliged to flee for his life. True, however, to his profession, he claims the credit of having assassinated three of the Ķoreish by the way, and a fourth he brought prisoner to Medīna.[3]

Bedawi tribes gained over

During this year and the following, Moḥammad made an important advance in gaining over certain Bedawi tribes lying between Medīna and Mecca. These did not, indeed, as yet make profession of Islām, but they entered into friendly relations; and the assistance, or at least neutrality, of all the tribes upon the road might now be counted on.

'The ten' of the Beni 'Abs

About this time, ten men of the Beni 'Abs, a small but warlike clan in Nejd, joined the faith and settled at Medīna. They distinguished themselves in battle under the title of

[1] For repeated robberies, the hands and feet may all, one after another, be cut off, rendering the criminal a helpless cripple. It may be noticed that putting out of the eyes is not recognised among the legal punishments.

[2] Ibn Hishām, p. 992; Aṭ-Ṭabari, i. 1437 ff.; Ibn Sa'd, p. 68.

[3] He is the same who, escaping from the massacre at Bi'r Ma'ūna, assassinated the two travellers for whom Moḥammad paid compensation (p. 271). He is stated by Al-Wāķidi to have been before Islām a '*professional* assassin'; so that the people of Mecca, recognising him, immediately understood what his errand was.

'the Ten,' and Moḥammad gave them a banner, which in the Syrian conquests became famous as the 'Absite ensign.

Thus steadily did the influence of Moḥammad, partly through religious motives, and partly from motives of rapine and conquest, extend and become consolidated.

CHAPTER XIX

PILGRIMAGE TO AL-ḤODEIBIYA[1]

Dhu'l-Ḳa'da, A.H. VI.—*March*, A.D. 628

SIX years had now passed since Moḥammad, and those who emigrated with him, had seen their native city, worshipped at the Holy House, or joined in the yearly pilgrimage, which from childhood they had regarded as an essential part of their social and religious life. They longed to revisit these scenes, and once more join in the solemn rites of the Ka'ba. Anxiety to perform pilgrimage to Mecca

No one shared these feelings more earnestly than the Prophet himself. It was, moreover, of great importance that he should show practically his attachment to the ancient faith of Mecca. He had, indeed, in the Ḳor'ān, insisted upon that faith as an indispensable element of Islām; upbraided Ḳoreish for obstructing the approach of pious worshippers to the House of God; and denounced them, because of their idolatrous practices, as not its rightful guardians, in such words as these:— Political considerations

> And what have they to urge that God should not chastise them, seeing that they have hindered His servants from the sacred Temple; and they are not the guardians thereof,—verily, none are its guardians save the pious. But the greater part of them do not consider. And their prayers at the Temple are nought but whistling through their fingers, and clapping of their hands. Taste, therefore, the punishment of your unbelief. Sūra viii. 34 f.

Yet something more than this was needed to show his attachment to the ancestral faith and observances of Ḳoreish. If he made no effort to visit the Holy Places, and fulfil the sacred rites, he would lay himself justly open to the charge of lukewarmness and neglect. Precept must needs be supported by example.

[1] Ibn Hishām, p. 740 ff.; Aṭ-Ṭabari, i. 1528 ff.; Al-Wāḳidi, p. 241 ff.; Ibn Sa'd, p. 69 ff.

Inducements for making Lesser Pilgrimage in Dhu'l-Ḳa'da, A.D. VI.

Musing thus, Moḥammad had a vision in the night. Followed by his people, he dreamed that he entered Mecca in security, and having made the circuit of the Ka'ba, and slain the victims, completed thus the ceremonies of the pilgrimage. The dream was communicated to his followers, and every one longed for its realisation. It foretold nothing of fighting or contest; the entrance was to be quiet and unopposed. Now the sacred month of Dhu'l-Ḳa'da was at hand, in which observance of the Lesser Pilgrimage was specially meritorious. There would, moreover, be less chance of collision with hostile tribes, than at the Greater Pilgrimage in the succeeding month. Furthermore, in the month of Dhu'l-Ḳa'da, war was unlawful throughout Arabia, much more within the inviolate precincts of Mecca. If Moḥammad and his followers, therefore, should at this time approach the Ka'ba in the peaceful garb of pilgrims, Ḳoreish would be bound by every pledge of national faith to leave them unmolested. On the other hand, should Ḳoreish oppose their entrance, the blame would rest with them; and even so, the strength of the pilgrim band would secure its safety,—if not the victory. So soon as this was resolved upon, the Citizens as well as Refugees responded to the call, and made haste to prepare themselves for pilgrimage. To swell the camp and render it more imposing, the Arab tribes around, who had entered into friendly relations with Moḥammad, were also summoned. But few responded to the call; there was, in fact, little inducement for them on the score of booty, and most part alleged that their occupations and families prevented them from leaving home.[1]

Surrounding tribes invited to join, but most decline

Moḥammad and his followers set out from Medina. A.H. VI. February, A.D. 628

Early in Dhu'l-Ḳa'da, therefore, arrangements for the journey being now completed, Moḥammad entered his house, bathed himself, and put on the two pieces of cloth which constitute the pilgrim garb. He then mounted Al-Ḳaṣwā, and led the cavalcade of 1,500 pilgrims to Dhu'l-Ḥuleifa, the first stage on the road to Mecca. There they halted, and Moḥammad with the rest consecrated themselves to the service by repeatedly uttering the cry, *Labbeik! Labbeik!* which signifies, 'Here am I, O Lord! Here am I!' The victims were then set apart for sacrifice; their heads having

[1] A few of the Beni Aslam joined, and they are consequently reckoned among the 'Refugees.'

been turned towards Mecca, ornaments were hung about their necks, and a mark affixed upon their right sides. Seventy camels were thus devoted; amongst them was the camel of Abu Jahl, taken on the field of Bedr. This done, the pilgrims moved forward by the ordinary stages. A troop of twenty horse marched in advance to give notice of danger. The pilgrims carried no arms but such as are allowed by custom to the traveller, namely, each a sheathed sword, a bow and well-filled quiver. The Prophet took his wife Um Selama with him.

Ḳoreish oppose advance of Moḥammad

Tidings of Moḥammad's approach soon reached Mecca; and, notwithstanding the pious object and unwarlike attitude of the pilgrims, filled Ḳoreish with apprehension. They did not credit their peaceful professions, and suspected treachery. The citizens of Mecca, joined by the surrounding tribes, were quickly under arms, and took up ground on the Medīna road, resolved to perish rather than allow Moḥammad to enter. A body of 200 horse, under Khālid and 'Ikrima, son of Abu Jahl, was pushed forward in advance.

Moḥammad leaves road, and encamps at Al-Ḥodeibiya

Moḥammad had nearly reached 'Osfān, the second stage from Mecca, when a scout returned with this intelligence: 'Ḳoreish,' he said, 'are encamped at Dhu Ṭowa, clothed in panthers' skins;[1] their wives and little ones are with them; and they have sworn to die rather than let thee pass.' Shortly after, the Meccan cavalry came in sight, and Moḥammad's horse went forward to hold them in check. Further advance on the high road was now impossible without a battle, and for this Moḥammad was not yet prepared. He halted, and, having procured a guide, turned to the right by a route safe from the enemy's horse, and, after a fatiguing march through devious and rugged pathways, reached Al-Ḥodeibiya, an open space on the verge of the sacred territory encircling Mecca. Here his camel stopped, and, planting her fore legs firmly on the ground, refused to stir another step. 'She is weary,' said the people, as they urged her forward. 'Nay,' exclaimed Moḥammad, 'Al-Ḳaṣwā is not weary; but the same hand restraineth her as aforetime held back the Elephant,'—alluding to the invasion of Abraha. 'By the Lord!' he continued, 'no request of

[1] Expressive symbolically of the fixed resolution of Ḳoreish to fight to the last, like beasts of prey.

Ḳoreish this day, for the honour of the Holy Place, shall be denied by me.' So he alighted, and all the people with him, at Al-Ḥodeibiya. Some wells were on the spot, but, being choked with sand, there was little or no water in them. Moḥammad, taking an arrow from his quiver (the only implement at hand), made one of his followers descend a well, and with it scrape away the obstructing sand. Abundance of water soon accumulated.[1]

Negotiations between Ḳoreish and Moḥammad

The road from Al-Ḥodeibiya led by a circuitous route to lower Mecca.[2] Ḳoreish no sooner learned that the pilgrims had taken this direction, than they fell back on the city for its defence, and began sending deputations to ascertain the real intentions of Moḥammad. Al-Ḥodeibiya being only a short stage distant, the communications were rapid and frequent. Budeil, a Khozā'ite chief, with a party of his tribe, was the first to approach. He acquainted Moḥammad with the excited state of Ḳoreish, and their resolve to defend the city to the last. The Prophet replied, that it was not for war he had come forth: 'I have no other design,' he said, 'but to perform the pilgrimage of the Holy House: and whosoever hindereth us therefrom, we shall fight against them.' 'Orwa, a chief from Aṭ-Ṭā'if, and son-in-law of Abu Sufyān, was the next ambassador. He came, saying that the people of Mecca were desperate. 'They will not suffer this rabble of thine to approach the city; I swear that even now I see thee as it were, by the morrow, deserted by them all.' At this Abu Bekr started up and warmly resented the imputation. 'Orwa, not heeding him, became still more earnest in his speech, and (according to the familiar Bedawi custom) stretched forth his hand to take hold of Moḥammad's beard. 'Back!' cried a bystander, striking his arm. 'Hold thy hands from off the Prophet of God!' 'And who is this?' said 'Orwa, surprised at the interposition of a red-

[1] This has been magnified into a miracle. As soon as the arrow was *planted* in the hitherto empty well, the fountain gushed up so rapidly that the people sitting on the brink could draw water at ease. By another account, Moḥammad spat into the well, on which a spring immediately bubbled up. According to a third tradition, he thrust his hand into a vessel, on which the water poured forth as it were from between his fingers, and all drank therefrom: 'The stream would have sufficed for a hundred thousand people.'

[2] It probably joined the Jidda road, some little distance from the city.

haired ungainly youth. 'It is thy nephew's son, Al-Moghīra.' 'O ungrateful!' he exclaimed (alluding to his having paid compensation for certain murders committed by his nephew), 'it is but as yesterday that I redeemed thy life.' These and other scenes at the interview struck 'Orwa with a deep sense of the reverence and devotion of the Muslims towards their Prophet; and this he endeavoured to impress upon Ḳoreish, when he carried back to them a message resembling that taken by Budeil. But Ḳoreish were firm. Whatever his intentions, Moḥammad should not approach the city with any show of force, and thus humble them in the eyes of all Arabia. 'Tell him,' they said, 'that this year he must go back; but in the year following he may come, and having entered Mecca then perform the pilgrimage.' One of their messengers was chief of the Bedawi tribes around Mecca. The goodly row of victims, with their sacrificial ornaments, and the marks of having been long tied up for this pious object, at once convinced him of the sincerity of Moḥammad's peaceful professions. But Ḳoreish, on his return, refused to listen. 'Thou art a simple Arab of the desert,' they said, 'and knowest not the devices of other men.' The Bedawi chief was enraged at the slight, and swore that, if they continued to oppose the advance of Moḥammad, he would retire with all his Arabs. The threat alarmed Ḳoreish. 'Have patience for a little while,' they said, 'until we can make such terms as are needful for our security.' Negotiations were then in earnest opened.

Deputation of 'Othmān to Ḳoreish

The first messenger from the Muslim camp Ḳoreish had seized and treated roughly; they maimed the camel on which he rode, and even threatened his life. But the feeling being now more pacific, Moḥammad desired 'Omar to go as his ambassador. 'Omar excused himself on account of the personal enmity of Ḳoreish; he had, moreover, no influential relatives in the city who could shield him from danger; and he pointed to 'Othmān, who belonged to one of the most powerful families in Mecca, as a fitter envoy. 'Othmān consented, and was at once despatched. On entering the city, he received the protection of a cousin, and went straightway to Abu Sufyān and the other chiefs. 'We come,' said 'Othmān, 'to visit the Holy House, to honour it, and to perform worship there. We have brought victims with us, and after slaying them we shall depart in peace.' They replied that 'Othmān, if he chose, might visit the Ka'ba and worship there; but as for Moḥammad, they had sworn that this year he should not enter the precincts of their city. 'Othmān declined the offer, and retired carrying their message to the camp.

The Pledge of the Tree on report of 'Othmān's murder

During his absence, there was great excitement at Al-Ḥodeibiya. Some considerable delay having occurred, a report gained currency that he had been murdered at Mecca. Anxiety and alarm overspread the camp. Moḥammad, himself began to suspect treachery; taking his stand under the thick shade of an acacia tree, and surrounded by the whole body of the pilgrims, he required a pledge from them of faithful service, and that they would stand by 'Othmān to the death. When all had taken thus the solemn oath, striking each one the palm of his hand on that of the Prophet, he himself struck his own right hand upon his left in token that he would stand by his absent son-in-law. While war and revenge thus breathed throughout the pilgrim camp, their fears were suddenly relieved by the reappearance of 'Othmān. But 'the Pledge of the Tree' is a scene to which the Prophet ever after loved to revert; for here the strong feelings of devotion and sympathy between him and his followers had found fitting and ardent expression. Their martial spirit and religious fervour had been excited to the highest pitch; and they were prepared at once to rush upon the enemy with resistless onset. It was one of those romantic occasions so congenial to an Arab's spirit, and which survives for ever in his memory.

Treaty between Moḥammad and Ḳoreish

After some further interchange of messages, Ḳoreish deputed Suheil,[1] and other representatives, with power to conclude a treaty of peace. The conference was long, and the discussion, especially on the part of 'Omar, warm. But at last the terms were settled. A ten years' truce, on the one hand, secured the safety of the Syrian caravans; while, on the other, it gave free liberty to converts passing over to the Muslim side. Moḥammad summoned 'Alī to write from his dictation. And thus he began:—

'IN THE NAME OF GOD, MOST GRACIOUS AND MERCIFUL!'—'Stop!' said Suheil. 'As for God, we know Him; but

[1] See the incident regarding him after the battle of Bedr, p. 233.

this new name, we know it not. Say, as we have always said, *In thy name, O God!*' Moḥammad yielded. 'Write,' he said—

'IN THY NAME, O GOD! *These are the conditions of peace between Moḥammad the Prophet of God and*'—'Stop again!' interposed Suheil. 'If thou wert what thou sayest, I had not taken up arms against thee. Write, as the custom is, thine own name and thy father's name.' 'Write, then,' continued Moḥammad, calmly,—'*between Moḥammad son of 'Abdallah, and Suheil son of 'Amr.* War shall be suspended for ten years. Whosoever wisheth to join Moḥammad, or enter into treaty with him, shall have liberty to do so; and likewise whosoever wisheth to join Ḳoreish, or enter into treaty with them. If one goeth over to Moḥammad without the permission of his guardian, he shall be sent back to his guardian; but should any of the followers of Moḥammad return to Ḳoreish, they shall not be sent back. Moḥammad shall retire this year without entering the City. In the coming year, Moḥammad may visit Mecca, he and his followers, for three days, during which Ḳoreish shall retire and leave the City to them. But they may not enter it with any weapons, save those of the traveller, namely, to each a sheathed sword. *The witnesses hereof are Abu Bekr,*' &c.[1] A copy duly attested, was made over to Suheil and his comrades, who taking it, departed. The original was kept by Moḥammad.

Deputies of Ḳoreish depart

Though unable to enter Mecca, Moḥammad resolved to complete such ceremonies of the pilgrimage as the nature of the spot admitted. So he sacrificed the victims, and concluded the solemnities by shaving his head. The rest of the pilgrims having followed his example,[2] the assembly broke

Moḥammad and his followers sacrifice their victims

[1] Here follow eight other names, viz.—'Omar, 'Abd ar-Raḥmān, Sa'd ibn Abi Waḳḳāṣ, 'Othmān, Abu 'Obeida, Moḥammad ibn Maslama, Ḥuweiṭib ibn 'Abd al-'Ozza, and Mikraz ibn Ḥafṣ (the last two Ḳoreish), and below the signatures these words: 'The upper part of this was written by 'Alī' (meaning probably the text of the treaty above the signatures).

[2] Some *cut* their hair instead of shaving it. There is a great array of tradition to prove that Moḥammad blessed the 'Cutters,' as well as the 'Shavers,' of their hair. Among the miracles mentioned on the occasion is this, 'that the Lord sent a strong wind which swept the hair of the Pilgrims into the sacred Territory,' within a stone's throw of the camp;—thus signifying acceptance of the rite, notwithstanding its performance on common ground.

up, and, after a stay at Al-Ḥodeibiya of ten or fifteen days, began their homeward march.

Although people disappointed, treaty gave Moḥammad great advantages

The people, led by the Vision to anticipate an unopposed visit to the Ka'ba, were crestfallen at the abortive result of their long journey. But, in truth, a great step had been gained by Moḥammad. His political status, as an equal and independent Power, was acknowledged by the treaty: the ten years' truce would afford opportunity and time for the new religion to expand, and to force its claims upon the conviction of Ḳoreish; while conquest, material as well as spiritual, might be pursued on every other side. The stipulation that no one under the protection of a guardian should leave Ḳoreish without his guardian's consent, though unpopular at Medīna, was in accordance with the principles of Arabian society; and the Prophet had sufficient confidence in the loyalty of his own people and the superior attractions of Islām, to fear no ill effect from the counter clause that none should be delivered up who might desert his standard. Above all, it was a great and manifest success that free permission was conceded to visit Mecca in the following year, and for three days occupy the city undisturbed. A Revelation appeared accordingly, to place in a clear light this view of the treaty, and raise the drooping spirits of the pilgrims.

In Ḳor'ān it is styled a *Victory*

At the close of the first march, the pilgrims might be seen hurrying across the plain, urging their camels from all directions, and crowding round the Prophet. 'Inspiration hath descended on him,' passed from mouth to mouth throughout the camp. Standing upright upon his camel, Moḥammad recited the Sūra entitled 'The Victory,' which opens thus:—

Sūra xlviii. 1 f.

> Verily We have given unto thee an evident Victory;—
> That God may pardon thee the Sin that is past and that which is to come, and fulfil His favour upon thee, and lead thee in the right way; and that God may assist thee with a glorious assistance.

Bedawīn denounced for not joining pilgrimage

After this opening pæan, and reference to future recompense in heaven and hell, Moḥammad proceeds with a scathing denunciation of the Arabs of the desert, who, by false pretences had excused themselves from the pilgrimage. Their brave words would shortly be tested in battle with 'a people terrible in war.'[1] Meanwhile, as the penalty for malingering (a penalty hateful to the Bedawīn), they are forbidden to join, or share in the plunder of any marauding excursion whatsoever:—

The Arabs who stayed behind will say to thee,—*Our Possessions and our Families engaged us; wherefore ask thou Pardon for us.* They say that with their tongues which is not in their hearts;—Say;—And who could procure for you any other thing from God, if He intended against you Evil,—or if He intended for you Good. Verily God is acquainted with that which ye do. Truly ye thought that the Apostle and the Believers would not return to their Families again for ever; this thought was decked out in your hearts; ye imagined an evil Imagination; and ye are a corrupt people. * * * Those that stayed behind will say when ye go forth again for the Spoil, *Suffer us to follow you.* They seek to change the word of God. Say;—*Ye shall not follow us!* for thus hath God already spoken. And they will say;—*Nay but ye grudge us* (a share in the booty). By no means. They are a People that understandeth little. Say unto the Bedawīn that stayed behind, Ye shall hereafter be called out against a People of great might in war, with whom ye shall fight, or else they shall profess Islām. Then if ye obey, God will give you a fair reward; but if ye turn back as ye have turned back heretofore, He shall chastise you with a grievous chastisement.

Sūra xlviii. 11 ff.

v. 15

The pilgrims who took the solemn oath under the Acacia tree are then applauded for their faithfulness. It was the hand of God himself, not the hand of His Apostle merely, which then was struck.[2] Victory and great spoil should be their reward:—

Further notices of this expedition in the Ḳor'ān

Verily God was well pleased with the Believers, when they pledged themselves to Thee under the Tree. He knew what was in their hearts, and He caused Tranquillity[3] to descend upon them, and granted them a speedy Victory;—And Spoils in abundance, which they shall take.[4] God hath promised you great Spoil, which ye shall seize; and He hath sent

Sūra xlviii. 18 ff.

---

[1] The meaning apparently is that these Arabs would first have to prove themselves in real and severe fighting (perhaps in Syria or elsewhere) before they were again allowed to join in easy expeditions for booty.

[2] The hand of God is upon their hands, v. 10.

[3] Sekīna (Shechina), Divine influence overshadowing the heart. According to Sprenger, the tree having been mentioned in the Ḳor'ān, 'Omar had it cut down, lest it should become an object of worship.

[4] Moḥammad had no doubt Kheibar, and other expeditions northward, in his mind's eye at the moment: the prospect also would no doubt aggravate the chagrin of the Bedawīn at the loss of so fine a prize.

this (truce) beforehand. He hath restrained the hands of men from you,
that it may be a sign unto the Believers, and that He may guide you into
the right way. And yet other (Spoils are prepared for you), over which
ye have as yet no power. But God hath encompassed them ; for God
is over all things powerful. If the Unbelievers had fought against you,
v. 24 verily they had turned their backs. * * * It is God that restrained their
hands from you, and your hands from them, in the valley of Mecca, after
that He had already made you superior to them ; and God observed that
which ye did. These are they which disbelieve, which hindered you
from visiting the holy Temple ; and the Victims also, which were kept
back, so that they reached not their destination. And had it not been
for believing men, and believing women, whom ye know not, and whom
ye might have trampled upon, and blame might on their account
unwittingly have fallen upon you (God had not held thee back from
entering Mecca ; but he did so) that God might cause such as He
pleaseth to enter into His Mercy. If these had been separable, verily
WE had punished those of them (the inhabitants of Mecca) that disbelieve,[1] with a grievous punishment. When the Unbelievers raised
scruples in their own hearts,—the scruples of the Ignorance,—then God
sent down Tranquillity upon His Apostle, and upon the Believers, and
fixed in them the word of Piety ;[2] and they were the best entitled to it,
and worthy of the same ;—for God comprehendeth all things.

Now hath God verified unto His Apostle the Vision in truth ;—Ye shall surely enter the Holy Temple, if it please God, in security, having your heads shaven and your hair cut. Fear ye not : for He knoweth that which ye know not. And He hath appointed for you after this a speedy Victory besides. It is He who hath sent His Apostle with Guidance, and the true Religion,—that He may exalt it above every other.

Nature and effects of the 'Victory.'

The 'evident Victory,' with which the Sūra opens, has puzzled many of the commentators, who apply it to other occasions ; but their applications are all far-fetched. When the passage was ended, a bystander inquired : 'What ! is *this* the Victory ?' 'Yea,' Moḥammad replied, 'by Him in whose hand is my breath, it is a Victory.' Another reminded him of the promise that they should enter Mecca unmolested. 'True ; the Lord indeed hath promised this,' said the Prophet ; 'but did He ever promise it for the present year ?' The comments of Az-Zuhri, though somewhat exaggerated,

[1] That is, the unbelieving Ḳoreish. Moḥammad thus makes it appear that there were numerous Believers at Mecca unknown to him, and that God held him back from attacking Mecca lest these should have been involved in the common destruction.

[2] This refers to the words in the preamble of the treaty objected to by Ḳoreish, and is in effect an apology for having yielded to Suheil in respect of the epithets there used.

are much to the purpose. 'There was no previous Victory,' he says, 'in Islām, greater than this. On all other occasions there was fighting: but here war was laid aside, tranquillity and peace restored; the one party henceforward met and conversed freely with the other, and there was no man of sense or judgment amongst the idolaters who was not led thereby to join Islām. And truly in the two years that followed, as many persons entered the Faith as there belonged to it altogether before, or even a greater number.' 'And the proof of this,' adds Ibn Hishām, 'is that, whereas Moḥammad went forth to Al-Ḥodeibiya with only fifteen hundred men, he was followed two years later, in the attack on Mecca, by ten thousand.' [1]

Beni Khozā'a enter into alliance with Moḥammad

One of the first effects of the treaty was that the tribe of Khozā'a, who had long shown favour to the new faith, entered immediately into alliance with Moḥammad. The Beni Bekr, another tribe resident in the vicinity of Mecca, on the other hand, adhered to Ḳoreish. The stipulation for the surrender of converts at the instance of their guardians soon gave rise to one or two peculiar incidents. The son of Suheil, the representative of Ḳoreish who had just concluded the treaty, rushed into the Muslim camp at Al-Ḥodeibiya, and desired to follow Moḥammad.[2] But his father claimed him under the compact already ratified, and, although the lad earnestly remonstrated, the claim was admitted. 'Have patience, Abu Jandal!' said Moḥammad to him as he was dragged away,—'put thy trust in the Lord. He will work

Suheil's son given up by Moḥammad

[1] Ibn Hishām, p. 751. The truth is, that tradition depreciates the treaty in the light of subsequent events. It appeared strange in after days that he, who within two years was supreme at Mecca, could now be suing for permission to enter it, and that he was not only satisfied with the scanty terms obtained, but could even call them a 'Victory.' His present weakness was overlooked in the consideration of later triumphs. Hence the vaunting speech at Al-Ḥodeibiya put into 'Omar's mouth, that 'had these terms been settled by any other than by Moḥammad himself,—even by a commander of his appointment, he had scorned to listen to them'; and the indignant conversation he is said to have held with Abu Bekr: 'What! Is not Moḥammad the Prophet of God? Are we not Muslims? Are not they Infidels? Why then is our divine religion to be thus lowered?' Hence also the alleged unwillingness of the people to kill their victims at Al-Ḥodeibiya: for, says Ibn Hishām, they were like men dying of vexation.

[2] Aṭ-Ṭabari, i. 1547 ff.

out for thee, and for others like-minded with thee, a way of deliverance.'[1]

Abu Baṣīr gathers band of marauders and harasses Ḳoreish

Some little time after Moḥammad had returned home, Abu Baṣīr, a young convert, effected his escape from Mecca, and appeared at Medīna.[2] His guardians sent two servants with a letter to bring the deserter back. The obligation of surrender was at once admitted, and Abu Baṣīr was led away. But he had travelled only a few miles, when he seized the sword of one of the servants and slew him. The other fled back to Medīna; Abu Baṣīr himself followed, the naked sword in his hand still reeking with blood. Both soon reached the presence of Moḥammad; the servant to complain of the murder, Abu Baṣīr to plead for his freedom. The youth contended that as the Prophet had once for all fulfilled the letter of the treaty in delivering him up, he was now free to remain behind. Moḥammad gave no direct reply. His answer was enigmatical; but after an exclamation in praise of his bravery,[3] he added aside: '*What a kindler of war, if he had but with him a body of adherents!*' Thus encouraged, Abu Baṣīr quitted Medīna and, accompanied by five other Meccan youths, took up his position by the seashore on the caravan road to Syria. The words of Moḥammad were not long in becoming known at Mecca, and the restless youth of Ḳoreish, receiving them as a suggestion to follow the same example, set out to join Abu Baṣīr, who was soon surrounded with about seventy followers desperate as himself. They waylaid every caravan from Mecca (for since the truce, traffic with Syria had again sprung up) and spared the life of no one. Ḳoreish were at length so harassed by these attacks,

[1] The story is told with much over-colouring. Abu Jandal came up just as the treaty was completed, having escaped from Mecca *in his chains*. His father beat him and dragged him away. He screamed aloud to the Muslims to save him: but Moḥammad said that he could not diverge from the terms of the treaty just concluded. 'Omar walked by the lad as he was being led back, and comforted him with such words as these: 'The blood of these infidels is no better than the blood of dogs.' The whole story is so exaggerated, that it is difficult to say what degree of truth there is in it. But it must have had *some* foundation on fact.

[2] Ibn Hishām, p. 751 f.; Aṭ-Ṭabari, i. 1551 f.; Al-Wāḳidi, p. 261 f.

[3] 'Alas for his mother!' signifying that his bravery would surely lead him to be killed in some daring conflict.

that they solicited the interference of Moḥammad, and, on condition that the outrages were stopped, waived their right to have the deserters delivered up. Moḥammad acceded to the request, and summoned the marauders to desist. Abu Baṣīr was on his death-bed when he received the order; but the rest returned and took up their abode at Medīna.[1]

The stipulation for the surrender of deserters made no distinction as to sex.[2] A female having fled to Medīna, her brothers followed and demanded her restoration under the terms of truce. Moḥammad demurred. The Oracle was called in, and it gave judgment in favour of the woman. Women who came over to Medīna were to be 'tried,' and, if their profession was found sincere, to be retained. The unbelief of their husbands had, in fact, dissolved their marriage; they now might legally contract fresh nuptials with Believers, provided only that restitution were made of any sums expended by their former husbands as dower upon them. The marriage bond was similarly annulled between Believers and their wives who had remained behind at Mecca;—their dowers, moreover, might be reckoned in adjusting the payments due to Ḳoreish on account of the women retained at Medīna. Though the rule is thus laid down at length in the Ḳor'ān, few instances are cited by tradition.[3]

Rule as to women who fled from Mecca to Medīna

[1] The whole story is probably exaggerated; for Moḥammad, though within the letter of the treaty, was bound by its spirit to promote amity and peace.

[2] Ibn Hishām, p. 754 f.; Aṭ-Ṭabari, i. 1553 f.

[3] Al-Wāḳidi, p. 262 f. The woman here mentioned as coming over to Medīna was Um Kulthūm, daughter of 'Oḳba, so cruelly executed by Moḥammad after Bedr. Another similar refugee is noticed by C. de Perceval as married to 'Omar. On the other hand, 'Omar divorced Ḳoreiba, his wife, who remained at Mecca, and thereafter was married by Mu'āwiya, son of Abu Sufyān. Another similar case is cited by Ibn Hishām.

The rule is given in the 60th Sūra, which opens with strong remonstrances against making friends of unbelievers; and proceeds thus:—

'O ye that believe! When believing women come over unto you as Refugees, then try them; God well knoweth their faith. And if ye know them to be Believers, return them not again unto the infidels; they are not lawful (as wives) unto the infidels; neither are the infidels lawful (as husbands) unto them. But give unto them (the infidels) what they may have expended (on their dowers). It is no sin for you that ye marry them, after that ye shall have given them (the women) their dowers. v. 10 ff.

Moḥammad's dream of universal conformity to Islām

The pilgrimage to Al-Ḥodeibiya is the last event of importance during the sixth year of Moḥammad's residence at Medīna. But towards its close a new and singular project occupied his attention. It was nothing less than to summon the sovereigns of the surrounding States and Empires to listen to his teaching. The principles of Moḥammad had been slowly but surely tending towards this end. Wherever his arms had reached, the recognition of his Mission had been peremptorily demanded. Throughout the Peninsula it was his object that there should be no other religion than Islām. An exception indeed was made in favour of Jews and Christians; but even these, if they retained their faith, must pay tribute, as an admission of inferiority. He now dreamed of something even beyond Arabia. It may seem a chimerical and wild design in the Prophet of Medīna,—scarcely able as yet to maintain his own position, helplessly besieged twelve months before, and forced but lately to retire from Mecca with the purpose of pilgrimage unfulfilled,—that he should seek to extend his Mission to Egypt, Abyssinia,

And retain not the patronage of the unbelieving women; but demand back that which ye have spent (in their dowers); and let the infidels demand back what they have spent (on the women which come over to you). This is the judgment of God, which He establisheth between you; and God is knowing and wise.

'And if any of your wives escape from you unto the infidels, and ye have your turn (by the elopement of their wives unto you), then give to those whose wives have gone (out of the dowers of the latter) a sum equal to that which they have expended (on the dowers of the former); and fear God in whom ye believe. O Prophet! when believing women come unto thee, and plight their faith unto thee that they will not associate any with God, that they will not steal, neither commit adultery, that they will not kill their children, nor promulgate a calumny forged between their hands and their feet, and that they will not be disobedient unto thee in that which is reasonable,—then pledge thy faith unto them, and seek pardon of God for them. For God is gracious and merciful.'

Stanley (on 1 Cor. vii. 1-40) quotes the above passage, and says that the rule it contains 'resembles that of the Apostle.' But there is really no analogy between them; the Christian inculcation differs *toto cœlo* from that of Moḥammad: 'If any brother hath a wife that believeth not, and she be pleased to dwell with him, let him not put her away';—and similarly the case of a believing wife with an unbelieving husband (1 Cor. vii. 12-16). Whereas Moḥammad declares the marriage bond *ipso facto* annulled by the unbelief of either party, which indeed was only to be expected from the ideas he entertained regarding the marriage contract.

and Syria, nay even to the Roman and Persian Empires. But so it was. Apart from the steadfast and lofty conviction which he had of his duty as the Apostle of God, it is not to be supposed that one so sagacious and discerning should have failed to perceive an ominous disintegration in the signs of the times. The Roman Empire, broken and wearied by successive shocks of barbarous invasion, was now wasted by a long and devastating war with Persia. Schism had rent and paralysed the Christian Church. The Melchites and the Jacobites, the Monothelites, and the Nestorians, regarded each other with a deadly hatred, and were ready to welcome any intruder who would rid them of their adversaries. The new faith would sweep away all the sophistries about which they vainly contended: still holding fast the groundwork of previous Revelations, it would substitute a reformed and universal religion for the effete and erring systems which man had overlaid them with. Superstition, Mariolatry, and every form of Polytheism would fall, and the claims of truth in the end prevail. Such probably were the thoughts of Moḥammad, when he determined to send embassies to the Kaiser and the Chosroes, to Abyssinia, Egypt, Syria, and Al-Yemāma.

Seal engraved; and despatches prepared for foreign princes

It was suggested by one of his followers that the kings of the earth accepted no communication unless attested by a seal. Accordingly Moḥammad had one made of silver, and engraved with the words MOḤAMMAD THE APOSTLE OF GOD.[1] Letters were written and sealed, and six messengers simultaneously despatched to their various destinations on the opening of the new year, as shall be further related in the following chapter.

[1] We are told that his messengers, 'like the Apostles of Jesus,' were immediately endowed with the faculty of speaking the language of the country to which they were deputed. But Moḥammad evidently selected for the purpose men who, as travellers, merchants, or otherwise, had before visited the respective countries. Thus Diḥya was sent to Syria. (See *ante*, p. 346.) Less trustworthy authorities make these embassies to have started from Medīna, on various dates. But Ibn Sa'd states distinctly that all set out *on the same day*, in Moḥarram, A.H. VII.

CHAPTER XX

EMBASSIES TO VARIOUS SOVEREIGNS AND PRINCES[1]

A.H. VII.—A.D. 627

Struggle between the two empires, A.D. 609-627

FROM a period as far back as the assumption by Moḥammad of the prophetic office, the Roman and Persian kingdoms had been waging with each other a ceaseless deadly warfare. Until the year A.D. 621 unvarying success attended the Persian arms. Syria, Egypt, and Asia Minor were overrun. Constantinople itself was threatened. At last, Heraclius awoke from his inglorious lethargy; and, about the time of Moḥammad's flight from Mecca, was driving his invaders from their fastnesses in Asia Minor. In the second campaign he carried the war into the heart of Persia. During the three years in which the Kaiser was by this brilliant stroke retrieving the fortunes of the Empire, Moḥammad was engaged in his doubtful struggle with Ḳoreish. Then came the critical siege of Constantinople by the Avars and Persians which preceded by little more than half a year the siege of Medīna known as the battle of the Ditch. It is curious to remark that while the Muslims attributed the sudden departure of Abu Sufyān and his Arab hosts to the interposition of the Almighty, the Greeks equally ascribed their signal deliverance from the hordes of the Chagan to the favour of the Virgin. In the third campaign, 627 A.D., Heraclius followed up his previous success, and at the close of the year achieved the decisive victory of Nineveh. In this action the forces of Persia were irretrievably broken; the Chosroes fled from his capital; and, early in the following year, was murdered by his son Siroes, who ascended the throne and concluded a treaty of peace with the Emperor.

A.H. I. A.D. 622

A.H. II.-IV. A.D. 623-625

July, A.D. 626

March, A.D. 627

A.H. VI. A.D. 627

February, March, A.D. 628

[1] Ibn Hishām, p. 971 f.; Aṭ-Ṭabari, i. 1559 ff.

About the same period Moḥammad was at Al-Ḥodeibiya ratifying his truce with the chiefs of Mecca.

I. Despatch of Moḥammad to Heraclius. A.H. VII. A.D. 628

During the autumn, Heraclius, in fulfilment of his vow for the splendid success which had just crowned his arms, performed on foot the pilgrimage from Edessa to Jerusalem, where the 'True cross,' recovered from the Persians, was with solemn pomp restored to the Holy Sepulchre. While preparing for this journey, or during the journey itself, an uncouth despatch, in the Arabic character, was laid before him. It was forwarded by the Governor of Boṣra, into whose hands it had been delivered by an Arab envoy. The epistle was addressed to the Emperor himself, from 'Moḥammad the Apostle of God,' the rude impression of whose seal could be deciphered at the foot. In strange and simple accents, like those of the Prophets of old, it summoned Heraclius to acknowledge the mission of Moḥammad, to cast aside the idolatrous worship of Jesus and his Mother, and to return to the Catholic faith of the one only God.[1] The letter was probably cast aside, or preserved, it may be, as a strange curiosity, the effusion of some harmless fanatic.[2]

II. Despatch to Ghassānid Prince

Not long after, another despatch, bearing the same seal,

[1] The terms of this and the other despatches are altogether uncertain. The drafts given by tradition, with the replies, are apocryphal, and tinged with the idea of universal conquest, as yet existing (if at all) only in embryo. The ordinary copy of the letter to Heraclius contains a passage from the Ḳor'ān which, as shown by Weil, was not revealed till the Ninth year of the Hijra. Diḥya was desired by Moḥammad to forward this despatch through the Governor of Boṣra.

[2] Here is another tradition. 'Now the Emperor was at this time at Ḥimṣ, performing a pedestrian journey, in fulfilment of the vow which he had made that, if the Romans overcame the Persians, he would travel on foot from Constantinople to Ælia (Jerusalem). So having read the letter, he commanded his chief men to meet him in the royal camp at Ḥimṣ. And thus he addressed them: "Ye chiefs of Rome! Do ye desire safety and guidance, so that your kingdom shall be firmly established, and that ye may follow the commands of Jesus son of Mary?" "And what, O King! shall secure us this?" "Even that ye follow the Arabian Prophet," said Heraclius. Hearing this they all started aside like wild asses of the desert, each raising his cross and waving it aloft in the air. Whereupon, Heraclius, despairing of their conversion, and unwilling to lose his kingdom, desisted, saying that he had only wished to test their constancy and faith, and that he was now satisfied by this display of firmness and devotion. The courtiers bowed their heads; and so the Prophet's despatch was rejected.'

and couched in similar terms, reached the court of Heraclius. It was addressed to Al-Ḥārith VII., prince of the Beni Ghassān, who forwarded it to the Emperor, with an address from himself, soliciting permission to chastise the audacious impostor.[1] But Heraclius, regarding the ominous voice from Arabia beneath his notice, forbade the expedition, and desired that Al-Ḥārith should be in attendance at Jerusalem, to swell the imperial train at the approaching visitation of the Temple. Little did the Emperor imagine that the kingdom which, unperceived by the world, this obscure Pretender was founding in Arabia, would in a few short years wrest from his grasp that Holy city, and the fair provinces which, with so much toil and so much glory, he had just recovered from the Persians!

III. Despatch to King of Persia

The despatch for the King of Persia reached the court probably some months after the accession of Siroes. It was delivered to the Monarch, who, on hearing the contents, tore it in pieces. When this was reported to Moḥammad, he prayed and said: 'Even thus, O Lord! rend thou his kingdom from him!'

Conversion of Bādhān, Governor Yemen. A.H. VI. A.D. 628

An incident of date somewhat earlier, in connection with the Court of Persia, was followed by results of considerable importance.[2] A few months before his overthrow, the Chosroes, receiving strange reports of the Prophetical claims

[1] In the account of these events, it is difficult to say what grains of truth mingle with fiction. The messenger of Moḥammad found Al-Ḥārith in the gardens of Damascus, busied with preparations for the reception of the Emperor shortly expected on his way to Jerusalem. He waited at the gate of Al-Ḥārith three or four days, audience being granted at certain intervals. During this delay, the Porter having been instructed about Moḥammad and his doctrine, wept and said: 'I read the Gospel, and I find therein the description of this Prophet exactly as thou tellest me:' thereupon he embraced Islām, and desired his salutation to be given to the Prophet. On a set day, Al-Ḥārith, sitting in state, called for the messenger, and had the despatch read. Then he cast it aside and said: 'Who is he that will snatch my kingdom from me? I will march against him, were he even in the Yemen.' He became very angry, and, having called out his army in battle array, said to the messenger: 'Go, tell thy Master that which thou seest.' The messenger, however, was afterwards permitted to wait for the reply of Heraclius: on its receipt, Al-Ḥārith dismissed him with a present of one hundred mithcals of gold. When it was reported to the Prophet, he said that the kingdom had departed from Al-Ḥārith; and so Al-Ḥarith died the following year.

[2] Ibn Hishām, p. 46 f.; Aṭ-Ṭabari, i. 1572 f.

of Moḥammad, and of the depredations committed on the Syrian border by his marauding bands, had sent orders to Bādhān, the Persian Governor of the Yemen, to despatch two envoys to Medīna, and thus procure trustworthy information regarding the Pretender. Bādhān obeyed, and with the messengers sent a courteous despatch to Moḥammad. By this time, however, tidings had reached the Prophet of the deposition and death of the Persian Monarch. When the letter, therefore, was read before him, Moḥammad smiled at its contents, and summoned the envoys to embrace Islām. He apprised them of the murder of the Chosroes, and accession of his son: 'Go,' said he, 'inform your master of this, and require him to tender his submission to the Prophet of the Lord.' The glory of Persia had now departed. Long ago she had relaxed her grasp upon Arabia; and the Governor of the Yemen was now free to choose a protectorate more congenial to his people. Bādhān therefore gladly recognised the rising fortunes of Islām, and signified his adhesion to the Prophet. From the distance, however, his allegiance was at the first little more than nominal; but the accession served as a point for further action, and meanwhile added fresh prestige to the Prophet's name.

IV. Despatch to Governor of Egypt

The envoy sent by Moḥammad to Egypt was courteously received by the Muḳauḳis, the Roman Governor, but dismissed with a gentle and evasive answer. While declining to admit the claims of the Prophet, he gave substantial proof of friendly feeling in valuable presents which he forwarded with this reply:—'I am aware that a prophet is yet to arise; but I am of opinion that he will appear in Syria. Thy messenger hath been received with honour. I send for thine acceptance two sisters, such as are prized among the Copts, a present of raiment, and a mule for thee to ride upon.' Though Moḥammad ascribed the unbelief of the Muḳauḳis to fear lest the government should slip from his hands, yet he willingly accepted the gifts. The two slave girls, indeed (strange present from a Christian prince), were well suited to his tastes. Mary, the fairest, was retained for his own ḥarīm; Sīrīn, the other, was presented to Ḥassān, the Poet, who, since his reconciliation with 'Ā'isha, had regained the Prophet's favour. The mule was white,—a rarity in Arabia; it was greatly prized, and was constantly ridden by Moḥammad.

V. Despatch to King of Abyssinia

The court of Abyssinia stood in a different relation to Moḥammad from that of the other kingdoms to which he addressed his apostolic summons. There his followers had long ago found a secure and hospitable retreat from the persecutions of Ḳoreish; and although about forty had rejoined the Prophet after his flight to Medīna, there still remained fifty or sixty enjoying the protection of the Abyssinian Prince. 'Amr ibn Omeiya was now the bearer of two despatches to him.[1] One was couched in language like that addressed to the other Christian kings; and to this the Negus replied in terms of humble acquiescence,—embracing the new faith, and mourning over his inability to join in person the standard of the Prophet.[2] In the second despatch, the Prophet begged that his remaining followers might now be sent to Medina; and the request was added that, before their departure, the Prince would betroth to him Um Ḥabība, daughter of Abu Sufyān, whose early charms, though she was now five-and-thirty years of age, still held a place in his imagination.[3] Her former husband, 'Obeidallah, one of the 'Four Inquirers,' after emigrating a Muslim to Abyssinia, had there embraced Christianity, and died in its profession. By this alliance Moḥammad at once gratified his desire for fresh nuptials (he had been now a whole year without adding any new inmate to his ḥarīm); and, perhaps, further hoped to make Abu Sufyān, the father of Um Ḥabība, more favourable to his cause.[4] The prince performed with readiness the part assigned him in the ceremony. He also provided two ships for the exiles, in which they all embarked, and in the autumn reached Medīna safely.

Um Ḥabība betrothed to Moḥammad

Abyssinian refugees reach Medīna. August, A.D. 628

[1] Mentioned above, p. 351.

[2] I have before, p. 92, given grounds for doubting the conversion of the Negus. It was quite possible for a Christian Prince, more especially if he held Arian or Nestorian views, and had seen only certain portions of the Ḳor'ān (those for example containing attestations of the Jewish and Christian Scriptures, and exhortations against idolatry), to have expressed an assent to the terms of Moḥammad's epistle. For the efforts of the various Christian sects to gain over the Abyssinians, see Gibbon, chapter xlvii.

[3] Aṭ-Ṭabari, i. 1570.

[4] Sprenger questions this view, and thinks that, with the Arab sentiments regarding women, Moḥammad's marriage with his daughter must, so long as he was unconverted, have been a mortification to Abu Sufyān, rather than a satisfaction. Um Ḥabība survived Moḥammad some thirty years, and died during the Caliphate of her brother Mu'āwiya.

VI. Despatch to Chief of Al-Yemāma

The sixth messenger was sent to Haudha, chief of the Beni Ḥanīfa, a Christian tribe, in Al-Yemāma.[1] He was hospitably entertained; and the chief, having presented him with change of raiment and provisions for the journey home, dismissed him with this reply for his master: 'How excellent is that Revelation to which thou invitest me, and how beautiful! Know that I am the Poet of my tribe, and an Orator. The Arabs revere my dignity. Grant unto me, therefore, a share in the rule, and I will follow thee.' When Moḥammad had read the answer, he said: 'Had this man asked of me but an unripe date, as his share in the land, I would not have given it. Let him perish, and his vainglory with him!' Thus cursed, Haudha died, we are told, in the following year.

[1] Ibn Hishām, p. 971; Aṭ-Ṭabari, i. 1560 f.

CHAPTER XXI

THE CONQUEST OF KHEIBAR[1]

A.H. VII.—*August and September*, A.D. 628

ÆTAT. 60

Expedition against Kheibar

ON his way back from Al-Ḥodeibiya, in the spring of the year, Moḥammad, as we have seen, had foretold 'a speedy victory and spoils in abundance elsewhere.' The summer passed quietly, and it was autumn before measures were taken to fulfil the promise. The destined prey was the Jewish settlement of Kheibar on the way to Syria.

Army marches. A.H. VII. August, A.D. 628

The army marched from Medīna, 1,600 strong; being about the same number as had followed the Prophet on his pilgrimage to Al-Ḥodeibiya. But the force was greatly more powerful in cavalry, the number being estimated at above a hundred, while it had never before exceeded thirty. Many of the citizens and the Bedawīn who had neglected the former summons, would gladly now have joined the tempting expedition; but, according to the divine injunction, they were not permitted, and their mortification was great at being left behind. Um Selama was again the favoured companion of the Prophet.

Kheibar surprised

The distance, about a hundred miles, was accomplished in three forced marches. So quick was the movement, and the surprise so complete, that the cultivators of Kheibar, issuing forth in the morning to their fields, suddenly found themselves confronted by a great army, and rushed back to the city in dismay. The rapidity of the approach cut off all hope of timely aid from the Beni Ghaṭafān.[2]

[1] Ibn Hishām, p. 755 ff.; Aṭ-Ṭabari, i. 1575 ff.; Al-Wāḳidi, p. 264 ff.; Ibn Sa'd, p. 77 ff.

[2] According to Ibn Hishām, Moḥammad took up a position so as to cut off their assistance, and he adds that the Ghaṭafān did go forth to aid

The rich vale of Kheibar was studded with villages and fortresses rudely built but posted strongly on the rocks or eminences which here and there rose from amidst the luxuriant date-groves and fields of corn. One by one, before any opposition could be organised, these forts were attacked and carried. '*Kharibat Kheibar*,' cried Moḥammad, with a jubilant play upon the name, as he passed from one stronghold triumphantly to another; '*Kheibar is undone. Allah Akbar! Great is the Lord! Truly when I light upon the coasts of any People, woe unto them in that day!*' From the villages first attacked, which were gained with little loss, Moḥammad proceeded to the strong fortress of Al-Ḳamūṣ. Here the Jews, who now had time to rally round their chief Kināna (the successor of his grandfather, Abu Rāfi', assassinated some months before), posted themselves in front of the citadel, resolved on a desperate struggle. After some vain attempts to dislodge them, Moḥammad planned a general attack: 'I will give the Eagle,' he said—'the great black Flag,—into the hands of one that loveth the Lord and His Apostle, even as he is beloved of them; he shall gain the victory.'[1] Next morning the flag was placed in 'Alī's hands, and the troops advanced. At this moment, a soldier stepped forth from the Jewish line, and challenged his adversaries to single combat: 'I am Marḥab,' he cried, 'as all Kheibar knoweth, a warrior bristling with arms when the war fiercely burneth.' The first Muslim who answered the challenge, aimed a blow at the Jewish champion with deadly force, but the sword recoiled upon himself, and he

The fortresses one by one fall before Moḥammad

General action before the fort of Al-Ḳamūṣ

their allies, but returned on a rumour that their own homes were being attacked. The fact, however, is that Moḥammad's advent was totally unexpected. 'When the Muslim army alighted before Kheibar, they did not stir that night, nor did a fowl cackle at them, till the sun arose. At dawn, the inhabitants opened their fortresses as usual, and went forth with their cattle, their spades, hoes, and other instruments of husbandry; suddenly perceiving the army in front they fled back into their forts, screaming: "*It is Moḥammad and his hosts!*"'

[1] There had been no great standard like this before. It is said to have been made out of a black mantle worn by 'Ā'isha,—a gallant device, and was called 'Oḳāb, the 'Black Eagle.' There were two other smaller banners of white, held, one by Al-Ḥobāb, the other by Sa'd ibn 'Obāda, both Citizens.

fell fatally wounded.[1] Marḥab repeating his vainglorious challenge, 'Alī advanced saying:—'I am he whom my mother named *the Lion;* like a lion of the howling wilderness, I weigh my foes in the giant's balance.' The combatants closed, and 'Alī cleft the head of Marḥab in two. Marḥab's brother having rashly renewed the challenge, Az-Zubeir went forth and slew him.[2] The Muslim line now made a general advance, and, after a sharp conflict, drove back the enemy. In this battle, 'Alī performed great feats of prowess. Having lost his shield, he seized the lintel of a door, which he wielded effectually in its stead. Tradition has magnified the shield into a gigantic beam, and the hero into a second Samson.[3] The victory was decisive, for the Jews lost 93 men; while of the Muslims, only 19 were killed throughout the whole campaign.

Jews beaten back with loss

Kināna tortured and put to death

After this defeat, the citadel of Al-Ḳamūṣ surrendered, on condition that the inhabitants were free to leave the country, but that they should give up all their property to the conqueror. With the rest, came forth Kināna, chief of Kheibar, and his cousin. Moḥammad accused them of keeping back, in contravention of the compact, some part of the treasure, and notably the marriage portion Kināna had obtained with his bride Ṣafīya, whose father perished in the slaughter of the Beni Ḳoreiẓa. 'Where are the vessels of

[1] The people cried out 'He hath killed himself: his works are vain' (because of his suicidal death). 'Nay,' said Moḥammad, 'he shall have a double reward!' On the road to Kheibar, this man had recited some martial verses before Moḥammad, who thanked him, saying: 'The Lord have mercy on thee!' It is said that this mode of blessing from Moḥammad, invariably portended impending martyrdom. The verses, by the way, are the same as those ascribed to Moḥammad at the battle of the Ditch.

[2] As Az-Zubeir walked forth to the combat, his mother Ṣafīya ran up to Moḥammad in alarm, crying out that her son would be killed: 'Not so, my Aunt!' replied Moḥammad; 'he will slay his fellow, if the Lord will!' Many women went from Medīna on this campaign to minister to the wounded. A story, very illustrative of the combined simplicity and coarseness of Arab manners, is given in the conversation of Moḥammad with a young woman of the Beni Ghifār, who rode on the same camel, and confided to him certain of her ailments.

[3] The story is in the ordinary cast of exaggerated tradition. Abu Rāfi', Moḥammad's servant, went after the battle to see the beam, in company with seven others, who together tried to *turn it over*, and were unable.

gold,' he asked further, 'the vessels ye used to lend to the people of Mecca?' They protested that they no longer possessed them. 'If ye conceal anything from me,' said Moḥammad, 'and I should gain knowledge of it, then your lives and the lives of your families shall be at my disposal.' They answered that it should be so. A recreant Jew, having divulged to Moḥammad the place in which some of the valuables lay hid, he sent and fetched them. On their appearance, Kināna was subjected to cruel torture—'fire being placed upon his breast till his breath had almost departed'—in the hope that he would confess where the remainder was concealed. Moḥammad then gave command, and the heads of both chief and cousin were severed from their bodies.

Marriage of Moḥammad with Ṣafīya, Kināna's bride

On this, Bilāl was sent to fetch Kināna's bride, Ṣafīya, a damsel some seventeen years of age, whose beauty was probably well known at Medina.[1] He speedily performed his errand, and finding her with her cousin, brought them both across the battlefield strewed with the dead, and close by the corpses of Kināna and his cousin. At the ghastly sight, Ṣafīya's companion screamed wildly, beating her face, and casting dust upon her head. 'Take that she-devil hence,' said Moḥammad, angrily: but aside he chided Bilāl for his want of consideration in taking them by the bodies of their relatives. 'Truly,' said the heartless negro, 'I did it of purpose, to see their anger and their fright.' But Moḥammad was moved by tenderer feelings; turning to Ṣafīya, he cast his mantle over her, in token that she was to be his own, and then made her over to the care of Bilāl. One of his followers had coveted this Jewish beauty; but Moḥammad contented him with her cousin.

Consummated at Kheibar

Ṣafīya, nothing loth, transferred her affections to the conqueror, who tarried not to take her to himself.[2] The

[1] No doubt this was the case, because (1) she was the daughter of a chief who had long lived at Medīna, and was well known there; and (2), because Moḥammad, immediately upon Kināna's execution, sent for her and cast his mantle over her.

[2] The interval is not stated anywhere, but it could not have been of long duration. Ibn Hishām says the marriage took place at Kheibar, or on the way returning from it, and other traditions imply no delay. [Al-Wāḳidi (p. 291 f.) says on the return journey at Wādi al-Ḳora.] I have met no credible tradition intimating Ṣafīya's conversion, as is commonly

wedding was celebrated by an abundant feast of dates, curdled milk, and butter. Earth was heaped up into the shape of tables; on these the viands were spread, and the guests ate and made merry. Meanwhile the Prophet had charged a female attendant suitably to array the bride, and make her ready for him. When the repast was ended, the people prepared for the march; and they watched Moḥammad, saying: 'We shall see now whether he hath taken her for his wife or as a slave girl.' So when he called for a screen to hide her from the public gaze, they knew that he had taken her as his wife. Moḥammad lowered his knee to help her to ascend the camel: and she, after some coy demur, placed her foot upon his bended knee, while he (a bridegroom now of sixty years of age) raised her into the litter, and seating himself thus before her, guided the camel in the evening to the bridal tent. In the morning he heard the noise of one rustling at the curtain of the tent. It was Abu Eiyūb, who had kept watch there all night with his drawn sword. 'What has brought thee here?' asked Moḥammad, surprised at the inopportune presence of his friend: 'O Prophet!' he replied, 'I bethought me that the damsel is young; it is but as yesterday that she was married to Kināna, whom thou hast slain. And thus, distrusting her, I said to myself, *I will watch by the tent and be close at hand, in case she attempt anything against thee.*' Moḥammad blessed him for his careful though ill-timed vigilance, and desired him to withdraw in peace. The precaution was unnecessary; for while Moḥammad was evidently enamoured of his bride, she not the less readily accommodated herself to the new alliance. It is related that she bore the mark of a bruise upon her eye; when the Prophet asked her tenderly the cause, she told him that, being yet Kināna's bride, she saw in a dream as if the moon had fallen from the heavens into her lap; and that when

Safīya's dream

supposed, before her marriage. Anyhow, it is clear that the period before marrying a woman previously the wife of another was not observed. Either such ordinance had not yet been imposed, or Moḥammad exempted himself from its operation. Um Suleim (mother of the Prophet's servant Anas) bathed Ṣafīya, dressed her hair, and, having arrayed her in bridal attire, carried her to Moḥammad. Ṣafīya's dower was her freedom.

she told it to Kināna, he struck her violently, saying: 'What is this thy dream but that thou covetest the new king of the Ḥijāz, the Prophet, for thy husband!' The mark of the blow was the same which Moḥammad saw.[1]

Moḥammad partakes of a poisoned kid

But all the fair sex of Kheibar were not so fickle and so faithless. The nuptials of Moḥammad were damped by the revenge of Zeinab, sister of the warrior Marhab, who had lost her husband, as well as father and brothers, in the battle. She dressed a kid with dainty garnishing, and, having steeped it in poison, placed the dish with fair words before Moḥammad at his evening repast.[2] Graciously accepting the gift, he took for himself the shoulder, his favourite piece, and distributed portions to Abu Bekr and other friends, including one called Bishr, who sat next him. 'Hold!' cried Moḥammad, as he swallowed the first mouthful, 'surely this shoulder hath been poisoned;' and he spat forth what remained in his mouth.[3] Bishr, who had eaten more than Moḥammad, at once changed colour, and stirred neither hand nor foot until he died. Moḥammad was seized with excruciating pain, and caused himself, and all those who had with him partaken of the dish, to be freely cupped between the shoulders. Zeinab, when put upon her defence answered bravely:—'Thou hast inflicted grievous injuries on my people; thou hast slain my father, and my uncle, and my husband. Therefore I said within myself, if he be a Prophet he will reject the gift knowing that the kid is poisoned; but if a mere pretender, then we shall be rid of him, and the Jews again will prosper.' She was put to death.[4] The effect of the poison was felt by Moḥammad to his dying day.[5]

[1] Ṣafiya survived Moḥammad forty years, and died A.H. 52.

[2] Ibn Hishām, p. 764 f.; Aṭ-Ṭabari, i. 1583

[3] Moḥammad, according to the favourite tradition, cried out, 'The shoulder *tells* me' (lit. *lets me know*) 'that it is poisoned.' But, however this story may have grown up, the statement is clear that he 'swallowed' the first mouthful before he perceived the evil taste.

[4] Some say that she was set free upon making this exculpatory statement. But the balance of tradition is according to the text. Certain traditions state that she was made over to the relatives of Bishr, to be put to death judicially for having poisoned him.

[5] Hence the conceit that Moḥammad had the merit of a 'martyr'; and the same is also said of Abu Bekr.

Remaining fortresses, with Fadak, capitulate

After the victory of Al-Ḳamūṣ, the only remaining strongholds, Al-Waṭīḥ and Sulālim, were invested, and, seeing no prospect of relief, capitulated.[1] Both were thus saved from being sacked; but, like the rest of Kheibar, their lands were subjected to a tax of half the produce. Fadak, a Jewish town, not far from Kheibar, profited by the example, and, having tendered a timely submission, was admitted on the same terms. On his march homeward, Moḥammad laid siege to the Jewish settlement of Wādi al-Ḳora, which, after a resistance of one or two days, surrendered upon like conditions.[2] The authority of Moḥammad was thus established over all the Jewish tribes north of Medīna.

Siege of Wādi al-Ḳora. A.H. VII. September, A.D. 628

Division of the rich plunder

The plunder of Kheibar was rich beyond experience. Besides vast stores of dates, oil, honey and barley, flocks of sheep and herds of camels, the spoil in treasure and jewels was very large.[3] A fifth was as usual set apart for the Prophet's use and for distribution at will among his family and the destitute poor. The remaining four-fifths were sold by outcry, and the proceeds, according to the prescribed rule, divided into 1,800 shares, being one for a foot soldier, and three for a horseman.

Territory, how disposed of

The villages and lands were disposed of in another way. One half, embracing all the places which surrendered without fighting, was reserved for Moḥammad, and constituted thereafter a species of Crown domain. The other moiety was allotted in freehold plots, by the same rule as the personal booty. A large and permanent reward was thus secured for all who had given proof of their faith and loyalty by accompanying Moḥammad to Al-Ḥodeibiya, and the promise made on that expedition thus amply redeemed. The Prophet, too, had now an ample revenue at his disposal. From this he made liberal assignment for the maintenance of his wives in so many measures yearly to each of dates and barley. The poor also were not forgotten. The remainder formed a reserve for the entertainment of visitors, support of

[1] Ibn Hishām, p. 764; Aṭ-Ṭabari, i. 1582 f. [2] Aṭ-Ṭabari, i. 1584 f.

[3] Ibn Hishām says that, from the time of Kheibar, *slaves* became very plentiful among the Muslims. I do not, however, find that, excepting the family of Kināna, any mention is made of slaves taken at Kheibar. But money, which the victors obtained plentifully at Kheibar, could purchase them cheaply in any part of Arabia.

auxiliaries, and other purposes of State. The power of Moḥammad no longer rested on spiritual resource alone, but on the more substantial basis also of the thews and sinews of war.

Jewish cultivators left in occupation

Even where the lands having been gained by storm were apportioned as private property, it was found expedient, in the absence of other cultivators, to leave the Jews in possession, on the same condition as with the public lands, namely, surrendering half the produce. An appraiser was deputed yearly to assess the amount, to realise the rents, and bring them to Medīna.[1] This arrangement continued till the Caliphate of 'Omar,[2] when, there being no longer any scarcity of Muslim husbandmen, the Jews were expatriated, and entire possession taken of the land.[3]

Special ordinances promulgated at Kheibar

Some special ordinances were promulgated in this campaign. The flesh of the domestic ass (which the army on their first approach to Kheibar were driven by want of other food to eat) was forbidden, as well as that of all carnivorous animals.[4] Some restrictions were laid upon the

[1] 'Abdallah ibn Rawāḥa first performed this duty, being a sort of arbiter between the Jewish cultivators and the Muslim proprietors. Whenever the former charged him with exceeding in his estimate, he would say: 'If it seem good unto you, take ye the estimated sum and give us the crop, or give us the estimated sum, and keep ye the crop.' The Jews greatly esteemed his justice. He was killed the year following at Mūta.

[2] Ibn Hishām, p. 779; Aṭ-Ṭabari, i. 1590.

[3] Such is the reason assigned by Al-Wāḳidi. Advantage was naturally taken by 'Omar, when he decided on the expatriation of the Jews, of the fact that his son 'Abdallah had been wounded in his possessions at Kheibar; but it is admitted that there was no proof as to who committed the outrage. 'Omar concluded that it must have been the Jews, simply because it was the second instance of the kind. The previous case was one of murder; but the perpetrator was not discovered, and therefore Moḥammad justly paid the blood-money as a public charge.

Two other grounds to justify 'Omar's expulsion of the Jews are given by tradition, (1) Moḥammad had stipulated that the Jews were to hold possession, pending his pleasure,—they were mere tenants-at-will. (2) Moḥammad said on his death-bed that no religion but Islām was to be permitted throughout the peninsula. According to Sprenger, 'Omar paid the Jews of Kheibar half the value of their lands as compensation. See the *Caliphate*, p. 156.

[4] See similar prohibitions in the Ḳor'ān as to what is torn, or dieth of itself, &c. (Sūra v. 1 ff.). There are some curious traditions on this part

immediate liberty of cohabitation heretofore enjoyed in respect of female captives; but, of whatever nature, it is clear that they did not fetter Moḥammad in his marriage with the captive Ṣafīya.[1] The most stringent rules were issued to prevent fraudulent appropriation from the common stock of booty. 'No Believer shall sell aught of the spoil, until it has been divided; nor shall he take a beast therefrom and, after riding upon it until it become lean, return it to the common stock; nor shall he take and wear a garment, and then send it back threadbare.' A follower was convicted of the theft of two sandal-straps; the articles were insignificant; yet, said the Prophet to the thief: 'Verily there shall be cut out for thee hereafter two thongs like unto them of fire.' When the army alighted before Wādi al-Ḳora, one of Moḥammad's servants was shot by an arrow while in the act of taking the litter down from one of the camels. 'Welcome to Paradise!' exclaimed the bystanders. 'Never,' said Moḥammad, 'by Him in whose hand my life is! Even now his vestment is burning upon him in the fire of Hell; for he pilfered it before Kheibar from amongst the booty.'[2]

A martyr gains Paradise who had never prayed

As a counterfoil, the following tradition assumes the certainty of Paradise by the mere profession of Islām. Al-

of the narrative; the soldiers were everywhere boiling asses' flesh in their pots throughout the camp, when the order was given, and forthwith they all overturned their pots. Horseflesh is allowed.

[1] The subject is one into which, from its nature, I cannot enter with much detail. Some traditions hold that Moḥammad now prescribed that the '*istibrā*,' or interval required of a woman before re-marriage, was to be equally observed with respect to women taken in war. The Sunna has fixed this period for female slaves at half the interval required for free women,—that this, two months (or possibly a month and a half), before the lapse of which, consorting with slave girls so captured (supposing the restriction to apply to such) would be unlawful. Some traditions make the prohibition delivered on the present occasion to apply to pregnant women only. Certainly, in the campaigns of the Caliphate, female captives were immediately consorted with by their captors even on the field of battle.

[2] Ibn Hishām, p. 765; Al-Wāḳidi, p. 292. The story is very possibly exaggerated, it being an object among the Muslims to make the general right of the army in all the booty taken by it as sacred as possible. But it shows the tendency and spirit of the system, under which a tradition of this nature could be put into the mouth of the Prophet, and, as such, gain currency.

Aswad, shepherd of one of the Jews of Kheibar, came over to Moḥammad, and declared himself a believer. Abandoning his flock, he straightway joined the Muslim army and fought in its ranks.[1] He was struck by a stone and killed, before he had as yet offered up a single prayer. But he died fighting for the faith, and had secured the Martyr's crown. Surrounded by a company of his followers, Moḥammad visited the corpse, which had been laid out for him to pray over. When he drew close to the spot, he stopped and modestly looked aside. 'Why dost thou thus avert thy face?' asked those about him. 'Because,' said Moḥammad, 'two black-eyed "Houries" of Paradise are with the Martyr now; they wipe the dust from off his face, and fondly solace him.'[2]

Moḥammad welcomes Ja'far and other Abyssinian exiles. Autumn, A.H. VII. A.D. 628

On the way home, Moḥammad had the pleasure of welcoming his cousin Ja'far, who, with some of the exiles just returned from Abyssinia, went out to meet him.[3] 'I know not,' said Moḥammad on this occasion, 'which of the two delighteth me the most, the conquest of Kheibar or the return of Ja'far.' The army, no less pleased, acceded cheerfully to his proposal that Ja'far and his companions should share equally with them in the spoil of Kheibar.

And marries Um Ḥabība

On his return to Medīna, Moḥammad took to wife Um Ḥabība, daughter of Abu Sufyān, thus consummating the marriage which the Negus had contracted for him in Abyssinia. There were now nine wives, besides two female slaves, in the ḥarīm of the Prophet.

Moḥammad bewitched by Jews

Before closing this chapter, which contains the last notice of the Jews, I ought to mention the tale of Moḥam-

[1] Ibn Hishām, p. 769 f. It is said that he asked Moḥammad what he was to do with his flock. On the principle that a believer must first discharge all his trusts and obligations, even those contracted with idolaters, before joining the standard of Islām, the Prophet desired him to throw a handful of gravel in the face of his sheep and goats, and they all ran off forthwith to their owner in the fortress. On the same principle, it is said that 'Alī and other converts first scrupulously discharged the trusts which Ḳoreish had committed to them, before leaving Mecca to join Moḥammad at Medīna.

[2] 'Whenever a martyr is slain in battle,' so runs the tradition, 'his two black-eyed "Houries" embrace him, wipe the dust from his face, and say,—"*The Lord cast dust on the face of him who hath cast dust on thine, and slay him who slew thee!*"'

[3] Ibn Hishām, p. 781 ff.; Al-Wāḳidi, p. 282.

mad's having been bewitched by a Jewish spell. On his return from Al-Ḥodeibiya, the Jews still remaining at Medīna (ostensibly converted but hypocrites at heart) bribed the sorcerer Labīd and his daughters to bewitch Moḥammad. This they did by secretly procuring hairs combed from the Prophet's head, and tying eleven knots with them on a palm-branch, which was then sunk in a well and covered with a large stone. The enchantment took effect. Moḥammad began to pine away, to fancy he had done things which in reality he never had done, to lose his appetite and neglect his wives. At last, Gabriel having told him the secret, the well was emptied, and the knots untied. Immediately the spell broke, and the Prophet was relieved.

Sūras cxiii., cxiv.

I confess myself unable to say what portion of the tale is likely to be true, or whether it has any foundation in fact at all. The common tradition is, that the last two Sūras in the Ḳo'rān were revealed on this occasion, containing a charm (still used as such) against spells and incantations; and that, during the recitation of the eleven verses which they contain, the knots unravelled themselves one by one till the whole were unloosed, and the charm dissolved. One of these Sūras is as follows :—

Sūra cxiii.

> Say :—I flee for Refuge to the Lord of the Daybreak,—from the evil of that which he hath created ; and from the evil of the darkness when it overshadoweth ; and from the evil of the Women that blow upon the knots ; and from the evil of the Envious man when he envieth.

Considerations as to credibility of the tale

The story may possibly have grown out of the penultimate verse of this Sūra, in which Moḥammad prays to be delivered 'from the evil of women blowing upon knots.' Or, on the other hand, it may be founded on suspicions actually entertained by Moḥammad against the Jews, of sorcery by the tying of knots and other forms of incantation ; and these suspicions may have led to the composition of the Sūra.

Its credibility partly sustained

The latter alternative is the more likely, as Moḥammad had already suspected the Jews of bewitching the Muslim women into barrenness.[1] On the present occasion, he is said to have caused the well into which the mysterious knots were cast to be dug up, and another sunk in its place. After visiting the garden watered by the well, he told 'Ā'isha that 'the

[1] *Vide supra*, p. 199.

date-trees in it were like devils' heads, and the water dark as a decoction of Henna.' She inquired whether the incident might with propriety be spoken of; he replied that it would be better not to divulge it, lest the evil of witchcraft should spread amongst his people. The well was filled up.[1]

[1] Some traditions say that the sorcerer was put to death; but the more reliable account is, that Moḥammad let him go free, but turned with aversion from him. Al-Wāḳidi has a profusion of traditions on the episode. Some say it was Labīd's *sisters* who aided him; and that it was *two angels* that revealed the plot to the Prophet.

CHAPTER XXII

THE FULFILLED PILGRIMAGE[1]

A.H. VII.—*February*, A.D. 629

Expeditions in autumn and winter. A.H. VII. A.D. 628

THE remainder of the Seventh year of the Hijra, that is, the autumn and winter of 628 A.D., was passed by Moḥammad at Medīna. Several expeditions were, during this period, despatched, under different leaders, in various directions. Beyond the chastisement and plunder of some offending tribes, and an occasional reverse, they were not attended by any important results. But they served to extend the influence of Moḥammad and bring him gradually into relations, hostile or friendly, with surrounding and even distant tribes.[2]

Moḥammad sets out on Lesser Pilgrimage. A.H. VII. February, A.D. 629

The month at length came round when Moḥammad, according to treaty, might visit Mecca and fulfil the 'Omra or Lesser Pilgrimage, from the rites of which he had been in the previous year debarred. Besides those who had made the unsuccessful pilgrimage to Al-Ḥodeibiya, many others accompanied him, so that the cavalcade numbered now about 2,000 men. Each was armed, according to stipulation, only

[1] Ibn Hishām, p. 788 f.; Aṭ-Ṭabari, i. 1594 f.; Al-Wākidi, p. 300 ff.; Ibn Sa'd, p. 87 f.

[2] Abu Bekr and 'Omar were among the commanders, and the expeditions were to distant parts; one beyond Mecca towards Nejrān, the others to Nejd in the east, and towards Kheibar in the north. One of the parties consisting of thirty men was cut to pieces, the leader only escaping. On another occasion many prisoners were taken, and among them (according to Sprenger) a female of great beauty who was sent to Mecca in ransom for certain prisoners; it seems doubtful, however, whether there were now any Muslim prisoners there. In another expedition, Moḥammad chid Osāma, son of Zeid, for killing an antagonist who shouted aloud the Muslim creed: 'What! didst thou split open his breast to see whether he told the truth or not?' Osāma promised not to do the like again.

with a sword; but, as a precaution against treachery, a heavy reserve of armour was carried separately. Moḥammad, son of Maslama, with a hundred horse, marched in advance of the pilgrims. Sixty camels for sacrifice were also driven in front. At Marr aẓ-Ẓahrān, a stage from Mecca, Moḥammad sent forward the store of armour to a valley outside the sacred territory, where it remained guarded by 200 men, while the rest advanced to the Ka'ba. The victims were also sent forward to a spot in the immediate vicinity of Mecca.

Precautionary arrangements before entering Mecca

Meanwhile, Ḳoreish, apprised of Moḥammad's approach, according to agreement evacuated the city in a body; and ascending the adjacent hills, expected with curious eye the Exile so long the troubler of their city. At last the cavalcade was seen emerging from the northern valley. At its head was Moḥammad, seated on Al-Ḳaṣwā; 'Abdallah ibn Rawāḥa, on foot in front, held the bridle; around on every side crowded the chief Companions; and behind, in a long extended line, the rest of the pilgrims on camels and on foot. Seven years had passed since Moḥammad and the Refugees last saw their native valley, and now with quickened step and long-repressed desire, they hastened forward and, as the Holy Temple came in view, raised high the pilgrim cry, *Labbeik! Labbeik!* Still mounted on his camel, the pilgrim mantle drawn under his right arm and thrown over the left shoulder, Moḥammad approached the Ka'ba, touched the Black Stone reverentially with his staff, and made the seven circuits of the sacred spot. The people followed, and, at the bidding of Moḥammad, to show Ḳoreish they were not weakened (as their enemies pretended) by the climate of Medīna, they ran the first three circuits at a rapid pace. Just then 'Abdallah, as he led the Prophet's camel, shouted at the pitch of his voice warlike and defiant verse. But 'Omar checked him; and Moḥammad said:—'Gently! son of Rawāḥa! Recite not this. Say rather, *There is no God but the Lord alone! It is He that hath upholden His servant, and exalted His people! Alone hath He put to flight the hosts of the Confederates.*' 'Abdallah proclaimed the words accordingly: and the people taking them up shouted the cry aloud as they encircled the Ka'ba, till the mighty sound rang round the valley.

Moḥammad enters Mecca; performs circuit of Ka'ba;

And slays the victims

The circuits completed, Moḥammad, still upon his camel, proceeded to the adjoining eminences of the Ṣafa and Merwa, and rode seven times from one to the other, according to ancient custom. The victims having then been placed in line at the Merwa, were sacrificed; Moḥammad calling aloud: 'This is the place of sacrifice, and so is every open valley of Mecca.' Then he shaved his head, and thus ended the ceremonies of the Lesser Pilgrimage. His next care was to relieve his followers on guard over the weapons at Yājaj, who then fulfilled their pilgrimage after the same example.

Guard over weapons do the same

Public prayer performed at the Ka'ba

On the morrow, Moḥammad ascended the inner chamber of the Ka'ba and remained there till the hour of prayer. Notwithstanding that the Temple was still garnished with the emblems of idolatry, Bilāl, mounting its roof, summoned the pilgrims with the usual cry to mid-day prayer. They crowded round from every quarter; and so under the shadow of the Holy House the service was led by the Prophet in the same form as in the Mosque of Medīna.

Singular sight presented at Mecca

It was surely a strange sight which at this time presented itself in the vale of Mecca—a sight, one might almost say, unique in history. The ancient city is for three days evacuated altogether by its inhabitants, and every house deserted. As they retire, the exiles, many years banished from their birthplace, accompanied by their allies, fill the valley, revisit the empty homes of their childhood, and within the short allotted period fulfil the rites of pilgrimage. The ousted citizens with their families, climbing the heights around, take refuge under tents or rocks amongst the hills and glens; and, clustering on the overhanging peak of Abu Ḳobeis, thence watch the movements of the visitors beneath, as with the Prophet at their head they perform the sacred rites—anxiously scanning every figure, if perchance to recognise among the worshippers some long-lost friend or relative.[1] It was a scene rendered possible only by the throes that gave birth to Islām.

[1] Her Highness the Begum of Bhopal thus describes the hill Abu Ḳobeis: 'The ascent of this hill is only about one mile from the base. The view from its summit of the house of God, its enclosure, and of the whole district comprised within the sacred boundary, is very distinct and picturesque. It is possible even to see distinctly the worshippers employed at their devotions within the holy shrine.'—*Pilgrimage to Mecca*, p. 204.

Moḥammad takes Meimūna to wife

While at Mecca, Moḥammad entered none of the houses there, but lived in a tent of leather pitched for him near the Ka'ba. Yet he held friendly converse with several of the citizens. Nor was he deterred either by his sacred errand, his advancing years, or having lately welcomed three new inmates to his ḥarīm, from negotiating another marriage. Meimūna, the favoured lady, six-and-twenty years of age, was sister-in-law of his uncle Al-'Abbās, into whose keeping since her widowhood she had committed the disposal of her hand. Moḥammad must have listened to the overtures of marriage the more readily as two of her sisters had already married into his family; but in truth the proposal of the young and charming widow who now offered herself as his bride was too congenial to the Prophet's tastes to require much pressure on the uncle's part.

Moḥammad warned to leave Mecca

Moḥammad endeavoured to turn the present opportunity for conciliating the citizens of Mecca to the best effect, and, as the sequel will show, not without success. But the time was short. Already the stipulated three days were ended, and he had entered on a fourth, when Suheil and Ḥuweiṭib, chief men of Ḳoreish, appeared before him and said: 'The period allowed thee hath elapsed: depart now therefore from amongst us.' To which the Prophet courteously replied: 'And what harm if ye allowed me to stay a little longer, celebrate my nuptials in your midst, and make for the guests a feast at which ye too might all sit down?' 'Nay,' they roughly answered; 'of any food of thine we have no need. Withdraw from hence!' Moḥammad gave immediate orders for departure: and by night not one of the pilgrims was left behind. Placing his bride in charge of his servant Abu Rāfi', he himself proceeded at once to Sarif, distant from the city eight or ten Arabian miles. In the evening, Meimūna having come up, the marriage was there consummated. Early next morning, the march was resumed, and the *cortège* returned to Medīna. Meimūna survived the Prophet fifty years, and was, by her desire, buried on the spot on which she had celebrated her marriage with him.[1]

Consummates his marriage with Meimūna

[1] Ibn Hishām, p. 790; Aṭ-Ṭabari, i. 1595. She died A.H. LXI., aged eighty. Burton states that her tomb is still visited at this place in the Wādi Fāṭima. The following anecdote may be of interest to the reader:

Number of his ḥarīm now complete

The ḥarīm of Moḥammad had now reached its limit; for this was the last marriage contracted by him. There were in it at this time ten wives, besides two servile concubines. but Zeinab, daughter of Khozeima, died before him; so that the number was then reduced to nine, or, including concubines, eleven. Some other women are mentioned by tradition, whose intended marriage was at the last stage broken off. The details in most instances are obscure. Of one case, at any rate, there can be no doubt: for a few years afterwards 'Ikrima, having married the lady in question, was subjected to grave animadversion by his troops, as if a slight had thereby been cast on the Prophet's memory. Abu Bekr, however, relieved him of all blame, on the ground that the marriage had been broken off by the Prophet before it was consummated.[1]

Sister and niece of his bride accompany him to Medīna

Moḥammad carried with him his bride's sister, Salma, widow of Ḥamza (who, apparently, had not accompanied her husband to Medīna), and 'Omārah, her unmarried daughter. Ja'far, 'Alī, and Zeid, each contending for the honour of receiving the damsel into his family, Moḥammad decided in favour of Ja'far, because he was married to her aunt Asmā.

Khālid, 'Amr, and 'Othmān ibn Ṭalḥa go over to Moḥammad

Another sister of Meimūna was the mother of Khālid, the famous warrior who had turned the tide of the battle at Oḥod against the Muslims. Not long after the marriage of his aunt to the Prophet, Khālid repaired to Medīna, and gave in his adhesion to the cause of Islām.[2] Two others followed

A deputation from a certain tribe came to Medīna, asking Moḥammad for help to discharge a debt, which he promised to give when the tithes came in. A nephew of Meimūna, being with this party, went to see his aunt. Moḥammad coming suddenly into the place, was disconcerted at the sight of a young man in such a place; his visage showed marks of wrath, and he turned to go away. 'It is only my sister's son,' cried Meimūna after him. So he returned. Then he took the young man into the Mosque for the mid-day prayer; and dismissed him with a blessing, placing both hands upon his head, and drawing them over his nose.

[1] See *Caliphate*, p. 40. The details regarding these unfulfilled marriages are not very edifying; neither, since they are in none of our early biographies, are they very trustworthy. A paper will be found with details of the wives, concubines, and broken-off marriages, by J. D. Bate, *Indian Antiquary*, April 1878.

[2] Al-Wāḳidi, p. 303 ff.

him. One, his friend, the equally famous 'Amr, whose poetic talents had often been used for the annoyance and injury of Moḥammad. Of versatile ability and weighty in council, he had been employed by Ḳoreish in their embassy to Abyssinia.[1] The other was 'Othmān, son of Ṭalḥa, a chief of some note, and custodian of the Ka'ba. He had, no doubt, in that capacity, attended with the keys of office to give Moḥammad admittance to the Holy House; and, perhaps, like many others, who gazed from a respectful distance on that memorable scene, was gained over by the devotion of the Prophet to the national shrine, and the elevation and beauty of the services which he there performed.

Moḥammad's position at Mecca improving

The position of Moḥammad at Mecca was greatly strengthened by the accession of such leading men. The balance was already wavering; it required little now to throw it entirely on the side of Islām. To what extent persons of less note and influence about this time came over to Medīna or remaining at Mecca declared in favour of Moḥammad, is not told to us. But there can be no doubt that the movement was not confined to those just mentioned, but was wide and general; and that the cause of Islām was gaining popularity day by day.

Coup d'état becoming possible

His visit to Mecca enabled Moḥammad thus to see and estimate the growth of his own influence there, as well as the waning power and spirit of Ḳoreish. The citizens of Mecca were weary of intestine war and bloodshed. The advocates of peace and compromise were growing in numbers and in confidence. Among Ḳoreish there were no chiefs of marked ability or commanding influence. A bold and rapid stroke might put an end to the struggle which for so many years had depressed and agitated Mecca. A *coup d'état* was fast becoming possible.

[1] Ibn Hishām, p. 716 f.; Aṭ-Ṭabari, i. 1601 f. [His name is often, but wrongly, written Amru or Amrou, because the Arabs add a *w* to it to distinguish it from the name 'Omar, which has the same consonants. This *w*, however, is never pronounced.] He was one of the envoys sent by Ḳoreish to Abyssinia; *vide supra*, p. 92.

CHAPTER XXIII

BATTLE OF MŪTA, AND OTHER EVENTS IN THE FIRST EIGHT MONTHS OF A.H. VII.—A.D. 629

ÆTAT. 61

Unfortunate expedition against Suleim. A.H. VII. April, A.D. 629

DURING the spring and summer of the Eighth year of the Hijra, several military excursions were undertaken, some of which ended disastrously. About a month after returning from pilgrimage, Moḥammad despatched a party of fifty men to the Beni Suleim, under a converted chief of their own, with the view apparently of winning them over to the faith. But, suspicious of their designs, they received the strangers with a cloud of arrows. Most of them were slain, and the leader with difficulty escaped. The tribe, however, must have seen cause to change their views, for we find them amongst those who shortly after sent embassies of submission to the Prophet, and also contributed an important contingent in the coming attack on Mecca.[1]

Marauding party sent against Beni Leith. A.H. VIII. June, A.D. 629

A month or two later an expedition was planned against a petty branch of the Beni Leith, on the road to Mecca, the object of which is not stated. The encampment was surprised, and their camels plundered. But the marauders were in their turn pursued, and only saved by rapid flight.[2] In the preceding winter, a small party, sent by Moḥammad towards Fadak, had been cut to pieces by the Beni Murra. A detachment of 200 men was now despatched to inflict chastisement upon them: 'If the Lord deliver them into thy hands,' said Moḥammad to the leader, 'let not a soul of them escape.' The commission was executed with success. All who fell within the reach of the avenging force were slain, and their camels carried off in triumph to Medīna.[3]

Beni Murra chastised

[1] Al-Wāḳidi, p. 303; Ibn Sa'd, p. 89.

[2] Al-Wāḳidi, p. 307 f.; Ibn Sa'd, p. 89 f.

[3] Al-Wāḳidi, p. 297 f.; Ibn Sa'd, p. 91.

Mishap at Dhāt Aṭlāḥ. A.H. VIII. July, A.D. 629

Soon after, a party of fifteen men was sent to Dhāt Aṭlāḥ, on the borders of Syria.[1] There they found a great multitude assembled, who were called upon to embrace Islām. A shower of arrows was the decisive answer. The Muslims fought desperately; one man alone survived to tell the tale. Moḥammad was much afflicted by this calamity, and planned an expedition to avenge it.[2] But tidings reached him that the place had been deserted, and he relinquished the idea for the moment. As in the case of similar mishaps, this reverse is described by tradition with enigmatical brevity, so that it is difficult to determine the object of the expedition. It may have been an embassy to certain tribes, or a secret mission to spy out the cause of rumoured gatherings on the Syrian frontier.

Perhaps the cause of the attack on Mūta

Army marches from Medīna upon Mūta. A.H. VIII. September, A.D. 629

This disaster not improbably paved the way for the grand attack directed shortly after against the border-districts of Syria. The cause, however, ordinarily assigned for this invasion of the Roman territory was the murder by the chieftain Shuraḥbīl, at Maāb or Mūta, of a messenger on his way with a despatch from Moḥammad, to the Ghassānid prince at Boṣra. It was immediately resolved to punish the offending chief.[3] A general call of all the fighting men was made, and a camp of 3,000 soldiers formed outside the city at Al-Jurf. A white banner was mounted; and the Prophet, placing it in the hands of his adopted son Zeid, bade him march to the spot where his messenger had been slain, summon the inhabitants to embrace Islām, and, should they refuse, then in the name of the Lord to draw the sword against them. If Zeid were cut down, then Ja'far was to command; if Ja'far, then 'Abdallah ibn Rawāḥa; and if he too were disabled, then the army should choose their own commander. Moḥammad accompanied them as far as the *Mount of Farewell*, a rising ground some little distance from Medīna; and, as they passed onwards, blessed them thus: 'The Lord shield you from every evil, and bring you back in peace, laden with spoil!'

[1] Ibn Hishām, p. 983; Aṭ-Ṭabari, i. 1601; Al-Wāḳidi, p. 308; Ibn Sa'd, p. 92.

[2] Ibn Hishām, p. 791 ff.; Aṭ-Ṭabari, i. 1610 ff.; Al-Wāḳidi, p. 309 ff.; Ibn Sa'd, p. 92 f.

[3] [Ibn Hishām does not mention Shuraḥbīl.]

Preparations made by Syrian tribes for its repulse

Tidings of the coming army reached Shuraḥbīl, who forthwith summoned to his aid the tribes of the vicinity. The hostile incursions from time to time against the Syrian border, the repeated attacks on Dūmat al-Jandal, the conquest of Kheibar, and the generally aggressive attitude of Moḥammad towards the north, had no doubt led to precautionary measures along the frontier. Thus, upon the alarm of invasion, there quickly rallied round Shuraḥbīl a large and (compared with the troops of Medīna) a well-appointed army.[1] Zeid first received the startling intelligence on reaching Maan. The enemy, he heard, was encamped at Maāb; and his apprehension was increased by the rumour that cohorts were with the force, and that the Kaiser himself was at their head. He halted. A council of war was called, and for two days the Muslim chiefs discussed the difficulties of their position. Many advised that a letter should be sent to Moḥammad; he had not contemplated an encounter with the Imperial forces; they were sent only to avenge the treachery of a petty chief, and ought not to risk battle with an enemy so vastly their superior: at least, the Prophet should be apprised of the new aspect of affairs, and fresh instructions asked. 'Abdallah, on the contrary, urged an immediate advance: 'What have we marched thus far for,' he cried indignantly, 'but for this? Is it in our numbers, or in the help of the Lord, that we put our trust? Victory or the martyr's crown, one or other, is secure. *Then forward!*' Overcome by the fervid appeal, they all responded: 'By the Lord! The son of Rawāḥa speaketh truth. Let us hasten onwards!' And so the camp advanced.

Council of war held by Muslims at Maan

Battle of Mūta

On entering the Belḳā, by the southern shore of the Dead Sea, they suddenly found themselves confronted by an enemy in numbers and equipment surpassing anything they had ever seen before.[2] Alarmed at the glittering array, they fell back on the village of Mūta. There, finding advan-

[1] A passage in Theophanes makes it probable that this great army was brought together by Theodorus, brother of Heraclius, which may account for the rumour reaching the Muslim camp that the Kaiser himself was in the field with 200,000 men.

[2] The Syrian army was composed partly of Greek troops, partly of the semi-Christian tribes of the desert—the Bahrā, Balī, Wā'il, Bekr, Lakhm, and Judhām.

tageous ground, they halted, and, forming front, resolved to offer battle. The Roman phalanx, with its cloud of Arabs on either flank, moved steadily down upon them. Zeid, seizing the white flag, led his columns forward, till, fighting bravely at their head, he fell. Then Ja'far leaped from his horse, and, maiming it in token of either death or victory, raised aloft the banner, and urged forward the attack. Soon covered with wounds, he yet fought on, till a Roman closing with him dealt the fatal blow.[1] Seeing Ja'far fall, 'Abdallah seized the standard, but he, too, speedily met the same fate. Then a Citizen rescuing the ensign planted it in the ground, and cried aloud,—*Hither, ye Muslims, hither!* and there was a temporary rally. The leadership being now vacant, a council hastily called together fixed their choice on Khālid, who forthwith assumed the command. But the chance of victory had passed away. The ranks were broken; and the Romans in full pursuit were already making havoc amongst the fugitives. It remained for Khālid but to save the dispersed columns from destruction, and even this taxed his skill and prowess to the utmost. By a series of ingenious and rapid movements, he drew off the shattered remains of the army to a safe retreat. But he dared not linger longer in the dangerous vicinity, and so, without further attempt to retrieve the day, he marched back straightway to Medīna. As they drew nigh the city, the people came out hooting at them, cast dust in their faces, crying out: 'Ah ye runaways, who flee before the enemy when fighting for the Lord!' 'Nay,' cried Moḥammad, who had ridden out to meet them on his mule, carrying the little son of Ja'far before him, 'Nay, these are not runaways: they are men who will yet again return to battle, if the Lord will.'

Khālid saves the force

The loss of Ja'far, brother of 'Alī, and of Zeid the faithful and beloved friend of five-and-thirty years, affected Moḥammad deeply. On the first intelligence of the reverse, and of their death, which he received early in the day, through a

Moḥammad's grief at death of Ja'far and Zeid

[1] The song with which Ja'far led the attack is no doubt apocryphal, but it strongly illustrates the fanatical feeling now rapidly growing up: *Paradise!* he cried, amid the glare and heat of the dusty battlefield,—'*Oh Paradise! how fair a resting-place! Cold is the water there, and sweet the shade. Rome, Rome! thine hour of tribulation draweth nigh. When I close with her, I will hurl her to the ground.*'

confidential messenger, he went to the house of Ja'far. His widow, Asmā, had just bathed and dressed her little ones when the Prophet entered, embraced the children tenderly, and burst into tears. Asmā guessed the truth, and sobbed aloud. A crowd of women soon gathering round her, Moḥammad silently left the place, and returning home, desired them to send provisions to Ja'far's house. 'No food,' he said, 'will be prepared there this day; for they are sunk in grief at the loss of their master.'[1] He then went to the house of Zeid; and Zeid's little daughter rushed into his arms, crying bitterly. Moḥammad was overcome, and wept with her. A bystander, thinking to check his grief, said to him: 'Why thus, O Prophet?' 'This,' he replied, 'is not forbidden grief; it is but the fond yearning in the heart of friend for friend.'[2]

Martyrdom of Farwa

In connection with Mūta, may be mentioned here the story of the Arab Farwa, Governor of Maan, represented by tradition (though upon imperfect evidence) as one of the early martyrs.[3] He sent a despatch announcing his conversion to Moḥammad, with several presents,—a white mule, a horse, an ass, and raiment inwrought with gold. The presents were graciously acknowledged in a letter from the Prophet, which contained directions for the spiritual guidance of the convert. The Roman government, hearing of his defection, sought, by offers of promotion, to bribe his return to the Christian faith. He refused, and was put to death.[4]

[1] Asmā afterwards married Abu Bekr, and on his death 'Alī, and bore sons to both.

[2] Next morning, he entered smiling into the Mosque, and when the people accosted him he said: 'That which ye saw in me yesterday was because of sorrow for the slaughter of my Companions, until I saw them in Paradise, seated as brethren, opposite one another, upon couches. And in some I perceived marks, as it were wounds of the sword. And I saw Ja'far as an angel with two wings, covered with blood,—his limbs stained therewith.' Hence Ja'far is known as 'the winged martyr.'

[3] Ibn Hishām, p. 958; (Aṭ-Ṭabari, 1783 f.).

[4] The tradition which is given both by Al-Wāḳidi and Ibn Hishām is surrounded by much that is marvellous; but there must have been some foundation of fact for the story. Farwa's reply is in the usual style:—'I will not quit the faith of Moḥammad. Thou knowest well that Jesus prophesied before of him. But as for thee, the fear of losing thy kingdom deterreth thee.' And so he was crucified.

Theophanes mentions about this period the secession of the Arabs

'Amr and Abu 'Obeida restore prestige on Syrian border. A.H. VIII. October, A.D. 629

The repulse at Mūta affected the prestige of Moḥammad among the northern tribes. There were rumours that the Bedawīn of the neighbourhood had assembled in great force, and even threatened a descent upon Medīna. 'Amr, the late convert, was therefore placed at the head of 300 men, including 30 horse, with instructions to subjugate the hostile tribes and incite those whom he found friendly, to harass the Syrian border.[1] The name of 'Amr justified the selection; connected, moreover, with the Beni Balī, a powerful tribe in the vicinity, he was possessed of personal influence which might aid in effecting the objects of the campaign. In the event of serious opposition, he was to call upon the Arabs in that quarter who had already tendered their submission to come to his aid. After a ten days' march he encamped at a spring near the Syrian confines. There he found that the enemy were assembled in great numbers, and that he could look for little aid from the local tribes. He halted and despatched a messenger for reinforcements. Moḥammad at once complied, and sent 200 men (among whom were both Abu Bekr and 'Omar) under command of Abu 'Obeida. On joining 'Amr, Abu 'Obeida wished to assume the leadership of the whole force, or at least retain the chief authority over his own detachment; but 'Amr, giving promise of the decision which characterised him in after days, insisted on retaining the sole command. Abu 'Obeida, a man of mild and pliant temper, succumbed. 'If thou refusest to acknowledge my authority,' he said, 'I have no resource but to obey thee; for the Prophet charged me to suffer no altercation, nor any division of command.' 'Amr replied imperiously; 'I am the chief over thee. Thou hast only brought a reinforcement to my army.' 'Be it so,' said Abu 'Obeida. 'Amr then assumed command of the united troops, and led their prayers; for thus early were the spiritual functions in Islām blended with the political and

employed in guarding the Syrian frontier, as occasioned by the refusal of a Greek officer to pay them their perquisites, on which they are said to have organised an attack on Gaza. Such a movement may have occurred in connection with the numerous accessions to Moḥammad's cause about this time, and the expedition to Tebūk the following year.

[1] Ibn Hishām, p. 984 f.; Aṭ-Ṭabari, i. 1604 f.; Al-Wāḳidi, p. 315 f.; Ibn Sa'd, p. 94 f.

military.[1] Thus strengthened, 'Amr again advanced, dispersed the hostile gatherings, and confirmed the friendly tribes. He had then the satisfaction of despatching a messenger to announce the complete success of his first campaign, and the re-establishment of the Prophet's influence on the frontier of Syria. Having accomplished this important object, he returned to Medīna.

Expedition of the Fish. A.H. VIII. November, A.D. 629

In the month following, to compensate Abu 'Obeida for his disappointment in giving up the command to 'Amr, Moḥammad sent him at the head of 300 men to chastise a refractory branch of the Juheina on the seacoast.[2] There was no fighting in this expedition, but it has become famous from the occurrence of a curious incident. Provisions failed, and the troops were already well-nigh famished, when to their joy a prodigious fish was cast opportunely on the shore, so large that it sufficed amply to relieve their hunger.[3] One other petty expedition during the winter, against a tribe of the Ghaṭafān in Nejd, yielded large plunder in camels, flocks, and prisoners.[4] The object is not stated. A fair damsel fell to the lot of the leader. He presented her to Moḥammad, who again gave her to one of his followers.

Raid on Nejd. December, A.D. 629

Various tribes tender their submission

Besides the Syrian tribes gained over by the success of 'Amr, several others, as the Beni 'Abs, Murra, and Dhubyān, now gave in their adhesion; and the Fezāra with their chief 'Oyeina, who had so long caused anxiety and alarm at Medīna, at last tendered submission. The Suleim also, who had taken part in the siege of Medīna, joined the cause about this time, and engaged to bring, when called on, a thousand men into the field. Most of the tribes in the

[1] It is interesting to notice in each of these commanders the same character already showing itself at this early period as after the death of Moḥammad marked their career in the Syrian wars. The same may be said of Khālid and other Companions, and is a satisfactory confirmation of the credibility of our authorities.

[2] Ibn Hishām, p. 992; Aṭ-Ṭabari, i. 1605 f.; Al-Wāḳidi, p. 317 f.; Ibn Sa'd, p. 95. [Aṭ-Ṭabari places these two expeditions before that of Mūta.]

[3] So Al-Wāḳidi. Ibn Hishām deals in extravagances; the whole army, which had been reduced to a famishing state, fed for twenty days upon it, and from being lean and famished became strong and fat. One of its bones, being set up as an arch, a camel with its rider passed under without touching it, &c.

[4] Al-Wāḳidi, p. 318 f.; Ibn Sa'd, p. 96.

vicinity of Medīna had already recognised the supremacy of Moḥammad.[1] The courteous treatment which the deputations which now began to come in from all directions experienced from the Prophet, his ready attention to their grievances, the wisdom with which he composed their disputes, and the politic assignments of territory by which he rewarded early declaration in favour of Islām, made his name to be popular, and his fame as a great and generous Prince to spread throughout the Peninsula. The accession of so many tribes, moreover, enabled him, whenever occasion might arise, to call into the field a far more imposing force than he had ever before aspired to command.

[1] The Beni Ashja', who had joined in the siege of Medīna, gave in their adhesion shortly after the massacre of the Beni Ḳoreiẓa; they told Moḥammad that they were so pressed by his warring against them, that they could stand out no longer. In the Secretary's chapter of 'Deputations from the Tribes,' &c., we learn that the Beni Ash'ar from Jidda, the Khushain, and the Daus, came to Moḥammad during the campaign of Kheibar, the latter with sixty or seventy followers, to whom were assigned shares in the booty. The Beni Sa'd ibn Bekr came over, A.H. V.; and the Beni Tha'laba, A.H. VIII. The Beni 'Abd al-Ḳeis (partly at least Christian) from Al-Baḥrein, in the same year. The Beni Judhām (see *ante*, p. 346) also in that year. The chief of the latter tribe carried back a letter from Moḥammad, of this tenor: 'Whoever accepteth the call to Islām, he is amongst the confederates of the Lord: whoever refuseth the same, a truce of two months is allowed him for consideration.' The tribes of the vicinity all accepted the invitation.

CHAPTER XXIV

CONQUEST OF MECCA[1]

Ramaḍān, A.H. VIII.—*January*, A.D. 630

ÆTAT. 61

Pretext arises for advance upon Mecca

THE truce of Al-Ḥodeibiya had been now nearly two years in force, when the alleged infraction of its terms afforded Moḥammad a plausible reason for the grand object of his ambition, the conquest of Mecca. Acting on the discretion allowed by the treaty, the Khozā'a and Beni Bekr tribes, inhabiting Mecca and its neighbourhood, declared their adhesion, the former to Moḥammad, the latter to the Ḳoreish. There had been sanguinary feuds of old standing between them, and, though these paled before the excitement of the war with Moḥammad, the blood which had been shed on either side caused hatred still to rankle in their breasts. The peace of Al-Ḥodeibiya allowed the Beni Bekr again to brood over their wrongs, and they sought opportunity to make reprisals. Aided by a party of the Ḳoreish in disguise, they attacked by night an unsuspecting encampment of Khozā'a, and slew several of them.[2] A deputation of forty men from the injured tribe, mounted on camels, hastened to Medīna, spread their wrongs before the Prophet, and pleaded that the treacherous murders might be avenged. Entreaty was little needed. The opportunity long expected had at last arrived. Starting up, with

Beni Bekr attack Beni Khozā'a A.H. VIII. December, A.D. 629

Khozā'a appeal to Moḥammad, who promises aid

[1] Ibn Hishām, p. 802 ff. ; Aṭ-Ṭabari, i. 1618 ff. ; Al-Wāḳidi, p. 319 ff. ; Ibn Sa'd, p. 96 ff.

[2] Weil thinks the outrage to have been in consequence of the defeat at Mūta, which emboldened the enemies of Islām.—*Einleitung*, p. 27. Belādhuri gives other instances of Ḳoreish having abused Moḥammad and encouraged his enemies, p. 30.

raiment yet ungirded, he thus pledged himself to the suppliants: 'If I help you not in like wise as if the wrong were mine own, then let me never more be helped by the Lord! See ye not yonder cloud? As the rain now poureth from it, even so shall help descend upon you speedily from above.'

Ḳoreish, hearing of this deputation, were thrown into great alarm. They despatched Abu Sufyān to protest against the imputed breach, and maintain the compact of peace. On his way, he met Budeil, chief of the Khozā'a, returning from Medīna after his interview with Moḥammad.[1] The mission of Abu Sufyān was not followed by any satisfactory result. He could gain from Moḥammad no promise, nor any assurance of pacific designs. Foiled in his endeavours, he took the only course open to him of expressing the desire of Ḳoreish to maintain friendly relations. Standing up in the court of the Mosque, he cried aloud: 'Hearken unto me, ye people! Peace and protection I guarantee for all.' To which Moḥammad answered: 'It is thou that sayest this, not we, O Abu Sufyān!' Thereupon he departed home, and reported the affair to Ḳoreish. They perceived that they were in evil plight, but did not suspect how imminent the hostile designs of their enemy at the moment were;[2] for Moḥammad had already resolved on an

Unsuccessful mission of Abu Sufyān to Medīna

[1] It will be seen below that there is reason for suspecting collusion between Abu Sufyān and Budeil; it may possibly have begun at this interview.

[2] 'Abbāsid tradition, in its hatred of the Omeiyads, delights to cast contumely on Abu Sufyān. On the present occasion it turns him into a laughing-stock; but, from what follows, there is room for conjecturing that communications of a less unfriendly character than those here represented passed between him and the Prophet.

The following narrative is strongly tinged with 'Alid tendencies: Arrived at Medīna, Abu Sufyān entered the house of his daughter Um Ḥabība, Moḥammad's wife. He was about to seat himself on the carpet or rug spread upon the floor, when she hastily drew it away and folded it up. 'My daughter!' he said, 'whether is it that thou thinkest the carpet is too good for me, or that I am too good for the carpet?' 'Nay, but it is the carpet of the Prophet,' she replied; 'and I choose not that thou, an impure idolater, shouldst sit upon the Prophet's carpet.' 'Truly, my daughter, thou art changed for the worse since thou leftest me' So saying, he went to Moḥammad, but could get nothing satisfactory from his lips. 'Omar, to whom he next addressed himself, received him with indignation. 'Alī was more cordial: 'Let me not go back unsuccessful as I came,' urged Abu Sufyān; 'intercede for me with the Prophet.'

Preparations for attacking Mecca

immediate and grand attack upon his native city. But the design was kept secret even from his closest friends as long as it was possible.[1] Meanwhile he summoned his allies from amongst the Bedawi tribes to join him at Medīna, or at certain convenient points upon the road. But he held their destination hid, and, to divert attention, despatched a small body of men in another direction. At the last moment he ordered his followers in the city to arm themselves, announced his project, and enjoined on all the urgent command that no hint regarding it should by any possible way reach Mecca. To this effect he prayed:—'*O Lord! Let not any spy carry tidings to Ḳoreish: blind their eyes and take their sight away until that I come suddenly upon them and seize them unawares!*' Such was the petition daily offered up by him in the Mosque.

Ḥātib's endeavour to communicate intelligence frustrated

Notwithstanding this injunction, Ḥāṭib, one of Moḥammad's most trusted followers, secretly despatched a female messenger with a letter to Mecca containing intimation of the intended assault. Information of this coming to the Prophet's ear, he sent 'Alī with Az-Zubeir in pursuit. They overtook the messenger, and after a long search discovered the letter carefully hidden in her locks. Ḥāṭib excused himself by the natural desire he had to save his unprotected family at Mecca; and the plea, in view of his former services, was graciously accepted.

'Alas for thee!' said 'Alī; 'truly, the Prophet hath resolved on a thing concerning which we may not speak with thee.' Then Abu Sufyān adjured Fāṭima ('Alī's wife) to let her little son Al-Ḥasan take him under his protection, 'and he will be the lord of the Arabs till the end of time.' But she told him that no one could be his protector against Moḥammad. On this, he besought 'Alī for his advice. 'Alī said that he saw no other course for him but to arise and call aloud that he took all parties under the guarantee of his protection: 'But will this benefit me at all?' 'Nay, I do not say so, but I see nothing else for thee.' Having followed this advice, Abu Sufyān returned to Mecca, and told Ḳoreish what he had done. 'But did Moḥammad sanction thy guarantee?' asked they. He replied in the negative. 'Out upon thee!' they cried; 'this will not benefit us at all; the man meant only to make sport of thee.' 'I know it,' said Abu Sufyān, 'but I could think of nothing else that I could do.'

[1] Even Abu Bekr was kept in ignorance. Entering 'Ā'isha's house, found her busy preparing the accoutrements of the Prophet; and, inquiring the cause, was told that an expedition had been resolved on, but she did not know in what direction.

On January 1, A.D. 630, the army commenced its march. It was the largest force Medina had ever seen. The tents of the Bedawi auxiliaries darkened the plain for miles around, and heavy contingents joined the Prophet on the line of march. Two of these, the Muzeina and Suleim, contributed as many as 1,000 soldiers each. Moḥammad now found himself at the head of between eight and ten thousand men. Az-Zubeir with two hundred men led the van. Zeinab and Um Selama were the Prophet's companions on the march,[1] which was made with such rapidity that within a week the army encamped at Marr Aẓ-Zahrān, but a single stage from Mecca.

Army marches. A.H. VIII. January, A.D. 630

Al-'Abbās, secretly apprised, had already quitted Mecca and joined Moḥammad on the road. The 'Abbāsids claim him as having been long a true Believer, and indeed number him among the Refugees, whose favoured ranks were now about to close. But Al-'Abbās was only worldly wise. He had waited till the supremacy of his nephew was beyond a doubt; and now, at the last moment, when there was no merit in the act, openly espoused his cause. Nevertheless, he was welcomed by the Prophet with favour and affection.[2]

Al-'Abbās joins Moḥammad

And now we come to a curious and somewhat mysterious passage. Moḥammad commanded his followers to kindle every one a fire that night on the heights above the camp. The Prophet trusted that this first intimation of his approach

Abu Sufyān visits camp of Moḥammad

[1] Um Selama seems to have been the favourite companion of Moḥammad on his marches. 'Ā'isha is not mentioned as accompanying him after the affair in the expedition against the Beni'l-Musṭaliḳ.

[2] He is said to have joined Moḥammad near Rābigh, about half-way between Medīna and Mecca. It is possible that he came by previous appointment. 'Abbāsid tradition naturally makes everything as favourable as possible. The truth is that he always sailed with wind and tide. It is, indeed, quite possible that ever since the Treaty, and especially since the Pilgrimage, he may have been in correspondence with Moḥammad, and secretly forwarding his cause at Mecca.

Two others appeared on the march to tender allegiance: Abu Sufyān, son of Moḥammad's uncle Al-Ḥārith; and 'Abdallah, brother of his wife Um Selama. Um Selama interceded for them; but Moḥammad at first refused to receive them. Both had incurred his severe displeasure,—the former for his satires; and the latter as a keen opponent. Abu Sufyān, being repulsed, declared that he would go forth into the desert with his little son, and that there they would both die of hunger; whereat Moḥammad relented.

would burst upon the city with alarming grandeur, and prove the hopelessness of opposition. No certain information of the march from Medīna had yet reached Ḳoreish, so carefully had all sources of intelligence been cut off. At last the chief men, uneasy at the portentous calm, broken only by vague reports of the coming storm, sent forth Abu Sufyān to reconnoitre. In the evening, accompanied by Ḥakīm (Khadīja's nephew, who had shown kindness to Moḥammad when shut up with Abu Ṭālib) and Budeil the Khozā'ite chief, Abu Sufyān sallied forth on the Medīna road. Ten thousand fires were by this time blazing on the mountain tops, and appearing in full sight engaged their speculations, when suddenly, in the dark, a stranger approaching thus accosted Abu Sufyān: 'Abu Ḥanẓala![1] is that thy voice I hear?' 'Yes, I am he,' said Abu Sufyān, 'but what hast thou left behind thee?' 'Yonder,' replied the stranger, 'is Moḥammad encamped with 10,000 followers. See ye not the myriad fires which they have kindled above their camp? Believe; cast in thy lot with us, else thy mother and thy house shall weep for thee!' It was Al-'Abbās who spoke. Mounted on the Prophet's white mule, he had issued forth, hoping that he might meet some wayfarer on the road, and send him to Ḳoreish, if haply they might come and sue for peace, and thus save Mecca from destruction. 'Seat thee upon the mule behind me,' continued Al-'Abbās; 'I will conduct thee to the Prophet, and thou shalt seek for quarter from him.' They were soon at the tent of Moḥammad. Al-'Abbās entered, and announced the welcome news of the arrival of his distinguished friend: 'Take him to thy tent, Al-'Abbās,' replied the Prophet, 'and in the morning come to me with him again.' In the morning accordingly they sought the Prophet's tent: '*Out upon thee Abu Sufyān!*' exclaimed Moḥammad as the Ḳoreishite chief drew near; '*hast thou not yet discovered that there is no God but the Lord alone?*' 'Noble and generous Sire! Had there been any God beside, verily he had been of some avail to me.' '*And dost thou not acknowledge that I am the Prophet of the Lord?*'

[1] Abu Sufyān, so called after his son, Ḥanẓala. Belādhuri represents him as having been now taken prisoner, and 'Omar as threatening to kill him.

continued Moḥammad, 'Noble Sire! As to this thing, there is yet in my heart some hesitancy.' 'Woe is thee!' exclaimed Al-'Abbās; 'it is no time for hesitancy, this. Believe and testify forthwith the creed of Islām, or else thy neck shall be in danger!' It was, indeed, no time for idle pride or scruple; and so Abu Sufyān, finding no alternative, repeated the formula of belief in God and in Moḥammad as his Prophet. What a moment of exultation when the conqueror saw his great antagonist a suppliant Believer at his feet! 'Haste thee to Mecca!' he said; for he knew well when to show forbearance and generosity;—'haste thee to the city: no one that taketh refuge in the house of Abu Sufyān shall be harmed this day. And hearken! speak unto the people, that whoever closeth the door of his house, the inmates thereof shall be in safety.' Abu Sufyān hastened to retire. But before he could quit the camp, the forces were already under arms, and were being marshalled in their respective columns. Standing by Al-'Abbās, he watched in amazement the various tribes, each defiling with the banner given to it by Moḥammad, into its proper place. One by one the different clans were pointed out by name, and recognised. 'And what is that black mass,' asked Abu Sufyān, 'with dark mail and shining lances?' 'It is the chivalry of Mecca and Medīna,' replied Al-'Abbās—'the favoured band that guards the person of the Prophet.' 'Truly,' exclaimed the astonished chief, 'this kingdom of thy Nephew's is a mighty kingdom.' 'Nay, Abu Sufyān! he is more than a king—he is a mighty Prophet!' 'Yes, thou sayest truly; now let me go.' 'Away!' said Al-'Abbās; 'and speed thee to thy people!' Abu Sufyān hurried back to Mecca, and, as he entered, shouted at the pitch of his voice: 'Ye Ḳoreish! Moḥammad is close upon us. He hath an army which ye are not able to withstand. Whoever entereth the house of Abu Sufyān shall be safe this day; and whoever shutteth his door upon him shall be safe; and whosoever entereth the Holy House he shall be safe!' So the people fled in all directions to their homes, and to the Ka'ba.

Abu Sufyān carries message of quarter to Mecca

Such is the tradition. But, beneath it, there are symptoms of a previous understanding between Moḥammad and Abu Sufyān. Whether there was any collusion so early as the visit of Abu Sufyān to Medīna, whether Al-'Abbās

Was there collusion between Abu Sufyān and Moḥammad?

was charged by the chiefs of Mecca with the conduct of negotiations with the Prophet, and from which side the overtures first came, can be matter for conjecture only. But there seems reason to believe that the meeting by night of Abu Sufyān with Al-'Abbās was a concerted measure, and not mere accident. That Abu Sufyān, wearied with the long struggle about to be renewed with all the prospects of internecine strife, assured also that the chances of victory lay on Moḥammad's side, and anxious to avert bloodshed, should now have conspired to lull alarm and prevent Mecca rising against the invader, seems perhaps hardly less probable. As hereditary leader he possessed more influence for that object than any other chief at Mecca, and of his influence Moḥammad willingly availed himself. To the treason, or one might rather say the patriotism, of Abu Sufyān, it is mainly due that the submission of Mecca was thus peaceably secured. Such at least is the conclusion which may be drawn from the uncertain tale of tradition.

The army moves forward upon Mecca

We return to the camp. The army was now in full march on Mecca. The anxieties of a lifetime crowded into the moment. But as the city opened on the Prophet's view it became evident that his precautions had been effectual. Had any general opposition been organised, it was here that a stand would have been made; yet no army appeared in sight. In token of his gratitude, he bowed low upon his camel, and offered up thanksgiving to the Lord. The troops were told off in four divisions, and to each was assigned a different road, by which simultaneously to advance. From Dhu Ṭowa they separated to perform their several parts, with strict injunctions not to fight excepting in the last extremity, nor offer violence to any one. Az-Zubeir, leading the left battalion, was to enter from the north. Khālid, with the Bedawi marshalled on the right, was to make his way into the southern or lower suburb. The men of Medīna under Sa'd ibn 'Obāda were to force their way into the western quarter. The mild but vigilant Abu 'Obeida, commanding the Refugees and followed by Moḥammad himself, took the nearest road skirting Jebel Hind. This disposition of his forces was wisely made: if opposition were offered anywhere, one of the other divisions would be at hand to take the enemy in the rear. As Sa'd led on the citizens of Medīna, he sang: 'To-day is the day of slaughter; there is no safety this day for Mecca!' Hearing these martial and threatening words, and fearing evil from the fiery temper of Sa'd, Moḥammad took the Medīna banner from his hands, and gave it to his son Ḳeis—a man of towering stature, but of gentler disposition than his father.

Abu Ḳoḥāfa watches advance of Muslim army

Just then, an old man, blind and decrepit, might be seen climbing, with the help of his daughter, over the heights of Abu Ḳobeis which overhang the city. It was Abu Ḳoḥāfa, the aged parent of Abu Bekr. To his frequent inquiry whether anything was yet in sight, the maiden at last replied: 'A dark moving mass has just emerged from yonder valley.' 'It is the army!' said the aged man. 'And now I see a figure hasting to and fro amid the columns of that mass.' 'This is the leader marshalling the force.' 'But the blackness is dispersing rapidly. It spreads'—continued the girl. 'Ah! then the army is advancing! Haste thee, my daughter, and lead me home.' It was full time, for the troops were already sweeping along the approaches to the town on every side; and a rude assailant snatched the maiden's silver necklace from her neck while she was yet guiding her father's tottering steps toward their house.

Khālid encounters opposition

The several columns entered peaceably, excepting that of Khālid. The southern quarter, assigned to him, was inhabited by Moḥammad's bitterest enemies and those most deeply implicated in the attack upon the Beni Khozā'a; these had now taken up a defensive position, or perhaps in despair were preparing for hasty flight. They were led by Ṣafwān, Suheil, and 'Ikrima, son of Abu Jahl. As the battalion, composed of Bedawīn, difficult at any time to hold in hand, appeared in view, it was saluted by a shower of arrows. But Khālīd, ready to receive his opponents, soon put them all to flight. Flushed with success, and unmindful of the Prophet's order, he pursued with his wild troops the fugitive Ḳoreish into the streets of Mecca. The leaders escaped; but eight-and-twenty Citizens were killed in the conflict. Khālid lost only two men, and those because they missed their way. While this encounter was going forward, Moḥammad, following the column of the Refugees, crossed an eminence from whence the full view of the vale and city burst upon him. But his pleasure at the grateful prospect was turned into concern as

Moḥammad's concern at the encounter

his eye caught the gleaming of swords on the farther side of the city, and the troops of Khālid in pursuit. 'What!' he cried in surprise and anger, 'did I not strictly command that there should be no fighting?' The cause was soon explained, and Moḥammad said: 'That which the Lord decreeth is the best.'

Moḥammad reposes in his tent

From the pass, Moḥammad descended into the valley at a spot not far from the tombs of Abu Ṭālib and Khadīja. He was there joined by the division of Az-Zubeir, and, having assured himself that Mecca was now wholly at his will, directed his tent of leather to be pitched in the open space to the north of the city.[1] 'Wilt thou not alight at thine own house?' inquired his followers. 'Not so,' he said 'for have they left me yet any house within the city?' The great banner was planted at the door of his tent, and he retired to repose therein, and to reflect on the accomplishment of his life's dream. The abused, rejected, exiled Prophet now had the rebellious city at his feet. Moḥammad was Lord of Mecca.

Worships at the Ka'ba, and destroys its idols

But he did not long repose. Again mounting Al-Ḳaṣwā, he proceeded to the Ka'ba, reverently saluted with his staff the Sacred Stone, and made the seven circuits of the temple. Then, pointing with his staff to the idols one by one that stood around, he commanded them to be hewn down. '*Truth hath come*,' he cried in the words of the Ḳor'ān, as the great image of Hubal, reared in front of the Ka'ba, fell with a crash;—'*Truth hath come, and falsehood gone; for falsehood verily vanisheth away*.'[2] Advancing now to the *Station of*

[1] See map facing Chapter I. The pathway north of Jebel Hind brought him into the valley near the burying-ground; a little below this he pitched his tent, and in the same vicinity the two northern divisions of the army encamped. The two other divisions probably occupied ground to the south of the city. The tradition of the Prophet's route is still retained, though loose and inaccurate. 'Mounting our animals,' says Burton, iii. 349, 'we followed the road to the Jannat al-Maala, the sacred cemetery of Mecca. A rough wall, with a poor gateway, encloses a patch of barren and grim-looking ground at the foot of the chain which bounds the city's western suburb; and below El Akabah, the gap through which Khālid bin Walid entered Meccah with the triumphant Prophet.' As regards Khālid, this is a mistake.

[2] Sūra xvii. 82. Tradition says there were 360 idols ranged round the Ka'ba, and that as Moḥammad pointed to each in succession with his staff, reciting this verse, the idol of its own accord fell forwards on its face. The use of metaphorical language in describing the actual scene would easily give rise to such tales.

Abraham, twenty or thirty paces from the Ka'ba, he bowed himself in worship; and, sitting down, sent Bilāl to summon 'Othmān ibn Ṭalḥa with the key of the temple. Ascending the steps of the threshold, and unlocking the door, he entered the sacred hall, and there again performed devout prostrations. He then returned to the doorway, and, standing upon its elevated step, caught hold of the two rings attached to the door, and gazed in thankfulness on the thronging multitude below. 'Othmān ibn Ṭalḥa!' he cried, naming the hereditary Guardian of the Temple,—'Here, take back the key to be kept a perpetual charge by thee and thy posterity. None shall take it from thee save the unjust. And thou Al-'Abbās,' turning to his uncle, 'I confirm thee in the giving drink from out of the well Zemzem to the pilgrims: it is no mean office this that I give now unto thee.'

Mohammad's attachment to Mecca

Having destroyed the images and obliterated the pictures of Abraham and the angels painted on the walls of the Ka'ba, Moḥammad desired Bilāl to sound the call for prayer from the top of the Ka'ba, and worship was performed by the surrounding multitude, as it has been ever since, according to the ritual of the Mosque of Medīna. A crier was then sent through the city with this proclamation;—'Whoever believeth in God, and in the day of Judgment, let him not leave in his house any image whatever that he doth not break in pieces.' The Prophet likewise deputed a party of the Knozā'a to repair the boundary pillars around the sacred territory.[1] Thus he gave practical proof that, while determined to uproot idolatry from the land, he was equally resolved to uphold the sanctity of Mecca, and the obligation of its worship. He won the hearts of the inhabitants by his ardent declaration of attachment to their city: 'Thou art the choicest spot on the earth unto me,' he said, 'and the most delectable. If thy people had not cast me forth, I never had forsaken thee!' The Citizens of Medīna now began to express their fear that, as the Lord had given him

[1] Pillars were then, as at the present day, placed at the limits of the sacred territory on either side of all the main roads leading to Mecca. They had probably become neglected or injured, as Moḥammad must have observed in passing. The distance of these landmarks from Mecca varies in different directions. On the Jidda road they are nine miles from Mecca; towards Al-'Omra, only three.

the victory over his native city, he would not return to Medīna as his home. He overheard it, and, calling them around him, assured them he would never quit Medīna: 'God forbid it,' he said; 'where ye live, there will I live, and there too shall I die.'

Abu Bekr brings his father to visit Moḥammad

He now retired again into his tent. Soon after, Abu Bekr approached the door leading his father, Abu Ḳoḥāfa, now bowed down with great age, and his locks 'white as the flower of the mountain grass.'[1] Moḥammad accosted him kindly: 'Why didst thou not leave thine aged father in his house, Abu Bekr? and I would have gone and seen him there.' 'It was more fitting that he should visit thee, O Prophet, than that thou shouldst visit him.' Moḥammad seated the aged man beside him, and, affectionately pressing his hand upon his bosom, invited him to make profession of the Muslim faith, which he readily did.

Citizens proscribed

Al-Ḥuweirith and Habbār: the former executed

Two murderers and a singing girl put to death

From the amnesty extended to the Citizens of Mecca, Moḥammad excluded ten or twelve persons. Of these, however, only four were actually put to death. Al-Ḥuweirith and Habbār were proscribed for their ruffianly attack on his daughter Zeinab, when she escaped from Mecca. The former was put to death by 'Alī. The latter concealed himself; and some months later, appearing at Medīna, a repentant convert, was forgiven. The next two were renegade Muslims who, having shed blood at Medīna, had fled to Mecca and abjured Islām. They were both slain, one as he clung to the curtain of the Ka'ba; and also a singing girl belonging to them, who had been in the habit of annoying the Prophet with her satires.

Ibn abi Sarḥ, an apostate, escapes

The rest escaped. Among these was another apostate, Abdallah ibn abi Sarḥ, whom Moḥammad had employed at Medīna in writing down passages of the Ḳo'rān from his dictation. His foster-brother 'Othmān sheltered him till quiet was restored, then brought him forward and implored forgiveness. The Prophet, unwilling to pardon so great an offender, for some time held his peace; but at last granted him quarter. When 'Abdallah retired, Moḥammad thus addressed the Companions about him: 'Why did not one of

[1] The fine image is spoiled by the addition that Moḥammad desired him to dye his snow-white hair. He lived to see his son Caliph, and died A.H. XIV., aged 97.

you arise and smite 'Abdallah on the neck. I remained silent expecting this.' 'But thou gavest no sign unto us,' replied one. 'To give signs,' said Moḥammad, 'is treachery; it is not fitting for a Prophet in such fashion to ordain the death of any.'[1] Ṣafwān and 'Ikrima, after eluding the pursuit of Khālid, fled towards the seashore; they were on the point of embarking, when the assurance of forgiveness reached them and they were persuaded to return.[2] Hind, the wife of Abu Sufyān, and Sāra, a singing girl who had in the discharge of her profession given offence to Moḥammad, escaped the sentence of death by opportunate submission.[3]

Safwān, 'Ikrima, Hind, and Sāra escape

The proscriptions were thus comparatively few; and capital sentence, where actually carried into effect, was (with perhaps the exception of the singing girl) justified probably by other crimes than mere political antagonism. The magnanimity with which Moḥammad treated a people who had so long hated and rejected him is worthy of all admiration. It was indeed for his own interest to forgive the past, and cast into oblivion its slights and injuries. But this did not the less require a large and generous heart.[4] And Moḥammad had his reward, for the whole population of his native city at once gave in their adhesion, and espoused his cause with alacrity and apparent devotion. Whatever the strength

Treatment of Mecca magnanimous and forbearing

[1] We shall hear more of him in connection with his foster-brother's Caliphate.—*Caliphate*, p. 203.

[2] 'Ikrima was brought back by his wife, who, having obtained pardon from Moḥammad, hurried after him to Jidda. C. de Perceval tells a romantic story of her reaching the shore just as he had embarked, and waving her scarf to bring him back 'Omeir, a Meccan chief, sought out Ṣafwān, taking as a pledge the red striped turban worn by Moḥammad around his head as he entered Mecca. He asked for two months' quarter; Moḥammad gave him four.

[3] Waḥshi, the Abyssinian slave who slew Ḥamza, fled to Aṭ-Ṭā'if, and eventually obtained pardon in company with its inhabitants. Um Hāni', daughter of Abu Ṭālib, gave refuge to two men of her husband's tribe whom her brother 'Alī wished to kill. She asked quarter for them of Moḥammad, who received her graciously, saying: 'I give protection to whomsoever thou dost give protection.' A curious scene is here described of Moḥammad's camp life; the Prophet, wearied and covered with dust, had retired to a corner of the tent across which Fāṭima held a screen; thus veiled, he bathed himself, and then came forth to meet the persons waiting for him.

[4] Moḥammad is said to have compared himself in his treatment of Mecca to Joseph forgiving the injuries of his brethren.

or weakness of religious conviction, there were no 'disaffected' inhabitants at Mecca nor any relapse even in the rebellion that followed the Prophet's death. Within a few weeks we find two thousand of the citizens fighting faithfully by his side.

Bloodshed prohibited

On the night after the occupation of Mecca, certain of the Khozā'a, to gratify an old-standing enmity, rose upon a neighbouring tribe, and put one of them to death. The day following, Moḥammad took advantage of the incident to address the congregation assembled in front of the Ka'ba for mid-day prayer: 'Verily the Lord hallowed Mecca in the day that he created the heavens and the earth. Nor was it common unto me but for a single watch of the day; then it returned to its sacredness as before. Neither was the plunder thereof lawful unto me. Let him that is present tell it unto him that is absent. Ye Beni Khozā'a! withdraw your hands from shedding blood. The man whom ye have killed, I will myself pay compensation for him; but whoso slayeth any man after this, verily the blood of him that is murdered shall be required at the murderer's hands.'

Parties sent out to destroy images

During the succeeding fortnight, while occupied in the arrangement of public affairs at Mecca, Moḥammad sent forth several armed parties to destroy the idolatrous shrines in the vicinity, and secure the submission of surrounding tribes. Khālid demolished the fane of Al-'Ozza at Nakhla, the famous goddess of the Meccan tribes; 'Amr broke in pieces Suwā', an image adored by Hudheil; and Manāt, the divinity worshipped at Ḳodeid, was destroyed by a band of the citizens of Medīna who had formerly been especially devoted to its service.[1]

Cruelty of Khālid to Beni Jadhīma

On his return from Nakhla, Khālid was sent with a detachment to require the adhesion of the Jadhīma, a tribe

[1] Curious stories are told about these deities. When Khālid returned from Nakhla, Moḥammad asked him what he had seen. He replied, 'Nothing.' 'Then thou hast not yet destroyed the goddess? Return and do so.' On his going back, a naked female, black, and with dishevelled hair, rushed out, and Khālid cut her in pieces. '*That* was Al-'Ozza,' said the Prophet, when it was reported to him. A similar tale is told of Manāt.

The servitor of one of these images, after suspending his sword about its neck, retired to an adjoining hill, and cried out to the image to wield the sword and save itself.

which dwelt a day's march south of Mecca. They tendered immediate submission, professed themselves converts, and, at the bidding of Khālid, laid down their arms. But Khālid, actuated by an ancient enmity, and thus giving early proof of the sanguinary temper which afterwards gained for him the title of *The Sword of God*, made them all prisoners and gave command for their execution. A portion were put to death by his Bedawi followers, but fortunately there were also present some Citizens of Medīna and Refugees, who interposed and saved the rest. Moḥammad, grieved at the intelligence, raised his hands to heaven, and said: 'O Lord! I am innocent in thy sight of that which Khālid hath done.' To prove the sincerity of his displeasure, he sent forth 'Alī with money to make compensation for the slain, and for the plunder.

CHAPTER XXV

THE BATTLE OF ḤONEIN[1] AND SIEGE OF AṬ-ṬĀ'IF

Beni Hawāzin assemble against Moḥammad;

A STORM that lowered in the east cut short the Prophet stay at Mecca. The great Hawāzin tribe occupied (as the still occupy) the ranges and slopes of the hill country soutl east of Mecca; and with their numerous branches an affiliated clans, spread themselves over the wide steppe beyond Aṭ-Ṭā'if. That city, inhabited by the Beni Thaḳ of the same descent, was their centre, and its inhabitant devoted to idol worship, and closely connected with Mecc feared not unnaturally that the iconoclastic conqueror woul strike his next blow at their faith and liberties. According they sent an urgent summons to all the branches of th Hawāzin stock to assemble, with the view effectively to chec the arrogant assumptions of Moḥammad, now too plain developing his scheme of conquest and universal supremac Having appointed a rendezvous at Auṭās, a valley in th mountain range north-east of Aṭ-Ṭā'if, they began rapidly t assemble there.

Who is therefore obliged to leave Mecca

This movement obliged Moḥammad to cut short his sta at Mecca. Although the city had cheerfully accepted h authority, all its inhabitants had not yet embraced the ne religion, nor formally acknowledged his prophetic clair Perhaps he intended to follow the course he had pursued Medīna, and leave their conversion to be gradually accon plished without compulsion. However this may have bee the threatening intelligence called him suddenly away fro Mecca. Mo'ādh ibn Jebel, a young citizen of Medīna, we skilled in the Ḳor'ān and all questions of religious practic was left behind to instruct the people of Mecca in the tene

[1] Ibn Hishām, p. 840 ff.; Aṭ-Ṭabari, i. 1654 ff.; Al-Wāḳidi, p. 354 ff Ibn Sa'd, p. 108 ff.

and requirements of Islām; and 'Attāb, a youthful Ḳoreishite, of the house of 'Ạbd Shams, placed over the secular administration of the city.

Moḥammad sets out for Ḥonein. A.H. VIII. January 28, A.D. 630

Four weeks had just elapsed since quitting Medīna, when Moḥammad marched forth from Mecca at the head of all his forces, swelled now, by the addition of 2,000 auxiliaries from Ḳoreish, to the number of 12,000 men. Ṣafwān, at his request, made over to him one hundred suits of mail and stand of arms complete, and as many camels. The array of tribes, each with a banner waving at its head, was so imposing that Abu Bekr broke forth in admiration as they passed:—We shall not this day be worsted by reason of the smallness of our numbers!' Moḥammad smiled with a complacent assent. His vainglorious attitude was remembered by the Prophet afterwards with self-reproach. In three or four marches the army arrived near the entrance of the valley of Ḥonein.

Hawāzin also advance on Ḥonein

The Hawāzin, gathered in great force at Auṭās under their chief Mālik, had meanwhile also been advancing upon the same valley. The women and children of the tribe, with their herds and flocks, followed in the rear. Mālik hoped thus to nerve his troops to victory. Doreid, an aged warrior who accompanied the army in his litter, protested against the fatal measure. But the youthful leader derided his advice. During the night of Moḥammad's arrival at Ḥonein, Mālik drew up his men in a masked recess, commanding the steep and narrow defile which formed the entrance to the valley, and awaited there in silence the enemy's approach.[1]

Battle of Ḥonein, February 1 A.D. 630

At early dawn, while it was yet dark, the sky being overcast with clouds, the Muslim army was in motion.

[1] Mālik was only thirty years of age. Doreid was a famous chief in his day. After the battle, he was cruelly put to death by a youth of the Suleim, who captured him as he was endeavouring to escape in his camel-litter. The first cut of the youth's sword took no effect. 'How badly has thy mother furnished thee!' said the old man, cold and unmoved at the prospect of death. 'There, take that sword hung up behind my litter, and strike just between the spine and the head. It was thus I used to slay the adversary in my day. Then go and tell thy mother that thou hast killed Doreid. Many are the days in which I have saved the lives of the women of thy tribe.' He had, in fact, saved the lad's mother, and his two grandmothers. The skin of his legs resembled paper, from constant riding on the bare backs of horses.

Mounted on his white mule and clad in panoply as on the dɛ of Oḥod, Moḥammad followed in the rear. The vanguard the Beni Suleim, led by Khālid, were defiling leisurely up tl steep and narrow pass, when on a sudden the Hawāzin sprar from their ambuscade, and charged impetuously dov upon them. Staggered by the unexpected onslaugh column after column fell back and choked the narrow pas Aggravated by the obscurity of the hour, and the straitne of the rugged road, panic seized the army. They all turne and fled. 'Whither away?' cried Moḥammad, as troop aft troop they hurried past him. 'Whither away? Tl Prophet of the Lord is here! Return! return!' But h words had no effect, excepting that a band of devoted followe gathered round him.[1] The confusion increased, the multitu of camels jostling wildly one against the other; all w noise and clamour, and the Prophet's voice was lost amid tl din. At last, seeing the Medīna column hurrying down the common flight, he bade Al-'Abbās who held his mule, cry aloud:—'Citizens of Medīna! Ye men of the Pledge the Tree of Fealty! Men of the Sūrat al-Baḳara![2] A 'Abbās forthwith shouted these words over and over again the pitch of his stentorian voice, till they reached far ar near. At once they touched a chord in the heart of tl Citizens. Arrested in their flight, 'like she camels who bowels are stirred over their young,' they flew to Moḥamma crying aloud, '*Ya Labbeik!* Here we are, ready at thy call A hundred of these devoted followers, disengaged wit difficulty from the camels that jammed the road, threw them selves across the gorge, and stayed the downward rus Relieved of the pressure from above, the army rallie gradually, and returned to the battle. The conflict wa severe; and the issue, from the nature of the ground an the impetuosity of the Bedawi foe, for some time doubtfu

Moḥammad's army surprised and driven back, but eventually rallied

[1] The following stood firmly by Moḥammad:—Al-'Abbās and his sc Al-Faḍl, 'Alī, Abu Bekr, 'Omar, Osāma, Aiman. The last two we sons of Moḥammad's slave Um Aiman by different husbands. Tl latter was among the slain.

[2] Alluding to those who took the oath of fealty under the Acacia tre at Al-Ḥodeibiya; and to Sūrat al-Baḳara, the chapter of the Ḳor'ān fir revealed at Medīna. The double allusion would thus remind them once of their conversion, and of their oath to defend Moḥammad to tl death. [Ibn Isḥāḳ omits the expression, p. 847.]

Moḥammad from an eminence watched the struggle. Excited by the spectacle, he began loudly to cry out:—'*Now is the furnace heated: I am the Prophet that lieth not; the seed of 'Abd al-Muṭṭalib!*' Then bidding Al-'Abbās pick him up a handful of gravel, he cast it at the enemy. '*Ruin seize them! I swear they are discomfited,*' he shouted eagerly, as he saw them wavering. 'By the Lord of the Ka'ba, they yield! God hath cast fear into their hearts.' The moment was critical, but in the end the steadiness of the Medīna band, and the enthusiasm of the rest when once recalled, had won the day. The enemy fled; and the rout was so complete, and so fierce the pursuit, that some even of the women and children were killed, an atrocity strictly forbidden by the Prophet.

The Beni Hawāzin beaten back

Mālik, taking his stand, with the flower of his army, at the upper end of the valley, covered the escape of his broken forces; but he was unable to rescue the women and children, who fell into the conqueror's hands, with the camp and all that it contained. The spoil included 24,000 camels, 40,000 sheep and goats, and 4,000 ounces of silver. The prisoners, 6,000 in number, with the booty, were removed to the neighbouring valley of Al-Ji'rāna, and sheltered there, awaiting the return of the army from Aṭ-Ṭā'if. Moḥammad knew that Hawāzin would seek to regain their families, and an opportunity was skilfully left thus open for negotiation. The fugitive army was pursued with slaughter as far as Nakhla; from thence part fled back to Auṭās, and part to Aṭ-Ṭā'if. The former entrenched themselves in their previous camp. A strong detachment was sent to dislodge them, which after severe fighting was accomplished. The dispersed fragments found refuge in the surrounding hills.

Their families and camp captured

Pursuit of fugitive columns

The victory was thus complete, but not without some considerable loss on the part of Moḥammad. Only a few of his immediate followers are named among the slain.[1] But some of the auxiliaries, who being in the van bore the brunt of the enemy's onset, suffered severely, and two tribes are spoken of as almost annihilated. For these Moḥammad offered up a special prayer, and said: 'O Lord! recompense them because of their calamities!'

Loss on Moḥammad's side

In the passages which treat of this battle, the reverse sus-

[1] Al-Wāḳidi names only five; others ten.

Victory ascribed to angelic aid

tained at the outset is attributed to the vainglorious trust in their numbers with which the army set out from Mecca, while the eventual success is ascribed to the invisible hosts which fought against the enemy ;—

Sūra ix. 25 f.

> Verily God hath assisted you in many battlefields ; and notably on the day of Ḥonein, when ye rejoiced in the multitude of your host. But the multitude did not in any wise benefit you : the earth with all its spaciousness became too strait for you.[1] And so ye turned your backs and fled. Then after that the Lord caused His peace to descend upon His Prophet and on the Faithful, and sent down Hosts which ye saw not, and thereby punished the Unbelievers. And such is the end of them that disbelieve. Then God will be turned hereafter unto whom He pleaseth ; for God is gracious and merciful.[2]

Siege of Aṭ-Ṭā'if. February, A.D. 630

As soon as the detachment had returned from Auṭās, Moḥammad pushed forward his army by way of Nakhla, and laid siege to Aṭ-Ṭā'if.[3] But the battlements were strong, the city well provisioned, and a plentiful supply of water within the walls. The besiegers were received with showers of arrows, so thick and well sustained that they darkened the sky like a flight of locusts. Twelve men were killed, and many wounded, among whom was a son of Abu Bekr. The camp was therefore speedily withdrawn out of range ; and tents of red leather were pitched by it for Um Selama and Zeinab, who both had followed their lord through all the dangers of the way. On a spot between the two Moḥammad performed the daily prayers; and here eventually was built the great Mosque of Aṭ-Ṭā'if.

Testudos and catapults tried without success

The siege did not advance, for no one dared expose himself before the galling archery from the walls. This had been anticipated, and a novel remedy already sought. The Beni Daus, a tribe one or two days south of Mecca, were famous for the use of the testudo and catapult. Aṭ-Ṭofeil, one of

[1] That is to say, in the narrow and precipitous pass, their great numbers, of which they had been vaingloriously proud, only added to the difficulty.

[2] The last verse is generally construed as referring to the mercy afterwards shown to the Beni Hawāzin ; but it more probably means forgiveness for the vainglory and cowardice just described. As usual, the angels are a favourite subject of tradition. On this occasion they wore *red uniform.* A cloud was seen to fill the valley as it were a swarm of ants : this was the angelic troop.

[3] Ibn Hishām, p. 869 ff. ; Aṭ-Ṭabari, i. 1669 ff. ; Al-Wāḳidi, p. 368 ff. ; Ibn Sa'd, p. 114 f.

their chiefs, having joined Moḥammad at Kheibar, was despatched to secure the allegiance of his people, and seek their aid. They accepted the summons; and Aṭ-Ṭofeil, having burned their famous tutelary image, joined Moḥammad four days after siege had been laid to Aṭ-Ṭā'if.[1] Besieging engines were speedily prepared, and parties pushed forward to undermine the walls. But the citizens, prepared for the stratagem cast down balls of heated iron from the battlements, and set the machines on fire. The party under their shelter fled in alarm, and a discharge of archery opened on them. Some were killed and many wounded before they got beyond the range. The testudo and catapult were not tried again.

Vineyards cut down and liberty offered to slaves of garrison

Seeing no other way of bringing the city to terms, Moḥammad gave command to cut down and burn to their roots the far-famed vineyards which surrounded it.[2] This was being done, as the unfortunate citizens could descry, with merciless vigour, when they succeeded in conveying to Moḥammad an earnest expostulation that he would, 'for the sake of mercy and of God,' desist. He listened to the appeal, and stayed further destruction. But in place of it he caused a proclamation to reach the garrison which grievously displeased them, that if any slaves came forth from the city, they would receive their freedom. Some twenty escaped, and became eventually valiant followers of their liberator.

Siege raised, army returns to Al-Ji'rāna, end of February, A.D. 630

Half a month passed thus without effect. The army became impatient to share the spoil in store for them at Al-Ji'rāna. Moḥammad took counsel with the principal men. 'What thinkest thou,' said he to a Bedawi leader, 'of this stubborn city?' 'A fox in its hole,' replied the astute sententious chief;—'sit long enough and ye will catch it: leave it alone, and it will not harm you.' A dream of the Prophet ratified the adage.[3] It was not the divine will that

[1] Aṭ-Ṭofeil, but on doubtful authority, is said to have been converted at Mecca, before the Hijra. So Ibn Hishām, p. 252 ff.

[2] These charming gardens, with their rills of running water, lie at the foot of the low mountains encircling the sandy plain in the middle of which Aṭ-Ṭā'if stands. They are still as famous as they were 1,200 years ago. The nearest is 'now about a half or three-quarters of an hour from the city.' *Vide supra*, p. 109 f.

[3] Moḥammad dreamed that a bowl of cream was presented to him, which a hen pecked at and spilled. Abu Bekr interpreted the dream to

operations should be continued. The siege was raised, and the army marched back to Al-Ji'rāna, which it reached about the end of February.

Scene between Moḥammad and his foster-sister

Here occurred the interesting incident already noticed in the opening chapter. An aged female among the captives, roughly treated like the rest, warned the rude soldiery to beware,—'For,' said she, 'I am the foster-sister of your Chief.' Hearing this, they carried her to Moḥammad, who recognised in the complainant the little girl Sheimā, who used, when he was nurtured by Ḥalīma among the Beni Sa'd, to tend and carry him. He seated her affectionately beside him, and offered to take her to Medīna. But as she preferred remaining with her tribe, he dismissed her with a handsome present.[1]

Prisoners of Beni Hawāzin given up

Encouraged by the kind treatment of their kinswoman, a deputation from the various tribes of the Hawāzin presented themselves before the Prophet, among whom was an aged man who claimed to be his foster-uncle. They professed submission to their conqueror, recounted the calamities that had befallen them, and thus urged their claim upon his favour;—'There, in these huts among the prisoners, are thy foster-mothers and foster-sisters,—they that have nursed thee and fondled thee in their bosoms. We have known thee a suckling, a weaned child, a youth generous and noble: and now thou hast risen to this dignity. Be gracious therefore unto us, even as the Lord hath been gracious unto thee!' Moḥammad could not withstand the appeal. Turning kindly to them, he said: 'Whether of the two, your families or your property, is

mean that he would not at this time obtain his desire against Aṭ-Ṭā'if, and Moḥammad thought so too. A story told of 'Oyeina, chief of Fezāra, illustrates the feelings and motives of Moḥammad's Bedawi auxiliaries. 'Oyeina was lauding the garrison for their brave and determined resistance. 'Out upon thee, 'Oyeina!' said his neighbour; 'dost thou praise the enemies of the Prophet,—the very people whom thou hast come to aid him in destroying?' 'Verily,' said the Bedawi chief, 'I had another object in coming hither. I hoped that, if Moḥammad gained the victory, I should obtain one of the damsels of Aṭ-Ṭā'if; then should I have had worthy issue; for truly the tribe of Thaḳīf are a warlike, noble race.'

[1] See *ante*, p. 7. The mark of the bite, recognised by Moḥammad as having been inflicted by himself when a child on Sheimā's back, may be a traditional embellishment.

the dearer to you?' 'Our women and our children,' they replied; 'we would not take anything in exchange for them.' 'Then,' continued the Prophet, 'whatsoever prisoners fall to my portion and that of my family, I give them up unto you; and I will presently speak unto the people concerning the rest. Come again at the mid-day prayer when the congregation is assembled, and ask of me to make intercession with them for you.' At the appointed time they appeared and made their petition. The citizens of Medīna, and those of Mecca also, cheerfully followed the example of Moḥammad; but some of the allied tribes, as Fezāra, with 'Oyeina at their head, declined to do so. Moḥammad urged the claims of his new converts, and promised that such of the allies as were unwilling to part with their share of the prisoners should be recompensed hereafter from the first booty the Lord might give into their hands, at the rate of six camels for every captive. To this they agreed, and the prisoners were all released.

Moḥammad presents slave girls to 'Alī, 'Othmān, and 'Omar

Among the captives were three beautiful women, who were brought to Moḥammad. One was presented by him to Alī, another to 'Othmān, and the third to 'Omar. 'Omar transferred the one allotted him to his son 'Abdallah, who returned her as she was, with the rest of the prisoners.[1] Whether the other two were restored likewise, is not stated: but, be this as it may, it throws a curious light on the domestic history of Moḥammad, that he should have presented such gifts as slave girls to the father of one of his wives, and the husbands of two of his own daughters.

Moḥammad is mobbed on account of the booty

Having arranged for the restoration of the prisoners, Moḥammad had already mounted his camel and was proceeding to his tent, when the people, fearing lest the spoil, as well as the prisoners, should slip from their grasp, crowded round him;—'Distribute to us the spoil,' they cried, 'the camels and the flocks!' So rudely did they jostle, that he was driven to seek refuge under a tree, with his mantle torn from his shoulders. 'Return to me my mantle, O man:' cried Moḥammad, who had now secured a more free position, extricating himself with some difficulty from the crush;—'Return my mantle: for I swear by the

[1] 'Abdallah had sent the girl to be kept in readiness for him after he had visited the Ka'ba; but meanwhile the prisoners were surrendered.

Lord that if the sheep and the camels were as many as the trees of the forest in number, I would divide them all amongst you. Ye have not heretofore found me niggardly or false.' Then plucking from his camel's hump a hair, he held it aloft and said;—'Even to a hair like this, I would keep back nought but the Fifth; and even that I will divide amongst you.' They were pacified, and Moḥammad went on his way.

Present made to Meccan and Bedawi chiefs

He took an early opportunity of making good his promise, and at the same time of gaining, by a princely liberality, the hearts of the leading chiefs of Mecca and of the Bedawi tribes. To the most powerful he presented each one hundred camels. Among them we find Abu Sufyān, with his two sons, Yazīd and Mu'āwiya, Ḥakīm ibn Ḥizām, Ṣafwān, Suheil, Ḥuweiṭib, 'Oyeina, and others who but a few weeks before were his deadly enemies. To the lesser chiefs he gave fifty camels each. And so liberal was he that in some cases where discontent was expressed, the gift was without hesitation doubled.

Discontent among older followers

Although taken from the Prophet's Fifth, these largesses to new and doubtful converts gave umbrage to his veteran followers. Thus one complained that such Bedawi chieftains as Al-Aḳra' and 'Oyeina received each one hundred camels, while a faithful believer like Jo'eil got nothing at all. 'And what of that?' replied the Prophet; 'I swear that Jo'eil is the best man that ever stepped on earth, were it filled never so full of Al-Aḳra's and 'Oyeinas; but I wished to gain over the hearts of these men to Islām, while Jo'eil hath no need of any such inducement.' A Bedawi follower, who watched the proceeding, openly impugned its equity. Moḥammad became angry, and said: 'Out upon thee! If justice and equity be not with me, where will ye find them?' But what concerned Moḥammad the most was the murmurs of the Citizens of Medīna. 'Truly (thus they spake among themselves) he hath now joined his own people and forsaken us.' The discontent became so serious that Sa'd ibn 'Obāda thought right to represent it to the Prophet, who bade him call the murmurers together. He then addressed them thus;—'Ye men of Medīna,[1] it hath been reported to me that ye are disconcerted, because I have

[1] *Anṣār*, 'Helpers,' as before explained; and so throughout this address.

given unto these Chiefs largesses, and have given nothing unto you. Now speak unto me. Did I not come unto you whilst ye were wandering, and the Lord gave you the right direction? needy, and He enriched you;—at enmity amongst yourselves, and He hath filled your hearts with love and unity?' He paused for a reply. 'Indeed, it is even as thou sayest,' they answered; 'to the Lord and to his Prophet belong benevolence and grace.' 'Nay, by the Lord!' continued Moḥammad; 'but ye might have answered (and answered truly, for I would have vouched for it myself)—*Thou camest to Medīna rejected, and we bare thee witness; a fugitive, and we took thee in; an outcast, and we gave thee an asylum; destitute, and we fed thee.* Why are ye disturbed in mind because of the things of this life wherewith I have sought to incline these men unto the faith in which ye are already stablished? Are ye not satisfied that others should have the flocks and herds, while ye carry back with you the Prophet of the Lord? Nay, I will never leave you. If all mankind went one way, and the men of Medīna another way, verily I would go the way of the men of Medīna. The Lord be favourable unto them, and bless them, and their sons and their sons' sons for ever!' At these words they wept, till the tears ran down upon their beards; and they cried with one voice: 'Yea, we are well satisfied, O Prophet, with our lot!'

Notwithstanding this touching return of kindly feeling, a grave misdemeanour had been committed by those who had found fault with the distribution, and a passage was revealed bearing a divine reprimand accordingly. The legitimate recipients of public charity had already been laid down as the 'poor and needy and the wayfarer,' and certain other deserving classes. It was needful now for the Prophet to justify his stepping beyond these limits; and so a new class is added as proper recipients of public gifts;— Subject noticed in Ḳor'ān

There are that blame thee in thy (distribution of the) alms;[1] if they receive therefrom they are well pleased, but if they do not receive a part they are angry. Now, if they had been well pleased with whatever God and his Apostle gave unto them, and had said,—'God will suffice for us; Sūra ix. 58

[1] That is, they complained that the Prophet's Fifth destined for charity, &c., along with the tithes, had been diverted by Moḥammad from its proper use.

God will give unto us of his bounty, and his Prophet also,—verily unto God is our desire,'—(it had been better for them). Verily, Alms are for the poor and the needy, and for the collectors of the same, *and for them whose hearts are to be gained over*, and for captives, and for debtors, and for the service of God, and for the wayfarer. It is an ordinance from God; and God is knowing and wise.

Mālik, the Hawāzin chief, gained over

Thus Moḥammad made no attempt to hide the motive which dictated these munificent gifts, and the chiefs who received them were ever known as 'those *whose hearts had been gained over*.' Mālik, the chief who had led the Hawāzin, was still in Aṭ-Ṭā'if. Moḥammad, desiring to gain him over also, directed his tribe to make it known that if he embraced Islām his family and property would be restored, and a present of one hundred camels besides bestowed upon him. He soon joined Moḥammad and became an exemplary Believer. Confirmed in his chiefship, he entered on a constant warfare with the citizens of Aṭ-Ṭā'if, cut off their cattle whenever they were sent away to graze, and reduced them to great straits.

Booty distributed, February, March, A.D. 630

Moḥammad spent about a fortnight at Al-Ji'rāna, during which period the booty captured at Ḥonein was all distributed. Four camels, and forty sheep or goats, fell to the lot of each foot soldier, and three times that amount to every horseman. The distribution ended, Moḥammad, having taken upon him the pilgrim vows, started for Mecca, where he fulfilled the rites of the Lesser Pilgrimage. But he made no stay there. He returned to Al-Ji'rāna that same night; and thence, striking through the valleys, took the direct route homewards to Medīna.

Moḥammad performs Lesser Pilgrimage

'Attāb left in the government of Mecca

The youthful 'Attāb was confirmed in the government of Mecca, and an allowance assigned him of one dirhem a day.[1] The annual pilgrimage followed shortly afterwards, but Moḥammad did not go up to it. 'Attāb presided; and Idolaters were still permitted to mingle freely with Believers in performance of its ceremonies. Mo'ādh was left behind to complete the spiritual instruction of the city.

Despatches to Al-Baḥrein, &c.

On his return to Medīna, Moḥammad despatched letters to the Chiefs of Al-Baḥrein, 'Omān, and the Yemen, the result of which will be told in the narrative of the following year.

[1] 'Attāb was content with this moderate allowance. He said: 'Let the Lord make hungry that man's liver, who is hungry upon a dirhem a day. The Prophet hath appointed that as my sustenance. I have not further claim on any one.'

CHAPTER XXVI

MARY, THE COPTIC MAID, AND HER SON IBRĀHĪM

A.H. VIII.-X.—A.D. 630, 631

ÆTAT. 61, 62

Death of Zeinab, Mohammad's daughter

In the Ninth year of the Hijra, Moḥammad lost his daughter Zeinab, who had never recovered the ill-treatment which she suffered on her escape from Mecca. Um Kulthūm, whom 'Othmān married after Roḳeiya's death, had also died, so that of his family Fāṭima alone was left. His heart was now for a brief space to be solaced by another child.

Mary, the Coptic maid

We have already seen that the Muḳauḳis sent two Coptic maids, Sīrīn and Mary, as a gift to Moḥammad. They were both comely; but it was not lawful, according to his own strict precept, for the Prophet to place two sisters in his ḥarīm. The beauty of Mary, whose fair complexion and delicate features were adorned by a profusion of black curling hair, fascinated Moḥammad. So he kept Mary, and gave her sister to another. Um Suleim, the wife of his servant Abu Rāfi' (the same that adorned Ṣafīya for him at Kheibar), was entrusted with the new charge. Mary was not at once placed in the ḥarīm at the Mosque, but a garden house was prepared for her in Upper Medīna, where, in the heat of the summer and the date harvest, she used to receive the visits of the Prophet.[2] Originally a Christian, she had no doubt by this time gone over to Islām.

[1] Ibn Hishām, p. 121 ; Aṭ-Ṭabari, i. 1591, 1686.

[2] According to Belādhuri (p. 18), it was one of seven properties escheated from the Beni an-Naḍīr, and given to Mukheirīk the Jew, and on his death left by him to Moḥammad. Burton (ii. 323 f.) tells us it is shown to the present day. It lies in the quarter called Ambarīya, on the S.E. side of the city, where the road emerges to Yenbo' and Mecca ; it is

Presents Moḥammad with a son. A.H. VIII. April, A.D. 630

A singular fortune elevated Mary to a dignity which her charms alone could not have secured. In course of time she gave promise of becoming a mother; and the aged Selma, who had long ago attended the birth of Khadīja's children, was now engaged to perform the same office for Mary. Shortly after the return from Aṭ-Ṭā'if, a son was born, and Um Burda was selected from amongst many candidates to be the infant's nurse. His name was called Ibrāhīm.[1] More than five-and-twenty years had elapsed since the birth of Moḥammad's last child, and his numerous marriages at Medīna had not given promise of any progeny. His joy, therefore, at the birth of a son in his old age was very great. On the seventh day, following the example of Khadīja, he sacrificed a kid; and, having shaved his head, he distributed silver among the poor to the weight of the hair, which then was buried.[2] He used daily to visit the house of the nurse (where according to custom Ibrāhīm was brought up), and calling for the little child would embrace him in his arms and kiss him fondly.

Jealousy of Moḥammad's wives

The wives of Moḥammad were envious of Mary, who as the mother of Ibrāhīm was now advanced beyond the position of a slave, and enjoyed peculiar favour. As the infant grew and throve, Moḥammad one day carried him to 'Ā'isha and with pride exclaimed: 'Look, what a likeness it is to me!' 'I do not see it,' said 'Ā'isha, who would gladly have put Mohammad out of conceit with the little Ibrāhīm. 'What!' rejoined he; 'canst thou not see the likeness, and how fair and fat he is?' 'Yes,' she replied; 'and so would

separated from the rest of the town by the stream and low intervening land. A Mosque called Masjid Mashrabat Um Ibrāhīm, 'the Mosque of the summer house of the mother of Ibrāhīm,' still marks the spot. At what period Moḥammad provided this garden for her is not certain; possibly *after* the birth of Ibrāhīm, or on her becoming *enciente*. Certainly it was an honour one would not have expected to be conferred on a slave-girl, without some special cause. Sprenger thinks that Moḥammad kept her in a neighbour's house at first, and transferred her to the garden only after the affair of Ḥafṣa.

[1] The name, I need hardly say, is the Arabian form of *Abraham*. Another tradition says that the child was given to be nursed by the wife of a blacksmith, who used to be blowing his forge when Moḥammad came to see the child, and the house was consequently full of smoke.

[2] The weight must have been trifling, as he had only shaved his head a month or six weeks before, at the Lesser Pilgrimage.

be any other child that drank as much milk as he.' A flock of milch goats was kept for the especial service of the child.

But the jealousy of Mary's 'Sisters' showed itself in a more serious way, and led to an incident in the Prophet's life which the biographers pass over in decent silence; and I should gladly have followed their example if the Ḳor'ān itself had not accredited the facts and stamped them with unavoidable notoriety.

Affair with Mary creates scandal in Moḥammad's ḥarīm

It once happened that Ḥafṣa paid a visit to her father on the day which, in due course, Moḥammad was passing in her house.[1] Returning unexpectedly, she surprised the Prophet in her own private room with Mary. She was indignant at the wrong. The affront was the more intolerable from the servile position of her rival. She reproached her lord bitterly, and threatened to make the occurrence known to the whole sisterhood. Afraid of the exposure, and anxious to appease his offended wife, Moḥammad begged of her to keep the matter quiet, and promised to forego the company of Mary altogether. Ḥafṣa, however, did not care to hide her wrong. She told it all to 'Ā'isha, who boiled with indignation at the tale. The scandal throughout the harīm spread apace, and Moḥammad soon found himself received by his wives with coldness and reserve.

Moḥammad's displeasure with his wives

As in the affair of Zeinab, a heavenly message interposed, which disallowed the promise to refrain from Mary's company, chided the chief offenders for their insubordination, and hinted at the possibility of the whole harīm being divorced in favour of other consorts more loyal and complacent. Having delivered this warning, the Prophet withdrew from the society of his wives, and for a whole month lived alone with Mary. 'Omar and Abu Bekr were mortified at the scandal and at the desertion of their daughters for a menial concubine. At length Moḥammad, unwilling longer to continue the disgrace of his wives, or impatient at his self-imposed seclusion from them, listened to their prayer. Gabriel, he said, had spoken well of Ḥafṣa, the chief offender, and desired that he should take her back again. So he

[1] As before explained, Moḥammad divided his time equally among his wives. He would say: '*This* (*i.e.* living in rotation with each) I have power to do; but Thou, O Lord, art the master over that in respect of which I have no power' (meaning love in the heart).

forgave them all and returned to their apartments as before.

Notice of affair in Ḳor'ān

The passage in the Ḳor'ān relating to the affair is as follows:—

Sūra lxvi. 1 f.

O Prophet! Why hast thou forbidden thyself that which God hath made lawful unto thee, out of desire to please thy Wives; for God is forgiving and merciful? Verily God hath sanctioned the revocation of your oaths; and God is your Master. He is knowing and wise.

The Prophet had entrusted as a secret to one of his wives a certain affair; and when she disclosed it (to another), and God made known the same unto him, he acquainted (her) with a part thereof, and withheld a part.[1] And when he had acquainted her (Ḥafṣa) therewith, she said, *Who told thee this?* He replied, *He told it to me, the Knowing and the Wise.*

If ye both turn with repentance unto God (for verily the hearts of you both have swerved)—Well. But if ye combine with each other against him, surely God is his Master; and Gabriel and (every) good man of the Believers, and the Angels, will thereafter be his supporters.

Haply, his Lord, if he divorce you,[2] will give him in your stead Wives better than ye are, submissive unto God, believers, pious, repentant, devout, fasting;—both women married previously, and Virgins.[3]

There is surely no grotesquer utterance than this in the 'Sacred Books of the East'; and yet it has been gravely read all these ages, and is still read, by the Muslim, both in public and private, as part of the 'eternal' Ḳor'ān. It is equally remarkable that the affair did not in any perceptible degree affect either the reputation and influence of the Prophet, or the credit of his revelation.

[1] The passage is enigmatical. The meaning is apparently this: Moḥammad told a part,—that is, a part of what he had supernaturally learned that Ḥafṣa had said to 'Ā'isha; and withheld a part, *i.e.* refrained from upbraiding her with a part of what he had thus learned:—the one part perhaps relating to Moḥammad's affair in Ḥafṣa's room; the other, to his promise that he would not consort with Mary again. According to another tradition, Moḥammad, with the view of appeasing Ḥafṣa, told her that Abu Bekr, and after him her father 'Omar, were to succeed him; this being the part which, from fear of its getting abroad, he did not mention; but such an interpretation is altogether unlikely.

[2] 'You' in the plural, not as before in the dual number,—implying that all his wives were involved in his displeasure.

[3] The Sūra, a short one of only thirteen verses, is a curiosity from beginning to end. It ends with a warning allusion to two wicked women, who, though the wives of Noah and Lot, were yet condemned to hell,—signifying that his own wives, unless they repented, might possibly find themselves in the same category; and to two good women the wife of Pharaoh, and the Virgin Mary, examples of virtue and piety.

I turn gladly to a more edifying scene. A year and more had passed; and the child Ibrāhīm was now advanced to an age at which the innocent prattle and winning ways of infancy stole away the heart of Moḥammad. His hopes and affections centred for awhile in his little son. There is, indeed, no ground for supposing that Moḥammad ever contemplated the succession of princely office in his own family. The prophetical dignity was personal, and his political authority exercised solely in virtue of it. But he regarded his children with a loving and partial eye; he no doubt also rejoiced in the prospect, dear to every Arab, of having his name and memory perpetuated by male issue; and he might naturally expect that his son would be cherished and honoured by all followers of Islām. But his expectations, of whatever nature, were doomed to an early blight. When but fifteen or sixteen months old, Ibrāhīm fell sick, and it was soon seen that he would not survive. He was laid in a palm-grove near the house of his nurse. There Mary, with her sister Sīrīn, tended his dying bed; and there too was Moḥammad in deep and bitter grief. Seeing that the child was soon to breathe his last, he folded him in his arms and sobbed. The bystanders tried to comfort him. They reminded him that he had counselled others to moderate their grief. 'Nay,' said Moḥammad, calming himself as he hung over the expiring child;—'It is not this that I forbade, but wailing and fulsome laudation of the dead. This that ye see in me is but the working of love and pity in the heart: he that showeth no pity, unto him no pity shall be shown. We grieve for the child: the eye runneth down with tears, and the heart swelleth inwardly; yet we say not aught that would offend our Lord. Ibrāhīm! O Ibrāhīm! if it were not that the promise is faithful, and hope of Resurrection sure, if it were not that this is the way to be trodden by all, and that the last of us shall rejoin the first, I would grieve for thee with a grief sorer even than this!' But the spirit had already passed away, and the last fond words of Moḥammad fell on ears that could no longer hear. So he laid down the little body, saying: 'The remainder of the days of his nursing shall be fulfilled in Paradise.'[1]

Sickness of Ibrāhīm

His death, A.H. X. June or July, A.D. 631

[1] Moḥammad held *two years* as the proper period for the suckling of a child.

Then he comforted Mary and Sīrīn, and bade them, now that the child was gone, to be silent and resigned.

Burial of the child

Moḥammad, with his uncle Al-'Abbās, sat by while Al-Faḍl, son of the latter, washed and laid out the body. It was then carried forth upon its little bier. The Prophet, as was his wont, prayed over it, and then followed the procession to the graveyard. He lingered at the grave after it was filled up; and calling for a skin of water, caused it to be sprinkled over the spot. Then, observing some unevenness, he smoothed it with his hand, saying to the bystanders: 'When ye do this thing, do it carefully, for it giveth ease to the afflicted heart. It cannot injure the dead, neither can it profit him; but it giveth comfort to the living.'

Eclipse

An eclipse of the sun occurred on the same day, and the people spoke of it as a tribute to the death of the Prophet's son. A vulgar impostor would have accepted and confirmed the delusion; but Moḥammad rejected the idea. 'The sun and the moon,' he taught them, 'are amongst the signs appointed by the Lord. They are not eclipsed on the death of any one. Whensoever ye see an eclipse, then betake yourselves to prayer until it passeth away.'

The nurse rewarded

In gratitude for her services he gave Um Burda, the nurse, a parcel of ground planted as an orchard with palm-trees.

General history anticipated

In this chapter I have anticipated the march of events by about a year, in order to bring under one view the story of Mary, the Coptic maid, and of her little son.

CHAPTER XXVII

EMBASSIES TO MEDĪNA[1]

FIRST HALF OF THE NINTH YEAR OF THE HIJRA

April 20 *to September*, A.D. 630

Political supremacy attained by conquest of Mecca

THE conquest of Mecca opened a new era in Islām. It practically decided the struggle for supremacy in Arabia. Followed by the victory of Ḥonein, it not only removed apprehension of future attack upon Medīna, but elevated Moḥammad to a position in which it was natural for him to assert an authority paramount over the whole Peninsula. It is true that no such authority had ever vested in the chiefs of Mecca. Neither had the Byzantine empire pretended to any influence beyond the confines of the Syrian desert. The suzerainty of Arabia, enjoyed in remote times by the Kings of Ḥimyar, had, it is true, been transferred to the dynasty of Al-Ḥīra as representing the court of Persia. But Al-Ḥīra had fallen to the rank of an ordinary Satrapy; and the Chosroes, long before discomfited in a decisive battle by the Arabs themselves, and humbled now by the Roman arms, no longer commanded respect.[2] There was thus at the moment no power even nominally paramount throughout the Peninsula. Besides Moḥammad himself, no one could lay claim to the dignity, or even dream of aspiring to it. The possession of Mecca now imparted a colour of right; for Mecca was the spiritual centre of Arabia, and to Mecca the tribes from every quarter yielded a reverential homage.

[1] Ibn Hishām, p. 933 ff.; Aṭ-Ṭabari, i. 1710 ff.

[2] In the battle of Dhu Ḳār, fought A.D. 611, just before Moḥammad assumed the prophetic office, the Persians were completely routed by the great tribe of the Beni Bekr, inhabiting the N.E. of the Peninsula; and thereafter Al-Ḥīra sank in importance. See Introd., p. xcvi., and p. 370.

The conduct of the annual pilgrimage, the custody of the Holy House, the intercalation of the year, and the commutation at will of the sacred months—institutions affecting all Arabia, belonged by ancient privilege to Ḳoreish, and were now in the hands of Moḥammad. Throughout Arabia, who could advance pretensions to the supreme authority beside the Prophet of Medīna and Conqueror of Mecca?

Possession of Mecca increased Moḥammad's spiritual power;

Moreover, it had been the special care of Moḥammad to interweave with the reformed faith all essential parts of the ancient ceremonial. The one had become an inseparable portion of the other. It was not, indeed, till the expiry of another year that full advantage was taken of this, by admitting none but adherents of Islām to the Ka'ba and its rites. Yet the spiritual power which the Prophet gained by combining the Pilgrimage with the new faith was felt throughout from the moment that Mecca submitted to his arms. There remained but one religion for Arabia, and that was Islām.

Which, in its turn, involved absolute secular authority

Again, the new creed was so deftly bound up with the civil polity, that the recognition of Moḥammad's spiritual power necessarily involved a simultaneous submission to his secular jurisdiction. It lay at the root of Islām that the convert should not only submit to its teaching, its ritual and its code of ethics, but also that he should render an implicit obedience in all things 'to the Lord *and to his Prophet*,' and that he should pay Tithes annually (not indeed as a tribute, but as a religious offering that sanctified the rest of his wealth) towards the charities and expenses of Moḥammad and his growing empire.[1] It was the privilege of believing tribes alone, to pay the tithe: from Jews, Christians, and heathen tribes, it was not tithe but *Tribute* that was taken, and that in token of their servitude.

Collectors deputed to gather tithes. A.H. IX. April 20, A.D. 630

It was under these circumstances that, on his return from Al-Ji'rāna, at the opening of the Ninth year of the

[1] Tithes and voluntary almsgiving are called by two names of Jewish derivation, *Zakāt* and *Sadaḳāt;* the former signifying 'purification' (see Luke xi. 41), the latter 'righteousness,' as in Matt. vi. 1. The tribute from unbelievers is called *Kharāj* or *Jizya.*

For the purposes to which Moḥammad applied the tithes, see the passage quoted at p. 423. Moḥammad assisted debtors from the fund. A debtor once applied for aid: 'Wait,' said Moḥammad, 'till the tithes come in, and then I will help thee.'

Hijra, the Prophet demanded from the tribes which had tendered their adhesion, the prescribed offerings or Tithes. Collectors were deputed by him in every direction to assess a tenth part of the increase, and bring it in as tithe to Medīna.[1] They were well received, and accomplished their mission without obstruction, excepting only one or two cases.

Beni Temīm attacked for driving away tax-gatherer

A branch of the Beni Temīm chanced to be encamped close at hand when the tax-gatherer arrived to gather the tithes of an adjoining tribe. While the herds and flocks of their neighbours were being collected for the tenth, Temīm, anticipating a like demand, came forward armed with bows and swords and drove the tax-gatherer away. Moḥammad resolved on a prompt example of the offenders. 'Oyeina, with fifty of his Arab horsemen, travelling with haste and secrecy, fell unexpectedly upon them, and making above fifty captives—men, women, and children—carried them off to Medīna, where they were kept by Moḥammad in confinement.[2]

Beni Temīm send deputation for release of prisoners

The Beni Temīm, some of whom had fought by the side of Moḥammad at Mecca and Ḥonein, and been munificently rewarded at Al-Ji'rāna, lost no time in sending a deputation, of eighty or ninety chief men, to beg for their brethren's release. As they passed through the streets of Medīna, the captive women and children, recognising their friends, raised a loud cry of distress. Moved by the sight, the party hastened onwards to the Mosque. After waiting impatiently for a little in its spacious court, they at last called out (for they were rude children of the desert) in a loud and familiar voice to Moḥammad, who was in one of his wives' apartments adjoining the hall of audience:—'O Moḥammad, come forth unto us!' The Prophet was displeased at their roughness and importunity, for he loved to be addressed in low and submissive accents. But, as the mid-day prayer was at hand, he came forth; and while Bilāl was summoning the people, entered into discourse with the strangers and listened to their application.

[1] Nine such parties are mentioned as having started on the first day of the new year to various tribes. They were instructed to take only the best and unblemished part of the increase, but not to interfere with the capital.

[2] Ibn Hishām, p. 983; Aṭ-Ṭabari, i. 1711; Al-Wāḳidi, p. 385; Ibn Sa'd, p. 116.

Their poet and orator worsted by Thābit and Ḥassān

The prayers ended, Moḥammad seated himself in the court of the Mosque, when a scene occurred illustrative at once of Arab manners and of the successful readiness with which Moḥammad adapted himself to the circumstances of the day. The Chiefs sought leave to contend for the palm of victory in rhetoric and poetry with the orators and poets of Medīna.[1] It was hardly the proper issue for Moḥammad on which to place his cause; but to have refused would have injured him in the eyes of these wild Bedawīn; and the Prophet was confident in the superior eloquence of his followers. So he gave permission. First arose 'Otārid, the orator of his tribe, and, in an harangue of the ordinary boastful style, lauded his own people for their prowess and nobility. When he had ended, Moḥammad motioned to Thābit ibn Ḳeis that he should reply. Thābit descanted on the glory of Moḥammad as a messenger from Heaven, on the devotion of the Refugees, and on the faithful and generous friendship of the Citizens; and wound up by threatening destruction against the enemies of Islām. Then Zibriḳān the Bedawi bard arose, and recited poetry, in which he dilated on the greatness and unequalled hospitality of Temīm. When he sat down, Ḥassān the son of Thābit, by Moḥammad's command, followed in glowing and well-measured verse. After the more ordinary topics, he ended thus:—

Children of Dārim! strive not with us; Your boasting will turn to your shame.

Ye lie when ye contend with us for Glory. What are ye but our Servants, our Nurses, and our Attendants?

If ye be come to save your lives, and your property, that it may not be distributed as booty,

Then make not unto God an equal, embrace Islām, and abandon the wild manners of the Heathen.

The strangers were astonished at the beauty of Ḥassān's poetry, and abashed at the force and point of his concluding verses. 'By the Lord!' they said, 'how rich is this man's fortune! His poet, as well as his orator, surpasseth ours in

[1] Al-Aḳra' said: 'Give us permission to speak; for, verily, from me praise is an ornament and reproach a disgrace.' 'Nay,' replied the Prophet, 'thou speakest falsely; that may be said of the Great and Almighty God alone.'

eloquence. Moḥammad liberated the prisoners, and, having entertained his visitors hospitably, dismissed their Chief with rich presents and provisions for the way. All the branches of the tribe which had not yet given in their adhesion were now converted.[1] But the Prophet did not forget the first rude and impatient address of the deputation. To guard against such familiarity for the future, the following passage was revealed:—

Moḥammad liberates their prisoners

Notice of deputation in the Ḳor'ān

O ye that believe! Go not in advance (in any matter) before the Lord and his Prophet; and fear God, for God heareth and knoweth. O ye that believe! Raise not your voices above the voice of the Prophet; nor speak loudly in discourse with him as the loud speech of one of you with another, lest your works become vain, and ye perceive it not. Truly, they that lower their voices in the presence of the Apostle of God, are those whose hearts God hath disposed unto piety; these shall have pardon and an abundant reward. Verily as to those that call unto thee from outside of the private apartments, the most part of them understand not. If they had waited patiently, until thou wentest forth unto them, it had been better for them. But God is forgiving and merciful.

Sūra xlix. 1 ff.

The tax-gatherer deputed to gather the tithes of the Beni'l-Musṭaliḳ, on approaching their encampment, was encountered by an assemblage who went forth on camels to meet him. Apprehending violence, he fled back to Medīna; and Moḥammad was preparing a party to avenge the affront, when a deputation appeared to explain the circumstance. They had in reality held steadily to the profession of Islām, and what had been mistaken for hostile preparations, were, they said, marks of joy and welcome. The deputation was received with courtesy. The tax-gatherer was reprehended, and his misconduct deemed not unworthy of a special revelation. Another of his followers was then deputed by Moḥammad to levy the tithes and to instruct the people in their religious duties.[2]

Deputation from Beni'l-Musṭaliḳ. May, A.D. 630

[1] Sprenger gives an anecdote which, though of doubtful authority, illustrates the spirit of the times. One of the prisoners was a beautiful female, to whom Moḥammad offered terms of marriage, which, however, she declined. When her husband came with the deputation, he turned out to be a black and ill-favoured person; whereupon the Muslims were so displeased at her refusal of the Prophet, that they began to abuse and curse her. But Moḥammad interfered to excuse her, and bade them refrain.

[2] The passage relating to this incident is in continuation of that just quoted, and runs as follows: 'O ye that believe! if an evil man come

Expeditions during summer of A.H. IX. A.D. 630

During the summer several lesser expeditions were undertaken for the chastisement of rebellious or recusant tribes Marked only by the ordinary features of surprise and capture of prisoners and plunder, it is unnecessary to burden the page with their details. The largest was directed against a combination of the Abyssinians with the people of Jidda, the nature of which is not clearly explained. It was, however, regarded by the Prophet as of sufficient importance to require the services of an army of 300 men. The force reached an island on the shore of the Red Sea which the enemy had made their rendezvous, and forced them to retire.[1]

Abyssinians attacked at Jidda. July

Campaign against Beni Ṭai'

About the same time, 'Alī was sent, in command of two hundred horse, to destroy the temple of the Beni Ṭai', a tribe divided between the profession of Idolatry and the Christian faith. He performed his mission effectually, and returned laden with plunder and with many prisoners. Amongst these prisoners was the daughter of Ḥātim of Ṭai', the Arab Chieftain so famous for his generosity, but now for some time dead. His son 'Adī, having on the first alarm of 'Alī's approach, fled to Syria, his sister now prostrated herself at the Prophet's feet, and told her plaintive tale. She was at once released, and presented with a change of raiment and a camel, on which, joining the first Syrian caravan, she went in quest of her brother. At her solicitation, 'Adī made his way to the Prophet's presence, and, having embraced Islām, and been confirmed in the chiefship of his tribe, distinguished himself hereafter in the Muslim wars.[2]

Conversion of son of Ḥātim of Ṭai'. July.

Conversion of the poet Ka'b ibn Zuheir

The submission of the poet Ka'b, son of Zuheir, took place about the same time.[3] His father was one of the most

unto you with intelligence, make careful inquiry, lest ye injure a people through inadvertence, and afterwards repent of what ye have done. And know that, verily, the Apostle of God is amongst you. If he were to listen to you in many matters, ye would surely fall into sin (by leading him into a misunderstanding).'—Sūra xlix. 6 f.

[1] Ibn Sa'd, p. 117 f. The circumstance is remarkable, and not the less so on account of the brevity of the Secretary and the silence of the other biographers. *Apparently*, a body of Abyssinians had crossed the Red Sea to join the Arabs of Jidda in opposing Moḥammad. Was the Negus now disappointed to find that Mohammad no longer supported Christianity?

[2] Ibn Hishām, p. 948; Aṭ-Ṭabari, i. 1706 ff.; Ibn Sa'd, p. 118.

[3] Ibn Hishām, p. 887 ff.

distinguished poets of Arabia; and the poetical mantle descended on several members of his family. After the capture of Mecca his brother wrote from thence to warn Ka'b of the fate which had overtaken certain of the poets there, and urged him either to sue for terms at Medīna, or else seek for himself secure asylum elsewhere. Ka'b was imprudent enough to reply in verses significant of displeasure at his brother's conversion. Moḥammad, highly incensed, gave utterance to threats ominous for the safety of Ka'b. Again the poet was warned, and urged by his brother to delay no longer. At last, in despair, he resolved to present himself before Moḥammad and seek for pardon. As a stranger appearing one day unexpectedly in the Mosque, he thus addressed the Prophet;—'Ka'b son of Zuheir cometh unto thee repentant and believing; wilt thou give him quarter if I bring him to thee?' The promise having been vouchsafed, the speaker made known that he himself was Ka'b. To signalise his gratitude, Ka'b composed the famous 'Poem of the Mantle,' in which he lauded the generosity and glory of his benefactor. When reciting it in the assembly, he came to this verse,—

Poem of the Mantle

> Verily, the Prophet is a light to illuminate the world,
> A naked sword from out of the armoury of God,—

Moḥammad, unable to restrain his admiration and delight, threw his mantle from off his shoulders upon the poet. The precious gift (from which the poem derived its name) was treasured up with care. It passed into the hands of the Caliphs, and was by them preserved, as one of the regalia of the empire, until Baghdad was sacked by the Tartars; and, under the name of the *Khirḳa Sharīfa*,[1] a relic is even now exhibited at Constantinople as from the self-same mantle. To gain over such a poet was no empty triumph, for Ka'b wielded a real power which was now thrown as a fresh weight into the scale of Islām.

Deputations from Arab tribes. A.H. IX., X. A.D. 630, 631

The Mosque of Moḥammad was now the scene of frequent embassies from all quarters of Arabia. His supremacy was everywhere recognised; and from the most distant parts of the Peninsula, from the Yemen and Ḥadramaut, from Mahra,

[1] The *Noble Remnant*. The poem was published by Freytag with Latin translation (*Halæ*, 1823). The mantle was bought by one of the Caliphs from Ka'b's heirs for 40,000 pieces.

'Omān, and Al-Baḥrein, from the borders of Syria and the outskirts of Persia, the tribes hastened to prostrate themselves before the rising potentate, and by an early submission secure his favour. They were uniformly treated with consideration and courtesy. Their representations were heard publicly in the court of the Mosque, which formed the hall of audience; and there whatever matters required the commands of Moḥammad, such as the collection and transmission of tithes and tribute, grant of lands, recognition or conferment of authority and office, or adjustment of international disputes, were discussed and settled. Simple though its exterior, and unpretending its forms and usages, more absolute power was exercised, and affairs of greater importance transacted, in the courtyard of the Mosque of Moḥammad than in many an Imperial palace.

Mode in which they were treated

The messengers and embassies were quartered by Moḥammad in the houses of the chief Citizens, by whom they were hospitably entertained. On departure they received an ample sum for the expenses of the road, and generally some further present corresponding with their rank. A written treaty often guaranteed certain privileges to the tribe, and not unfrequently a 'Reader' was sent back with the embassy to instruct the people in the duties of Islām, and to see that every remnant of idolatry was obliterated. A large amount of independence was left to the rulers of powerful tribes, and to such distant provinces as Al-Baḥrein and 'Omān; but, though allowed themselves to collect the tithes, the amount must nevertheless, as a rule, be remitted to Medīna. In some cases this demand created discontent; but before the Prophet's death the irresistible combination of temporal with spiritual power had overcome all opposition.

The Ninth year of the Hijra, called year of Deputations

These embassies having commenced in the Ninth year of the Hijra, it is styled in tradition 'the Year of Deputations'; but they were almost equally numerous in the Tenth year, under which they will be further mentioned.

CHAPTER XXVIII

CAMPAIGN OF TEBŪK;[1] AND OTHER EVENTS IN THE SECOND HALF OF THE NINTH YEAR OF THE HIJRA

October, A.D. 630, *to April*, A.D. 631

Gathering of Roman feudatories on Syrian border

DURING the summer of the year A.D. 630, an expedition was despatched towards the Syrian frontier, directed, apparently, against certain disaffected clans of the Beni ʻOdhra and Balī, who since the operations of Khālid in that quarter were now, at least nominally, adherents of Moḥammad. Whether to guard against the recurrence of such marauding inroads, or in consequence of Moḥammad's growing power and pretensions, the Emperor, said to have been then at Ḥimṣ, directed the feudatory tribes of the border to assemble for its protection. Rumours of this movement were magnified by travellers and traders from Syria into the assemblage of a great and threatening army; a year's pay (they said) had been advanced by the Kaiser, for the necessities of a long campaign; the Syrian tribes, Lakhm, Judhām, and Ghassān, were flocking around the Roman eagles, and the vanguard was already at the Belḳā. Moḥammad resolved to meet the danger with the largest force he could collect. His custom at other times had been to conceal to the very last the object of an intended march, or by seeming preparations for a campaign in some other direction, to lull the suspicions of his enemy. But the journey now in contemplation was so distant, and the heat of the season so excessive, that timely warning was deemed necessary in order that the necessities of the way might be foreseen and provided for.

Moḥammad projects counter-expedition. Autumn, A.H. IX. A.D. 630

Backwardness of Bedawīn and some Citizens

All his adherents and allies, the inhabitants of Mecca as well as the Bedawi tribes, received from Moḥammad an

[1] Ibn Hishām, p. 893 ff.; Aṭ-Ṭabari, i. 1692 ff.; Al-Wāḳidi, p. 390 ff.; Ibn Saʻd, p. 118 ff.

urgent call to join the army. But the Arabs of the desert, ever loose and fickle in their loyalty, and even Citizens of Medīna, showed little alacrity in obeying the command. Anticipated hardships of the journey, long-continued drought and overpowering heat, and perhaps memory of the Roman phalanx at Mūta, made them loth to quit the ease and shelter of their homes. Multitudes pleaded inability and other frivolous excuses. The plea was generally accepted when tendered with colourable ground by the men of Medīna; for Moḥammad, conscious of the debt he owed their city, always treated them with tenderness. But coming from the Bedawīn it was altogether disallowed.

Exemplary zeal of true Believers

On the other hand, extraordinary eagerness pervaded the ranks of loyal and earnest Muslims. Tithes and free-will offerings poured in from every quarter, while the leading Companions vied with one another in the costliness of their gifts. The contribution of 'Othmān surpassed all others, and amounted to a thousand golden pieces. From these sources carriage and supplies were provided for the poorer soldiers; but they did not suffice for all who longed to share in the merit, haply also in the spoils, of the campaign. A party for whom, after every effort, Moḥammad could make no provision, retired in tears, and their names are embalmed in tradition under the title of *The Weepers*.[1]

Arrangements at Medīna on Moḥammad's departure

At last the army was marshalled in the outskirts of the city, and Abu Bekr appointed to conduct prayers in the encampment until the Prophet himself should assume command. Moḥammad, son of Maslama, was placed in charge of the city; 'Alī also was left behind to take care of the Prophet's family, as well as to check any rising of disaffection. 'Abdallah ibn Obei pitched a separate camp for his numerous adherents hard by the main army; but eventually, as it would appear with the consent of Moḥammad,[2] he remained behind.

March for Tebūk. September, October, A.D. 630

The army, with all these drawbacks, was probably the largest force ever before put in motion in Arabia. Its

[1] *Bakkā'ūn*. See Judges ii. 1, 5, where a place is named *Bochim*, or 'Weepers,' because the children of Israel wept there; also Ps. lxxxiv. 6, 'the valley of *Baca*,' or weeping. *The Weepers* are specially noticed in Sūra ix. 93, in allusion to the present occasion.

[2] Weil doubts this. *Einleitung*, p. 32.

numbers are given, though probably with some exaggeration, at 30,000, of whom no less than 10,000 were cavalry. After a hot and thirsty march, the force reached the valley of Al-Ḥijr, whose rocky sides were hewn out (according to local tradition) into dwellings, by the rebellious and impious Thamūdites. Having alighted there, drawn supplies from the refreshing fountains, and already begun to prepare their food, suddenly proclamation ran through the ranks that none should drink of the water or use it for their ablutions, that the dough which had been kneaded should be given to the camels, and that no one should go forth alone by night. And the reason assigned was because of the ominous surroundings of the fateful valley;—'Enter not the houses of the Transgressors, except with lamentation, less that overtake you which happened unto them.' On the morrow, a plentiful shower of rain, ascribed to the miraculous intervention of the Prophet, compensated for the loss of the wells of Al-Ḥijr.[1]

Valley of Al-Ḥijr

Having reached Tebūk, where was plenty of shade and water, the army halted. The rumours of invasion had by this time melted away. There was nothing at the moment to threaten the border. So Moḥammad contented himself with sending a strong detachment under Khālid to Dūma, and with receiving the adhesion of the Jewish and Christian tribes on the shores of the Ælanitic Gulf, towards the east of which he was now encamped. To the chief of these, John, Prince of Ayla,[2] Moḥammad addressed a letter, summoning him to

Halt at Tebūk: communications with surrounding tribes

Treaty with John, Christian Prince of Ayla

[1] The story, however, is not confirmed by Al-Wāḳidi, and Ibn Hishām deals greatly in the marvellous. Two men, neglecting Moḥammad's caution, went out by night alone, and were maltreated by the evil spirits,—one having his neck wrenched, and the other being carried away by the wind to the hills of the Beni Ṭai'. Again: By the way, they came to a trickling fountain, at which hardly two or three men could have slaked their thirst. Moḥammad bade none to touch it before himself. But the prohibition was not attended to. Coming up, he found it empty, and cursed the men who had disobeyed him. Then he took up a little of the water, and, sprinkling the rock, wiped it with his hand and prayed over it. Floods immediately gushed forth, with a noise as it had been thunder, and all drank thereof. Moḥammad said: 'Whosoever of you shall survive the longest, will hear of this valley being greener with trees and verdure than any other round about;'—meaning that the great stream now created would be permanent. Ibn Hishām, 898 f.

[2] Ibn Hishām, p. 902; Aṭ-Ṭabari, i. 1702; Al-Wāḳidi, p. 405.

submit on pain of being attacked.[1] The Prince, with a cross of gold upon his forehead, hastened to the camp, and, offering the present of a mule and a shawl, bowed himself reverentially in the Prophet's presence. He was received with kindness, and Bilāl commanded to entertain him hospitably. The following treaty was concluded with him:—

'*In the name of God the Gracious and Merciful:* A compact of Peace from God, and from Moḥammad the Prophet and Apostle of God, granted unto Yuḥanna, son of Ru'ba, and unto the people of Ayla. For them who remain at home, and for those that travel by sea or by land, there is the guarantee of God and Moḥammad the Apostle of God, and for all that are with them, whether of Syria or of the Yemen or of the seacoast. Whoso contraveneth this treaty, his wealth shall not save him; it shall be the fair prize of him that taketh it. Now it shall not be lawful to hinder the men of Ayla from any springs which they have been in the habit of frequenting, nor from any journey they desire to make,

[1] I have no reason to doubt the genuineness of this letter; its purport is as follows: *To John ibn Ru'ba and the Chiefs of Ayla* (or Al-Akaba). Peace be on you! I praise God for you, beside whom there is no Lord. I will not fight against you until I have written thus unto you. Believe, or else pay tribute. And be obedient unto the Lord and his Prophet, and unto the messengers of his Prophet. Honour them and clothe them, specially Zeid, with excellent vestments, not with inferior raiment. As long as my messengers are pleased, so likewise am I. Ye know the tribute. If ye desire to have security by sea and by land, obey the Lord and His Apostle, and he will defend you from every demand, whether by Arab or foreigner, saving the demand of the Lord and his Apostle. But if ye oppose and displease them, I will accept nothing from you, until I have fought against you and taken captive your little ones and slain the elder; for I am the Apostle of the Lord in truth. Believe in the Lord and in his Prophets. And believe in the Messiah, son of Mary; verily he is the Word of God: I believe in him that he was a Messenger of God. Come then, before trouble reach you. I commend my messengers to you. Give to Ḥarmala three measures of barley; and indeed Ḥarmala hath interceded for you. As for me, if it were not for the Lord and for this (intercession of Ḥarmala), I would not have sent any message at all unto you, until ye had seen the army. But now, if ye obey my messengers God will be your protector, and Moḥammad, and whosoever belongeth unto him. Now my messengers are Shuraḥbīl, &c. Unto you is the guarantee of God and of Moḥammad his Apostle, and peace be unto you if ye submit. And convey the people of Maḳna back to their land.

whether by sea or by land. The writing of Juheim and Shuraḥbīl, by command of the Apostle of God.[1] In token of approbation, Moḥammad presented the Christian Prince with a mantle of striped Yemen stuff, and dismissed him honourably. The tribute was fixed at the yearly sum of a golden piece for every family, or three hundred for the whole town of Ayla.

He is dismissed honourably

At the same time deputations from the Jewish settlements of Maḳna, Adhruḥ and Jarbā presented themselves with a tender of submission to the Prophet. To each was given a rescript, specifying the amount of their tribute, and binding them to afford refuge and aid to any Muslim travellers or merchants who might stand in need of their good offices.[2]

Terms made with Jews of Maḳna, Adhruḥ and Jarbā

Having concluded these matters, Moḥammad quitted Tebūk after having halted there for twenty days, and returned to Medīna. He reached home, after a prolonged absence, in the beginning of Ramaḍān, or December, A.D. 630.

Moḥammad returns to Medīna. A.H. IX. December, A.D. 630.

Meanwhile Khālid had been travelling across the desert from Tebūk to Dūma, with 420 horse, the flower of the army.[3] So rapidly did he march, and so unexpectedly appear before Dūma, that Okeidir, the Christian chief, was surprised

Khālid conquers Dūma, and takes Chief prisoner to Medīna

[1] The treaty is evidently genuine. The original was, no doubt, retained as a precious charter of right by the chiefs of Ayla. We are told that ʻOmar II. refrained from raising the tribute, which was below the proper amount, in deference to the guarantee given in this treaty.

[2] Wellh. p. 405. These treaties are genuine and interesting. The following was copied by Al-Wāḳidi, apparently from the original: ʻIn the name of God, &c. This writing is from Moḥammad the Prophet to the people of Adhruḥ. They are included in the truce of God and in the truce of Moḥammad. They are to pay one hundred dinars every year, in Rajab, full weight and good money. And God is their guarantee that they shall behave towards the Muslims with probity and kindness. Whoever of the Muslims taketh refuge with them from danger and in quest of assistance, in case there should be ground of fear for such Muslims, and they are themselves in security, they are to protect them until they hear that Moḥammad is preparing to set out for their aid.' A proof of the authenticity of this document is that Moḥammad is mentioned throughout by his simple name *Moḥammad* without either the affix *Prophet* or *Apostle*, or the reverential addition, ʻPrayers and blessings be on him.' Such affixes are, in general, later additions by the pious transcriber.

[3] Ibn Hishām, p. 903; Aṭ-Ṭabari, i. 1702 f.; Al-Wāḳidi, p. 403 ff.; Ibn Saʻd, p. 119 f.

by him while hunting the wild cow. Khālid pursued the party, and after a short struggle, in which the chief's brother was killed, took Okeidir captive. His life was spared on condition that the gates of Dūma should at once be thrown open. The city was ransomed at 2,000 camels, 800 sheep, 400 suits of mail, and as many stand of arms. With this booty, and carrying with him Okeidir and a brother, Khālid returned to Medīna. The Christian chief, wearing a golden cross, and clad in brocade, inwrought with gold, to the admiration of the simple Citizens, was brought to the Prophet, who pressed him to embrace Islām. The inducements of the new religion proved too strong for his faith. He surrendered the Gospel for the Ḳor'ān and was admitted to the terms of a favoured ally.[1]

The Chief embraces Islām

Malingerers chided in Ḳor'ān

When Moḥammad returned to Medīna, many who had remained behind without permission came forward to exculpate themselves from the heavy charge of malingering. Moḥammad reserved his reproaches for a special revelation. He thus avoided the odium attaching to a personal rebuke, while the admonition came with all the force of a message from Heaven. In the 9th Sūra, the latest of all in chronological order, the vials of wrath are discharged against the Disaffected generally still lingering in Medīna, and against those in particular who had neglected to join in the

[1] Al-Wāḳidi says he took the following copy *from the original at Dūma:* 'In the name of God, &c.—from Moḥammad the Prophet of God to Keidar (when he accepted Islām and put away from him the images and idols, by the hand of Khālid, the Sword of God), regarding Dūma of the waters of Al-Jandal and its environs: to Moḥammad belongeth the unoccupied land with its streams and fountains, its unenclosed and fallow ground, and the armour, weapons, camels, and forts; and to you belongeth the occupied land with the fruit-bearing date-trees, and springs of water, after payment of the fifth. Your cattle shall not be molested in grazing on the waste lands; that which is ordinarily exempt from tithe shall not be taxed; the old date-trees shall not be taxed,—excepting the tenth thereof; so as they observe prayer regularly, and pay the tithes faithfully. A true and faithful treaty. God is witness thereto, and all that are present of the Muslims.' This may be taken as a type of the treaties made with converted tribes. Okeidir revolted after Moḥammad's death. The 'images and idols' may have been either those in use amongst the heathen part of the community, or such as belonged to the worship of Jesus and the Virgin. The title 'Sword of God' was no doubt added later on.

late expedition. The following passage will suffice as examples :—

O ye that believe! What ailed you that when it was said unto you, *Go forth to war in the ways of God*, ye inclined heavily towards the earth? What! do ye prefer the present life before that which is to come? If ye go not forth to war, He will punish you with a grievous punishment, and He will substitute another people for you: and ye shall not hurt Him at all; for God is over all things powerful. * * * Sūra ix. 38 f.

If it had been plunder near at hand, and an easy journey, they had surely followed thee. But the way seemed long unto them. They will swear unto thee by God, *If we had been able we had surely gone forth with you.* They destroy their own souls, for God knoweth they are liars. The Lord pardon thee! Wherefore didst thou give them leave, until thou hadst distinguished those that speak the truth, and known the liars?[1] * * * v. 41

If they had gone forth with thee, they had only added weakness to you, and had run to and fro amongst you, stirring up sedition. And amongst you, some had listened to them; for God knoweth the unjust. Verily they thought to stir up sedition aforetime; and they disturbed thine affairs until the Truth came, and the command of God was made manifest, although they were averse therefrom.[2] Among them there is that saith, *Give me leave to remain, and throw me not into temptation.* What! have they not fallen into temptation already? Verily, Hell shall compass the unbelievers round about.[3] v. 47

The hypocrites also chided

The hypocrites who privately scoffed and jested at the Faith and at those who spent their money in its propagation, are reprobated bitterly. Moḥammad might pray for them seventy times; it would avail nothing with God for their pardon :—

They said, *Go not forth to war in the heat.* Say, the fire of Hell is a fiercer heat, if they understood. Wherefore they shall laugh little and weep much, for that which they have wrought. v. 82

Moḥammad not to pray for them on their death

Nevermore shall these unfaithful and stiffnecked followers be allowed the opportunity of going forth to fight. 'Neither v. 85

[1] From this it would appear that Moḥammad repented (or appeared to repent) afterwards that he had so easily and indiscriminately accepted the excuses of those to whom he did give permission to remain behind.

[2] Alluding to the conduct of the 'Disaffected' at the battle of Oḥod, or perhaps to the affair at the Beni'l-Muṣṭaliḳ expedition.

[3] Tradition assigns this last verse to the case of a man who begged Moḥammad to excuse him from the campaign, as he feared the attractions of the Greek women. But a great number of the stories belonging to this campaign may be suspected (on the analogy of similar traditions regarding other texts) to have been fabricated for the purpose of illustrating the text of the Ḳor'ān.

do thou ever (so runs the heavenly Oracle) pray over any of them that shall die, nor stand over his grave; for they do reject God and his Prophet, and they shall die transgressors.'

Bedawin specially reprobated

The Arabs of the desert, who were the chief offenders, because they had stayed away notwithstanding the distinct refusal of leave, are censured unsparingly for their disobedience; — ignorant, stubborn, unbelieving, fickle, — 'they
v. 96 watched but the changes of fortune.' 'Turn from them. They are an abomination. Their resting-place shall be Hell-fire, the reward of that which they have wrought.'

Such as confessed, more leniently treated

Those Believers who had not dissembled their fault, but honestly confessed it, were the most leniently dealt with:—

Sūra ix. 103 f.

> And others have acknowledged their offences; they have mingled a good action with another that is evil. Haply God will be turned unto them, for God is forgiving and merciful. Take offerings of their substance, that thou mayst cleanse them and purify them thereby; and pray for them, for thy prayers will restore tranquillity unto them. And there are others waiting the command of God, whether He will punish them, or whether He will be turned unto them, for God is knowing and wise.

Ka'b and his two companions: ban put upon them

The last verse refers to Ka'b ibn Mālik, the poet, who had done good service to Moḥammad, and to two other Believers who had incurred his special displeasure. They had no pretext to offer for their absence, and their bad example had encouraged the hesitating and disaffected in their neglect of the Prophet's summons; the latter could not with any show of justice be reprimanded or punished, if the far more serious offence of these his professed followers were passed over. A ban was therefore placed upon them. They were cut off from all intercourse with the people, and even with their own wives and families. Fifty days passed thus miserably, and the lives of the three men became a burden to them. At length Moḥammad relented; and, by the delivery of the following revelation, received them back into his favour:—

Sūra ix 118 f.

> Verily, God is reconciled unto the Prophet, and unto the Refugees and Citizens who followed him in the hour of difficulty, after that the hearts of a part of them had nearly swerved. Thereafter He turned to them, for He is compassionate unto them and merciful. And He is likewise reconciled unto the Three;—they that stayed behind, until that

the earth with all its spaciousness became straitened unto them, and their souls became straitened within them, and they saw no refuge from God otherwise than by fleeing unto Him ;—then He turned unto them, for God is easy to be reconciled, and merciful.

After the promulgation of this passage, Ka'b was again treated by Moḥammad as before with kindness and consideration.

Ka'b received back into favour

The displeasure of the Prophet was also at this time kindled against a party at Ḳobā, who had built a mosque there, and desired Moḥammad that he would come and consecrate it by praying in it himself. As he was at the moment about to start for Tebūk, he deferred their request until his return. Meanwhile he received information that the new Mosque was built with a sectarian bias, to draw off men from the original Mosque at Ḳobā, and even afford shelter to certain of the Disaffected. On his return, therefore, he not only sent a party to destroy the new edifice, but promulgated this severe denunciation :—

Moḥammad destroys a Mosque at Ḳobā

Sūra ix. 108 f.

There are men who have builded a Mosque with evil purpose, out of unbelief, to make divisions among the Unbelievers, and as a lurking-place for him that hath fought against God and his Apostle aforetime.[1] Yet they will swear, *Verily we intended nothing but good.* God beareth witness that they are Liars. Stand not up (for prayer) therein for ever. There is a Mosque which from the first day hath been founded upon Piety.[2] It is more just that thou shouldest stand up therein ;—Therein are men that love to be purified : and God loveth the Pure. What, therefore ? Whether is he better that hath builded his foundations upon the fear of God and His good pleasure, or he that hath built his foundations upon the brink of a crumbling bank, to be swept away with him into the fire of Hell : for God doth not guide the race of transgressors. The building which they have built shall not cease to be a cause of doubting in their hearts, until their hearts be cut in pieces. And God is knowing and wise.

About two months after the return of the army from Tebūk, 'Abdallah ibn Obei, the leader of the disaffected party, died. Moḥammad had throughout followed the advice given him on his first arrival, to deal tenderly with this chief. Excepting the rupture which occurred in the affair of the Beni'l-Musṭaliḳ, and one or two other occasions when 'Abd-

Death of 'Abdallah ibn Obei

[1] The biographers do not mention who is here alluded to. The *Commentators* specify Abu 'Āmir the hermit, who, after the battle of Ḥonein, is said to have fled to Syria ; but this is doubtful.

[2] The 'Mosque of *Godly fear*,' *vide* p. 169.

allah openly took part with his Jewish confederates, the Prophet was careful to avoid any harsh or humiliating treatment which might have driven him, with his numerous adherents, into open and active opposition. This forbearance he observed to the last. He even followed the bier, and prayed over the grave, thus recognising his once powerful antagonist as having been a true believer. After 'Abdallah's death there was no one left in the ranks of the Disaffected possessing power or influence. There was none whom Moḥammad needed longer to treat with delicacy or caution. The faction had died out. Those who had hitherto been lukewarm or disloyal soon embraced, heart and soul, the cause of Islām, and the power of Moḥammad became fully and finally consolidated in Medīna.

Faction of the disaffected dies with him

War to be carried on by Islām till Antichrist appear

The campaign to Tebūk was the last undertaken during the Prophet's lifetime. His authority was now unquestioned northwards to the Syrian confine, equally as it was to the south as far as the still recusant Aṭ-Ṭā'if. It seemed almost as if the need of fighting had gone by. The following tradition shows how little the real spirit of Islām, aggressive and tending necessarily to universal conquest, had yet dawned upon the people;—although indeed the principles from which such a conclusion was legitimately to be deduced had long been inculcated by Moḥammad. Looking around them, and seeing no enemy remain,—the Greeks even having retired and left them alone in their deserts,—the followers of the Prophet, we are told, began to sell their arms, saying: 'The wars for religion now are ended.' But Moḥammad saw better into the future. When it was told him, he forbade the sale, saying: 'There shall not cease from the midst of my people a party engaged in fighting for the truth, until Antichrist appear.' At the same time it is interesting to note that, though warfare was recognised as the normal state, provision was yet made for the maintenance of students and teachers of religion, as we learn from the following verse:—

Provision made for study of theology

Sūra ix. 123

> It is not necessary that the whole body of Believers should go forth to war. If a certain number from every party go not forth to war, it is that they may give themselves to study in religion, and may admonish their people when they return unto them (from the wars), so that they may take heed unto their ways.

CHAPTER XXIX

EMBASSY FROM AṬ-ṬĀ'IF; AND PILGRIMAGE OF ABU BEKR

A.H. IX.—*December*, A.D. 630, *to March*, A.D. 631

At-Ṭā'if still hostile

IT was now ten months since Moḥammad had raised the siege of Aṭ-Ṭā'if. The citizens, still wedded to idolatry, maintained a sullen isolation.

Martyrdom of 'Orwa. A.H. IX. A.D. 630

'Orwa ibn Mas'ūd, the chief already noticed as one of those sent by Ḳoreish to the Muslim camp at Al-Ḥodeibiya, was absent during the siege of his native city, having gone to the Yemen to learn the use of warlike engines for its defence.[1] On his return, finding that all Mecca and the surrounding tribes, excepting Aṭ-Ṭā'if, had submitted to Moḥammad, and being himself favourably impressed with what he had seen at the truce of Al-Ḥodeibiya, 'Orwa went in quest of the Prophet to Medīna, and there embraced Islām. His first generous impulse was to return to Aṭ-Ṭā'if, and invite his fellow citizens to share in the blessings of the new faith. Moḥammad, well knowing their bigotry and ignorance, warned him of the danger he would incur; but, presuming on his popularity at Aṭ-Ṭā'if, he persisted in the design. Arriving in the evening, he made public his conversion, and called upon the people to join him. They retired to consult upon the matter. In the morning, ascending his roof, he cried out at the pitch of his voice the call to prayer, on which the rabble surrounded the house, and shot arrows at him, by which he was mortally wounded. His family and friends rallied around him, but it was too late. He had offered up, he said, his blood to its Master for the sake of his people; he blessed God, with his dying breath, for the honour of martyrdom, and prayed his people to bury him by

[1] (Ibn Hishām, p. 869); Aṭ-Ṭabari, i. 1687 f.; Al-Wāḳidi, p. 381.

2 F

the side of the Muslims who had fallen at Ḥonein. When the tidings reached Moḥammad, he lauded the memory of the martyr:—'He may be compared,' was his exclamation, 'to the prophet Al-Yāsīn, who summoned his people to believe in the Lord, and they slew him.'

At-Ṭā'if sends embassy to Moḥammad. A.H. IX. December, A.D. 630

The martyrdom of 'Orwa compromised the inhabitants of Aṭ-Ṭā'if, and forced them to continue the hostile course they had been pursuing. But they began to suffer severely from the marauding attacks of the Hawāzin under Mālik, who, according to his promise, had maintained an unceasing warfare against them. The cattle were cut off in their pasture lands, and at their watering-places; and at last no man's life was safe beyond the walls of the city. 'We have not strength,' they said among themselves, 'to fight against the Arab tribes all round who have plighted their faith to Moḥammad, and bound themselves to fight in his cause.' So they sent a deputation of six chiefs with some twenty followers, who reached their destination a fortnight after the return of the army from Tebūk. Al-Moghīra (nephew of the martyr 'Orwa), meeting the embassy in the outskirts of the city, hastened to announce their approach to the Prophet, who received them gladly, and pitched a tent for their accommodation close by the Mosque. Every evening after supper he visited and instructed them in the faith, till it was dark. They freely communicated their apprehensions to him. As for themselves, they were quite ready at once to destroy their great idol (ṭāghiya) Al-Lāt; but the ignorant amongst them, and especially the women, were devoted to the worship, and would be alarmed at its demolition. If the fane were left but for three years, and the people meanwhile familiarised with the requirements of Islām, the wishes of the Prophet might then without difficulty be carried into effect. But Moḥammad would not consent. Two years,—one year,—six months,—were asked successively, and successively refused. 'The grace of one month might surely be conceded;' but Moḥammad was firm. Islām and the idol could not co-exist. The idol must fall without a single day's delay. They then begged to be excused performance of the daily prayers, and that some one else might be deputed to destroy the image. 'As for the demolition of the idol with your own hands,' replied Moḥammad, 'I will dispense with that; but prayer is indispensable. Without prayer religion were naught.' 'In that case,' said they, 'we shall perform it, though it be a degradation.' They also pleaded hard that the forest of Wajj, a famous preserve for the chase in the vicinity of Aṭ-Ṭā'if, should be declared inviolate. To this Moḥammad acceded; and the embassy, having finally tendered their allegiance, were dismissed with a rescript to the effect 'that neither the trees nor the wild animals of Wajj should be meddled with. Whoever was found transgressing should be scourged, and his garments seized. If he transgressed again, he should be sent to the Prophet. This was the command of Moḥammad the Apostle of God.'[1]

Their idol is destroyed by Al-Moghīra

Abu Sufyān and Al-Moghīra, both friends of the tribe, were deputed by Moḥammad to accompany the strangers, and destroy their idol. Al-Moghīra, wielding a pickaxe, and surrounded by a guard of his relatives, attacked the great image, and, amid the cries and wailing of the women, with his own hand hewed it to the ground. The debts of the martyr were defrayed from the jewels and spoil of the temple. Aṭ-Ṭā'if was the last stronghold that held out against the authority of Moḥammad. It is remarkable also as the only place where the fate of an idol excited the sympathy of the people. Everywhere else the images seem to have been destroyed by the people themselves without a pang.

Moḥammad stays away from yearly pilgrimage. A.H. IX. March, A.D. 631

The closing month of the Arabian year, the month of Pilgrimage, again drew near. Moḥammad had hitherto abstained from being present at its ceremonies because the great mass of the pilgrims still were heathens, and idolatrous practices mingled with the holy rites. The same cause kept him away in the present year. But he resolved that it should be the last in which the Pilgrimage was desecrated by unworthy customs, and the Holy places by the presence of unbelievers. He was now strong enough to banish heathenism for ever from the Sanctuary. When thus purged, but not till then, without compromising his prophetic office, the sacred ceremonies might be presided over by himself.

Abu Bekr's pilgrimage. The 'Release' committed to 'Alī for publication

The caravan of pilgrims from Medīna was therefore limited to 300 men, with Abu Bekr as their chief.[2] Shortly

[1] Al-Wāḳidi, p. 385.

[2] Ibn Hishām, p. 919 f.; Aṭ-Ṭabari, i. 1722 f.; Al-Wāḳidi, p. 416; Ibn Sa'd, p. 121.

after its departure the Oracle spoke, and a passage was promulgated to carry out the object which Moḥammad had in view. It is called the Discharge or Release, because the Prophet is therein discharged, after the lapse of four months, from his obligations towards the heathen Arabs. This important declaration was committed to 'Alī, who was despatched after the caravan. On coming up with it, and communicating the nature of his errand, Abu Bekr inquired whether the Prophet had put him in command over the pilgrimage. 'No,' replied 'Alī; 'but he hath directed me to recite the divine behest in the hearing of all the people.'

The *Release.* 10th Dhu'l-Ḥijja, A.H. IX. March 20, A.D. 631

Towards the close of the pilgrimage, therefore, on the great day of sacrifice, at the place of casting stones near Mina,[1] 'Alī read aloud, to the multitudes that crowded in the narrow pass around him, the heavenly command, as follows:—

Sūra ix. 1 ff.

A DISCHARGE [*Barā'a*] by God and his Apostle, in respect of the Heathen with whom ye have entered into treaty. Go to and fro in the earth securely in the four months to come. And know that ye cannot hinder God, and that verily God will bring disgrace upon the Unbelievers ;—

And an ANNOUNCEMENT [*Adhān*] from God and his Apostle unto the People, on the day of Pilgrimage, that God is discharged from (liability to) the Heathen,—and his Prophet likewise. Now, if ye repent, that will be better for you ; but if ye turn your backs, know that ye cannot hinder God ; and acquaint those who disbelieve with the tidings of a grievous punishment ;—Excepting those of the Heathen with whom ye have entered into treaty, and who thereafter have not failed you in any thing, and have not helped any one against you. Fulfil unto these their engagements, until the expiration of their term ; for God loveth the pious.

And when the forbidden months are over, then fight against the Heathen, wheresoever ye find them ; take them captive, besiege them, and lie in wait for them in every ambush ; but if they repent, and establish Prayer, and give the Tithes, leave them alone, for God is gracious and merciful. And if any of the Heathen ask a guarantee of thee, give it unto him, until he shall have heard the Word of God ; then convey him back unto his place of security. This because they are a people that do not understand. * * *

v. 28 O ye that believe ! Verily the Unbelievers are unclean. Wherefore, let them not approach the Holy Temple after this year. And if ye fear poverty, God will enrich you of His abundance, if He pleaseth, for God is knowing and wise.

'Alī announces Prophet's commands

Having finished the recitation of this passage, 'Alī expounded the edict thus:—'I am ordered to declare unto

[1] See the picture of the spot facing page 470.

you that no Unbeliever shall enter Paradise. No Idolater shall after this year perform the pilgrimage; nor shall any make the circuit of the Holy House unclothed. Whosoever hath a treaty with the Prophet, it shall be respected till its term expire. Four months are given to the tribes that they may return to their homes in security. After that the obligations of the Prophet cease.'

Concourse breaks up quietly

The vast concourse listened peaceably. Then they broke up and departed every man to his home, publishing throughout the Peninsula the inexorable ordinance which they had heard from the lips of 'Alī. Thus was completed the system of Moḥammad so far as concerned its relations with idolatrous tribes and races. The few cases of truce excepted, uncompromising warfare was declared against them all. To the utmost bounds of Arabia, and wheresoever prevailed the worship of the Ka'ba, idolatry was doomed, and Islām was to be henceforth the nation's faith.

Annihilation of idolatry now the declared mission of Islām;

And reduction of Judaism and Christianity to dependent position

Side by side with this deliverance (though revealed on a different occasion) is another affecting Jews and Christians. For some years, the Oracle which used to teem with testimonies to the faith of both, had ceased to mention either, or make quotations, as had so constantly been done before, from their Sacred Books. After long neglect and silence, the Jewish and Christian tribes of the Peninsula are noticed now, only to be condemned to a perpetual vassalage:—

Sūra ix. 29 ff.

Fight against those who do not believe in God nor in the last day, and who forbid not that which God hath forbidden, and profess not the true religion,—those, namely, who have received the Scriptures (that is both Jews and Christians) until they pay tribute with the hand, and are humbled. The Jews say that Ezra is the Son of God, and the Christians that the Messiah is the Son of God. This is their saying, with their mouths. They imitate the saying of the Unbelievers before them. God destroy them! How have they devised lying vanities! They take their Priests and their Monks for lords besides God,—and also the Messiah, son of Mary. Yet they were not bidden but to worship the one God alone;—There is no God but He, far exalted above that with which they associate Him! They seek to extinguish the light of God with their mouths. But God refuseth to do otherwise than make His light perfect, even though the Unbelievers be averse therefrom. He it is that hath sent His Apostle with the true guidance, and the religion of truth, that He may make it superior to all other religions, even though the Idolaters be averse therefrom. O ye Faithful! Verily many of the Priests and Monks devour the substance of men in vanity, and obstruct the way of God. They that treasure up gold and silver, and spend it not in the way of God, announce unto them a grievous punishment;—On the day on which it (their gold and silver) shall be heated in the fire of Hell, and their foreheads and their sides and their backs shall be seared therewith (while it is said unto them),—This is that which ye have treasured up for yourselves, wherefore taste ye of the same!

Judaism and Christianity cast contemptuously aside

Thus, with threats of abasement and cruel words, Moḥammad parted finally from both Jews and Christians, whom he had so long entertained with professions of attachment to their Scriptures, and from whose teaching he had borrowed that which was most valuable in his own. Having reached the pinnacle of his ambition, he now cast contemptuously aside the means by which he reached it. Yet even here a broad distinction is drawn between their treatment and that of the Heathen. These are not tolerated even on submission. Failing to embrace Islām, Idolaters must be fought with to the death. But Jews and Christians are permitted to continue such. They are, indeed, to be warred against; but, on submission and 'payment of tribute with their hand,' they are to be left, though humbled, in the undisturbed profession of their faith.[1]

[1] It is important, however, to note that the passage quoted, as combined with the 'Discharge,' is like it, applicable, in its original intention, only to the peoples of Arabia. But after Islām had burst the borders of the Peninsula, it was held to be of universal application. Consequently all over the world the followers of the Prophet, adopting the precedent set in Arabia, while holding themselves bound, by his example and precept, utterly to destroy idolatry root and branch, hold themselves equally bound to tolerate the Jewish and Christian religions, even when they fall before their arms, on condition that their professors submit and become tributary.

[The toleration extended to the Jews and Christians embraced a third faith, that of the Ṣabians (Sūras ii. 59; v. 73). This name is derived from an Aramaic root meaning to 'baptise,' and the Ṣabian religion was characterised largely by lustration. In fact, the first Muslims were called Ṣabians because of their frequent ablutions. The Ṣabians of the Ḳor'ān are the Mandæans, the so-called 'Christians of St John.' The name Ṣabian is not to be confused with Sabæan, which denotes the people of Saba or the Yemen (Chwolson, *Die Ssabier und der Ssabismus*). It should be added that the two passages cited above are said to have been abrogated by later revelations.]

CHAPTER XXX

EMBASSIES OF SUBMISSION RECEIVED AT MEDĪNA

A.H. IX. AND X.—A.D. 630, 631

ÆTAT. 62, 63

THE life of Moḥammad was drawing to a close; but his work was also near completion. The proof is amply seen in the stream of submissive embassies which from all quarters of Arabia now flowed uninterruptedly towards Medīna.

Numerous embassies during Tenth year of Hijra

The adhesion of Aṭ-Ṭā'if and destruction of its famous idol enhanced the Prophet's fame throughout the south and east of the Peninsula. Before the close of the Ninth year of the Hijra, many chiefs and princes of the Yemen and Mahra, of 'Omān, Al-Baḥrein, and Yemāma, had signified by letter or by embassy their conversion to Islām and submission to the Prophet.

Embassies from south and east. A.H. IX. and X. December, A.D. 630, to March, A.D. 631

Some of them had been converted even earlier. On his return from Aṭ-Ṭā'if, towards the close of the Eighth year of the Hijra, Moḥammad sent 'Amr with a despatch to Jeifar, King of 'Omān, summoning him to make profession of the faith. At first the king and his advisers gave answer 'that they would be the weakest among the Arabs, if by paying tithe they made another man possessor of their property.' But as 'Amr was about to depart, they repented, and, calling him back, embraced Islām. The people followed their lead, and without demur paid tithe to 'Amr, who continued till the Prophet's death to be his representative in 'Omān. He was supported by a 'Reader,' who instructed the people in the Ḳor'ān and superintended the assessment of the tithes. This province, which had hitherto been under the suzerainty of Persia, was so distant

Conversion of 'Oman; A.H. VIII. February, A.D. 630

[1] Ibn Hishām, p. 971; Aṭ-Ṭabari, i. 1686.

that Moḥammad allowed the Prince to distribute the tithes among his own poor—a concession which, no doubt, facilitated the introduction of the new faith.

Conversion of Ḥimyarite princes of Mahra and the Yemen;

At the same time, another legate was deputed to the Ḥimyarite princes professing the Christian faith in the Yemen. He carried with him a letter in which Moḥammad expressed his belief in Moses and Jesus, but denied the Trinity and the divinity of Christ. Their reply, accepting the new religion with all its conditions, reached the Prophet after his return from Tebūk; and he acknowledged it in a despatch, praising the alacrity of their faith, setting forth the legal demands of Islām, and commending his tithe collectors to their favour.[1]

[1] The instructions given to the envoy are curious. He was to be specially careful in his purification and prayers on reaching the country. He was to take the Prophet's despatch in his right hand and place it in the right hand of the princes. He was to recite Sūra xcviii. and then call upon them to submit, saying that he was able to refute every argument and book they could adduce against Islām. Then he was to repeat the passage in Sūra xlii., in which it is asserted that there is no real controversy between Moḥammad and Christians. A strange part of the instructions was, to call upon the people, after they believed, to produce three sticks,—two gilded white and yellow, and one a black knotted cane,—which they used to worship. These he was to burn publicly in the market-place. The people, who spoke the Ḥimyar tongue, were to translate their creed, &c., into Arabic. Moḥammad's despatch is as follows: '*From Moḥammad the Apostle of God to Al-Ḥārith, &c.* I praise God on your behalf,—that God beside whom there is no other. Now, your messenger hath reached me at Medīna, on my return from the land of Greece; and he hath conveyed to me your letter, and given me intelligence regarding your conversion and your fighting against the Idolaters. Now, verily hath the Lord guided you with the right direction, that ye should amend your lives, obey God and his Apostles, set up prayer, pay the tithes, and from your booty set aside a Fifth as the share of God and his Apostle.' Then follows a detail of the tithes. 'This is what is obligatory, and whoever exceedeth it will be for his merit. Every one that shall fulfil this, and believe in Islām, and assist the Believers against the Idolaters, verily he is one of the Faithful: he shall share in what they share, and be responsible for that for which they are responsible. Thus it shall be with all Jews and Christians who embrace Islām. But such as will not abandon Judaism and Christianity shall pay tribute, every adult male and female, whether bond or free, a full golden dīnār, or its equivalent in cloth. Whosoever payeth this, shall be embraced in the guarantee of God and his Apostle: whoever refuseth shall be their enemy.'

Then he commends his messengers, readers, and tithe collectors to

And of Al-Bahrein and Hejer

Simultaneously with the mission of 'Amr, or a little later, Moḥammad sent Al-'Alā, son of the Ḥaḍramite, towards the Persian Gulf with a letter to Al-Mundhir, chief of Al-Baḥrein.[1] Al-Mundhir at once embraced Islām, and forwarded a reply to Moḥammad, saying, 'that of the people of Hejer to whom he had read the Prophet's letter, some were delighted with the new religion, others displeased with it; and that among his subjects there were Jews and Magians, regarding whom he solicited instructions.' A rescript was granted by Moḥammad securing Al-Mundhir in the government of his province so long as he administered it well, and directing that tribute should be levied from the Jews and Magians. To the Magians he dictated a separate despatch, inviting them to believe in the Ḳor'ān: 'If they declined, toleration would be extended to them on the payment of tribute; but in such case, their women would not be taken in marriage by Believers, nor would that which they killed be lawful as food to any Muslim.'[2] Al-'Alā remained in Al-Baḥrein as the representative of Moḥammad at the court of Al-Mundhir.

Embassies from Beni Ḥanīfa and other Christian tribes. End of A.H. IX. Beginning of A.D. 631

Among the peoples of the same region which sent embassies to Medīna before the close of the Ninth year of the Hijra, were the Beni Bekr, who had so gloriously overthrown the forces of Persia about twenty years before; and the Beni Ḥanīfa, a Christian branch of the same, inhabiting Al-Yemāma.[3] One of the Beni Ḥanīfa party

the Princes' good offices,—specifying Mo'ādh as their chief, and desiring that the tithe and tribute should be made over to him. He forbids oppression, 'for Moḥammad is the protector of the poor as well as of the rich amongst you.' The tithe is not for Moḥammad or his family: it is a means of purifying the rest of the giver's property, and is to be devoted to the poor and the wayfarer.

The deputation of Hamdan sang as they approached Moḥammad: 'We have come to thee from the plains of Ar-Rīf; in the hot whirlwinds of summer and Kharīf' (*i.e.* 'autumnal harvest,' a word, *Khureef*, familiar to the Indian administrator). Moḥammad's reply secured to them their hills and dales, &c. Ibn Hishām, p. 963.

[1] Ibn Hishām, p. 945; Aṭ-Ṭabari, i. 1561, 1600, 1737.

[2] This passage refers to the distinction made by Moḥammad in favour of the Jews and Christians, whose women may be taken in marriage, and also what is killed and cooked by them eaten, by the Muslims. These privileges are refused to the Magians.

[3] Ibn Hishām, p. 945; Aṭ-Ṭabari, i. 1737 f.

was Museilima, who, from what he then saw, conceived the idea that he too might successfully set up pretensions to be a Prophet. When the customary presents were distributed amongst them, the deputies solicited a share for him, saying that he had been left behind in charge of the baggage. Moḥammad commanded that he should have the same as the rest,—'for his position,' he said, 'is none the worse among you because of his present duty.' These words were afterwards converted by Museilima to his own ends. On the departure of the Beni Ḥanīfa, the Prophet gave them a vessel with some water in it remaining over from his ablutions, and said to them: 'When ye reach your country, break down your church, sprinkle its site with this water, and in place of it build up a Mosque.' These commands they carried into effect, and abandoned Christianity without compunction.

Christian tribe desired to demolish its church

Beni Taghlib not to baptise

Another embassy, partly Christian, came from the Beni Taghlib. It was composed of sixteen men, some Muslims and some Christians. The latter wore crosses of gold. The Prophet made terms with them, stipulating that they might themselves continue in the profession of their religion, but that they should not baptise their children into the Christian faith.[1]

Rescript to Church of Nejrān

The ancient Church of Nejrān,[2] in the centre of Arabia, was granted more favourable terms. Among the despatches of the year we find one addressed to the Bishop, Priests, and Monks of Nejrān guaranteeing that everything small and great should continue as it then stood in their Churches, their Services, and their Monasteries. 'The pledge of God and of his Prophet' (such are the terms of another Rescript) 'is given that no Bishop shall be removed from his bishopric, nor any Monk from his Monastery, nor any priest from his priesthood; their authority and rights shall not be interfered with, nor anything that is customary amongst them;—so long as they conduct themselves peaceably and uprightly. They shall not be oppressed, neither shall they themselves oppress.[3]

[1] We find the Caliph 'Omar, A.H. XVII., making a similar stipulation with another branch of the same tribe.—*Caliphate*, p. 151.

[2] See reference to them in the *Introduction*, p. lxxxi.

[3] The Rescript is signed by Al-Moghīra. Al-Wāḳidi gives still another treaty, probably the final one. Their tribute of fruit and captives

The embassy of this people to Medina is in itself curious, and has an additional interest from being referred to in the Ḳor'ān.[1] A deputation of fourteen chief men from Nejrān repaired to Moḥammad in the Tenth year of the Hijra. Among them was 'Abd al-Masīḥ of the Beni Kinda, their chief, and 'Abd al-Ḥārith, Bishop of the Beni'l-Ḥārith. On reaching Medīna, they entered the Mosque, and prayed turning towards the east. Then Moḥammad called them; but when they came, the Prophet turned away and would not speak with them, because of the silken lining of their garments. So they departed, and in the morning appeared in their monastic dress. The Prophet now returned their salutation, and invited them to accept Islām, but they refused; on which words and disputation increased between them. Then Moḥammad recited to them passages from the Ḳor'ān, and said: 'If ye deny that which I say unto you, *Come let us curse each the other;*' so they went away to consider the matter. On the morrow 'Abd al-Masīḥ, with two of the chief men, came to Moḥammad and said: 'We have determined that we shall not curse with thee; wherefore command regarding us whatsoever thou wilt, and we shall give it, and enter into treaty with thee.' So he made a treaty with them and they returned to Nejrān.[2] Such is

Embassy from Nejrān. A.H. X.

Moḥammad challenges them to curse

was generously commuted to a half-yearly contribution of 1,000 suits of raiment worth each an ounce of silver, in lieu of all claims; the collectors to be entertained for three weeks. When there was war in the Yemen, 30 suits of armour, 30 horses, and 30 camels were to be lent by them, —any of which lost in the war to be made good. It ends with this curious condition: 'Whosoever taketh interest shall be excluded from the guarantee of Moḥammad.' Signed by Abu Sufyān and five others.

[1] Ibn Hishām, p. 401 f.

[2] Their subsequent history is thus traced by Al-Wāḳidi. They continued in possession of their lands and rights under the above treaty, during the rest of Moḥammad's life and the whole of Abu Bekr's Caliphate. Then they were accused of taking usury, and 'Omar expelled them from the land, and wrote as follows:—

'The despatch of 'OMAR, the Commander of the Faithful, to the people of Nejrān. Whosoever of them emigrates is under the guarantee of God. No Muslim shall injure them;—to fulfil that which Moḥammad and Abu Bekr wrote unto them. Now to whomsoever of the chiefs of Syria and Al-'Irāḳ they may repair, let such chiefs allot them lands, and whatever they cultivate therefrom shall be theirs; it is an exchange for their own lands. None shall injure or maltreat them; Muslims shall

the tradition regarding the interview, the purport of which is thus alluded to in the Ḳor'ān:—

Affair described in the Ḳor'ān. Sūra iii. 52 ff.

Verily, the analogy of Jesus is, with God, like unto the analogy of Adam. HE created him out of the dust; then HE said unto him BE, and he was. This is the truth from thy Lord: wherefore be not thou amongst the Doubters. And whosoever shall dispute with thee therein, after that the true knowledge hath come unto thee; say—*Come let us call out* (the names) *of our sons and your sons, of our wives and your wives, of ourselves and yourselves; then let us curse one the other, and lay the curse of God upon those that lie!* Verily this is a true exposition. There is no God but the Lord, and verily God is mighty and wise. And if they turn back, verily God is acquainted with the evil doers. SAY:—Oh ye people of the Book! come unto a just judgment between us and yourselves, *That we shall not worship aught but God, and that we shall not associate any with Him, nor shall we take any of us the other for lords besides God.* And if they turn back, then bear witness, saying;—Verily, we are the true Believers.

Proof of Moḥammad's earnestness

It was surely a strange manner of settling the question between Islām and the Christian faith, which the Arabian Prophet here proposed, and we have no reason to be ashamed of the Christian embassy for declining it. Still we cannot but see throughout the earnestness of Moḥammad's belief, and his conviction that a spiritual illumination had been vouchsafed to him, bringing with it knowledge and certainty where to the Christian, as he conceived, all was speculation and conjecture.

Christianity allowed to exist on sufferance

These narratives confirm the conclusion of the preceding chapter, that the conditions upon which Moḥammad permitted Christianity to exist were those of sufferance. Christianity, indeed, was less obnoxious to him than Judaism because he did not experience from it such persevering and active hostility. The clergy and monks are even spoken of in expressions of comparative praise.[1] But, not the less, the

assist them against oppressors. Their tribute is remitted for two years. They will not be troubled except for evil deeds.'

Some of them alighted in Al-'Irāḳ, and settled at Nejrānīya (so called after them) near to Al-Kūfa. As they decreased in number, their tribute of raiment was correspondingly lightened.—See *Caliphate*, p. 155.

[1] 'And We caused Jesus, son of Mary, to succeed them, and We put into the hearts of those that followed him compassion and mercy; and the monastic state,—they framed it for themselves (We did not command it unto them) simply out of a desire to please God.'—Sūra lvii. 27.

So also Sūra v. 85 f.: 'And thou wilt find the most inclined amongst them to the Believers, those who profess Christianity;—This because

object of Moḥammad was entirely to *supersede* Christianity as well as Judaism.

It is no wonder that Christianity, which never had obtained in Arabia a firm and satisfactory footing, now threatened, and, where her adherents remained faithful, reduced to tribute, her distinctive rite prohibited wherever the professors were passive and careless, her churches demolished and their sites purified before they could be used again for worship by the Muslim converts;—it is no wonder that Christianity, thus, at the closing stage of the Prophet's mission, insulted and trampled under foot, should have languished, and soon altogether disappeared.[1]

Deputations from south. A.H. X. April and May, A.D. 632

The Tenth year opened with fresh deputations from the south. Among the earliest were embassies from the sea-coast of the Yemen, from the Beni Khaulān who lived in the hilly country of that name, from the Beni Bajīla, and many others. The Bajīla at Moḥammad's command, and with the aid of an armed party deputed by Moḥammad, destroyed the famous image of Dhu'l-Kholaṣa, of which the Temple, from the popularity of its worship, was called the 'Ka'ba of the Yemen.'[2] About the same time, some twenty men of the Beni Azd from the Yemen presented themselves, with their chief Ṣurad,[3] to whom, as ruler of his clan, Moḥammad gave a commission to war against the heathen of his neighbourhood. After besieging Jorash, the chief city of the idolaters, for more than a month without success, Ṣurad made the feint of retiring to a hill. The enemy falling into the snare pursued him, and in a pitched battle sustained a

Submission of Beni Azd and people of Jorash

there are amongst them Clergy and Monks, and they are not proud; and when they hear that which hath been revealed unto the Prophet, thou shalt see their eyes flow with tears, because of what they recognise therein of the truth,' &c.

[1] The following tradition is illustrative of Moḥammad's relations with our faith at this period. Among the Beni 'Abd al-Ḳeis was a Christian named Al-Jārūd. He said: O Prophet, I have hitherto followed the Christian faith, and I am now called on to change it. Wilt thou be *Surety* for me in the matter of my religion!' 'Yea,' replied Moḥammad, 'I am thy surety that God hath guided thee to a better faith than it.' On this Al-Jārūd and his comrades embraced Islām. Ibn Hishām, p. 944 f.; Aṭ-Ṭabari, i. 1736 f.

[2] Ibn Hishām, p. 55.

[3] Ibn Hishām, p. 954 f.; Aṭ-Ṭabari, i. 1729 f.

signal defeat. The people of Jorash immediately sent an embassy of submission to Medīna.

Chiefs of Beni Kinda from Ḥadramaut visit Medīna

From Ḥaḍramaut, two princes of the Beni Kinda, Wā'il, chief of the coast, and Al-Ash'ath, chief of the interior, visited the Prophet at the head of a brilliant cavalcade, arrayed in garments of Yemen stuff lined with silk.[1] 'Will ye embrace Islām?' said Moḥammad to them, after he had received their salutations in the Mosque. 'Yea; it is for that end that we have come.' 'Then why all this silk about your necks?' The silken lining was forthwith torn off and cast aside.[2] To mark his delight at the arrival of the embassy, Moḥammad desired Bilāl to call aloud the summons for general prayer.[3] When all were assembled, the Prophet introduced the strangers to the congregation: 'O People!' he said; 'this is Wa'il ibn Ḥojr, who hath come unto you from the region of Ḥaḍramaut, out of desire to embrace Islām.' He then presented Wā'il with a patent securing him in his rights, in terms as follows: 'Since thou hast believed, I confirm thee in possession of all thy lands and fortresses. One part in every ten shall be taken from thee: a just collector shall see to it. I guarantee that thou shalt not be injured in this respect so long as the faith endureth. The Prophet, and all Believers, shall be thine allies.' Mu'āwiya, son of Abu Sufyān, was desired to escort Wā'il to his house and entertain him there. On his way, the haughty Prince displayed what Moḥammad styled 'a remnant of heathenism.' He would not allow Mu'āwiya to mount behind him: the ground was scorching from the mid-day sun, yet he refused to let him have the use even of his sandals, so that he was obliged to walk barefooted by the camel: 'What would my subjects in the Yemen say,' he exclaimed in disdain, 'if they heard that a common man had worn the sandals of the king! Nay, but I will drive the camel gently, and thou shalt walk in my shade.' Such insolent demeanour was altogether foreign to the *brotherhood* of Islām; and was only tolerated by Moḥammad since the accession of such a chief was too valuable to be imperilled.

Wā'il

[1] Ibn Hishām, p. 953; Aṭ-Ṭabari, i. 1739 f.

[2] Moḥammad disapproved of silk and velvet for men's attire.

[3] *I.e.* the same as for the Friday service, at which all attended, joined in the 'common' prayer, and heard the address.

The other visitor, Al-Ash'ath, sealed his adhesion to the cause of Moḥammad by entering into a contract of marriage with Um Farwa, Abu Bekr's sister. The marriage was not at the time consummated, her parents declining that the bride should leave them for so distant a home as Ḥaḍramaut.[1]

Al-Ash'ath marries Abu Bekr's sister

The supremacy of Islām being thus widely recognised in the south of Arabia, Moḥammad sent forth a band of officers charged with the instruction of the people, and the collection of the public dues. Over them he placed Mo'ādh, who had by this time fulfilled his mission at Mecca. 'Deal gently with the people,' said the Prophet to Mo'ādh, as he dismissed him to his new scene of labour, 'and be not harsh. Scare them not, but rather cheer. Thou wilt meet with Jews and Christians who will ask thee: What is the key of Paradise? Reply: *Verily the key of Paradise is to testify that there is no God but the Lord alone. With Him there is no partner.*'[2] These Envoys were invested to some extent with a judicial authority. Acceptance of the new faith implied of necessity the simultaneous recognition of its civil institu-

Mo'ādh sent forth with band of collectors and teachers to southern Arabia

[1] Al-Ash'ath joined the rebellion which broke out upon the death of Moḥammad, but subsequently returned to his allegiance, was pardoned, and then received Um Farwa, the Caliph's sister, for his wife.—See *Caliphate*, p. 40.

A member of the royal family in the deputation besought Moḥammad to pray that his stammer might be removed. This the Prophet did, and appointed him a portion from the tithes of Ḥaḍramaut. Another tradition relates that this man was seized with a paralytic affection on his way home. His followers came and told Moḥammad, who desired them to heat a needle and pierce his eyelid with it; and this remedy healed him. Moḥammad attributed the illness to something wrong which the chief must have said after leaving Medīna.

[2] Mo'ādh was inextricably involved in debt, and his creditors had been clamorous before Moḥammad for payment. Mo'ādh surrendered all his property, but it fell far short of the claims. When Moḥammad therefore sent him away, he said: 'Go, and perchance the Lord will relieve thy wants.' Mo'ādh would appear to have made good use of his position, for 'Omar, when shortly after he met him at Mecca performing the pilgrimage, reprimanded him for the state in which he appeared, followed by a retinue of slaves, &c. He is said to have been very particular in following the practice of Moḥammad, and never spat on his right side. He was lame, and obliged to stretch out his legs at prayer. The people (as they always imitated the Imām in all his postures) did the same, till he forbade them.

tions. Every dispute must be brought to the test of the Ḳor'ān or of the instructions given by Moḥammad; and the exponents of these became, therefore, the judges of the land.[1]

Nejrān submits to Khālid. A.H. X. June, A.D. 631

Towards the close of the Prophet's life, the sound of war had almost died away. During this Tenth year, only two expeditions of a hostile character were undertaken. The first, under command of Khālid, was directed against the Beni'l-Ḥārith of Nejrān, during summer.[2] A section of these, as we have seen, had already obtained terms of security on payment of tribute. Khālid was now instructed to call on the rest to embrace Islām; if they declined he was, after three days, to attack and force them to submit. Having reached his destination, he sent mounted parties in all directions, with this proclamation: 'Ye people! embrace Islām, and ye shall be safe.' They all submitted, and professed their belief in the new faith.[3] Moḥammad, delighted with Khālid's report, summoned him to return along with a deputation from the tribe, which accordingly visited Medīna, and were received with courtesy.

Campaign of 'Alī in the Yemen against Beni an-Nakha', &c. A.H. X. December, A.D. 631

As the Beni an-Nakha' and some other tribes in the Yemen still held out, 'Alī was sent in the winter at the head of 300 horse, to reduce them to submission.[4] Yemen had repeatedly sent forth armies to subdue the Ḥijāz; this was the first army the Ḥijāz had ever sent forth to conquer the Yemen. 'Alī met with but feeble opposition. His detachments ravaged the country all around, and returned with spoil of every kind—women, children, camels, and flocks. Driven to despair, the people drew together, and attacked 'Alī with a general discharge of stones and arrows. The

[1] Moḥammad asked Mo'ādh, before he left, how he would adjudicate causes: 'By the book,' he replied. *But if not in the Book?* 'Then by thy precedent.' *But if there be no precedent?* 'Then I will diligently frame my own judgment; and I shall not fail therein.' Thereupon Moḥammad clapped him on the breast and said: 'Praise be to God, who hath fulfilled in the messenger sent forth by his Apostle, that which is well pleasing to the Apostle of the Lord!'

[2] Ibn Hishām, p. 958 f.; Aṭ-Ṭabari, i. 1724 f.

[3] Ibn Hishām tells this naïvely: 'So they, being worsted, believed, and embraced the invitation to profess the new faith. Thereupon Khālid began to teach them the nature of Islām, and the word of God, and the regulations of the Prophet.'

[4] Ibn Hishām, p. 999; Aṭ-Ṭabari, i. 1731 f., 1868; Al-Wāḳidi, p. 417 ff.; Ibn Sa'd, p. 122.

Muslim line put them to flight with slaughter. 'Alī held back his troop from pursuit, and again summoned the fugitives to accept his terms. This they now hastened to do. The chiefs did homage, and pledged that the people would follow their example. 'Alī accepted their promise; he then retraced his steps with the booty, and, reaching Mecca in the spring, joined Moḥammad in the Farewell pilgrimage. The Beni an-Nakha' fulfilled their pledge, and submitted themselves to Mo'ādh, the Prophet's envoy in the Yemen. Two hundred of them set out to tender a personal allegiance to Moḥammad. It was the last deputation received by him. They reached Medīna at the beginning of the Eleventh year of the Hijra.

Numerous embassies and despatches

Numerous other embassies are described by Ibn Sa'd, who has devoted a long chapter to the subject, as well as a chapter to the despatches and rescripts of the Prophet. Those which I have already described will afford a sufficient idea of the whole; further detail would be tedious and unprofitable. But one or two incidents of interest connected with them may be mentioned.

Beni 'Amir

The part played by the Beni 'Āmir at the massacre of Bi'r Ma'ūna will be in the memory of the reader.[1] This tribe had taken little share with the rest of the Hawāzin (of which they formed a branch) in the battle of Ḥonein. It maintained, under its haughty chieftain 'Āmir, an independent neutrality.

Abu Berā applies to Moḥammad for a cure

The aged chief of the tribe, Abu Berā, still exhibited friendly feelings towards Moḥammad, but with advancing years his influence had passed away. Labouring under an internal ailment, he sent his nephew Labīd, the poet of the tribe, to the Prophet, with the present of a beautiful horse, and an urgent request that he would point out a cure for his disease. Moḥammad declined the gift, saying courteously: 'If I could ever accept the offering of an idolater, it would be that of Abu Berā.' Then taking up a clod of earth, he spat upon it, and directed that Abu Berā should dissolve it in water, and drink the mixture. When he had done this, we are told, he recovered from his sickness.[2]

[1] *Ante*, p. 279.

[2] Labīd is famous for his Mo'allaḳa, or 'Suspended' poem. According to another tradition, Moḥammad gave Labīd a leather bottle of honey, of which Abu Berā ate, and so recovered.

Interview of 'Āmir ibn Aṭ-Ṭofail with Moḥammad. Conversion of the Beni 'Āmir. A.H. X. A.D. 631, 632

The following year 'Āmir, at the solicitation of his tribe, presented himself before Moḥammad and sought to obtain from him advantageous terms.[1] 'What shall I have,' he asked, 'if I believe?' 'That which other Believers have,' replied Moḥammad, 'with the same responsibilities.' 'Wilt thou not give me the rule after thee?' 'Nay, that is not for thee nor for thy tribe.' 'Then assign unto me the Bedawi tribes; and do thou retain the rest.' 'This,' said Moḥammad, 'I cannot do; but I will give thee the command over the cavalry, for thou excellest as a horseman.' 'Āmir turned away in disdain: 'Doth this man not know,' he cried, 'that I can fill his land from one end to the other with troops, both footmen and horse?' Moḥammad, alarmed at the threat, for the Beni 'Āmir were a formidable tribe, prayed thus for deliverance: 'O Lord! defend me against 'Āmir, son of Aṭ-Ṭofail. O Lord! guide his people unto the truth; and save Islām from his stratagems!' The haughty chieftain never reached his home; he sickened by the way, and died miserably in a deserted hut. The Beni 'Āmir shortly after gave in their adhesion to the Prophet.

Prejudices of Ben Jo'fi

The Beni Jo'fi, a tribe inhabiting the Yemen, had a deeply-rooted prejudice against eating the heart of any animal. Ḳeis, one of their chief men, came to Moḥammad with his brother, and professed belief in the Ḳor'ān. They were told that their faith was imperfect until they broke through their heathenish scruples, and a roasted heart was placed before them. Ḳeis took it up and ate it, trembling violently. Moḥammad, satisfied with the test of his sincerity, presented him with a patent, which secured him in the rule over his people. But before Ḳeis and his brother left the presence of Moḥammad, the conversation turned upon the guilt of infanticide: 'Our mother Muleika,' said they, 'was full of good deeds and charity; but she buried a little daughter alive. What is her condition now?' 'The burier and the buried both in hell,' replied the Prophet. The brothers turned away in wrath. 'Come back,' Moḥammad cried; 'mine own mother, too, is there with yours.' They would not listen. 'This man,' they said, as they departed, 'hath not only made us to eat the heart of animals, but saith that our mother is in hell: who would follow him?' On

Two of their chiefs cursed

[1] Ibn Hishām, p. 939 f.; Aṭ-Ṭabari, i. 1745 f.

their way home, they met one of Moḥammad's followers returning to Medīna with a herd of camels which had been collected as tithe. They seized the man, left him bound, and carried off the camels. Moḥammad was greatly offended; and he entered the names of the robbers in the commination already mentioned (the repetition of which seems still to have been kept up) against the perpetrators of the massacre at Bi'r Ma'ūna. A second deputation from the same tribe visited Moḥammad, and was well received. We do not hear more of Ḳeis.[1]

[1] Moḥammad is said to have healed the hand of the leader from a protuberance which had prevented him holding his camel's rein, by striking an arrow on it and then stroking it, when it disappeared. He changed the name of this chief's son from '*Azīz* (glorious) to 'Abd ar-Raḥmān;—saying: 'There is none *glorious* but the Lord.'

CHAPTER XXXI

THE FAREWELL PILGRIMAGE[1]

Dhu'l-Ḥijja, A.H. X.—*March*, A.D. 630

ÆTAT. 63

Farewell pilgrimage, A.H. X. March, A.D. 630

THE month of Pilgrimage was again at hand, and nought remained to hinder Moḥammad from going up to it. Nothing would now offend the eye, nor any pagan by his presence pollute the sacred precincts. Every vestige of an image or heathen rite had been swept away; and after the warning of the previous year, Believers alone might venture near. With nothing left to offend him, the Prophet, therefore, announced his intention of going up to the coming festival. It is called the *Farewell Pilgrimage*, because it was the last. He had not performed the Greater pilgrimage since his Flight from Mecca, and now he was about to bid a last farewell to the city of his birth, and to the Holy House, over which and its surroundings a halo of blessedness rested in his soul.

Moḥammad's journey from Medīna to Mecca

Five days before Dhu'l-Ḥijja, the month of pilgrimage, the Prophet assumed the pilgrim's garb; and, followed by vast multitudes,[2] set out on the journey to Mecca. All his wives accompanied him. One hundred camels, marked by his own hands for sacrifice, were led in solemn order. Mosques had already sprung up at the various halting-places, and there the people daily prayed, Moḥammad leading the devotions. On the tenth day, he reached Sarif, an easy stage from Mecca; there he rested for the night, and on the morning, having bathed, and mounted Al-Ḳaṣwā, proceeded towards Mecca.

[1] Ibn Hishām, p. 966 ff.; Aṭ-Ṭabari, i. 1751 ff.; Al-Waḳidi, p. 421 ff.; Ibn Sa'd, p. 124 ff.

[2] Weil says not less than 40,000.—*Einleitung*, p. 34.

He entered the upper suburbs by the same route which he had taken two years before; and, passing down the main street, approached the Ka'ba. As he passed through the Beni Sheiba gate, with the Holy Temple full in view, he raised his hands to heaven, and invoked a blessing on it: '*O Lord! add unto this House in the dignity and glory, the honour and the reverence, which already thou hast bestowed upon it. And they that for the Greater pilgrimage, and the Lesser, frequent the same, increase them much in honour and dignity, in piety, goodness, and renown.* Then, mounted as he was on his camel, he performed the prescribed circuits with other preliminary rites, and afterwards retired to a tent pitched for him in the valley.

Most of his followers perform Lesser pilgrimage only

The greater part of the pilgrims had brought no victims with them. These were directed by Moḥammad, after completing the customary forms of the Lesser pilgrimage, to divest themselves of the pilgrim garb. They accompanied the Prophet and the others who had brought victims in the farther procession to Mina and 'Arafāt, but only as spectators. 'Alī, meanwhile, having returned from the Yemen, received the same directions as those who had no victims: 'Go,' said Moḥammad, 'encircle the Holy House; then divest thyself of the pilgrim's garb as thy fellows have done.' But 'Alī was anxious to fulfil the full rites of the yearly festival; 'for,' said he, 'I have taken upon me vows to perform the same pilgrimage as the Prophet shall perform, whatever that might be.' Moḥammad yielded, and allowed him to fulfil the Greater pilgrimage, and for this end to share in the victims he had brought for himself.[1]

[1] The sacrifice of victims is an essential part of the Greater pilgrimage, but not of the Lesser. The pilgrim must *resolve*, before he assumes the pilgrim's garb, which pilgrimage he will perform. In connection with this custom, there is a great mass of varying tradition as to whether Moḥammad set out from Medīna with the vows upon him of the Lesser pilgrimage, or the Greater, or of both together; and the question is very warmly discussed.

When Moḥammad desired those who had no victims to conclude their pilgrimage with the 'Omra, or Lesser festival, they objected, saying: 'How then can we go on with thee to Mina, after quitting the holy state of a pilgrim and returning to the impurities of the world?' Moḥammad told them that there was no harm in doing so, for that, if similarly circumstanced, he would have done it himself; and that if he

Mohammad's pilgrimage to 'Arafāt. 8th Dhu'l-Ḥijja

On the 7th of Dhu'l-Ḥijja, the day preceding the opening rites of the Greater pilgrimage, Moḥammad, after the midday prayer, preached to the concourse assembled around the Ka'ba. Next day, followed by myriads of devotees, and shaded from the sun's glare by Bilāl, who walked at his side with a screen (a staff with a piece of cloth attached), he set out for Mina, where he performed the ordinary prayers, and slept in a tent. The following morning at sunrise, he moved onwards and, passing Al-Muzdelifa, reached 'Arafāt, an abrupt conical hill, a couple of hundred feet in height, in the middle of the valley, which, though elsewhere narrow, and on the farther side pent in by lofty granite peaks, here spreads out bare and stony to the breadth of nearly a mile.[1] On its summit, the Prophet, standing erect upon his camel, said: 'The entire valley of 'Arafāt is the holy station for pilgrimage, excepting only the vale of 'Orana.' Then bowing low in prayer, he recited certain passages, regarding the ceremonies

had foreseen these objections, he would not have brought any victims. Perhaps it was Moḥammad's wish to show that visiting Mecca at the time of the Greater pilgrimage did not necessarily involve participation in the pilgrimage, the observance of which was reserved for special occasions.

[1] Pictures of the hill are given by Ali Bey, Burton, and Dozy. The latter describes it thus: 'A mass of coarse granite split into large blocks, with a thin coat of withered thorns, about one mile in circumference, and rising abruptly from the low gravelly plain (a dwarf wall at the southern base forming the line of demarcation) to the height of one hundred and eighty or two hundred feet. It is separated by Batn Arna, a sandy vale, from the spurs of the Tayif hills. Nothing can be more picturesque than the view it affords of the blue peaks behind, and the vast encampment scattered over the barren yellow plain below.' So also Ali Bey:—'Arafāt is a small mountain of granite rock, the same as those that surround it; it is about one hundred and fifty feet high, and is situated at the foot of a higher mountain to the E.S.E., in a plain about three quarters of a mile in diameter, surrounded by barren mountains.' The 'Hadjy,' who has recently published an account of his pilgrimage in the *Bombay Times*, says: 'Round the foot of 'Arafāt, which is completely detached from the adjoining mountains, are a number of trees, a thick growth of underwood, and a little grass, which are nourished by the water that escapes from the canal of Mecca which passes behind the hill.' But before the canal was made, the place must have been wild and bare of any growth but thorny bushes.

The popular tradition for the exclusion of the vale of 'Orana (or Arna) is given thus by Burton: 'This vale is not considered "standing ground," because Satan once appeared to the Prophet as he was traversing it.'

of pilgrimage, and concluded with the verse: '*This day have I perfected your Religion unto you, fulfilled my mercy upon you, and appointed for you Islām to be your faith.*' Sūra v. 5

Moḥammad returns to Al-Muzdelifa. 9th Dhu'l-Ḥajja

As the sun was going down, Moḥammad quitted the sacred mount on his way back; and with Osāma, son of Zeid, seated on the camel behind him, travelled hastily by the bright moonlight along the narrow valley to Al-Muzdelifa, where he said the sunset and evening prayers both at once; in this, and every other point, his example has been closely imitated by pilgrims to the present day. He passed the night at Al-Muzdelifa, and very early in the morning sent forward the women and the little children, lest the crowds that followed should impede their journey:[1] but, touching one and another on the shoulder as they went, he said: 'My children, have a care that ye throw not the stones at the corner pass of Al-'Aḳaba until the sun arise.'

Moḥammad completes the pilgrimage at Mina. 10th Dhu'l-Ḥijja

At the dawn he arose to perform the matin prayer; after which, mounted on his camel, he took his stand on a certain spot, saying: 'This, and the whole of Al-Muzdelifa, is the station of pilgrimage, excepting only the vale of Muḥassir.'[2] Then, with Al-Faḍl, son of Al-'Abbās, seated behind him, he proceeded onwards amid a heavy fall of rain to Mina, shouting as he went the pilgrim's cry:—

Labbeik! O Lord! Labbeik! Labbeik!
There is none other God but Thee. Labbeik!
Praise, blessing, and dominion be to Thee. Labbeik!
No one therein may share with Thee. Labbeik! Labbeik![3]

He ceased not to utter these ejaculations till he entered the

The last pilgrimage is regarded as the type of all succeeding ones: there is accordingly a tendency to make Moḥammad foresee that it was the last, and provide anticipatory instructions on all possible points. Such traditions must be received with caution: take, *e.g.*, the following: Moḥammad, as he went through the various rites, said: 'Observe, and learn of me the ceremonies which ye should practise, for I know not whether after this I shall ever perform another pilgrimage.'

[1] The 'Hadjy gives a vivid description of the utter confusion which prevails on the hurried return of the multitude from 'Arafāt to Al-Muzdelifa; and it would seem that the same prevailed even in the time of Moḥammad.

[2] I do not know the origin of the allusion here to this valley; it is according to Burton on the road to Mina. A picture of Al-Muzdelifa will be found in Ali Bey.

[3] For this expression, see *ante*, p. 354.

valley of Mina, and here cast stones at the 'Devil's corner,' a projecting rock at the entrance of the station.[1] Then he slew the victims brought for sacrifice, and ended the pilgrimage by shaving the hair of his head, partly also of his face, and paring his nails. The hair and parings he ordered to be burned.[2] The Iḥrām, or scanty pilgrim garb, was now exchanged for his ordinary dress, perfumes were burned, the flesh of the victims and other cattle distributed for food; and 'Alī, riding the Prophet's white mule, made proclamation that, the restrictions of the pilgrim state being over, it was now a day for eating and enjoyment, and for the remembrance of God. Moḥammad remained at Mina from the 10th to the 12th of the month, and every evening repairing as the sun declined to the prescribed spots at 'Aḳaba, repeated the rite of casting stones.

Parting exhortations at Mina. 11th Dhu'l-Ḥijja

On the second of these days, the Prophet mounted his camel, and from the widening centre of the Mina valley,[3] addressed a vast crowd of pilgrims in a memorable speech, which was looked upon by the people, and perhaps was felt by himself, to be his last farewell. He enjoined the sacredness of life and property and of domestic obligations thus:—

YE PEOPLE! Hearken to my words; for I know not whether, after this year, I shall ever be amongst you here again.[4]

---

[1] See pp. ci and 452. There are two or three spots at which stones are thus cast, called the greater and lesser Shaiṭān, or *devils*. The tradition is that Abraham here met the Devil and repulsed him by similar means. There are minute traditions as to the kind of stone to be used on this occasion. 'Abdallah, son of Al-'Abbās, picked up some gravel for Moḥammad to throw; and the Prophet said: 'Yes: just such as this is the kind to throw. Take care that ye increase not the size. Verily they that have gone before you have come to naught, because of thus adding to the rites of their religion.'

[2] According to another tradition the hair was all caught by his followers. This idea must have grown up in after days, when a single hair of the Prophet was treasured up as a relic and talisman.

[3] 'He stood between the two places for casting stones.' Burton mentions two such spots. Ali Bey's plan gives the chief one, or 'the Devil's house,' on the Mecca side of Mina, and 'two small columns raised by the Devil,' in the middle of the narrow street of the village of Mina. The position of Moḥammad while delivering this famous discourse was thus within Mina itself, but somewhat on the side of Mecca.

[4] So Ibn Hishām. The words, however, may be an afterthought of tradition. There is no other intimation that Moḥammad felt his strength to be decaying at this time, or that either he or his followers anticipated the nearness of his end.

Your Lives and Property are sacred and inviolable amongst one another until the end of time.

The Lord hath ordained to every man the share of his inheritance: a Testament is not lawful to the prejudice of heirs.

The child belongeth to the Parent: and the violator of Wedlock shall be stoned. Whoever claimeth falsely another for his father, or another for his master, the curse of God and the Angels, and of all Mankind, shall rest upon him.

Ye People! Ye have rights demandable of your Wives, and they have rights demandable of you. Upon them it is incumbent not to violate their conjugal faith, neither to commit any act of open impropriety;—which things if they do, ye have authority to shut them up in separate apartments and to beat them with stripes, yet not severely. But if they refrain therefrom, clothe them and feed them suitably. And treat your Women well: for they are with you as captives and prisoners; they have not power over anything as regards themselves. And ye have verily taken them on the security of God: and have made their persons lawful unto you by the words of God.

And your Slaves! See that ye feed them with such food as ye eat yourselves; and clothe them with the stuff ye wear. And if they commit a fault which ye are not inclined to forgive, then sell them, for they are the servants of the Lord, and are not to be tormented.

Ye people! hearken to my speech and comprehend the same. Know that every Muslim is the brother of every other Muslim. All of you are on the same equality; (as he pronounced these words, he raised his arms aloft and placed the forefinger of one hand, as an emblem of equality, on the forefinger of the other[1]); ye are one Brotherhood.

Know ye what month this is?—What territory this is?—What day? To which the People answered,—'The Sacred month,—the Sacred territory,—the Great day of pilgrimage.' At each reply, Moḥammad added: '*Even thus sacred and inviolable hath God made the life and the property of each of you unto the other, until ye meet your Lord.*'

Let him that is present tell it unto him that is absent. Haply, he that shall be told may remember it better than he who hath heard it.

Next he recited the passage which abolishes the triennial intercalation of the year, declaring it to be an unhallowed innovation on the Divine arrangement of the months:— Abolition of the intercalary year

Verily, the number of the months with God is twelve months, according to the Book of God, on the day in which He created the Heavens and the Earth. Of these, four are sacred:—this is the true Religion. Sūra ix. 36, 37

Verily, the changing of the months is an excess of infidelity, which causeth the Unbelievers to err. They make a month common in one year, and they make it sacred in another year, that they may equalise the

---

[1] Intending thereby to teach that all were absolutely upon the same level.

number which God hath made sacred. Thus do they make common that which God hath hallowed.

'And now,' continued Moḥammad, 'on this very day hath time performed its cycle, and returned to the disposition thereof existing at the moment when God created the Heavens and the Earth. Ye People! Truly Satan despaireth of being worshipped in your land for ever. But if in some indifferent matter, which ye might be disposed to slight, he could secure obedience, verily he would be well pleased. Wherefore beware of him!

Verily, I have fulfilled my mission. I have left that amongst you,—a plain command, the Book of God, and manifest Ordinances—which, if ye hold fast, ye shall never go astray.'

Moḥammad takes God to witness that he has fulfilled his mission

Then, looking up to heaven, he said: '*O Lord! I have delivered my message and discharged my Ministry.*' 'Yea,' cried all the people crowding round him, 'yea, verily thou hast.' '*O Lord! I beseech Thee bear Thou witness unto it.*' And with these words, the Prophet, having concluded his address, dismissed the great assembly.

Returns to Mecca. Further ceremonies there

After three days thus spent at Mina, the concourse broke up and returned to Mecca. Moḥammad desired the mass of the pilgrims to travel thither by day. He himself accompanied his wives on the journey by night. On reaching Mecca, he went straightway to the Ka'ba, and performed the seven circuits of it on his camel. He next visited the well Zemzem close by, and calling for a pitcher of its water, drank part of its contents; then rinsing his mouth with the rest, he desired that what remained in the pitcher should be thrown back into the well. After this, taking off his shoes, he ascended the doorway of the Holy temple, and prayed within its walls.[1] Having now ended all the ceremonies, and being fatigued with the journey, he stopped at the house of one who kept date-water for the pilgrims to drink, and desired the beverage to be furnished to him. The son of Al-'Abbās, who

[1] Moḥammad regretted that he had entered the Ka'ba on this occasion, and when asked the reason said: 'I have this day done a thing which I wish I had left undone. I have entered the Holy House. And haply some of the people, when on pilgrimage, may not be able to enter therein, and may turn back grieved in heart (*i.e.* at not having completed the pilgrimage fully after their Prophet's example). And, in truth, the command given unto me was only to encircle the Ka'ba: it is not incumbent on any one to enter it.' This appears to be founded upon the notion before explained, that Moḥammad *intended* this pilgrimage to be the final type and exemplar for all future pilgrims.

accompanied him, interposed: 'The hands of the passers-by,' he said, 'have been in this all day, and fouled it: come unto my father's house, where we have some that is clean and pure for thee.' But the Prophet, refusing to drink of any other, quenched his thirst upon the spot.[1]

Returns to Medīna

Three days more were spent at Mecca, and then Moḥammad with his followers returned to Medīna.

[1] Water in which dates or raisins have been steeped or washed is called Nabīdh. So accurately do the pilgrims follow their Prophet, that some regard the rites of the pilgrimage as not properly completed until Nabīdh be drunk as it was by Moḥammad.

CHAPTER XXXII

THE THREE PRETENDERS

Opening of A.H. XI.—*April and May*, A.D. 632

The year A.H. XI. opens peacefully. March 29, A.D. 632

THE Eleventh year of Moḥammad's residence at Medīna opened peacefully. Already the greater part of the Peninsula acknowledged his authority. The loose autonomy of the Arab tribes made it easy for Moḥammad to assert his suzerainty without interfering in their internal affairs. In the more distant provinces, also, the prerogative was vague, and as yet put to no sufficient test. Still, there was, almost everywhere, the outward form of submission to all that had been demanded. The days of the Prophet were now chiefly occupied in the reception of embassies, the issue of rescripts to his various delegates scattered over the land, and the consolidation of his power, secular as well as spiritual.

Death of Bādhān and division of his territories

Bādhān, the Persian governor who (as we have seen) had early submitted himself to Moḥammad, died about this time.[1] His son Shehr was continued in the government of Ṣan'ā and the surrounding district. But the other provinces hitherto combined under his authority, as Ma'reb, Nejrān, and Hamdan, were divided by Moḥammad among different governors, of whom some were natives of the several districts, while others were officers specially deputed from Medīna.

Three impostors arise, claiming prophetic office

But a new cause of danger began suddenly to darken the horizon. Three claimants of the prophetic office arose, in different quarters of Arabia, to dispute with Moḥammad the supreme authority.[2] Their assumptions were not, however, developed till near the close of his life, and the tidings which he received were hardly perhaps of so grave a nature as to raise serious uneasiness. Their history belongs to the Cali-

[1] Aṭ-Ṭabari, i. 1852 f. [2] *Op. cit.* i. 1795.

phate of Abu Bekr, and I shall not, therefore, do more in this place than very briefly notice these remarkable impostors.

Moment propitious for such pretentions

Besides the temptation to follow in the steps of Moḥammad arising from his marvellous success, the present moment was especially propitious for the assertion of such a claim. The Bedawi tribes, and distant peoples who had but lately succumbed to the new religion, began to find its rites irksome and its restraints unpalatable. How deep and general was the discontent, is evident from the rebellion which throughout Arabia followed immediately on the Prophet's death, and which probably never would have been effectually subdued had not the energies and passions of the Arabs been roused by foreign conquest. Moḥammad was now well stricken in years, and strangers might perceive in him the marks of advancing infirmity. His death could not be far distant. No provision had been made for a successor nor for the permanent maintenance at Medīna of a supreme control over the Peninsula. If one were bold enough to assert that he had received a divine commission like that of Moḥammad, why should the claim not be crowned with similar success?

Toleiha. His rebellion crushed by Khālid

The least important of the three impostors who now started with such notions was Ṭoleiḥa, chief of the Beni Asad, and a warrior of note and influence in Nejd.[1] His tribe once journeying through the desert were overpowered by thirst, when Ṭoleiḥa announced to them that water would be found at a certain spot. The discovery confirmed the claims to inspiration, or at least to divination, which he had already made. When the news of this reached Moḥammad, he sought, by aid of faithful converts in the tribe, to crush the Pretender. Subsequently, however, to the Prophet's death he broke out into open rebellion, and was defeated, after a severe engagement, by Khālid. On 'Omar's summoning the conquered tribe to join his standard, Ṭoleiḥa submitted, and afterwards with them fought bravely on the side of Islām.

Museilima. His advances indignantly rejected by Moḥammad

Museilima has already been noticed as having accompanied the deputation of the Beni Ḥanīfa to Medīna.[2] He was a man of small stature, in presence insignificant, but ready and powerful in speech. Following the example of Moḥammad, he gave forth verses professed to have been

[1] *Vide* p. 276. [2] Ibn Hishām, p. 945, 964.

received from heaven, and he pretended also to work miracles.[1] He claimed an authority and mission concurrent with that of the Prophet of Medīna; and he deceived the people of Al-Yemāma by alleging that the claim had been admitted.[2] Moḥammad, hearing the rumour of his insolent pretensions, sent him a summons to submit to Islām. Museilima returned reply that he, too, was a Prophet like Moḥammad himself: 'I demand therefore that thou divide the earth with me; as for Ḳoreish, they are a people that have no respect for justice.' When this letter was read before him, Moḥammad turned with indignation to the two envoys who ventured to urge their master's claim. '*By the Lord!*' he exclaimed, '*if it were not that Ambassadors are secure, and their lives inviolate, I would have beheaded both of you!*' Then he indited the following answer: 'Thine epistle, with its lies and its fabrications against the Lord, hath been read to me. Verily the earth is the Lord's, and He causeth such of His servants as He pleaseth to inherit the same. Peace be to him that followeth the true Direction!' The battle of Al-Yemāma, with its 'Garden of death,' in which Museilima lost his life, was a perilous day for Islām, but the story belongs to the Caliphate of Abu Bekr.

Rebellion of *Al-Aswad*

Al-Aswad, the 'Veiled Prophet' of the Yemen, differed from the other impostors in not only advancing his pretensions, but in casting off the Muslim yoke, while Moḥammad was yet alive.[3] A prince of wealth and influence in the South, he assumed the garb of a magician, and gave out that he was in communication with the unseen world. He prosecuted his claims at the first secretly, and gained over the chieftains in the neighbourhood dissatisfied with the distribution of power upon the death of Bādhān. About the close of the Tenth year of the Hijra, he openly raised the standard of rebellion, and drove out the officers of Moḥammad, who fled for refuge to the nearest friendly country. Advancing

[1] He had learned the art of sleight of hand, &c., from conjurers. One of his *miracles* was to slip an egg into a narrow-mouthed phial. None of the verses attributed to him are worth quoting. Sprenger says that the name, signifying 'the little Muslim,' was given him in contempt.

[2] See the words of Moḥammad which he is said to have drawn into this construction,—*ante*, p. 458.

[3] Aṭ-Ṭabari, i. 1795-8.

on Nejrān, which rose in his favour, he suddenly fell upon Ṣan'ā, where, having killed Shehr, the son of Bādhān, he put his army to flight, married his widow, and established himself in undisputed authority. The insurrection, fanned by this sudden success, spread like wildfire, and the greater part of the Peninsula lying between the provinces of Al-Baḥrein, Aṭ-Ṭā'if, and the coast, was soon subject to the Usurper.

Crushed about the time of Moḥammad's death

At what period intimation of this rebellion reached Moḥammad, and what the nature of the intelligence received, is not apparent. The accounts could not have been very alarming, for the Prophet contented himself with despatching letters to his officers on the spot, in which he desired them, according to their means, either to compass the death of the Pretender, or to attack him in the field. Fortunately for Islām, Al-Aswad, in the pride of conquest, had already begun to slight the commanders to whose bravery he was indebted for success. The agents of Moḥammad opened up secret negotiations with them; and, favoured by the tyrant's wife, who detested him, and burned to avenge her late husband's death, plotted his assassination. The Usurper was slain, according to tradition, on the very night preceding the death of Moḥammad. The insurrection ceased; and peace would immediately have been restored had not the tidings that the Prophet had passed away again thrown the province into confusion. The campaign that followed belongs to the reign of Abu Bekr.

CHAPTER XXXIII

SICKNESS AND DEATH OF MOḤAMMAD

Moḥarram, A.H. XI.—*June*, A.D. 632

ÆTAT. 63

Expedition to Syrian frontier

ABOUT two months after his return from the Farewell pilgrimage, Moḥammad, now sixty-three years of age, and to all appearance in his ordinary health, gave orders for an expedition to the Syrian frontier. The inroad upon Tebūk was the last occasion on which a general levy had been called. But the reverse at Mūta had not yet been sufficiently avenged. The present campaign was accordingly intended to strike terror into the tribes of the border, and wipe out the memory of the disaster, which still rankled in the Prophet's heart. On the day following the command just mentioned, it was announced that Osāma, son of Zeid, the beloved friend of Moḥammad slain at Mūta, was, notwithstanding his extreme youth (hardly yet twenty years of age) but the more clearly to mark the object of the expedition, appointed to lead the army. Having called him to the Mosque, the Prophet thus addressed him: 'March unto the place where thy father was killed, and let them destroy it utterly. Lo! I have made thee commander over this army. Fall suddenly at early dawn upon the men of Obna,[1] and devour them with fire. Hasten thy march so that thine onset may precede the tidings of thee. If the Lord grant thee victory, then shorten thy stay amongst them. Take with thee guides, and send before thee scouts and spies.'

Osāma appointed to command. A.H. XI. May 25, A.D. 632

Banner presented to him, and camp formed at Al-Jurf May 27

On the following day, being Wednesday, Moḥammad was seized with a violent headache and fever; but it passed off. The next morning he found himself sufficiently recovered to

[1] [Or Yubna, a village near Mūta.]

bind with his own hand the banner for the army; and thus he presented it to Osāma;—'Fight thou beneath this banner in the name of the Lord, and for His cause. Thus shalt thou discomfit and slay the people that disbelieveth in the Lord!' The camp was then formed at the Jurf; and the whole body of the fighting men, not excepting Abu Bekr and 'Omar, were summoned to join it.[1] But the attention of the city was soon occupied by a more engrossing subject, which suspended for a time the preparations of Osāma's force.

Mohammad attributes illness to poisoned meat eaten at Kheibar

Moḥammad had not hitherto suffered from any serious illness. About the close of the Sixth year of the Hijra (as has been already told), he ailed temporarily from loss of appetite and a pining depression of health and spirits, ascribed to the incantations of the Jews. Again, in the middle of the Seventh year, his system sustained a shock from partaking of poisoned meat at Kheibar, for which he was cupped, and the effects of which he complained of periodically ever after. Indeed, the present attack was attributed by Moḥammad himself to this cause. When he had been now for several days sick, the mother of Bishr (who had died from the effects of the same poison) came to inquire after his health; she condoled with him on the violence of the fever, and remarked that the people said it was an attack of pleurisy. 'Nay,' answered Moḥammad, 'the Lord would never permit that sickness to seize his Apostle, for it cometh of Satan. This, verily, is the effect of that which I ate at Kheibar, I and thy son. The artery of my back feeleth as though it would just now burst asunder.'

Circumstances affecting strength of his constitution

Whether his constitution was really impaired by the poison, or whether it was merely the Prophet's fancy, the frailties of age were now imperceptibly stealing upon him. His vigorous, well-knit frame had begun to stoop. Though frugal, if not abstemious in his habits, and in all things (the ḥarīm excepted) temperate, yet during the last twenty years of his life there had been much to tax both mind and body. At Mecca, hardship, rejection, persecution, confinement, exile; at Medīna, the anxieties of a cause for some years doubtful, and now the cares of a daily extending empire, all pressed heavily upon him. Nor must we forget the excite-

[1] Ibn Hishām, p. 970 and 999, 1006 ff.; Aṭ-Ṭabari, i. 1704, &c.; Al-Wāḳidi, p. 433 f.; Ibn Sa'd, p. 136 f.

ment and agitation (possibly of an epileptic character) which occasionally overpowered him in the moments of supposed inspiration and intercourse with his unseen visitants. 'Ah! thou that art dearer to me than father or mother!' exclaimed Abu Bekr to Moḥammad as he entered one day from his wives' apartments into the Mosque; 'alas! grey hairs are hastening upon thee'; and his eyes filled with tears as the Prophet raised his beard with his hand, and gazed upon it. 'Yes,' said Moḥammad, 'it is the travail of inspiration that hath done this. The Sūras *Hūd*, and the *Inevitable*, and the *Striking*, with their fellows, these have made white my hair.' But Moḥammad did not yield to the infirmities of old age. To the very last he maintained the severe simplicity of robuster years. 'The people throng about thee in the Mosque,' said his uncle Al-'Abbās to him;—'what if we make for thee an elevated seat, that they may not trouble thee?' But Moḥammad forbade it: 'Surely,' he said, 'I will not cease from being in the midst of them, dragging my mantle behind me thus,[1] and covered with their dust, until that the Lord give me rest from amongst them.'

Increasing infirmity

Conviction that his end was near

Moḥammad himself was latterly not unconscious (so we learn from 'Ā'isha) of the premonitions of decay. He used frequently to repeat the 110th Sūra, as follows:—

When the help of God shall come, and the Victory,
And thou shalt see men entering the religion of God in troops;
Then celebrate the praises of thy Lord, and ask pardon of Him, for He is merciful.

These expressions he would refer to the multitudes now flocking to the faith from the Yemen and the farther coasts of Arabia. He would furthermore declare that the sign received from the Lord of the completion of his work was thus fulfilled, and that it remained for him now only 'to busy himself in the praises of his Lord and to seek for pardon.'[2]

[1] *I.e.* hurrying along and being jostled by the crowd.

[2] The traditions of this period abound in anticipations of Moḥammad's decease. But few of these seem founded on fact. Take the following as a specimen. When the 110th Sūra was revealed, Moḥammad called Fāṭima, and said: 'My daughter! I have received intimation of my approaching end.' Fāṭima burst into tears. 'Why weepest thou, my child?' continued the prophet; 'be comforted, for verily thou art the first of my people that shall rejoin me.' Whereupon Fāṭima dried her tears and smiled pleasantly. As Fāṭima died within six months after

Attacked by illness, Moḥammad visits the burial-ground

When attacked by his last illness, Moḥammad, though probably feeling it to be serious, did not at the first succumb; for a day or two he still maintained the custom he had prescribed to himself of visiting his wives' apartments in rotation. One night lying restless on his bed, he arose softly, cast his clothes about him, and, followed only by a servant, walked to the burial-ground, in the outskirts of the city. There he rested long absorbed in meditation. At last winding up his thoughts, he prayed aloud for those who were buried there, apostrophising thus: '*Verily, both ye and I have received fulfilment of that which our Lord did promise us. Blessed are ye! for your lot is better than the lot of those that are left behind. Temptation and trial approach like portions of a dark night that follow one upon another, each darker than that preceding it. O Lord! have mercy upon them that lie buried here!*' With these words, he turned and departed to his house. By the way, he told his attendant that he too was himself hastening to the grave: 'The choice hath verily been offered me of continuance in this life, with Paradise thereafter, or to meet my Lord at once; and I have chosen to meet my Lord.'[1]

'Ā'isha's raillery when he seeks commiseration

In the morning, passing by the chamber of 'Ā'isha, who was suffering from a headache, he heard her moaning: 'My head!—oh, my head!'[2] He entered and said: 'Nay,

her father, it is easy to see how this tale grew up. Similar are the traditions in glorification of Fāṭima: *e.g.* where Moḥammad calls her 'the Queen of the women of Paradise after Mary, Mother of Jesus'; also the prediction of coming divisions, sects, intestine war, &c. A shade of the same tendency will be observed in the prayer (in the text above) at the burial-ground, which, notwithstanding, I have given entire.

[1] Ibn Hishām, p. 999 f.; Aṭ-Ṭabari, i. 1799 f.

[2] It may be necessary here to warn the reader that we have now reached a point in Moḥammad's biography which has become specially the arena for contending traditions of party and faction. *First*, 'Ā'isha, who had the closest opportunities by far of all others for watching the last moments of Moḥammad, has made the most of her position; throughout her statements there is a patent endeavour to exclude even the mention of 'Alī and his partisans. There is, *secondly*, the party of 'Alī, who (with the view of strengthening their dogma that the divine right of succession was vested in him and his posterity) attribute to him every important part in the scene. And, *lastly*, there are the 'Abbāsids (holding the right of succession to reside in their line), whose tendency is to magnify Al-'Abbās and his family. Every tradition is coloured more or less by these factions; and it is necessary to steer very cautiously between them.

'Ā'isha, it is rather I that have need to cry *My head, my head!*' Then in a tenderer strain: 'But wouldst thou not desire to be taken whilst I am yet alive; so that I might pray over thee, and wrapping thee, 'Ā'isha, in thy winding-sheet, myself commit thee to the grave?' 'That happen to another,' exclaimed 'Ā'isha, 'and not to me!' archly adding: 'Ah, that, I see, is what thou wishest for! Truly, I can behold thee, when all was over, returning straightway hither, and sporting with a new beauty in my chamber here!' The Prophet smiled at 'Ā'isha's raillery, but was too ill for a rejoinder; and so, again with a sad complaint of the grievous ailment in his head, passed on to the apartment of Meimūna, whose day it was. The fever returning upon him shortly with increasing violence, he called his wives around him, and said: 'Ye see that I lie very sick: I am not able to visit you in turn; if it be pleasing unto you, I will remain in the room of 'Ā'isha.' They agreed, and so, his clothes having been wrapped loosely about him, and his head bound round with a napkin, he walked with the support of 'Alī and Al-'Abbās to the apartment of 'Ā'isha. Hardly yet twenty years of age, and never before used to such a duty, she tended with affectionate solicitude the death-bed of her aged husband.

Moḥammad retires to 'Ā'isha's room

He chides the murmuring at Osāma's appointment

For seven or eight days the fever, although unchecked, did not confine Moḥammad entirely to the house. He was able to move into the Mosque (the door of his apartment opening into its courts) and lead, though feebly, the public prayers. He had been ill about a week, when perceiving that the sickness gained ground, with occasional fits of swooning, he resolved upon an effort to address his followers, whose murmurs at the appointment of the youthful Osāma to the command of the army for Syria had reached his ears. 'Fetch me,' he said, 'seven skins of water from as many different wells, that I may bathe and then go forth unto them.' They procured the water, and, seating him in Ḥafṣa's bathing vessel, poured it upon him from the skins till he held up his hand and cried 'Enough!' Meanwhile the people, both men and women, having assembled in the Mosque, it was told the Prophet that they had come together, and that many wept. Refreshed now by the bath, his head bandaged, and a sheet drawn loosely round him (for it was summer), he went forth at the hour of prayer into the Mosque; and, when the service was ended, seated himself upon the pulpit and proceeded thus:—'Ye people! What is this which hath reached my ears, that some amongst you murmur against my appointment of Osāma to command the Syrian expedition? Now, if ye blame my appointment of Osāma, verily heretofore ye blamed likewise my appointment of his father Zeid before him. And I swear by the Lord that he verily was well fitted for the command, and that his son after him is well fitted also. Truly Osāma is one of the men most dearly beloved by me, even as his father was. Wherefore, do ye treat him well, for he is one of the best amongst you.'

Private doors leading into the Mosque closed

Then after a pause; 'Verily, the Lord hath offered unto one of his servants the choice betwixt this life and that which is nigh unto Himself; and the servant hath chosen that which is nigh unto his Lord.' The people were slow to catch this his first expressed anticipation that the illness would prove his last.[1] But Abu Bekr saw it, and burst into tears. Moḥammad bade him not to weep, and immediately added a touching proof of his affection; for, turning to the people, he said: 'Verily the chiefest among you all for love and devotion to me is Abu Bekr. If I were to choose a bosom friend it would be he: but Islām hath made a closer brotherhood amongst us all. Now let every door that leadeth into the Court be closed, excepting only the door of Abu Bekr.' Accordingly the relatives of Moḥammad and Chief men whose houses skirted the quadrangle of the Mosque, closed their doors opening into it, that of Abu Bekr alone excepted. Thus the busy hum and tread were hushed as became the precincts of death, and the courts of the Mosque

[1] It is likely that the expression used by Moḥammad regarding the *choice* of death or life was of a more general nature, such as 'that he preferred to depart and be near his Lord' (something, perhaps, in the manner of Paul's words, Philip. i. 21);—which would easily be converted into the mysterious phrase 'that he had *made election* of Paradise.' Against the text it might be urged that after such a declaration the people ought to have been more prepared for the Prophet's death when it did happen. But the scene after his death was justified by the immediate circumstances, and is to my apprehension quite consistent with even a more explicit statement by Moḥammad than this, of his forebodings.

frequented only by worshippers at the hour of prayer, and by knots of whispering inquirers after the Prophet's health.[1]

Moḥammad commends Citizens to his Followers' care

As he was about to re-enter 'Ā'isha's room, Moḥammad turned again, and, in testimony of his gratitude to the people of Medīna, thus addressed them;—'Ye that are Refugees from Mecca and elsewhere, hearken unto me! Ye increase, and throng into the city daily. But the men of Medīna do not increase. They will remain ever as they are this day. And verily they are dear unto me, for amongst them it was that I found refuge. Wherefore honour their honourable men, and treat well their excellent ones.' Then, having urged the early departure of the Syrian expedition, he retired into the chamber of 'Ā'isha.[2]

Abu Bekr appointed to lead public prayers

The exertion and excitement of this address aggravated the Prophet's sickness. On the following day, when the hour of public prayer came round, he desired water for the customary ablutions; but, on attempting to rise, he found that his strength had failed, so he commanded that Abu Bekr should conduct the prayers in his stead; and having done so, fell back into a swoon. Quickly recovering, he inquired whether the commission had been conveyed to his friend. 'Ā'isha replied: 'O Prophet! Truly Abu Bekr is a man of a tender heart, and weepeth readily. The people would with difficulty hear his voice.' 'Command that he lead the prayers,' repeated Moḥammad in a loud and impatient tone. 'Ā'isha, still clinging to the hope that Moḥammad would be able himself to perform the duty, began again in a similar strain. Displeased and irritated, Moḥammad exclaimed: 'Truly, ye resemble the foolish women in the story of Joseph:[3] give command forthwith as I desire.' The command was given, and Abu Bekr conducted the public prayers during the few remaining days of the Prophet's life.[4]

[1] Ibn Hishām, p. 1005 f. [2] *Ibid.*, p. 1007.

[3] See Sūra xii. The Commentators refer this expression to the scene in which the women of Egypt cut their hands in astonishment at the beauty of Joseph.

[4] Ibn Hishām, p. 1008; Aṭ-Ṭabari, i. 1811 f. Tradition is quite unanimous as to the above account. The only point on which I have ventured to deviate from it, is the *motive* of 'Ā'isha. She herself says that she objected simply from the fear that people would ever after dislike her father for having stood up in the Prophet's place, and would attribute any evil that might happen to ill-luck arising out of such

Closely joined together as is spiritual authority in Islām with temporal command, the right of presiding at public prayer was from the very first recognised as the mark of chief secular authority. There can be little doubt, I think, that Moḥammad, by nominating Abu Bekr to this duty, intended the delegation of power to him while laid aside, if not to mark him also as successor after death. It is related that on one occasion Abu Bekr happened not to be present when the summons to prayer was sounded by Bilāl; and that 'Omar having received, as he erroneously believed, the command of Moḥammad to officiate in his room, stood up in the Mosque, and in his powerful voice commenced the *Tekbīr*, 'Great is the Lord!' preparatory to the daily service. Moḥammad, overhearing it from his apartment, called aloud with energy: 'No! No! No! The Lord and the whole body of Believers forbid it! None but Abu Bekr! Let no one lead the prayers but only he!'[1]

Moḥammad thus signified transfer to him as his deputy of ruling power

While thus unable to leave the room of 'Ā'isha, Moḥammad was too weak to attend to any public business. Yet the Syrian expedition weighed upon his mind; and he kept saying to those around him: 'Send off quickly the army of Osāma.' He also inquired about the embassies daily arriving at Medīna, and enjoined the same hospitable treatment and gift of similar largesses as he had been wont to bestow.

He urges despatch of Osāma's army

The sickness had now lasted nearly a fortnight when, on the night of Saturday, it began to assume a very serious aspect. The fever rose to such a pitch that the hand could hardly be kept upon him from the burning heat. His body

Increase of illness. Saturday night, 11th Rabī' I. A.H. XI. June 6, A.D. 632

usurpation. This I believe to be an afterthought. 'Ā'isha was ambitious enough, and no doubt rejoiced greatly at this indication of her father to the chief command. But she was also overcome at the moment by concern for her husband, and could not bear the admission that he was so dangerously ill as the nomination appeared to imply. It seemed to her to be a foreboding of his end:—an inauspicious forestalling of the future. Hence she deprecated the idea.

One set of traditions makes her to propose that 'Omar should conduct the prayers in her father's stead. This is unlikely; but supposing it to be true, her proposal may have arisen from the same cause;—she knew well that Moḥammad would not pass over Abu Bekr, and may from false modesty, or it may be real delicacy, have suggested that 'Omar, and not her father, should be nominated to the invidious post.

[1] Ibn Hishām, p. 1009.

was racked with pain; restless and moaning, he tossed about upon his bed. Alarmed at a severe paroxysm, Um Selama screamed aloud. Moḥammad rebuked her: 'Quiet!' he said; 'no one crieth out so but an unbeliever.' During the night, 'Ā'isha sought to comfort him, and suggested that he should seek for consolation in the lessons he had so often taught to others when in sickness: 'O Prophet!' she said, 'if one of us had moaned thus, thou wouldst surely have found fault with her.' 'Yes,' he replied, 'but I burn with the fever-heat of any two of you together.' 'Then,' exclaimed another, 'thou shalt surely have a double reward.' 'Yea,' he answered,—'for I swear by Him in whose hands is my life, that there is not upon the earth a Believer, sore afflicted with calamity or disease, but the Lord thereby causeth his sins to fall off from him, even as the leaves from a tree in autumn.' At another time he said: 'Suffering is an expiation for sin. Verily, if the Believer suffer but the scratch of a thorn, the Lord raiseth his rank thereby, and wipeth away from him a sin.' And again, 'Believers are tried according to their faith. If a man's faith be strong, so are his sufferings; if he be weak, they are proportioned thereunto. Yet in any case, the suffering shall not be remitted until he walk upon earth without the guilt of a single transgression cleaving to him.'

Sayings of Moḥammad on his death-bed

'Omar, approaching the bed, placed his hand on the sufferer's forehead, and suddenly withdrew it from the great heat: 'O Prophet!' he said, 'how fierce is the fever upon thee!' 'Yea, verily,' replied Moḥammad, 'but I have been during the night season repeating in praise of the Lord seventy Sūras, and among them the seven long ones.' 'Omar answered: 'Why not rest and take thine ease, for hath not the Lord (and here he quoted the Ḳor'ān) *forgiven thee all thy sins, the former and the latter?*' 'Nay,' replied Moḥammad, 'for wherefore should I not yet be a faithful servant unto Him?' An attendant, while Moḥammad lay covered up, put his hand below the sheet and, feeling the excessive heat, made a remark like that of 'Omar. On which the Prophet said;—'Just as this affliction prevaileth now against me, even so shall my reward hereafter be.' 'And who are they,' asked another, 'that suffer the severest trials?' 'The prophets and the righteous,' answered Moḥammad; and then he made mention of one prophet having been destroyed by lice, and of another who was tried with poverty, so that he had but a rag to cover his nakedness withal; 'yet each of them rejoiced exceedingly in his affliction, even as one of you having found great spoil would rejoice and be glad.'

Osāma visits him. Sunday, 12th Rabī' I. June 7

All Sunday he lay in a helpless and at times delirious state. Osāma, who had delayed his march to see what the issue might be, came in from the Jurf to visit him. Removing the clothes, he stooped down and kissed the Prophet's face, but there was no audible response. Moḥammad only raised his hands in the attitude of blessing, and then placed them on the young Commander's head, who then returned to the camp.[1]

Moḥammad physicked by his wives

During some part of this day, Moḥammad complained of pain in his side, and the suffering became so great that he became unconscious. Um Selama advised that physic should be given him. Asmā,[2] step-sister of Meimūna, prepared a draught after an Abyssinian recipe, and they forced it into his mouth. Reviving from its effects he perceived the unpleasant taste, and cried: 'What is this that ye have done to me? Ye have even given me physic!' They confessed that they had done so, and enumerated the simples of which Asmā had compounded it.[3] 'Out upon you!' he exclaimed angrily; 'this is a remedy for the pleurisy, which she hath learned in the land of Abyssinia; an evil disease is it which the Lord will not let attack me. Now shall ye all of you within this chamber partake of the same. Let not one remain without being physicked, even as ye have physicked me, excepting only my uncle, Al-'Abbās' So all the women arose, and they poured the physic, in presence of the dying Prophet, into each other's mouths.[4]

[1] Ibn Hishām, p. 1007. [2] See *ante*, p. 396.

[3] Indian wood and a little *Wars* seed mixed with some drops of olive oil.

[4] This scene is well attested. How strangely it must have contrasted with the solemnity of the Prophet's death-bed! Meimūna pleaded that she was under a vow of fasting, and could not, therefore, allow anything, even medicine, to pass her lips; but the excuse was unavailing. Another tradition represents Moḥammad as grounding his displeasure at being forced to take the physic, on the fact that 'he was then fasting.' He had, perhaps, made some vow to this effect in reference to his sickness.

Moḥammad in fever curses Jews and Christians

After this strange scene, the conversation turning upon Abyssinia, Um Selama and Um Ḥabība, who had both been exiles there, spoke of the beauty of the cathedral of *Maria* there, and of the wonderful pictures on its walls. Overhearing it, Moḥammad was displeased, and said; 'These are the people who, when a saint among them dieth, build over his tomb a place of worship, and then adorn it with their pictures;—in the eyes of the Lord, the worst part of all creation.' Restless and apparently delirious, he kept now drawing the bed-clothes up over his face, now casting them off again;—and in the excitement and perhaps wanderings of the moment, cried out;—'The Lord destroy the Jews and Christians![1] Let his anger be kindled against those that turn the tombs of their Prophets into places of worship! O Lord, let not my tomb be ever an object of worship! Let there not remain any faith but that of Islām throughout Arabia!'[2] About this time, recognising 'Omar, and some other chief Companions in the room, he called out: 'Fetch me hither pen and ink, that I may make for you a writing which shall hinder you from going astray for ever.' 'Omar said: 'He wandereth in his mind. Is not the Ḳor'ān sufficient for us?' But the women wished that the writing materials should be brought; and a discussion ensued. 'Come, let us ask him,' said one, 'and see whether he wandereth.' So they asked him regarding the writing he

Moḥammad calls for writing materials

[1] Some authorities omit the *Christians* from this tradition.

[2] Ibn Hishām, p. 1021. *Lit.*, 'Let there not remain two religions,' &c. See *ante*, pp. 381, 454, 460. The facts there given prove that there was no *command* recognised by his people as such, given by the Prophet for the expulsion either of the Jews or Christians from Arabia. Had there been, Abu Bekr and 'Omar would no doubt have made it their first obligation to fulfil the order,—existing treaties and engagements notwithstanding. A command of Moḥammad was never questioned during his life, much less after his death. The last sentence must therefore either be without foundation, or, what is more likely, having been uttered in delirium, was not felt to be binding. If uttered even in delirium, it is a significant index of the current of Moḥammad's thoughts.

According to some traditions Moḥammad said that he had three injunctions to deliver; one concerned the treatment of the embassies arriving at Medīna (see *ante*, p. 455); the second directed the ejection of Jews and Christians from Arabia; before he could explain the third, he became unconscious. Other injunctions are mentioned, as kindness to slaves; paying tithes; observing prayer, &c.

had spoken of; but he no longer had any thought of it. 'Leave me thus alone,' he said, 'for my present state is better than that which ye call me to.'[1] In the course of the day he called 'Ā'isha to him, and said: 'Where is that gold which I gave unto thee to keep?' On her replying that it was by her, he desired that she should spend it at once in charity. Then he dozed off in a half-conscious state, and some time after asked if she had done as he desired her. On her saying that she had not yet done so, he called for the money (apparently a portion of the tithe income); she placed it in his hand, and counted six golden pieces. He directed that it should be divided among certain indigent families; and then lying down he said: 'Now I am at peace. Verily it would not have become me to meet my Lord, and this gold still in my hands.'[2]

He distributes alms

All Sunday night the illness lay heavy upon him. He was overheard praying, in apparent anticipation of his approaching end;—'O my soul! Why seekest thou refuge elsewhere than in God alone?'[3] The morning brought relief. The fever and the pain abated; and there was some return of strength.

Improvement on Monday morning, 13th of Rabī' I. June 8

[1] Either speaking incoherently, or meaning that he did not feel equal to the task. Al-'Abbās lamented the irreparable loss of what Moḥammad intended to dictate through their quarrelling. But Moḥammad was evidently wandering when he called for the writing materials. According to another tradition, when the women were about to bring the writing materials, 'Omar chided them: 'Quiet!' he said. 'Ye behave as women always do; when your master falleth sick ye burst into tears, and the moment he recovereth but a little, then ye begin embracing him.' Moḥammad, jealous even on his death-bed of the good name of his wives, was roused by these words, and said: 'Verily, they are better than ye are;' which, if true, shows that Moḥammad was only partially delirious.

[2] The story is told in various ways, but the version in the text is probably correct. Some traditions unite the incident with one of those strange tales of 'Ā'isha, contrasting the Prophet's poverty with his benevolence; she was obliged (she says) to send to a neighbour to get oil for her lamp when Moḥammad was on his death-bed. There are many traditions to show Moḥammad's unwillingness to retain money in his possession. He used to give everything away in charity; and did not even like retaining money in his house over the night. But they are probably exaggerated.

[3] In all his previous illnesses, Moḥammad had prayed for his recovery. This prayer, according to tradition, signified that now his expectation was to depart.

Moḥammad comes out to morning prayer;

The dangerous accession of fever on the previous night having become known, the Mosque was crowded in the morning at the hour of prayer by anxious worshippers. Abu Bekr, as usual, led the devotions; as Imām he stood in the place of Moḥammad before the congregation, his back turned towards them.[1] He had ended the first *Raka'* (or prostration), and the people had just stood up for the second, when the curtain of 'Ā'isha's door (to the left, and a little way behind Abu Bekr) slowly moved aside, and Moḥammad himself appeared. As he entered the assembly, he whispered in the ear of Al-Faḍl, son of Al-'Abbās, who with a servant supported him:—'The Lord verily hath granted unto me refreshment[2] in prayer;' and he looked around him with a gladsome smile marked by such as at the moment caught a glimpse of his countenance.[3] That smile, no doubt, was the index of deep emotion in his heart. What doubts or fears may have crossed the mind of Moḥammad as he lay on the bed of death, and felt that the time was drawing nigh when he must render an account to that God whose Messenger he professed to be,—tradition affords us no grounds even to conjecture. The rival pretensions of Ṭoleiḥa, Al-Aswad, and Museilima may haply have suggested misgivings such as those which, at the opening of his mission, had long ago distracted his soul. If any doubts and questionings had arisen in his mind, the sight of the great congregation, in attitude devout and earnest, may have caused him comfort and reassurance. That which brings forth good fruit (he may have said to himself) must itself be good. The mission which had transformed debased idolaters into spiritual worshippers such as these, and which, wherever accepted and believed in, was daily producing the same wonderful change, must surely be divine, and the voice from within which prompted him to undertake it must have been the voice of the Almighty revealed through His ministering spirit.

[1] It will be remembered that in Moḥammadan prayers, the whole congregation, the Imām (leader) included, look towards Mecca. The people ranged in rows behind him follow all his movements.

[2] *Lit.*, 'Cooling of the eyes.'

[3] That is by the portion of the congregation in a line with the door, who were standing sideways to it, and by all behind them. Those in front had their backs partly towards him; but some of them also may probably have turned round to see the cause of the general sensation.

Perhaps it was some thought like this which, passing at the moment through the Prophet's mind, lighted up his countenance with a smile of joy that diffused gladness over the crowded court.

And takes his seat beside Abu Bekr

Having paused thus for a moment at the door of his apartment, Moḥammad, supported as before, walked softly to the front where Abu Bekr stood. The people made way for him, opening their ranks as he advanced. Abu Bekr heard the rustle (for he never turned at prayer or looked to the right hand or the left) and, guessing the cause, stepped backwards to vacate the leader's place. But Moḥammad motioned him to go on, and, taking his hand, moved forward towards the pulpit. There on the ground he sat by the side of Abu Bekr, who resumed the service, and finished it in customary form.

Abu Bekr goes to visit his wife at the Sunḥ

When the prayers were ended, Abu Bekr entered into conversation with Moḥammad. He rejoiced to find him to all appearance convalescent. 'O Prophet,' he said, 'I perceive that by the grace of God thou art better to-day, even as we desire to see thee. Now this day is the turn of my wife, the daughter of Khārija; shall I go and visit her?'[1] Moḥammad gave him permission. So he departed to her house at the Sunḥ, a suburb of the upper city.

Moḥammad speaks with the people around him

Moḥammad then sat down for a little while in the courtyard of the Mosque, near the door of 'Ā'isha's apartment, and addressed the people who, overjoyed to find him again amongst them, crowded round. He spoke with emotion, and with a voice still so powerful as to reach beyond the outer doors of the Mosque. 'By the Lord!' he said, 'as for myself, verily, no man can lay hold of me in any matter;[2] I have not made lawful anything excepting that which God hath made lawful; nor have I prohibited aught but that which God in his Book hath prohibited.' Osāma coming up to bid farewell, Moḥammad said to him: 'Go forward with

[1] This was the wife whom he had married at Medīna, from amongst the Beni'l-Ḥārith, see *ante*, p. 169. The Muslims all followed Moḥammad's custom of giving a day in succession to each of their wives.

[2] In this expression probably originated the highly improbable traditions that Moḥammad on this occasion called upon all claimants to state what demands they had against him; some creditors having claims of very trifling amount came forward, it is said, and he discharged their debts. The appeal somewhat resembles that of Samuel (1 Sam. xii. 3).

the army; and the blessing of the Lord be with thee!' Then turning to the women who sat close by: 'O Fāṭima, my daughter!' he exclaimed, 'and thou Ṣafīya, my aunt! Work ye out that which shall gain acceptance for you with the Lord: for I verily have no power with Him to save you in anywise.' Having said this, he arose and was helped back into the chamber of 'Ā'isha.[1]

Mohammad retires exhausted to 'Ā'isha's room.

It was but the flicker of an expiring taper. Exhausted, he lay down upon the pallet stretched upon the floor; and 'Ā'isha, seeing him to be very weak, raised his head from the pillow, and, as she sat by him on the ground, laid it tenderly upon her bosom. At that moment, one entered with a green toothpick in his hand.[2] Seeing that his eye rested on it, and, knowing it to be such as he liked, 'Ā'isha asked whether he would like to have it. He signified assent. Chewing it a little to make it soft and pliable, she placed it in his hand. This pleased him; he took it up and used it for the moment vigorously. Then he put it down again.[3]

The hour of death draws near

His strength now rapidly sank. He seemed to be aware that death was drawing near. Calling for a pitcher of water, and therewith wetting his face, he prayed thus: 'O Lord, I beseech thee assist me in the agonies of death!' Then three times earnestly;—'Gabriel, come close unto me!'

Mohammad dies reclining on 'Ā'isha's bosom

He now began to blow upon himself, perhaps in the half-consciousness of delirium, ejaculating the while a petition which in the sick-room he used to repeat over persons who were very ill. When, from weakness, he ceased, 'Ā'isha took up the task and continued to blow upon him and recite the same prayer. Then, seeing that he was very low, she took hold of his right hand and rubbed it (as he himself used to do with the sick), repeating all the while the earnest invocation.[4]

[1] [Ibn Isḥāḳ says Al-'Abbās invited 'Alī to come with him to Moḥammad to secure the chief rule for themselves, but 'Alī refused on the ground that to do so would, if the request were refused, ruin their prospects for ever. Ibn Hishām, p. 1011.

[2] In the east, the fresh and tender wood of trees is used for this purpose, cut into thin and narrow pieces.

[3] Ibn Hishām, p. 1011.

[4] The prayer was: '*Take away evil and misfortune, O thou Lord of mankind! Grant a cure, for thou art the best Physician. There is no cure besides thine; it leaveth nought of the disease behind.*'

I have omitted mention of Gabriel's incantation over the dying

But he could not now bear even this, saying;—'Take thy hand from off me; it cannot help me now.' After a little, in a whisper: 'Lord, grant me pardon; and join me to the companionship on high.' Then at intervals: 'Eternity in Paradise!' 'Pardon!' 'The blessed companionship on high!' He stretched himself gently. Then all was still. His head grew heavy on the breast of 'Ā'isha. The Prophet of Arabia was no more.

Softly removing his head from her bosom, 'Ā'isha placed

'Ā'isha replaces his head on the pillow

Prophet; the story of the Angel of Death asking permission to exercise his vocation upon him; the voices of unseen visitants wailing, &c. But the following tradition is illustrative of Moḥammadan ideas on the subject:—'Three days before the death of Moḥammad, Gabriel came down to visit him: "O Aḥmed!" he said, "the Lord hath deputed me thus as an honour and peculiar favour unto thee, that He may inquire concerning that which indeed He knoweth better than thou thyself: He asketh, *How thou findest thyself this day?*" "Gabriel!" replied the Prophet, "I find myself in sore trouble and agony." Next day, Gabriel again visited Moḥammad, and accosted him in the same words; Moḥammad replied as before. On the third day, Gabriel descended with the Angel of Death; and there also alighted with him another angel, Ismail, who inhabiteth the air, never ascending up to heaven, and never before having descended to the earth since its creation: he came now in command of 70,000 angels, each in command of 70,000 more. Gabriel, preceding these, addressed Moḥammad in the same words as before, and received the same reply. Then said Gabriel: "This, O Moḥammad! is the Angel of Death. He asketh of thee permission to enter. He hath asked permission of no man before, neither shall he ask it of any after thee." Moḥammad gave permission; so the Angel of Death entered the room, and stood before Moḥammad, and said: "O Aḥmed, Prophet of the Lord! Verily God hath sent me unto thee, and hath commanded me to obey thee in all that thou mayest direct. Bid me to take thy soul, and I will take it; bid me to leave it, and I will do accordingly." To which, Moḥammad replied; "Wilt thou, indeed, do so, O Angel of Death!" The angel protested that his mission was even so, to do only that which Moḥammad might command. On this, Gabriel interposed, and said: "O Aḥmed! verily the Lord is desirous of thy company." "Proceed, then," said Moḥammad, addressing the Angel of Death, "and do thy work, even as thou art commanded." Gabriel now bade adieu to Moḥammad: "Peace be on thee," he said, "O Prophet of the Lord! This is the last time that I shall tread the earth; with this world I have now concern no longer." So the Prophet died; and there arose a wailing of celestial voices (the sound was audible, but no form was seen) saying: "*Peace be on you, ye inhabitants of this house, and mercy from the Lord and his blessing! Every soul shall taste death,*"'—and so on.

it on the pillow. Then she rose and joined the other women as they beat their faces in loud and bitter lamentation.

It was still but a little after mid-day

It was yet little after mid-day. But a moment ago, as it were, Moḥammad had entered the Mosque cheerful, and to all appearance convalescent. He now lay cold in death.

CHAPTER XXXIV

THE EVENTS WHICH FOLLOWED ON THE DEATH OF MOḤAMMAD

13th and 14th of Rabī', A.H. XI.—*June* 8 *and* 9, A.D. 632

News of Moḥammad's death reaches Abu Bekr

THE news of the Prophet's death, spreading rapidly over Medīna, soon reached Abu Bekr in the suburb of the Sunḥ. Immediately he mounted his horse, and rode back to the Mosque in haste.

'Omar wildly declaims that Moḥammad had only swooned away

Meanwhile, a strange scene was being enacted there. Shortly after Moḥammad had breathed his last, 'Omar entered the apartment of 'Ā'isha, and, lifting up the sheet which covered the body, gazed wistfully at the features of his departed master.[1] All was so placid, so natural, so unlike death, that 'Omar could not believe the mournful truth. Starting up, he exclaimed wildly: 'The Prophet is not dead; he hath but swooned away.' Al-Moghīra, standing by, vainly sought to convince him that he was mistaken. 'Thou liest!' cried 'Omar, as, quitting the chamber of death, they entered the courts of the Mosque;—'the Apostle of God is not dead. Thine own seditious spirit hath suggested this imagination. The Prophet of the Lord shall not die until he have rooted out every hypocrite and unbeliever.' The crowd which, at the rumour of the Prophet's death, rapidly gathered in the Mosque, attracted now by the loud and passionate tones of 'Omar, flocked around him, and he went on haranguing them in similar strain;—'The hypocrites would persuade you, O Believers! that Moḥammad is dead. Nay! but he hath gone to his Lord, even as Moses, son of 'Imrān, who remained absent forty days, and then returned after his followers had said that he was dead. So, verily, by the Lord! the Prophet shall

[1] Ibn Hishām, p. 1012; Aṭ-Ṭabari, i. 1816 f.

return, and of a certainty shall cut off the hands and feet of them that dare say that he is dead.' 'Omar found a willing audience. It was but a little while before that the Prophet had been amongst them, had joined with them in prayer on that very spot, and had gladdened their hearts by hope of speedy convalescence. The echo of his voice was hardly yet silent in the courts of the Mosque. Sudden alternations of hope and despair disturb equilibrium of the mind, and unfit it for exercise of calm and dispassionate judgment. The events of the day had been pre-eminently calculated to produce such effect upon the people, who, now carried away by 'Omar's fervour, gladly persuaded themselves that he might be in the right.

Abu Bekr visits scene of death;

Just then appeared Abu Bekr. Passing through the Mosque, he listened for a moment to the frenzied words of 'Omar, and, without pausing further, walked onwards to the door of 'Ā'isha's chamber. Drawing the curtain softly aside, he asked leave to enter. 'Come,' they replied from within, 'for this day no permission needeth to be asked.' Then he entered, and, raising the striped sheet which covered the bed, stooped down and kissed the face of his departed friend, saying: 'Sweet wast thou in life, and sweet thou art in death.' After a moment, he took the head between his hands, and, slightly lifting it, gazed on the well-known features, now fixed in death, and exclaimed: 'Yes, thou *art* dead! Alas, my friend, my chosen one! Dearer than father or mother to me! Thou hast tasted the bitter pains of death; and (referring to 'Omar's wild words without) thou art too precious with the Lord, that he should give thee the bitter cup to drink a second time! Gently putting down the head upon its pillow, he stooped again and kissed the face; then replaced the covering and withdrew.

Convinces 'Omar and the people that Mohammad is really dead

Leaving the room, Abu Bekr went at once to the spot without, where 'Omar, in the same excited state, was haranguing the people. 'Silence!' cried Abu Bekr, as he drew near. ''Omar! sit thee down. Be quiet!' But 'Omar went on, not heeding the remonstrance. So Abu Bekr, turning from him, began himself to address the assembly; no sooner did they hear his voice open with the customary exordium, than they quitted 'Omar and gave attention to the words of Abu Bekr, who proceeded thus: 'Hath not the

Almighty revealed this verse unto his Prophet saying,—"*Verily thou shalt die, and they shall die*"? And again, after the battle of Ohod,—"*Mohammad is no more than an Apostle; verily the other Apostles have deceased before him. What then? If he were to die, or be killed, would ye turn back upon your heels?*" Let him then know, whosoever worshippeth Mohammad, that Mohammad indeed is dead: but whoso worshippeth God, let him know that the Lord liveth and doth not die.' The words of the Kor'ān fell like a knell on the ears of 'Omar and all who with him had buoyed themselves with the delusive hope of Mohammad's return to life. The quiet and reflecting mind of Abu Bekr had no doubt of late dwelt upon these passages during the Prophet's illness. To the people in general they had not occurred, at least in connection with the present scene. When they heard them now repeated, 'it was as if they had not known till that moment that such words existed in the Kor'ān'; and, the truth now bursting upon them, they sobbed aloud. 'Omar himself would relate: 'By the Lord! it was so that, when I heard Abu Bekr reciting those verses, I was horror-struck, my limbs trembled, I dropped down, and I knew of a certainty that the Prophet indeed was dead.'

Army at the Jurf breaks up and returns to Medīna

The greater part of the army, when the Prophet died, was still at the Jurf, three miles distant from Medīna. Encouraged by his seeming convalescence that morning in the Mosque, they had rejoined their camp. Osāma, mindful of his master's strict injunction, had given the order for immediate march, and his foot was already in the stirrup, when a swift messenger from his mother, Um Aiman, announced the Prophet's death. The army, stunned by the intelligence, at once broke up, and returned to Medīna. Osāma, preceded by the standard-bearer, went direct to the Mosque, and planted the great banner there at the door of 'Ā'isha's house.

Citizens of Medīna assemble

It was now towards the afternoon when one came running hastily towards the Mosque to say that the chief men of Medīna, with Sa'd ibn 'Obāda at their head, had assembled in one of the halls of the city, and were proceeding to choose Sa'd for their leader:[1] 'If ye, therefore (addressing Abu Bekr and others still in the Mosque), desire to have the command, come quickly thither before the matter shall have been

[1] Ibn Hishām, p. 1013 ff.; At-Tabari, i. 1817 ff., 1837 ff.

settled, and opposition become dangerous.' On hearing this report, Abu Bekr, after arranging that the family of the Prophet should be undisturbed while they washed the corpse and laid it out, hurried in company with 'Omar and Abu 'Obeida, to the hall where the people had assembled. There was urgent necessity for their presence. The men of Medīna, in anticipation of the Prophet's death, were brooding over their supersession by the once dependent strangers whom they had received as refugees from Mecca: 'Let them have their own chief,' was the general cry; 'but as for us, we shall have a chief for ourselves.' Sa'd, who lay sick and covered over in a corner of the hall, had already been proposed for the chiefship of the Citizens, when suddenly Abu Bekr and his party entered. 'Omar, still in a state of excitement, was on the point of giving vent to his feelings in a speech which he had in his mind, when Abu Bekr, afraid of his rashness and impetuosity, held him back, and himself addressed the people. 'Omar used in after days to say that Abu Bekr anticipated all his arguments, and expressed them in language the most eloquent and persuasive. 'Ye men of Medīna!' he said, 'all that ye speak of your own excellence is true. There is no people upon earth deserving all this praise more than ye do. But the Arabs will not recognise the chief command elsewhere than in our tribe of Ḳoreish. We are the *Ameers;* ye are our *Wazeers.*'[1] 'Not so,' shouted the indignant Citizens, 'but there shall be an Ameer from amongst us, and an Ameer from amongst you.' 'That can never be, said Abu Bekr; and he repeated in a firm commanding voice: '*We* are the Ameers; *you* are our Wazeers. We are the noblest of the Arabs by descent; and the foremost in the glory of our City. There! Choose ye whom ye will of these two (pointing to 'Omar and Abu 'Obeida) and do allegiance to him.'[2] 'Nay!' cried 'Omar, in words which rose high and clear above the growing tumult of the assembly; 'did not the Prophet himself command that *thou*, O Abu Bekr, shouldst lead the prayers? Thou art

Abu Bekr sworn fealty to, as Caliph

[1] *Ameer*, Chief. *Wazeer*, or *Vizier*, Deputy.

[2] There was nothing in the antecedents of Abu 'Obeida to sustain a claim to the Caliphate. He was simply named by Abu Bekr as being the only other Ḳoreishite present. He subsequently bore a conspicuous part in the conquest of Syria.

our Master, and to thee we pledge our allegiance—thou whom the Prophet loved the best amongst us all!' So saying he seized the hand of Abu Bekr, and, striking it, pledged faith to him. The words touched a cord that vibrated in every Believer's heart, and his example had the desired effect. Opposition vanished, and Abu Bekr was saluted *Caliph* (Successor) of the departed Prophet.[1]

Body of Moḥammad washed and laid out

Meanwhile 'Alī, Osāma, and Al-Faḍl, the son of Al-'Abbās, with one or two of the Prophet's servants, had been busily employed in the room of 'Ā'isha. There on the spot on which he breathed his last, they washed the body and laid it out.[2] The garment in which he died was left upon him: two sheets of fine white linen were wound around it; and over all was cast a covering of striped Yemen stuff. Thus the body remained during the night, and until the time of burial.

Speech of 'Omar. Allegiance publicly sworn to Abu Bekr. Tuesday, 14th Rabī' I. June 9

On the morrow, when the people had assembled in the Mosque, Abu Bekr and 'Omar came forth to meet them. 'Omar first addressed the great assemblage: 'O ye people! that which I spoke unto you yesterday was not the truth. Verily, I find that it is not borne out by the Book which the Lord hath revealed, nor by the covenant which we made with his Apostle. As for me, verily I hoped that the Apostle of the Lord would continue yet a while amongst

[1] Ibn Hishām, p. 1013 ff.; Aṭ-Ṭabari, i. 1819. Khalīfa (Caliph) signifies 'Successor.'

[2] As usual, when the name of 'Alī is introduced, tradition is overspread with fiction. A heavenly voice was heard ordering the attendants not to make bare the Prophet's body, for the eyes of any one that looked upon his nakedness would forthwith be destroyed. When 'Alī raised the limbs, they yielded to his touch, as if unseen hands were aiding him; another, essaying to do the same, found the weight insupportable. Thus Al-Faḍl, who had ventured on the task, was well nigh dragged down, and called out for help: 'Haste thee, 'Alī! Hold, for my back is breaking with the weight of this limb.' Al-'Abbās refused to enter the room at the time, 'because Moḥammad had desired always to be hid from him while he bathed.'

Besides the three named in the text (who, as the nearest and most intimate friends, naturally superintended the washing of the body), one of the Medīna Citizens, Aus ibn al-Khaula, was admitted by 'Alī into the room. Another son of Al-'Abbās is also named by some authorities as having been present The servants employed on the occasion were Shaḳrān and Ṣāliḥ. Ibn Hishām, p. 1018 f.

us, and speak in our ears a word such as might seem good unto him and be a perpetual guide unto us. But the Lord hath chosen for his Apostle the portion which is with Himself, in preference to that which is with you. And truly the Word, that same word which directed your Prophet, is with us still. Take it, therefore, for your guide and ye shall never go astray. And now, verily, hath the Lord placed your affairs in the hands of him that is the best amongst us; The Companion of His Prophet, the sole companion, *The second of the two when they were in the cave alone.* Arise! Swear fealty to him!' Forthwith the people crowded round, and one by one they swore allegiance upon the hand of Abu Bekr.

Speech of Abu Bekr on his inauguration

The Ceremony ended, Abu Bekr arose and said: 'Ye people! now, verily, I have become the Chief over you, although I am not the best amongst you. If I do well, support me; if I err, then set me right. In truth and sincerity is faithfulness, and in falsehood perfidy. The weak and oppressed among you in my sight shall be strong, until I restore his right unto him, if the Lord will; and the strong oppressor shall be weak, until I wrest from him that which he hath taken. Now hearken to me; when a people leaveth off to fight in the ways of the Lord, verily He casteth them away in disgrace. Know also that wickedness never aboundeth in any nation, but the Lord visiteth that nation with calamity. Wherefore obey me, even as I shall obey the Lord and His Apostle. Whensoever I disobey them, obedience is no longer binding on you. Arise to prayers! and the Lord have mercy on you!'[1]

Discontent of 'Alī and Fāṭima

The homage done to Abu Bekr was almost universal. Sa'd ibn 'Obāda, deeply chagrined at being superseded, is said by some to have remained aloof.[2] It is probable that 'Alī, while the people were swearing allegiance, remained in his own house or in the chamber of mourning. The doctrine of his party is that he expected the Caliphate for himself; but there was nothing whatever in his previous position, or in the language and actions of the Prophet

[1] Ibn Hishām, p. 1017; Aṭ-Ṭabari, i. 1829, 1835.

[2] It is even said that he retired in disgust to Syria, where he died. Aṭ-Ṭabari, on the other hand, relates that he submitted to Abu Bekr, and acknowledged his authority. I. 1842 ff.

towards him, which could have led to such anticipation. As the husband of Moḥammad's only surviving daughter, indeed, he felt aggrieved when Abu Bekr refused the claim of his wife to inherit her father's share in the lands of Fadak and of Kheibar. But Fāṭima failed in producing any evidence of her father's intention to bestow this property on her, and the Caliph justly held that it should be reserved for those purposes of State to which Moḥammad had in his lifetime devoted it. Fāṭima took the denial so much to heart that she held no intercourse with Abu Bekr during the short remainder of her life. Whether 'Alī swore allegiance at the first to his new chief, or refused to do so, it was certainly not till Fāṭima's death, six months after that of her father, that he recognised with any cordiality the title of Abu Bekr to the Caliphate.[1]

Fāṭima renounces society of Abu Bekr

[1] Some traditions say that he swore allegiance at the first, with the rest; others, that he refused to do so till after Fāṭima's death.

The traditions of Fāṭima's deep grief at the loss of her father, and of her joy at his prophecy that she would soon rejoin him in heaven, &c., hardly accord with the persistent manner in which she urged her claim to the property. 'On the day after her father's death,' we learn from Al-Wāḳidi, 'Fāṭima repaired with 'Alī to Abu Bekr, and said: "Give me the inheritance of my father the Prophet." Abu Bekr inquired whether she meant his household goods or his landed estates. "*Fadak* and *Kheibar*," she replied "and the tithe lands at Medīna,—my inheritance therein, even as thy daughters will inherit of thee when thou diest." Abu Bekr replied: "Verily, thy father was better than I am, and thou art better than my daughters are. But the Prophet hath said, *No one shall be my heir; that which I leave shall be for alms.* Now, therefore, the family of Moḥammad shall not eat of that property; for, by the Lord, I will not alter a tittle of that which the Prophet ordained; all shall remain as it was in his lifetime. But," continued he, "if thou art certain that thy father gave thee this property, I will accept thy word, and fulfil thy father's direction." She replied that she had no evidence excepting that of the maid-servant Um Aiman, who had told her that her father had given her Fadak. Abu Bekr, therefore, adhered to his decision.' [Aṭ-Tabari couples Al-'Abbās with Fāṭima—i. 1825.]

CHAPTER XXXV

THE BURIAL

Grave prepared in 'A'isha's house. Tuesday, 14th Rabī' I. June 9

WHEN Abu Bekr had ended his address, preparations were made for the burial. The people differed regarding the place most fitting for the grave. Some urged that the body should be buried in the Mosque close by the pulpit, and some, beneath the spot where as their Imām he had so long led the daily prayers, while others wished to inter him beside his followers in the graveyard without the city. Abu Bekr, with whom as Caliph the matter rested now, approved none of these proposals: for, said he, 'I have heard it from the lips of Moḥammad himself, that in whatsoever spot a prophet dieth, there also should he be buried.' He therefore gave command that the grave should be dug where the body was still lying within the house of 'Ā'isha.'[1]

Grave dug in vaulted fashion

Another question arose as to the form in which the tomb should be prepared. Two fashions prevailed in Arabia: in one kind, the bottom or pavement of the grave was flat; in the other, it was partly excavated for the reception of the body, a ledge being left on one side of the vault or cavity. The former was the plan followed at Mecca, the latter at Medīna; and for each there was a separate gravedigger. Both were now summoned. The man of Medīna first appearing, dug the grave in the vaulted form; and so this fashion is followed by all Moḥammadans to the present day.

Body visited by people. Orations of Abu Bekr and 'Omar

The body remained upon the bier for four-and-twenty hours, namely, from the afternoon of Monday to the same hour on the following day. On Tuesday it was visited by all the inhabitants of the city. They entered in companies

[1] Ibn Hishām, p. 1019; Aṭ-Ṭabari, i. 1830 ff.

by the door which opened into the Mosque; and, after gazing once more on the countenance of their Prophet and praying over his remains, retired by the opposite entrance. The room was crowded to the utmost at the time when Abu Bekr and 'Omar entered together. They are said to have prayed as follows: 'Peace be upon thee, O Prophet of God; and mercy from the Lord and his blessing! We bear testimony that the Prophet of God hath delivered the message revealed to him; hath fought in the ways of the Lord until that God brought forth his religion unto victory; hath fulfilled his words, commanding that he alone in his Unity is to be worshipped; hath drawn us to himself, and been kind and tender-hearted to Believers; hath sought no recompense for delivering to us the Faith, neither hath he sold it for a price at any time!' And all the people said, *Amen! Amen!* The women followed in companies, when the men had departed; and then the children and even the slaves crowded round the bier for a last look at their Prophet's face.

In the evening the final rites were paid to the remains. A red mantle, worn by him, was first spread as a soft covering at the bottom of the grave; then the body was lowered into its last resting-place by the same loving hands that had washed and laid it out. The vault was built over with unbaked bricks, and the grave filled up.[1] Burial

[1] There is wonderful rivalry, at least among the traditionists, as to which person was the last to quit the interior of the tomb. Al-Moghīra asserts that, having dropped his ring into the grave, he was allowed to go down and pick it up, and thus was the last. Others, hold that 'Alī sent down his son Al-Ḥasan to fetch the ring. Others, that 'Alī denied the story of the ring altogether. Some allege that one or other of the sons of Al-'Abbās was 'the first to enter, and the last to leave, the grave.' These variations form a good example of the rivalry of the 'Alid and 'Abbāsid traditions.

I must not omit a tradition which seems to me to illustrate the naturalness of 'Omar's scepticism regarding the Prophet's death. Um Selama says: 'I did not believe that Moḥammad was really dead, till I heard the sound of the pickaxes at the digging of the grave, from the next room.' 'Ā'isha also says that the sound of the pickaxes was the first intimation she had of the approaching interment. She had apparently retired, with the other wives, to an adjoining apartment. [Ibn Hishām, p. 1020, says they did not know about the burial of Moḥammad until they heard the mattocks in the middle of the night.]

'A'isha continued to occupy apartment next the grave

'Ā'isha continued as before to live in her house thus honoured as the Prophet's cemetery. She occupied a room adjoining that which contained the grave, but partitioned off from it. When her father died, he was buried close by the Prophet in the same apartment, and in due time 'Omar also. It is related of 'Ā'isha that she used to visit this room unveiled till the burial of 'Omar, when (as if a stranger had been introduced) she never entered unless veiled and fully dressed.[1]

[1] 'Ā'isha tells us, she once dreamt that three moons fell from the heavens into her bosom, which she hoped portended the birth of an heir. After her husband's death, Abu Bekr told her that the grave of Moḥammad in her house was the first and best of the moons; the other two were the graves of Abu Bekr himself and of 'Omar. She survived the Prophet forty-seven years.

Al-Wāḳidi says there was no wall at first round Moḥammad's house. 'Omar surrounded it with a low wall, which 'Abdallah ibn az-Zubeir increased.

CHAPTER XXXVI

CAMPAIGN OF OSĀMA ON THE SYRIAN BORDER; AND CONCLUSION

Campaign of Osāma. A.H. XI. June, July, A.D. 632

THE first concern of Abu Bekr, on assuming the Caliphate, was to despatch the Syrian army, and thus fulfil the dying wish of Moḥammad. But the horizon was lowering all around; and many urged that the Muslim force should not be sent just yet upon this distant expedition. Even 'Omar joined in the cry: 'Scatter not the Believers; rather keep our army here: we may have need of it yet to defend the city.' 'Never!' replied Abu Bekr; 'the command of the Prophet shall be carried out, even if I be left here in the city all alone, prey to the wolves and beasts of the desert.' Then they besought that a more experienced soldier might be appointed to the chief command. On this, the Caliph arose in wrath. 'Out upon thee!' he cried, as he seized 'Omar by the beard; 'hath the Prophet of the Lord named Osāma to the leadership, and dost thou counsel me to take it from him!' He would admit of no excuse and no delay; and so the force was soon marshalled again at the Jurf. Abu Bekr repaired to the camp, and, treating Osāma with the profound respect due to a commander appointed by Moḥammad himself, begged permission that 'Omar might be left behind at Medīna as his counsellor. The request was granted. He then bade Osāma farewell, and exhorted him to go forward in the name of the Lord, and fulfil the commission received at the Prophet's hands. The army marched; and the Caliph, with 'Omar alone, returned to Medīna.[1]

His triumphal return to Medīna

Within twenty days of his departure from the Jurf, Osāma had overrun the province of the Belḳā. In fire and blood, he avenged his father's death and the disastrous field of Mūta.

[1] Aṭ-Ṭabari, i. 1848 ff.

'They ravaged the land,' says the historian, 'with the well-known cry of *Yā manṣūr amit* ("Strike, ye conquerors!"), they slew all who ventured to oppose them in the field, and carried off captive the remainder. They burned the villages, the fields of standing corn, and the groves of palm-trees; and there went up behind them, as it were, a whirlwind of fire and smoke.'[1] Having thus fulfilled the Prophet's last command, they retraced their steps. It was a triumphal procession as they approached Medīna; Osāma rode upon his father's horse, and the banner, bound so lately by Moḥammad's own hand, floated before him. Abu Bekr and the Citizens went forth to meet him, and received the army with acclamations of joy. Attended by the Caliph, and the chief Companions, Osāma proceeded to the Mosque, and offered up prayer with thanksgiving for the success which had so richly crowned his arms.[2]

The rapid spread of Muslim conquest

With the return of Osāma's army to Medīna a new era opens upon us. The Prophet had hardly departed this life when Arabia was convulsed by the violent endeavour of its tribes to shake off the trammels of Islām, and regain their previous freedom. The hordes of the desert rose up in rebellion, and during the first year of his Caliphate Abu Bekr had to struggle for the very existence of the faith. Step by step the wild Bedawīn were subdued and forced to tender their submission. By a master-stroke of policy, they were induced again to take up their arms, and, aroused by the prospect of boundless spoil, to wield them on the side of Islām. Like bloodhounds eager for the chase, they were let forth upon mankind—the whole world their prey. They gloried in the belief that they were the hosts of God, destined

[1] Al-Wāḳidi represents Osāma as killing in battle the very man that slew his father.

[2] Ibn Sa'd, p. 137. The tidings of this bloody expedition alarmed Heraclius, and he sent a strong force into the Belḳā. The attention Abu Bekr had first to be directed nearer home. Reinforced by the army of Osāma, he had to quell the fierce spirit of insurrection rising all around. But a year had not elapsed, when he was again in a position to take the field in Syria, and to enter on the career of conquest which quickly wrested from the Empire that fair province.

for the conversion of His elect and for the destruction of His enemies. The cry of religion thus disguised or gilded every lower motive. The vast plunder of Syria and Al-'Irāḳ was accepted as but the earnest of a greater destiny yet in store. Once maddened by the taste of blood, the lust of spoil, and capture without stint of female slaves, into a wild and irresistible fanaticism, the armies of Arabia swept their enemies everywhere before them. Checked towards the north by the strongholds of Asia Minor and the Bosphorus, the surging wave spread to the east and to the west with incredible rapidity, till in a few short years it had engulfed in common ruin the earliest seats of Christianity and the faith of Zoroaster.

Lives of first two Caliphs an argument for Moḥammad's sincerity

But these are matters beyond the subject of this volume. I will merely add that the simplicity and earnestness of Abu Bekr, and of 'Omar also, the first two Caliphs, are strong evidence of their belief in the sincerity of Moḥammad; and the belief of these men must carry undeniable weight in the formation of our own estimate of his character, since the opportunities they enjoyed for testing the grounds of their conviction were both close and long-continued. It is enough that I allude to this consideration, as strengthening generally the view of Moḥammad's character which throughout I have sought to support.

CHAPTER XXXVII

THE PERSON AND CHARACTER OF MOHAMMAD

General review of Mohammad's character

It may be expected that, before bringing this work to a close, I should gather into one review the chief traits in the character of Mohammad, which at different stages of his life, and from various points of view, have in the course of the history been presented to the reader. This I will now briefly attempt.[1]

Personal appearance

The person of Mohammad, as he appeared in the prime of life, has been portrayed in an early chapter; and though advancing age may have somewhat relaxed the outlines of his countenance and affected the vigour of his carriage, yet the general aspect remained unaltered to the end. His form, though little above mean height, was stately and commanding. The depth of feeling in his dark black eye, and the winning expression of a face otherwise attractive, gained the confidence and love of strangers, even at first sight. His features often unbended into a smile full of grace and condescension. 'He was,' says an admiring follower, 'the handsomest and bravest, the brightest-faced and most generous of men. It was as though the sunlight beamed in his countenance.' Yet when anger kindled in his piercing glance, the object of his displeasure might well quail before it. His stern frown was the augury of death to many a trembling captive. In later years, the erect figure began to stoop; but the step was still firm and quick. His gait has been likened to that of one descending rapidly a hill. When he made haste, it was with difficulty that one kept pace with

His gait

[1] Most of the illustrations here given are taken from the section of Al-Wāḳidi on the 'appearance and habits of the Prophet.' In the Supplement also will be found a selection of traditions on the subject taken from the same section.

him. He never turned, even if his mantle caught in a thorny bush, so that his attendants talked and laughed freely behind him secure of being unobserved.

His habits thorough

Thorough and complete in all his actions, he took in hand no work without bringing it to a close. The same habit pervaded his manner in social intercourse. If he turned in conversation towards a friend, he turned not partially, but with his full face and his whole body. 'In shaking hands, he was not the first to withdraw his own; nor was he the first to break off in converse with a stranger, nor to turn away his ear.'

Simplicity of his life

A patriarchal simplicity pervaded his life. His custom was to do everything for himself. If he gave an alms he would place it with his own hand in that of the petitioner. He aided his wives in their household duties, mended his clothes, tied up the goats, and even cobbled his sandals. The ordinary dress was of plain white cotton stuff, made like his neighbours'; but on high and festive occasions he wore garments of fine linen, striped or dyed in red. He never reclined at meals. He ate with his fingers; and, when he had finished, he would lick them before he wiped his hands. The indulgences to which he was most addicted were 'Women, scents, and food.' In the first two of these, 'Ā'isha tells us, he had his heart's desire; and when she adds that he was straitened in the third, we can only attribute the saying to the vivid contrast between the frugal habits at the birth of Islām, and the luxurious living which rapidly followed in the wake of conquest and prosperity. Moḥammad, with his wives, lived, as we have seen, in a row of low and homely cottages built of unbaked bricks, the apartments separated by walls of palm-branches rudely daubed with mud, while curtains of leather, or of black haircloth, supplied the place of doors and windows. He was to all easy of access—'even as the river's bank to him that draweth water from it,'—yet he maintained the state and dignity of real power. No approach was suffered to familiarity of action or of speech. The Prophet must be addressed in subdued accents and in a reverential style. His word was absolute; his bidding law. Embassies and deputations were received with the utmost courtesy and consideration. In the issue of rescripts bearing on their representations, or in other matters of State,

Moḥammad displayed all the qualifications of an able and experienced ruler, as the reader will have observed from the numerous examples given. And what renders this the more strange is that he was never known himself to write; and, indeed, rather rejoiced (as his followers still do) in the title of *An-Nebī al-Ummī*, or the Illiterate Prophet.[1]

Urbanity and kindness of disposition

A remarkable feature was the urbanity and consideration with which Moḥammad treated even the most insignificant of his followers. Modesty and kindliness, patience, self-denial, and generosity, pervaded his conduct, and riveted the affections of all around him. He disliked to say *No.* If unable to answer a petitioner in the affirmative, he preferred silence. 'He was more bashful,' says 'Ā'isha, 'than a veiled virgin; and if anything displeased him, it was rather from his face, than by his words, that we discovered it; he never smote any one but in the service of the Lord, not even a woman or a servant.' He was not known ever to refuse an invitation to the house even of the meanest, nor to decline a proffered present however small. When seated by a friend, 'he did not haughtily advance his knees towards him.' He possessed the rare faculty of making each individual in a company think that *he* was the favoured guest. If he met any one rejoicing at success he would seize him eagerly and cordially by the hand. With the bereaved and afflicted he sympathised tenderly. Gentle and unbending towards little children, he would not disdain to accost a group of them at play, with the salutation of peace. He shared his food, even in times of scarcity, with others; and was sedulously solicitous for the personal comfort of every one about him. A kindly and benevolent disposition pervades all these illustrations of his character.

Friendship

Moḥammad was also a faithful friend. He loved Abu Bekr with the close affection of a brother; 'Alī, with the fond partiality of a father. Zeid, the Christian slave of Khadīja, was so strongly attached by the kindness of the Prophet, that he preferred to remain at Mecca rather than return home with his own father: 'I will not leave thee,' he said, clinging to his patron, 'for thou hast been a father and a mother to me.' The friendship of Moḥammad survived the

[1] The fact is noticed in the Ḳor'ān, Sūra vii. 157-8, and is largely used to the present day as an argument for its being inspired.

death of Zeid, and his son Osāma was treated by him with distinguished favour for the father's sake. 'Othmān and 'Omar were also the objects of a special attachment; and the enthusiasm with which, at Al-Ḥodeibiya, the Prophet entered into 'the Pledge of the Tree' and swore that he would defend his beleaguered son-in-law even to the death, was a signal proof of faithful friendship. Numerous other instances of Moḥammad's ardent and unwavering regard might be adduced. And his affections were in no instance misplaced; they were ever reciprocated by a warm and self-sacrificing love.

Moderation and magnanimity

In the exercise of a power absolutely dictatorial, Moḥammad was just and temperate. Nor was he wanting in moderation towards his enemies, when once they had cheerfully submitted to his claims. The long and obstinate struggle against his pretensions maintained by the inhabitants of Mecca might have induced its conqueror to mark his indignation in indelible traces of fire and blood. But Moḥammad, excepting a few criminals, granted a universal pardon; and, nobly casting into oblivion the memory of the past, with all its mockery, its affronts and persecution, he treated even the foremost of his opponents with a gracious and even friendly consideration. Not less marked was the forbearance shown to 'Abdallah and the Disaffected citizens of Medīna, who for so many years persistently thwarted his designs and resisted his authority, nor the clemency with which he received the submissive advances of tribes that before had been the most hostile, even in the hour of victory.

Cruelty towards enemies

But the darker shades, as well as the brighter, must be depicted by the faithful historian. Magnanimity or moderation are nowhere discernible in the conduct of Moḥammad towards such of his enemies as failed to tender a timely allegiance. On the field of Bedr he exulted over the dead, with undisguised and ruthless satisfaction; and several prisoners,—accused of no crime but that of scepticism or political opposition,—were deliberately executed at his command. The Prince of Kheibar, after being subjected to cruel torture for the purpose of discovering the treasures of his tribe, was, with his cousin, put to death for having concealed them, and his wife led captive to the conqueror's tent. Sentence of exile was enforced by Moḥammad with rigorous severity on two whole Jewish tribes residing at Medīna; and of a third, likewise his neighbours, the women and children were sold into captivity, while the men, amounting to six or eight hundred, were butchered in cold blood before his eyes.

Craft and artifice

In his youth Moḥammad earned amongst his fellows the honourable title of 'the Faithful.' But in later years, however much sincerity and good faith may have guided his conduct in respect of friends, craft and deception were not wanting towards his foes. The conduct of his followers at Nakhla, where the first blood in the internecine warfare with Ḳoreish was shed, although at the outset disavowed by Moḥammad for its treacherous breach of the sacred usages of Arabia, was eventually justified by a revelation from heaven. Abu Baṣīr, the freebooter, was countenanced by the Prophet in a manner scarcely consistent with the letter, and certainly opposed to the spirit, of the truce of Al-Ḥodeibiya. The plea on which the Beni an-Naḍīr were besieged and expatriated (namely, that Gabriel had revealed their design against the Prophet's life) was feeble and unworthy of an honest cause. When Medīna was beleaguered by the Confederate army, Moḥammad sought the services of No'eim, a treacherous go-between, and employed him to sow distrust amongst the enemy by false reports; 'for,' said he, 'what else is War but a game of deception?' In his prophetical career, political and personal ends were frequently compassed by *divine* revelations, which, whatever more, were certainly the direct reflection of his own wishes. The Jewish and Christian systems, at first adopted honestly as the basis of his own religion, had no sooner served the purpose of establishing a firm authority, than they were cast aside and virtually disowned. And what is perhaps worst of all, the dastardly assassination of political and religious opponents, countenanced, if not in some cases directed, by Moḥammad himself, leaves a painful reflection upon his character.

Domestic life; polygamy

In domestic life the conduct of Moḥammad (if we except the unchecked range of his uxorious inclinations) was exemplary. As a husband his fondness and devotion were entire, bordering at times upon jealousy. As a father he was loving and tender. In his youth he lived a virtuous life; and at the age of twenty-five married a widow forty years old, during whose lifetime for five-and-twenty years he was a faithful husband to her alone. Yet it is remarkable that during this period were composed most of those passages of the Ḳor'ān in which the black-eyed 'Houries,' reserved for Believers in Paradise, are depicted in such glowing colours. Shortly after the death of Khadīja, he married again; but it was not till the mature age of fifty-four that he made the dangerous trial of polygamy, by taking 'Ā'isha, yet a child, as the rival of Sauda. Once the natural limits of restraint were overpassed, Moḥammad fell a prey to his strong passion for the sex. In his fifty-sixth year he married Ḥafṣa; and the following year, in two succeeding months, Zeinab bint Khozeima and Um Selama. But his desires were not to be satisfied by the range of a ḥarīm already in advance of Arab custom, and more numerous than was permitted to any of his followers; rather, as age advanced they were stimulated to seek for new and varied indulgence. A few months after his nuptials with Zeinab and Um Selama, the charms of a second Zeinab were by accident discovered too fully before his admiring gaze. She was the wife of Zeid, his adopted son and bosom friend; but he was unable to smother the flame she had kindled in his breast; and, by divine command, she was taken to his embrace. In the same year he wedded a seventh wife, and also a concubine. And at last, when he was full threescore years of age, no fewer than three new wives, besides Mary the Coptic slave, were within the space of seven months added to his already well-filled ḥarīm. The bare recital of these facts may justify the saying of Ibn Al-'Abbās: 'Verily the chiefest among the Muslims (meaning Moḥammad) was the foremost of them in his passion for women;'—a fatal example imitated too readily by his followers, who here adopt the Prince of Medīna, rather than the Prophet of Mecca, for their pattern.

Thus the social and domestic life of Moḥammad, fairly and impartially viewed, is seen to be chequered by light and shade. While there is much to form the subject of nearly unqualified praise, there is likewise much which cannot be spoken of but in terms of reprobation.

Conviction of special Providence

Proceeding now to consider the religious and prophetical character of Moḥammad, the first point which strikes the biographer is his constant and vivid sense of a special and all-pervading Providence. This conviction moulded his thoughts and designs, from the minutest actions in private and social life to the grand conception that he was destined to be the Reformer of his people and of all Arabia. He never entered a company 'but he sat down and rose up with the mention of the Lord.' When the first-fruits of the season were brought to him, he would kiss them, place them upon his eyes, and say: 'Lord, as thou hast shown us the first, show unto us likewise the last.' In trouble and affliction, as well as in prosperity and joy, he ever saw and humbly acknowledged the hand of God. A fixed persuasion that every incident, small and great, is ordered by the divine will, led to the strong expressions of predestination which abound in the Ḳor'ān. It is the Lord who turneth the hearts of mankind: and alike faith in the believer, and unbelief in the infidel, are the result of the divine fiat. The hour and place of every man's death, as all other events in his life, are established by the same decree; and the timid believer might in vain seek to avert the stroke by shunning the field of battle. But this persuasion was far removed from the belief in a blind and inexorable fate; for Moḥammad held the progress of events in the divine hand to be amenable to the influence of prayer. He was not slow to attribute the conversion of a scoffer like 'Omar, or the removal of an impending misfortune (as the deliverance of Medīna from the Confederate hosts), to the effect of his own earnest petitions to the Lord. On the other hand, he was often the subject of superstitious dread. He feared to sit down in a dark place until a lamp had been lighted; and his apprehension was at times raised by the wind and clouds. He would fetch prognostications from the manner in which a sword was drawn from the scabbard. A special virtue was attributed to being cupped an even number of times, and on a certain day of the week and month. He was also guided by omens drawn from dreams: but these may, perhaps, have been regarded by him as intimations of the divine will.

Moḥammad's unwavering steadfastness t Mecca

The growth in the mind of Moḥammad of the conviction that he was appointed to be a Prophet and Reformer is intimately connected with his belief in a special Providence embracing the spiritual as well as material world; and out of that conviction arose the confidence that the Almighty would crown his mission with success. While still at Mecca, there is no reason to doubt that the questionings and aspirations of his inner soul were regarded by him as proceeding directly from God. The light which gradually illuminated his mind with a knowledge of the divine unity and perfections, and of the duties and destiny of man,—light amidst gross darkness,—must have emanated from the same source; and He who in his own good pleasure had thus begun the work would surely carry it through to a successful ending. What was Moḥammad himself but an instrument in the hand of the great Worker? Such, no doubt, were the thoughts which strengthened him, alone and unsupported, to brave for many weary years the taunts and persecutions of a whole people. In estimating the signal moral courage thus displayed, it must not be overlooked that for what is ordinarily termed *physical* courage Moḥammad was not remarkable. It may be doubted whether he ever engaged personally in active conflict on the battle-field. Though he often accompanied his forces, he never himself led them into action, or exposed his person to avoidable danger. And there were occasions on which (as when challenged by 'Abdallah to spare the Beni Ḳainuḳā', alarmed by the altercation at the wells of Al-Moraisī', or pressed by the mob at Al-Ji'rāna) he showed symptoms of a faint heart. Yet even so, it only brings out in higher relief the singular display of moral daring. Let us for a moment look to the period when a ban was proclaimed at Mecca against all citizens, whether professed converts or not, who espoused his cause or ventured to protect him; and when along with these, he was shut up in the *Shi'b* or quarter of Abu Ṭālib, and there for three years, without prospect of relief, endured want and hardship. Strong and steadfast must have been the motives which enabled him, amidst such opposition and apparent hopelessness of success, to maintain his principles unshaken. No sooner was he released from this restraint than, despairing of his native city, he went forth solitary and unaided to Aṭ-Ṭā'if, and there summoned its rulers and inhabitants to repentance, with the message which he said he had from his Lord; on the third day he was driven out of the town with ignominy, while blood flowed from wounds inflicted on him by the populace. Retiring to a little distance, he poured forth his complaint to God, and then returned to Mecca, there to resume the same outwardly hopeless cause, with the same high confidence in its ultimate success. We search in vain through the pages of profane history for a parallel to the struggle in which for thirteen years the Prophet of Arabia, in the face of discouragement and threats, rejection and persecution, retained thus his faith unwavering, preached repentance, and denounced God's wrath against his godless fellow-citizens. Surrounded by a little band of faithful men and women, he met insults, menace, and danger with a lofty and patient trust in the future. And when at last the promise of safety came from a distant quarter he calmly waited until his followers had all departed, and then disappeared from amongst an ungrateful and rebellious people.

And at Medīna

Not less marked was the firm front and unchanging faith in eventual victory, which at Medīna bore him through seven years of mortal conflict with his native city; and enabled him, sometimes even under defeat, and while his influence and authority were yet limited and precarious even in the city of his adoption, to speak and to act in the constant and undoubted expectation of victory.

Denunciation of polytheism and idolatry

From the earliest period of his religious convictions, the UNITY, or idea of ONE great Being guiding with almighty power and wisdom all creation, and yet infinitely above it, gained a thorough possession of his mind. Polytheism and idolatry, at variance with this grand principle, were indignantly condemned as levelling the Creator with the creature. On one occasion alone did Moḥammad swerve from this position, when he admitted that the goddesses of Mecca might be adored as a medium of approach to God. But the inconsistency was soon perceived; and Moḥammad at once retraced his steps. Never before nor afterwards did the Prophet deviate from the stern denunciation of idolatry.

Earnestness and honesty of Moḥammad at Mecca

As he was himself the subject of convictions thus deep and powerful, it will readily be conceived that his exhortations were distinguished by a corresponding strength and cogency. Master of eloquence, his language was cast in the purest and most persuasive style of Arabian oratory. His fine poetical genius exhausted the imagery of nature in the illustration of spiritual truths; and a vivid imagination enabled him to bring before his people the Resurrection and the Day of judgment, the joys of believers in Paradise, and the agonies of lost spirits in Hell, as close and impending realities. In ordinary address, his speech was slow, distinct, and emphatic; but when he preached 'his eye would redden, his voice rise high and loud, and his whole frame agitate with passion, even as if he were warning the people of an enemy about to fall on them the next morning or that very night.' In this thorough earnestness lay the secret of his success. And if these stirring appeals had been given forth as nothing more than what they really were, the outgoings of a warm and active conviction, they would have afforded no ground for cavil; or, yet a step further, should he have represented them as the teaching of a soul guided by natural inspiration, or even enlightened by divine influence,—such a course would not have differed materially from that trodden by many a sincere, though it may be erring, philanthropist in other ages and other lands. But, in the development of his system, the claims of Moḥammad to inspiration far transcended such assumptions. His inspiration was essentially *oracular*. The Prophet was but the passive organ which received and transmitted a heavenly message. His revelations were not the fruit of a subjective process in which the soul, burning with divine life and truth, sought to impress the stamp of its own convictions on those around. The process, on the contrary, was one which Moḥammad professed to be entirely external to himself—independent of his own reasoning, affections, and will. The words of inspiration, whether purporting to be a portion of the Ḳor'ān or a simple message of direction, were produced as a real and objective intimation, conveyed to him immediately from the Almighty or through the angel Gabriel His messenger. Such was the position assumed by Moḥammad. How far this conviction was fostered by epileptic or supernatural paroxysms (which do not, however, come prominently to view at least in the later stages of his career) or by cognate physiological phenomena, it is impossible to determine. We may readily admit that at the first Moḥammad did believe, or persuaded himself to believe, that his revelations were dictated by a divine agency. In the Meccan period of his life there certainly can be traced no personal ends or unworthy motives belying this conclusion. Moḥammad then was nothing more than he professed to be, 'a simple Preacher and a Warner'; he was the despised and rejected prophet of a gainsaying people, having no ulterior object but their reformation. He may have mistaken the right means for effecting this end, but there is no sufficient reason for doubting that he used those means in good faith and with an honest purpose.

At Medīna worldly motives mingle with spiritual objects

But the scene changes at Medīna. There temporal power, aggrandisement, and self-gratification mingled rapidly with the grand object of the Prophet's life; and they were sought and attained by just the same instrumentality. Messages from heaven were freely brought down to justify political conduct, in precisely the same manner as to inculcate religious precept. Battles were fought, executions ordered, and territories annexed, under cover of the Almighty's sanction. Nay, even personal indulgences were not only excused but encouraged by the divine approval or command. A special license was produced, allowing the Prophet many wives; the affair with Mary the Coptic bond-maid was justified in a separate Sūra; and the passion for the wife of his own adopted son and bosom friend was the subject of an inspired message in which the Prophet's scruples were rebuked by God, a divorce permitted, and marriage with the object of his unhallowed desires enjoined. If we say that such 'revelations' were believed by Moḥammad sincerely to bear the divine sanction, it can only be in a modified and peculiar sense. He surely must be held responsible for that belief; and, in arriving at it, have done violence to his judgment and the better principles of his nature.

Rapid moral declension the natural consequence

As the natural result, we trace from the period of Moḥammad's arrival at Medīna a marked and rapid declension in the system he inculcated. Intolerance quickly took the place of freedom; force, of persuasion. The spiritual weapons designed at first for higher objects were no sooner devoted to the purposes of temporal authority, than temporal authority was employed to give weight and temper to those spiritual weapons. The name of the Almighty imparted a terrible strength to the sword of the State; and the sword of the State yielded a willing return by destroying 'the enemies of God' and sacrificing them at the shrine of the new religion. 'Slay the unbelievers wheresoever ye find them,' was now the watchword of Islām. 'Fight in the ways of God until opposition be crushed and the Religion become the Lord's alone.' The warm and simple devotion breathed by the Prophet and his followers at Mecca, when mingled with worldly motives, soon became dull and vapid; while faith degenerated into a fierce fanaticism, or evaporated in a lifeless round of formal ceremonies. In its final evolution, Islām left far behind the toleration of early days when the men of Mecca were told that 'there should be no force in religion,' but that conscience alone must rule. And so also with the former Revelations which yielded the Prophet the first firm foothold for his aspiring step. The Jéwish faith, whose pure fountainhead was now so much more accessible than before, as well as the less familiar Gospel, having served his purpose, were in spite of all former protestations of allegiance, cast silently aside. Islām, now resting on the sword, had done with them.

Benefits of Moḥammadanism;

And what have been the effects of the system which, established by such instrumentality, Moḥammad has left behind him? We may freely concede that it banished for ever many of the darker elements of superstition for ages shrouding the Peninsula. Idolatry vanished before the battle-cry of Islām; the doctrine of the Unity and infinite perfections of God, and of a special all-pervading Providence, became a living principle in the hearts and lives of the followers of Moḥammad, even as in his own. An absolute surrender and submission to the divine will (the idea embodied in the very name of *Islām*) was demanded as the first requirement of the faith. Nor are social virtues wanting. Brotherly love is inculcated towards all within the circle of the faith; infanticide proscribed; orphans to be protected, and slaves treated with consideration; intoxicating drinks prohibited, so that Moḥammadanism may boast of a degree of temperance unknown to any other creed.

Outweighed by its evils

Yet these benefits have been purchased at a costly price. Setting aside considerations of minor import, three radical evils flow from the faith in all ages and in every country, and must continue to flow *so long as the Ḳor'ān is the standard of Belief.* FIRST: Polygamy, Divorce, and Slavery strike at the root of public morals, poison domestic life, and disorganise society; while the Veil removes the female sex from its just position and influence in the world. SECOND: freedom of thought and private judgment are crushed and annihilated. Toleration is unknown, and the possibility of free and liberal institutions foreclosed. THIRD: a barrier has been interposed against the reception of Christianity. They labour under a miserable delusion who suppose that Moḥammadanism paves the way for a purer faith. No system could have been devised with more consummate skill for shutting out the nations over which it has sway from the Christian faith; for there is in it just so much truth, truth borrowed from previous Revelations yet cast in another mould, as to divert attention from the need of more. *Idolatrous* Arabia (judging from the analogy of other nations) might have been aroused to spiritual life, and the adoption of the faith of Jesus; while *Moḥammadan* Arabia is, to the human eye, sealed against the benign influences of the Gospel. Many a flourishing land in Africa and in Asia which once rejoiced in the light and liberty of Christianity, is now crushed and overspread by darkness gross and barbarous. It is as if their day of grace had come and gone, and there remained to them 'no more sacrifice for sins.' That a brighter morn will yet dawn on these countries we may not doubt; but the history of the past, and the condition of the present, is not the less true and sad. The sword of Moḥammad, and the Ḳor'ān, are the most stubborn enemies of Civilisation, Liberty, and Truth which the world has yet known.

Inconsistencies run through the character of Moḥammad

In conclusion, I would warn the reader against seeking to portray for himself a character in all its parts consistent, as that of Moḥammad. On the contrary, the strangest inconsistencies were blent (as we so often find) throughout his life. The student will trace for himself how pure and lofty aspirations were first tinged, and then gradually lowered, by a half-unconscious self-deception. Nor will he fail to observe that simultaneously with the anxious desire to extinguish idolatry and promote religion and virtue in the world, there arose in his later years a tendency to self-indulgence; till in the end, assuming to be the favourite of Heaven, he justified himself by 'revelations,' releasing himself in some cases from social proprieties, and the commonest obligations of self-restraint. He will remark that while Moḥammad cherished a kind and tender disposition, 'weeping with them that weep,' and binding to his person the hearts of his followers by the ready and self-sacrificing offices of love and friendship, he could yet gloat over the massacre of an entire tribe, and savagely consign an innocent babe to the fires of hell. Inconsistencies such as these continually present themselves from the period of the Prophet's arrival at Medīna. It is by the study of them that his character must be rightly apprehended. And the key may be found, I believe, in the chapter on the doubts and difficulties that beset his first search after truth, and how he emerged therefrom. When once he dared to assume the name of the Most High as the seal and authority of his own words and actions, the germ was laid from which were developed the perilous inconsistencies of his later life.

Conclusion

MOḤAMMAD and the ḲOR'ĀN, the author of Islām and the instrument by which he achieved success, are themes worthy the earnest attention of mankind. If I have at all succeeded in contributing some fresh materials towards the formation of a correct judgment upon them, many hours of study, snatched not without difficulty from engrossing avocations, will have secured an ample recompense.

DESCRIPTION OF MOḤAMMAD FROM THE BIOGRAPHY OF IBN SA'D[1]

Extracts from Ibn Sa'd

In what follows I offer the reader a selection from Ibn Sa'd's chapter on the person and character of Moḥammad. The traditions will, I trust, prove interesting in themselves, as well as illustrate the style of the Prophet's biographers.

Prophecies regarding Moḥammad

Description of Moḥammad in the Old Testament and the Gospel.—Moḥammad was thus foretold: 'O Prophet! We have sent thee to be a Witness and a Preacher of good tidings, and a Warner, and a Defender of the Gentiles. Thou art my servant and my messenger. I have called thee *Al-Mutawakkil* (he that trusteth in the Lord). He shall not be one that doeth iniquity, nor one that crieth aloud in the streets; he shall not recompense evil for evil, but he shall be one that passeth over and forgiveth. His kingdom shall be Syria. Moḥammad is my elected servant; he shall not be

[1] Aṭ-Ṭabari, i. 1789 ff.

severe nor cruel. I shall not take him away by death, till he make straight the crooked religion; and till the people say, *There is no God but the Lord alone.* He shall open the eyes of the blind, and the ears of the deaf, and the covered hearts.' These are evident accommodations of passages in Isaiah xlii. and lxi. In one set of traditions from 'Ā'isha, she speaks of them as prophecies *from the Gospel*, in ignorance that they are quoted there (Matt. xii. 18) as applying to Jesus.

His disposition

His disposition.—When 'Ā'isha was questioned about Moḥammad, she used to say: 'He was a man just such as yourselves; he laughed often and smiled much.' *But how would he occupy himself at home?* 'Even as any of you occupy yourselves. He would mend his clothes, and cobble his shoes. He used to help me in my household duties; but what he did oftenest was to sew. If he had the choice between two matters, he would always choose the easier, so as that no sin accrued therefrom. He never took revenge excepting where the honour of God was concerned. When angry with any person, he would say, "*What hath taken such a one that he should soil his forehead in the mud!*"'

Humility

His humility was shown by his riding upon asses, by his accepting the invitation even of slaves, and when mounted by his taking another behind him. He would say: 'I sit at meals as a servant doeth, and I eat like a servant: for I really am a servant;' and he would sit as one that was always ready to rise. He discouraged (supererogatory) fasting, and works of mortification. When seated with his followers, he would remain long silent at a time. In the Mosque at Medīna, they used to repeat pieces of poetry, and tell stories regarding the incidents that occurred in the 'days of ignorance,' and laugh; and Moḥammad, listening to them, would smile at what they said. He hated nothing more than lying; and whenever he knew that any of his followers had erred in this respect, he would hold himself aloof from them until he was assured of their repentance.

Speech

His manner of speech.—He did not speak rapidly, running his words into one another, but enunciated each syllable distinctly, so that what he said was imprinted in the memory of every one who heard him. When at public prayers, it might be known from a distance that he was speaking by the motion of his beard. He never read in a singing or chanting style; but he would draw out his voice, resting at certain places. Thus, in the prefatory words of a Sūra, he would pause after *bismillāhi*, after *ar-Raḥmān*, and again after *ar-Raḥīm*. *His walking.*—One says that at a funeral he saw Moḥammad walking, and remarked to a friend how rapidly he moved along; it seemed as if he 'were doubling up the ground.' He used to walk so rapidly that the people half ran behind him, and could hardly keep up with him. *His eating.*—He never ate reclining, for Gabriel had told him that such was the manner of kings; nor had he ever two followers to walk behind him. He used to eat with his thumb and his two forefingers; and when he had done would lick them, beginning with the middle one. When offered by Gabriel the valley of Mecca full of gold, he preferred to forego it; saying, that when he was hungry he would come before the Lord lowly, and when full, with praise. *Excellence of his Morals.*—A servant maid being once long in returning from an errand, Moḥammad was annoyed, and said: 'If it were not for the law of retaliation, I should have punished you with this toothpick' (*i.e.* with an inappreciably light punishment).

Gait

Habits in eating

Moderation

Attitude at Prayers.—He used to stand for such a length of time at prayer that his legs would swell. When remonstrated with, he said: 'What! Shall I not behave as a thankful servant should?' He never yawned at prayer. When he sneezed he did so with a subdued voice, covering his face. At funerals he never rode; he would remain silent on such occasions, as if conversing with himself, so that the people used to think he was holding communication with the dead.

Customs at prayer

His personal appearance and habits.—He used to wear two garments. His *izār* (under-garment) hung down three or four inches below his knees. His mantle was not wrapped round him so as to cover his body, but he would draw the end of it under his shoulder. He used to divide his time into three parts: one was given to God, the second allotted to his family, the third to himself. When public business began to press upon him he gave up one-half of the latter portion to the service of others. When he pointed he did so with his whole hand; and when he was astonished he turned his hand over (with the palm upwards). In speaking with

Appearance, habits, &c.

another, he brought his hand near to the person addressed; and he would strike the palm of the left, on the thumb of the right, hand. Angry, he would avert his face; joyful, he would look downwards. He often smiled, and when he laughed his teeth used to appear white as hailstones. In the interval allotted for the purpose, he received all that came to him, listened to their representations, and occupied himself in disposing of their business and in hearing what they had to tell him. He would say on such occasions: 'Let those that are here give information regarding that which passeth to them that are absent; and they that cannot themselves appear to make known their necessities, let others report them to me in their stead; the Lord will establish the feet of such in the day of judgment.'

Refusal to make personal use of the tithes

While he accepted presents, he refused anything that had been offered as tithe (Ṣadaḳa); neither would he allow any one of his family to accept what was brought in tithe; 'for,' said he, 'tithes (or alms) are the impurity of mankind' (*i.e.* that which cleanses their impurity). His scruples were so strong, that he would not eat even a date picked up on the road, lest perchance it might have dropped from a tithe load. One day, little Al-Ḥasan was playing by his grandfather when a basketful of dates was brought in; on inquiry, Moḥammad found that they were tithe, and ordered them to be taken away and given to the poor Refugees. But Al-Ḥasan, having taken up one to play with, had already put it in his mouth; the Prophet, seeing this, opened the boy's mouth, and pulled it out, saying, 'the family of Moḥammad may not eat of the tithes.'

Food relished

Food which he relished.—Moḥammad had a special liking for sweetmeats and honey. A tailor once invited him to his house and placed before him barley bread, with stale suet; there was also a pumpkin in the dish; now Moḥammad greatly relished the pumpkin. His servant Anas used to say as he looked at the pumpkin: 'Dear little plant, how the Prophet loved thee!' He was also fond of cucumbers and of undried dates. When a lamb or a kid was being cooked, Moḥammad would go to the pot, take out the shoulder and eat it. Abu Rāfi' tells us: 'I once slew a kid and dressed it. The Prophet asked me for the forequarter and I gave it to him. "*Give me another,*" he said; and I gave him the second. Then he asked for a third. "O Prophet!" I replied, "there are but two forequarters to a kid." "*Nay*," said Moḥammad, "*hadst thou remained silent, thou wouldst have handed to me as many forequarters as I asked for.*" He used to eat moist dates and cooked food together. What he most relished was a mess of bread cooked with meat, and a dish of dates dressed with butter and milk. When he ate fresh dates he would keep such as were bad in his hand. One asked on a certain occasion that he would gave him the dates so rejected. '*Not so*,' he answered; '*what I do not like for myself, I do not like to give to thee.*' Once a tray of fresh dates was brought to him; he sat down on his knees, and taking them up by handfuls, sent a handful to each of his wives; then taking another handful, he ate it himself. He kept throwing the date stones on his left side, and the domestic fowls came and ate them up. He used to have sweet (rain) water kept for his use.

Food which he disliked.—On Moḥammad's first arrival at Medīna, Abu Eiyūb used to send him portions of baked food. On one occasion the dinner was returned uneaten, without even the marks of the Prophet's fingers. On being asked the reason, he explained that he had refrained from the dish because of the onions that were in it, for the angel which visited him disliked onions; but others he said might freely eat of them. So also with garlic; he would never allow it to pass his lips; '*for*,' said he, '*I have intercourse with one* (meaning Gabriel) *with whom ye have not.*' He disliked flour made of almonds, saying that it was 'spendthrift's food.' He would never partake of the large lizard, for he thought it might have been the beast into which a party of the children of Israel were changed; but he said there was no harm in others eating it. When drinking milk, Moḥammad once said, 'When a man eateth let him pray thus: *O Lord! grant Thy blessing upon this, and feed me with better than this!* But to whomsoever the Lord giveth milk to drink, let him say: *O Lord! grant Thy blessing upon this, and vouchsafe unto me an increase thereof;* for there is no other thing which combineth both food and drink save milk alone.'

Food disliked

Moḥammad's fondness for women and scents.—A great array of traditions are produced to prove that the Prophet

Women and scents

liked these of all things in the world the best. 'Ā'isha used to say: 'The Prophet loved three things—women, scents, and food; he had his heart's desire of the two first, but not of the last.' In respect to scents, traditions have been already quoted in Chapter XVII., p. 331 *n*.

Straitened means at Medīna

Narrowness of means at Medīna.—A long section is devoted to this subject, containing many such traditions as the following. Fāṭima once brought Moḥammad a piece of bread; it was the first that had passed his lips for three days. 'Ā'isha tells us that for months together Moḥammad did not get a full meal. 'Months used to pass,' she says again, 'and no fire would be lighted in Moḥammad's house either for baking bread or cooking meat. *How, then, did ye live?* By the "two black things" (dates and water), and by what the citizens used to send unto us; the Lord requite them! Such of them as had milch cattle would send us a little milk. The Prophet never enjoyed the luxury of two kinds of food the same day; if he had flesh there was nothing else; and so if he had dates; so likewise if he had bread. We possessed no sieves, but used to bruise the grain and blow off the husks. One night Abu Bekr sent Mohammad the leg of a kid. 'Ā'isha held it while the Prophet cut off a piece for himself in the dark; and in his turn the Prophet held it while 'Ā'isha cut off a piece for herself. "*What,*" exclaimed the listeners, "*and ye ate without a lamp!*" "Yea," replied 'Ā'isha; "had we possessed oil for a lamp, think ye not that we should have lighted it for our food?"'

Abu Hureira explains the scarcity thus: 'It arose,' he says, 'from the great number of Mohammad's visitors and guests; for he never sat down to food but there were some followers with him. Even the conquest of Kheibar did not put an end to the scarcity; because Medīna has an intractable soil, which is ordinarily cultivated for dates only, the staple food of its inhabitants. There did not exist in the country means of support sufficient for the greatly increased population. Its fruits are the commonest products of the soil, which want little water; and such water as was needed the people used to carry on their backs, for in these days they had few camels. One year, moreover, a disease (premature shedding) smote the palms, and the harvest failed. It is true that a dish used to be sent for the Prophet's table from the house of Sa'd ibn 'Obāda, every day until his death, and also in the same manner by other Citizens; and the Refugees used to aid likewise; but the claims upon the Prophet increased greatly, from the number of his wives and dependants.'

I have repeatedly noticed these stories, and have attributed them to the frugal habits of Moḥammad compared with the sudden growth of wealth and splendour in the Caliphate. The products of the surrounding country were, no doubt, at first inadequate to the wants of the great numbers who flocked with Moḥammad to Medīna. But it is evident that although Moḥammad, in the early years of the Hijra, may have been reduced to common fare, he could hardly have ever suffered *want*, especially with so many devoted followers about him. It is the vivid contrast between the luxury prevalent in the days when tradition was growing up, and the simple life of Moḥammad, which mainly gave rise to these ideas. Thus 'Abd ar-Raḥmān, when in after years he used to fare sumptuously on fine bread and every variety of meats, would weep while looking at his richly furnished table, thinking of the Prophet's straitened fare. Another upbraids his comrade who could not live without bread made of the finest flour: 'What!' said he; 'the Prophet of the Lord, to the last hour of his life, never had two full meals on the same day, of bread and of oil; and behold, thou and thy fellows vainly luxuriate on the delicacies of this life, as if ye were children!'

The 'Seal' of prophecy on the back of Moḥammad.—This, says one, was a protuberance on the Prophet's back of the size and appearance of a pigeon's egg. Ibn Sarjis describes it as having been as large as his closed fist, with moles round about it. Abu Rimtha, whose family were skilled in surgery, offered to remove it, but Moḥammad refused, saying: '*The Physician thereof is He who placed it where it is.*' According to another tradition, Mohammad said to Abu Rimtha *Come hither and touch my back;* which he did, drawing his fingers over the prophetical seal, and, 'behold there was a collection of hairs upon the spot.'[1] I have not before noticed this 'seal,' because it is so surrounded with supernatural tales that it is extremely difficult even to conjecture what it really

'Seal' of prophecy

[1] *Cf.* At-Ṭabari, i. 1790 f.

was. It is said to have been the *divine* seal which, according to the Scriptures, marked Moḥammad as the last of the Prophets. How far Moḥammad himself encouraged this idea it is impossible to say. From the traditions quoted above, it would seem to have been nothing more than a mole of unusual size, and the saying of Moḥammad that 'God had placed it there' was probably the germ of the supernatural associations which grew up concerning it. Had the Prophet really attributed any divine virtue to this mole, he would have spoken very differently to one who offered to lance or remove it.

Hair

On his hair.[1]—It reached, a follower tells us, to his shoulders; according to another to the tip of his ears. His hair used to be combed; it was neither curling nor smooth. He had, says one, four curled locks. His hair was ordinarily parted, but he did not care if it was not so. According to another tradition, 'The Jews and Christians used to let their hair fall down, while the heathen parted it. Now Moḥammad loved to follow the people of the Book in matters concerning which he had no express command. So he used to let down his hair without parting it. Subsequently, however, he fell into the habit of parting it.'

Cupping

On his being cupped.—Some of the many traditions on this head have been quoted elsewhere. It was a cure which Gabriel directed him to make use of. He had the blood buried lest the dogs should get at it. On one occasion, Moḥammad having fainted after being cupped, an Arab is said to have gone back from the profession of Islām.

Moustache

On his moustache.—Moḥammad used to clip his moustache. A Magian once came to him and said: 'You ought to clip your beard and allow your moustaches to grow.' 'Nay,' said the Prophet, 'for my Lord hath commanded me to clip the moustaches and allow the beard to grow.'

Dress

On his dress.—Various traditions are quoted on the different colours he used to wear,—white chiefly, but also red, yellow, and green. He sometimes put on woollen clothes. 'Ā'isha exhibited a piece of woollen stuff in which she swore that Moḥammad died. She said that he once had a black woollen dress; and she still remembered, as she spoke, the contrast between the Prophet's fair skin, and the black cloth. 'The odour of it, however, becoming unpleasant, he cast it

[1] *Cf.* Aṭ-Ṭabari, i. 1792 f.

off,—for he loved sweet odours.' He entered Mecca on the taking of the city (some say) with a black turban. He had also a black standard. The end of his turban used to hang down between his shoulders. He once received the present of a scarf to be worn as a turban; it had a figured or spotted fringe, and this he cut off before wearing it. He was very fond of striped Yemen stuffs. He used to wrap his turban many times round his head, and 'the lower edge of it would appear like the soiled clothes of an oil-dealer.' He once prayed in a silken dress, and then cast it aside with abhorrence, saying: '*Such stuff it doth not become the pious to wear.*' On another occasion, as he prayed in a figured or spotted mantle, the spots attracted his notice; when he had ended he said: '*Take away that mantle, for verily it hath distracted me in my prayers, and bring me a common one.*' His sleeve ended at the wrist. The robes in which he was in the habit of receiving embassies, and his fine Ḥaḍramaut mantle, remained with the Caliphs; when worn or rent these garments were mended with fresh cloth; and in after times the Caliphs used to wear them at the festivals. When he put on new clothes, whether an undergarment, a girdle, or a turban, the Prophet would offer up a prayer such as this: 'Praise be to the Lord, who hath clothed me with that which shall hide my nakedness and adorn me while I live. I pray Thee for the good that is in this raiment, and I seek refuge from the evil that is in the same.' Moḥammad had a piece of tanned leather which was ordinarily spread for him in the Mosque, to pray upon. He had also a mat of palm-fibre for the same purpose: this was always taken, after the public prayers, into his wives' apartments for use there.

Golden ring

On his golden ring.—Moḥammad had a ring made of gold, he used to wear it, with the stone inwards, on his right hand. The people began to follow his example and make rings of gold for themselves. Thereupon the Prophet, ascending the pulpit, sat down and, taking off the ring, said: *By the Lord I will not wear this ring ever again;* so saying, he threw it from him. And all the people did likewise. According to another tradition, he cast it away because it had distracted his attention when preaching; or, again, because the people were attracted by it. He then prohibited the use altogether

Silver ring

of golden signet rings. *On his silver ring.*—Already mentioned at p. lxvii.

Shoes

On his shoes.—His servant, Anas, had charge of his shoes and of his water-pot. After his master's death Anas used to show the shoes. They were after the Ḥaḍramaut pattern, with two thongs. In the year 100 or 110 A.H., one went to buy shoes at Mecca, and tells us that the shoemaker offered to make them exactly after the model of Moḥammad's, which he said he had seen in the possession of Fāṭima, grand-daughter of Al-'Abbās. His shoes used to be cobbled. He was in the habit of praying with his shoes on. On one occasion, having taken them off at prayers, all the people did likewise; but Moḥammad told them there was no necessity, for he had merely taken off his own because Gabriel had apprised him that there was some dirty substance attaching to them (cleanliness being required in all the surroundings at prayer). The thongs of his shoes once broke and they mended them for him by adding a new piece; after the service Moḥammad desired the shoes to be taken away and the thongs restored as they were before; 'for,' said he, 'I was distracted at prayer thereby.'

Toothpicks

His toothpicks.—'Ā'isha tells us that Moḥammad never lay down, by night or by day, but on waking he applied the tooth-pick to his teeth before he performed ablution. He used it so much as to wear away his gums. The toothpick was always placed conveniently for him at night, so that, when he got up to pray, he might use it before his lustrations. One says that he saw him with the toothpick in his mouth, and that he kept saying '*ā*, '*ā*, as if about to vomit. His toothpicks were made of the green wood of the palm-tree. He never travelled without one. *Articles of toilet.*—Already noticed at p. 331. He very frequently oiled his hair, poured water on his beard, and applied antimony to his eyes. The Prophet used to snuff *simsim* (sesamum), and wash his hands in a decoction of the wild plum-tree. When he was afraid of forgetting anything, he would tie a thread on his finger or his ring.

Articles of toilet

Armour

Armour.—Four Sections are devoted to the description of his armour—swords, coats of mail, shields, lances, and bows.

Horses

His horses, &c.—The first horse which Moḥammad ever possessed was one he purchased of the Beni Fezāra, for ten

[1] Aṭ-Tabari, i. 1782 ff.; Ibn Ḳoteiba, p. 73 f.

ounces of silver, and he called its name *Es-Sekb* (running water), from the easiness of its paces. Moḥammad was mounted on it at the battle of Oḥod, when there was but one other horse from Medīna on the field. He had also a horse called *Sabaha;* he raced it and it won, and he was greatly rejoiced thereat. He had a third horse named *Al-Murtajis* (neigher). When the white mule Duldul arrived from the Muḳauḳis, Moḥammad sent it to his wife Um Selama; and she gave some wool and palm-fibre, of which they made a rope and halter. Then he brought out a garment, doubled it fourfold, and throwing it over the back of the mule, straightway mounted it, with one of his followers behind him. This mule survived till the reign of Mu'āwiya. Farwa (the Syrian governor said to have died a martyr) sent the Prophet a mule called *Fiḍḍa* (Silver) and he gave it to Abu Bekr; also an ass, which died on the march back from the Farewell pilgrimage. He had another ass called *Ya'fūr.* 'Alī was anxious to breed a mule similar to that of Moḥammad; but Moḥammad told him that 'no one would propose so unnatural a cross save one that lacked knowledge.' *Riding camels.*—Besides Al-Ḳaṣwā, Moḥammad had a camel called *Al-Aḍbā,* which in speed outstripped all others. Yet one day an Arab passed it when at its fleetest pace. The Muslims were chagrined at this; but Moḥammad reproved them, saying: 'It is the property of the Lord, that whensoever men exalt anything, or seek to exalt it, then He putteth down the same.' *Milch camels.*—Moḥammad had twenty milch camels, the same that were plundered at Al-Ghāba. Their milk was for the support of his family: every evening they gave two large skinsful. Um Selama relates: 'Our chief food when we lived with Moḥammad was milk. The camels used to be brought from Al-Ghāba every evening. I had one called *Al-'Arīs,* and 'Ā'isha one called *As-Semrā.* The herdman fed them at Al-Jauwānīya and brought them to our homes in the evening. There was also one for Moḥammad. Hind and Asmā, two herdmen, used to feed them, one day at Dhu'l-Jedr, the other at Al-Jemmā. They beat down leaves from the wild trees for them, and on these the camels fed during the night. They were milked for the guests of the Prophet, and his family got what was over. If the evening drew in and the camels' milk was late in being brought, Moḥammad would

Riding camels

Milch camels

say: 'The Lord make thirsty him who maketh thirsty the family of Moḥammad at night.' *Milch flocks.*—Moḥammad had seven goats which Um Aiman used to tend (this probably refers to an early period of his residence at Medīna).[1] His flocks grazed at Dhu'l-Jedr and Al-Jemmā alternately, and were brought back to the house of the wife whose turn it was for Moḥammad to be in her chamber. A favourite goat having died, the Prophet desired its skin to be tanned. He attached a peculiar blessing to the possession of goats. 'There is no house,' he would say, 'possessing a goat, but a blessing abideth thereon; and there is no house possessing three goats, but the angels pass the night there praying for its inmates until the morning.' *Moḥammad's servants.*—Fourteen or fifteen persons are mentioned who served the Prophet at various times. His slaves he always freed.[2]

Milch flocks

Servants

Houses

The houses of his wives.—'Abdallah ibn Yazīd relates that he saw the houses in which the wives of the Prophet dwelt, at the time when 'Omar ibn 'Abd al-'Azīz, governor of Medīna, (about A.H. 100) demolished them. They were built of unburnt bricks, and had separate apartments with partitions of palm-branches, daubed (or built up) with mud; he counted nine houses, each having separate rooms, in the space extending from the house of 'Ā'isha to the house of Asmā daughter of Al-Ḥosein. Observing the dwelling-place of Um Selama, he questioned her grandson concerning it; and he told him that when the Prophet was absent on the expedition to Tebūk, Um Selama built up an addition to her house with a wall of unburnt bricks. When Moḥammad returned, he went in to her and asked what new building this was. She replied: 'I purposed, O Prophet, to shut out the glances of men thereby!' Moḥammad answered: 'O Um Selama! verily, the most unprofitable thing that eateth up the wealth of a believer is building.' A citizen, present at the time, confirmed this account, and added that the curtains (Anglo-Indicé, *Purdas*) of the doors were of black hair-cloth. He was present, he said, when the despatch of the Caliph 'Abd al-Mālik (A.H. 86-88) was read aloud, commanding that these houses should be taken down and the site brought within the area of the Mosque, and he never witnessed sorer weeping than there was amongst the people that day. One

[1] *Cf.* At-Tabari, i. 1786. [2] *Cf.* Ibn Ḳoteiba, p. 70 f.

exclaimed: 'I wish, by the Lord! that they would leave these houses alone just as they are; then would those that spring up hereafter in Medīna, and strangers from the ends of the earth, come and see what kind of building sufficed for the Prophet's own abode, and the sight thereof would deter men from extravagance and pride.' There were four houses of unburnt bricks, with apartments partitioned off by palm-branches; and five houses made of palm-branches built up with mud and without any separate apartments. Each was three yards in length. Some say that they had leather curtains for the doors. One could reach the roof with the hand. The house of Ḥāritha was next to that of Moḥammad. Now whenever Moḥammad took to himself a new wife, he added another house to the row, and Ḥāritha was obliged successively to remove his house, and to build on the space beyond. At last this was repeated so often that the Prophet said to those about him: 'Verily, it shameth me to turn Ḥāritha over and over again out of his house.'

Properties

Moḥammad's private property.—There were seven gardens which Mukheirīk the Jew left to Moḥammad. 'Omar ibn 'Abd al-'Azīz, the Caliph, said that, when governor of Medīna, he ate of the fruit of these, and never tasted sweeter dates. Others say that these gardens formed a portion of the confiscated estates of the Beni an-Naḍīr. They were afterwards dedicated perpetually to pious purposes. Mukheirīk is said to have been a learned Jewish priest and a leader of the Beni Ḳainuḳā', who 'recognised Moḥammad by his marks, and identified him as the promised Prophet.' But the love of his own religion prevailed, so that he did not openly join Islām. Nevertheless, on the day of Oḥod he put on his armour, notwithstanding it was the Sabbath day, and went forth with the Muslims and was killed. His corpse was found and was buried near the Muslims; but he was not prayed over, nor did Moḥammad beg mercy for his soul then or afterwards; the utmost he would say of him was, '*Mukheirīk, the best of the Jews!*' He had large possessions in groves and gardens, and left them all to Moḥammad.[1]

Moḥammad had three other properties:—I. The confiscated lands of the Beni an-Naḍīr. The produce of these was appropriated to his own wants. One of the plots was called

[1] Aṭ-Tabari, i. 1424.

Mashrabat Um Ibrāhīm, the 'summer garden of (Mary) the mother of Ibrahim,' where the Prophet used to visit her. II. Fadak; the fruits of this were reserved as a fund for indigent travellers. III. The fifth share, and the lands received by capitulation, in Kheibar. These were divided into three parts. Two were devoted for the benefit of the Muslims generally (*i.e.* for State purposes); the proceeds of the third, Moḥammad assigned for the support of his own family; and what remained over he added to the fund for the use of the Muslims.

Wells

Wells from which Moḥammad drank.—A variety of wells are enumerated out of which Moḥammad drank, and on which he invoked a blessing, spitting into them. One night as he sat by the brink of the well called Gharsh, he said: 'Verily, I am sitting beside one of the fountains of Paradise.' He praised its water above that of all other wells, and not only drank of it but bathed in it. He also drank from the fountain of Buḍā'a, taking up the water in both his hands and sipping it. He would send the sick to bathe in this fountain, 'and when they had bathed, it used to be as if they were loosed from their bonds.' The well called Rūma belonged to a man of the Beni Muzeina. Moḥammad said that it would be a meritorious deed if any one were to buy this well and make it free to the public. 'Othmān, hearing this, purchased the well for 400 dīnārs, and attached a pulley to it. Moḥammad, again happening to pass the well, and apprised of what 'Othmān had done, prayed the Lord to grant him a reward in Paradise, and calling for a bucket of water drank therefrom, and praised the water, saying that it was both cold and sweet.

INDEX